Elizabethan America

© 2011 by James Alan Egan.
All Rights reserved.

ISBN_10:1467967858
ISBN-13:9781467967853
LCCN:

Published by
Cosmopolite Press
152 Mill Street
Newport, Rhode Island 02840

For more information, visit:
newporttowermuseum.com

Printed in the United States of America

Elizabethan America

The John Dee Tower of 1583

A Renaissance horologium*
in Newport, Rhode Island

*A horologium is a building that keeps track of time.

BY
James Alan Egan

"Citizen of the World"
(Cosmopolite is a word coined
by John Dee, from the Greek
words cosmos meaning "world"
and politēs meaning "citizen")

Cosmopolite Press
Newport, Rhode Island

*This book is dedicated to my
supportive wife, Lucinda*

Contents

1	Enlightening clues found in the Tower
15	Various theories about who built the Tower?
37	Two words provide an illuminating clue
43	The History of the Camera Obscura
53	John Dee and the Elizabethan colonization effort of 1583
71	John Dee's mathematical cosmology, expressed in architecture
79	The *Monas Hieroglyphica* (Dee's most cherished work)
91	John Dee and Buckminster Fuller thought alike
109	Robert Marshall finds Symmetry in Number
155	Dee's ideas about vision
167	A brief history of clocks in city-centers
169	From Vitruvius to Vegas: the long tradition of circular temples
179	Giovanni de Verrazanno's Voyage of 1524
191	The Dutch theory about the origin of the name Rhode Island
195	"Mad Jack" Oldham and Narragansett Bay in 1634
197	How Rhode Island got its name?
233	(What I call) "The Riddle of the Royal Ring" in John Dee's *The Limits of the British Empire*
247	A deeper look at the title of John Dee's work: *The Limits of the British Empire*
259	Did the English name for the state of "Rhode Island" come from the mind of John Dee?
299	The "shibboleth" (or "watchword") for the first Elizabethan colony in America, at the Dee River
309	Did John Dee have the word "RODE" cryptically concealed in the fabric of the Tower?
325	A deeper clue: In ancient Greece, the lowercase *eta* meant EIGHT
351	Why John Dee selected January 15 to be the Coronation Date for Queen Elizabeth I
a	Books written by John Dee
c	Bibliography
h	Who is Jim Egan?

Introduction

TO UNDERSTAND THE WORKS OF A RENAISSANCE MAN, ONE MUST THINK LIKE A RENAISSANCE MAN.

They were polymaths

In our complex modern world, there is pressure to specialize. What's your major? What kind of doctor are you? What department of the company do you work in?

The great thinkers of earlier times, from Plato, Aristotle, and Archimedes, to "Renaissance Men" like Leonardo da Vinci, Leon Battista Alberti, and Copernicus, and even onward, to men like Isaac Newton, Thomas Jefferson and Benjamin Franklin, were **"polymaths."**

(in Greek *polymathe*, means "having learned much.")

Renaissance polymaths didn't merely become masters of different subjects. They explored the **interconnections** between those branches of knowledge. They saw science, art and mathematics as an indivisible whole.

The writings, illustrations, and architectural work of the particular Elizabethan "Renaissance Man" we explore in this book are all fascinating. But it's how he has woven all these things together that is truly astounding.

They saw numbers differently than we do

"One is not a number."

This idea might sound absurd to the modern mind. But none of the great Hindu, Egyptian, Roman, Greek, Neo-Platonic, Medieval, or Renaissance mathematicians considered "one" to be a number. As D. E. Smith writes in his book *History of Mathematics*, even up until the late 1700's, "school arithmetics" still taught that "one was not number."

Even knowing this history, the idea still sounds ridiculous. Why do I have a "one" on my cell phone? And on my calculator? If I have 2 apples and eat one, how many are left? No number?

This concept perplexes most moderns because we don't see numbers the way our predecessors did. We see numbers as "quantities." Earlier mathematicians explored the "qualities" of the numbers (particularly the single digits, out of which all numbers are made).

Just because they didn't consider "one" to be a number, doesn't mean they felt it was unimportant. Quite the contrary. They felt "one" was the "source" or "wellspring" of all numbers. All numbers (the single-digit numbers, the two-digit numbers, all the way up into the trillions-of-digits numbers) are derived from **"one."**

Whether we moderns are "right," or our predecessors were "right," is not what's important here. The key point is that when we study the history of mathematics, science, art, or philosophy, we must try to **think like our predecessors**. When we think like they thought, the subtle, intended meanings of their works becomes clearer.

In this book, we'll explore what this "one is not a number" concept is all about. Suddenly the doors will open and you will see "perfect symmetries" in the realm of number. Symmetries which would otherwise be invisible.

They loved riddles

Nowadays, many consider riddles to be child's play. But in the days of old, adults delighted in them. And brilliant minds put great effort into devising them. This book solves a series of small riddles that are all interrelated in one giant riddle.

The solution is a spider's web, with strands of geometry, number, architecture, geography, art, optics, and more – even politics and theology. Some of the brain teasers involve secret codes, symbols, literary references and even jumbled-word clues. Only a truly interdisciplinary Renaissance man could have conceived of such a grand puzzle.

An interdisciplinary approach to solving the puzzle

Nowadays, there is so much to learn, someone attempting to be a "jack of all trades" might become a "master of none." A modern solution is a multidisciplinary approach in which experts from various fields collaborate, each providing a piece of the puzzle.

This book explores the mind of a Renaissance polymath by combining the discoveries of several modern-day experts: a geometer, a numbers-whiz, an astronomer, and a photographer (an artist who studies vision and optics). Only by seeing the all these fields as interrelated can we understand the cosmology this Renaissance man was expressing in his words, drawings, and architecture.

So, put on your thinking caps and fasten your seatbelts. We're in for a wild ride through European history, the geometry of space, and the "part-natural and part-supernatural" realm of number.

(But don't be afraid you'll get lost in the mathematics.
It's so easy fifth graders have understood it.)

James A. Egan,
Newport, Rhode Island,
January 15, 2011

[This book is a synopsis of 9 separate books (over 2000 pages) that I have written on the history of the Newport Tower. If it appears as though I have not "connected the dots" well enough, please refer to the longer text for a fuller explanation See the bibliography at the end of this book.]

Enlightening clues found in the Tower

The city of Newport, Rhode Island is at the mouth of Narragansett Bay. In a small park above the harbor stands the 28-foot tall stone-and-mortar Tower. Its eight sturdy pillars support a tall cylinder that is several feet thick.

Even though it's unlike any other building in America, historians still debate about who actually built it.

In 1942, historian Philip Ainsworth Means wrote the 300-page book titled *Newport Tower,* and he draws this conclusion:

"The circular arcaded tower at Newport continues to be the most enigmatic and puzzling single building in the United States, a building which may hold the very key to the early Christian history of the Western Hemisphere."

In the 1800's, vines were allowed to grow on the Tower, to give it an aura of antiquity.

At that time, the huge mansions along Bellevue Avenue were privately owned summer cottages. One of Newport's main attractions was the "Old Stone Mill."

(from old postcard, Metropolitan News Co. Boston)

The Tower was a popular subject for postcards of Newport in the early 1900s.

You can get a sense of the Tower's roundness by walking around it, but its circularity is much more striking when seen from above.

Before houses were built on the west side of Touro Park, the Tower had a panoramic view of Newport Harbor, Goat Island, the island of Jamestown, and even the mainland of South County.

2

Let's take a quick tour of the Tower
(searching for subtle clues in the architecture)

During his 1948 excavation, William Godfrey, a graduate student at Harvard University, found that there was a 4-foot tall footing under each of the eight pillars. Down near the bedrock, these footings are about 8 feet in diameter. They taper upwards to a platform 4 feet in diameter. On top of each footing was a 4-foot diameter "drum" (or pillar base).

About 1 foot of the drums is buried underground, leaving only about 6 inches visible

These drums are each a foot-and-a-half tall. Over the years, about a foot of fill has been brought into the park for various gardens, so only about 6 to 8 inches of the drums are above ground today. Godfrey writes:

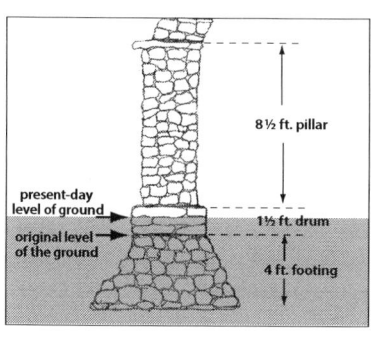

"The addition of these bases to the columns materially alters the appearance of the Tower and makes it architecturally a more satisfying structure."

(Godfrey, 1948 Excavation, *Initial Report*, Sept. 24, 1948, p. 2)

Above the drums, 8 symmetrical pillars rise about 8 ½ feet to small capitals. Connecting the pillars are the 8 arches which support the upper cylinder.

The outer diameter of the cylinder is about 24 feet, and the inner diameter is about 18 ½ feet.

This cylinder is about 3 feet thick just above the pillars and about 2 feet thick near the upper rim. This baby is solid. It was built to last.

The interior of the Tower

Inside the Tower are 8 beam sockets that once held beams about 20 feet long by about 1-foot-by-1-foot square. The four massive beams crisscrossed in a tic-tac-toe pattern. Where they crossed, they were probably mortise-and-tenoned together like Lincoln logs.

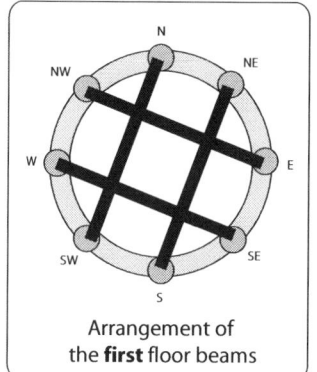

Arrangement of the **first** floor beams

I think the floor sat directly on the beams, at the same height as the tops of the arches (12 feet above ground level)

Resting on top of the beams would have been a 2-inch thick subfloor, and then a 2-inch thick floor. Thus, the first floor was at the same height of the tops of the arched openings: 12 feet above the original ground level.

Looking west, the two other beam sockets and the "running mortise" are clearly visible

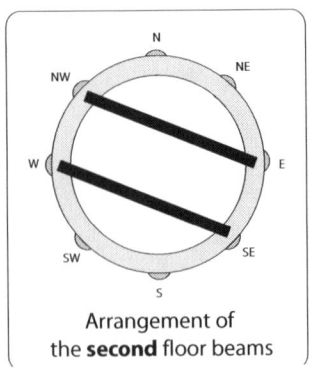

Arrangement of the **second** floor beams

The room on the first floor has a fireplace and 3 main windows. It's clearly a room, as the beam sockets for the second floor are still visible.

At the same height as the tops of these beam sockets is a "running mortise" or a small ledge that runs around the whole interior of the Tower.

The walls of the second floor rise about another 6 feet. They probably once rose even higher. It's most likely the Tower once had a roof, but it has long since disappeared.

close-up view of the "running mortise" on the southeast part if the interior

The Unusual Fireplace

The 3-foot-wide by 4-foot-tall fireplace recessed about two feet into the eastern wall is peculiar in several ways. Philip Means calls the fireplace the "strangest exant feature of the tower."

The first thing is its placement on the wall. If the level of the first floor is at the height of the arched openings, that means that the fireplace is about 2 feet above floor level.

That's quite unusual. Have you ever seen a "wall fireplace"? In most colonial fireplaces, the hearths are at floor level.

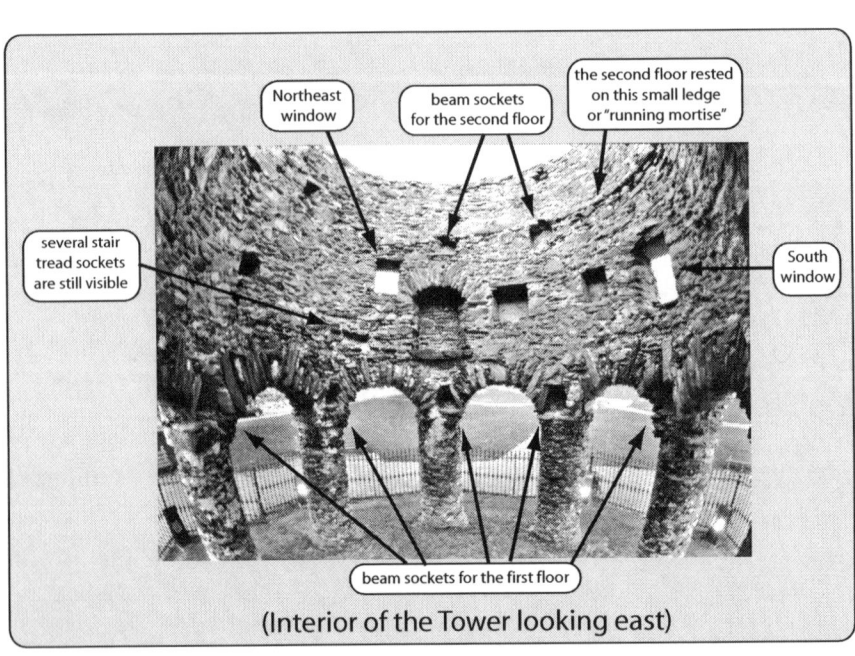

(Interior of the Tower looking east)

The second unusual feature is that it has two flues. One rises from the upper left corner of the firebox and the other right upper right corner. Each of the flues is about 7" x 7" square. The flues rise up inside the wall and exit out the exterior about 2 feet from the top rim.

Interoir of the Tower, showing where the 2 flues run through the middle of the thick wall

Exterior view of Tower showing the 2 flue venting holes

That's unusual, too. Have you ever seen a fireplace with two flues? Most fireplaces have one big flue that funnels the smoke, ensuring there's a sufficient draft for venting.

Furthermore, as hot air rises, most fireplaces exit upwards to the sky. Why do these two flues exit out the side of the Tower?

The third unusual fact is that the fireplace has an arch above it. Most fireplaces have a lintel, a horizontal support across the top. Structurally, an arch is stronger than a lintel, but it needs support on both ends.

On the right side this arch has plenty of support. **But, on the left side, precisely where it needs all its support, there's a window.** Why didn't these obviously talented stone masons simply position the window over to the left a little more? (More about this clue in a moment.)

Why put a window so close to the end of the fireplace arch?

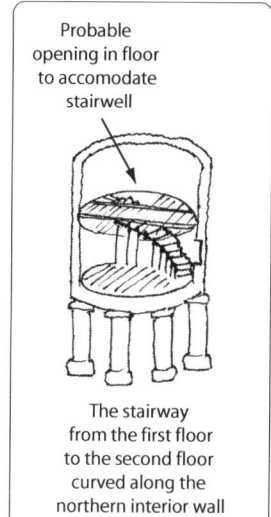

Probable opening in floor to accomodate stairwell

The stairway from the first floor to the second floor curved along the northern interior wall

Below the window are horizontal sockets that once held the step treads of a stairway that spiraled up the northern interior wall to the second floor.

Traces of more step sockets were visible in the late 1800's, but parts of the northern wall have subsequently been remortared to seal cracks.

Unwrapping the Tower

This composite photo of the exterior shows the asymmetrical arrangement of the 3 windows.

They are all different sizes, different heights above the ground.
And none of them aligns directly above either a pillar or an arch.

If the eight pillars and eight arches are so perfectly symmetrical,
why would the windows be arranged so asymmetrically?

This interior composite shows the relative positions of the
beam sockets, niches, windows, peepholes, and the fireplace.

One of the shelves that jut out above the pillars

On the exterior of the building, the whole upper cylinder of Tower rests on the inner two-thirds of the pillars. At the top of each pillar is a shelf that juts out about 7 inches.

Some historians have theorized that these shelves held horizontal beams which radiated outwards to vertical posts. They envision the Tower as a "round church" with an outer ambulatory, an enclosed area in which the priests would walk around the Tower, saying their prayers.

I respectfully disagree with this thesis for several reasons. First, a beam simply resting on a shelf can slide to the left, or to the right, or even pull outwards. Why wouldn't the builders have used beam sockets like they did on the inside of the Tower?

Secondly, why would they make the shelf out of slate, a stone which can easily be broken? And why would they "cantilever" the slate outwards, making it even more susceptible to chipping off?

Finally, so rain and snow doesn't get into the open areas where the arches are, such an ambulatory would require a roof that skirted the building. But there is no evidence of any rafter sockets higher up on the exterior wall. (These eight exterior shelves are definitely clues, but determining their purpose will require some creative thinking.)

The "Sun Stone" and the "Rock with Shoulders"

"Sunstone" above the stone with "shoulders"

northwest-west arch (exterior view of tower)

The entire Tower is made from local fieldstone, mostly dark-gray slate, tan-colored granite, blue-grey colored bluestone (and the occasional white quartz and other rocks). But there is one rock in the west-northwest arch that is most unusual. We call it the "Sun Stone" because it's fairly round, it's reddish in color, and it has tiny crystals in it that reflect sunlight, making it sparkle.

Just below it is a rock with "shoulders." It's quite distinct and appears to have been crafted by man.

The combination of the two rocks appears to be some sort of a symbol. As the "shouldered" rock is somewhat tapered, some historians have referred to it as a "keystone."

However, true keystones are always in the exact center of the arch. This one is clearly to the right of center. A true keystone is a centralized V-shaped rock that "locks" the two sides of the arch.

True keystones are important in "ashlar" masonry (when all the stones are square-cut with smooth sides). But the arches of this Tower are all simply flat stones of varying thicknesses. Furthermore, none of the other arches in the tower has a central rock that could be called a true keystone. (We'll return to the "Sun Stone" and the "Rock with Shoulders" in a moment.)

On the interior of the northwest and northeast pillars are large sections of the plaster that once covered the entire building inside and out. It's the same material that was used for the white mortar that holds all the rocks together (crushed seashells, gravel and sand). Plaster was even found in the beamsockets.

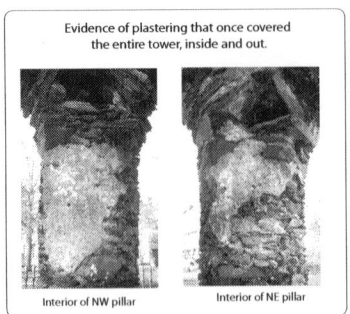

Would the builders have left the structure to look like a white elephant? I don't think so. In Medieval and Renaissance times, they would plaster over a building, then paint it to look like brickwork or stonework. They would paint in rock edges and shadow effects, even words and pictures. Examples of this "sgrafitto" technique can still be seen all over Europe today (especially in Eastern Europe).

The Windows

The first floor room of the Tower has three main windows. The Northeast window is about 2 feet tall by 2 ½ feet wide. Not only is this the window built so unusually close to the fireplace arch, it's also about 6 feet above the level of the floor. **That's so high up, most people couldn't even see out of it!**

The West window (which again is a few degrees off of due west) is the largest of the 3 windows, (about 2 ½ feet tall by 3 feet wide). And strangely, this window is only about 2 ½ feet above the level of the first floor.

That's so low, one would have to bend over to look through it!

The South window (it's actually a few degrees away from exactly facing south) is squarish, about 2 ½ feet tall by 2 ½ feet wide. It's sill is about 4 feet above the level of the first floor.

8

All three windows are different sizes, different proportions, and are different heights above the first floor. After building the eight symmetrical columns and arches, why would the builders place the windows in such an asymmetrical fashion?

Furthermore, none of the three windows is aligned vertically above either a pillar or an arch. Smells like a clue to me.

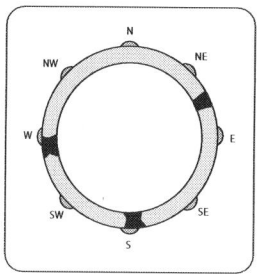

The three windows are different in other ways. The West window is the only one with a relieving arch above its lintel. The other two windows have lintels, but no relieving arches above them.

The sides of the West window are quite splayed. The sides of the South window are slightly splayed. But the sides of the Northeast window are not splayed at all.

Peepholes and Niches

In addition to the 3 windows, there are 4 "peepholes," each about a foot square. And there are seven "niches" or shallow recesses built into the interior walls. Finding traces of wood in the plaster of the niches, Philip Means suggests they were made by constructing the masonry around a box mold.

Two niches on the interior of the Southeast wall

Professor Penhallow's astronomically important discoveries

Professor Penhallow makes a reading with his astrolabe

In the early 1990's, Professor William Penhallow, a professor of astronomy and physics at the University of Rhode Island, found several astronomical alignments in the windows of the Tower.

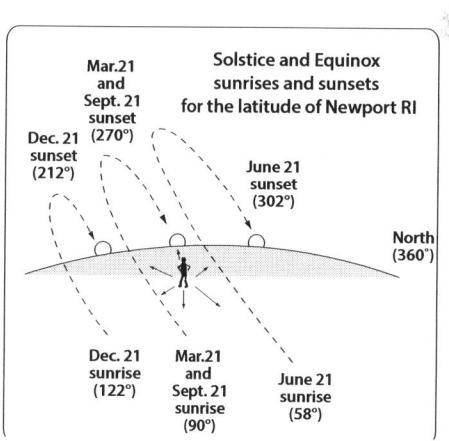

The most obvious alignment involves the arc the sun makes across the sky at various times of the year. The arc is low in the winter, high on the summer, and right in-between on the equinoxes (when the sun sets precisely due west).

Standing on the northeast corner of the park,
you can look through the West window,
through the interior of the Tower,
through the South window and
see a small section of the sky.

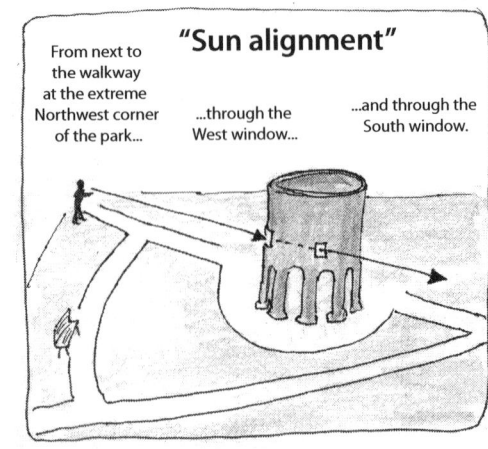

winter solstice 1999

But here's the special part:
On and around the Winter Solstice,
the rising sun can be seen right
through these two windows!
(About a half-an-hour after dawn.)

I have photographed this event
several times over the years and
it always happens–like clockwork.

winter solstice 2007

Throughout the rest of the year, the sun makes a higher arc
through the sky, and it is not visible through these two windows.

In addition to the "Sun alignment," Penhallow also found an important "Moon alignment."

From a different position in the park (approximately west-southwest of the Tower) you can see through the West window, through the interior of the Tower and out the Northeast window.

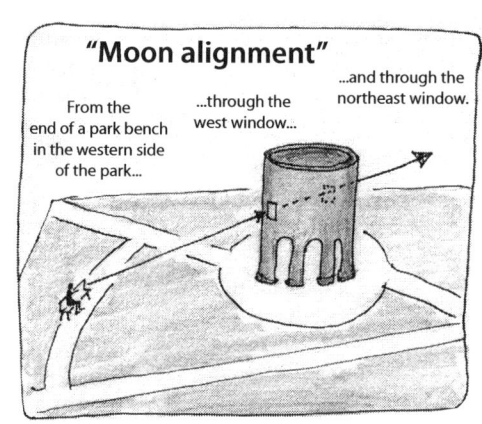

Approximately 20 minutes after the alignment, the moon becomes visible to the right of the Tower.

Penhallow calculated that on the evening of December 25, 1996, (and only on that night only) the full moon, rising in the east, would be visible through these two windows. (My wife's Christmas present to me that year was to let me see if Penhallow was right.)

This dotted line shows the path of the moon that night.

And here's the full moon seen through the West and Northeast windows. Penhallow was right!

Lunar Minor alignment through two windows, December 25, 1996

11

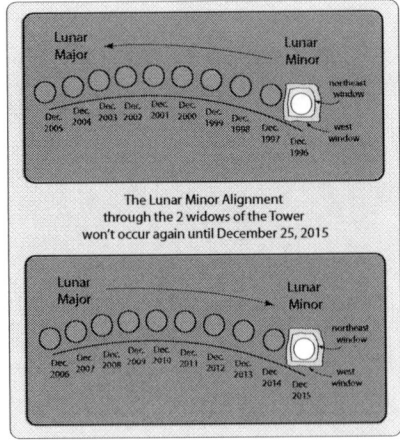

The Lunar Minor Alignment through the 2 widows of the Tower won't occur again until December 25, 2015

The special thing about this event is that it only happens once every 18.6 years. It marks the Lunar Minor standstill position of the Moon (the most southerly of all the northernmost risings of the moon).

For the next 9.3 years, the Moon's northernmost risings arc further north in the sky, and the moon is not visible through these windows. Then, for the next 9.3 years, the northernmost risings work their way back southward. This "Moon alignment" event will happen again in the year 2015.

Note that West window (the only one with a relieving arch above it) is used for both the Sun alignment and the Moon alignment.

The second window involved in the Moon alignment is the Northeast window.

Interestingly, that's the window that was built so close to the arch that spans the fireplace!

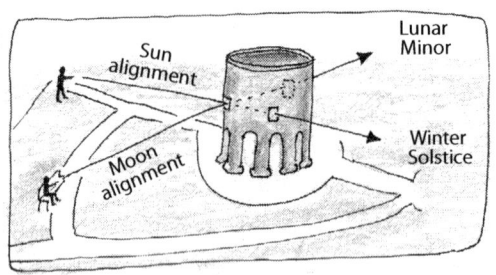

The Northeast window is the one that's 6 feet above floor level, too high to look through. And the West window is the one which is about 2 1/2 feet above the floor level, too low to look through!

It was becoming clear to Penhallow that the Tower was built for **"archeoastronomy."**

The Tower had celestial alignments that were built right into the stone-and-mortar fabric of the building.

The "North Star alignment"

WILLIAM PENHALLOW

Penhallow found another dramatic alignment. Standing just south of the Tower you can see through the South window and out a small peephole in the northern wall. Penhallow found that this alignment might help the builders use the stars to find true North.

Boy Scouts and Girl Scouts can tell you that Polaris, (the pole star) can help you find north if you get lost. But Polaris (which is in the tail of the Little Dipper) is hard to locate because it's not that bright,

To locate Polaris, first find the much more prominent Big Dipper. The outer edge of the bowl of the Big Dipper is made from two very bright stars, Merak (at the bottom of the bowl) and the vey bright Dubhe (at the top of the bowl).

Merak and Dubhe "point" to the North Star. Measure out about five "Merak-to-Dubhe-lengths," and you'll find Polaris.

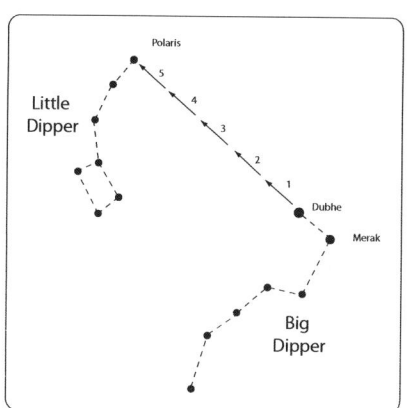

What the Scouts might not know (but what astronomers and navigators know) is that Polaris is **not exactly due north**. It's about 1° away from a dark place in the sky that is exactly due north.

One degree out of 360° doesn't seem that significant. But, because of the precession of the equinoxes, about 400-500 years ago, Polaris was about 5° away from the north. (The apparent diameter of the Moon is about one half of a degree, so five degrees is quite significant.)

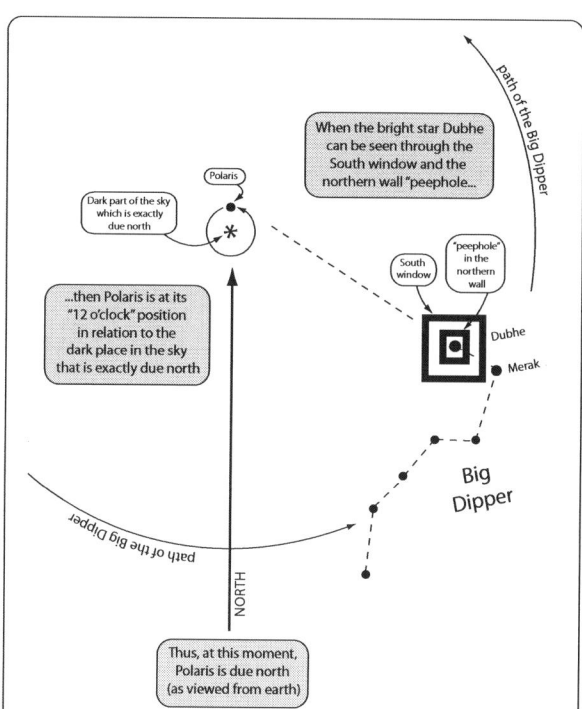

But because Polaris rotates around this dark place in the sky, when it is "above" that dark place
(at what might be called the "12 o'clock position," or its uppermost culmination),
then Polaris is exactly due north.
(Polaris is also due north when it is in the "six o'clock" position or its lowermost culmination.)

What Penhallow found was that when the bright "pointer" star, Dubhe, is visible through the South window and the peephole, then Polaris is exactly due north.

Why is finding exact north so important? When astronomers and navigators are trying to determine the position (azimuth and declination) of other celestial objects, it's important to have a fixed reference to start from.

Because of the "procession of the equinoxes," this Dubhe alignment is not visible today. Penhallow calculates that Dubhe was only visible through these two windows from around 1200 AD to around 1600 AD.

(This suggests that the Tower was not built during Colonial times. Also, this Dubhe alignment works in the summer and fall, when the Big Dipper is visible, but not during winter and spring when the Big Dipper is below the horizon)

Suddenly, we have a building that is aligned to the Sun, the Moon, and the Stars. Someone wanted to connect Heaven and Earth. This is not really that unusual. It's what a church spire does.

But the Tower does it in a clever "internal" way, in which the light rays from celestial objects **pass right through the structure**. Who would have devised such an ingenious arrangement?

The "egg-shaped" rock alignment

During the Winter Solstice of 1997, after photographing the "Sun alignment" through the West-and-South windows, I decided to stick around and see what happened next, particularly inside the Tower.

   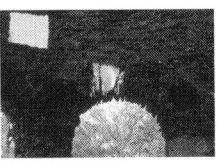

After passing through the west window, the patch of light creeps along the western interior wall and illuminates an egg-shaped rock in the west-northwest arch.

Streaming through the South window, the patch of light slowly inched its way across the western interior wall, heading downward and to the right.

About an hour later, at around 9:00 AM, this patch of light illuminated a large "egg shaped" rock in the west-northwest arch.

It looked quite dramatic—as if there was a spotlight on the rock.

patch of light from the south window spotlighting the "egg-shaped" rock

This egg-shaped rock is **not** in the center of the arch, so I don't consider it to be a keystone.

But here's the fascinating part: Directly behind this "egg shaped" rock is the "Sun Stone" and the "Rock with Shoulders."

This whole arrangement seemed far from accidental.

Somebody was trying to tell us something.

But who?
And what was the architect trying to say?

Various Theories About Who Built the Tower

Over the years many theories have been put forth about who built the Newport Tower.

The Viking tower theory

In 1841, the Danish antiquarian Charles Christian Rafn asserted the Tower was built by the Vikings in the year 1120 AD. (Though he never actually saw the Tower, only some not-very-accurate illustrations of it.) Henry Wadsworth Longfellow romanticized Rafn's theory in a poem about a pair of Viking lovers:

> "There for my lady's bower
> Built I the lofty tower,
> Which to this very hour,
> stands looking seaward."

Rafn's ideas, fueled by Longfellow's famous poem, still linger in the mythos of modern-day of Newport: Viking Automotive, Viking Cleaners, Hotel Viking, Newport Vikings Pop Warner Football Team, even the Viking Tuxedo Company.

The Templar Round-Church theory

In 1921, Dr. F. J. Allen wrote about how similar the Tower was "in form and dimension" to the Church of the Holy the Sepulchre, built in his hometown of Cambridge, England by the Templars in the 1100's.

Modern Templar enthusiasts claim the Newport Tower was built by the Scottish Earl Henry Sinclair during an expedition led by Antonio Zeno in 1398.

The Chinese Lighthouse theory

British historian Gavin Menzies suggests the Tower was built by the Chinese navigator Zheng-He in 1421. He asserts the Chinese sailed around the southern coast of Africa in large ships and built the Tower as a pagoda-lighthouse.

The Portuguese Watchtower theory

Edmund Delabarre and Dr. Manuel DaSilva assert the Tower was built as a church-watchtower by the early Portuguese navigator Miguel Corte-Real. Miguel set sail 1501 and was never heard from again. His brother even came to the New World in search of Miguel, to no avail. DaSilva suggests that the otagonal rotunda of the Castle of Tomar, in Tomar, Portugal was the prototype for the Newport Tower.

The Governor Benedict Arnold Windmill theory

But the most popular theory is that the Tower was built as a windmill by Benedict Arnold, the first governor of Rhode Island. (No, this is not the infamous Revolutionary war traitor Benedict Arnold. Yes, they were related. But the Governor Benedict Arnold was the traitor's great-great-great-grandfather. They lived a full century apart.)

In his 1677 Will, Governor Benedict Arnold writes that he wants to be buried in the small cemetery on:

"ye Lyne or Path from my Dwelling House to my Stone-built Wind-Mill'n."

Benedict's house was on Thames Street (near the corner of Pelham Street). Walk up Pelham Street and you can still visit Governor Benedict Arnold's grave site. It's exactly halfway between his mansion and his Tower.

A Mindmill? Who are you trying to kid?

colonial windmill still standing in Eastham, Mass., on Cape Cod

But there are reasons to suspect that Benedict might have been "shading the truth" by calling the it a "Windmill." Philip Means calls the Tower **"the most un-windmill-like structure I have ever seen."**

To start with, every other windmill built in the 1600's in New England was made from wood. There were dozens of colonial windmills up and down the coast, but this would have been the only one made from stone. The typical wooden windmill shown here was originally built in 1680, in Plymouth, and was later moved to Eastham on Cape Cod.

(photo by C. Holmes, wikipedia)

Second, all windmills taper towards the top so the turret can be smaller than the base. The turret must be rotated frequently so the four large blades always face the wind. (Most turrets could be moved by a human, but to rotate a 24-foot diameter turret would require the force of an ox, or a team of oxen.)

Third, in a windmill there is a horizontal shaft, geared to a vertical shaft, which rotates one grinding-stone against another. Below the stones the flour was collected. If you have a good strong wind needed to power the sails, all your flour would blow away! Why build a windmill be with an open arcade?

From an engineering point of view, a solid base would have handled torque better than eight tall pillars. If, as some suggest, the grinding and flour collection was all done the enclosed first-floor room, where is the stairway needed to bring sacks of corn up and sacks of flour down? Even if there was a solid ladder, it's awkward to carry heavy sacks when ascending and descending.

But the most damning evidence is this: The last thing you would want in a windmill is a fireplace. Flour powder is more explosive than gunpowder. Spontaneous combustion is enough of a problem, but one small spark and **Ka-boom**! The while mill would explode!

The Viking, Templar, Portuguese, and Chinese theorists all must think that Benedict Arnold was lying about his "windmill." Their conjectured dates of construction are well before 1677. But apparently none of these theorists ever bothered ask several obvious questions:

Out of all the early colonists of Rhode Island, why did the
Tower "just happen" to be owned by the first governor?

And why, in 1663, did King Charles II appoint
Benedict Arnold to be the first governor?
Why didn't he appoint Roger Williams?

Roger Williams

Roger was always portrayed as playing the leading role in the history of colonial Rhode Island. In Providence, there's a Roger Williams Park, a Roger Williams National Memorial, and a huge statue of Roger in Prospect Park overlooking the city. There's Roger Williams Medical Center, Roger Williams University, Roger Williams Park Zoo, and even Roger Williams Auto Repair on Roger Williams Avenue.

Dozens of books have been written about Roger Williams. He is often referred to as the founder of Providence. I won't deny he was a key player in the founding of Rhode Island, but why has no book ever been written about the Rhode Island's first governor, Benedict Arnold?

Unfortunately, Benedict Arnold has a name which is synonymous with "traitor" in the minds of most Americans. Would you want to be married in Benedict Arnold Park, attend Benedict Arnold University, or have surgery at Benedict Arnold Hospital?

And it's too bad, because the name Benedict Arnold is actually a nice sounding name with symbolic meaning: Benedict means "blessed," and Arnold means "strong as an eagle."

The actions of one of his descendents should not cloud the fact that Governor Benedict Arnold played a key role in the history of Rhode Island. I dare say Benedict was just as important as Roger Williams and John Clarke in the birth of this state.

I noticed something else about the existing theories about the Tower.
Scandinavians scholars think the Scandinavians built it.
Portuguese historians think the Portuguese built it.
Templar enthusiasts think the Templars build it.
And a student of Chinese history thinks the Chinese built it.

Might their theories possibly be colored by their own interests?
It appeared as though none of them ever made and in-depth study of Rhode Island history.
So I decided to explore the history of the Tower from the inside-out, not the outside-in.

Curiously, no full biography has ever been written about Governor Benedict Arnold.
So first, I searched the historical archives for every reference I could find on him.

Aside from the Arnold family records, details of his role in the early development of Rhode Island can be found in several well-documented texts. Many clues can be found in Glenn W. LaFantasie's *The Correspondence of Roger Williams 1629–1653*. Perhaps the finest scholarship on early Rhode Island history is Dennis Allen O'Toole's *Exiles, Refugees, and Rogues: The Quest for Civil Order in the Towns and Colony of Province Plantations 1636-1654*.
(I found this typewritten thesis to be a gold mine of information on birth of Rhode Island, but it only been checked out of the library several times in the last 40 years. So I contacted the author, who now lives in New Mexico, and we have brought the 480-page text back to light in book form.)

Roger Williams is often depicted as a lone man, banished from Salem, trudging through the winter snows to found Providence. But he wasn't alone. He was actually accompanied by at least 4 other men when he founded Providence in the Spring of 1636.

In addition, 10 members of the Arnold Clan were there **at the exact same time**, as Benedict Arnold later wrote,

"We came to Providence to Dwell the 20th of April in 1636."

William Arnold was been born in 1587, during Elizabethan times. He and his his wife Christian had 5 children. The couple also raised the children of William's sister who had died. Together with a few spouses, the Arnold Clan totaled 10 people.

Benedict Arnold and his cousin Thomas Hopkins were 19 years old at the time, fresh out of school and full of energy.

The Arnold Clan in 1635

The clan arrived in Hingham, Massachusetts in 1635. Unhappy with the politics of that town, they headed west to Narragansett Bay in search of opportunity.

Like Roger Williams, Benedict Arnold befriended the Narragansetts and learned to speak their native Algonquin dialect. Roger and Benedict were the only two Englishmen to sign this facsimile of the original deed of Providence.

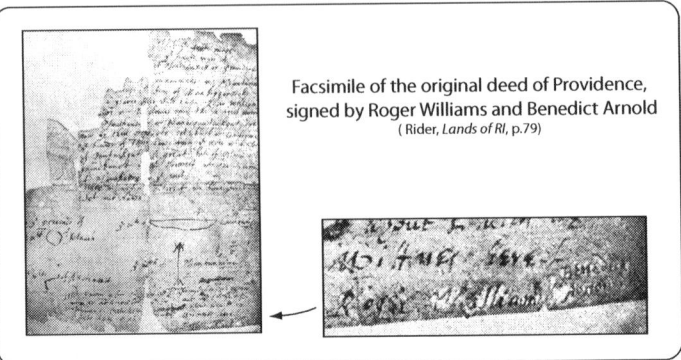

Facsimile of the original deed of Providence, signed by Roger Williams and Benedict Arnold
(Rider, *Lands of RI*, p.79)

The friendly Narragansetts deeded English settlers all the lands and meadows upon the two fresh rivers called Moshassuck and the Woonasquatucket. The parcel went from what is now the city of Pawtucket (on the north) to what is now Pawtuxet Village, Cranston (on the south). To the west the boundary went just beyond Neutaconkanut Hill (near what is now the eastern Johnston).

Several years later, the land hungry William Arnold apparently "spin-doctored" the deed, claiming it included all the lands between the Pawtucket River and the Pawtuxet River and extending westward about 20 miles.

Arguments ensued, and soon William Arnold and several associates left Providence and built homes further south along the northern bank of the Pawtuxet River.

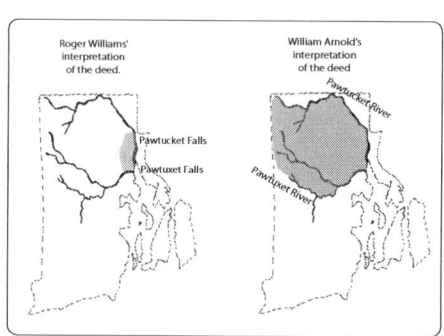

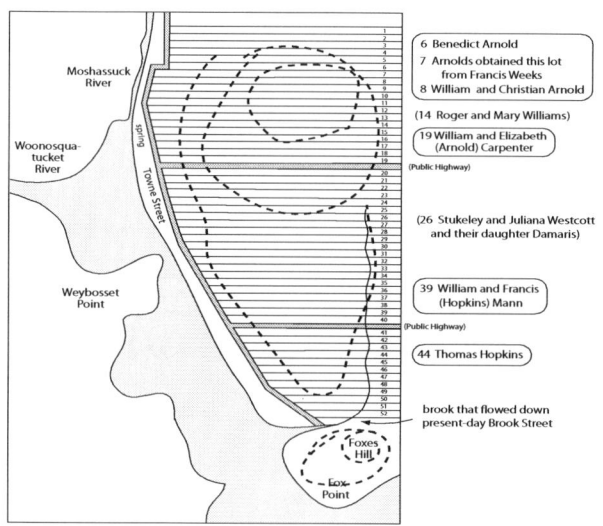

Benedict fell in love with another settler's daughter, Damaris Westcott, and they continued to live in Providence.

His property spanned three house-lots on top on Prospect Hill (ironically the property includes Prospect Park, where the statue of Roger Williams now stands).

Benedict started a cattle ranch near present-day Olneyville. Even today, Benedict Street still leads towards Benedict Pond (although the marshy pond has since been filled in).

The enterprising Arnolds started making their own land deals with the Narragansetts. They bought all the land from what is now Green State Airport in Warwick to the Warwick Mall and eastern Cranston, up to Olneyville and eastern Johnston.

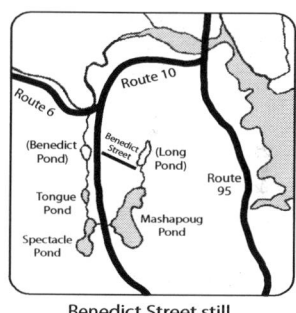

Benedict Street still goes to Benedict Pond (but it's no longer there)

Then the cantankerous Samuel Gorton came to town. Gorton was an outspoken theologian who didn't believe in baptism, communion, or that any religious training was required for someone to become a preacher. He had already been kicked out of Plymouth and Boston. Now his "railing and turbulent" rantings were agitating the people of the Providence.

Roger Williams and William Arnold became "two unlikely allies" in squeezing Gorton out of town. But Gorton had picked up a few followers, and they moved to Warwick Neck, just south of William Arnold's Pawtuxet home. This really ticked off the Arnolds.

19

After the early trader John Oldham had been murdered in 1636, the Arnolds become the key middlemen, handling the trade between between the Narragansetts, the largest tribe in New England, and the Massachusetts Bay colony.

On one of their trading forays they brought along all their deeds and put themselves under the jurisdiction of the Massachusetts Bay Colony. That's right: Cranston, Rhode Island was once a part of Massachusetts.

The Mass. Bay Colony militia attacking Gorton's garrison

Then the Arnolds asked the authorities of Boston to send 40 soldiers down to put an end to Gorton's slander and his trespassing. Gorton and his men were holed up in their garrison. Shots flew back and forth. Eventually Gorton surrendured. The prisoners were forced to walk to Boston in manacles.

The Massachusetts Bay Colony sentenced them to a year of hard labor, chained to posts in various town centers. (Later, Gorton actually returned to found the town of Warwick, Rhode Island)

Colonial shallop

Meanwhile, the Arnolds developed a trading monopoly in Narragansett Bay. Roger Williams became a part owner of Prudence Island, and had opened a small trading post at Wickford. But Williams had been banished from Boston. He couldn't travel there, even on a trading mission.

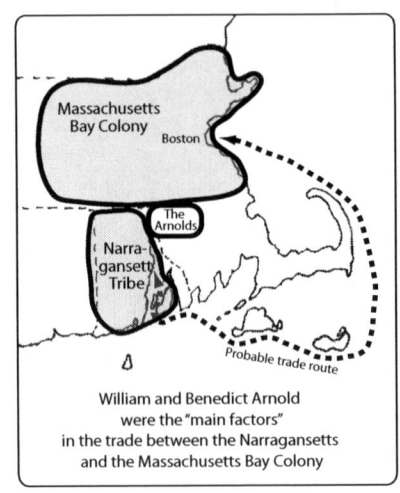
William and Benedict Arnold were the "main factors" in the trade between the Narragansetts and the Massachusetts Bay Colony

In the early days, the road between Providence and Boston was still an Indian path. And there weren't many horses available to transport goods.

The Arnolds probably had a fleet of shallops that plied the coast from Narragansett Bay, around Cape Cod, to Boston.

(A shallop is a small boat that can be rowed or sailed)

Benedict Arnold became an interpreter for the United Colonies (which consisted of Plymouth, Massachusetts Bay, Hartford, and New Haven) in their negotiations with the Indians. Benedict learned how to handle being in the hot seat. He must have made promises that weren't kept because, at certain times, his life was threatened, and Roger Williams was called in to do the interpreting.

Providence was not a member of the United Colonies. It had its own (more harmonious) relationship with Canonicus and Miantonomi, the great sachems of the Narragansetts.

During the long, harsh winter of 1647, the Narragansetts were close to starvation. There had been a steady decline in game in the woods and they had sold off too much of their winter corn supply to the English. Massachusetts Bay records reveal that Benedict requested permission to sell corn back to the Indians.

In 1647, the four towns on the bay, Providence, Warwick, Portsmouth and Newport assembled to form a "democratical" government and legal system. The Arnolds were **left their choice, whether they will have Providence, Portsmouth, or Newport.**"

The independent-minded William Arnold didn't want to be part of any of them. He opted to remain a part of the Massachusetts Bay colony.

But Benedict realized that his trading business depended on being a part of the local government. Narragansett Bay was his home port. Could he make the hard decision to break with his trading partners? Could he break with his father? (What is this, a colonial soap-opera?)

Providence 2nd Sept. 1650 A Towne Rate			
[Providence]	£.	s.	d.
Arthur ffennor	01	13	4
William Wickenden	00	10	0
Thomas Sucklinge	00	05	0
Thomas Roberts	00	13	4
William Hawkings	00	13	4
James Austine	00	10	0
Joshua Winsor	00	03	4
Robert West	00	13	4
Thomas Hopkings	00	13	4
Widdow Sayers	00	16	8
Nicholas Powers	01	00	0
Nathaniell Dixings	00	13	4
Widdow Man	00	06	8
William Barrowes	00	13	4
Adam Goodings	00	03	4
Thomas Harris	01	00	0
George Sheppard	00	10	0
John ffeild	01	00	0
William ffeild	03	00	8
George Ricketts	00	05	0
Widdow Browne	00	06	8
Robert Williams	01	00	0
Stew: Westcote	00	13	4
Hugh Bewitt	00	06	8
Richard Waterman	02	10	0
Tho: Angell	01	00	0
Tho: Olnye	01	13	4
Edward Manton	01	00	0
Peter Greene	00	01	8
Henry Right	01	00	0
Roger Williams	01	13	4
Richard Scotte	03	06	8
John Throckmorton	01	13	4
John Elderkine	00	03	4
Benedicke Arnold	**05**	**00**	**0**
Pardon Tillinghurst	00	03	4
Grigory Dexter	01	00	0
John Browne	00	03	4
Ch Smith	00	03	4
William ffenner	00	06	8
Widdow Smith	02	10	0
John Jones	00	03	4
	41	8	4
[Pawtuxet]			
Tho: Clements	00	06	8
Tho: Slowe	00	13	4
William Harris	01	06	8
William Arnold	03	06	8
Robert Coles	03	06	8
William Carpender	03	06	8
Stephen Arnold	01	00	0
Zachery Rodes	01	00	0
Ch: Hawkhurst	00	10	0
	14	16	8
[Total]	56	05	0

The Providence tax roll for 1650 reveals just how successful Benedict Arnold's trading business was. He was the only citizen who was charged 5 pounds (apparently the maximum). Even though there were 50 other men and women on the tax roll, Benedict paid almost 10 percent of the total.

But as Dylan sings, "The times they are a-changin'." In the 1640's, much money was to be made in the fur trade. But beavers, who don't migrate very far and are not highly reproductive, soon became extinct in many locales. Fur trading declined in the 1650's and was "practically defunct by 1660."

(Bernard Bailyn, *The New England Merchants of the Seventeenth Century*, p.56-59)

Benedict Arnold and other merchants looked for other opportunities, like iron mining and trading with other colonists from places like Virginia and the West Indies. For ocean trade, Benedict knew that Newport harbor was the place to be.

In April of 1649, Benedict was a main player in a controversial Newport business deal. Along with Newporter Captain Jeremy Clarke and several others, Benedict purchased the contents of the Spanish vessel, the *Saint Lewis*, that the Dutch had seized in the West Indies. The Dutch Captain Philip Vander Euiden sold them the cargo of Campechey wood (Mexican logwood), West Indies hides, and Cochineal (a red dye made from Central American insects).

This infuriated Peter Stuyvesant, the Governor of New Netherlands (the early Big Apple). The prize had been taken after Spain's treaty with the Dutch and had the potential of setting off a huge diplomatic fiasco.

Stuyvesant appealed to the United Colonies for restitution of the cargo, but to no avail. Benedict pretty much did as he pleased.

The founding of the town of Newport

In 1638, Anne Hutchinson, William Coddington, John Clarke, and their associates left the rigid theocratic government of Boston. Roger Williams helped them purchase all of Aquidneck Island from the Narragansett Indians. But curiously, they settled in a rather nondescript place called Pocasset at the north end of the island (now part of Portsmouth). Why didn't they decide to settle in the beautiful natural harbor of Newport? (This appears to be a clue).

In 1639, Coddington, Clark, and others broke with Portsmouth to found Newport.

In 1650, the power-hungry William Coddington went to England and convinced the authorities to make him the Governor of Aquidneck Island for life. The citizens of Newport were aghast, but didn't quite know what to do. They wanted to be able to elect their own leaders, but they were afraid to challenge the authorities in England.

So who do they ask to come to their rescue? The bold Benedict Arnold.

On November 19, 1651, Benedict Arnold, his wife Damaris, and their 4 young children moved from Providence to Newport. Even though all the lands of Newport had been subdivided during the previous 12 years (from 1639–1651), Benedict somehow managed to obtain most of what is now downtown Newport.

His land extended from modern-day Church Street to Bellevue Avenue, to Harrison Avenue, and all the way down to Brenton Cove.

What had previously been a common grazing land called "South Meadow" (from King's Park southwards) now became Benedict's "Limington Farm," named after his hometown in Somerset, England.

(What is now Ida Lewis Rock was once called "Lime Rock" after the name of Benedict's farm.)

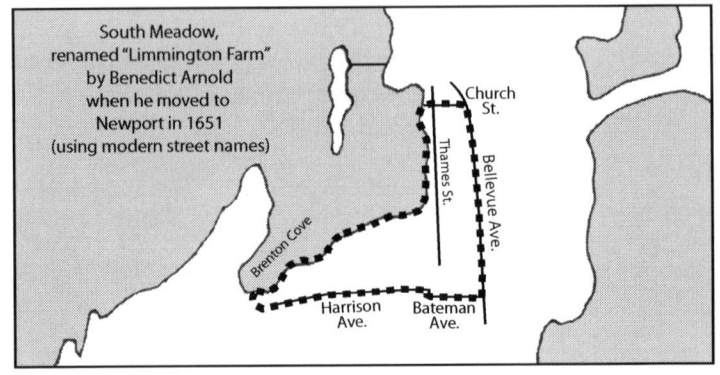

To me, this is another fat clue. I suggest that Benedict had been using Newport Harbor as a trading post ever since he first arrived in Narragansett Bay in 1636. And I believe he had "claimed" the Tower to be his own, perhaps using it for storage, or as a resting-over place for his shipping crew. (I'll explain more reasons why I make this conjecture later.)

I suggest that Benedict had a 3-day shipping route. The first day from Providence or Pawtuxet to Newport. The second day from Newport to Nantucket. And the third day around Cape Cod to Boston. Then back in three more days.

The Arnold family's store in Pawtuxet was the only place the planters of Providence could buy English-made goods like tools, cooking utensils, guns, ammunition, liquor, and clothes.

Benedict really began to shine as a leader. Four times his fellow citizens around Narragansett Bay elected him to be the President of the Colony of Providence Plantations.

As President of the Colony is 1657, Benedict responded to his old comrades in Massachusetts when they demanded that Quakers not be allowed to settle in Newport:

"We have no law among us whereby we punish any for declaring by words their minds and understandings concerning the things and ways of God as to salvation and external condition."

[This is basically the first amendment of the U.S. Constitution, asserted by a government official, 134 years before the Bill of Rights was ratified in 1791.]

Presidents of Providence Plantations		
	1654	Nicholas Easton and Roger Williams
	1655	Roger Williams
	1656	Roger Williams
	1657	**Benedict Arnold**
	1658	**Benedict Arnold**
	1659	**Benedict Arnold**
	1660	William Brenton
	1661	William Brenton
	1662	**Benedict Arnold**
Governors under the Royal Charter		
	1663	**Benedict Arnold**
	1664	**Benedict Arnold**
	1665	**Benedict Arnold**
	1666	William Brenton
	1667	William Brenton
	1668	William Brenton
	1669	**Benedict Arnold**
	1670	**Benedict Arnold**
	1671	**Benedict Arnold**
	1672	Nicholas Easton
	1673	Nicholas Easton
	1674	William Coddington
	1675	William Coddington
	1676	Walter Clarke
	1677	**Benedict Arnold**
	1678	**Benedict Arnold**

Benedict the rose to such prominence that when King Charles II granted "The Colony of Rhode Island and Providence Plantations" its charter in 1663, Benedict was appointed the first Governor.

The people of Rhode Island re-elected him 7 more times. When he died in 1678, over 1000 people attended his funeral.

Historian Samuel Arnold writes about Benedict:

"Throughout his long and useful life, he displayed talents of a brilliant order which were ever employed for the welfare of his fellow men."

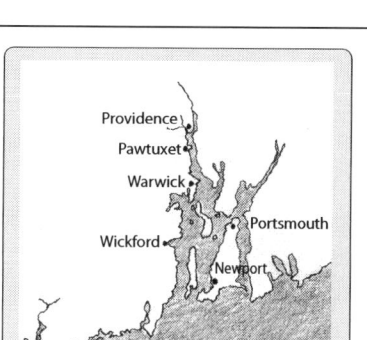

The four earliest towns and two outposts (Pawtuxet and Wickford)

23

In a *Providence Journal* article written in 1936
(exactly 300 years after Providence's founding in 1636),
J. Earl Clauson writes about Benedict Arnold:

"It's hardly to be gainsaid that he was one of the self-seeking settlers. They were
they all self-seeking in one way or another; some were after enlargement purely
on the spiritual side and some after this world's goods. The latter was Arnold's line.

Though a brilliant negotiator he must have been, he was also a 'wheeler-dealer,'
who had no qualms of twisting the truth slightly for his own purposes.

Brilliant no doubt he was, and strong-willed, a main chancer,
and perhaps a shade overbearing, but he served the colony well."

As Glenn LaFantasie puts it,

"Arnold, who was fluent in local Algonquian dialects,
was often asked by the Commissioners of the United
Colonies to act as interpreter and messenger in their
transactions with the Indians of Narragansett Bay.

The Narragansett sachems, however, suspected Arnold of
distorting their meaning in his translations, and preferred
to rely on Roger Williams' services whenever they could.

(LaFantasie, *Letters* p. 253)

J. Earl Clauson's assessment is a bit harsher:

"Indians kept their knives ground to a keen edge for the time when they
should meet up with Benedict…he gave inaccurate and unfavorable
translations of their speech…and gypped them in land deals."

(Clausen, *Prov Journal*, Feb 12, 1936)

With these insight into Benedict's character, it's easier see why I suggest Benedict
might easily have been "shading the truth" when he called the Newport Tower a "Windmill."
Benedict was not above distorting the truth a bit, as a means to an end.

Benedict Arnold was land hungry

The Indians respected Arnold not only because he spoke their language, and traded with
them, but because the they knew he was a great leader among the English. Arnold respected the
Indians as well, but he still felt Indians should share their lands with the English.

As Benedict's descendant James N. Arnold writes (around 1900)
in his historical magazine *Book Notes* Benedict Arnold,
"was land hungry. First, last, and all the time, he wanted the earth."

Historian Sidney Rider called Benedict,
"an inveterate land grabber" during the **"wild craze for land in 1658."**
(Tompkins, *Benedict Arnold: First Governor of Rhode Island*, p.16) and (Rider, *Lands*, p.289)

Benedict Arnold's mansion stood on the "old wide line" of Thames Street, between what is now Mill Street and Pelham Street. It was a classic Rhode Island style "stone-ender." George Mason reports that the whole south end of the house, which included a massive chimney, was all made from stone. (The house was probably 2 ½ stories tall.) (Mason, in Downing and Sculley, p.28)

Hamilton B. Tompkins reports that it had a "stately fence in front of it, with tall images on the gate posts."

(Tompkins, *Benedict Arnold: First Governor of Rhode Island*, p.18)

From his windows, Benedict had a clear view of the activity in his warehouses and wharf, which were just across Thames Street.

Conjectured view of Benedict Arnold's Mansion on the "old wide line" of Thames Street

In England, the wealthiest and most influential men owned large estates. Benedict wanted to acquire land not only for his descendants, but for the future prosperity of the growing colony over which he presided. If he and his colleagues didn't acquire it first, wealthy investors from Boston or Connecticut would move in and purchase it.

Gravestone of one of Benedict Arnold's descendants...

...in an Arnold family cemetery overlooking Mackerel Cove.

Looking south down Mackerel Cove from "Parting Beach"

On April 17, 1657, Benedict Arnold, William Coddington, William Brenton, and 100 others bought **Conanicut Island** (the island of Jamestown). Arnold got almost half of the Island–over 1,400 acres. His portion includes what he called "Cajaset," (most of the land south of the present-day village of Jamestown) and all of Beavertail (so-named because it is the shape of a beaver's tail). His eldest son, (Benedict Jr.) had a farm just west of what is now called Mackeral Cove Beach.

That same month, Benedict Arnold and William Coddington bought **Dutch Island**, just north of Beavertail.

On May 22, 1657, Benedict Arnold and John Green acquired **Goat Island** (in the middle of Newport Harbor) and **Coaster's Island**, (now the site of the Naval War College).

(The southern part of Goat Island was lengthened in the 1900's, but the middle and northern parts were always there. The island was an ideal location for fortification, and later, Fort George was built there.)

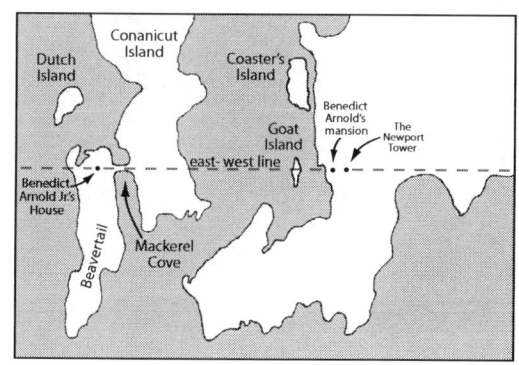

Mapping Benedict's properties, I noticed something peculiar.
They seemed to form an east-west line.

In 1657, a group of men from Newport and the wealthy mint-master John Hull (from Boston) bought a huge chunk of the mainland called the Pettisquamicutt Purchase.

This included all of the present towns of South Kingstown and Narragansett. Benedict was not one of the original group, but a few years later he owned one-seventh interest in the company.

(In 1657, Benedict was President of the Colony, so it appears he kept his name out of the negotiations to make it seem there was no conflict of interest.)

One of his parcels was a large ranch, now a turf farm in **West Kingston,** (near where Route 138 crosses Route 2). Several other parcels border what is now called Point Judith Pond, including all of present day Matunuck and Jerusalem, Harbor Island, and Buttonwood Point.

(Buttonwood is another name for the sycamore tree.)

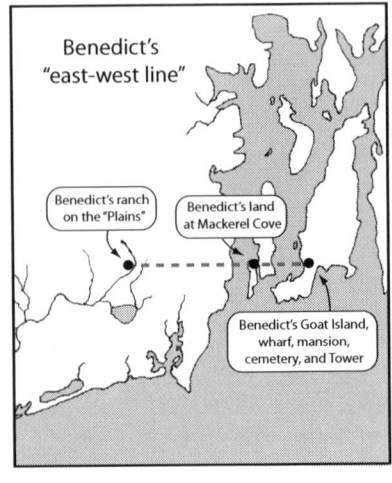

In 1997, archaeologist and researcher Jim Whitall of the Early Sites Society did a preliminary excavation of house foundation located in the woods of North Stonington, Connecticut.

It was a "stone-ender." This is a style of construction unique to early Rhode Island in which one wall of the house is made up of a massive stone chimney.

(Elsewhere in New England colonists primarily built center-chimney houses.)

The tall exterior face of the Chimney

The 6-foot-wide fireplace

The massive hearthstones | Interleafing of stonework in the rear corner of the fire place

Whitall concluded that this might very well be the remains of Benedict Arnold's trading post or garrison. In the 1640's, North Stonington was still within the bounds of the Rhode Island Charter of 1644.

(It was east of the westernmost tributary of the Pawcatuck River.)

Not only would this be a convenient location for trading with the Indians, it would be a perfect location to keep an eye on the western frontier. It is adjacent to the "Narragansett Indian Trail" where the land of the Narragansetts met the land of the Pequots.

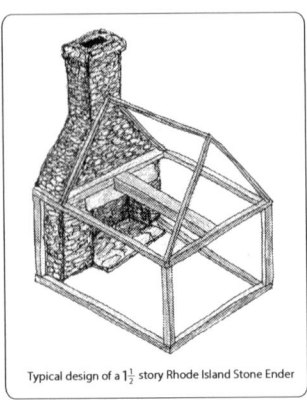
Typical design of a 1½ story Rhode Island Stone Ender

Interestingly, this site was also on what I call "Benedict Arnold's east-west line."

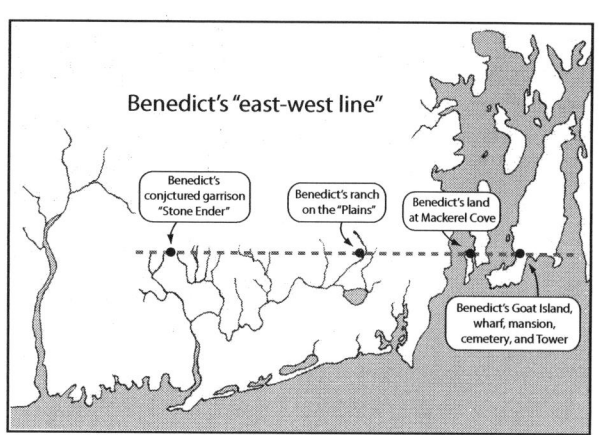

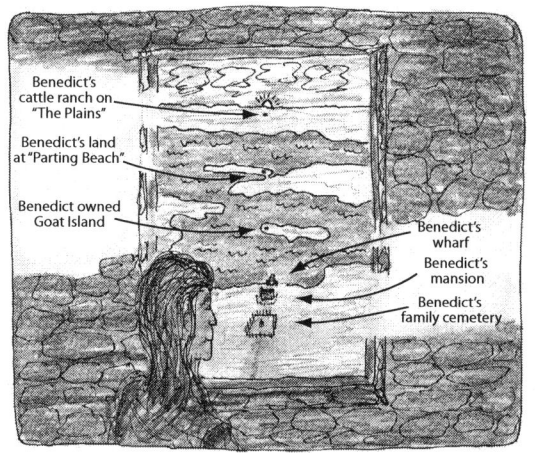

Benedict looking at his properties out the West window of the Tower

To visualize this from a different perspective, here is my conjectured illustration of Benedict looking out the West window of the Tower over all his properties.

If he happened to be looking out on the afternoon of the Spring equinox, he would also see the sun setting due west along his line. This is March 21, the first of Aries.

I'll admit this scenario sounds conjectural, but as a creative historian, I set it forth as a hypothesis. How was I find more corroborating clues?

In 2005, the original 7-page land agreement to purchase a Jamestown Island from the Indians came up for sale at an auction house in New York City. At the last minute, a magnanimous donor purchased the agreement and gave it to the Jamestown Historical Society. The article in the newspaper mentioned the date, March 10, 1657, when 80 colonists including Benedict Arnold and William Coddington signed their names on it.

Something caught my eye about March 10th. The English (including the New Englander colonists) were still using the Julian Calendar at that time. To get the corresponding day in the Gregorian Calendar, you must add 10 days. Thus, the agreement was signed on **March 21, the Spring Equinox. The first of Aries. The day the sun sets over Benedict's properties!**

This certainly helped to support my hypothesis, but if I was right, I knew there were more clues to be found.

Benedict Arnold's Charter Chair of 1663

The first Governor's chair, before restoration

During my research, I noticed an old photo of the "charter chair" that the first Governor, Benedict Arnold, received in 1663. It still existed, but it was in tough shape. The top rail and the back-panel were missing, but the side rails, the seat, and the legs were still intact.

I tracked it down. It was in storage in the basement of the Redwood Library. Cheryl Helms and Lisa Long were kind enough to bring it up into the Harrison Room so I could inspect and photograph it.

The top rail and the back-panel had been replaced, but the two outer side-panels (to which the arms are connected) were both original.

(Judging from the curved arms and the detailing of the base rails, it appeared as though this was originally a "wainscot chair," and the top should have been much fancier than the horizontal piece that was used to repair it.)

The Governor's chair given to Benedict Arnold by the King Charles II in 1663

The inscribed mark on the upper right part of the chair

At the top of the right side-panel, carved deeply into the wood, was a curious design. Three circles, each about two and one-eighth inches in diameter, had been inscribed by carpenter's compass. (It appears as though a scribing compass with two metal tips was used, as the central pivot points of the circles were still visible). One deeply incised straight line cuts diagonally across the three overlapping circles.

The chair had been in various homes of Arnold's descendants over the centuries. One idea was that these marks were made by mischievous children. (There are also some smaller circles inscribed on the inside surface of the chairs arms.) Lisa Long suggested it looked like a "mason's mark" or a "merchant's mark," a trader's symbolic signature.

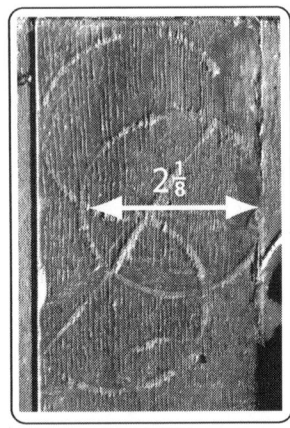

28

I took a close-up photo of the mark. Upon returning home, I tried to duplicate it on a similar piece of hardwood, using a strong carpenter's compass (the kind with two metal points).

It took a lot of pressure and quite a few turns before the wood was sufficiently grooved. This didn't seem like child's play. **This was done by an adult**.

And who would have the temerity to carve a geometric design on the first Governor's throne? **Only the bold Benedict himself!**

Replicating the design on paper using a geometer's compass (the kind with one point and a pencil), I drew 3 conclusions about the design:

Conclusion 1: The person who inscribed this symbol had a basic grasp of geometry.

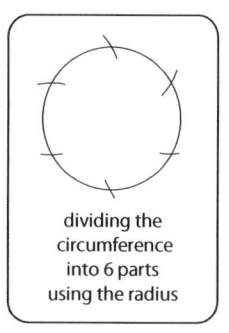

First, the designer knew how to divide the circumference of a circle into 6 equal parts.

Keeping the compass set to the width of the radius, you can "walk around" the circle with a compass in exactly 6 steps.

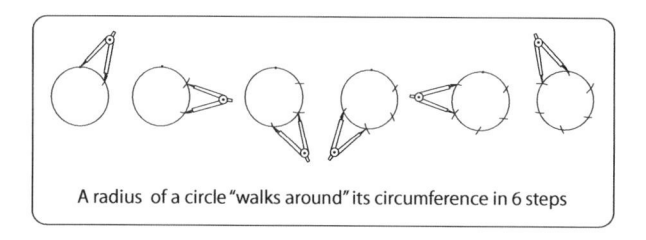

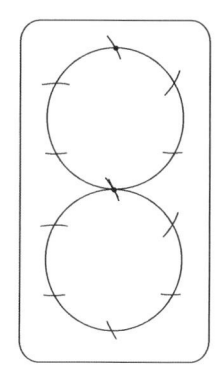

dividing the circumference into 6 parts using the radius

A radius of a circle "walks around" its circumference in 6 steps

The upper and lower circle of the design are tangent to each other.

So let's make another circle, and divide it into 6 parts as well.

Next, let's connect the center points of the two circles and draw a radius out to the upper right point of the lower circle.

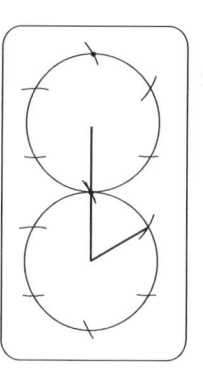

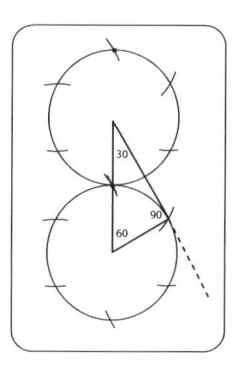

Adding a "tangent line" drawn from the center of the upper circle and tangent to the lower circle, makes a 30-60-90 triangle.

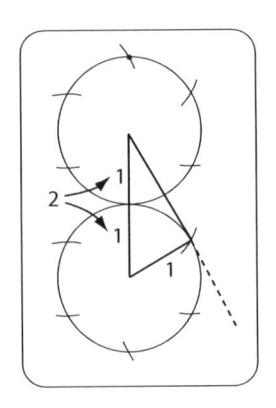

In any 30-60-90 triangle, the sides are in the ratio of 1: 2: √3. The carving does a simple job showing the 1:2 part of this ratio.

(One side of the triangle is a **radius** of the lower circle. And another side of the triangle is the **radius** of the lower circle, **plus** an equal-sized **radius** of the upper circle.)

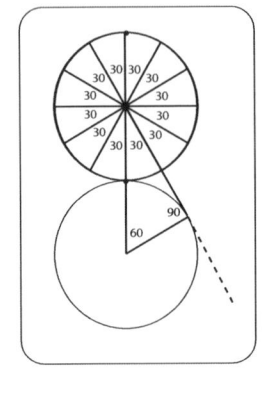

In other words, the upper 30° angle of the triangle represents one twelfth of the upper circle (as 30° x 12 = 360°).

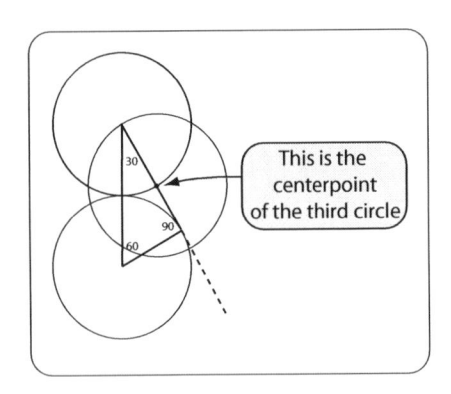

Using the point where the "tangent line" crosses the upper circle as a center-point, let's draw one more same-sized circle.

**Voila!
We have the three circles
in Benedict's mark.**

In the actual mark, the first two circles are not oriented vertically.

The lower one is slightly to the left and even runs off the edge of the sideboard.

(However, the geometric analysis just shown still applies. The **whole** geometric assembly of the 3 circles is simply rotated a few degrees clockwise.)

The 3 circles inscribed on the first Governor's chair

So my first conclusion was that the inscriber of these marks knew his geometry. A simpler approach would be to divide the upper circle into 6 peices of pie and then bisect one of the pieces. However it was done, it's clear that the inscriber knew how to divide a circle into **not just 6 parts, but 12 parts as well.**

Conclusion 2: The hidden Initials

My second conclusion involves the line which slashes diagonally through parts of the circles (adding to the confusion). The line not perfectly straight. It's a little crooked in places, suggesting it was inscribed freehand and not with a straightedge.

But just with a little imagination the straight line can be seen as the vertical stem of a capital letter B. (The rounded parts are made from the two lower circles).

Seen another way, the lower half of it might be seen as the left leg of a capital letter A. The rounded left leg is made from the lowest circle. And the cross-arm is made from the middle circle.

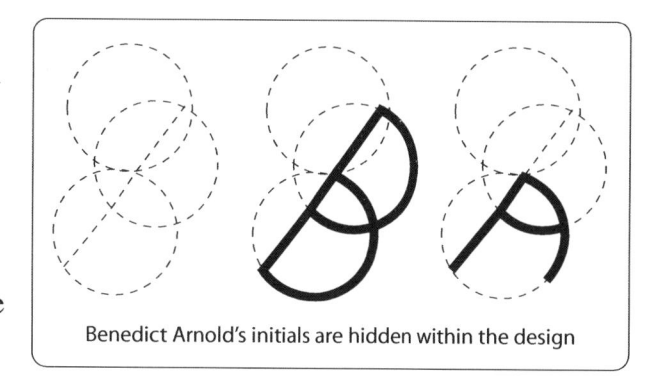

Benedict Arnold's initials are hidden within the design

Benedict Arnold seems to have **cryptically hidden his initials, B.A., in his mark**!

Conclusion 3 The special thing about the diameter of the circles

My third conclusion has to do with the scale of the mark. Benedict could have made had three circles smaller. Smaller circles would have fit into the width of the panel much more comfortably and still would have expressed the same geometric relationships.

Instead, these circles, each about two-and-an-eighth inches in diameter, awkwardly extend beyond the edges of the wooden side-panel. It seems as though the 3 circles were drawn this size on purpose.

[Can you figure out what that reason might be?
I'll explain at the end of the next chapter.]

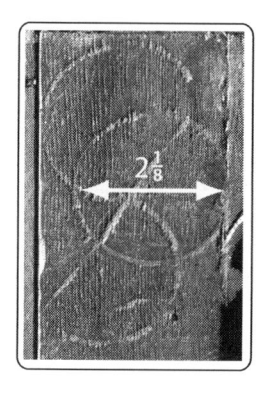

The Arnold Children

The 9 Children of Benedict and Damaris Arnold

Born in Providence:

Benedict II	Feb. 10, 1641	(named after Benedict Arnold I)
Caleb	Dec. 19, 1644	
Josiah	Dec. 22, 1646	
Damaris	Feb. 23, 1648	(named after Damaris Wescott Arnold)
William	Oct. 21, 1651 – Oct. 23, 1651	

Born in Newport:

Penelope	Feb. 10, 1652	
Oliver	July 25, 1655	(probably named after Oliver Cromwell, Lord Protector of England at that time)
Godsgift	Aug. 27, 1658	
Freelove	July 20, 1661	

When Governor Benedict Arnold died, Benedict II, Josiah, and Oliver inherited various parcels on the island of Jamestown.

Caleb inherited the ranch on the Plains of what is now West Kingston.

All of the Governor's daughters (except for his youngest daughter) married influential Newporters.

Benedict's daughter marries well

Benedict and Damaris Arnold's youngest daughter had a name that might have been given to a hippie-child in the psychedelic 1960s: Freelove.

She was 16 when her father died, and 17 when her mother died. In days of primogeniture, the eldest son usually inherited the most of the estate. But Benedict gave his mansion, the Tower, the wharves, and the surrounding farmland to his young Freelove, apparently in hope that she would be able to attract a good husband. And indeed she did. She married the Harvard educated, Edward Pelham, one of the few men in New England with Royal peerage. The Pelham bloodline goes back through families like the Wests, the Knollys, the Carys, the Spencers (Lady Diana was a Spencer), and all the way back to King Henry III in the 1200s.

Edward Pelham's father, Herbert Pelham, had been the Treasurer of Harvard College in 1643. In 1646, Herbert was chosen as one of the two Massachusetts Bay Commissioners of the United Colonies. (In this position he worked with Benedict Arnold, the interpreter for the peace treaties with the Narragansetts.)

Around 1647, Herbert returned to England to help "attend to the service of the Countrie of England" in the fermenting Civil War. In 1654, he represented Essex in Cromwell's Puritan Parliament. (Colket 3, p.142)

Edward and Freelove had a son named Edward (Jr.).

Edward Jr.'s Will of 1740 refers to the tower as "an Old Stone Mill."(Means, P. 26) If Governor Benedict Arnold had built around 1660, the mill would only be 80 years old. Would Edward Jr. have referred to it as "old" if it was still in use as a windmill? Why wouldn't he just have called it the "Stone Mill?" Did he also know some "family secret" about the Tower?

Edward Pelham (Jr.), had two daughters, **Hermoine and Elizabeth**. Hermoine (a name which is the female form of Hermes) married John Bannister and inherited Benedict's Governor's mansion and the Tower.

Elizabeth married a dashing young merchant who it sailed into Newport one day–**Peter Harrison**. Harrison had been tutored in architecture by an English Lord and had traveled all across Europe studying classical buildings.

Peter Harrison the "First American Architect"

Biographer Carl Bridenbaugh calls Peter Harrison, the "First American Architect." Among Harrison's many works are the King's Chapel in Boston, and the Touro Synagogue, the Redwood Library, and the Brick Market Building in Newport.

Certain clues in the proportions of the Redwood Library floor plan lead me to suspect that Peter Harrison knew about the astronomical alignments in the Tower.

For example, the 30-60-90 triangle appears to be the starting point of Harrison's floor plan.

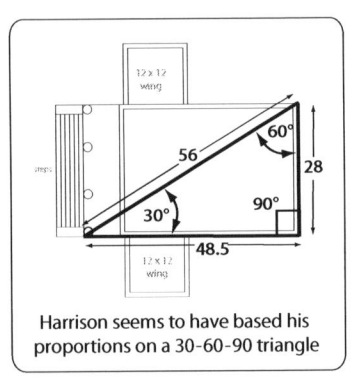

Harrison seems to have based his proportions on a 30-60-90 triangle

32

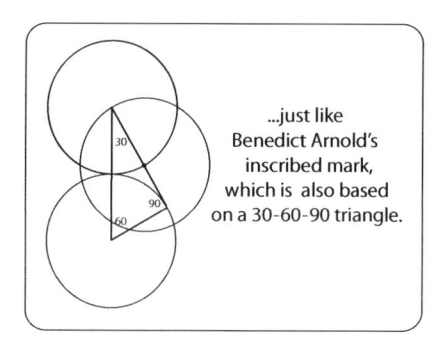

...just like Benedict Arnold's inscribed mark, which is also based on a 30-60-90 triangle.

This was the same geometric shape that Benedict Arnold used for for the basis of his inscribed mark on his Governor's chair.

It seemed like Arnold and Harrison were on the same wavelength, but this was hardly proof that Harrison knew what Benedict knew about the Tower.

The Redwood Library is right around the corner from the Tower. But you can't see one from the other because of more recently constructed buildings on Mill Street and Bellevue Avenue.

However, I recalled being able to see the four prominent pillars of the Redwood Library while measuring the top rim of the Tower.

The Redwood Library is still visible from the top of the Newport Tower

I found that the compass bearing from the Tower to the Redwood was around 58°. This is the angle of the Summer Solstice Sunrise! (If you are looking northeast from the Tower at dawn on June 21, the sun will rise right behind the Redwood Library.)

It seemed likely that Peter Harrison in the other key members of the 1730 Philosophical Society who started the Redwood Library were savvy to this alignment. Perhaps these distinguished scholars (mostly Anglicans, but some Jews and Quakers) also knew there was something special about the Tower.

Confirming this alignment on a US geological survey map, I noticed something else. From the Tower, the Trinity Church was at 302° or (or 58° west of north). This is the angle of the Summer Solstice Sunset. Houses currently block the view from the Tower to the church. But from the Tower, on June 21 the sun will touch the horizon line directly behind the Trinity Church.

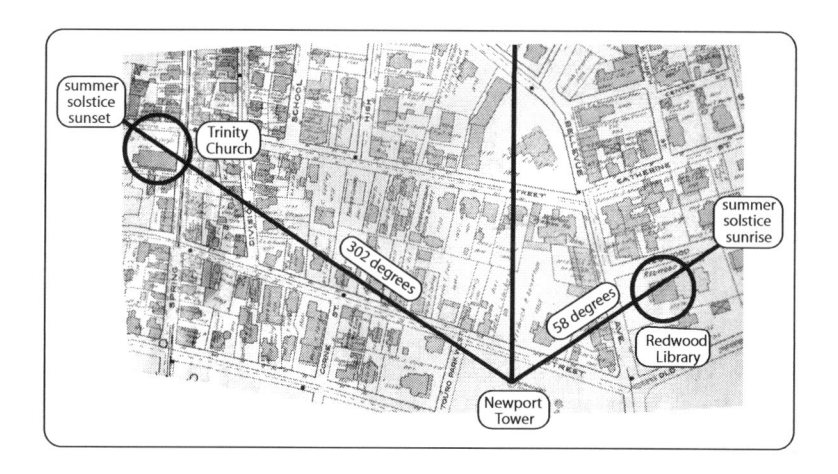

I double checked these alignments on an aerial photo of Newport.
Again they seemed right on.

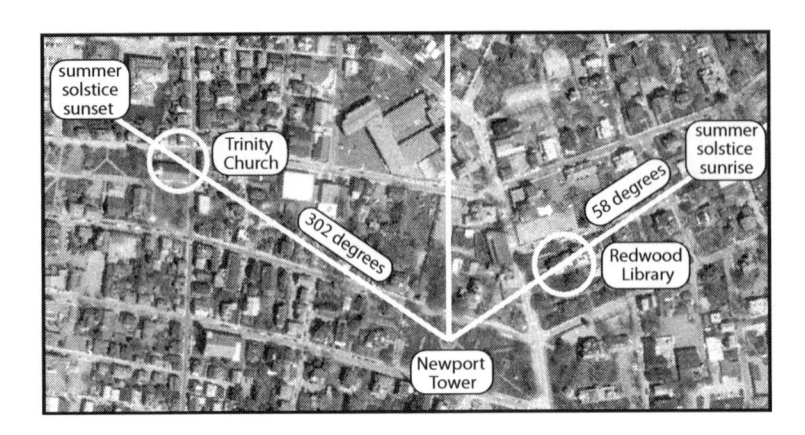

Peter Harrison had been a parishioner at Trinity Church, and had helped fund the 1762 expansion, (this is why it is so close to the sidewalk on Spring Street). However, he wasn't even in Newport when the church was constructed in 1726.

Besides, there was an earlier Trinity Church which it stood just to the north of the present one (where the part of the church graveyard and Church Street are now). Being so close, this earlier church would also have been on that summer-solstice-sunset line!

The Anglican congregation had begun to gather in 1698 and the early, smaller church was built in 1700.

From Benedict Arnold's death in 1678 to 1698 is only 20 years. It appeared to me a whole privileged group of Newport residents might have been aware that the Tower had certain astronomical alignments.

Benedict Arnold: prime suspect. But was he unqualified?

As I proceeded in my detective work, it still seemed like Benedict was the prime suspect. But something didn't ring true. Sure, Benedict knew geometry and might have been able to figure out how to Tower functioned, but he just didn't seem capable being able to conceive of such an ingenious structure.

Benedict Arnold probably knew Latin and Greek. These would have been a standard part of his education back in Somerset, England around 1630. I suggest that Benedict picked up the native Algonquin tongue so speedily because he had previous experience in learning languages. He was one of the few New England colonists who owned a watch, so he might have been fascinated with time. (On the other hand, money can buy watches.)

It seemed to me that Tower was designed by a master: someone who thoroughly understood astronomy, optics, horometry (timekeeping), and architecture. Someone who knew these subjects so well, he could playfully integrate them into a soaring sculpture of stone-and-mortar. Someone who knew that his creative philosophy would forever be an integral part of the Tower– locked in for centuries–available for anyone to decode –yet invisible to most. Someone who could put something right in front of your eyes, yet still make it invisible.

No, I don't think the brash, brazen, (type A–personality) Benedict Arnold could have designed such a Tower. He was a salesman and skilled negotiator, not an architect. But it certainly seemed that he knew who did design it. And he used his political and financial power (and his penchant for shading the truth) to conceal his knowledge of the Tower, seemingly to protect it.

Why would he do such a thing? What was he hiding?

Remember, in his will Benedict calls it "my Stone–built Wind–mill'n." He doesn't say he built it—only that he owned it.

At the John Carter Brown Library in Providence, I was able to inspect Benedict's original will of 1677. I noticed that there were **five asterisks** which appeared to be surrounding the reference to the "my Stone-built Wind-Mill'n." These asterisks did not refer to anything in the margin. They follow a seemingly random group of words or phrases. And these five are the only asterisks in his entire 12-page will.

Was this Benedict way of indicating he is shading the truth a bit? (Sort of like* crossing your fingers* behind your back* when you tell* a harmless little white lie*.)

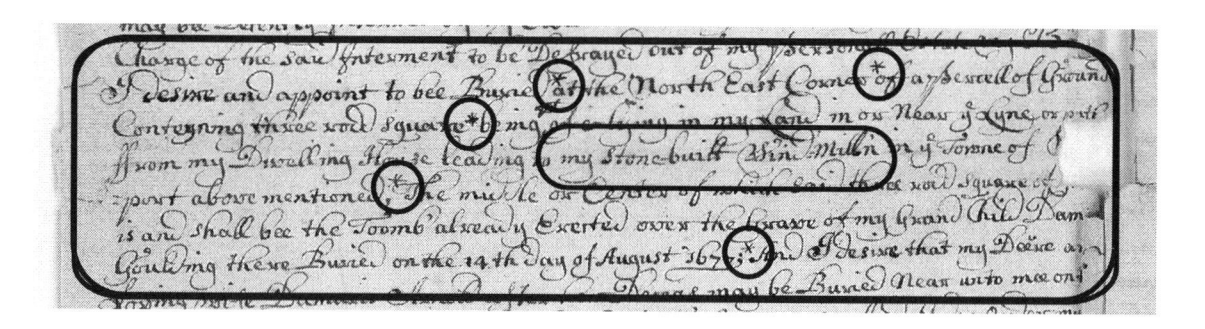

What happened to this special knowledge about the Tower?

Basically, the American Revolution wiped the slate clean.

When Peter Harrison's brother was called back to England, Peter moved to Connecticut to assume his brother's position as tax collector for New Haven. Unfair taxation is what sparked the American Revolution. The Burning of the Gaspee. The Boston Tea Party. Being a tax collector was risky business, but Harrison remained loyal to the Crown.

Just before the revolution, all the Loyalists were chased out of Newport. Harrison was about to be chased out of New Haven, when suddenly he died from natural causes. But this didn't stop an angry mob from burning his house and his archive of architectural drawings. Americans were past their boiling point.

England got the message, but they were not happy with their petulant offspring in America. British forces attacked and captured Newport. Many of the locals fled the island. During their three-year stay in Newport, the British took over the finest houses in town and tore down others to use for firewood. They trashed the place.

Before retreating from Newport, the British Army ignited the gunpowder they had been storing in the Tower

But after a severe trouncing in the Battle of Rhode Island, the British were forced to leave town in a hurry. They had been storing their gunpowder in the Tower, and so the powder would not be confiscated by the American forces, they ignited it. This probably blew the top off the Tower and caused a fire, burning the wooden floors and beams.

(Since that time, the remaining top has been re-pointed to make it level, and a cap of cement protects the upper rim.)

The British also absconded with the early records of Newport, and the ship they left town on was later sunk by American forces in Long Island Sound. More knowledge of the Tower was lost.

Newport after the American Revolution

For decades after the American Revolution, Newport's prosperity declined. Almost all the wealthy Anglicans and Jews had left town, never to return. Maritime trade diminished. Americans had no interest in "things English" like the Tower.

In the 1800's, goods started to be transported via roads and railroads instead of ships, but there were no bridges connecting Aquidneck Island to the mainland. Providence's economy boomed, while Newport's economy dwindled. Furthermore, there was no waterpower on Aquidneck Island to power the new factories.

It wasn't until the late 1800s when super-rich businessmen from New York and Philadelphia started building their "cottages" (read as huge mansions) on Bellevue Avenue that Newport's star started to shine brightly again. Tourists came from all around to see this antique Tower. But the memory of who built it, and why, was long gone.

Was the Tower in Newport meant to be like the "Tower of the of the Winds" in Athens?

The Tower of the Winds still stands in Athens, Greece

It was beginning to seem like the Newport Tower was once a symbolic "city-center," a place that also kept track of time for the community. The Tower of the Winds, in the Plaka district of Athens, is a octagonal building made from white marble. It was built around 50 BC as a horologium, a building that kept track of time.

Metal gnomons project from the outer walls with sundial marks below them. In the interior was a clepsydra or water clock. The peak was surmounted with a weathervane that pointed to bas-relief sculptures of the 8 main dieties of the winds.

Writing about the orientations of streets in a new city, the Roman architect Vitruvius describes the Tower of the Winds. He also writes that temples should be built "on the highest point commanding a view of the greater part of the city." Was the builder of the Tower aware of this ancient tradition of putting a grand timekeeping device in a city-center? (Vitruvius, *Book 1*, Chapters 4 and 6)

Two Words Provide an Illuminating Clue

One day, while giving tour of the Tower, Professor Penhallow offhandedly remarked, "That first floor room was probably a **camera obscura**."
I was taken aback. What did he mean?

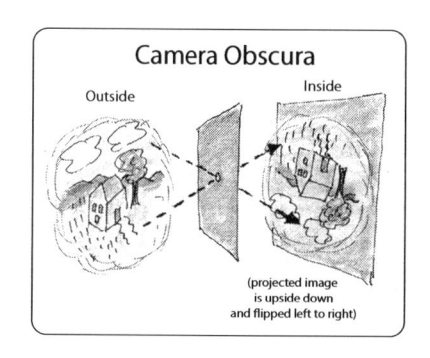

A camera obscura is simply a dark room with one small hole in the wall. Magically, the image of what's outside appears upside-down and reversed left-to-right on the interior wall. (In Latin, *camera* means "room" and *obscura* means "dark.")

As a professional photographer, I had used a camera obscura every day. A camera is a mini-camera obscura. And an eye is even smaller camera obscura.

Perplexed, I asked the retired astronomy professor to elaborate, "Do you mean that that Tower acted like some kind of a movie theater?"

He replied, "Centuries ago, people kept track of time by following the movement of the solar disc. If the scene outside a camera obscura includes the sun, then inside you will see the circular image of the sun moving slowly across the floor or wall. It's like an inside-out sundial that can be used to tell time."

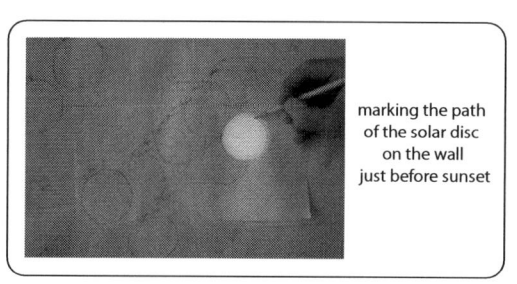

marking the path of the solar disc on the wall just before sunset

A week later, at the end of a long day photographing, I noticed a spot of yellowish-orange light on the wall of my darkened studio.

It was a perfect circle, about 2 1/8 inches in diameter.

My studio was acting as a large camera obscura room and this circle was the image of the sun in the projected scene.

As the circle of light slowly moved upwards on the wall, every minute I drew a circle around its perimeter. After a while, it was only three quarters of the circle. Then it was half-circle. Then just a pinpoint of light. Then it vanished. Outside the west-facing window opposite the wall, the sun had just set, leaving the soft glow of twilight.

Several days later, the path of the solar disc (just before sunset) had shifted a bit to the right.

I traced the path of solar disc
a week later and found that it
had shifted shifted dramatically.

So for the next year, I marked
the ever-changing position of
the solar disc (just before sunset.)

On the spring and fall equinoxes,
the solar disc set in the kitchenette.

At the summer solstice it was
about 25 feet to the right.

At the winter solstice it was
about 25 feet to the left.

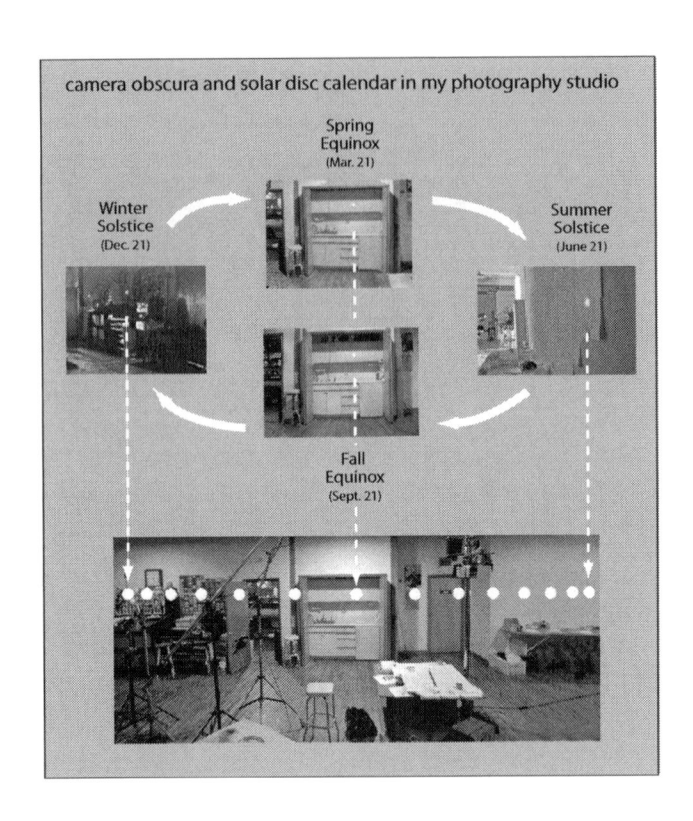

camera obscura and solar disc calendar in my photography studio

Spring Equinox (Mar. 21)
Winter Solstice (Dec. 21)
Summer Solstice (June 21)
Fall Equinox (Sept. 21)

I calculated all the angles of my
"solar disc-at-sunset calendar room."

Then I transferred that data to
the interior of the Tower. (This overhead
view even looks like an eyeball.)
Note that the horizontal line marks the
equinoxes.

If the West window of the Tower
was all blocked up except for one small
hole, the solar disc would be projected
just to the right of the fireplace.

I couldn't help but think: Why
didn't the builders arrange things so it set
right in the middle of the fireplace? That
would have been a lot cooler.

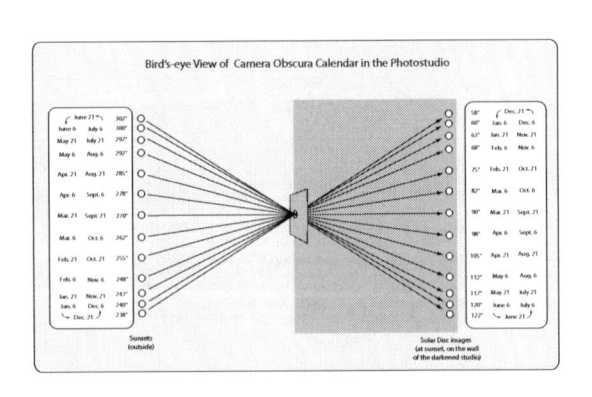

Bird's-eye View of Camera Obscura Calendar in the Photostudio

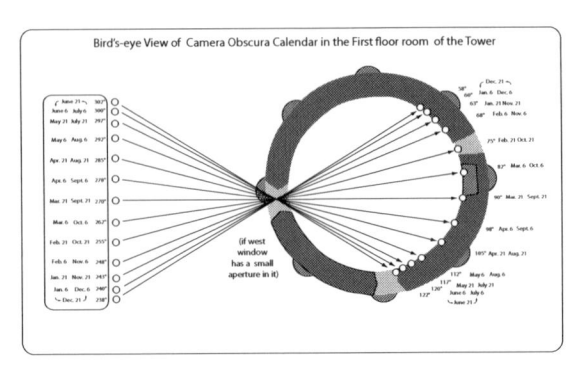

Bird's-eye View of Camera Obscura Calendar in the First floor room of the Tower

38

In this digital simulation, the cenral circle, just to the right of the fireplace, is where the solar disc would be just before sunset on both the spring and fall equinoxes.
(The outermost circles represent the solstices.)

Digital simulation of the solar disc at sunset at various times of the year.

It wasn't feasible to re-create a camera obscura in the Tower. The floors and roof are long gone. And besides, houses now block the Tower's view of the harbor..

So my photo assistant, John Tavares, and I scouted for a location that had a view similar to the one the Tower once had.

We spotted a small room at the top of old fire station tower on lower Mill Street. The owners, a marketing company, kindly let us set up a long roll of seamless paper and block up the window (except for one small hole).

The projected image was astounding.
You could see all the way from the Newport/Pell Bridge to Fort Adams.
Cars were moving along America's Cup Avenue.
Boats cruised through the harbor.

Amid the blue sky and clouds, the solar disk was quite bright. So we made the aperture smaller, to make the edges of the solar disc sharper.

We noticed another spot that was just as bright as the sun. It wasn't round, but it was shimmering like a disco mirror-ball. Do you know what was creating that bright spot?

It was the reflection of the sun off the choppy waters of Newport Harbor.

Ironically, the water looked like it was **on fire**.

Looking west over water in the late afternoon, this "fiery water" can be seen as scattered pinpoints of light. But about a half an hour before sunset, the reflection is so intense, you can't even look at it – not even with sunglasses. Then, as the sun approaches the horizon (and it must pass through more of the lower atmosphere) it dims down considerably, and thus the brightness of the "fiery water" reflection also slowly dies down.

Back around 1660, the scientist Robert Boyle was fascinated by this visual phenomenon:

> "In a darkened room, I used a convex lens to project the image of a river (about a quarter of a mile away) which is being shined upon by the sun.
>
> Observing the projected image from about 8 feet away, the river appeared like a white object.
>
> But observing it up close, I could see that this whiteness came from innumerable white reflections made from the waves on the water's surface.
>
> It looked like millions of shining fish scales, which sparkled as the Sun, Wind, and River changed."
>
> (My transliteration of Robert Boyle's observations from around 1660.)

The Equinox alignment

Professor Penhallow had calculated that on the equinox a patch of light coming through the West window would set just to the right of the fireplace. This time lapse sequence shows the patch of light moving slowly up and to the right.

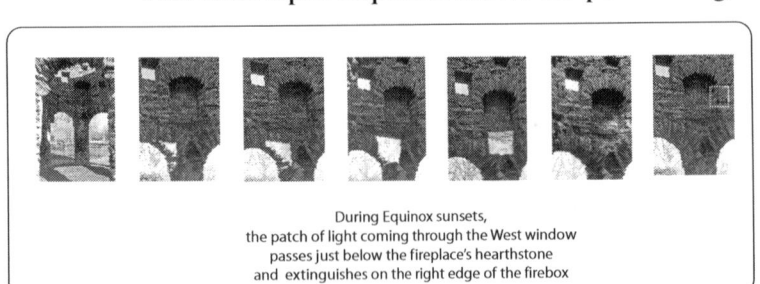

During Equinox sunsets, the patch of light coming through the West window passes just below the fireplace's hearthstone and extinguishes on the right edge of the firebox

At one point the patch is directly below the fireplace. But then the patch fades because it is blocked by the houses at the west end of the park.

But if the houses weren't there, at the moment of sunset, the patch would be **just to the right of the fireplace**.

40

If the West window was all blocked up except for one small hole, this is the path the resulting solar disc would take on the late afternoon of the equinox.

Just as Penhallow calculated, at sunset it would be just to the right of the fireplace.

But a half hour before sunset (at 5:15), it would be just below the hearthstone of the fireplace.

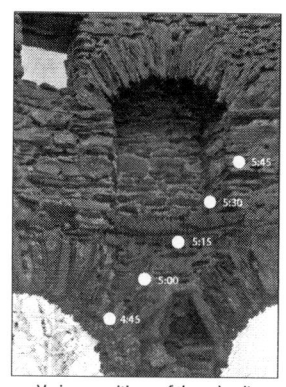

Various positions of the solar disc during the Equinox sunset

In Photoshop, I have digitally blocked out the West window (except for one hole), and drew in where the solar disc would a half hour before sunset.

If the West window was blocked up, except for a small hole, during the Equinox sunset a small solar disc would creep up the eastern interior wall

Suddenly I realized how all these puzzle pieces fit together!
(Drumroll, please.)

If the solar disc was below the fireplace...

... that means the firebox would be ablaze with Fiery Water!

Sun and Fiery Water image superimposed on fireplace

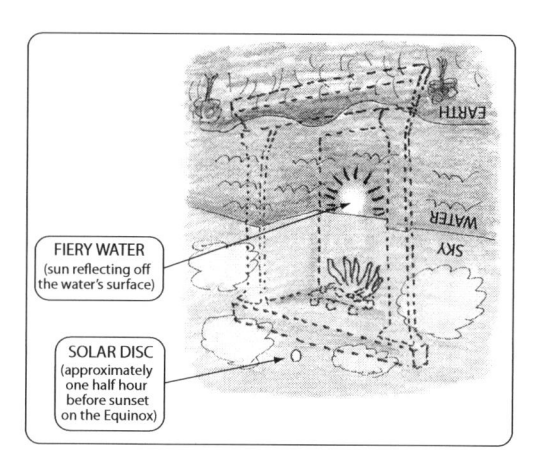

FIERY WATER (sun reflecting off the water's surface)

SOLAR DISC (approximately one half hour before sunset on the Equinox)

This illustration shows the whole upside-down image of the sky, earth, and bay–and the fiery water.

Imagine someone starting up an actual fire at this moment to celebrate this first day of Spring, the day the sun sets precisely due west.

Having the "fiery water" *in* the fireplace on the Equinox was a lot more exciting than just having the solar disc set to the right of the fireplace.

Zodiacally speaking, the Spring Equinox, March 21, is the beginning of the sign of Aries, commonly called the '**first of Aries**.' And in astrology, **Aries is a Fire sign**!

(Aries is one of the three Fire signs, along with Leo and Sagittarius).

Over the years, many cultures have celebrated the Spring Equinox. In fact, some of the ancients even felt the whole world **began** on the "first of Aries."

(I'm not suggesting you have to believe in astrology to consider this noteworthy. What's key is that most Medieaval and Renaissance philosophers studied astrology.)

The clue in the size of the solar disc

The size of the image in a camera obscura varies depending upon the distance from the aperture hole to the projection wall. Thus, the size of the solar disc (the image of his sun), varies depending on this distance.

If the projection wall is about 4 feet from the hole, the solar disc is only about 1/2 inch in diameter. If the projection wall is 8 feet from the hole, the solar disc is about 1 inch in diameter.

In the first floor room of the Tower, the distance between the West window (where the aperture hole would be) and the eastern interior wall (where the projected image would be) is 18 1/2 feet. And at this distance, the size of the solar disc would be about 2 1/8 inches in diameter.

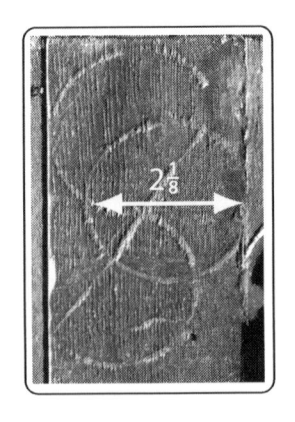

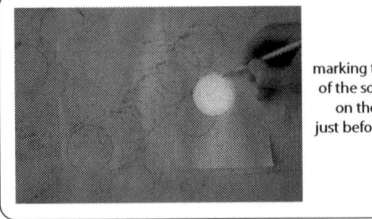

Hey! That's a diameter of each of the three circles in Benedict Arnold's symbol.

marking the path of the solar disc on the wall just before sunset

[How did this happen to occur to me? Well, my photo studio was also about 18 1/2 feet wide, so I had been observing 2 1/8 diameter solar discs for quite a while.]

It seemed to me that Benedict Arnold knew that the first floor room functioned as a solar-disc-at-sunset calendar room.

Here is my conjectured illustration of what might have transpired during an equinox sunset in the mid 1600's when Benedict owned the Tower.

Could it be that on the equinox Benedict actually situated the chair facing the West window, with his back to the fireplace? The solar disc might have actually projected onto his symbol. Perhaps he even shared his knowledge with his fellow leaders.

My conjectured illustration of Governor Benedict Arnold and fellow leaders watching the solar disc on the Governor's chair during an equinox sunset.

Astronomical alignments of the **Sun, Moon, and Stars**.
"**Fiery water**" in the **fireplace**, on the equinox, the day the "**Fire sign**" of Aries begins ?
Could Benedict Arnold have devised such a clever piece of architecture?

For more clues, I decided study the history of the camera obscura and the solar disc calendar room.

THE HISTORY OF THE CAMERA OBSCURA

The history of the camera obscura goes hand-in-hand with the history of ideas about **vision**. The Greeks debated whether vision resulted from rays emanating from the eye or rays emanating from the object seen.

Aristole couldn't figure out why sunlight, passing through a square aperture, made a round circle of light. (The circle of light he saw was the solar disc, the image of the sun, and the sun is round.)

Around 875 AD, a monk named Helperic, living in a monastery in Auxerre, France, described how to make a camera-obscura solar-disc-at-sunrise calendar-room:

"note each day at sunrise where sunbeams, passing through an aperture, fall on the western wall of a room."
(McCluskey, *Astronomies and Cultures in Early Medieval Europe*, p. 151)

Helperic was doing the same thing at **sunrise** that I did in my photography studio at **sunset**. (Only about 1140 years earlier.)

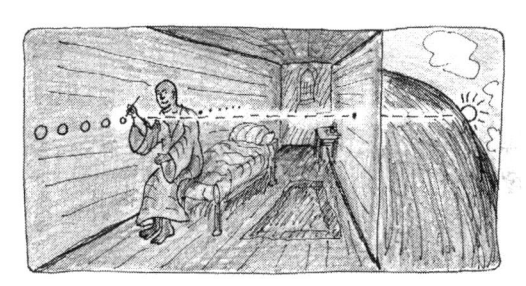

Helperic marks the position of the solar disc at sunrise

Around 1000 AD, the great Arab scientist Alhazen used a camera obscura room to demonstrate that light travels in a straight line.

When he extinguished the fifth candle in one room, the first candle in the other room would go out.

43

In the 1200's, English scientists like Robert Grossteste, Roger Bacon, and John Peckham wrote about camera obscuras. Arnold of Villanova would amuse his friends and patrons by darkening a room and having actors perform a play outside, which was projected on a translucent screen inside. To simulate a hunting scene, he put actors in animal costumes. To make a thunderstorm the crew banged on metal barrels. It was a medieval movie theatre, With Sensurround sound.

During the Renaissance, the camera obscura was described in detail by many Italian scholars like Cornelius Agrippa, Cesare Cesariano, Giovanni Battista Della Porta, and Danielo Barbaro. Girolamo Cardano even recommends using a lens to make the image sharper.

Leonardo da Vinci succinctly describes the camera obscura:

**"I say that if the front of a building – or any open piazza or field –
which is illuminated by the sun has a dwelling opposite to it, and if,
in the front which does not face the sun, you make a small round hole,
all the illuminated objects will project their images through that hole
and be visible inside the dwelling on the opposite wall which may
be made white; and there, in fact, they will be upside down."**

Leonardo adds, **"and so it is with the pupil."**
He even knew the eye was a mini-camera obscura.

(da Vinci, in J. P. Richter, 1970, Vol I, p. 44, no. 70, in Mary Sayer Hammond, p. 124-5)

Not only was the camera obscura "cutting edge" technology in both science and art, it served as a bridge between the two. The camera obscura was used to explain the art of perspective. In fact the name for the study of optics was called *Perspectiva* (from the Latin word *perspicio* meaning "to look at").

Northern European scholars were also well aware of the camera obscura. In the Netherlands, Regnier Gemma Frisius drew the first illustration of a camera obscura. He used it to view an eclipse of the sun in 1544. One of Gemma Frisius' students was the Elizabethan polymath John Dee.

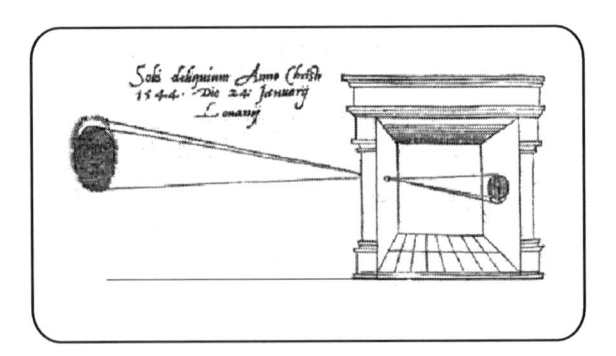

In his book *Brief Lives*, English biographer John Aubrey reports that John Dee had a camera obscura room in his house in Morklake, just west of London:

**"Old Goodwife Faldo (a Native of Mortlake in Surrey) did know Dr. Dee
and told me that he did entertain the Polonian [Polish] Ambassador at
his house in Mortlake and died not long after; and that he showed
the Eclipse with a darke Room to the said Ambassador."**

In the 1700s, artists like Vermeer (in Delft) and Canaletto (in Venice) used a small camera obscura-in-a-box as an to drawing.

a camera obscura-in-a-box used as a drawing aid

In the 1800s, Louis Daguerre, W.H. Fox Talbot, and Nicephore Niepce inserted light-sensitive plates and invented photography.

Nicéphore Niépce used a camera obscura and a sensitized plate to make the first photograph

In 1900, George Eastman introduced the famous Brownie Box Camera.

George Eastman's Kodak "Brownie" box camera

Through the century companies like Leica, Canon, Nikon and Polaroid made huge advances in camera technology.

modern cameras are simply camera obscuras

And now we take pictures with smart phones. But even a smart phone has a miniature camera obscura in it. All cameras are essentially "dark rooms" with one small hole.

(After camera obscuras and photography came movie cameras, then television, and now computers. Two of the scholars who have followed this important thread of optical science, are Friedrich Kittler in "Optical Media" and Anne Freidburg in "The Virtual Window: From Alberti to Microsoft

even cell phone cameras are camera obscuras.

45

The long history of the camera obscura provides a subtle clue about who might have built the Tower. If you examine the data, it's apparent there was a huge spike of interest in camera obscuras during the Renaissance.

There's another factor to consider. The Italians were pretty outspoken about describing this natural behavior of light. But Northern Europe and England were still undergoing religious upheavals, spreading a dark cloud of paranoia.

Camera obscuras could be risky business. If word got out you were sitting in a dark room watching upside-down horses-carts driving by, birds flying, and even inverted miniature people walking along the interior walls of your darkened house, you might be branded as a conjurer or magician and quite possibly find your life terminated in an abrupt and unpleasant fashion.

"The Sun in the Church"
The camera obscura is used to keep track of time

The Italians used the camera obscura in another important way. As J. L. Hielbron explains in his book *The Sun in the Church: Cathedrals as Solar Observatories*, astronomers would place a pinhole high up in the dome of a church and follow the progress of the solar disc on the floor.

In 1472, Paolo Toscanelli placed a pinhole in the Duomo in Florence.

Toscanelli's pinhole and solstice mark inside the Duomo in Florence

overhead view of Toscanelli's pinhole and solstice mark

Ignazio Danti made a "meridiana line" (a bronze north-south line embedded in the floor) on the floor of the Basilica of San Petronio in Bologna, and another in a small tower in the Vatican. Both of these can still be seen today.

The meridiana line in the Basilica of San Petronio, Bologla, Italy

Danti also installed one in the Santa Maria Novella Church in Florence.

He marked where the solar disc crossed the meridiana line (or noon line) every day for a year.

By counting the number of days between the equinoxes and the solstices, he (along with Christopher Clavius and others) convinced Pope Gregory that the Julian Calendar was out-of-sync from the sun by 10 days, leading to the **Gregorian Calendar Reform of 1582**.

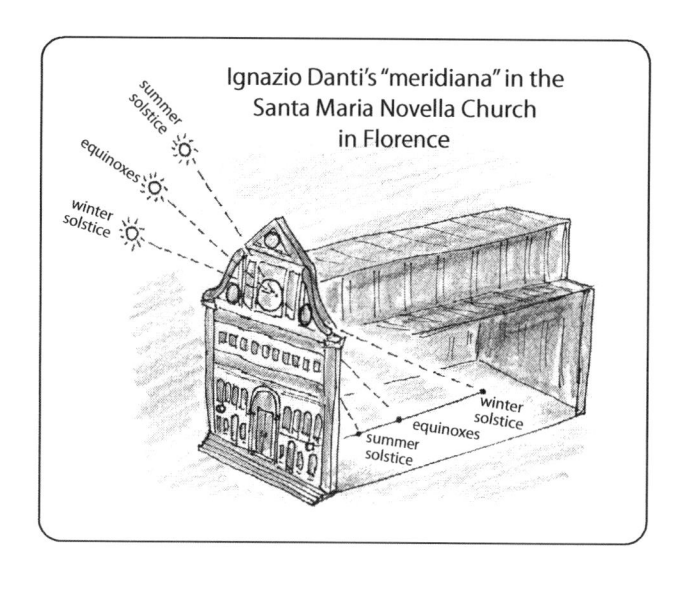

Ignazio Danti's "meridiana" in the Santa Maria Novella Church in Florence

Ignazio Danti studying the solar disc as it crosses the meridiana line

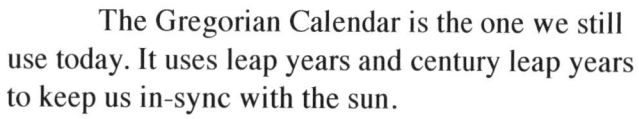

The Gregorian Calendar is the one we still use today. It uses leap years and century leap years to keep us in-sync with the sun.

The Julian calendar had been instituted by Julius Caesar in 45 BC. Every 128 years it became one more day out-of-sync with the sun, so by the 1500s, it was 10 days off.

Another beautiful noon-line that still can be still see today is Bianchinis' 1703 meridiana in Santa Maria Angeli in central Rome. Bianchini called it a "heliometer," glorifying it as,

> **"an image of the heavens serving as a floor in the house of God."**

[heliometer means "sun measurer"]

Aperture

Meridiana Line

47

The Art of Creative Thinking

If I was going to crack the puzzle of the Tower, I had to think creatively. So I studied the art of creativity. Like any other art, science, or sport, the art of creativity can be learned with practice.

I read books like *How To Think Like Leonardo da Vinci: Seven Steps to Genius Every Day*, by Michael J. Geib; *Thinkertoys: a Handbook of Creative Thinking Techniques*, by Michael Michalko; and *A Whack on the Side of the Head*, by Roger von Oech.

According to John Briggs, author of *Fire in the Crucible: Understanding the Process of Creative Genius*, creative people achieve breakthroughs by considering opposing viewpoints simultaneously.

Briggs gives several examples. Expressionist sculptor Louise Nevelson called herself and "architect of shadow" as well as an "architect of light." Perfume is often made of "such contrary substances as skunk oil and flowers."

Briggs sites Alan Rothenberg's comment that Mona Lisa's smile has been described as both "both good and wicked," and as well as both "compassionate and cruel." (Briggs, pp. 183, 112, 113)

Creative thinkers don't "flip from one opposite to the other," nor do they "reconcile" the opposites to make a "synthesis." Instead they have the ability to view both of the opposites at the same time. They can accept that the paradox is unresolvable, yet still express both sides in the same breath.

Rothenberg calls this "janusian" thinking, after the Roman god Janus who could observe all comings and goings. His image was frequently carved on gate posts and doorways.

Janus was also the god of "endings and beginnings." They named the month of January after him, as he looks backwards to the old year and forward to the new one.

A Roman coin with the two faces of Janus

from Oscar Seyffert's 1899 Dictionary of Classical Antiquities

The physicist **David Bohm** saw "omnivalence" as the "space between opposites" : "If you say north and south, then there's a whole range in between. Therefore you have to tremendously enrich the field to a new level in order to resolve the opposites." He continues, "if you hold these opposites together, then you must suspend thought and your mind must move to a new level. The suspension of thought allows intelligence beyond thought to act. Then you can create a new form." (Briggs' interview with Bohm, in Briggs, p.114-115)

I was particularly inspired by Tom Monahan's book, *The Do-It-Yourself Lobotomy: Open Your Mind to Greater Creative Thinking*. Having been the creative director in a highly successful Providence ad agency, Tom is able to provide practical tools for the job of creative thinking.

Tom's calls one of his tools,
"180 degree thinking: a tnereffid way to ideate."

tnereffid

"To break free of predictable patterns and find new ideas, look in a different place: Direct your thought process in the exact opposite direction of where conventional wisdom would suggest you go.
If conventional wisdom says **soft**, think **hard**.
If conventional wisdom says **warm**, think **cold**."

(The word "**tnereffid**" is "**different**," spelled backwards.)

Tom recommends "**Ask a better question**," to trigger your own curiosity. "Curiosity means putting yourself in the place you don't know." (So with regards to the Tower, we might ask, "Which one of the existing suspects is most likely to have built it?" But, a better question might be, "Who else might have built the Tower?)

Tom also advises: "**Ask the question early**." This gets your imagination perking so the subconscious mind can work on the problem. "At a conscious rate we can only process 120–130 bits of data every second, but on a subconscious or superconscious level, we can process billions of bits of data.

Quick tips on creative research

Like Leonardo, **take notes**. Write down what comes into your mind. And not just words– a **quick sketch** can express things words cannot. Think visually.

Computer search engines are great tools for creative research. Nowadays, the texts of many books can be found online. But to really squeeze the wisdom of the book, I recommend **buying a used paperback so you can "customize" it**. Write notes in the margin. Make bright red asterisks. Use a yellow marker when you read a passage that excites you.

If you find a hot clue, or if one particular sentence "says it all," circle it with a blue pen. Then, on the inside back cover of the book, jot down the page number and few key words describing the clue. Several months later, when you want to refer back to that special clue, you'll find this personalized index super-handy.

Some academic books are unavailable or too expensive to buy online. But you can go to a good library and photocopy the full book for about 10 to 20 dollars. (This is legal if it's for your own reference purposes.) Put the copies in a three-ring binder and you have your own copy, free to "customize" with pencil and yellow marker.

But there's another great reason for going to the library. Browsing. When you locate the book you are looking for, inspect the books immediately to its left and right. They are all in the same category and you'll be shocked by the new, pertinent information you will discover.

As Louis Pastuer wrote: "Chance favors the prepared mind"

When you creatively focus on the problem for a while, something else very special happens:
Serendipity. Good fortune. A happy accident. Lady Luck.

I was in the Newport Historical Society library searching for clues about Governor Benedict Arnold. The head librarian went downstairs to retrieve a manuscript from the vault. He said was I was free to browse the stacks while I waited.

In the local history section, I noticed a book called *Newport Begins* by Lloyd Robson. The book was a the Historical Society's compilation of numerous articles Robson had written for the *Newport History Journal* in 1964 and 1965. I had not come across it in other libraries, because it had never been published in book form.

From numerous maps and documents, Lloyd Robson had compiled a list of the various names people have called Narragansett Bay over the years:

> **Historical Names for Narragansett Bay**
> (from Lloyd Robson's 1958 *Newport Begins*)
>
> Refugio (Maiollo, Maggiolo, 1527)
> Gulf del Refugio (Verrazano, 1529)
> Bay de Sanct. Baptista (Chavez, 1537)
> Port de Refugio (Gastaldi, 1548)
> John Dee Bay and River (1583)
> Bay of Nassaw (Delaet, 1630)
> Narragansetts Bay (William Wood, 1634)

One name caught my eye: **John Dee**. Where had I heard that name?

Hey, he's the guy John Hammond mentioned in his *History of the Camera Obscura*. John Aubrey in *Brief Lives* had quoted Goodwife Faldo as saying John Dee had shown the Polish Ambassador an eclipse of the sun in a darkened room.

(Dee was the only Elizabethan that Hammond mentioned in his whole book)

But what did John Dee have to do with Narragansett Bay?

Eagerly I started to do research on John Dee. Unlike researching Benedict Arnold, where I had to piece together bits of clues to get a picture of his life, finding info on Dee was easy.

There were older biographies like:

> (1968) Richard Deacon — John Dee
> (1972) Peter J. French — The World of an Elizabethan Magus
> (1909) Charlotte Fell Smith — John Dee (1527-1608)
> (1842) J.O. Halliwell-Phillips — The Private Diary of Dr. John Dee
> (1969) Frances Yates — Theatre of the World

An a number of newer books about Dee like:

```
(1978) Wayne Shumaker and J.L. Heilbron   John Dee on Astronomy – Propaedeumata Aphoristica
(1981) Graham Yawbrey        John Dee and the Sidney Group (thesis paper)
(1988) Nicholas H. Clulee    John Dee's Natural Philosophy: Between Science and Religion
(1995) William H. Sherman    John Dee The Politics of Reading and Writing in the English Renaissance
(1996) Gerald Suster         John Dee: Essential Readings
(1999) Deborah E. Harkness   John Dee's Conversations with the Angels:
                                    Cabala, Alchemy and the End of Nature
(1990) R.J. Roberts and Andrew G. Watson   John Dee's Library Catalogue
(1998) Dr. Robert Poole      Time's Alteration: Calendar Reform in Early Modern Europe
(1998) Edward Fenton         The Diaries of John Dee
(2001) Hâkan Hâkanson        John Dee and Renaissance Occultism
(2001) Benjamin Woolley      The Queen's Conjurer, The Science and Magic of Dr. John Dee,
                                    Adviser to Queen Elizabeth I
(2003) Joseph H. Peterson    John Dee's Five Books of Mystery
(2004) György Szonyi         John Dee's Occultism
```

and more books were published as I began to study him:

```
(2004) Ken MacMillan and Jennifer Abeles   John Dee: The Limits of the British Empire
(2007) Stephen Clucas, ed.   John Dee Interdisciplinary Studies in Early Renaissance Thought
(2009) James Geoffrey        Enochian Evocation of Dr. John Dee
```

Dee was also a popular character with modern fiction writers:

```
(1927) Gustav Meyrink     The Angel at the West Window
(1993) Peter Ackroyd      The House of Doctor Dee
(2002) Lisa Goldstein     The Alchemist's Door
```

"Oh no! What am I getting into?" I thought, "Angels, alchemy, cabala, occultism!" What could all this strange stuff have to do with Narragansett Bay? or with the Tower?

The more I read about this fascinating Elizabethan who lived from 1527 to 1608, the more I realized that his life seemed to be divided into two parts.

In his later life, from 1583-1608, he was fascinated with the supernatural. He and his hired scryer, or crystal-ball-reader, Edward Kelley, journeyed to Prague and were involved with all sorts of intrigue involving Rudolf II, the Holy Roman Emperor and King of Hungary and Bohemia.

But in his early life, from 1527 to 1583, Dee was one the most learned and well-respected scholars in Elizabethan England. He wrote dozens of books on mathematics, navigation, astronomy, and other sciences. (But after 1583, at age 56, he hardly wrote anything.)

In the centuries following his death he was mostly remembered as a mystic. But recently, many books have been written on scholarly texts and his influence in the Elizabethan court..

John Dee 1527-1608

As György Szony puts it, "Researchers have been perplexed by the apparent sudden turn which transformed the venerable scientist into as eccentric enthusiast."
(Szonyi, p.11)

**What happened in 1583,
the year Narragansett Bay was named after him?**

John Dee and the Elizabethan Colonization Effort of 1583

John Dee was a mathematician, astronomer, and an expert on navigation and cartography. He had a library of over 4000 books at his house in Mortlake, on the River Thames, just west of London. This "largest private library in England" housed a wide array of Greek, Roman, Neoplatonic, Arabic, Medieval and Renaissance books and manuscripts. Many had been inexpensive to obtain after Henry VIII's dissolution of the monasteries, but Dee also imported numerous rare books from the continent.

He provided navigational advice to all the great Elizabethan explorers. He contributed greatly to the revival of interest in mathematics and classical architecture in England.

Dee lived a time when science was separating from magic. Astronomy with separating from astrology. Alchemy was becoming chemistry, botany and medicine. It was also a time when Protestants and Catholics were at loggerheads.

John Dee lived in tumultuous times

For over 450 years, England had been Catholic (from 1066 to 1547). For the past 450 years (from 1559 until now), England has been Protestant. John Dee's lifetime spanned that turbulent changeover period.

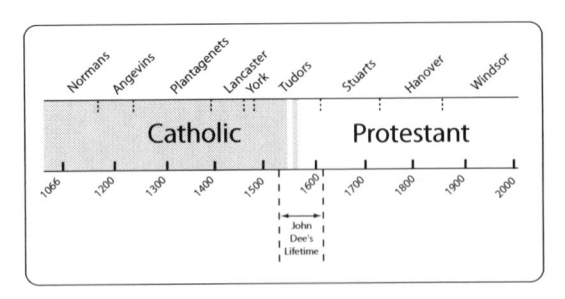

When the Pope would not grant Henry VIII a divorce from Catherine of Aragon, Henry split off the English Church from the Roman Church. From 1537 to 1540, as Supreme Head of the Church of England, Henry dissolved all the monasteries in his realm. After having 6 wives, Henry died in 1547. At this time John Dee was studying at St. John's College in Cambridge.

Saint John's College in Cambridge

Henry's son, Edward VI, came to the throne. Under the the 9-year-old "boy king," England became Protestant. John Dee was busy absorbing the knowledge of the Northern Renaissance. Dee studied at the Louvain in the Netherlands under Renier Gemma Frisius, who had recently redesigned the Astronomer's Ring Dial.

GEMMA FRISIUS

Dee's best friend was Gerard Mercator the famous cartographer. He gave Dee a handmade terrestrial globe and a celestial globe, each about 16 inches in diameter.

Dee taught geometry in Paris and became friends with great scholars all across Europe. Then he returned to England to share his knowledge with the English courtiers. He dedicated two works on astronomy to the young king.

GERARD MERCATOR

Dee presents King Edward IV with two of his books, Practical Uses for the Celestial Globe and Distances of the Planet, Fixed Stars...

After five years, Edward VI suddenly died, and his half-sister Mary I came to the throne. Bloody Mary was a staunch Catholic and was not tolerant of Protestantism. She rounded up the unruly Protestant bishops and chopped off their heads.

John Dee had been friends with Mary's sister, Elizabeth, and was thrown into jail. One day they took away Dee's cell mate, Bartlett Greene, and executed him. But Dee somehow convinced the authorities he could be of great use to them, as he was quite learned in theology. John Dee actually became a Catholic priest for several years. On January 15, 1556, Dee wrote a proposal to Queen Mary recommending she start a "Royal Library." Unfortunately, she rejected the idea.

In 1556, Dee writes a "Supplication" to Queen Mary, recommending the establishment of a Royal Library

But in 1558, when Elizabeth came to the throne, not only was Dee instantly Protestant again, the Queen asked Dee to select the most propitious day for her coronation. He selected January 15, 1559.

[As we'll see, the date January 15 involves certain numbers that are important in Dee's mathematical cosmology].

54

John Dee is asked to determine the date for Queen Elizabeth I's Coronation January 15,1558

Dee saw first-hand how this seesaw of religion was tearing his country apart and sought to find peaceful ways to encourage cooperation.

As Dee biographer Benjamin Woolley writes, "Dee was a deeply committed Christian… but he refused to accept that Protestants or Catholics, or the Bible, or the Pope had the monopoly of knowledge. He believed that God's truth was in the world of nature and learning as well. It was to the movement of the stars and the pages of ancient text that humanity must look to find the common ground upon which the church had originally been built." (Woolley, p. 46.)

Henry VIII	Edward VI	Mary I	Elizabeth I
Catholic	Protestant	Catholic	Protestant

- 1542: Dee studied in Cambridge, England
- 1547: Dee studied at the Louvain, in the Netherlands, then returned to tutor the English Courtiers
- 1553: Dee thrown in prison, then becomes a Catholic Chaplain under Bishop Bonner
- 1558: Dee writes his mathematical works, and becomes "the Queen's philosopher"

John Dee in his library at Mortlake, ca. 1560

QUEEN ELIZABETH I

During Elizabeth's reign, Dee was prolific. He wrote books on astronomy, navigation, mathematics and science. The Queen referred to him as "my philosopher" and frequently called upon him for sage advice.

The Queen had problems. Some of her Catholic subjects were relentlessly plotting to kill her. In 1581, she passed the Recusancy Act (a "recusant" means a "refuser").

Anyone who refused to attend the Church of England, or who held a private mass in their house, was fined 20 pounds a month. If they couldn't pay, their landowner had to pay. And if no one paid, both were thrown into jail.

Many of the wealthy Catholics were moving to Europe, taking their money with them. Not only was this draining England's economy, is was aiding the Catholic cause on the continent.

Elizabeth had external problems as well. Spain was becoming a superpower by importing gold from Mexico and silver from Peru. Spain had over 200 ships in its fleet. England had but 22. England needed get its act together, or it would soon be in deep trouble.

John Dee wrote a series of 8 books for Queen Elizabeth recommending a course of action for England. The first four books were entitled *General and Rare Memorials to the Perfect Arte of Navigation*.

Dee's Paradoxical Compass and his Book of Tables for Navigation

Dee recommended that England should immediately build 60 to 80 large ships and hire over 6000 seamen to build the "Petty Navy Royal."

He invented the "Paradoxical Compass" that allowed sailors navigate at the northernmost latitudes, where the longitude lines converged (and a thick book of tables that accompanied it).

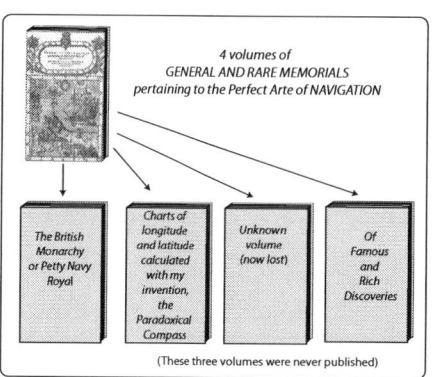

4 volumes of GENERAL AND RARE MEMORIALS pertaining to the Perfect Arte of NAVIGATION

- The British Monarchy or Petty Navy Royal
- Charts of longitude and latitude calculated with my invention, the Paradoxical Compass
- Unknown volume (now lost)
- Of Famous and Rich Discoveries

(These three volumes were never published)

The Title page of Dee's book is chock full of hidden clues.

Dee even tells us, "More is hidden than meets the eye" (written in Latin, around the lozenge shape at the top).

Dee calls his illustration, "A British Hieroglyphic" (written in Greek around the illustration).

Elizabeth has her hand on the tiller, guiding the "ship of state" (on the rudder is the Royal Coat of Arms). Her courtiers are aboard, and her allies from Europe are by her side (Europa is written in Greek).

The kneeling woman repesents the people of England pleading, **"Send forth a sailing expedition...to make a steadfast watch post."**

Above the sturdy walls of the watch post stands Lady Occasion, or Lady Opportunity. This metaphor stems from the classical era: If you grab a lock of Lady Luck's flowing hair you will have good fortune and grasp the crown of victory. Lady Occasion is offering crown of victory to Queen Elizabeth. And the Queen is reaching out for it.

Above Lady Occasion is the Archangel Michael, who is Angel number 42 in the *Shemhamphorasch*, the 72 Names of the Angels.

In the upper right, the Hebrew letters YHVH (the "unspoken" name of God) beam down beneficial rays. The sun, moon, and stars all shine down on the fleet of five ships anchored at the mouth of a river in the New World.

Some of the settlers are trading. At the bottom, a pair of them are walking to the right, towards a "new city" that appears to be prospering.

In short, Dee is painting a picture of the future for the Queen. If she "seizes opportunity by the forelock," all these wonderful things can happen. But if she doesn't...danger lurks! (Notice the half-skull peeking out from the lower right border.)

56

Dee's other large 4-volume set is entitled *The Limits of the British Empire*. It contained top-secret material meant only for the eyes of the Queen and the Privy Council. (This manuscript, which was only rediscovered in 1977, sheds new light onto Dee's pivotal role in Elizabethan exploration.)

Dee was encouraging the Queen to think not just in terms of the island of England, but of a **British Empire**. This is the first written usage of the term the "The British Empire," which later grew to be the largest Empire the world has ever known. At its height, it incorporated about one quarter of the world's population and one quarter of the world's land mass.

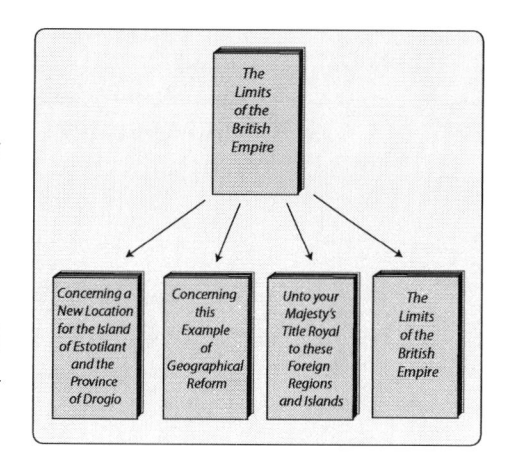

In the first text, Dee notes that Spanish travel writers (following Antonio and Nicolo Zeno's narrative) called the large land mass of North America "Estotiland" and a large island off the coast "Drogio." But Dee found they had misinterpreted the Zeno narrative and had their terminology backwards. Estotiland was the island (now Baffin Island) and Drogio was the mainland (now Labrador). Dee asserts that if Spain couldn't even get the names of these lands straight, they certainly couldn't lay claim to them.

The second text encourages the exploration of the Northwest and Northeast passages, (which I have labled and marked with arrows on John Dee's 1581 *Circumpolar Projection of the Northern Hemisphere*). Dee felt trade with Japan and China would bring great wealth to England.

The third text reviews the voyages of early English explorers like King Arthur, Saint Brendan, Prince Madoc and John and Sebastian Cabot. Dee writes that these Englishmen had already claimed various parts of North America for the British Crown.

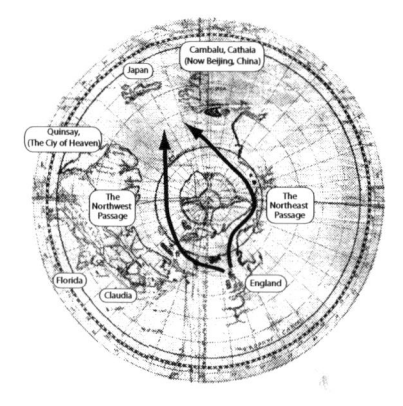

Dee's grand assertion is that because of "Jure Gentium, Jure Civilis, and Jure Divino" (Law of Nations, Civil Law, and Divine Law) Queen Elizabeth has a legal right to all of North America, except for Florida because the Spanish already had settlements there.

Ken MacMillan, who has written two scholarly books on Dee's key role in Elizabethan exploration concludes: "Dee's *Limits of the British Empire* like so many of his other works, confirms the polymathic abilities of one of the most remarkable figures in the English renaissance."

(Ken MacMillan, with Jennifer Abeles, *John Dee: Limits of the British Empire*, p..27)

The Elizabethan colonization effort of 1583

Dee was the navigational advisor for almost every Elizabethan voyage of discovey. He instructed Richard Chancellor and Hugh Willoughby before their expedition in search of the Northeast Passage.

Dee gave Martin Frobisher and the members of the Muscovy Company a two-week cram course just before Frobisher's first journey to find the Northwest Passage.

Upon sighting land, Frobisher named the huge peaks along the Greenland coast "**Mr. Dee his Pinnacles**."

Over the course of several days in the spring of 1578, Dee presented his "*Limits of the British Empire*" proposal to the Queen and the leaders of the Privy council.

One month later, the Queen awarded one of her most courageous generals, Sir Humphrey Gilbert, letters patent to all of North America. All he had to do was build a fort, settle a colony, and remain there for for a year. He was given 6 years, after which time the patent would expire.

For all his legal and cartographical assistance, **Gilbert granted Dee all the lands north of the 50th parallel.** That's pretty much all of modern day Canada and Alaska. These guys thought big.

In the summer of 1580, Sir Humphrey Gilbert sent Simon Fernandez on a reconnaissance mission across the Atlantic. Fernandez was only gone for 3 months, so wherever he went, he didn't stay long.

On November 20, 1580, **Simon Fernandez brought his map of his voyage to John Dee at Mortlake**. Dee had one of his assistants copy it, as on the map is written: "The Counterfeit of Mr. Fernando Simon his Sea carte, which he lent unto my Master at Mortlake, Anno 1580, November 20. The same Fernando Simon is a Portugale, and borne in Tercera, being one of the Isles called AZORES."

(Quinn, Voyages, Vol II, p. 239, footnote 2)

Sir Humphrey Gilbert departed with 5 ships in 1578, but after a harsh winter at sea, they all returned back to England. For the next several years, Gilbert was recommissioned as a General, leading English forces against the rebels in Ireland. In addition, he was having a hard time gathering funds for another voyage.

By 1581, the time limit on Gilbert's letters patent was half over. This was the same year the Crown was enforcing the "Recusancy Laws" against the English Catholics.

The Queen called upon her Secretary of State, Sir Francis Walsingham to deal with England's internal religious strife. Walsingham came up with a creative solution. He made a proposal to one of the wealthiest Catholic sympathizers, Sir George Peckham of Buckinghamshire. Sir George's father had been Master of the Mint under Henry VIII and had served in Queen Mary's Privy Council, but had moved to Rome during Elizabeth's reign.

Walsingham told Peckham that if he would fund Gilbert's expedition to the New World, all the settlers in the new colony would be free to worship as they pleased. It was a win-win-win situation. Gilbert would get North America, the English Catholics would get religious freedom, and the civil turmoil in England would be quelled.

Shortly thereafter, Sir Humphrey Gilbert deeded Sir George Peckham and his associate, Sir Thomas Gerard, 3.5 million acres in exchange for money to hire ships, crew, and to buy supplies.

Dee wrote in his Diary,
"on July 16, 1582, at 3:30 in the afternoon, came Sir George Peckham to me, to know the title for Norombega in respect of Spain and Portugal parting the whole world's discoveries.

He promised me his gift out of his patent 5000 acres of the new conquest, and thought to get so much of Mr. Gerard's gift, to be sent me with seal, within a few days."
Dee was to get 10,000 acres in total in this new colony.

The foremost authority on Elizabethan exploration in the New World, David Beers Quinn, writes about this meeting:
"Eventually, Dee assured Peckham that Spain had no rights in the area; on the maps it was but not occupied.

Moreover, Dee was able to point out to them on the large map of North America he had drawn in 1580 the precise place he thought their settlement should lie.

Verrazzano had stayed for some time on Narragansett Bay in modern Rhode Island, which he called his "Refugio," and there it was decided that Peckham should lay out his seignory."
(Quinn, *England and the Discovery of America*, p..376)

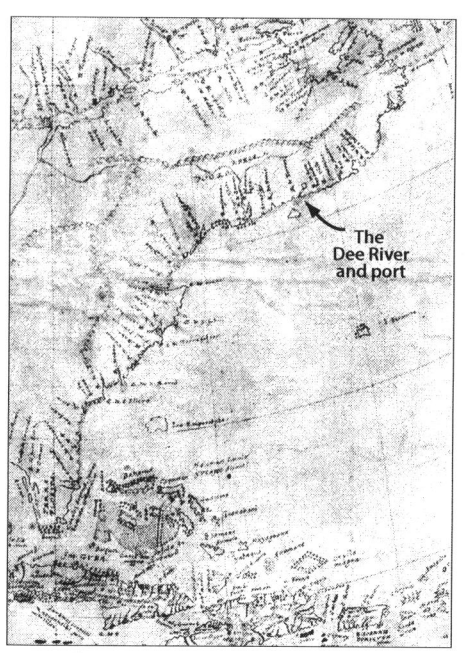

Part of John Dee's 1580 map of North America

59

On February 28, 1583, an agreement was signed between Sir Humphrey Gilbert and Sir George Peckham (and also his son, George Peckham Jr, who replaced Sir Thomas Gerard, as Gerard had been thrown back in prison.) Gilbert deeded the Peckhams:

"...all that river or porte called by Master John Dee, Dee Ryver, which Ryver by the discripcion of John Verarzanus a Florentyne lyeth in Septontrionall latitude about fortye twoo degrees and hath his mouth lyinge open to the South halfe a league brode or there aboute and enteringe within the saide Baye between the Easte and the Northe encreaseth his breadith and contynuteth twelve leagues or there aboutes and then maketh a gulf of twentie leagues compasse or thereabouts and conteyneth in it selfe five small Islandes newlie named the Cinque Isles.

And the saide gulfe and the five Isles therein and all other Isles lyinge within the saide Ryver or gulfe together with fyfteene hundred thousande acres of ground within the supposed continent lyinge nexte adjoininte upon the saide river gulfe and five Isles at the choice of the saide Sir George and George his yongeste sonne their heires deputies or assignes or any of them."

This Elizabethan English is challenging to read, so here's an abbreviated transcription.

" all that river or port called by Master John Dee,
the Dee River,
which lies at about 42 degrees North latitude,
according to Giovanni Verrazzano of Florence.

The river's mouth lies open to the South, about a half a league wide.

The river widens and heads Northeast for about 12 leagues.
and then makes a gulf about 20 leagues in circumference, in
which there are 5 small islands, recently named the Cinque Isles.

This grant also includes 1,500,000 acres adjacent to the gulf and 5 islands."

This is a perfect description of Narragansett Bay. It's about at 42 degrees latitude (Newport is actually at 41 ½ degrees). It has a mouth which opens to the south, about a half a league wide. (As they used the "French league," that's about a mile wide, the approximate width of the "East Passage" of the bay at Newport).

Then the bay continues northeast for about 12 leagues (about 23 miles), and opens to a gulf 20 leagues in circumference (38 miles), containing 5 small islands (Prudence, Patience, Hope, Dyer, and Hog islands). **Scholars have known that the Dee River is Narragansett Bay since 1935**, when William B. Goodwin wrote an article in the Journal of the Rhode Island Historical Society entitled *The Dee River of 1538 (Now called Narragansett Bay) and its relation to Norumbega*.

In the same year, in an article entitled, *Narragansett Bay and the Dee River, 1583*, historian Fulmer Mood agreed with Goodwin's findings.

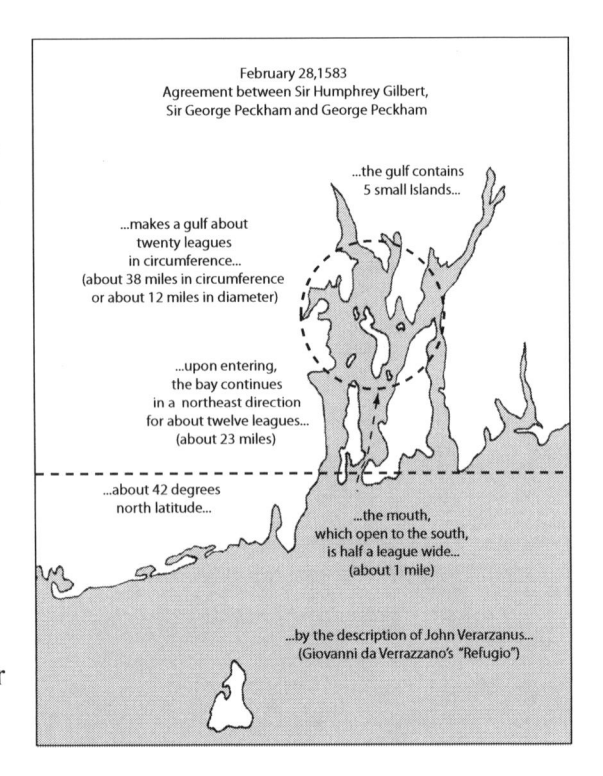

February 28,1583
Agreement between Sir Humphrey Gilbert,
Sir George Peckham and George Peckham

...the gulf contains 5 small Islands...

...makes a gulf about twenty leagues in circumference...
(about 38 miles in circumference or about 12 miles in diameter)

...upon entering, the bay continues in a northeast direction for about twelve leagues... (about 23 miles)

...about 42 degrees north latitude...

...the mouth, which open to the south, is half a league wide... (about 1 mile)

...by the description of John Verarzanus... (Giovanni da Verrazzano's "Refugio")

The exact acreage of the settlement is clearly also spelled out,

"Fifteen hundred thousand [or 1.5 million] **acres of ground extending along the sea coast westward towards the River of Normbega** [which is probably the Hudson River] **not more than 60 English miles in length "**

(This is basically most of present day Rhode Island and almost half of Connecticut.)

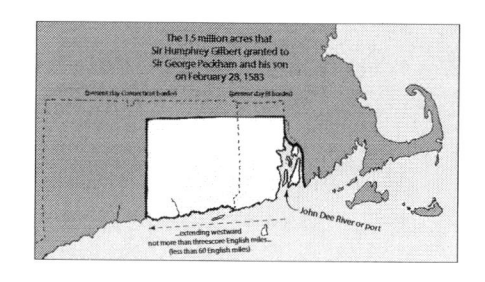

The deed even mentions that it is using Verrazzano's description. Here's a modernized transcription from Verrazzano's 1525 report:

"The shore of the land runs from west to east. The mouth of the port, (which we call Refugio, on account of its beauty), faces south, and is a half a league wide.

From its entrance it extends for 12 leagues in a northeasterly direction and then widens out to form a large bay of about 20 leagues in circumference.

In this bay are five small islands, very fertile and beautiful, full of tall and spreading trees. Any large fleet could ride safely among them, without fear of tempest or other dangers."

Sir Humphrey Gilbert's ill-fated voyage

On July 11, 1583, five ships under the command of Sir Humphrey Gilbert departed from Plymouth Harbor, England.

Unfortunately, after only one day out at sea, the men on the Bark Raleigh, (captained by Sir Humphrey Gilbert's half-brother, Sir Walter Raleigh) caught a contagious disease and headed back home. (It might have been a mutiny.) Gilbert had lost his largest ship and more than half of his supplies.

Instead of taking the southerly route to the Dee River, Gilbert decided to take a northerly route and stock up on supplies in Newfoundland.

When they arrived in Saint John's harbor they were greeted by several dozen European fishing vessels. Sir Humphrey took out his letters patent and claimed the land in the name of the Queen, thus founding the British Empire.

This plaque on Water Street in Saint John's commemorates Gilbert's claim to Newfoundland. Gilbert is quite famous throughout Canada, but very few Americans have ever heard of him.

More of his men got ill (or fed up with their oft-arrogant commander), so Gilbert left a ship for the sick men to return to England. The mission to the Dee River continued with only 3 vessels.

Granted, Gilbert did "found Britain's overseas empire," as the plaque says, but he hardly colonized St. Johns. He was only there for two weeks.

The 3 ships headed down the coast towads Nova Scotia and Maine, but off the coast of Sable Island, they hit a tempest. Gilbert's second-largest supply ship, *The Delight*, got stuck on a sandbar and was crushed by the pounding waves.

Disheartened, and with only two small ships left, Gilbert decided to return to England. But he was determined to set sail again the following spring with more men and supplies.

Unfortunately, off the coast of the Azores they met up with another hurricane. Gilbert's ship got his ship, the *Squirrel*, swallowed up by huge "pyramidlike" waves. Courageous to the end, his final words were, "We are as near to heaven by land as by sea," a quote from Sir Thomas More's book *Utopia*. The vision Gilbert and Dee had of their Elizabethan utopia at the Dee River went down with the ship.

Sir George Peckham tried to keep the enthusiasm for the colony alive, but unfortunately was soon thrown in jail on recusancy charges. The colonization effort (shown at the top here: Gilbert/Peckham/Dee) hit a dead-end.

Dee then teamed up with Sir Humprey Gilbert's younger brother, Adrian Gilbert, and the explorer John Davis, but their North American colonization proposal was rejected by the Crown. Exasperated, Dee left for Europe in September of 1583.

Then a new group was formed. John Dee was replaced by the half-brother of Sir Humphrey and Adrian Gilbert: Sir Walter Raleigh.

(Now there's a name Americans are familiar with.)

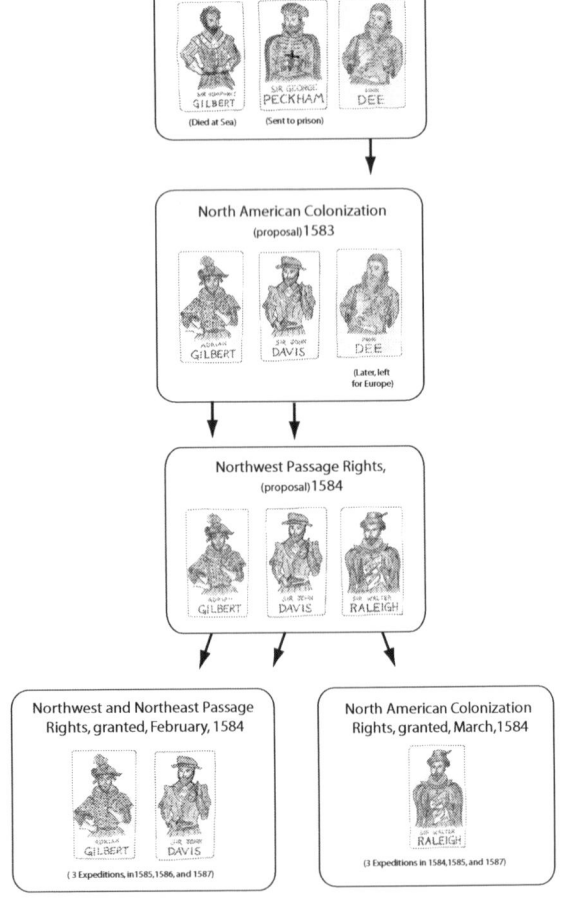

The Queen split up the new trio. She gave Adrian Gilbert and John Davis the rights to discover the Northwest and Northeast passages. Davis made three expeditions to what is now called the Davis Strait, but didn't find the passageway to the Orient.

Sir Walter Raleigh was given Sir Humphrey's grant to settle North America, but the three expeditions he sent in 1584, 1585, and 1587 failed to settle a permanent colony at what is now Roanoke Island, North Carolina.

More clues about Anthony Brigham's journey
–from the Spanish Ambassador's espionage reports

David Beers Quinn was a great researcher. After finding all he could in the archives in London, he went to Madrid. He found that the Spanish ambassador to London, the sneaky Don Bernadino de Mendoza, had written letters back to King Philip II of Spain reporting that there was a "preliminary voyage" in 1582, a year **before** Sir Humphrey left in 1583.

On July 25, 1582, Mendoza writes to the King:

"As to the ships which as I previously wrote to your majesty the Catholics were getting ready here, it turns out that not more than two are going this year with Hongigibert [Humphrey Gilbert] to reconnoiter the place where they can land next year.

These ships are already riding in Sotamton [Southampton] harbour, only waiting for the weather to set sail, and with them a pinnace.

Incidentally, 142 of the documents pertaining to this Elizabethan colonization effort were published by Quinn found in a two-volume set entitled *The Voyages and Colonizing Enterprises of Sir Humphrey Gilbert*. (London, Hakluyt Society, 1940).

Historians have known about this colonization effort for 60 years, but no one ever pieced it together that might have something to do with the Tower in Touro Park (on the Dee River).

This 1582 preliminary voyage was led by **Anthony Brigham**. These "two ships and a pinnace," with approximately 80 men, stayed in the New World for at least nine months.

It's known Brigham returned to England by March of 1583, as he met with Sir Francis Walsingham, who then sent a fundraising letters to the wealthy men of London regarding "the discovery of America."

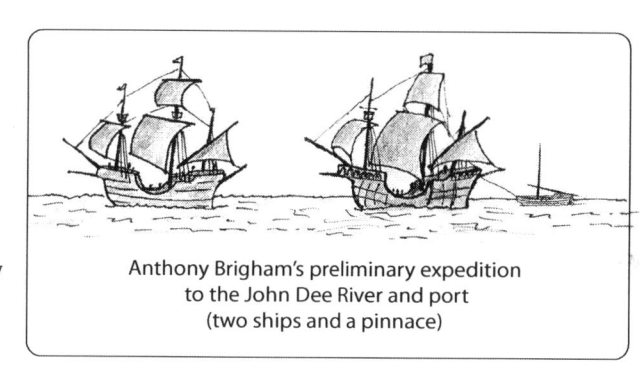

Anthony Brigham's preliminary expedition to the John Dee River and port (two ships and a pinnace)

It's not known exactly what Brigham did on his mission. It was top-secret because Mendoza had threatened:
"the settlers of the new colony would immediately have their throats cut, as happened to the French who went with Joan Ribao."

(Indeed, in 1565, the Spanish had slaughtered 140 men in Jean Ribault's French Colony at Fort Caroline, where Jacksonville, Florida is today.)

David Beers Quinn (writing about 75 years ago, in 1940) wasn't certain where Anthony Brigham went, or even who we was.

Modern research reveals that Peckham and Brigham families were quite close. Under Henry VIII, Sir George Peckham (the elder) was Master of the Mint and Anthony Brigham (the elder) was Peckham's clerk (or assistant). Both men became quite wealthy watching over the King's money and making sure England's currency flowed smoothly.

Sir George Peckham (the elder) owned a large manor in Denham, Buckinghamshire on the River Coine, about 10 miles west of London.

Anthony Brigham (the elder) lived in Caversham, Oxfordshire on the River Thames and about 25 miles west of London. After dissolving the monasteries, Henry VIII had sold him the ancient abbey in Caversham called "Cane End."

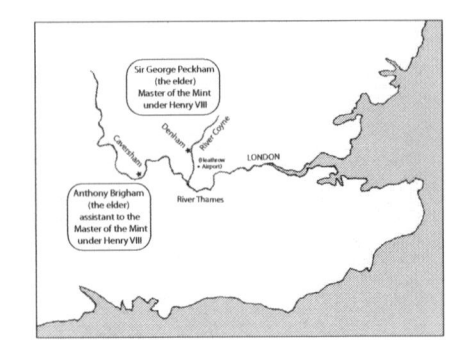

The two families were so close, Sir George Peckham (the elder) and his eldest son Robert Peckham were even trustees of Anthony Brigham (the elder's) estate at Caversham.
Their sons, Sir George Peckham (the younger) and Anthony Brigham (the younger) were both born around 1530 and had probably been chums from boyhood (like the Gilbert/Raleigh/Davis boys on the River Dart).

So while the "next generation" of Peckhams and the Brighams tried to abide by new rules of the Protestant regime, their long family traditions of Catholicism still held their hearts.

It became obvious to me that the destination of Anthony Brigham's preliminary expedition was the Dee River, the site of Sir George Peckham's soon-to-be colony.

In addition to the 80 men on Brigham's mission, 280 men were soon to follow with Sir Humphrey Gilbert. Furthermore, Mendoza reports that 10,000 men were to follow after that "to conquer the territory and safeguard the court." (Mendoza may have been fed false information or was exaggerating for dramatic effect, but its clear a large-scale, long-range project was in the works.)

(Quinn, *Voyages*, p. 244)

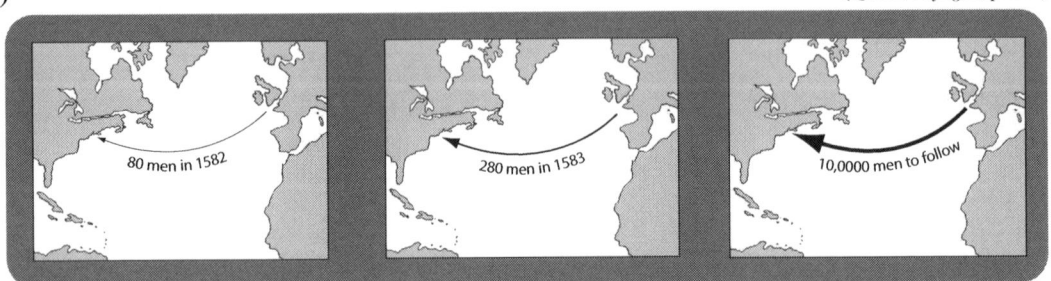

This Elizabethan colony at the Dee River was to be the first, central port, eventually seeding other English colonies up and down the East Coast from Florida to Newfoundland. The official church of this new colony was still the Protestant Church of England, but Catholicism was to be tolerated.

The great Elizabethan travel writer Richard Hakluyt includes "Antonie Brigham" on the third page of his 1583 book, "*The Principal Navigations, Voyages, Traffiques and Discoveries of the English Nation.*" He lists "The names of certain recent travelers, both by sea and land, which also, for the most part, have written of their own travels and voyages."

Note the final entry on the list: **1582 Humphrey Gilbert Knight, Edward Heyes, Antonie Brigham, Englishmen.**

Hakluyt was so anxious to get his work printed to promote the colonization effort, he wrote that Gilbert and Hayes left in 1582. (They were actually delayed until 1583).

But Anthony Brigham (who definitely did not sail in Gilbert's fleet of 5 ships) did go to the New World with 2 ships in 1582.

Brigham's name is the very last name on a list of heavy hitters like Marco Polo, Christopher Columbus, and Francis Drake. Hakluyt was dramatizing the importance of Sir Humphrey Gilbert's project.

my conjectured illustration of "two Ships and a pinnace" at the Dee River and port in 1582

I assert that the Tower that still stands in Touro Park was built by Anthony Brigham and his 1582 "preliminary expedition." It was to be the city center of this grand first Elizabethan colony.

It was the fort Sir Humphrey Gilbert was required to build to fulfill the requirements of his letters patent. It was to have been the "Statue of Liberty" that would greet the thousands of settlers who were expected to follow in the ensuing years.

Why build a Tower?

An obvious question is: Why wouldn't the new settlers build houses or some kind of shelter first instead of a tall tower?

When the Pilgrims arrived in Plymouth, they built crude houses and toiled simply to get enough food to survive. About half of the 105 settlers died the first year. They certainly didn't have time or energy to build a Tower. Why would a similarly-sized colony spend all this effort on a Tower? (And indeed, about 40 years earlier.)

Well, the Pilgrims were a group of relatively poor English refugees who came to the New World with few worldly goods. The Elizabethan colonization effort of 1583 was different. It was a project which involved the highest levels of English government—the Queen and her closest circle of advisers. It was funded by some of the wealthiest men in the country. It was considered to be the England's first foothold, its "steadfast watch post" in the New World.

This new colony was of international importance. It was to be the first seed of the British Empire. With 80 men, and 280 men to follow, then 10,000 more to follow, this was no Plymouth Plantation. It was also risky business. This colony would challenge Spain's claim to the North America, a move that just might precipitate war.

The way I see it, Dee also knew a monumental classical Tower would be good PR. Once English forces had the bay well defended, word would get back to England of this beautiful port. And in its city center was a grand monument commemorating the birthplace of the British Empire in America.

The Blueprint for the Tower

I suggest that the main purpose of Brigham's "preliminary expedition" was to build this Tower. The master masons and master carpenters who took this project on were probably promised large parcels of land in the new colony. I think they probably brought along oxen and carts to transport all the stones. They might have lived on the boats, in tents, or even in the Tower after it had been partially constructed. They would have had masonry and carpentry tools, ropes, nails, but most importantly, they would have had a detailed blueprint.

I believe this blueprint was conceived and drawn by John Dee. As you can see walking around the Tower today, it was built with great intent and forethought. The builders knew enough to make 4-foot tall underground foundations sitting on bedrock because they knew this building was going to be tall. The idea of eight symmetrical pillars is not one they came up with on the spot. The architecture was well thought out. And to involve the intricate astronomical alignments that Penhallow found, it must have been designed by a very wise person.

Who was the "Queen's philosopher"?
Who convinced her she had a legal right to North America?
Who was the navigational and cartographical expert planning the mission?
Who named the site of the new colony after himself?
Who was given 10,000 acres in the new colony?

(answers, D, D, D, D, D)

I think Dee designed the Tower not only as a city center, but as a horologium–a building that keeps track of time. And not just "externally" with the sun, moon, and star alignments that Penhallow found, but "internally" as well, with "camera-obscura solar-disc calendar rooms."

And I think it was a classical building that functionally and visually encapsulated John Dee's mathematical cosmology. Fortunately, Dee wrote several key texts that explain his mathematical worldview.

Unfortunately, Dee wrote in a cryptic style that has made his works perplexing to historians.

But fortunately, with a little creative thinking, Dee's riddles can be solved. And as it turns out, Dee left an abundance of clues about what the Tower might have originally looked like.

John Dee and the (almost) English Calendar Reform

The year 1582 was famous for another monumentous event. Pope Gregory XIII enacted the Gregorian Calendar Reform. Italy, Spain, Portugal, and the Netherlands all eliminated 10 days to make their calendars "in sync" with the sun.

In England, Queen Elizabeth was perplexed. She certainly didn't have to obey the Pope's decree, but she wondered whether England should change its calendar as well? So, who did she ask? Her wise philosopher, John Dee.

John Dee wrote a 62-page treatise entitled:

> "***An advice and discourse for her Majesty about the Reformation
> of the Vulgar Julian year, by her Majesty's and the right
> Honorable Council, their commandment.***"

Dee recommended that, indeed, the English calendar **should** be changed. Not only could the reasons for the change be demonstrated in a camera-obscura solar-disc calendar-room, but Dee had numerous texts in his library that confirmed the need for change.

For three centuries, astronomers like Johannes de Sacrabosco, Roger Bacon, Nicholas of Cusa, and Regiomontanus had been urging the Church to reform the calendar. One of the prime motivations for change was that, in some years, Easter was being celebrated on the wrong day.

(Heilbron, *Sun in the Church*, pp.37-39)

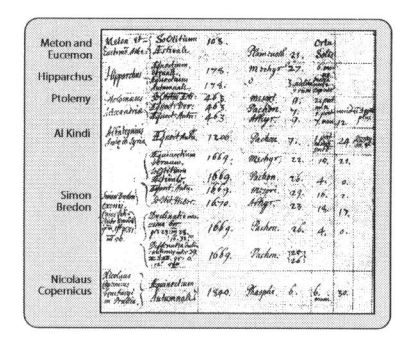

The accuracy of the calendar depends on what is considered to be the precise length of a year.

Dee compiled a list of various astronomers' calculations about year length – from the Greeks, to the Arabs, to Copernicus' newly published data.

To dramatize his proposal, Dee illustrates (what I call) "The Circle of Time." Curiously, it goes all the way back to Adam (at the bottom, in the 6:00 position). Then it goes clockwise through Enoch, Noah, the Exodus, the Greeks, Jesus, Mohammed, Al Kindi, and Copernicus. (Sort of "mankind's greatest hits.")

Dee's "Circle of Time"

Dee's "Circle of Time" from Adam to Queen Elizabeth I

1583 Queen Elizabeth the Reformer of the Year for the next Christian epoch

The final entry is, "**Queen Elizabeth the Reformer of the year for the next Christian epoch.**" And that new era was begin in "1583" (the same year in which I believe the Tower was completed.)

Dee felt England would be using "The Elizabethan Calendar," not "The Gregorian Calendar," and the Queen would be forever famous for putting England "in sync" with the sun.

It was the great astronomer Sosigenes who designed the Julian calendar for Julius Caesar in 45 BC. Dee concludes his treatise with a poem comparing Queen Elizabeth and John Dee to Julius Caesar and Sosigenes:

"As Caesar and Sosigenes, The vulgar calendar did make.
So Caesar's Peer, our true Empress, To Dee, his work she didt betake...

Elizabeth our Empress bright, Who in the year of eighty three,
Thus made the truth come to light, And Civil year with heaven agree..."

(In 1582, Dee was working feverishly to complete his proposal, which was to take effect in 1583.)

67

The Queen promptly approved Dee's calendar reform proposal. The Privy Council approved it as well. But Edward Grindall, the Archbishop of Canterbury, head of the Church of England, vetoed the proposal outright. He claimed the whole idea of changing the calendar was Papist. Furthermore he asserted that the Protestant calendar could only be changed with approval of all the Protestant churches on the continent, (which he knew very well would take years).

(Woolley, p. 173; Poole, p. 66; Clullee, p. 178).

Dee was enraged. In his mind, it was a no-brainer. He was shocked his countrymen couldn't comprehend the importance of re-aligning themselves with the cosmos, especially at this momentous time when the British Empire was about to be born.

For the next **169** years, the English Calendar remained out of sync with European calendars. If you went from Dover to Calais you has to add 10 days. And returning, subtract 10 days.

It wasn't until **1752** that the English finally made the change to the Gregorian Calendar. The whole era of the Pilgrims and the Puritans, almost to up to the time of the American Revolution, England's calendar differed from European calendars (and from the sun). All because they didn't listen to Dee.

In 1582, things were going great for John Dee.
Anthony Brigham and his eighty men were at the Dee River, building (I suggest) the Tower which Dee had designed. Sir Humphrey Gilbert's five ships and 280 men were about to set sail to join them. Dee had helped find a solution to England's religious infighting.

His calendar proposal had been approved by the Queen and the Privy Council. Dee had synchronized the beginning of the new "Elizabethan Calendar" time with the beginning of the British Empire (Dee was an awesome master-planner.) He had also been granted two rectories for which he was to receive 1000 pounds a year for life.

But in 1583, things changed drastically.
Almost half of Sir Humphrey Gilbert's expedition had returned to England. Dee sensed the mission had failed. John Dee, Adrian Gilbert, and John Davis had made a proposal to the Privy Council to discover the Northwest passage. It was rejected. Edward Grindall had vetoed Dee's calendar reform proposal.

(England was finally made the calendar change in 1752. That's 169 years after Dee's recommendation. He was way ahead of his time.)

Dee had been so absorbed in writing his calendar treatise, he neglected to get the official Seal of the Crown afffixed to his rectorship documents within the specified time period. Grindall took both rectory appointments away from Dee (about 1000 pounds per year). Dee was infuriated by all these rejections of his sage advice.

68

Frustrated that his fellow countrymen couldn't settle a simple colony in New World or comprehend the virtues of being "in sync" with the sun, he decided to leave the country. He felt his wisdom might be better appreciated on a larger stage: the continent of **Europe.**

In 1582, Edward Kelley walked into Dee's life. Kelley demonstrated to Dee that he had the power to communicate with the Angels. Dee was fascinated and he employed Kelley for the next five years. Though Dee never claims to have seen the Angels himself, he took copious notes on Kelley's "conversations." Dee's diary has survived and provides many clues as to what was on his mind during these times. (But, alas, this why many historians fail to Dee more scholarly works seriously.)

Later in 1582, the Polish ambassador Albert Lasky sailed into London. The flamboyant Lasky (he always wore red) promised Dee and Kelley a large annual stipend and if they were to return with him to Poland. (The angels, through Kelley, had foretold that told Laski would shortly be made the King of Poland.)

September 22, 1583 was the wedding day of Sir Philip Sidney and Sir Francis Walsingham's daughter, Frances.

The evening before, while all of London was making preparations and partying, Laski, Kelly (and his wife) and Dee (and his wife and children) surreptitiously sailed down the Thames under the cover of darkness. For the next six years they visited the courts of various kings and princes from Kraków to Prague.

surreptitiously sailing down the Thames

A momentous event: the Fiery Trigon of 1583

In 1583, Saturn and Jupiter were in conjunction and entering a Fire Sign for only the seventh time since man walked the face of the earth! This might not seem significant to most people nowadays, but to Elizabethans it was a momentous event.

Since the days of the ancients, **Saturn** and **Jupiter** have been known as the "great Chronocrators" (or markers of time). These are the two superior planets known at the time. Unlike Mercury, Venus, and Mars their orbits around the sun are outside the Earth's orbit (thus they were considered to be closer to heaven).

It takes Saturn 29 years to orbit the sun. It only takes Jupiter 13 years. Thus, every 20 years they are conjunct, or right next to each other, in the night sky. They had been conjunct in 1543, in 1563, and it was about to happen again in 1583. However, this 1583 conjunction was special.

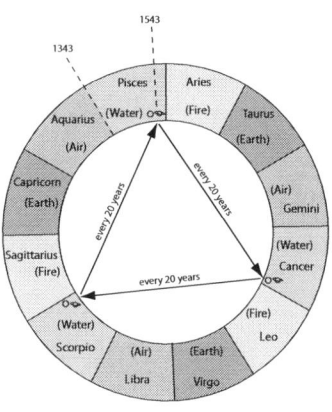

For 240 years (or 12 times) these conjunctions will always appear in a sign represented by the same kind of "Element." Since around 1343 AD, the con-junctions had always appeared in a **Water Sign**, either Pisces, Cancer, or Scorpio. (240 years was their best approximation. We now know it happens every 198 years and 265 days)

The special 1583 conjunction marked the beginning of the next 240-year period when the conjunctions would all be in a **Fire Sign**, either Aries, Leo, or Sagittarius. This is why it's called the Fiery Trigon of 1583. (trigon means "tri-angle")

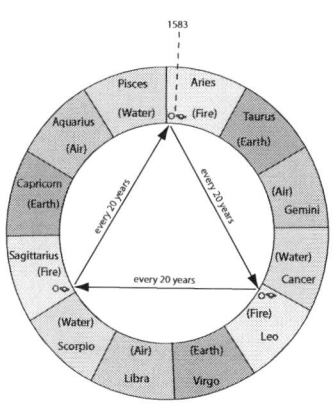

Watery Trigons from 1343 to 1543

the Fiery Trigons start in 1583

69

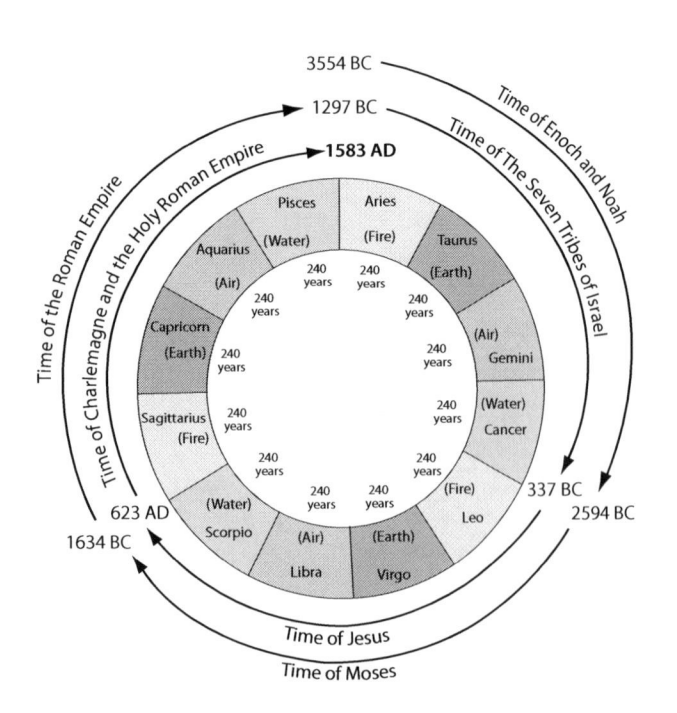

But the 1583 conjunction was even more super-duper special! The conjunction had not entered a Fire Sign since 623 A.D. It takes 960 years for the conjunction to return to the same "Element."

(240 years x 4 elements = 960 years)

It had been 960 years since the conjunction had entered a Fire Sign. The most recent time prior to that was around 623 AD, when it ushered in the great reign of Charlemagne.

The time before that, around 337 BC, it heralded the Time of Jesus. Before that, the Times the of the Seven Tribes of Israel, then the Times of the Roman Empire, then the Times of Moses, and finally the time of Enoch and Noah.

In short, it was well known that there had only been six times in the history of man when the conjunction had entered a Fire Sign. **And the seventh time was to occur in 1583!**

There's another reason Europeans in particular were anticipating great changes in 1583. In his influential work *Tetrabiblos* (first printed around 150 AD), Ptolemy associated the four Elements with the four quadrants of the world. Air Signs affected the Northeast (Russia and China). Earth Signs affected the Southeast (from Greece to India). Water signs affected the Southwest (Africa). And Fire Signs affected the Northwest (Europe from Italy to Britain). (Woolley, p. 141, and Ptolemy, *Tetrabiblos*, J.M. Ashmond, pp. 43-52)

In the 1400s, Regiomontanus had predicted the world would end after this 1583 conjunction (he actually calculated to it to be 1588). After witnessing a new star that was born in Cassiopeia in 1572, astronomer Tycho Brahe predicted at 1583 conjunction would have an even more magnified effect.

In his 1564 text, *On the Most Extraordinary Conjunction of the Superior Planets*, Prague astrologer Cyprus Leowitz predicted an end of the World, and a second coming of Christ. In England, Richard Harvey paraphrased Leowitz: "We are most likely to have a new world, by some sudden, violent, and wonderful strange alteration. This has happened before when one Trigon ended and another began. But it is especially likely now because a Watery Trigon is being followed by its opposite, a Fiery Trigon. This has only happened twice before."

(He's referring to the events that happened around 1297 BC and around 3554 BC on my time chart.)

John Dee bought Leowitz's book when it was first printed in 1564, and annotated it extensively.

(Roberts and Watson, *John Dee's Library Catalogue*, book #631; Margaret E. Aston, "The Fiery Trigon Conjunction: An Elizabethan Astrological Prediction," *Isis*, volume 61, (1970), p. 167, and pp.159-187. Also Deborah Harkness, *John Dee's Conversations with Angels*, pp.69-71)

The specialness of 1583 was in the air and Dee wanted to harness its energy. Indeed, 1583 was a year of big changes for John Dee. Remember, 1583 was also the year I suggest his Tower was completed. Besides marking the birth of the British Empire, and the "New Time" of the proposed Elizabethan Calendar, 1583 also was ushering in a whole new 240-year era of Fiery conjunctions of Saturn and Jupiter. Again, such astrology all might seem like petty superstition to many modern minds. But the point is, this was definitely a big deal to Elizabethans, and especially to John Dee.

JOHN DEE'S MATHEMATICAL COSMOLOGY, EXPRESSED IN ARCHITECTURE

I claim Dee was the architect of the Tower, yet he isn't noted as an architect. No building in London has ever been attributed to him.

However, in the Renaissance, they didn't have the specialized job category of "architect" as we know it today. Back then, an architect was a learned person involved in many fields of study. For example, Michaelangelo, Raphael, and da Vinci are well known for their paintings, but they were great architects as well.

You can see from the Title pages of Dee's 1558 *Propaedeumata Aphoristica* (Preparatory Aphorisms) and his 1564 *Monas Hieroglyphica* (Sacred Symbol of Oneness) that he was familiar with classical architecture.

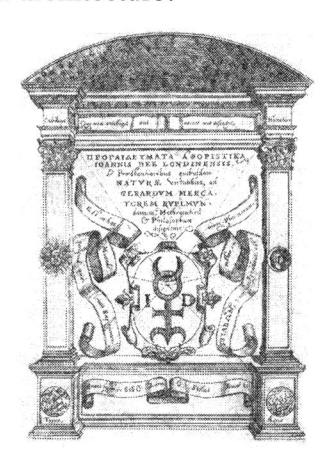

At the bottom of each of these illustrations is a solid foundation, with short pedestals. Above that rise two classical pillars (the Title page on the left has Corinthian columns). Resting on the columns is a thick horizontal entablature. On top of that is a dome festooned with stars.

Dee actually explains his ideas about architecture in his 1570 *Preface to Euclid*. Dee was As aan expert on many subjects, but his strong suit was mathematics.

After attending Saint John's College in Cambridge, he became a reader in Greek at Trinity College. Then he went to the Louvain in the Netherlands, studying under Regnier Gemma Frisius, one of the most noted mathematicians and astronomers of the Northern Renaissance. Dee's best friend was the cartographer Gerard Mercator. They were inseparable, philosophizing for days on end. In 1550, at age 22, Dee lectured to standing-room-only crowds at Rheims College in Paris. He explained each of the over 465 propositions of Euclid's famous book *The Elements of Geometry*.

In 1570, when a rich London merchant named Henry Billingsley funded a project to translate Euclid's *Elements of Geometry* into English, Dee wrote over 150 corollaries and addendums to Euclid's work. He also wrote the *Preface* to the translation. It's not simply a short introductory statement. It's a 50-page exposition defining all the major arts and sciences.

At the bottom of his "ground plat" or summary chart, he lists them and provides a one sentence definition. At the top of the chart, Dee emphasizes that all these arts and sciences derive from two things: Geometry and Arithmetic.

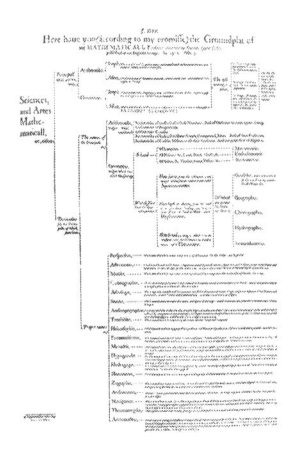

His term "Mathematical Arts" might sound like an oxymoron to modern ears. I doubt you'll find any college nowadays where the math department and the art department are even in the same building. But in Dee's time, Art, Mathematics, and Science were all interrelated parts of "Natural Philosophy," the study of how Nature works.

Dee wasn't just a mathematician, he was a mathematical philosopher. He felt everything was dependent upon geometry and number.

In the *Preface*, Dee quotes Boethius: **"All things (which from the very first original being of things, have been framed and made) do appear to be formed by the reason of Numbers. For this was the principal example or pattern in the mind of the Creator."**

Then Dee enthusiastically remarks: **"O comfortable allurement, O ravishing persuasion, to deal with a Science whose subject is so ancient, so pure, so excellent, so surmounting all creatures, and so used by the Almighty and incomprehensible wisdom of the Creator in the distinct creation of all creatures. The distinct parts, properties, natures, and virtues of all creatures are ordered and, by most absolute number, brought from Nothing to the Formality of their being and state."**

(Dee felt that all of Creation was based on Number. Now there's some powerful insight into his Renaissance mind.)

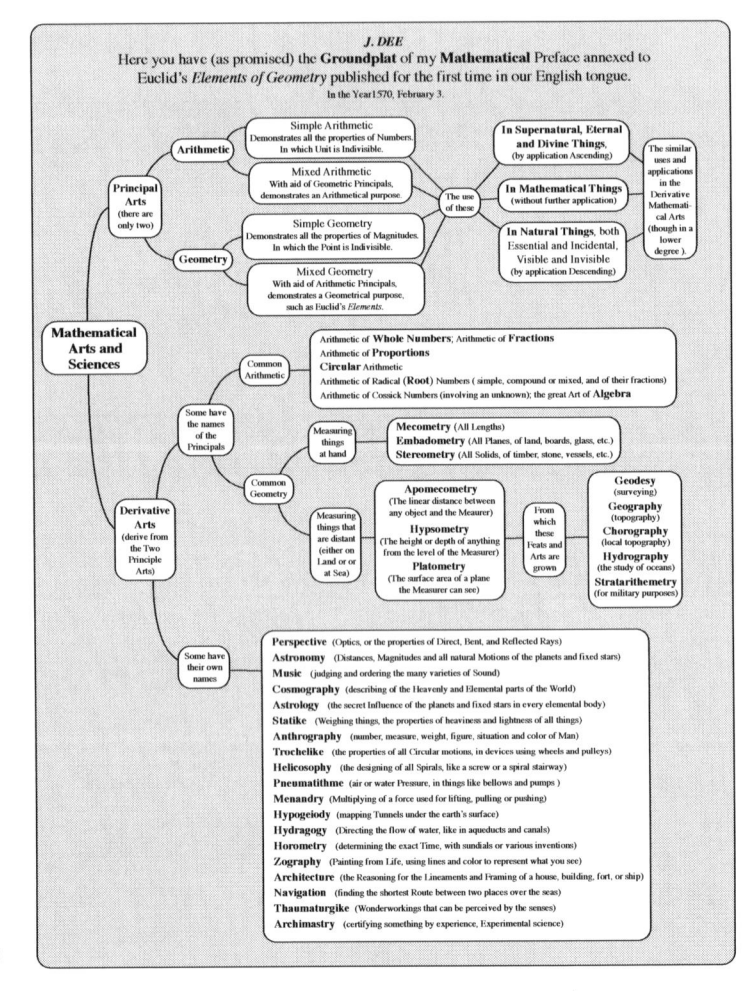

72

Some of Dee's Mathematical Arts, like Astronomy, Architecture, Navigation and Music are familiar to us. But others, like Trochilke (the study of pulleys and wheels), Statike (the science of weights), and Zography (the art of painting and sculpture) have names which Dee coined from Greek words. At the very top of the list is the Art of Perspective.

Nowadays, "perspective" means "seeing the effect of distance on the appearance of objects," like the way railroad tracks appear converge as they get further from the eye. When an artist draws a building "in perspective" it means depicting 3-D shape on a 2-D piece of paper. The "perspective" lines meet at a vanishing point.

But in the Renaissance, "Perspective" incorporated the whole science of sight.

(In Latin "per" means "through" and "specere" means "to look," so perspective means "to look through or to inspect.")

Dee is emphatic. To become proficient in any of the arts and sciences, one must first learn Perspective. And he gives three good reasons: (Dee, *Preface*, page b.j.)

First, "**Without understanding Perspective, perfect knowledge of Astronomical Appearances cannot be attained.**"

Second, Perspective deals with light, and "**Light is the First of God's Creatures.**"

Third, it deals with, "**The Eye, the light of our body, and his Sense most mighty, and his organ most Artificial and Geometrical.**"

Note that a "camera-obscura solar-disc calendar-room" is a perspective tool that involves each of these three topics. The solar disc moving across the floor or wall is an "Astronomical Appearance."

By the phrase "Light is the First of God's Creatures," Dee is referring to "Let there be light," in the first book of Genesis. Aside from a dark room and a hole, the only thing required for a camera obscura is "Light."
(This means camera obscuras were around, in some cave with one small hole, before plants, beasts, or Man.)

"Let there be light"

Dee glorifies the "Eye" as the "light of our body." That's a profound idea. He considers the eye to be the mightiest of all five senses.

(When he says it is our most "artificial" organ, he doesn't mean "fake," he means the "most artfully or skillfully" constructed.)

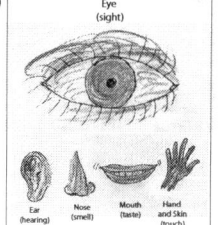

Note that Dee also calls the eye "geometrical." As the eye is a camera obscura, this implies that the camera obscura is "geometrical."

(This is a key clue to understanding Dee's cosmology. Can you figure out what geometric shape, or shapes, best describe the geometry of the behavior of light in a camera obscura?)

Dee breaks Perspective into several parts:
The main principle of "**Direct Radiation**" is that light travels in straight lines.
"**Broken Radiation**" means Refraction, or why an oar in water looks bent.
"**Reflected Radiation**" is Catoptrics, the study of flat, concave, and convex mirrors.

73

After explaining these types of Perspective, Dee concludes:
**"The Art of Perspective is excellent but no man
would easily believe it without actual proof.
Without perspective Natural Philosophy cannot be fully understood."**

(Trust me, I've tried to explain how a camera obscuras works to many people, but folks don't
believes it works until they actually stand inside one and witness the projected image with their own eyes.)

Dee adds:
**"But before you have learned enough about the power of Nature and Art,
you might not fully comprehend some parts of Perspective
and slip into light Judgement of them, so I shall
refrain from explaining them all here."**

(The "light Judgement" Dee means accusations, like dealings with the supernatural, that some uninformed fanatics
would make if Dee claimed he could show things walking, sailing, or flying around the walls of a dark room.)

Dee's **Art of Zography** incorporates the art of painting and the art of sculpture.
(In Greek, *zöos* means "living things" and *graphos* means "to paint or draw,"
so Dee's Mathematical Art of Zography means "painting from life.")
As a subcategory of Zography, Dee briefly explains the **Art of Althalmasat**.

[In addition] **To these two Arts** [painting and sculpture]
**... is a certain odd Art, called Althalmasat, much
more beholding than the common Sculptor,
Entayler** [Intaglio artist]**, Kerver** [Carver]**,
Graver** [Engraver]**, Founder** [Moldmaker]**,
or Painter (& etc.) know their Art,
to be commodious** [useful]**.**

Althalmasat was the slightly cryptic term Dee coined for a camera obscura. The root word in the middle of "Althalmasat" is the Greek word *thalamus*, meaning a "room" or a "chamber." *Thalamus* is much like the Latin word *camera,* which also means a "room" or a "chamber."

The word *thalamus* is related to the Greek word *tholos*, a round building with a conical roof, like this tholos in southern Italy. Dee even depicts a tholos on the front cover of his *Monas Hieroglyphica*.

In Dee's day, artists were starting to use miniature camera-obscura rooms and camera obscuras in small boxes, as aids to drawing. The 3-D image of a scene was projected onto a 2-D screen and the scene could be drawn quite accurately.

an illustration of a **tholos** on the Title page

Also, using an Althalmasat, 2-D artwork could be enlarged or reduced, like the "lucy" machine (short for *camera lucida*) used by graphic artists in the 1900s.

Dee probably sensed that the Althalmazat machines would develop over the centuries into amazing devices. Indeed they have. From drawing-aid boxes, to 8-by-10 view cameras, to 35 mm cameras, to video cameras, to 3D holography cameras. And trust me, the Althalmazat machines will continue to evolve.

Dee provides other cryptic references to the camera obscura in his "advice to the 14 various professions" in his Letter to Maximillian in the *Monas Hieroglyphica*. For example, here is he gives this advice to experts on Weights:

"And will not he, who has devoted all the Time of his life to making exacting measurements with WEIGHTS, judge just how well his Labors and costs have been invested, when here, the Magistery of our MONAD will teach him, most assuredly by actual Experience, that the Element of Earth can float above that of Water?"

This passage is not as mystical as it sounds– he's talking about an **Althalmazat.**

To demonstrate, here's my graphic depiction of John Dee's study at Mortlake. Outside, his children are playing in the dirt of the riverbank and beyond them is the River Thames. Inside, the Element of Earth floats above that of above Water.

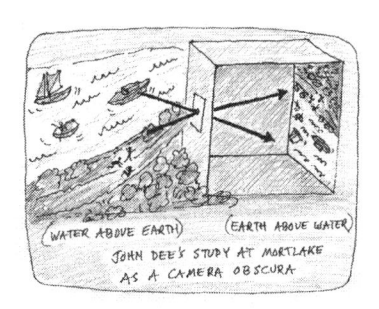

Dee gives this cryptic advice to Astronomers:

"And won't the ASTRONOMER regret all his sleepless vigils and cold labors he has suffered under the Open Sky, when here, without any Discomfort from the Air, Under his own roof, with windows and Doors Shut on all sides, at any given Time, he is able to observe the movements of the heavenly bodies?

And, indeed, without any Mechanical Instruments made from Wood or Brass?"

"With windows and Doors shut on all sides" pretty much implies a "dark room." The solar disc (and even the lunar disc) is visible in a camera obscura. The stars are only visible if a focusing lens is used. But Dee doesn't say anything about not using glass, only wood and brass.

In the Preface to Euclid, immediately following the Art of Zography and Althalmasat, Dee writes about the Art of Architecture. He tells us his two all-time favorite architects are Vitruvius (from around 25 BC) and Leon Battista Alberti (from around 1450).

When Vitruvius' text, *Ten Books on Architecture,* was rediscovered in the Renaissance, it inspired a revival of classical Greek and Roman architecture. All great Italian architects like Donato Bramante, Leon Battista Alberti, Sebastiano Serlio, and Andrea Palladio based their ideas on Vitruvius. Dee paraphrases Book 1, Chapter 1 of Vitruvius' classic text:

"An Architect must be familiar with various Languages, skillful in Painting, well instructed in Geometry, not ignorant of Perspective, equipped with knowledge of Arithmetic, familiar with History, a diligent student of Philosophy, have skill in Music, be not ignorant of Medicine, understand rules of Law, and have a firm grasp on Astronomy and the courses of Celestial objects."

Dee elaborates:

**"Likewise, by Perspective the Lights of Heaven are well-led
in the buildings, from certain quarters of the world."**

Hey, this is exactly what Professor Penhallow found in the Tower! The "Lights of Heaven," (or the sun, moon, and stars) are "well-led" throught the windows from various parts of the sky.

Dee continues, again paraphrasing Vitruvius:

**"As for Astronomy, the Architect must know East, West, South and North,
and the design of the heavens, the Equinox, the Solstices, and the course of the stars.
Anyone who lacks knowledge of these matters will be unable
to understand the Art of Horology."**

Further on, Dee explains Horology (the science of time) or Horometry (the measurement of time).

"Horometry is a Mathematical Art which demonstrates how, for any
given location, the exact designation of time may be known.
In antiquity, part of this Art was called **Gnomonica**.
More recently it was called **Horologiographia**.
And in English, it is called **Dialing**.

It takes more than a talented Painter to prescribe the path of the Sun's shadow,
(down to a hair's-width), for any regular surface in any given location.

In my youth, I invented a way to accomplish this feat of determining how,
using any Horizontal Dial [like a dial on a floor], Mural Dial [wall dial]
or Equinoctial Dial [tilted dial], at any given hour (provided the
Sun is shining), to determine the Sign and Degree ascendant."

"Man's affairs often require knowledge of time at moments when neither
the Sun, Moon, or Stars can be seen. So, industrious Mechanics invented
a way to keep track of time using a consistent flow of Water.
Vitruvius rightfully praises to the skies the famous Inventor Ctesibius.

Later, hours were measured by running Sand.

Then, using gears and by weights.

And lately, using gears without weights, using a Spring instead.

But all these methods require corrections over time...
because of the inaccuracy of their own Operation.

There remains, among the Philosophers, a more excellent, more commodious   **A**
and more marvelous way than all these to imitate the motion of the Primovant **perpetual**
(or the first equinoctial motion) by using Nature and Art, which you shall   **motion**
understand more of, by further search in weightier studies."

Dee writes in the margin, "**A perpetual motion.**" Mankind has yet to invent a perpetual motion machine, but Dee saw that the "camera-obscura solar-disc calendar-room" was a perpetual motion timepiece. It's always on time. It has worked since "Light" was made. And it will continue work forever, or at least as long as there is "Light."

He notes that water clocks, hourglasses, weight-driven clocks, and even spring-driven watches all need to be reset every so often. What did they use to reset them? The "camera-obscura solar-disc calendar-room."

Dee enthusiastically calls it "more excellent, more commodious, and more marvelous" than other ways to imitate the movements of the heavens. But he suggests the reader will have to study a little bit more to understand how it all works.

Why didn't Dee simply say: Make a dark room, put a hole on one wall, and follow the movement of the solar disc across the floor.

Well, along with the image of the sun, you also get an image of the sky, trees, the street scene, and anything else visible outside the hole. If someone happened to be inside Dee's house and saw images of birds flying, horse carts driving, or people walking across the walls of his study, they would accuse him of being a conjurer and lock him up. The citizens of England weren't as enlightened about the fine line between magic and science as Dee's scholarly friends on the continent were.

Next, Dee quotes Leon Battista Alberti's 1450 book,
De Re Aedificatoria, (On the Art of Building):

""'The whole Feat of Architecture in building consists of Lineaments
[its distinctive lines or proportion] and Framing [its physical structure].
The whole intent and purpose of Lineaments lies in determining the best
way of coordinating and joining all the lines and angles that define all the
faces of the building.

The function of the lineaments is to prescribe an appropriate
location, precise numbers, proper scale, and elegant order for
the whole building as well as for its various parts.

Thus the entire form and appearance of a building may depend upon the Lineaments.
Lineaments have nothing to do with the particular material the building is made from.

Building made from different materials can have the same lineaments
if they share similar siting, order, and all the lines and angles are similar.
Thus, Lineaments are all the precise and correct lines and angles of a building,
first conceived in the mind, and then perfected by inspired vision and learned intellect.'

We thank you, Master Alberti. By setting aside the material stuff of the building,
you have appropriately given your Art (and your description of it)
a Mathematical perfection that involves thinking about
order, number, form, figure, and symmetry."

This idea that a building's mathematical proportions are more important than the material from which it is made is important concept to keep in mind as we try to visualizing what Newport Tower originally looked like.

A classical building need not be ashlar (made from large pre-cut stones) but instead might made from fieldstones, plastered over, and then *sgraffitoed* (faux painted) to look ashlar. Classical columns might be wooden, yet painted to look like marble. What really matters are the lineaments, or proportions, which are "perfected by inspired vision and learned intellect."

an example of Renaissance sgraffito

Dee also informs us what he thought of architecture with regards to mathematics:

"But to those whom Nature has bestowed such ingenuity, skillfulness, and a good Memory that they have mastered Geometry, Astronomy, Music and the other Arts, and who have surmounted and passed the calling and state of Architects can finally become Mathematicians."

Dee was one of the top mathematicians in England, so obviously he felt he had even surpassed the requirements to be an architect.

In my mind, Dee was a perfect candidate for someone who could design a tower with clever astrological alignments and camera obscura rooms. Benedict Arnold might have appreciated how it functioned, but to me, he didn't seem capable of being the architect.

Dee's 1558 *Propaedeumata Aphoristica.*

Between 1550 (when Dee lectured in Paris) and 1570 (when he wrote his famous *Preface to Euclid*), Dee wrote two other books in which he encapsulated his vast knowledge of astronomy, geometry, number, and perspective.

In 1558, Dee published his *Propaedeumata Aphoristica*. This is Greek for "Preparatory Aphorisms." He lists 120 concepts that must be understood before you could grasp what he's talking about in his next book, the 1564 *Monas Hieroglyphica*.

One of Dee's Aphorisms reads:

"Whatever is in the Universe possesses order, agreement, and similar form with something else."

Another Aphorism reads:

"Observe and contemplate the wonders of the many fracturings of the heavenly rays in the air, the clouds, and the water and you will be impelled to praise the infinite goodness and Wisdom of God."

The "fracturings" (or reflections) of the heavenly rays on "the water."
Hey, here's a guy who's actually acclaiming the beauty of "fiery water"
(which blazes in the Tower's fireplace on the equinox).

The Monas Hieroglyphica
(Dee's most cherished work)

The *Monas Hieroglyphica* (Sacred Symbol of Oneness) has puzzled scholars for centuries. Gerald Suster, in *John Dee, Essential Readings* writes:

"Certainly Dee regarded it as his masterpiece, the summary and crowning synthesis of all the knowledge and wisdom he had acquired."

But in the past few centuries, no one has been able to figure out what it all means. Dee scholar Francis Yates writes that Dee's text **"leaves the reader thoroughly bewildered."**

Suster adds:

"Commentators agree that the key is no longer with us, that key being Dee's oral explanation; or perhaps we are too far removed from sixteenth-century intellectual sensibilities to perceive implications deeply significant to intelligent men of that time."

This wasn't about to stop me. The wise Dee was expressing something very important in the *Monas*. If I could figure out Dee's cosmology, the design of the Tower would become clear. I literally had to think like a Renassance guy.

I tracked down and studied all the existing translations of Dee's work. A library in Edinborough, Scotland sent me a copy of a handwritten translation done in 1691. A library near Prague provided me with a copy (in Latin) handwritten by Dee in the late 1580's. Then, with the help of a Latin expert, I made my own translation.

Most scholars see the *Monas Hieroglyphica* as an alchemical text that somehow involves numbers. To me the *Monas Hieroglyphica* was a mathematics text written in alchemical language to slightly obscure some kind of important math concepts he had discovered. He wanted to share his wisdom but only with those wise enough to figure out what he was talking about.

Dee's discovery must be important because he dedicated his book to King Maximillian, the Holy Roman Emperor. In the *Letter to Maximillian* that preceeds the 24 Theorems of the *Monas*, Dee says he has a "rare gift" for the King.

Now, you don't promise the King a rare gift if you don't have one to give. The King had all the riches he wanted. What did Dee have that's so special it was fit for a King?

(I'll give you a hint. It's a number. But I could give you 12 million guesses and you still might not guess it.)

Dee flatters himself by suggesting that only one in a million philosophers could have discovered what he has found. But he adds that his findings will be useful to 14 different professions. [His admonishions to the 14 professions are each little riddles.]

Dee tells Maximillian that "his mind was pregnant with the *Monas* continuously for the past 7 years." [This is actually a numerical clue.] Dee even informs the reader that he likes to use Gematria, Notariacon and Tzyruph. Don't be put off by these strange words. They're really quite simple [and fun].

14 professions
(that Dee claims will find the information in the Monas Hieroglyphica useful)
1 Grammarians
2 Arithmeticians
3 Geometers
4 Musicians
5 Astronomers
6 Opticians
7 Experts on Weights and Measures
8 Experts on Matter and Space
9 Cabbalists
10 Magicians
11 Physicians
12 Scryers
13 Refiners of Gold
14 Alchemists

Gematria
certain letters represent certain numbers

Notariacon
first letters of a phrase combine to spell a new word,
(like an acronym)

Tzyruph
certain letters, jumbled, form different words

In short, Dee's book is an amalgam of word games, number codes, metaphors, parables and brainteasers. I call it a "The Book of 100 Riddles."

When it was published in 1564, **Queen Elizabeth** summoned Dee to court to explain it to her. When he journeyed to Prague, he explained it to Maximilian's son, **King Rudolph II**.

[I have explained the riddles more thoroughly in 3 other books, but what follows is the gist of Dee's work, enough to explain what it has to do with the Tower, and of course his "rare gift" to the King. I encourage you to read a translation of Dee's work first and try to solve it yourself. At least you'll see that it's Dee who sounds crazy, not me.]

Dee has encapsulated his cosmology into one simple graphic figure: the **Monas symbol**.

At first glance it may look like a stick figure of a one-eyed person, squatting, with outstretched arms, and horns or a crown. But it's so much more.

Dee writes that the
astrologocal symbols of all the 7 planets
[Saturn, Jupiter, Moon, Mercury, Mars, Venus and Sun]
can be made from various parts, and presents them in an egg, in a square, and on 7 circuits of a spiral.

He fashions several parts into a mortar and pestle, and other parts into a distilling vessel and collecting bowl.

He even **inverts** the symbol, and **separates** its parts in various ways.

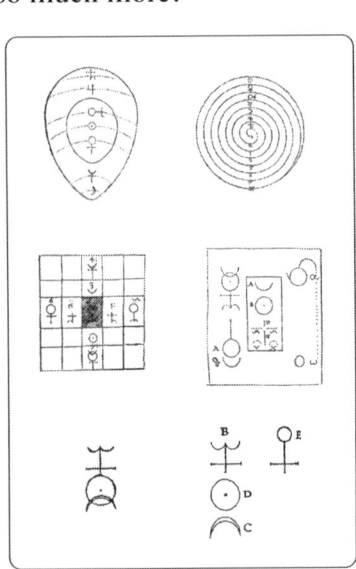

80

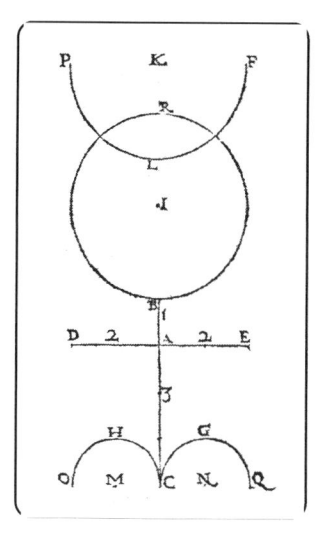

Proportions of the
Monas Symbol

Dee insists all component parts be drawn
in the proper geometric proportions.
There is only one correct way to draw the symbol.

He starts in the middle with the short line AB.
If that is 1 unit, the lower part of the vertical line of the Cross is 3 units.
And the arms of the Cross are each 2 units.

The diameter of the Sun must equal the diameter of the Moon.
The diameter of each of the Aries half-circles equals the radius of the Sun.

The entire shape works out to be a 9:4 height-to-width propoportion.

He is also gived a detailed description
of how it should look "for Ornament,"
like when it is engraved in a ring or a seal.

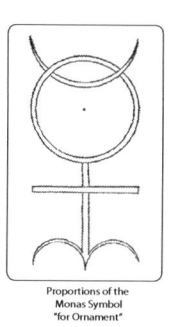

Proportions of the
Monas Symbol
"for Ornament"

The Monas symbol has four main parts:
At the top is the half-circle of the **Moon**.

Below it is the symbol of the **Sun**. Dee explains
that the point in the center represents earth.

Below that is what Dee calls the **Cross of the Elements**.
The cross obviously has theological meaning, but Dee
emphasizes its geometry, The cross is "offset,"
the horizontal arm crosses the vertical spine
exactly one quarter of the way up from the top.

At the bottom of the Monas symbol is Dee's
sign for **Aries**, the zodiacal month that begins
at the Spring Equinox, around March 21st.

The first 5 short Theorems will
give you a feel for Dee's writing.

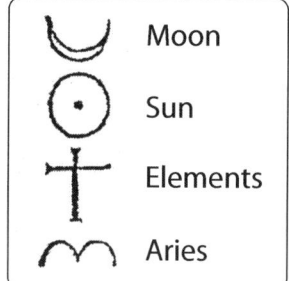

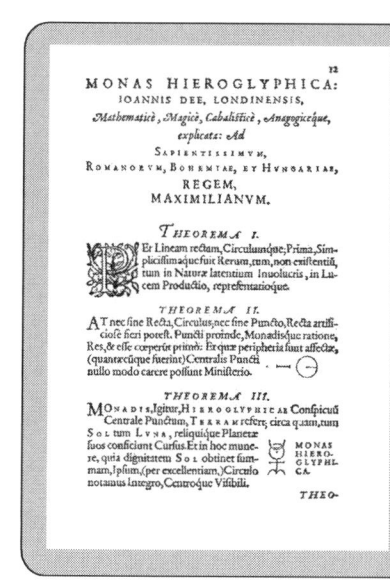

81

SACRED SYMBOL OF ONENESS

JOHN DEE OF LONDON
Mathematically, Magically, Cabalistically, and Anagogically
Explained To
MAXIMILLIAN
Most Wise
KING
of The Romans, Bohemia, and Hungary

THEOREM 1

The very First and most Simple Representation, of not only existing things, but also things hidden in the Folds of Nature, and also in the exhibition of the Bringing Forth of Light, is made by means of a straight Line and a Circle.

THEOREM 2

However, a Circle cannot be skillfully crafted without the Line. Likewise, the Line cannot be crafted without the Point. Thus, Things come into being by way of the Point and a Monad. And things related to the circumference (regardless of how big they may be) cannot exist without the Service of the Central Point.

THEOREM 3

Thus, the Central Conspicuous Point of the HIEROGLYPHIC MONAD refers to the EARTH, around which both the Sun, as well as the MOON, and the rest of the Planets complete their Courses. And in this gift, since the Sun possesses the greatest dignity (because of its excellence) we represent It by a Complete Circle with a Visible Center.

MONAS HIEROGLYPHICA.

THEOREM 4

The Semicircle of the Moon is shown here to be Above the Circle of the Sun. Nonetheless, the Moon obeys the SUN as her Master and King.

The Moon seems to rejoice in the Sun's Shape and proximity so much that she emulates him in the Size of her Radius (at least, as it appears to the common man). Finally she longs to be imbued by the SOLAR RAYS so much that she becomes Transformed into him. Then she disappears from the Sky altogether. After a few Days she reappears as a horned-shaped figure, exactly as we have depicted her.

THEOR. 5

And most certainly, one Day was Made out of Evening and Morning by the joining of the Lunar Half-Circle to its Solar complement. Thus, it was on this first Day that the LIGHT of the Philosophers was made.

[Dee's word "Anagogically" means "making a spiritual interpretation from a literal statement."
Medieval scholars interpreted the Bible in 4 ways: "Literally, Allegorically, Morally, and Anagogically."
Dee had created his own "4 ways."
Most significantly that he has replaced the first word ,"Literally," with "Mathematically."]

Here's a visual summary of the first 5 Theorems.

Theorem 1

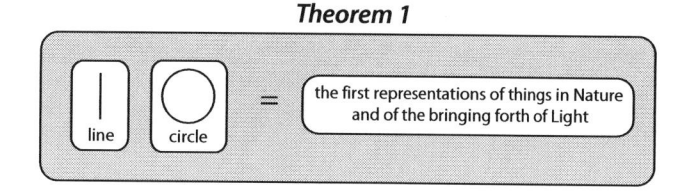

| line | circle | = | the first representations of things in Nature and of the bringing forth of Light |

The first two Theorems read like the beginning of a geometry text, explaining "point, line and circle."

Theorem 2

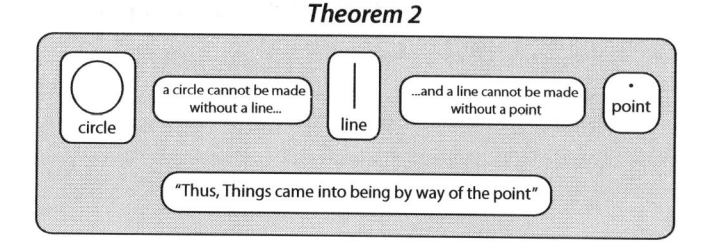

circle — a circle cannot be made without a line... — line — ...and a line cannot be made without a point — point

"Thus, Things came into being by way of the point"

Dee was well-versed in Copernicus' sun-centered ideas, and probably knew Copernicus was right, but he wasn't about to get embroiled in such a sensitive issue.

[However, one of Dee's best students, Thomas Digges, was not afraid to espouse his own heliocentric beliefs.]

Theorem 3

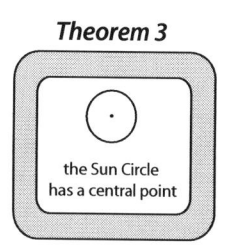

the Sun Circle has a central point

In Theorem 4, Dee explains that the Moon emulates the Sun and, during the full Moon, they appear to be the same size.

(To show this, I have added a dotted line to the top of the Moon.)

Indeed, even though they are at dramatically different distances from earth (250,000 miles verses 93,000,000 miles), the moon and sun each appear to subtend or angle of about a half of a degree.

Theorem 4

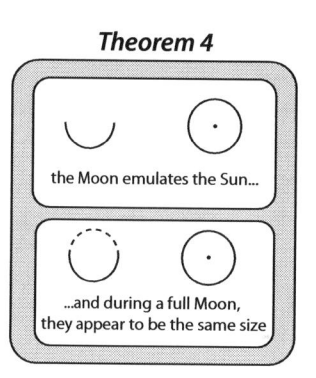

the Moon emulates the Sun...

...and during a full Moon, they appear to be the same size

Evening and Morning, light and dark, Moon and Sun. These are all opposites. Can you guess what Dee means by the "Light of the Philosophers"?

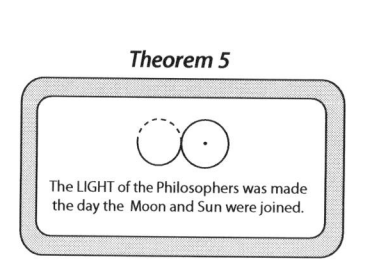

It's a camera obscura.
Light on the outside, dark on the inside.
Even if humans weren't around to observe it, on the very "first Day," when the sun first started to shine, a camera obscura could have been be created in a cave that had one small hole.

Theorem 5

The LIGHT of the Philosophers was made the day the Moon and Sun were joined.

All it takes is light. In fact, in any dark room with a small hole, you can't get the camera obscura effect **not** to happen.

The Title page has two columns,
the **Sun** column and the **Moon** column.

At the top of the central emblem are what Dee refers to as Solar Mercury and Lunar Mercury.

Mercury, the messenger god of the Romans, had wings on his feet and carried a caduceus or staff.

The two Mercuries are visual reflections of each other and they are aiming their pointed wands to **a hole** in the top of the shield.

They form a triangle with a strange crustacean.
That's Dee humself,
Cancer the Crab.
[Dee's birthday was July 13]

At the bottom of the large egg-shape is Leo the Lion, King Maximillian's birthsign.
Like a lion, Maximillian was also figuratively the "king of the jungle."

Theorem 11

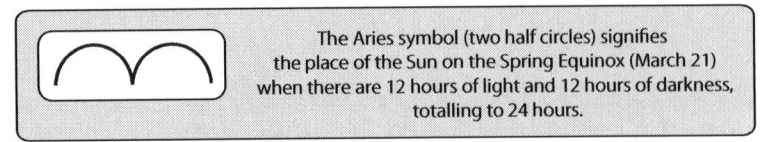

The Aries symbol (two half circles) signifies the place of the Sun on the Spring Equinox (March 21) when there are 12 hours of light and 12 hours of darkness, totalling to 24 hours.

Here, Dee is inferring that the two half circles of the Aries symbol are "12" each, totalling "24".
As we shall see, Dee was aware of the vital importance of
12 and 24 in both geometry and in the realm of number.

From these clues (and others) I was able to decipher the main theme of the *Monas Hieroglyphica:*
The Union of Opposites.

[This is exactly what the present-day researchers had found in the nature of creative people.
They could grasp both sides of a problem simultaneously and come up with a novel idea.]

*The principle of the "Union of Opposites"
certainly doesn't start with Dee, by any means.*

As far back as 600 BC, the Chinese sage
Lao Tzu expressed it in the Yin Yang symbol.

Plato, Socrates and their buddies had prolonged discussions about oppositeness.

Aristotle put his spin on what he knew about the Pythagoreans by providing a table of 10 opposites (based on the sacred number of the Pythagorean tetraktys).

Aristotle's table of
10 Pythagorean opposites.
Limited Unlimited
Odd Even
Unity Plurality
Right Left
Male Female
At Rest In Motion
Straight Curved
Light Darkness
Good Evil
Square Oblong

As we've seen, the Romans expressed the Union of Opposites in their two-headed God, ***Janus***.

A Roman coin with the two faces of Janus

In Medieval days, philosophers expressed the Union of Opposites as an ***ouroborus***, a serpent biting its own tail, making a circle.

The alchemists expressed it as
fire (an upright triangle) and **water** (an inverted triangle), uniting in a 6 pointed star (or hexagram).

The called the Union of Opposites
"coincidentia oppositorum."

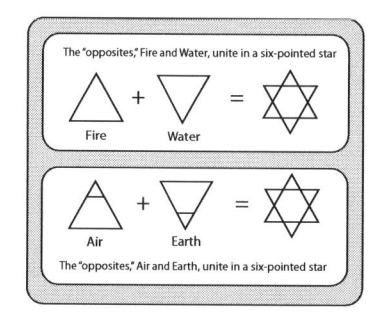

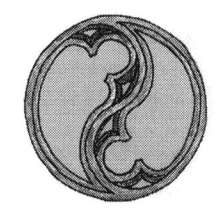

The "opposites," Fire and Water, unite in a six-pointed star

Fire + Water = ✡

Air + Earth = ✡

The "opposites," Air and Earth, unite in a six-pointed star

The visual oppositeness of yin and yang symbol can even be seen in Gothic Window design.
(Beidermann, *Symbols*, p. 393)

Since Dee's time, many authors have written about "opposites," including:

Immanuel Kant (1724–1804)
Georg Hegel (1770–1831)
Neils Bohr (1885–1962)
Jiddu Krishnamurti (1895–1986)
Claude Levi-Straus (1908–2009)
David Bohm (1917–1992)

Even modern-era poets express the Union of Opposites. Wallace Stevens writes:

"Among twenty snowy mountains, the only moving thing was the eye of a blackbird."

Among the implied opposites in this simple sentence are black-white, small-large, one-many, moving-still, living-nonliving, round-angular. All in one word image!

tnereffid

When creative consultant Tom Monahan writes about "tnereffid" way to ideate, he is encouraging "thinking about opposites."

In Theorem 5, Dee tells us that the day of the Moon and Sun were joined, "the LIGHT of the Philosophers was made."

I've portrayed them as two circles touching, but the Union of Opposites is not a static result, it's an ongoing process.

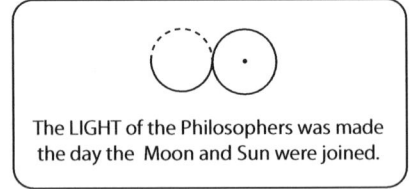

The LIGHT of the Philosophers was made the day the Moon and Sun were joined.

Two things are becoming one,
and that one thing is becoming two.
(concurrently and continuously)

Dee calls this process "Conjunctio" and "Separatio."
Theorem 5 might be visualized this way:

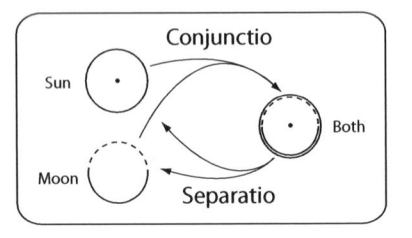

John Dee was well-read and knowledgeable about many things from navigation to law, but above all else, he was a mathematician.

In the *Propaedeumata Aphoristica*, Dee asserts:

"Whatever is in the Universe possesses order, agreement, and similar form with something else."

In the *Monas Hieroglyphica*, Dee drops hints about looking for the idea of Union of Opposites in geometry and in the realm of number.

A simple example is the geometric opposite-ness Dee found in the cross.

In Theorems 8 and 16, Dee equates the Pythagorean tetraktys (1+2+3+4=10),
to an X (Roman numeral for 10),
to an equilateral cross,
to his offset cross.

(In Dee's mind, they these 3 versions of the cross all have the same potency.)

Theorems 8 and 16

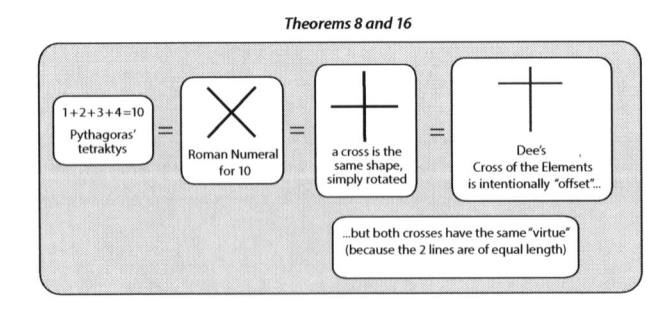

1+2+3+4=10 Pythagoras' tetraktys = Roman Numeral for 10 = a cross is the same shape, simply rotated = Dee's Cross of the Elements is intentionally "offset"...

...but both crosses have the same "virtue" (because the 2 lines are of equal length)

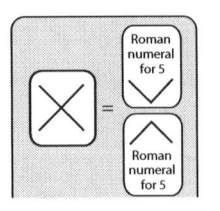

He says the X might be seen as two V's (the Roman numeral for 5).

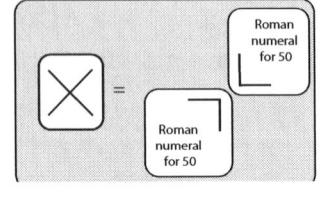

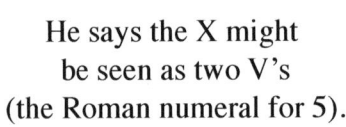

Or even into two L's (the Roman numeral for 50).

86

Theorem 17

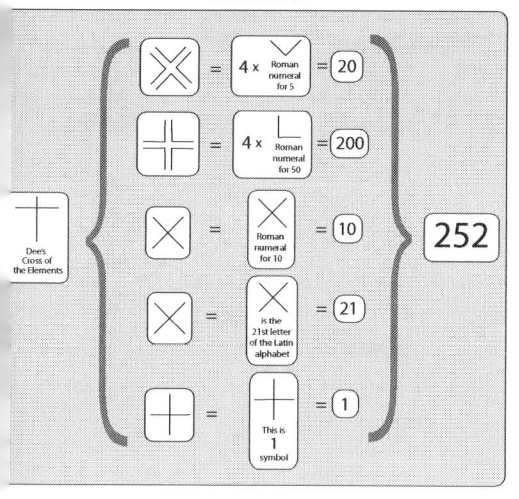

In Theorem 17, Dee explains the cross can represent 20, 200, 10, 21, or 1.
These numbers sum to 252.

From the information in his book, Dee wants us to figure out "2 other logical ways" to arrive at 252.

Here Dee is punning that the cross, as an X, or two V's, or as two L's, can spell LVX (or LUX, the Latin word for light).

Dee says there are "2 other logical ways" that 252 can be derived "from our premises"

He wants the reader to think about how X separates into either two L's or two V's "because then a LIGHT (**LVX**) will appear."

Aesop's Fable of the "Eagle and the Dung Beetle"

Cast of Characters:
The hero: A Scarab Beetle who rolls its eggs in cow dung or horse dung making spherical dungballs.
The villian: An Eagle who lays spherically shaped eggs.
Also starring (with a bit part): A Rabbit
And (playing himself): Jupiter, the chief god of the Romans, (synonymous with the chief Greek god Zeus)

A Rabbit, being chased by an Eagle, begged the Scarab Beetle for help. The Beetle warned the Eagle not to touch the Rabbit. But the Eagle brushed the Beetle away with the sweep if its wing, seized the Rabbit in its talons, and devoured it.

Enraged, the Beetle flew up to the Eagle's nest. Being quite practiced in rolling spherical dungballs, the Beetle rolled the eggs over the lip of the nest and they shattered on the rocks below.

When the Eagle returned to its nest, she was distraught with grief and anger. The following season, the despairing Eagle implored Jupiter to provide her with a safe place to keep her eggs. The great Jupiter allowed her to place the eggs in his lap.

The wily Beetle flew up and deposited some of its spherical dungballs among the the eggs. Jupiter noticed the filthy dungballs, was startled, and stood up abruptly. Once again, all the Eagle's eggs were shattered on the ground.

To resolve the whole dispute, Jupiter commanded that the Eagle lay its eggs in early spring, when the Beetles are still asleep in the ground.

In the midst of all this unusual geometry and astronomy, Dee relates one of Aesop's parables [which I have paraphrased above].
The moral of the story is that the weak can find clever ways to avenge the powerful, but differences can be resolved. Following the fable, Dee writes: "**I am not trying to play Aesop, But Oedipus.**"

Oedipus is famous for his "Riddle of the Sphinx:"
"What goes on four legs in the morning, on two legs at noon, and on three legs in the evening"?
[The answer: A man, who crawls on all fours as a baby, walks on two legs as an adult, and walks with a cane in old age.]

Dee is telling the reader he is using the fable as a riddle (Oedipus), not for its moral message (Aesop).
[Hint: Dee wants the reader to think about how the spherical eggs and dungballs naturally arrange themselves in Jupiter's lap.]

The Greek playwright Aristophanes alludes to Aesop's fable (probably written around 550 BC) in his play *Peace* [written around 400 BC]. While attending Saint John's College in Cambridge [from 1542–1545], Dee was the stage manager for a production of *Peace*.

Using a system of hidden ropes and pulleys, Dee had the hero (on the back of a giant Beetle) fly off the stage and up into the rafters. Some of the astonished audience members suspected Dee had used magic.

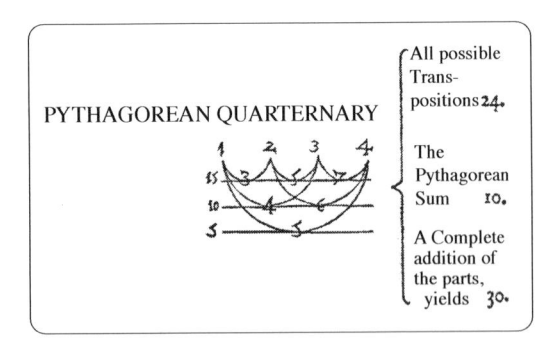

PYTHAGOREAN QUATERNARY

All possible Transpositions 24.
The Pythagorean Sum 10.
A Complete addition of the parts, yields 30.

In Theorem 23, Dee compares two "Quaternaries."
The **Pythagorean Quaternary** is **1, 2, 3, and 4**.

These mumbers multiply to 24, they sum to 10, and the sum of all the pairings of the parts sums to 30.

Dee has devised his own "**Artificial Quaternary**" which is "1, 2, 3, and then 2 again."

(To reiterate, nowadays, artificial means fake or unnatural, but in Dee's time it meant artful, skillful, or well-crafted.)

Dee wants us to discover what's so artful about **1, 2, 3, 2**.

They multiply to 12, they sum to 8, and the complete addition of the parts sums to 24.

[Here are those numbers 12 and 24 again. Dee even notes that 24 karats is pure gold.]

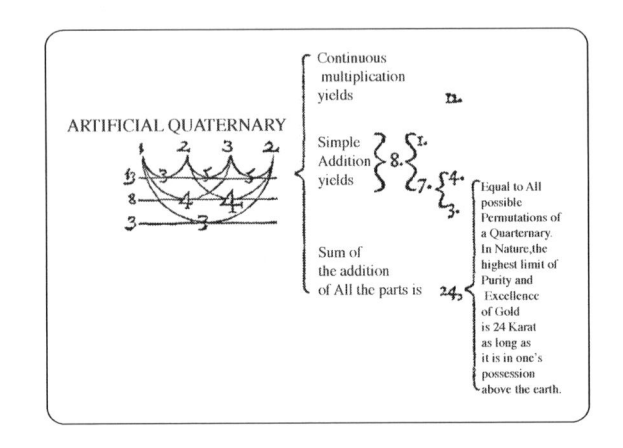

ARTIFICIAL QUATERNARY

Continuous multiplication yields 12.
Simple Addition yields 8. {1, 4, 7, 3}
Sum of the addition of All the parts is 24.

Equal to All possible Permutations of a Quaternary. In Nature, the highest limit of Purity and Excellence of Gold is 24 Karat as long as it is in one's possession above the earth.

On the left side of what I call the "Artificial Quaternary chart," Dee emphatically claims there are "**certain and Fixed Limits**" in the realm of number.

In the middle are three categories Virtue, Weight, and Time, which incorporate various arrangements of numbers.
Note that Dee list includes 1, 2, 3, 4, 5, 6, 7, 8, 12, 13, 24, and 25.
Why does he omit 9, 10, and 11?

Way down at the bottom is Dee's "Magistral" number or Master number, **252**.

"Lapidification and Fermentation" is Dee's clever was of hinting the "Philosopher's Stone" of number is 252.

What's so special about 252?

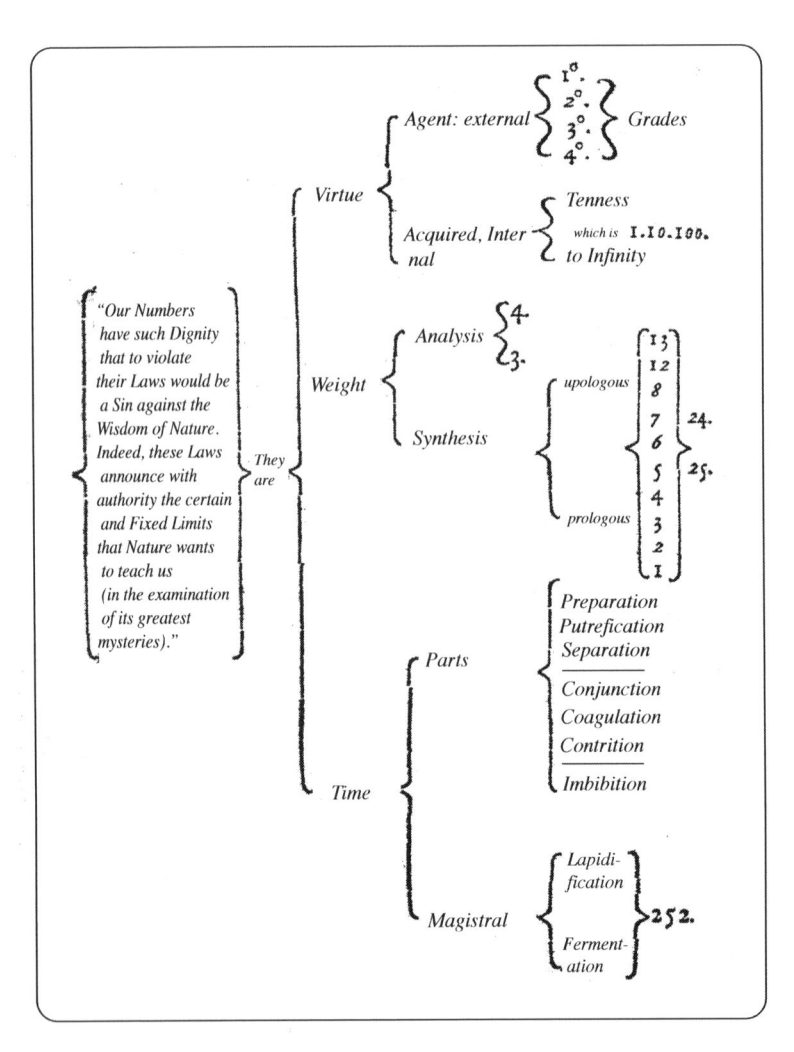

"Our Numbers have such Dignity that to violate their Laws would be a Sin against the Wisdom of Nature. Indeed, these Laws announce with authority the certain and Fixed Limits that Nature wants to teach us (in the examination of its greatest mysteries)."

They are

- Virtue
  - Agent: external {1°, 2°, 3°, 4°} Grades
  - Acquired, Internal { Tenness which is 1.10.100. to Infinity
- Weight
  - Analysis {4, 3}
  - Synthesis { upologous {13, 12, 8} 24. {7, 6, 5} 25. prologous {4, 3, 2, 1}
- Time
  - Parts { Preparation, Putrefication, Separation / Conjunction, Coagulation, Contrition / Imbibition
  - Magistral { Lapidification, Fermentation } 252.

88

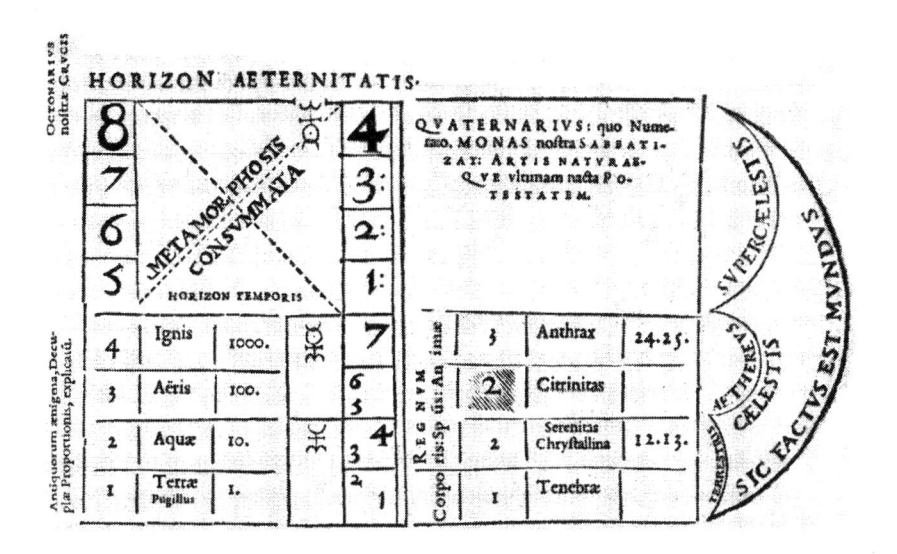

At the end of Theorem 23, Dee presents a chart entitled "Thus the World Was Created."

[How many people do you know that would even attempt to summarize the Creation of the World in a chart?]

The bottom half of the chart (labeled Terrestrial and Aetheic Celestial) is the "Below" part of the world. The upper half (labeled Supercelestial) is the "Above" part of the world.

In the "Above" section, Dee lists, (in bold) **1, 2, 3, 4**, then **5, 6, 7,** and **8**.
But in the "Below" section, he only lists 1 through 7.

He also lists various quaternaries, like the Pythagorean Quaternary, the 4 Elements, "1, 10, 100, 1000," his Artificial Quaternary, the colors of 4 alchemical stages, as well as those numbers 12 and 24 (along with 13 and 25).

He uses words like METAMORPHOSIS and CONSUMMATA.

Along the top is the HORIZON OF ETERNITY.

In the upper right, he uses the peculiar word SABBATIZAT.

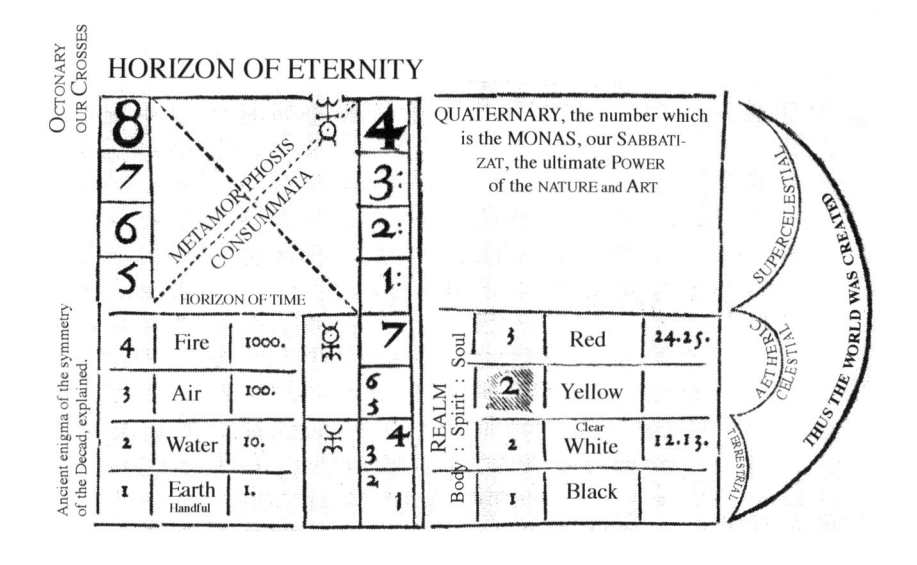

In Theorem 24, he reiterates that the day and night of the equinox total exactly 24 hours, that 1 x 2 x 3 x 4 = 24. He also relates several cryptic ways Saint John refers to the number 24 in *Revelations*.

Dee signs his work with an equilateral triangle, his code symbol for himself.

Delta (triangle) is the fourth Greek letter.

The fourth Latin letter is D, pronounced "Dee."
John Dee was a consummate punster and riddlemaker.

> Δ
> Dee's signature
> Delta, the fourth Greek letter
> like D(ee) is the fourth Latin letter

After much study, I was finally able to understand what this chart (and the whole *Monas Hieroglyphica*) is all about and it's really quite clever. It expresses various rhythms or symmetries found in geometry and number.

Just as Dee suggests, the key to unlocking this puzzle is the number 252. Fortunately, to figure out what 252 meant, I had a tool that historians in the 1800's and 1900's did **not** have.

You know what that tool was?

I googled 252.

I figured if 252 was so important in Dee's cosmology, it might be important in someone else's cosmology.

And guess who popped up when I googled "252 spheres"?

Buckminster Fuller, the geometer and architect who invented the geodesic dome. Unfortunately, Bucky sounded more confusing than Dee:

> "Thus by experimental evidence we may identify the electron with the volume of the regular, unit-vector-radius-edge tetrahedron, the simplest symmetrical structural system in Universe. We may further identify the electron tetrahedral with the maximum possible symmetrical aggregate of concentrically packed, unit-radius spheres symmetrically surrounding a single nucleus – there being [8] new potential nuclei appearing in the three-frequency shell of 92 spheres, which three-frequencies shell, when surrounding embraced by the four-frequency shell of 162 spheres, buries the [8] candidate new nuclei only one shell deep, whereas qualifying as full-fledged nuclei in their own right requires two shells all around each, which [8], newborn nuclei event calls for the fifth-frequency shell of **252 spheres**."

[Warning: the next 2 chapters involve geometry and mathematics. But fear not! It's all quite simple. Even if you don't feel you have a knack for math, or feel you have forgotten all the geometry you learned in school, you will still be able to understand the next 2 chapters [5th-grade students have undersoood it).

The following chapters might seem like a grand diversion from this story, but they are actually it's essence. In the *Monas Hieroglyphica*, Dee actually left us a blueprint for the design if the Tower. But it will be totally invisible unless you first understand the startling discoveries Dee made about geometry and number.]

John Dee and Buckminster Fuller thought alike

Richard Buckminster Fuller (1895-1983) was an inventor, philosopher, engineer, and architect. Called by some the Leonardo da Vinci or Benjamin Franklin of the Space Age, he was one of the most important thinkers of the 20th century.

He worked globally and worked fervently suggesting ways "to make man a success in Universe." Born in Milton, Massachusetts in 1895, Bucky got kicked out of Harvard twice for partying and "lack of ambition." Bucky explains he was more excited about exploring novel ideas than "memorizing facts."

Bucky became a management trainee at the meat-packing firm Armour and Company in Manhattan. After serving in the Navy during World War II, he got married and went into business with his father-in-law, building houses from a compressed-fiber block they had invented.

In 1927, the company lost its financial backing. Bucky was out of a job. Soon all of his savings were gone and he was falling further and further into debt. Down and out, he started drinking and carousing on the streets of Chicago.

One cold fall night he walked to the shore of Lake Michigan and considered jumping in, swimming as far out as he could far out in the cold water, and ending his life. Suddenly something clicked. "You don't have the right to eliminate yourself. You do not belong to you. You belong to the Universe." He decided to start a fresh new life, thinking less about himself, and assessing how he could best help all of humanity.

He took a vow of silence for 2 years, speaking only to his wife and daughter. They rented a small room in a cheap hotel in the city's ghetto area. It had with one closet and an alcove with a stove and a sink.

(Sieden, *Buckminster Fuller's Universe: His Life and Work*, pp.22, 88)

He studied great thinkers like DaVinci and Gandhi. To see how nature expressed itself, he studied astronomy, physics, biology, and mathematics. He sensed that nature had certain "pattern integrities," that might not be detectable by the physical senses, but that might be expressed with tangible models.

Bucky set out to find the geometry of universe,
"Nature's one comprehensive coordinate system."

And he found it!

Bucky went on to design cars, maps, houses, buildings, and of course, domes. He is most well-known for inventing the geodesic dome, like Spaceship Earth at Walt Disney World in Orlando.

During the 1960's and 1970's, Bucky gave hundreds of lectures every year at colleges and conferences all over the world. By 1971, he had circumnavigated the globe 37 times.

In 1975, Bucky wrote his 876-page opus **SYNERGETICS**, *Explorations in the Geometry of Thinking*. It is a synthesis of his discoveries about Nature's coordinate system.

Realizing he still had more to say, in 1979 he followed it up with his 592-page *Synergetics 2*.

Bucky's "Spaceship Earth" at Epcot Center

Studying the almost 1500 pages of "idiosyncratic, hyphenated prose" of Bucky-speak in the 2 volumes of *Synergetics* is a daunting task. Fortunately, one of his students, Amy Edmondson has done a superb job of summarizing his ideas in ***A Fuller Explanation**, The Synergetic Geometry of R. Buckminster Fuller*.

It soon became clear to me that John Dee and Buckminster Fuller had both discovered the same thing. It's not that surprising. They were each great geometers. And they were each searching for the same thing, "Nature's operating system."

The world changed has dramatically in the 4 centuries between the mid-1500's and the mid-1900's, but the "Laws of Nature" have stayed the same. They never change.

Nature's operating system

Take one circle.
How many same-sized circles will fit around it?
For example, if put a quarter on a tabletop, how many
quarters can you fit around it, so they all touch and fit snugly?

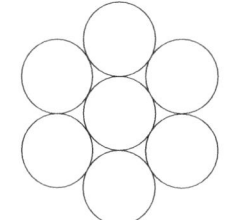

The answer is exactly 6.
Five quarters is not enough
and 7 is too many,
but 6 fit perfectly around 1.

Now let's put a sphere on a flat surface. How
many same-sized spheres will fit around it?

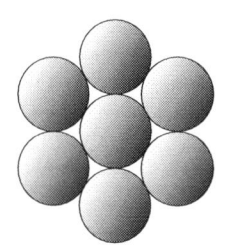

Again the answer is 6. This holds true whether
the spheres are marbles, ping-pong balls,
bowling balls or planet earths.

Now, instead of using a flat surface, imagine a
sphere suspended in space. How many same-sized
spheres fit perfectly around it in all directions?

Now the answer is 12.
Eleven is too few, thirteen is too many.
12 spheres fit perfectly around 1.

An easy way to envision this is to start with the 6-around-1 arrangement.
Then, put three spheres in the nests they create on the top
and three more in the nests on the bottom.

(These trios on top and bottom **must** be arranged in opposite direction.
For example, here the top triangle of spheres points forwards
and the bottom triangle of spheres points backwards.)

93

Next, imagine the centerpoints of each of the 12 spheres connecting with the centerpoints of all each of their neighboring spheres (and also with the central sphere).

Let's zoom in for a close up.
Notice that the 12 central radiating lines are the same length as the lines comprising the outer shell (of which there are 24.)

(In other words, I made this model by hot-gluing 36 lollipop sticks that were each 4 inches in length.)

Because the radiating vectors and the outer vectors are equal, Bucky named this shape the "**Vector Equilibrium**."

Bucky loved this shape.
He considered it:
"Nature's operating system."
He even designed a logo for it.

In the closest packing of spheres arrangement, some sides are triangular (made from 3 spheres) and some sides are square (made from 4 spheres).

Notice that each of the 12 outer spheres are "shared" by triangular and square faces.

In total, this shape has
8 triangular faces and 6 square faces.
What Bucky called the Vector Equilibrium, other geometers call a cuboctahedron.
This shape was known long before Bucky.
And long before Dee.
Heron informs us that even Plato knew about it.

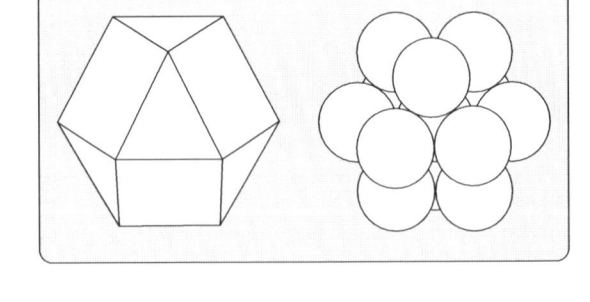

There are only five 3-D geometrical figures which have only one kind of face-shape.
They are called the "regular solids" or the "Platonic Solids."

The tetrahedron has 4 triangular faces.
The cube has 6 square faces.
The octahedron has 8 triangular faces.
The dodecahedron has 12 pentagonal faces.
The icosahedron has 20 triangular faces.

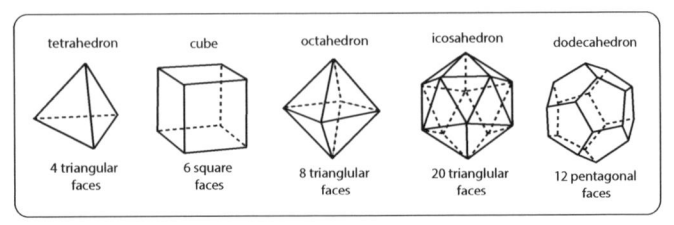

94

Archimedes helped identify a group of "semi-regular solids," which have only 2 or 3 kinds of face-shapes.

As you can see, the cuboctahedron is one of the simplest of the Archimedean Solids.

	types of faces		edges	radiating vertices	total faces
5 "Platonic Solids"	4 triangles	tetrahedron	6	4	4
	8 triangles	octahedron	12	6	8
	20 triangles	icosahedron	30	12	20
	6 squares	cube	12	8	6
	12 pentagons	dodecahedron	30	20	12
13 "Archimedean Solids"	**8 triangles and 6 squares**	**cuboctahedron**	**24**	**12**	**14**
	20 triangles and 12 pentagons	icosidodecahedron	60	30	32
	4 triangles and 4 hexagons	truncated tetrahedron	18	12	8
	8 triangles and 6 octagons	truncated cuboctahedron	36	24	14
	6 squares and 8 hexagons	truncated octahedron	36	24	14
	20 triangles and 12 decagons	truncated dodecahedron	90	60	32
	12 pentagons and 20 hexagons	truncated icosahedron	90	60	32
	8 triangles and 18 squares	rhombicuboctahedron	48	24	26
	12 squares and 8 hexagons and 6 octagons	great rhombicuboctahedron	72	48	26
	20 triangles and 30 squares and 12 pentagons	rhombicosidodecahedron	120	60	62
	30 squares and 20 hexagons and 12 decagons	great rhombicosidodecahedron	180	120	62
	32 triangles and 6 squares	snub cube	60	24	38
	80 triangles and 12 pentagons	snub dodecahedron	150	60	92

length of edge vector / length of radiating vector

1.6329931619	tetrahedron	
1.4142135624	octahedron	**5 "Platonic Solids"**
1.0514622242	icosahedron	
1.1547005384	cube	
0.7136441795	dodecahedron	
1.0000000000	**cuboctahedron**	
0.6180339887	icosidodecahedron	
0.8528028654	truncated tetrahedron	
0.5621692754	truncated cuboctahedron	
0.6324555320	truncated octahedron	**13 "Archimedean Solids"**
0.3367628118	truncated dodecahedron	
0.4035482123	truncated icosahedron	
0.7148134887	rhombicuboctahedron	
0.4314788105	great rhombicuboctahedron	
0.4478379596	rhombicosidodecahedron	
0.2629921751	great rhombicosidodecahedron	
0.7442063312	snub cube	
0.4638568806	snub dodecahedron	

But, here's the remarkable thing: Of all the Platonic and Archimedean Solids, **only** in the cuboctahedron are the length of the edge vector equal to the length of the radiating vector.

edge vector = radiating vector

(As we'll se, this is because it is actually an assembly of eight tetrahedra)

The cuboctahedron derives its name from the fact it is the intersection of a cube and an octahedron.

Envision joining these two shapes together, then cutting off all the pointy stellations.

What remains is a cuboctahedron.

(It inherits its six square faces from the character of the cube, and its eight triangular faces from the character of the octahedron.)

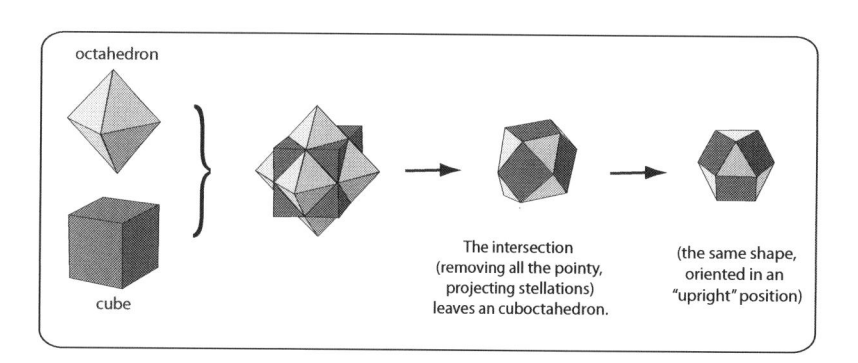

octahedron

cube

The intersection (removing all the pointy, projecting stellations) leaves an cuboctahedron.

(the same shape, oriented in an "upright" position)

95

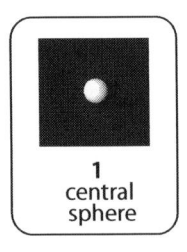

We've seen that starting with one sphere ...

1 central sphere

... 12 fit perfectly around it.

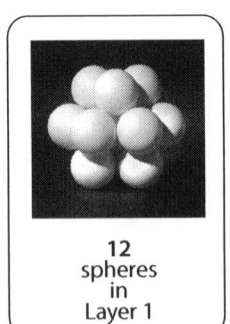

12 spheres in Layer 1

Now, how many spheres do you think will fit perfectly around this cluster of 13 spheres?

This is a littler harder to guess.
The answer is exactly **42**.
But notice it makes an even more well-defined cuboctahedron.

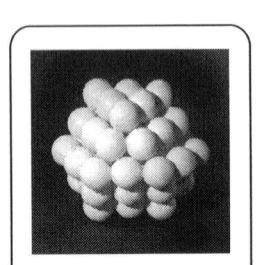

42 spheres in Layer 2

A cluster of 55 total spheres makes the central sphere a "true nucleus."

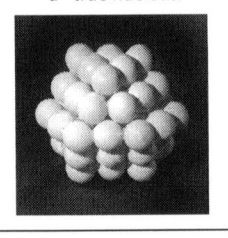

Starting with 1 sphere, plus 12, plus 42 more, makes a total of 55 spheres in this cluster. According to Bucky, at this stage the central sphere finally has become a "true nucleus."

(When only Layer 1 surrounds the central sphere, that nucleus sphere is visible through the gaps between the 12 outer spheres. But after Layer 2 (of 42 more spheres) has been added, the central sphere is **not** visible, and has now become a "true nucleus.")

Now, how many spheres will there be in layer 3?

The answer is **92**.
And it still makes a cuboctahedral shape.

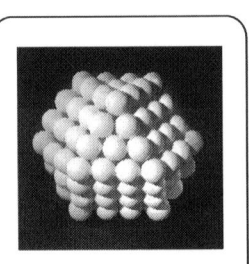

92 spheres in Layer 3

How about the next layer?
The answer is **162**, and again the cuboctahedral shape is maintained.

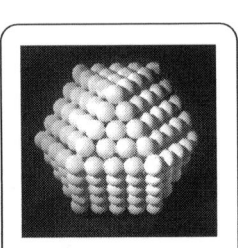

162 spheres in Layer 4

Do you notice anything peculiar about these numbers?
Well, they all end in 2. But ignoring the final digit 2 for a moment, the other digits are 1, 4, 9, 16.

Hey, these are the squares of 1, 2, 3, and 4.

Layer 1	12
Layer 2	42
Layer 3	92
Layer 4	162

The great mathematician Leonhard Euler discovered this around 1750, and devised this formula for the number of spheres per layer:

Take the layer number,
square it,
multiply it by 10,
and add 2.

Leonhard Euler

Euler's Formula
for the number of
spheres-per-layer
in the
closest-packing-of-spheres

$$(10 L^2) + 2$$

L= Layer number

In layer 1, 10 x 1 is 10, plus 2 is 12.
In layer 2, 10 x 4 is 40, plus 2 is 42.
In layer 3, 10 x 9 is 90, plus 2 is 92.
In layer 4, 10 x 16 is 160, plus 2 is 162.
Now, [drum roll, please], how many spheres will there be in layer 5?

	Ten times (the Layer number "squared")...	...Then add 2.
Layer 1	10 x 1 = 10	10 + 2 = 12
Layer 2	10 X 4 = 40	40 + 2 = 42
Layer 3	10 X 9 = 90	90 + 2 = 92
Layer 4	10 X 16 = 160	160 + 2 = 162

	Ten times (the Layer number "squared")...	...Then add 2.
Layer 5	10 x 25 = 250	250 + 2 = 252

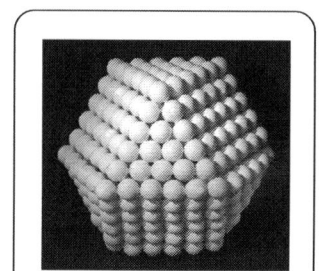

252 spheres in Layer 5

5 squared is 25.
10 times 25 is 250,
then adding 2 makes **252**.

Hey, that's Dee's magistral number!
(It has appeared quite naturally in this basic growth pattern.)

You can tell the cuboctahedral shape will continue if even more layers are added
(to 362, 492, 642, ... etc).

But there's something special about layer 5.

Spheres-per-Layer in closest-packing-of-spheres

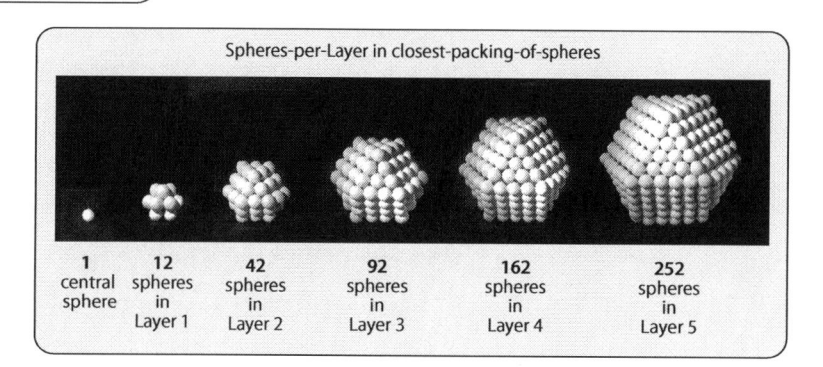

| 1 central sphere | 12 spheres in Layer 1 | 42 spheres in Layer 2 | 92 spheres in Layer 3 | 162 spheres in Layer 4 | 252 spheres in Layer 5 |

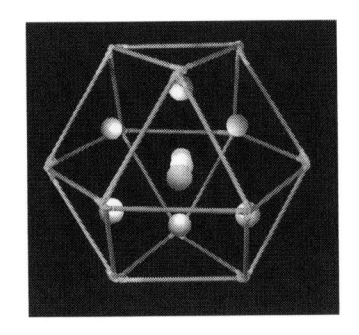

When layer 5 has been reached, eight of the spheres from layer 3 have enough spheres around them that they are now "true nuclei." It's hard to see their positions without x-ray vision, so I've simulated their positions digitally, along with the original central sphere.

[This is what Bucky was explaining in that confusing paragraph I found when I had googled "252 spheres." If you reread it now, it will make much more sense. It's at the end of the previous chapter]

As we'll see shortly, there's a whole lot more "eightness" going on here than simply these eight new nuclei.

Four "Bucky bowties" make a cuboctahedron

Bucky didn't like the term "Platonic solids."
He didn't see these shapes as solid at all.
He saw them as *energy events*.

Bucky didn't like the word "cuboctahedron" because it defines the shape by its faces. Bucky was more interested in the "vectors."
A vector is simply a line connecting two points.

[The term "vector" is used because technically a "line" extends in 2 directions endlessly.]

And as we've seen, only in the cuboctahedron are the radiating vectors and the edge vectors the same length.

To understand what Bucky means by "equilibrium" [a state in which opposing forces are balanced], let's first start in 2-dimensions.

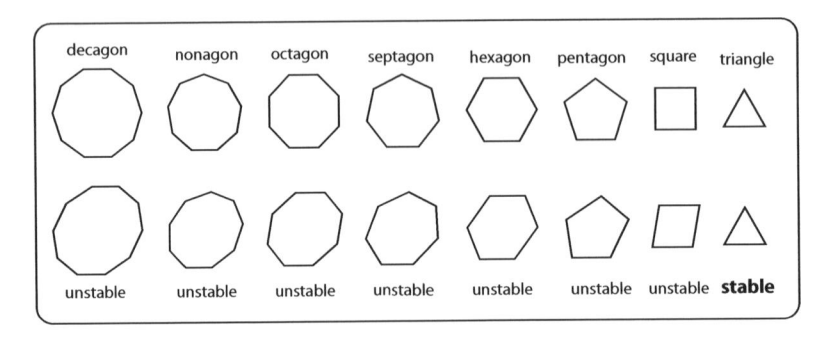

Of all the polyhedra (many-sided shapes), only the triangle is stable.

Using same-sized lollipop sticks and hot glue, if you make models of the triangle, square, pentagon, hexagon, septagon, octagon, etc., you can feel that **only the triangle is completely rigid**.

The others will move at the joining points.
They will not hold their shape.

The equilateral triangle is the simplest 2-D shape.

[Hint: Geometer Dee clearly recognized the wonder of the equilateral triangle–he used it as his name.]

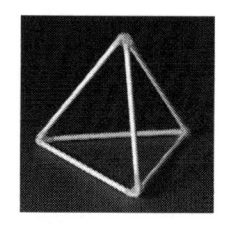

In 3 dimensions, the simplest shape that can be made from triangles is the tetrahedron. In Greek, *tetra* means "four" and *hedron* means "sides." The tetrahedron has 4 identical faces that are each perfect equilateral triangles.

Sometimes the tetrahedron is called a "pyramid," but be aware that it's not the same thing as what I call a "Pyramid of Giza," which has a square base and 4 triangular faces.

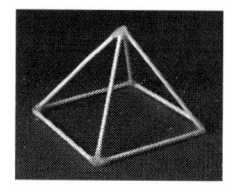

Bucky loved the tetrahedron. He called it the **"simplest structure"** or **"first and simplest subdivision of Universe"** or **" Nature's most economical shape**."

He succinctly declares,
"Six vectors are required for complete multidimensional stability."
(Fuller, *Synergetics 1*, Fig 621.10, p. 339)

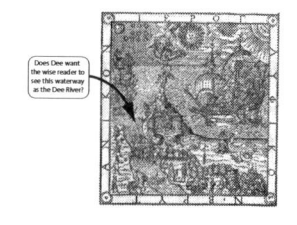

[Incidentally, John Dee saw the wonders of the tetrahedron as well. He shows Lady Occasion standing on a tetrahedron in the Title page illustration of *General and Rare Memorials pertaining to the Arte of Navigation*.]

One tetrahedron is nice, but Bucky realized to make an "energy event," two tetrahedra are required. And they must be tip-to-tip, with one point in common.
(In the Union of Opposites, it takes two to tango.)

As Bucky frequently wore a Bow tie, I call this shape a "Bucky bowtie."

Bucky frequently wore a bowtie

In a Bucky bowtie, the two tetrahedra **must** be oriented so their edges align making **three long lines** that each pass through a common point in the middle.

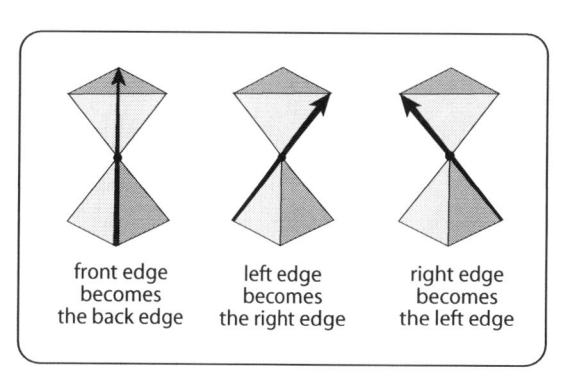

front edge becomes the back edge

left edge becomes the right edge

right edge becomes the left edge

99

What Bucky means by the term "energy event"
In Synergetics I, Bucky writes:

Plunging the elastics through the metal triangle

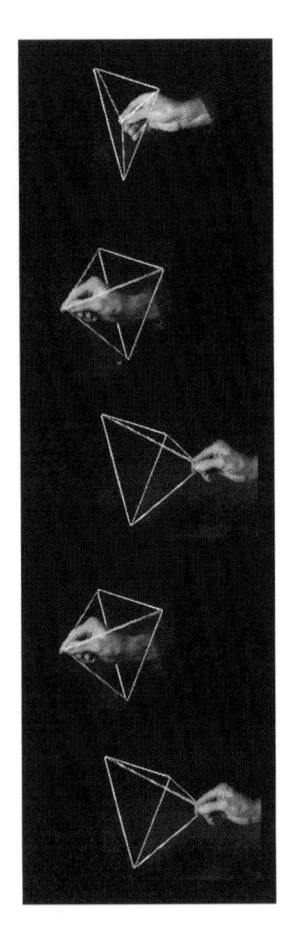

> "The tetrahedron is the only polyhedron, the only structural system that can be turned inside out and vice versa by one energy event."

To demonstrate this concept, Bucky welded three steel rods into a triangle (like the percussion instrument, only fully closed). He attached rubber bands to each of the three corners, then interconnected the bands in the center of the triangle.

Holding that center conjunction point in his fingers, he would plunge his hand deep into the triangle forming a tetrahedron (made from 3 rubber band edges and 3 steel edges).

Then he would quickly pull his hand back out of the triangle, making a tetrahedron pointed in the opposite direction.

He would plunge his hand back and forth, continuously "inside-outing" the tetrahedron. This pumping action formed what he called "positive and negative tetrahedra" and demonstrated "the essential twoness of a system."
(Fuller, Synergetics 1, 624.01- 02, p.341)

Inside-outing a three-petaled flower   Here's another way Bucky demonstrated the "inside-outing" of a tetrahedron. One tetrahedron splits apart at the seams and "opens up like a three-petaled flower bud." In this sequence, the "upward pointing" white tetrahedron morphs into a "downward pointing" black tetrahedron.

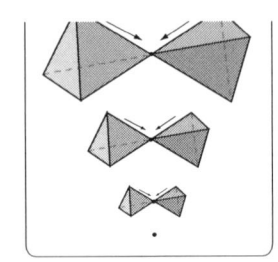

The pumping of an accordion

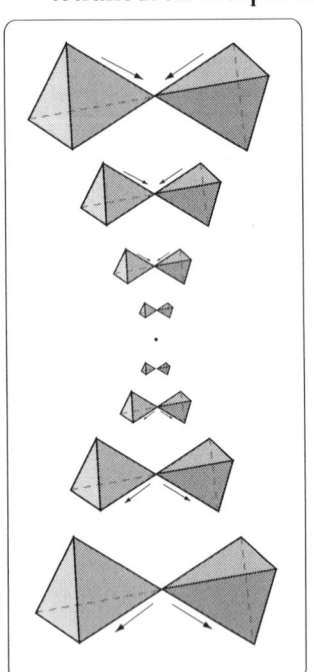

But I think the most insightful way Bucky demonstrates the energy event is with one tetrahedron shrinking, shrinking, shrinking, to a point, then coming out the other side and enlarging into the "opposite" tetrahedron. At the same time, the opposite tetrahedron does the same thing.

You can get a good feel for the "energy event," this two way pumping action of what he calls "convergence and divergence."

Envision this pumping action as rapid continuous, and going in both directions. It's like an accordion whose two sided shrink to a point, and then expand again, over and over again, every instant, eternally.

Bucky's "pumping" or "convergence and divergence"

100

Four Bucky bowties with a common center point

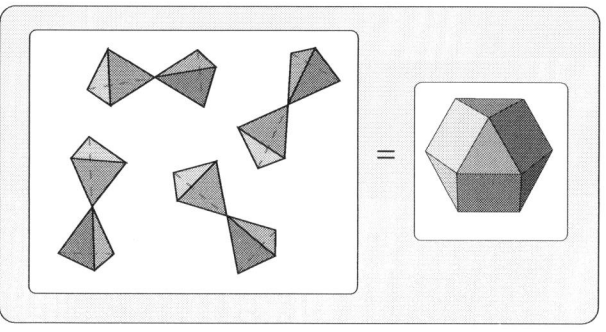

4 pairs of tip-to-tip tetrahedra assemble into a cuboctahedron

4 Bucky Bowties make a vector equilibrium

Now here's the important part.

Four of these Bucky bowties form a cuboctahedron!

(The tops and bottoms of the Bucky bowties make the 8 triangular faces of the cuboctahedron and the spaces between them make the 6 square faces.)

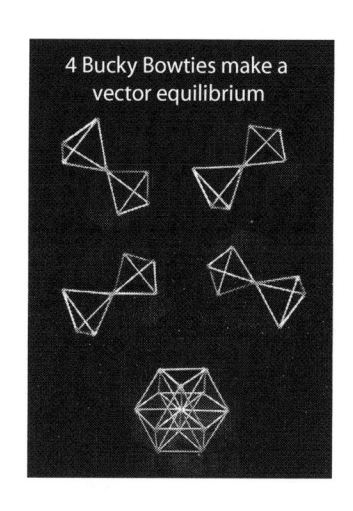

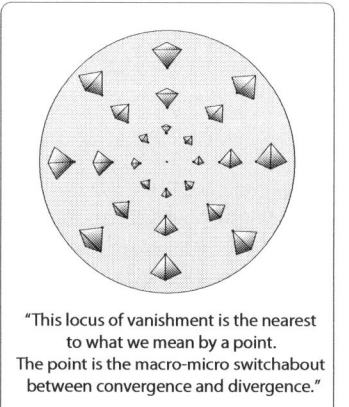

"This locus of vanishment is the nearest to what we mean by a point. The point is the macro-micro switchabout between convergence and divergence."

(Fuller, *Synergetics 1*, 1012.33)

Imagine four Bucky bowtie accordians, all pumping, all contracting, then expanding, all at the same time, through one point in the common center.

Four simultaneous, continual, and eternal enrgy events passing through a point so infinitesimally small you can't even see it with an electron misroscope.

Bucky poetically calls this center point the **"locus of vanishment."**

Eight tip-to-tip tetrahedra, all shrinking to nothingness at the same time. This glorious event is what Bucky uses to define the simplest thing in all of geometry: **a point.**

(A point is infinitely small.)

Most people might see the cuboctahedron as just another 3-D shape, perhaps an interesting ornament for a Christmas tree. But to Bucky it was the essence of how Nature's operates.

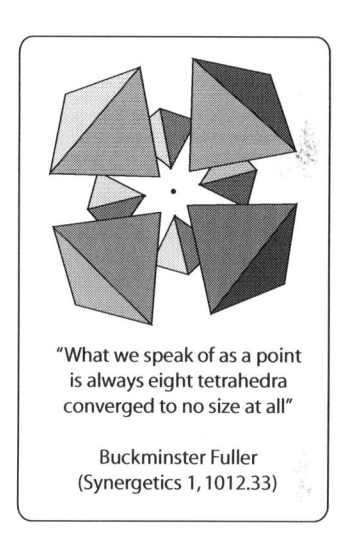

"What we speak of as a point is always eight tetrahedra converged to no size at all"

Buckminster Fuller
(Synergetics 1, 1012.33)

"A happening is an involuntary experience. You cannot program 'happen.' The vector equilibrium is the minimum operational model of happenings."

(Fuller, *Synergetics 1*, sec. 503.01 and 503.03, p. 224)

He even goes a step further with this astounding statement,

"Pulsation in the vector equilibrium is the nearest thing we will ever know to eternity and god."

(Fuller, *Synergetics 1*, sec. 502.52, p. 224)

Of all the things Bucky explored during his 88-year life on Spaceship Earth, the energy event of this simple shape was the ultimate experience. The quintessence of universe. Eternal and god-like. That's pretty profound.

Rhythm of Geometry = Rhythm of Number

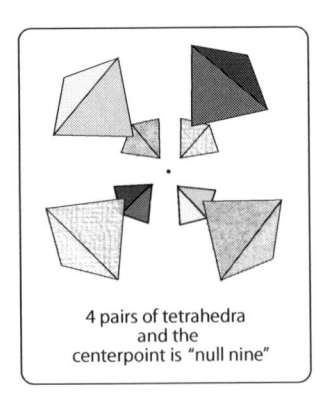

Bucky pondered the rhythm of the geometry of the vector equilibrium: Four positive tetrahedra and four negative tetrahedra make an octave of tetrahedra. Then he made a brilliant connection. This was the same rhythm he had seen when working with our Base Ten numbers.

Bucky saw geometry and number as two sides of the same coin. To him, the the "four positive" was like 1, 2, 3, 4, and the "four negative" was like 5, 6, 7, 8.

However, this doesn't account for all the single digits
(from which all other numbers are made)..

It's missing a digit: the number 9.

4 pairs of tetrahedra and the centerpoint is "null nine"

Bucky saw that common central point (the very heart of the vector equilibrium) **as the number 9.**

But that central point plays a different role than the 8 tetrahedra in this energy event. Bucky considers the 9 to be more like a "zero." More like a null thing or an empty place.

If all the radiating vectors in a vector equilibrium are like train tracks, that central point is the Grand Central Station, where they all meet up (or pass through).

Bucky asserts that the vector equilibrium has a **"+4, −4, octave; null 9"** rhythm.

In a chapter titled:
Nucleus as Nine = None = Nothing
Bucky writes:

"Nucleus as Nine
that is, non (Latin)
that is, none (English)
that is, nein (German)
that is, neuf (French)
that is, nothing..."

He's pretty clear about it: the center point of the vector equilibrium is the number 9.

He refers to 9 as "zero-nine" or "null nine," suggesting it acts like emptiness, or just plain zero. He calls the vector equilibrium the **"modular domain of the nine-zero-punctuated octave system."**

What fascinated Bucky was that he found this same "+4, −4, octave; null 9" in the realm of **number.** Bucky remembered a math trick he had learned when he was 25 years old. while training in the accounting department of Armour and Company (a large meat-packing facility in Manhattan). This was back in 1920, long before hand-calculators had been invented.

The technique called **casting out nines** was used to check if you had done a long multiplication problem correctly. [Perhaps you learned it in math class.]

Casting out nines involves boiling a number down to its "Digital Sum" (that is, the sum of the digits). Bucky called this process "indigging," or finding the "**Indig**" of a number (in**te**grating its **dig**its).

For example 375 indigs to 15, which further indigs to 6.

102

Examples of indigging:

24 indigs to 6

913 indigs to 4

90909 indigs to 0

6372815 indigs to 5

4678 indigs to 25, which further indigs to 7

Casting out nines is fun, easy, and useful:

1. Any time the digit 9 appears, cast it out (that is, ignore it, treat it like zero).
2. Any combination of digits that add up to 9 can also be crossed out.
3. Add up the digits that remain.
4. If the result is a two-digit number, add those two digits together (so it boils down to a single-digit number).

```
 ③⑦6         7
X  41      4+1=5       7x5=35    3+5=⑧
---                                        These two results
 376                                       should be the same
1504                                       if the original
-----                                      long multiplication
1⑤4̄16                         1+1+6 =⑧    was done correctly.
```

Here's a quick demo of **casting out nines**:

First, indig the two numbers involved in the multiplication problem.

Then multiply these two results together.

Finally, indig that result.
(In this example, the result is 8.)

Next, indig the **product** of the multiplication problem.
(In this example, 15416 also indigs to 8.)

If the two indigged results are equal, chances are your original long multiplication was done correctly.

(Amazingly, this "casting out of nines" procedure can also be used to check division, addition, and subtraction problems. The only time it doesn't work as a proving tool is if you make mistake which just happens to indig to the same number you would have arrived at with no mistake.)

Bucky summarizes,

"From this I saw that nine is zero."

Bucky then made a chart of the indigs in the normal Base-Ten flow of number and found the same "octave, null 9" rhythm he saw in the vector equilibrium.

On the left are all the single digits, and 9 is zero.

Next, the numbers 10 through 17 indig to 1, 2, 3, 4, 5, 6, 7, and 8, and the 18 indigs to zero.

At the bottom of the next column, 27 indigs to zero,

And in the next column, 36 indigs to zero.

This "octave, null nine" rhythm continues endlessly.

Indigging the normal flow of numbers reveals an "octave, null nine" rhythm.

1 = 1	10 = 1	19 = 1	28 = 1	37 = 1
2 = 2	11 = 2	20 = 2	29 = 2	38 = 2
3 = 3	12 = 3	21 = 3	30 = 3	(...)
4 = 4	13 = 4	22 = 4	31 = 4	
5 = 5	14 = 5	23 = 5	32 = 5	
6 = 6	15 = 6	24 = 6	33 = 6	
7 = 7	16 = 7	25 = 7	34 = 7	
8 = 8	17 = 8	26 = 8	35 = 8	
9 = 0	18 = 0	27 = 0	36 = 0	

Then Bucky made a chart of the **squares**
of the normal Base Ten flow of number:
1, 4, 9, 16, 25, etc.

The indigs flow "1407, 7041, zero,"
Then "1407, 7041 zero" again,
Then "1407, 7041 zero" again, endlessly.

Once again, he had found the "octave, null 9"
pattern.

Indigging the SQUARES
of the normal flow of numbers
reveals an "octave, null nine" rhythm.

1 = 1	100 = 1	361 = 1	784 = 1	1369 = 1
4 = 4	121 = 4	400 = 4	841 = 4	1444 = 4
9 = 0	144 = 0	441 = 0	900 = 0	(...)
16 = 7	169 = 7	484 = 7	961 = 7	
25 = 7	196 = 7	529 = 7	1084 = 7	
36 = 0	225 = 0	576 = 0	1089 = 4	
49 = 4	256 = 4	625 = 4	1156 = 0	
64 = 1	289 = 1	676 = 1	1225 = 1	
81 = 0	324 = 0	729 = 0	1296 = 0	

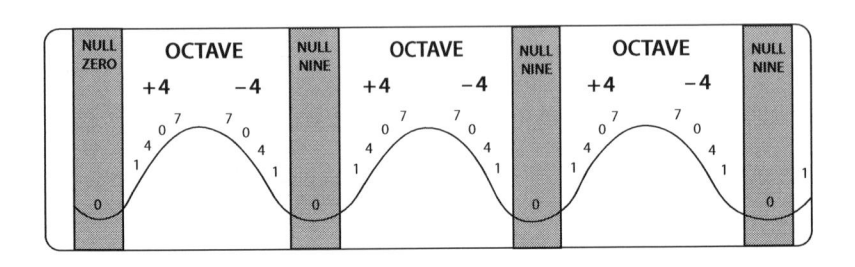

Here is a graphic depiction
of this rhythm found by
indigging the squares.

Bucky breaks the octave
into +4 and −4.

As Bucky puts it:
**"Indig congruences demonstrate that nine is zero
and that number system is inherently octave..."**
with an internal rhythm of
"four positive and four negative."

He calls it:

"The inherent +4, −4, 0, +4, −4, 0 ⟶ of number"

or the

"+4, −4, octave; null 9" rhythm of number

It's the same rhythm he saw in the vector equilibrium.
He saw how Geometry and Number were intrinsically related.

Similarly, John Dee, in his *Preface to Euclid*, emphasizes that all the arts and sciences derive
from only two "Principall Mathematical Artes." They are "Geometry" and "Arithmetic."

In short, Bucky discovered in the 1900s the same thing Dee discovered in the 1500's:
the closest packing of spheres and its cuboctahedron shape
synthesizes with the "+4,−4, octave;null nine" nature of number.
And they were each thrilled with their discovery.

104

How can I be certain Dee knew about the closest packing of spheres?

Johannes Kepler (in the early 1600s) is generally credited with being the first person to explore the closest-packing-of-spheres. But the wise philosophers of Europe had known about this arrangement for least 50 years.

Girolamo Cardano described the 12-around-1 closest-packing-of-spheres arrangement in his 1550 book about natural phenomena called *De Subtilitate* or "On Subtle Things."

(In 1552, Dee had a meeting with Cardano when the Italian mathematician was visiting London. Not only did Dee have two copies of Cardano's book in his library, he took one with him when he traveled to Prague in 1583. *Subtilitas* literally means "keenness, acuteness, or exactness." In his thick compendium, Cardano explains natural phenomena that go unnoticed by most people, including the behavior of light in a camera obscura.)

Dee cryptically refers to the closest-packing-of-spheres in his *Letter to Maxmillian*, in which he gives advice to those who have studied *Plenum and Vacuo* or "Space and Void."

"They have seen that the Surfaces of Elements, which are in close proximity are coordinated, connected, and Joined Together by a Law (decreed by God Almighty) and Bond (practically Unable to be Loosened) of Nature."

Dee's dramatic wording indicates this was an important concept in his cosmology.

Atomism

As we saw earlier, in Theorem 18 of the *Monas*, Dee relates one of Aesop's parables. A vengeful Scarab Beetle has deposited its dungballs in Jupiter's lap, where the Eagle had left its eggs for safekeeping. Dungballs and eggs (if all the same-sized spheres) will naturally arrange themselves in this closest-packing-of-spheres arrangement.

I'm not suggesting there were exactly 13 spheres in the cuboctahedral shape in Jupiter's lap. When any large quantity of same-sized spheres close-pack together, in the middle are of the pack are groupings of 13 spheres arranged in the cubocthedral shape.

Indeed, after relating the parable, Dee writes he is acting more like "Aesop" than "Oedipus."

(Oedipus was famous for the Riddle of the Sphinx).

Dee is hinting: This is not a parable, it's a riddle.

My interpretation of Dee's "eggs and dungballs" being "same-sized spheres" might seem conjectural, but not if you understand the bigger picture of Dee's philosophy:

Dee was an Atomist.

Atomism is simply the theory that the universe is made from atoms, which can neither be divided nor destroyed. Dee didn't invent this concept by any means. Atomism goes back to the Greek philosophers:

Anaxagoras (ca. 500 BC – 428 BC),
Leucippus (ca. 425 BC),
his student **Democritus** (ca. 375 BC),
and later, **Epicurus** (ca. 300 BC)

Democritus writes:

"In nature, there is nothing but 'atoma' (atoms)
and 'kenon' (void, space, emptiness).**"**

In the Renaissance, great thinkers like Nicholas of Cusa, Marcello Ficino, and Giordano Bruno were influenced by Lucretius' ideas on atomism.

As Andrew Pyle writes in *Atomism and its Critics: from Democritus to Newton*: during the late 1500s and early 1600s, "atomism was becoming very popular and widespread." By the year 1600, the Classical Atomic theory had been thoroughly revived and was the subject of heated controversy.   (A. J. Pyle, pp. 224-5)

Robert Kargon, in his 1966 book *Atomism in England, from Hariot to Newton*, prefaces his chapter on Dee's friend, Thomas Harriot, with a few words about John Dee. Kargon calls Dee the **"leading participant in the Platonic-Pythagorean revival of the English Renaissance."**

(Kargon, p. 8)

[Atoms are so small, Dee could never see one close up. But if he thought
atoms were spherical, then all close-packed matter would contain cuboctahedral shapes]

More evidence that Dee knew about the cuboctahedron

Besides writing the *Preface* to the 1570 first English Edition of Euclid's *Elements*, Dee provided over 150 corollaries and addendums to various propositions. The French expert on Euclid, Francois de Foix (also known as Flussas) provided some as well.

The whole translation of *Elements* is almost 1000 pages long. At the very end, after Book 16, is a *Brief Treatise* by Flussas.

In it, Flussas explains that the intersection of a cube and an octahedron is an "exoctahedron."

The prefix "ex" is short for "sex" which means "six." So this word, "ex," is simply another name for the six-sided cube. Thus, ex-octahedron means cube-octahedron.

Exoctahedron, Cuboctahedron, Vector Equilibrium;
they all refer to the exact same shape.

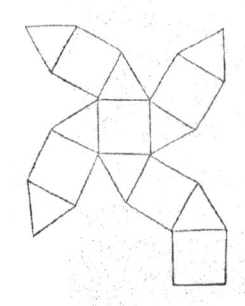

Along with Flussas's explanation is a flattened version that
can be cut out and shaped into a 3-D cuboctahedron.
Note that it has 8 trianglular face and 6 square faces.

Flussas also provides a geometric proof of how to make the shape
by cutting off the corners of a cube at the middle of its edges.

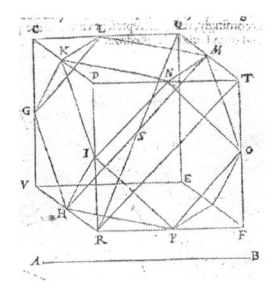

106

Dee gives several clues about the cuboctahedron in his "Thus the World Was Created" chart. He knew an astute geometer would recognize that **12, 13, 24,** and **25** are all numbers associated with the cuboctahedron:

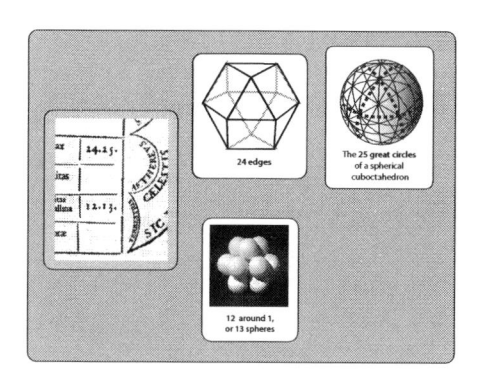

The cuboctahedron's **12** spheres-around-1 arrangement makes a cluster of **13** spheres.

The cuboctahedron has exactly **24** edges.

The 25 is a little trickier. If a cuboctahedron is blown up like a balloon, there are exactly **25** "great circles" that pass through the vertices, edge-midpoints, and face-centerpoints.

Dee and his fellow navigator friends were quite familiar with "great circles." They used them to find the shortest route between two places on the spherical globe of the earth.

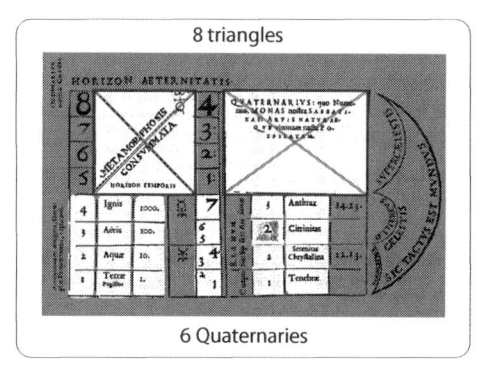

Alchemists like Paracelsus refer to the **"Earthly Quaternary"** and the **"Heavenly Ternary."**

Things "of Earth," are grouped in fours (like the 4 Elements). Things "of Heaven" are in groups of three (like the Holy Trinity).

In the "Below" half of Dee's chart are 6 "quaternaries," or lists containing 4 items.

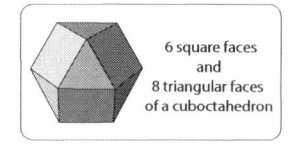

In the "Above" half of the chart, Dee has cryptically hidden 8 triangles.

This is Dee's clever way of hinting at the 6 square faces and the 8 triangular faces of a cuboctahedron.)

How can I be sure Dee knew about the "+4, –4 octave; null 9" nature of number?

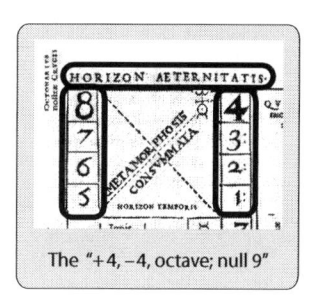

This one is easy to answer. Dee illustrated it in his "Thus the World Was Created" chart.

The Greeks called 9 the "Horizon Number" because, being the largest single digit, it is on the horizon of a vast sea of multiple-digit numbers.

The digits 1, 2, 3, and 4 are in one grouping. And 5, 6, 7, and 8 are in another. And the two groupings are connected with a large dotted-line X, a symbol of oppositeness.

To conclude, Dee and Bucky both saw the wonders of the cuboctahedron.

They each saw that it was made from 4 pairs of tip-to-tip tetrahedra, with a null ninth centerpoint.

107

One of Bucky's favorite maxims: "Unity is plural and at minimum two."

"Unity is plural" might seem like a contradiction in terms. "Unity" seems as though it means wholeness, or oneness. And "plural" is anything but oneness.

So let's take a sphere as an example. Bucky saw that in order for it to be a sphere, it has to have an outside and an inside. Outsidedness is convex, and insidedness is concave.

How you see the sphere depends on if you're outside it or inside it.

To humans, the surface of the earth is convex. But to an earthworm or a fish, the surface of the world is concave.

As another example, let's take a line, (in this case a lollipop stick). Most of us see a line as one thing.

But Bucky saw a line as a vector connecting two endpoints.

These endpoints are centers of two same-sized spheres that are tangent to each other.

To Bucky, a line was an energy event between two things.

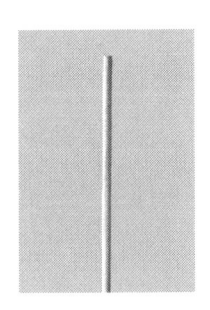

Bucky summarizes with an even shorter maxim:

"Unity = 2"

Well, this is exactly how Dee saw things.
The main theme of the *Monas Hieroglyphica* is the Sun and the Moon becoming one. The Union of Opposites.

Dee and Bucky were on the same wavelength. They both fervently searched to find Nature's laws. They were both skilled geometers. And they both found the same things.

Bucky called himself a "**comprehensivist**," someone who ties together various fields of knowledge.
Dee was a **polymath**, a philosopher wise in many fields of learning.

Bucky saw himself as a "**citizen of Spaceship Earth**."
Dee called himself a "**cosmopilite**," meaning "citizen of the world."
(Dee's birthday was July 13 and, curiously, Bucky's birthday was July 12).

Bucky was a brilliant, creative thinker.
And he had the advantage of 300 years of accumulated knowledge over Dee.
But next, we'll see that Dee actually discovered **more** about number than Bucky did!

Robert Marshall Finds Symmetry in Number

Fortunately, one of Bucky's followers, Robert Marshall, had a brain for seeing patterns in number and explained his findings to Bucky.

Bucky understood what Marshall had discoverd and was quite excited about it. He asked Marshall if he would publish his findings "in another edition of *Synergetics*." Unfortunately, in 1983, before the project came to fruition, Bucky passed away.

Again, I found Marshall through more googlification of 252. He was in his 70's and living in a small house in Northern California. We corresponded for 10 years until he died. He called his study of the symmetry of number "Syndex." He saw rhythms in number that are invisible to most people.

Marshall was thrilled. Few scholars besides Bucky were able to see the significance his work.

I was thrilled. I soon realized that Marshall saw numbers the same way Dee saw numbers. Dozens of puzzling parts of the *Monas* became crystal clear.

[It's explained more fully in my Book 5, *The Meaning of the Monas Hieroglyphica with Regards to Number*. But here is a brief synopsis.]

Marshall saw numbers differently than most people. As a child, he had a hard time grasping subtraction of digits.

But when he saw numbers as dots, and some dots were taken away, things were much clearer.

109

In the 1960's, Bob Marshall was a hippie living in the Haight-Ashbury district of San Francisco, the epicenter of many of the social and cultural changes that were swirling trough America.

While studying Eastern religion, he asked a visiting guru how he should proceed in his study of number. The guru was no mathematician, but he recommended that Bob study the number which had been sacred in Indian culture since the days of the ancients – the number 108.

108 SACRED HINDU NUMBER

The Hindus recite the names of 108 deities while counting their mala, a looped string with 108 beads.
There are 108 verses in the Rig Veda.
To the Hindus, 108 represents totality and wholeness.
Even today, some Hindus in India pay lots of rupees
to have 108 in their smartphone numbers.

(To my Western-educated mind, 108 seemed as random as 252.
It seemed like 100 would be a better candidate
to express wholeness than 108.)

mala
(108 beads)

Marshall made a huge spiral of numbers called the "108 Wheel."
The first circle of the spiral went from 1 to 108.
The next circle went from 109 to 216, and onward.
It had 60 cycles that went all the way out to the number 6480.

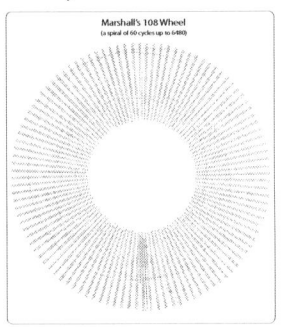

Marshall's 108 Wheel
(a spiral of 60 cycles up to 6480)

With the wheel as a starting point, Marshall found what he calls an "ancient canon of number." He was quick to add that he didn't discover it. He only claims to have "re-discovered" it, as he was able to discern that it was known to the Ancient Hindus, the Greeks, and even the authors of the Bible.

Why haven't other mathematicians seen what Marshall found? Well, Marshall had a different way of looking at number. Most people see Number as a one-way street. One, two, three, four … and off into infinity. Marshall saw **number as a two way street.** It goes forwards and backwards. [And backwards doesn't mean the "negative numbers" that go –1, -2, -3, -4, etc. Marshall only worked with the positive integers.]

Marshall found that at certain finite limits, there is **complete symmetry of number**. What does he mean by symmetry of number? [And could these be the same "fixed limits" of "Nature's Law" that Dee was referring to in his Artificial Quaternary chart?]

Also, Marshall did not consider 1 to be a number. This might sound strange to modern ears. If Joe has 5 apples and sells 4, he has one left. So, one **must** be a number. I live at 321 Main Street. Where am I supposed to tell people I live?

However, math historians will confirm that, up until around 1700, nobody thought one was a number. Greek, Medieval and Renaissance mathematicians saw that "1" acted differently than all the other digits.

Multiply one times any number and the result is the same number.
Divide one into any number and the result is the same number.
Add one to any number, then add another one, then another,
and the result is the natural sequence of number.

You can't say these things about 2, or 3, or 4, or any other digit.

As we'll soon see, early mathematician-philosophers considered one
to be the "fount" or source of all number.

Marshall's symbol for "retrocity" or "oppositeness"

Marshall also recognized a function that most other mathematicians ignore.
He calls it "**retrocity**." It expresses oppositeness.

(From the Latin word *retro*, meaning backwards)

To express it in mathematical notation, Marshall invented the "**retrocity symbol**."
He considered the retrocity symbol (which is read as, "is the opposite of") to be as
important as other function signs like "=" ("is equal to") or ">" ("is greater than").

To draw it, make a vertical line that ascends, then slowly
arches, then descends in the "opposite" direction.

Then add a horizontal line that suggests there is
an "interconnection," despite the "opposition."

Here's my artistic interpretation that emphasizes
its "Union of Opposites" character.

[There's a positive side and a negative side,
but they're united as one symbol.]

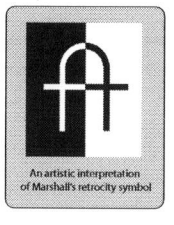

An artistic interpretation of Marshall's retrocity symbol

Here are some examples to show how simple it is.

The opposite of 29 is 92.

[As they mirror each other, Marshall
calls them "reflective mates."]

The reflective mate of 341 is 143.

The reflective mate of 27956 is 65972.

```
29 ⊕ 92
341 ⊕ 143
27956 ⊕ 65972
```

The "opposite" of a number which
contains all the same digits is "itself."
For example, the reflective mate of 22 is 22.

```
8 ⊕ 8
22 ⊕ 22
77777 ⊕ 77777
```

Here are the reflective mates of
some numbers that end in zero.

The reflective mate of 270 is 072 or simply 72.
The reflective mate of 27,000 is also 72.
The reflective mate of 35,000 is 53.

```
270 ⊕ 72
27000 ⊕ 72
35000 ⊕ 53
```

111

This might seem like a silly number game, but we'll shortly see
that it's essential to seeing the natural symmetry of number.

Plus, it's useful shorthand for expressing the
"oppositeness" found in many kinds of things.

Wet ⚡ Dry   Loud ⚡ Quiet
Hot ⚡ Cold
Rich ⚡ Poor   Up ⚡ Down
On ⚡ Off
Love ⚡ Hate   War ⚡ Peace

It's obvious that Hot and Cold are opposites, but they are
united in the sense they are both aspects of temperature.

Wet and Dry are both aspects of humidity.
Loud and Quiet are both aspects of sound.

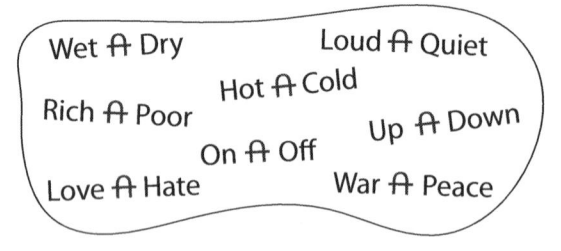

My initial reaction was that you can't simply ignore place value like that. For example,
the 2 in 29 really represents 20, not 2. Then I recalled how place value was ignored in the
"indigging" Bucky did in the "casting out of nines" to check long multiplication.

The idea of ignoring place value opens up a world of number not many people have explored.
And in it, wonderful symmetries can be seen. This might sound mysteriously mystical, but
perfect symmetry can be easily seen on the chart of numbers you learned in grade school.

	1	2	3	4	5	6	7	8	9
10	11	12	13	14	15	16	17	18	19
20	21	22	23	24	25	26	27	28	29
30	31	32	33	34	35	36	37	38	39
40	41	42	43	44	45	46	47	48	49
50	51	52	53	54	55	56	57	58	59
60	61	62	63	64	65	66	67	68	69
70	71	72	73	74	75	76	77	78	79
80	81	82	83	84	85	86	87	88	89
90	91	92	93	94	95	96	97	98	99

This square chart includes all the
single and double-digit numbers.

(Note that it ends with 99, because 100 is a triple-digit number.)

Across the horizontal rows are the single digits, then
the teens, the twenties, the thirties, etc.
Looking vertically, the first column of numbers all end
in 0, the next column of numbers end in 1, then 2, etc.

To see the perfect symmetry
more clearly, allow me to make a few
non-destructive adjustments to the chart.

First, let's look at it backwards, like
the way Hebrew or Chinese is read.

Now the 10, 20, 30, etc.
column is now on the right.

9	8	7	6	5	4	3	2	1	
19	18	17	16	15	14	13	12	11	10
29	28	27	26	25	24	23	22	21	20
39	38	37	36	35	34	33	32	31	30
49	48	47	46	45	44	43	42	41	40
59	58	57	56	55	54	53	52	51	50
69	68	67	66	65	64	63	62	61	60
79	78	77	76	75	74	73	72	71	70
89	88	87	86	85	84	83	82	81	80
99	98	97	96	95	94	93	92	91	90

Next, let's rotate it
45 degrees counter-clockwise,
making the square into a diamond.

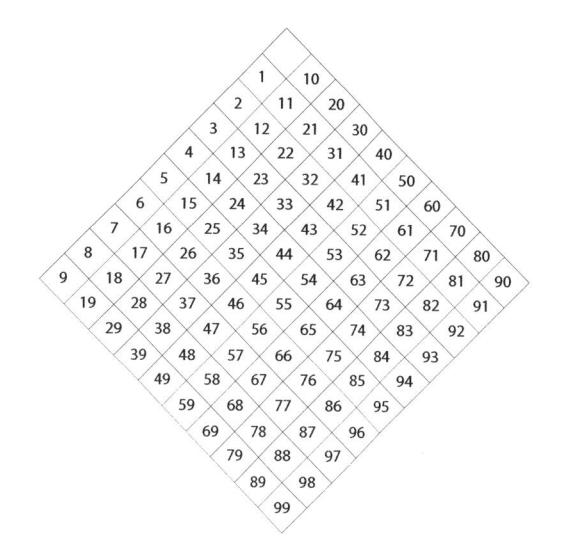

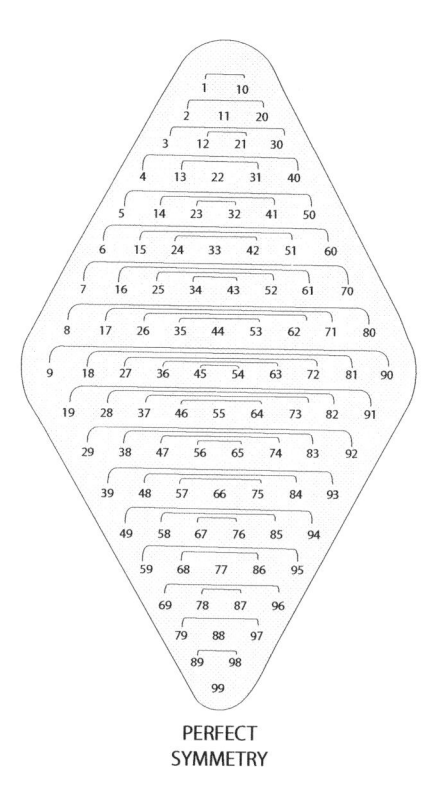

Then, let's stretch it vertically to
make room for brackets which
connect various reflective mates.

Look. Every number on the left side
of the chart has a reflective mate
on the right side!

PERFECT SYMMETRY

The chart has **perfect symmetry**!
Like the wings of a butterfly!

There is complete retrocity!

The numbers on the central vertical
spine of the chart (11, 22, 33, etc.)
don't have partners because they
are reflective mates of themselves!

(For example, the opposite of 77 is 77)

The numbers "11, 22, 33, 44, 55, 66, 77, 88, and 99" are all multiples of 11,
so I call them the "**11 Wave**".

Marshall refers to these numbers as **palindromes** (or palindromic numbers).

(They're similar to palindromic words, which read the same forwards as backwards, like "level," "kayak," or "racecar."

Marshall calls the reflective pairs which contain two different numbers "**transpalindromes**."

(If you put a mirror right down the spine of this chart, splitting the palindromes in half,
you can see the perfect symmetry of the whole chart.)

Who knew numbers had such splendor!

113

It appears as though the **11 Wave** rules the chart.
But not so fast. There's another wave that's just as important.

It's the **9 Wave**, which runs horizontally across
the middle of the chart (the multiples of 9).
On the far left is 9.
On the far right is 90.

In them between are 4 transpalindromic pairs,
(18 and 81), (27 and 72), (36 and 63), and (45 and 54).

Seeing the 90 as that "null 9th thing," Bucky's
"+4, –4, octave; null 9" rhythm is clearly evident.

The "9 Wave"

Marshall calls 9 the **transpalindromizer** and 11 the **palindromizer**.

9 10 **11**
nine ten eleven

Incidentally, similar symmetries can be found
in other Bases besides our Base Ten System.

The transpalindromizer is always one digit less than the Base number.

The palindromizer is always one more than the Base number.

[But only Base Ten makes this "octave, null 9" rhythm, and I believe it was for this reason Base Ten
was selected by the ancients. And not because man has 10 fingers. But that's a longer story]

The Cycloflex

The "northwest edge"
of the "butterfly chart"
expresses Bucky's rhythm
"+ 4, –4, octave; null nine"
(in the single-digit range of number).

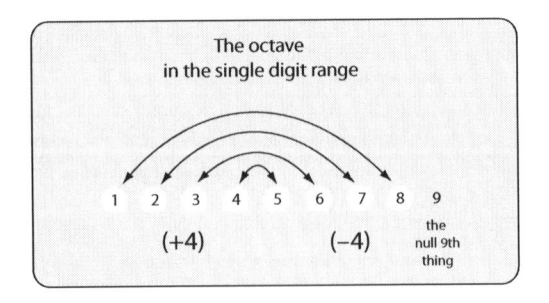

The octave
in the single digit range

1 2 3 4 5 6 7 8 9
    (+4)   (–4)   the
                        null 9th
                        thing

And the middle horizontal row
also expresses Bucky's rhythm
"+4, –4, octave; null nine"
(in the two-digit range of number).

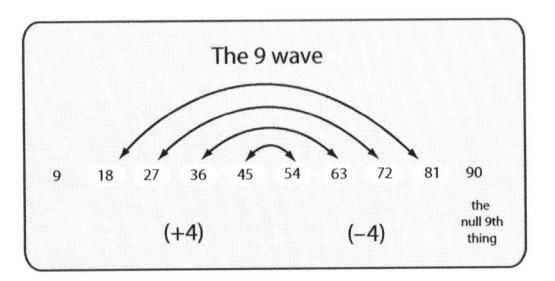

The 9 wave

9 18 27 36 45 54 63 72 81 90
         (+4)   (–4)   the
                                   null 9th
                                   thing

114

Multiplying 9 times 11 makes 99, which is the largest double-digit number.
The three-digit range of numbers is ruled by the multiples of 99:
198, 297, 396, 495, 594, 693, 792, 891 and 990,
or what I call the **99 Wave**.

You can see that
198 and 891 are reflective mates,
297 and 792 are reflective mates, etc.

They beat out the same
"+4, –4 octave, null nine" rhythm.

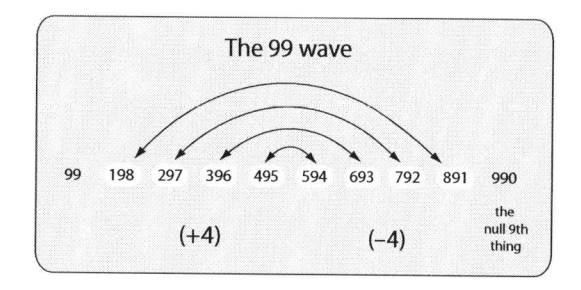

The 99 wave

99 198 297 396 495 594 693 792 891 990

(+4) (–4) the null 9th thing

What Marshall meant by
"number is a two-way street"
now becomes a lot clearer.

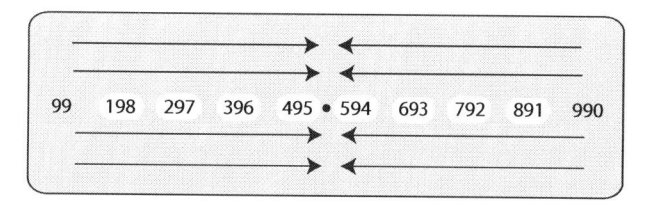

99 198 297 396 495 • 594 693 792 891 990

Next, 99 times 11 is 1089,
and the **1089 Wave** rules the
range of the 4-digit numbers.

However, a curious thing happens.
A "nave" or central-point is born.
It's the palindromic number 5445.

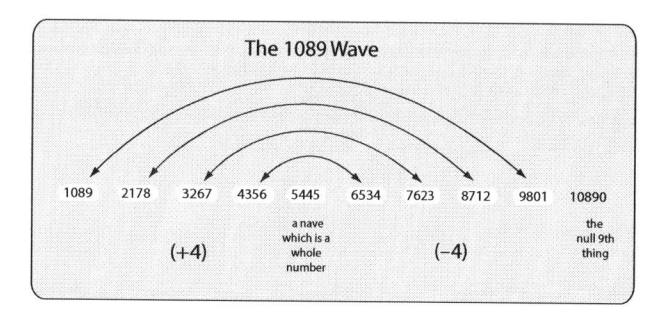

The 1089 Wave

1089 2178 3267 4356 5445 6534 7623 8712 9801 10890

(+4) a nave which is a whole number (–4) the null 9th thing

That nave of 5445 causes the
5-digit range to be ruled by 10890.

The **10890 Wave** also exhibits
perfect symmetry and has Bucky's
"+4, –4 octave; null nine" rhythm.

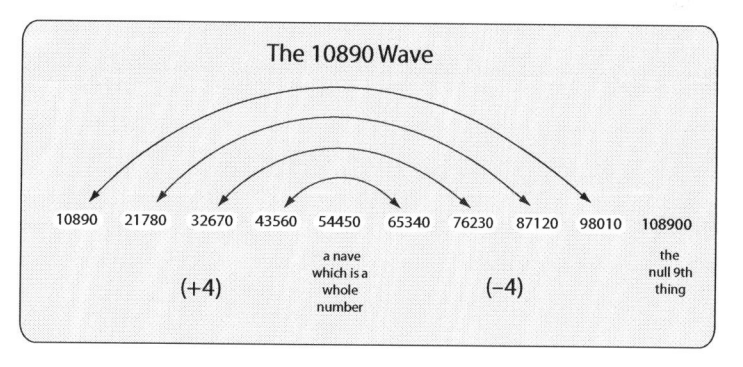

The 10890 Wave

10890 21780 32670 43560 54450 65340 76230 87120 98010 108900

(+4) a nave which is a whole number (–4) the null 9th thing

This same "+4, -4 octave; null nine" rhythm continues through the **108900 Wave**,
the **1089000 Wave**, the **10890000 Wave**, etc. (You get the picture).

Marshall referred to this number rhythm as the "**Cycloflex**."
As you **cycle** through the number ranges, numbers **flex** back on themselves.

(Dee called this number rhythm "Consummata," which is Latin for "to make perfect" or "to complete.")

What does all this have to do with Dee?

Note that of the single digit numbers are palindromes.
For example, the reflective mate of 6 is 6.
The reflective mate of the palindrome 11 is 11.
That makes 12 and 21 the "**first** transpalindromic pair."
And guess what **12 times 21** equals?

252

Dee's Magistral number.

Putting the hand calculator aside and doing this as "long multiplication" reveals how 252 is made from 12 and 24, two of Dee's favorite numbers.

Marshall explored 252 even deeper and found this amazing relationship. The squares of 12 and 21 are transpalindromes themselves:
144 and 441.

Also, the difference between 252 and 144 is 108.
Marshall calls this the relationship the "Syndex pretzel"

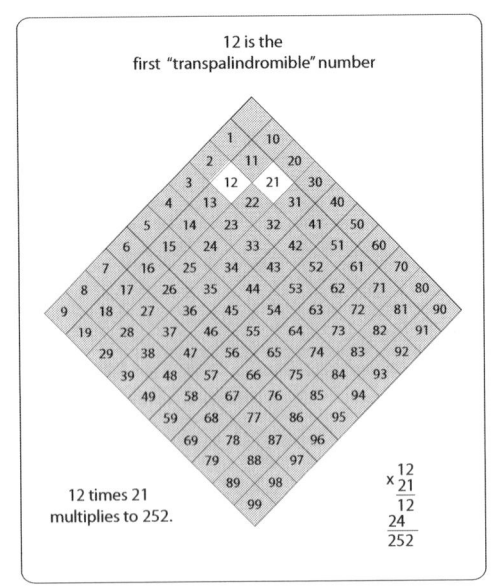

12 is the first "transpalindromible" number

12 times 21 multiplies to 252.

$$12^2 = 144$$
$$12 \times 21 = 252$$
$$21^2 = 441$$

the difference is 108
the difference is 189

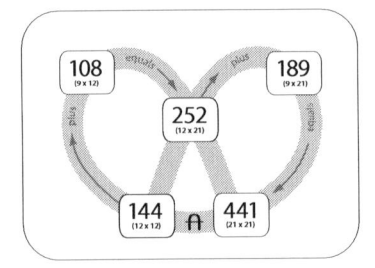

I call 252 a "nexus number," because its always in the middle of things. Mathematicians will want to explore its prominent position in what is called Pascal's Triangle.

(It was known long before Pascal, and Dee definitely knew about it. Dee even uses the "1, 7, 21, 35, 35, 21, 7, 1" row to calculate probabilities in Aphorism 116 of his 1558 *Propaedeumata Aphoristica*.)

When we separate even numbers from odd numbers, right in the center of the large triangular patch of even numbers is 252

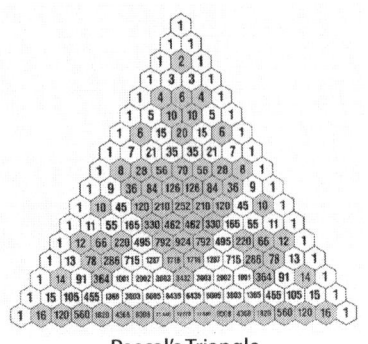

Pascal's Triangle

Pascal's Triangle
(with even numbers in grey)

The Holotomic Sequence

Marshall found **another** great sequence that flows through number whose members show the "symmetry of number" in a different way.

He calls them the "**Holotomes.**"

This word is a composite of the Greek word *holo*, which means "whole," and *tome*, which means "book."

Marshall sees them as "whole-books" because each is a complete "book" of numbers, which exhibits perfect symmetry.

Plus, contained within each holotome are the symmetries of all the holotomes which precede it.

(This will become clearer in a moment when we look at "number wheels.")

To find these symmetrical books of number we must "Think like a Renaissance man." And remember, Renaissance men didn't consider "one" to be a number.

One is Not a Number

In *History of Mathematics*, D.E. Smith declared:

"Not until modern times was unity considered a number. Euclid defined number as a quantity made up of units…"

(D.E. Smith, *History of Mathematics*, II, p. 26)

Aristotle wrote in *Physics*,

"The smallest number in the strict sense of the word 'number' is two."

(*Aristotle*, edited by Richard McKeon, *Physics*, Book 3, Ch. 11, Section 220, Line 27)

Nicomachus wrote that unity is not a polygonal number, but Boethius interpreted this as meaning that one was not a number. Following Boethius, great mathematicians in the Middle Ages like al-Kwârmizi (ca. 825), Michael Psellus (ca.1075) and Rolandus (ca. 1424) excluded one from the realm of number.

This viewpoint held fast during the Renaissance. The Italian mathmetician Luca Pacioli (ca. 1494) writes, "**…unita nō e numero…**"

The German mathematician Theodoricus Tzwivel (ca.1505), writes:
"Unitas em numeus non est. Sed fons et origo numerorum,"
"Unity is not a number, but the fount and origin of number."

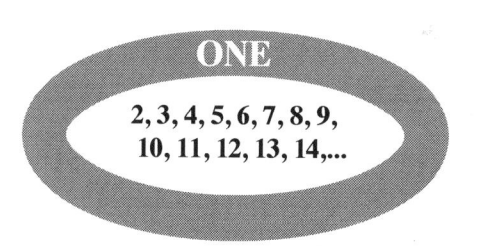

ONE
2, 3, 4, 5, 6, 7, 8, 9, 10, 11, 12, 13, 14,…

Dee writes in his 1570 *Preface to Euclid*,

"We consider a Unit to be a Mathematical thing, though it be no number, as it is indivisible."

(Dee, *Preface*, p. j.)

Humphrey Baker, one of Dee's contemporaries in England, writes,
"an unitie is no number, but the beginning and original of number."

Towards the end of the 1500's, mathematicians like Simon Stevin (1585) and Petrus Ramus debated whether it was all a question of semantics. Stevin writes,

"…if from 3 we take 1, 3 does not remain, hence 1 is not no number,"

[He used a "double negative" for emphasis]

Eventually, Stevins' admittedly logical train of thought caught on.
But to grasp why earlier mathematicians didn't consider one to be a number, we must explore the ultimate example of oppositeness.
Are you ready:

$$\boxed{\text{Nothing} \;\text{⊕}\; \text{Everything}}$$

"Nothing is the opposite of Everything"
Whoa. That's a pretty big concept.
(Don't worry, I'm not going to get all philosophical on you)
Let's look at it mathematically.

The "Nothing" (or the void) is 0.
The "Everything" is 1.
(As all numbers flow from the well-spring of 1.)

$$\boxed{0 \;\text{⊕}\; 1}$$

As Marshall writes,
**"You cannot have matter without space.
An object cannot exist unless it has a place to be.
And you cannot have both, then, without reversal."**

Marshall coined an term for this group of 3 things:
the **"Prenumerical Tertiary Singularity."**

"Prenumerical" in the sense that it comes "before numbers" (2, 3, 4...)
"Tertiary" because there are "3 things" involved.
And "Singularity" because "they all work together."

What we normally think of as "one,"
Marshall saw as a collection of three things:

"zero-retrocity-one"

He used a triangle to depict the
"Prenumerical Tertiary Singularity."

And to simplify, he shortened the mouthful "zero-retrocity-one" to the pithier term, "zero-one."

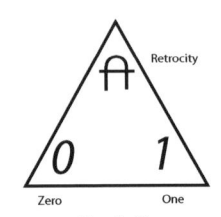

Marshall's
"Prenumerical Tertiary Singularity"

What I call "The Birth of Number"

Let's start with that first important step from "zero-one" to two.

The energy of the "zero-one" generates special number 2.
Marshall calls 2 the "symmetrical aspect" of "zero-one."
Let's label 2 as "symmetry."

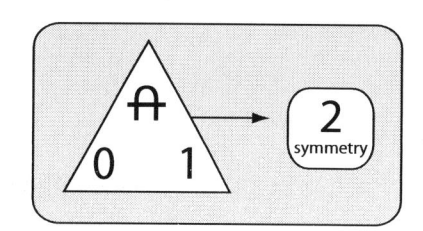

Envision this "symmetry" energy echoing
further out into the number realm,
to 4, 8, 16, 32, 64, 128 ... and beyond.

But let's confine this analysis to just the single digits
(out of which all other numbers are made)..

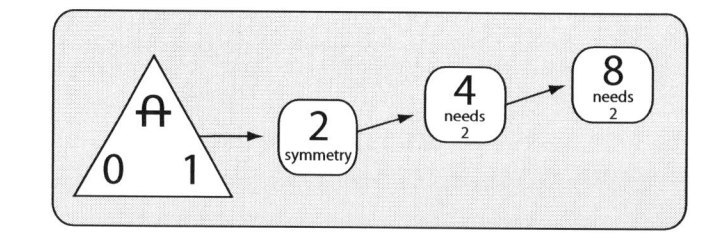

In making 4, number 2 already exists,
so (as I express it) 4 only "needs 2."

Similarly, as 4 now exists, 8 only "needs 2."

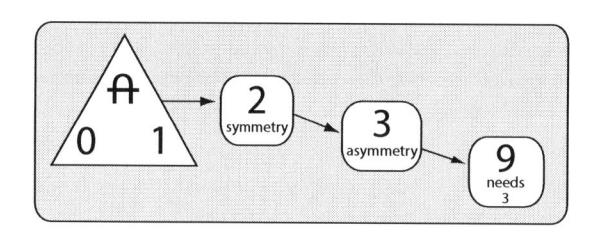

Now that 2 exists, it has another special power.
Along with "zero-one," it generates 3.
I call the number 3 "asymmetry."

[For example, if 3 people are playing tennis together, there
will always be an asymmetrical arrangement.]

This "asymmetrical 3" beams its
energy into the number realm,
making 9, 27, 81, 243, 729, 2187, ...

Again, let's restrict this study to the single-digits.
Because 3 now exists, 9 only "needs 3."

This leads to what I call the "tussle" between 3 and 4.

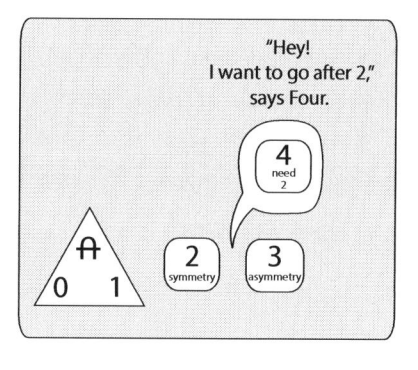

"Hey!
I want to go after 2,"
says Four.

The number 2 has generated two things:
2's close relative, 4,
and 2's neighbor, 3.

Both 4 and 3 are vying for position
to follow immediately after 2.

Both have good reasons
to claim the spot.

Who wins?

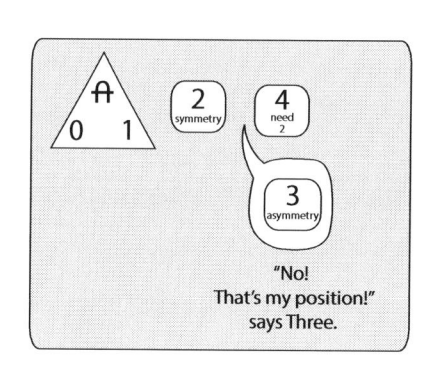

"No!
That's my position!"
says Three.

119

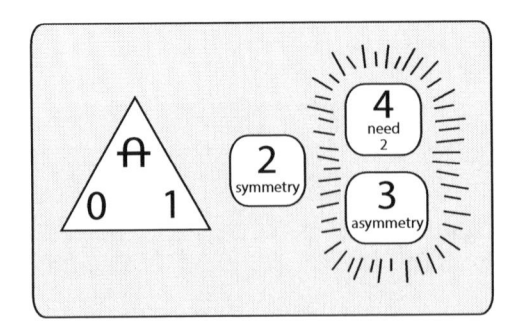

This interaction between the Quaternary and the Ternary has huge ramifications in geometry and number.

This tension between 3 and 4 can be seen physically in the cuboctahedron. The triangular faces "tussle" with the square faces.

(Also, there 6 square faces and 8 triangular faces or a 6:8 ratio, which reduces to a 3:4 ratio.).

The cuboctahedron is a display of 3 and 4 in a spherical wrestling match.

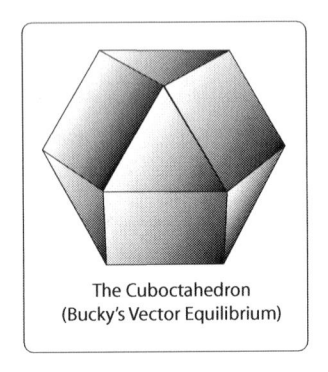

The Cuboctahedron
(Bucky's Vector Equilibrium)

In Theorems 6 and 20 of the *Monas*, Dee cryptically refers to this friendly tension between 3 and 4.

He says the Cross of his Monas symbol can be seen as either "Ternary" (two lines and their common point) or "Quaternary" (four lines).

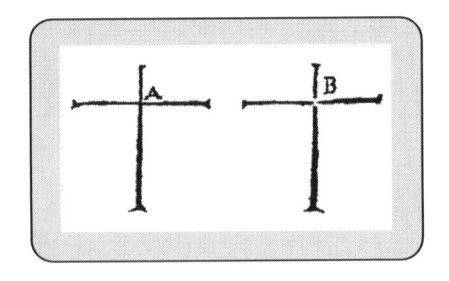

Dee tells us the results of the "tussle" in one of his favorite axioms:
Quaternarius Internario Conquiescens
"The Quaternary Rests in the Ternary."

(If the 4 had won the tussle, the Ternary would be resting in the Quaternary.)

(Dee, *Propaeaedeumata Aphoristica*, Title page of the 1568 edition)

Number historian Michael Schneider writes,

"A fundamental map of ourselves is found in the mathematical intimacy between the Triad and the Tetrad. The ancient mathematical philosophers saw themselves wherever three and four mingle."

[Schneider, Michael, *Beginner's Guide to Constructing the Universe, the Mathematical Archetypes of Nature, Art, and Science*, p. 89; (an enlightening book about the qualities of each of the single digits)]

So here's where the story now stands.

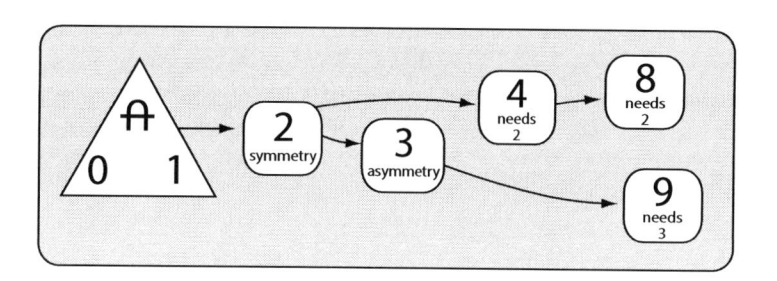

Next, we might add the number 6.
But, 2 and 3 already exist, and
2 x 3 = 6,
so 6 already exists.
In other words, 6 "needs nothing,"

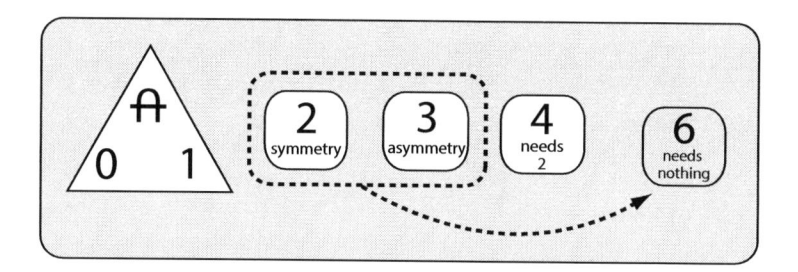

Then 8 and 9 battle it out for the next position.
The winner is 8, because it is related to 2,
which was born before 3 (the relative of 9).

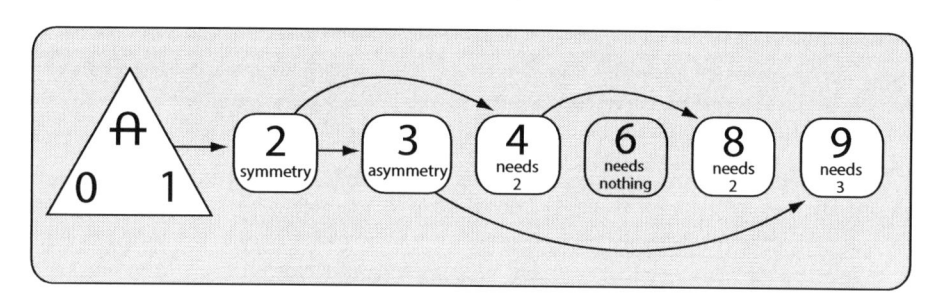

Finally, those prime numbers 5 and 7 can be added to the sequence.
They linger at the tail end because they are not related
to either symmetrical 2 or asymmetrical 3.
(And 5 beats out 7 because it's a lower number.)

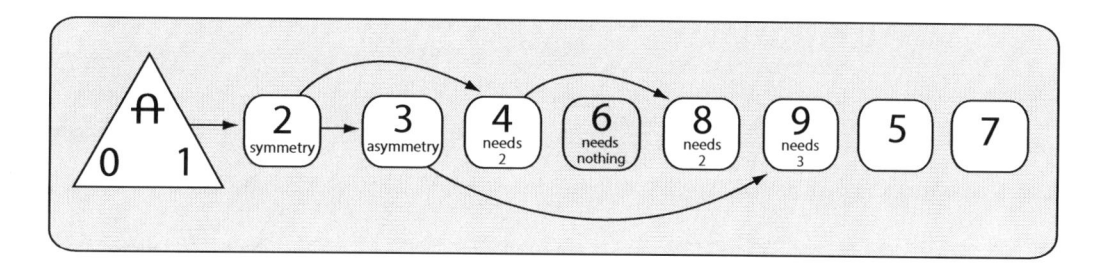

121

Now that we have accounted for all the single digits,
let's look only at their "essences," or only at what they "need."
Continuous multiplication of these "essences" generates the
beginning of what Marshall calls the Holotomic sequence:
12, 24, 72, 360, and 2520.

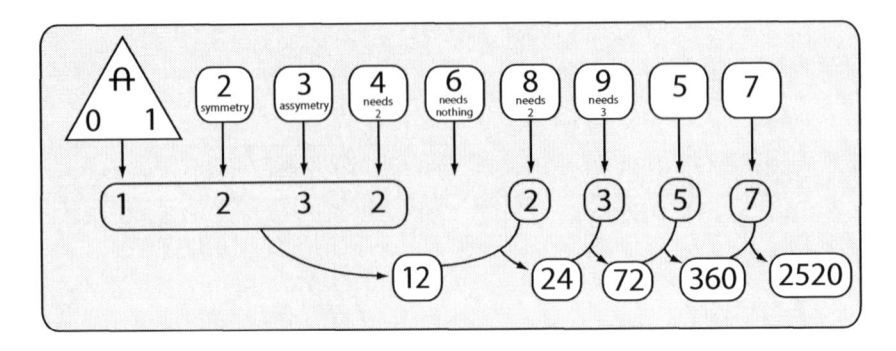

Why not just use the natural order of digits 1, 2, 3, 4, 5, 6 7, 8, 9?
Well, some of the numbers that result, (60, 420, and 840) are **not** Holotomes.
They do not symmetrically arrange the prime numbers they contain.

(More on how to see this in a moment.)

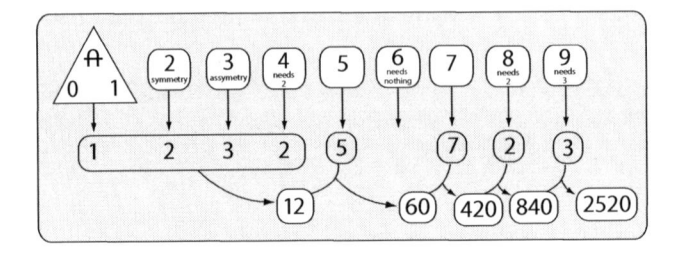

Here's a summary of the creation of the Holotomes:

From the source of retrocity, "zero-one,"
blossoms symmetrical 2 and asymmetrical 3,
and then their relatives (4, 6, 8, and 9),
and then the primes (5 and 7).

So the simplified recipe for the Holotomes is:
"12 times the primes."

Here's a more dramatic way of
envisioning the Metamorphosis sequence
It begins at the source, "zero-one," and it
spins its way out into the realm of number.

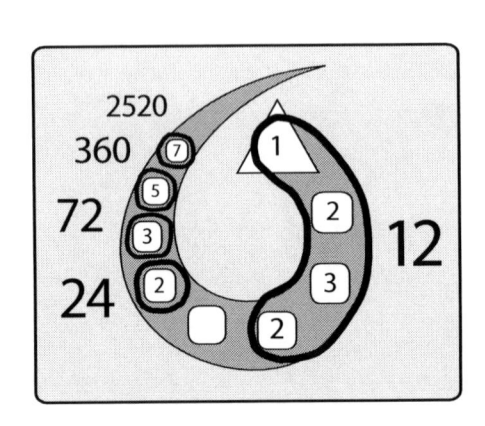

122

But the Holotomes don't stop at with 2520.
We can continue to multiply by the primes
(in their consecutive order).

Note that "Holotome H" (6126120)
is in the 6 million range.

Next "Holotome I" jumps into
the 116 million range.

And next, "Holotome J" is in the 2 billion range.
And they continue onward in giant steps.

12	Holotome A
12 x 2 = 24	Holotome B
24 x 3 = 72	Holotome C
72 x 5 = 360	Holotome D
360 X 7 = 2520	Holotome E
2520 x 11 = 27720	Holotome F
27720 x 13 = 360360	Holotome G
360360 x 17 = 6126120	Holotome H
6126120 x 19 = 116396280	Holotome I
116396280 X 23 = 2677114440	Holotome J

6126120	360
360360	72
27720	24
2520	12

The first octave
of Holotomes

As Bucky said,
numbers are organized in octaves,
so we can assume something special happens
when we have a "octave of Holotomes."
An octave of Holotomes brings us to 6126120.

Let's look at the "twelveness" inherent in the first few Holotomes.

24 is, of course, two dozen. 72 is half of 144 (which is 12 squared).

The ancients rounded off a year to 360 days and used 12 months of 30 days each.

The next Holotome, 2520, is perhaps the most spectacular of all.
You might have noticed that it is 10 times Dee's Magistral number, 252.

But even more importantly, seeing it with Marshall's "retrocity,"
the **reflective mate of 2520 is 0252**, or simply **252**.

But 2520 is even more important than that.

**2520 is the lowest number that is
divisible by all the single digits!**

Marshall admired it so much he called it the "Auric
Number," in the sense that it has a certain aura about it.

Here are all the single digits and the numbers
by which they need to be multiplied to arrive at 2520.

1 x 2520 = 2520
2 x 1260 = 2520
3 x 840 = 2520
4 x 630 = 2520
5 x 504 = 2520
6 x 420 = 2520
7 x 360 = 2520
8 x 315 = 2520
9 x 280 = 2520

Nature's most
economical number

2520

(the lowest number
be divisible by all the single digits
1, 2, 3, 4, 5, 6, 7, 8, and 9)

Dee loved the number 2520 and cryptically hid references
to it in several places in the *Monas Hieroglyphica*.

One of the most obvious is when he tells King Maximillian that his mind has
been pregnant with the ideas of the *Monas Hieroglyphica* for "seven years."

Rounding the year off to 360 days [the way the ancients did], **seven years is 2520 days**!

(Notice that "7 x 360 = 2520" is the exact same multiplication step used in the Holotomic Sequence.)

quem Annos prius continuos Septem, Mente gestaui mea,

"My mind has been pregnant with it continuously for the past 7 years"

Dee cryptically refers to 2520 as the "**Sabbatizat.**"
It's much like the Sabboth (the seventh day), only in years.

(You may be suspecting that 2520 is Dee's "rare gift" to Maximillian.
Think again. His gift is even **more** special than 2520.)

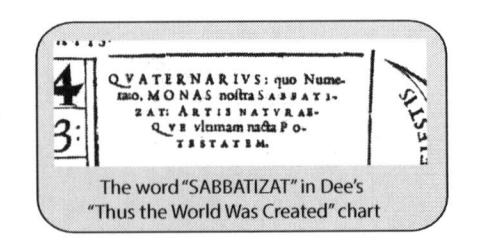

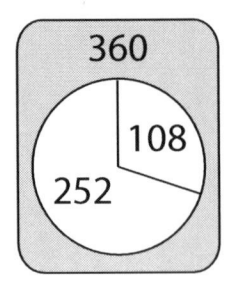

The word "SABBATIZAT" in Dee's
"Thus the World Was Created" chart

The Holotomic number 360 is pretty special as well. It's the number of degrees in a circle. It's also important in a way I call "**East meets West.**" Add that ancient Hindu number **108** to Dee's Magistral number **252** and what do you get?

The answer is **360**, a perfect circle. So, 108 and 252 are each essentially expressions of the same thing, the various rhythms and symmetries we are exploring here.

$$108 + 252 = 360$$

The perfect symmetry of the Holotomes can be seen in "number wheels"

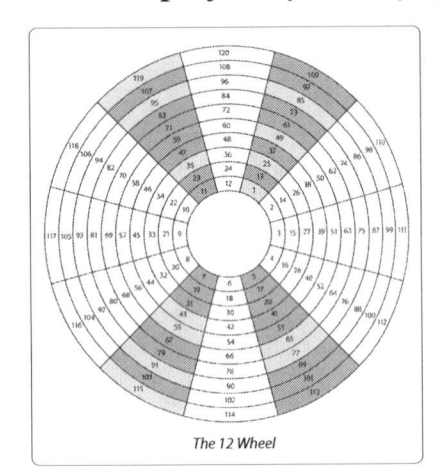

One way to see the symmetrical nature of the Holotomes is by depicting them as wheels. This is what I call the **12 Wheel**.

It's a spiral of numbers from 1 to 12, then the next circle goes from 13 to 24, then 25 to 36, etc. All the prime numbers in the chart have been shaded in **dark** gray. **All the primes fall in only 4 of the 12 radians.**

In these number wheels, the only two primes I do not shade in dark grey are 2 and 3. And as you can see, no other primes ever fall in their radians anyway.

The 12 Wheel

For the sake of comparison, here's the 18 Wheel. It **is** symmetrical across the vertical axis, but **not** across the horizontal axis. (The left side reflects the right side, but the top half does not reflect the bottom half.)

Number 18 **is not** a Holotome, but the number 12 **is** a Holotome.

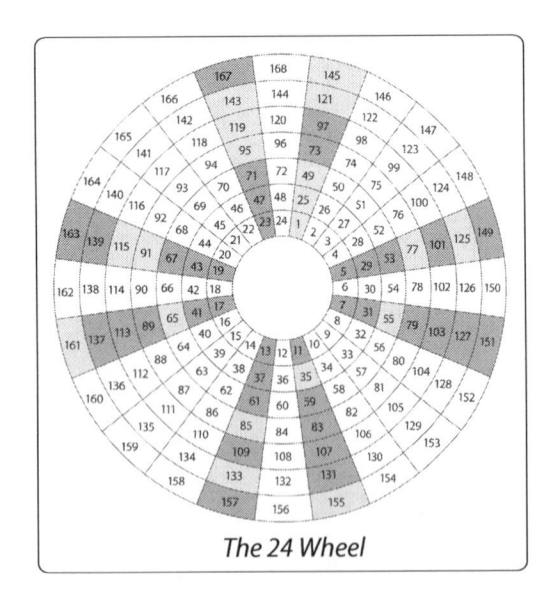

The 18 Wheel

The **24 wheel**.
is like a Maltese Cross,
with perfect horizontal
and vertical symmetry.

For comparison,
here is the 30 wheel.

It **is** symmetrical across
the vertical axis,
but **not** across the
horizontal axis (thus
30 is not a holotome).

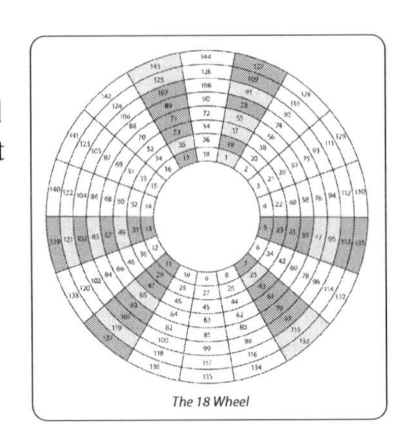

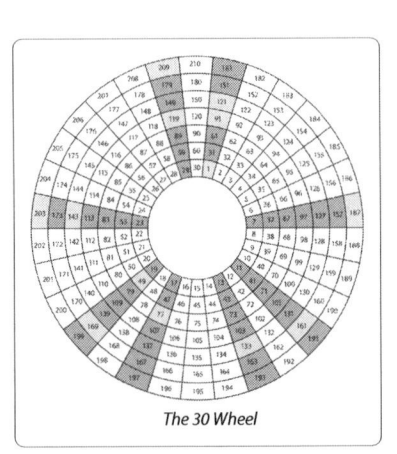

The 24 Wheel

The 30 Wheel

124

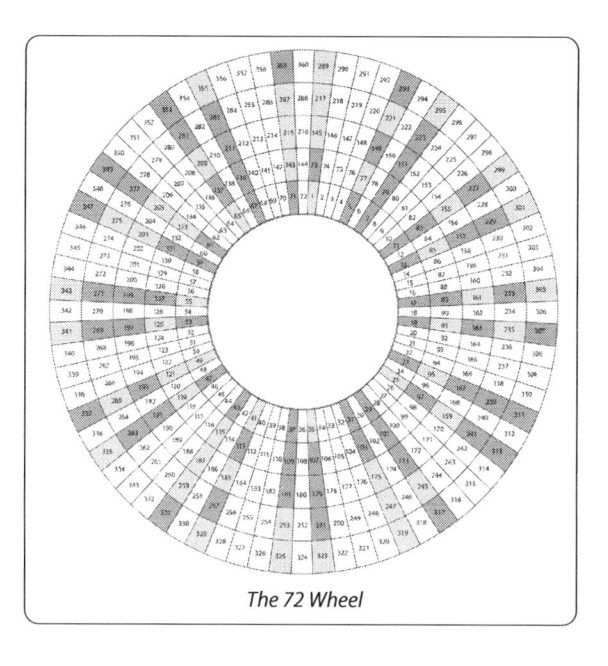

The symmetry of the **72 Wheel** is a little hard to discern.

So in this diagram, the radians which contain prime numbers are fully colored in gray.

It's a **sunburst** of perfect **symmetry**!

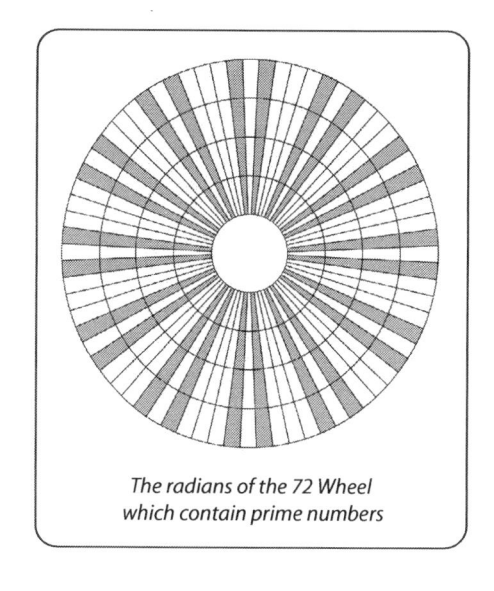

The 72 Wheel

The radians of the 72 Wheel which contain prime numbers

In my **360 Wheel** shown here, the radians are too thin to be able to include numbers, but you can see the perfect symmetrical distribution of the radians containing prime numbers.

The **2520 Wheel** is just as symmetrical. As are the Wheels for all the larger Holotomes.

As mentioned earlier, each Holotome incorporates all the symmetries of the Holotomes which precede it.

[Caveat: These wheels help us see the symmetrical nature of the Holotomes, but are not an empirical test as to whether a number is a Holotome or not. For example, because of the awesome symmetry in the 72 wheel, half of the 72 wheel or the "36 wheel" is also perfectly symmetrical. And twice the 72 wheel, or the "144 wheel" is perfectly symmetrical as well.]

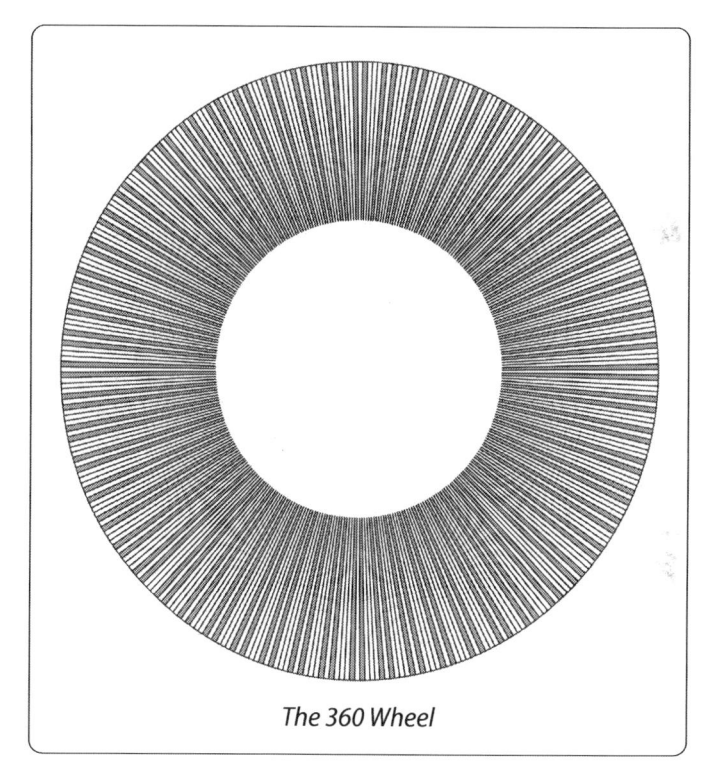

The 360 Wheel

**2520
The Great Eagle**

To celebrate the wonderful symmetry of the 2520 Wheel (which incorporates all the single digits), Marshall calls 2520 "**The Great Eagle**."

It's two wings of 1260 each are perfect reflections of each other.

125

This chart of the first octave of Holotomes shows little boxes with their divisors. Starting down on the bottom right, 12 is divisible by 2, 3, 4, and 6.

Through 24, 72, and 360 more divisors are added to the box, until at 2520 the box is filled with the first "octave, null nine" of number.

Proceeding upwards, more divisors get added until, at 6126120, the second "octave, null 9" of numbers, up to 18, is included.

Well, almost all. Look closely. Notice that the 16 is missing. The number 6126120 is evenly divisible by all the numbers from 1 to 18, **except 16**. How are we to deal with this fly in the ointment?

6126120	360
360360	72
27720	24
2520	12

6126120 divided by 16 is 382882.5
Because this result ends in .5, it's obvious that the number which is "2 times 6126120" **will** be divisible by 16 (and thus be divisible by all the numbers up to 18.)

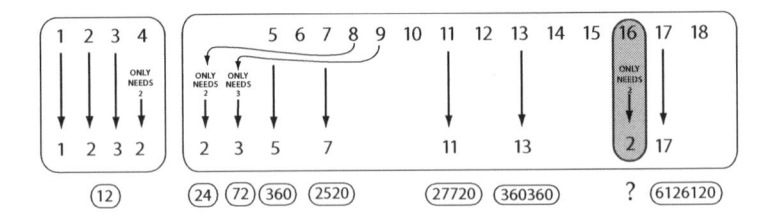

Now.... drum roll please... 6126120 times 2 is this glorious number:

12252240

Ignoring place value, look who we can find in here. There of two of Dee's favorite nimbers, the first two Holotomes, 12 and 24. And there's Dee's Magistral number 252.
(Or by using that zero, there's the Sabbatizat or the Great Eagle, 2520)

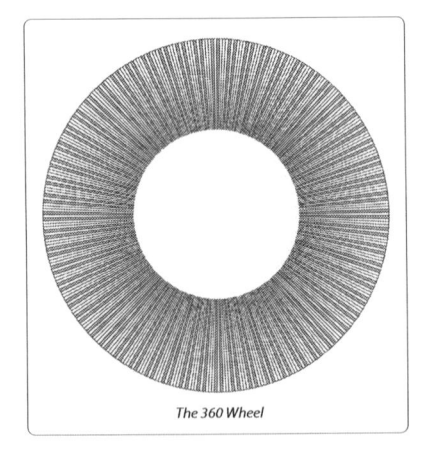

12 252 24 0

Try to imagine what the **12252240 Wheel** would look like. It would exhibit the same perfect symmetry like the 360 Wheel, only it would have over 12 million radians!

Being the lowest number divisible by all the numbers up to 18 (which is two "octave, null nines" of number).
Yes, 12252240 is truly a **rare** number.

The 360 Wheel

Indeed, I believe 12252240 is Dee's "rare gift" to Maximilian, the King of the Holy Roman Empire.

126

That's his gift to the King? A measly number? Well, yes, but it's no ordinary number.
To a mathematician who sees the symmetries in number, it's very, very special.
Dee even prefaces his *Letter to Maximillian* this way:

**"This gift is so extremely rare and of great goodness
that the warm feelings I have for your Majesty
should not be held in contempt,
even though it is so small in size."**

(By "small in size" Dee means its only a number, it's not something like a grand
sculpture made from gold and silver festooned with precious gems)

Here's a summary of how we
reached this glorious Number.

Marshall was so excited about 12252240,
he called it the **"Even Greater Eagle."**
[It has two symmetrical wings of 6216120 each.]

12252240
The Even Greater Eagle

12252240	
6126120	360
360360	72
27720	24
2520	12

Marshall also refers to 12252240 as the **"Encapsulation Number"**
because it symmetrically "encapsulates" two octaves of number.

In the *Preface to Euclid,* Dee cryptically refers to 12252240 as the
"Exemplar number of all things Numerable."
[An "Exemplar" is something which serves as an
excellent model (a fitting term for 12252240.]

The word numerable means "able to be counted."
[Of course, there are many numbers higher than 12252240. But this number, way up
in the 12 million range, is already pushing the limits of what a man could actually count.
There are about a million grains in a handful of sand. Try counting over 12 handfuls.]

127

To summarize, Dee (in the 1500's) saw the same thing Marshall saw (in the 1900's).
They just gave different names to what they found.

Two of the most puzzling words in Dee's
"Thus the World Was Created" chart
are "Metamorphosis" and "Consummata."

In his final chart, he places them along the dotted-line X,
prominent in the middle of his "1, 2, 3, 4 and 5, 6, 7, 8" octave.

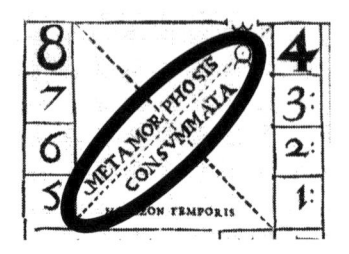

Marshall's Holotomic Sequence is what Dee calls METAMORPHOSIS.
Marshall's Cycloflex is what Dee calls CONSUMMATA.

Robert Marshall's names:		John Dee's names
Cycloflex	"+4, −4, octave; null 9" rhythm of the 9 Wave, 99 Wave, 1089 Wave,...	Consummata
Holotomes	12 times the primes 12, 24, 72, 360, 2520...	Metamorphosis
Auric number	2520	Sabbatizat
Encapsulation number	12252240	Exemplar number

The Cycloflex (9 Wave, 99 Wave, 1089 Wave,...)
and the Holotomes (12, 24, 72, 360, 2520...)
exhibit symmetry in different ways.

It might not seem like these two great sequences are related.
But they are!

This chart is but one way to see that the Holotomes and the Cycloflex are synchronous.

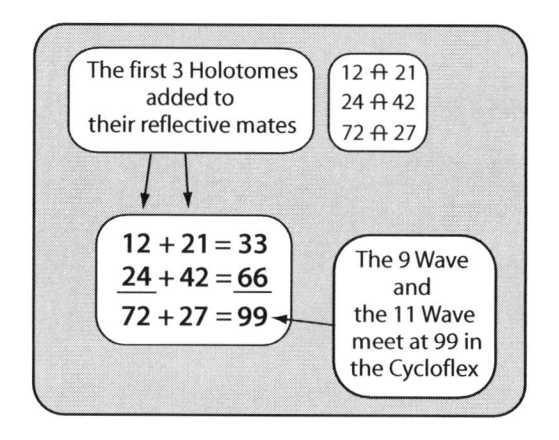

The first 3 Holotomes added to their reflective mates
12 ⚹ 21
24 ⚹ 42
72 ⚹ 27

12 + 21 = 33
24 + 42 = 66
72 + 27 = 99

The 9 Wave and the 11 Wave meet at 99 in the Cycloflex

The first 3 Holotomes (12, 24, and 72) are added to their reflective mates (21, 42, and 27).

12 + 21 makes 33
24 + 42 makes 66
33 + 66 total to 99

Amazingly, 72 + 27 also sum to 99.

We started with three **Holotomes,** and ended up with 99, a key number in the **Cycloflex**.

In the *Monas*, Dee's most obvious clue about the Metamorphosis numbers is his Artificial Quaternary (1, 2, 3, 2.)

Dee is teaching us how to look for the "essence" of number. Everyone knows the normal flow is "1, 2, 3, 4," but, as 2 already exists, the 4 "only needs 2."

Continue this line of thought with the rest of the single digits (as we did earlier) and the Metamorphosis sequence appears before your eyes.

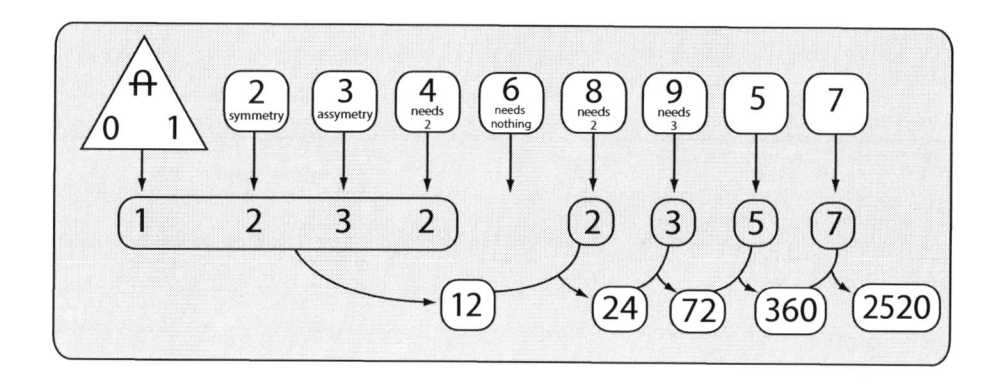

| ⚹ 0 1 | 2 symmetry | 3 assymetry | 4 needs 2 | 6 needs nothing | 8 needs 2 | 9 needs 3 | 5 | 7 |

1 2 3 2 → 12 → 2 3 5 7
                      24 72 360 2520

129

The Anient canon of number both Dee and Marshall "re-discovered" has been known for a long time

Dee wasn't the only person who understood the ancient canon of number involving 252, the Holotomes and the Cycloflex. The German metallurgist and alchemist Pantheus, writes that the "number of days" is 252. Dee heavily annotated his copy of Pantheus' *Voarchadumia* (*Gold Making*) and makes reference to the book in the *Monas Hieroglyphica*.

Robert Marshall found that the ancient Hindus knew about the canon and that's why number 108 was so special to them. The Yugas, the Hindu's long-calendar-time-periods, are all multiples of number 108.

108
SACRED HINDU NUMBER

Marshall asserts that Plato knew about 2520 cryptically refers to it in *Laws* where he recommends the population of his "Ideal City" be 5040 people (twice 2520) because the populace could be subdivided in so many ways.

In the Bible, Saint John seems to be making a cryptic reference to 2520 in *Revelation*, by writing that the "woman went into the wilderness" for 1260 days (half of 2520).

Marshall claims other authors of the Bible knew about the canon of number as well. In the last chapter of the Gospel of John (21:1–14), Jesus helps Saint Peter with the "miraculous catch of 153 fish. This seems like such a strange number to pick. Perhaps it's the actual fish count, but why not just say "about 150" or "three barrels."

With his vision for number symmetry, Robert Marshall recognized 153 as a number which relates to 252 and to the Cycloflex.

The reflective mate of 153 is 351.
Added together they make 504.
Divide by two, and their average is 252.
This averaging calculation involves an important aspect of the
Cycloflex, the number 99, the largest two digit number,
the product of 9 (of 9 Wave fame) and 11 (of 11 Wave fame).

In short, 153+99=252.
Furthermore, 252+99=351.

The transpalindromes, 153 and 351, are each 99 away from 252.

```
 153 (fish)
+ 99
─────
 252
+ 99
─────
 351
```

Dee also hints that he has figured out Plato's Number, an obscure reference to a number Plato makes in *Republic* (Book 8:546). The exclamation is too long to relate here, but Plato actually refers to two numbers. Following Dee, I have determined that Plato's "number of divine births" is 2520, and his "number of human births" is 360 (which Plato wittily refers to as "a geometrical number".) [See my Book 7, *Dee's Decad of Shapes and Plato's Number*]

Brief Visual Summary

The "+4, –4, octave; null nine" rhythm of CONSUMMATA:

"Cycloflex" Summary Chart

The METAMORPHOSIS sequence:

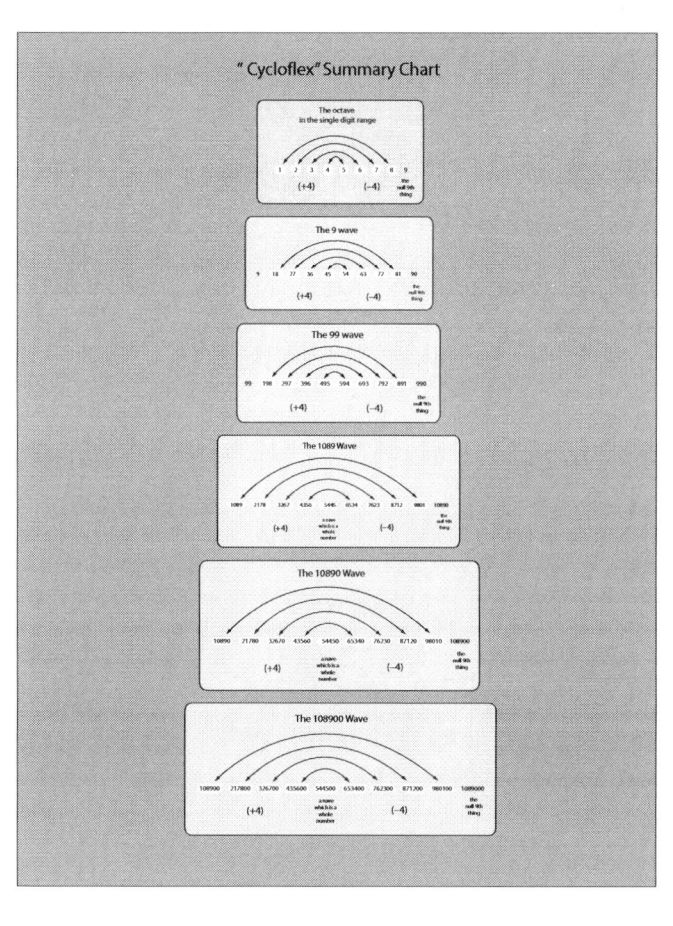

12	Holotome A
12 x 2 = 24	Holotome B
24 x 3 = 72	Holotome C
72 x 5 = 360	Holotome D
360 X 7 = 2520	Holotome E
2520 x 11 = 27720	Holotome F
27720 x 13 = 360360	Holotome G
360360 x 17 = 6126120	Holotome H
6126120 x 19 = 116396280	Holotome I
116396280 X 23 = 2677114440	Holotome J

You may be wondering what all this math has to do with the Tower. Trust me, it's essential for unraveling the *Monas Hieroglyphica* even further to find (what I call) "Dee's hidden blueprint for the Tower." But first we must explore of another facet of "1, 2, 3, 4."

It's an idea that was near and dear to both the ancient mathematicians and to Renaissance mathematicians like Dee.

The Story of 1, 2, 3, 4

Flashback to to around 500 BC. Legend has it Pythagoras was passing by a blacksmith's shop and heard a variety of different sounds caused by hammers banging away on anvils. He went inside and found the various sounds were produced by the variously sized anvils.

Returning to his house he experimented with various sized hammers, bells, glasses of water, strings under tension and flutes to find the most harmonious sounds and the numerical proportions they expressed.

He summarized his discoveries with his famous **tetraktys**, upon which the followers of Pythagoras would swear their oaths.

It's deceptively simple: a triangular shape with four rows of dots (1, 2, 3, 4), making a total of 10 dots in total.

(In Greek, *tetra* means four.)

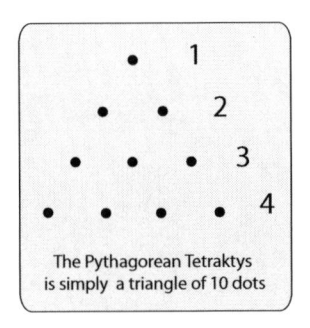

The Pythagorean Tetraktys is simply a triangle of 10 dots

Which, of course, Dee reminds us of in Theorem 23.

The middle result here is *Summa Pythagorica*, or "the Pythagorean Sum," 10.

(Another curious connection is that the tetraktys forms an equilateral triangle, the same symbol Dee used to sign his name.)

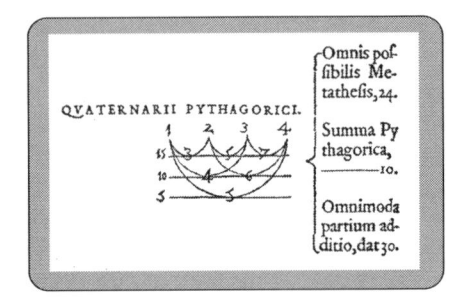

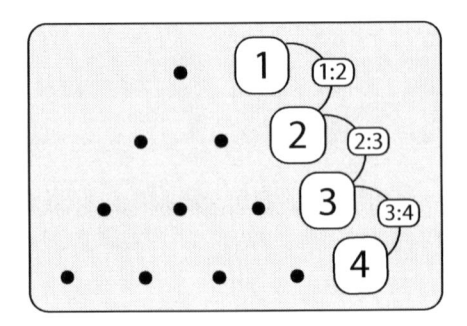

But what Pythagoras and Dee really want us to explore are the ratios between the various rows: (1 to 2), (2 to 3), and (3 to 4).

Nicomachus of Gerasa wrote the famous math text called *Introduction to Arithmetic* around 100 AD.

Around 500 AD, Boethius translated it into Latin. It became the **most popular math text for 1000 years**, from the Dark Ages, through the Middle Ages and into the Renaissance.

The *Introduction to Arithmetic* explains how Pythagoras and his followers felt the universe was arranged according to the attunement of the ratios (1:2), (2:3), and (3:4).

They could hear these beautiful harmonies in music as *diapason, diapente and diatessaron*, (the musical octave, the fifth, and the fourth, shown here on a modern keyboard)

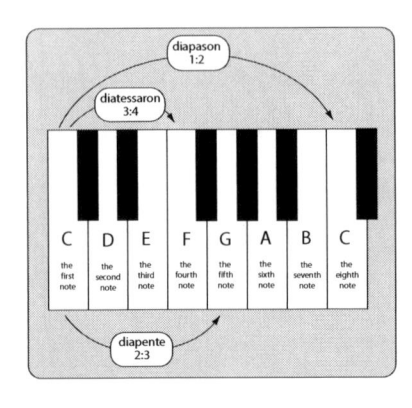

The "greatest and most perfect harmony"

In the last section of the last chapter in their texts,
Nicomachus and Boethius reveal what they call
the **"greatest and most perfect harmony."**
It involves the relationships between
the numbers **6, 8, 9,** and **12**.

(At the top here) The ratio **1:2** can be seen in 6:12
(At the bottom) The ratio **2:3** can be seen in both 6:9 and 8:12
(And in the middle) The ratio **3:4** can be seen in both 6:8 and 9:12
Pure harmony! Hmmmm!

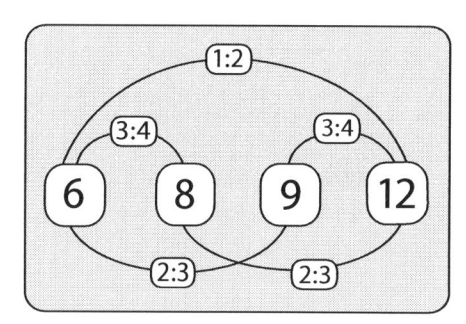

These 3 harmonies were important to
Renaissance artists and geometers as well.

Raphael's famous *School of Athens*, a 26-foot wide fresco
in the Vatican depicts all the "superstars" of antiquity.
Under the central arch are Plato and Aristotle.

Various groupings of students are clustered around
Epicurius, Socrates, Strabo, Euclid and Pythagoras.

Averroes
(Arab translator
of Greek works,
ca.1175 AD)

Hypatia of
Alexandria
(famous woman
mathmetician,
ca. 400 AD)

Boethius
holding his
*Introduction
to Arithmetic*
with 3 book
clasps visible
on the
back cover
(ca. 525 AD)

Nicomachus
peering
(ca. 125 AD)

Pythagoras
writing
(ca. 500 BC)

diagram of
"the greatest
and most perfect
harmony"

Let's zoom in on the
group of mathematicians.

Peering around the nearest shoulder
of Pythagoras is **Nicomachus**.

Standing on the right side, holding
his influential text, *Introduction
to Arithmetic*, is **Boethius**.

A young student is propping up
a tablet in front of Pythagoras.

Let's zoom in even closer.

133

close up view of
"the greatest and
most perfect harmony"

Written in Greek on the diagram are the words *diatessaron, diapente, and diapason.*

Across the top is *epogdoon*, or the 8:9 ratio, the ratio describing a single increment of "tone."

(The Greeks expressed it as 9:8, an octave plus an eighth-of-an-octave is nine)

At the bottom is the Pythagorean tetraktys along with an X, which is not Greek, but Latin, as X is the Roman Numeral for 10.

(My transcription)

(My simplification)

The tablet is a lot easier to visualize when the ratios are expressed with numerals.

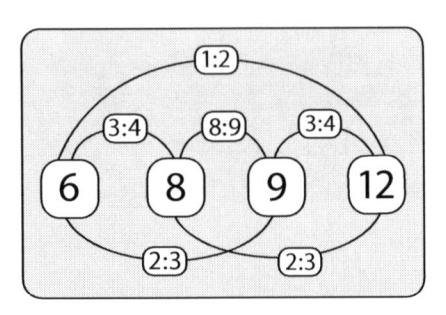

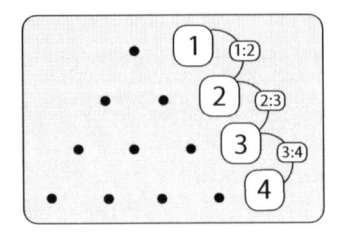

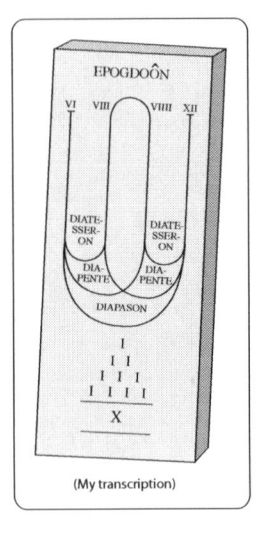

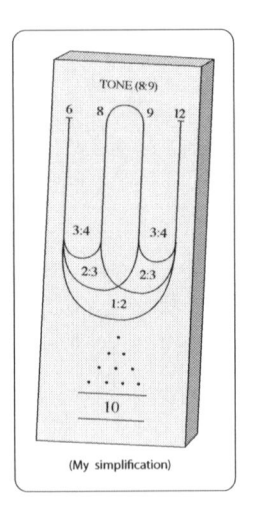

Raphael is depicting the same thing I show in my modern illustrations.

The 3 ratios the Pythagorean tetraktys are also implied by the greatest and most perfect harmony (comprised of the numbers 6, 8, 9, 12).

(It's likely that Raphael incorporated these ratios into the proportions of various parts of his fresco, and he was subtly providing us with his recipe.)

Raphael was not alone. Many great Italian Renaissance painters, sculptors, and architects glorified their works with these three harmonic ratios.

Not only did Dee include the Pythagorean Quaternary (1, 2, 3, 4) in the "Below" half of his "Thus the World Was Created" chart, he put (1, 2, 3, 4) in the "Above" half of the chart as well.

Dee makes a very subtle reference to the proportions (1:2), (2:3), and (3:4) by putting **colons** after the digits 1, 2, and 3 (but not after the 4).

Incidentally, Dee is credited as being the first mathematician to use a colon as a symbol to express proportion.

(Florian Cajori, *A History of Mathematical Notations*, p.168)

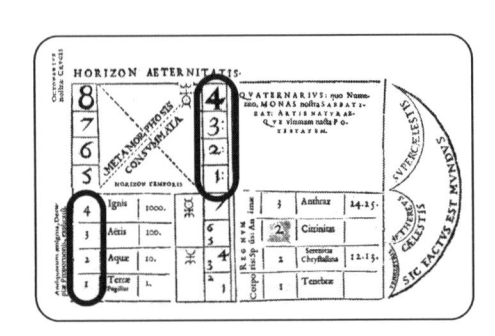

134

The Hidden Blueprint of the John Dee Tower

To see the hidden blueprint for the Tower in the *Monas Hieroglyphica,* you must be aware of the Metamorphosis sequence (12, 24, 72, 360, 2520, etc.) and those principal harmonies (1:2), (2:3) and (3:4).

Once I understood how important these three harmonious ratios were to Pythagoras, Nicomachus, and Boethius, I searched for traces of them in the *Monas Hieroglyphica*.

I didn't have to look very far. I noticed that the height-to-width proportion of the Title page illustration was 4:3.

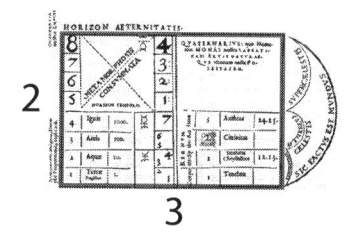

Then, I noticed that the rectangular part of Dee's summary chart was in the height-to-width proportion of 2:3.

Hurriedly, I flipped through the Dee's book to find an illustration in the proportion of 1:2, or 2:1. But none were to be found.

It seemed like the Monas symbol might be the proportion 2:1, but making a grid based on Dee's specifications, I found it was 9:4.

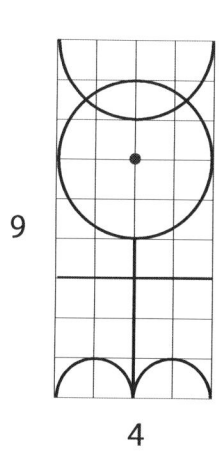

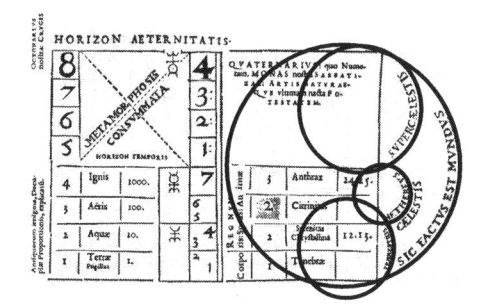

I thought that maybe if the large arc that bracketed the right end of the chart was completed, I could find the 1:2 proportion, but this was not the case.

I completed the arcs of the 3 smaller brackets, but still no 1:2 ratio. Then I noticed something unusual about the segments Dee had made.

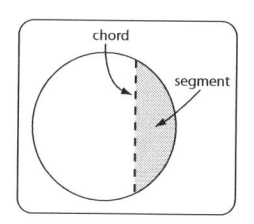

(A segment is the area within a circle that is cut off by a chord.)

The Terrestrial segment was unusually flat, especially when compared with the Aetheric Celestial segment, which was quite bulbous.

135

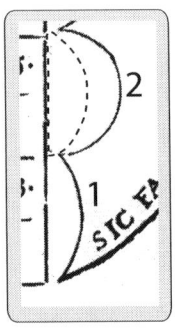

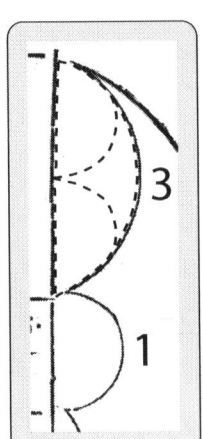

Throughout the *Monas*, Dee drops hints about 12 and 24.

Describing the Aries symbol in Theorem 11, he writes that on the first day of Aries (the Spring Equinox) there are exactly 12 hours of daylight and 12 hours of darkness, totaling to 24 hours.

I also knew that 12 and 24 were the first two members of the Metamorphosis sequence.

Eyeballing their areas, it seemed like I could fit two of the flat Terrestrial segments into the bulbous Aetheric Celestial segment. I had found a 1:2 ratio.

[But wait, there's more to Dee's geometric clue-game.]

Next, I discovered that the area of the Supercelestial segment was about 3 times the size of the Aetheric Celestial segment. This was following the recipe of the Metamorphosis sequence. (12 times 2 is 24), then (24 times 3 is 72).

This also made sense symbolically. Kabbalistic tradition holds that there are 72 angels, so this is certainly a fitting number for the Supercelestial realm.

As they are involved in the earth/sun dance, 12 and 24 are fitting numbers for the Terrestrial and Aetheric Celestial realms.

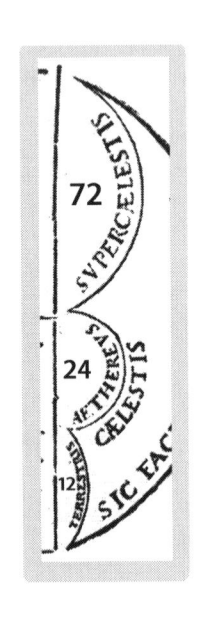

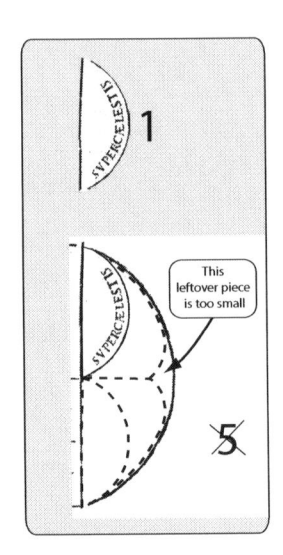

It seemed likely that the largest, encompassing bracket would make a segment 5 times the size of the Supercelestial segment.

But this time I was wrong.

No matter how I tried to estimate it, four Supercelestial segment areas fit fine, but there just was no way that five would fit.

I tried to determine just how large that large segment would have to be so that it would accommodate 5 Supercelestial segments.

I realized it needed to extend out to be a **complete half circle**.

Hey! A half-circle was Dee's symbol for the Moon!

(And it also makes the letter D, the sound of Dee's last name.)

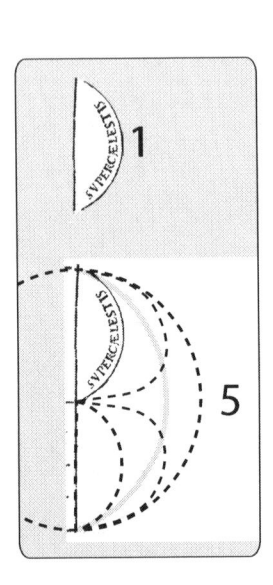

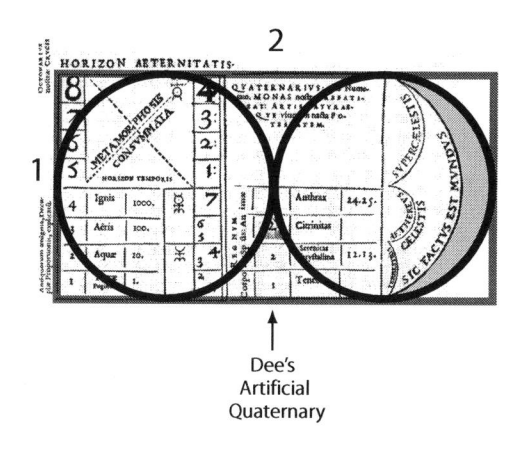

One of the main themes of the *Monas Hieroglyphica* involves the Sun and the (full) Moon, two circles. And now, two circles fit the proportions perfectly. I've "grayed-in" the area that I added. (It even looks like a crescent moon!)

I call my revised chart the "**ballooned Thus the World Was Created chart.**" Admittedly, I have changed the proportions of Dee's 450 year old chart, but this is what Dee wanted the reader to do. It's Dee's geometric riddle.

He left several confirming clues that this was his intent. The point of tangency of the two circles is aligned with his Artificial Quaternary. And in the Artificial Quaternary, the number 2 is curiously **larger** than the rest of the digits.

Dee's Artificial Quaternary

(Dee made the large "2" appear to be a mistake by putting hatch marks around it. But it was printed on the "engraving pass" through the press. The three other digits were printed on the "letterpress pass" through the press. The clever Dee made an "intentional mistake" to cryptically emphasize the 2, hinting at the 2 big circles he wants us to find)

When I found this next confirming clue,
I knew I was on the right track.
The sum of 12 + 24 + 72 is 108.

In order for whole segment area to be 360,
the rest of the area must be 252,
which is Dee's Magistral number!

It's clearly there, but cleverly
invisible to most readers.

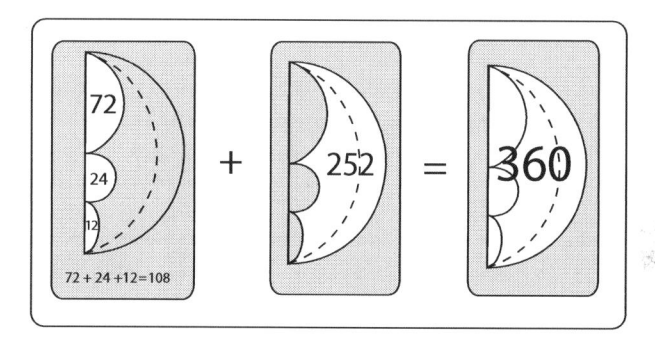

The "Two Circles" or "Two Rings"

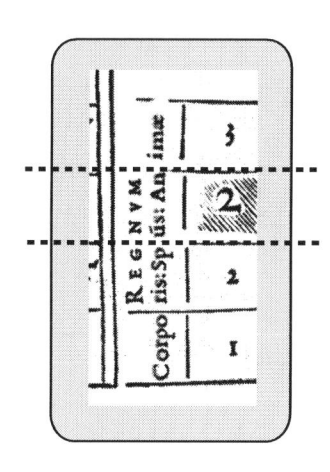

Immediately to the left of this "enlarged 2," Dee writes
"REGNUM: Corporis, Sp[irit]ūs, Animae"
(which means "REIGN: Body, Spirit, Soul")

Dee has omitted several letters and arranged it so
the letters "us:An" align with the "enlarged 2."

This is a jumbled-letter clue for the
Latin word *Anus* which means "ring"
(Anus is shortened version of the Latin word
Annulus, which also means "ring.").

The idea of "2 Rings" (like the 2 circles Dee wants us to find) relates to a famous parable in one of Dee's favorite books, Plato's *Republic*.

Plato relates the classic tale of the Ring of Gyges. A poor shepherd named Gyges finds a gold ring that has the power to make its owner invisible. He uses his power to kill the King, marry the Queen, usurp the throne, and become a tyrant.
(There actually was a King of Lydia named Gyges who is known as the "world's first tyrant.")

[Incidentally, J. R. R. Tolkien modernized the tale of the Ring of Gyges with the
"One Ring," a magic ring owned by Bilbo Baggins in *The Lord of the Rings*.]

Ring worn by the unjust man

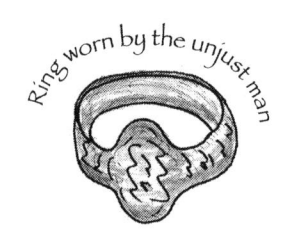

After relating the tale of the Ring of Gyges, Plato's character Glaucon debates with the wise Socrates.

What if there were two rings of invisibility?
One given to an unjust man,
The other given to a just man.

Ring worn by the just man

    The **unjust** man would use it to become rich. But if the **just** man had the power of invisibility and didn't use it, his comrades as would consider him to be a "most miserable and utter fool."

    In short, Glaucon asserts that anyone would be unjust given the opportunity and given immunity from getting caught. This leads to a long discussion between Glaucon and Socrates about justice and injustice.

    Throughout the *Monas*, there are subtle references to the tale of Gyges and the two rings of Glaucon. In the *Letter to Maximillian,* Dee rants about justice and injustice. He uses the word TYRANT (TYRANNOS) prominently in one of his illustrations.

    Dee even tells Maximillian he is "offering him a MAGIC **parable**" adding "...he who nourished the MONAD will First Go Away into a METAMORPHOSIS, and afterwards, **will very rarely be seen by the eyes of Mortals**. This, O Great King, is the true **INVISIBILITY** of the MAGI..."

    In short, the "**two rings of Glaucon**" are the "**two circles**"
Dee wants us to find. They are the overall design plan for his chart.

(And also perhaps the simplest possible geometric representation
of the Union of Opposites. The Sun and the Moon.)

Most importantly, two tangent circles fit in a rectangle
that is has a height-to-width proportion of **1:2.**

I had found the missing 1:2 ratio.

The Metamorphosis numbers were
the key that had unlocked the door.

Now I had a full inventory of those three
wonderful ratios (1:2), (2:3), and (3:4).

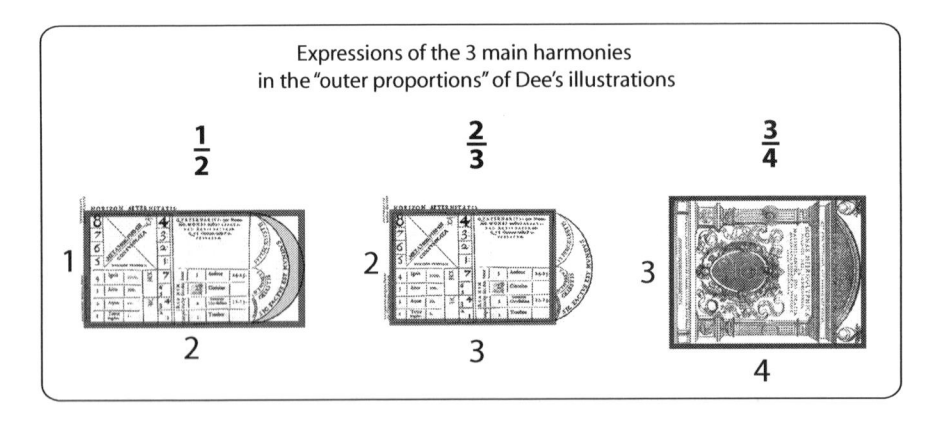

Expressions of the 3 main harmonies
in the "outer proportions" of Dee's illustrations

$\frac{1}{2}$ $\frac{2}{3}$ $\frac{3}{4}$

What size grid did Dee use for his Title page illustration?

Applying the 4:3 grid on the Title page emphasizes how geometric Dee's architecture is.

It occurred to me that he probably used a grid to keep everything symmetrical.

But this grid was not fine enough.

So I applied an 8 by 6 grid. Some correspondences became obvious.

Under the dome, grid lines delineated the top and bottom of the entablature.

At the bottom, grid lines defined the top of the base foundation, as well as the tops of the short pedestals.

The vertical grid lines defined the inner edges of the columns, **but not their outer edges**.

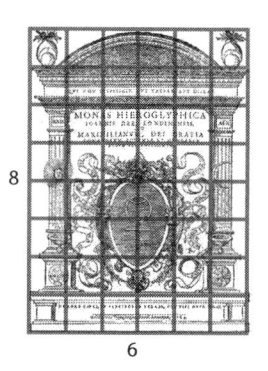

I made a tighter grid, this time 24 by 18. But still, no grid lines corresponded with the outer edge of the columns.

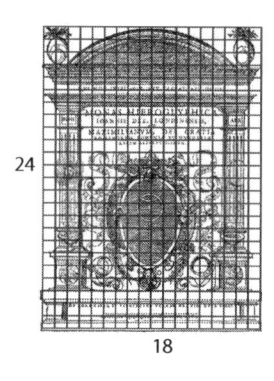

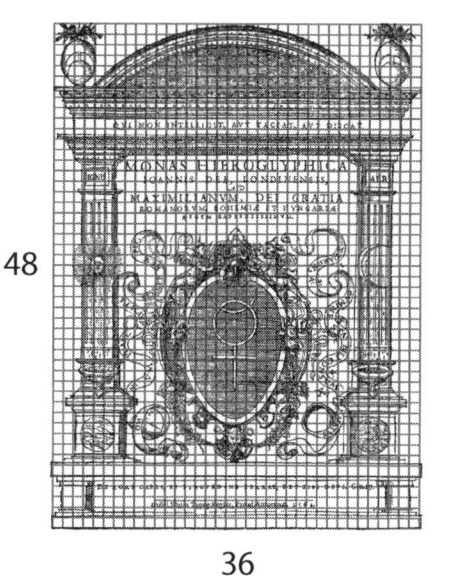

Finally, when I got to a 48 by 36 grid, both sides of the columns were delineated.

I tried a finer grid, 84 x 72, but this seemed **too** fine. 6048 little boxes would be way too many to deal with.

Indeed, the 48 x 36 grid, with 1728 boxes, seemed just right.

(And interestingly, 1728 is 12 times 12 times 12)

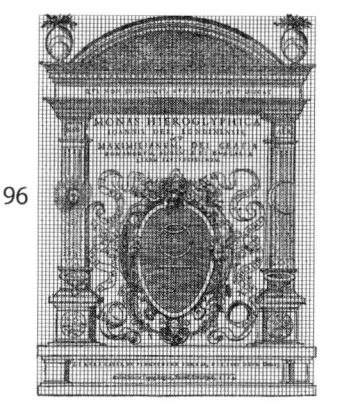

139

What grid did Dee use for the "Thus the World Was Created" chart?

If the Title page was made on a grid, it seemed likely the
"Thus the World Was Created" chart was made on a grid.
(Actually, it already looks somewhat gridded.)

A "2:4" grid emphasizes a top half of
the chart and bottom half of the chart.

What I call the "2:3 rectangular part of the chart,"
(the part **not** including the brackets on the right)
aligns nicely with this grid.

A finer "8:16" grid really showed promise.

The "1, 2, 3, 4, 5, 6, 7 boxes" on the bottom half
of the chart and the "1, 2, 3, 4, 5, 6, 7, 8 boxes"
on the top half of the chart fit the grid nicely.

However, there were other chart
lines that were not delineated.

With a "12:24" grid, the "1, 2, 3, 4, 5, 6, 7, 8 boxes"
on the Top half of the chart had lost their delineation.

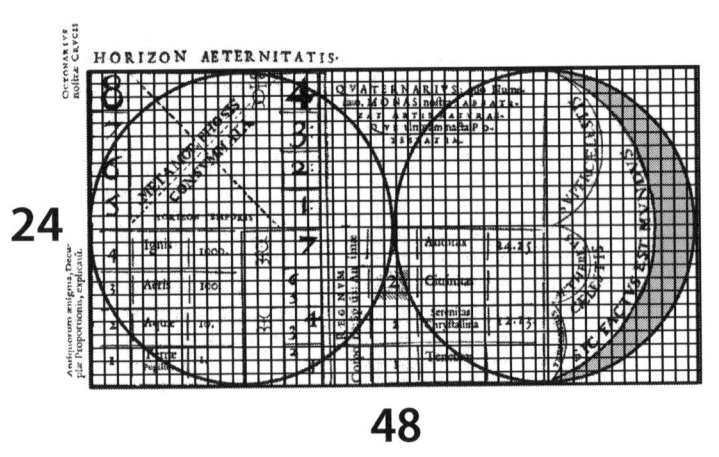

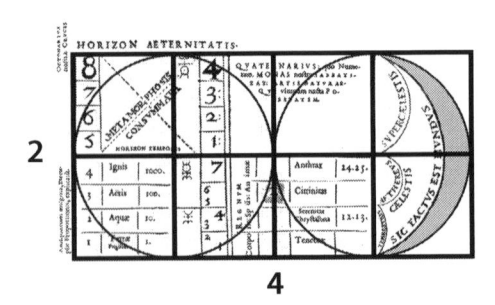

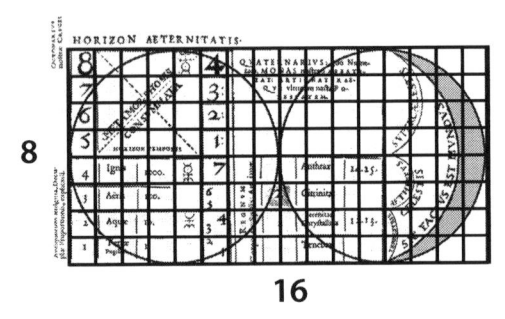

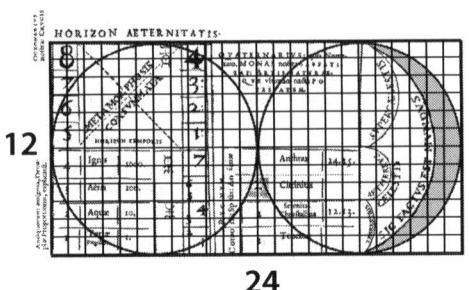

But with a "24 by 48" grid,
the boxes were nicely delineated.
Furthermore, the boxes containing the
large digits was subdivided into 3 rows of 3)
(See, for example, the box containing 8 on the upper left).

This grid seemed to accommodate all the lines in the chart
(except for a few short vertical lines which seem to have
drifted out of place during the letterpress printing process.)

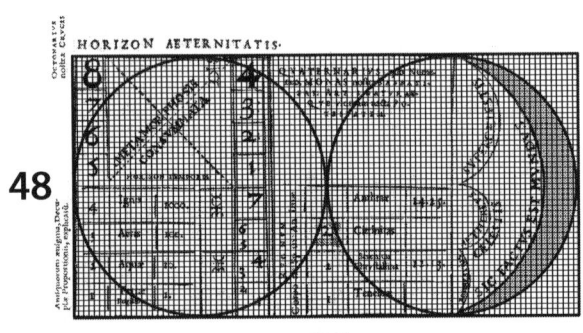

The tighter "48 by 96" grid, with
4608 grid squares was overkill.

Indeed, the "24 x 48" grid with its "1052 grid
squares" seemed to be the one Dee used.

140

Dee's chart probably went
through several working design phases.
(Summarizing the Creation of the World
in one chart is not a task taken lightly.)

I estimate Dee's working charts were
about 1 foot tall by 2 feet wide.

Even though the Title page is at the start
of Dee's book and the "Creation" chart was
way at the end, I wondered what the two
charts might reveal when superimposed.

Interestingly, the "ballooned Creation Chart"
was **exactly the same width as the Title page**!

(To visually simplify, I have deleted the
central emblem and inscriptions, leaving
only the bare bones of the architecture.)

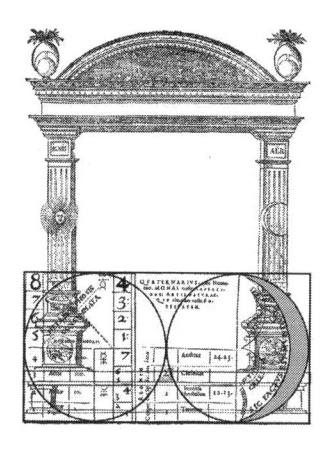

A horizontally oriented
superimposition

When verticalized, it went up to the bottom
edge of the entablature, as if it could support it
(the same way the columns and foundation do).

However, the "ballooned Creation chart"
seemed kind of wimpy compared to
the architecture of the Title page.

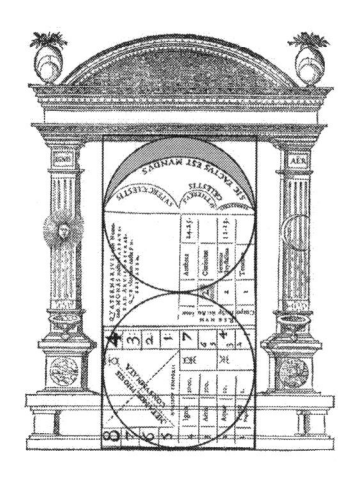

A vertically oriented
superimposition

So I enlarged it to the full height of the architecture, and to
my surprise, its width fit perfectly **between the columns**!

Also, one edge of the "360-segment" at the top
of the "ballooned Creation chart" was the
same height as the **bottom of the entablature**.

Furthermore, its "half-moon shape"
echoed the architectural **dome** behind it.

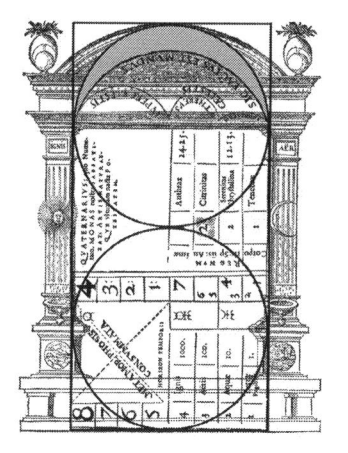

Enlarged 133% (or by 4/3) to
match height instead of width

141

This meant that the 2:3 rectangular part of the chart fit perfectly between the columns and under the entablature.

The 3 ratios (1:2), (2:3), and (3:4) seemed interrelated graphically.

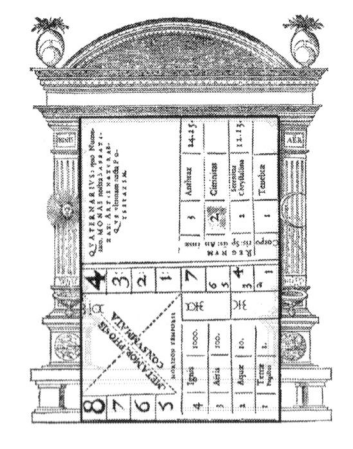

The 2:3 "rectangular part" of the chart fits perfectly between the columns and beneath the entablature

48

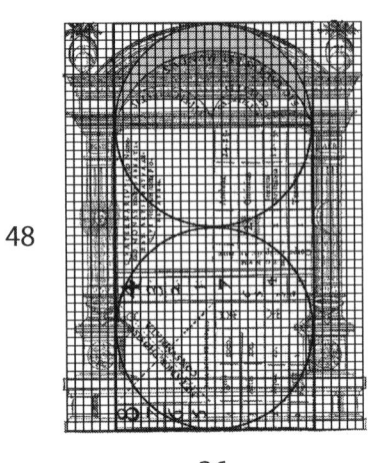

36

If the Title Page was done using a 48 by 36 grid...

Here, the 48 x 36 grid covers the whole Title page. But let's just look at that central area.

That central area is 48 tall by 24 wide.

48

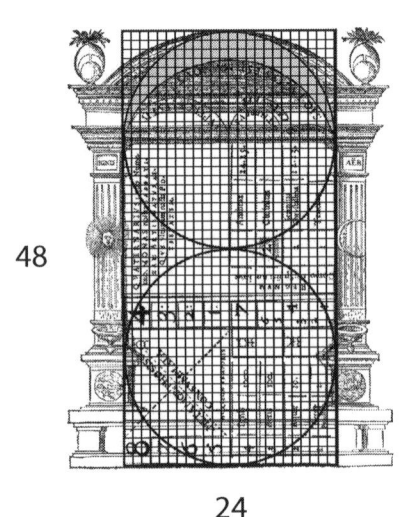

24

The 1:2 "ballooned" chart fits a grid of 48 by 24.

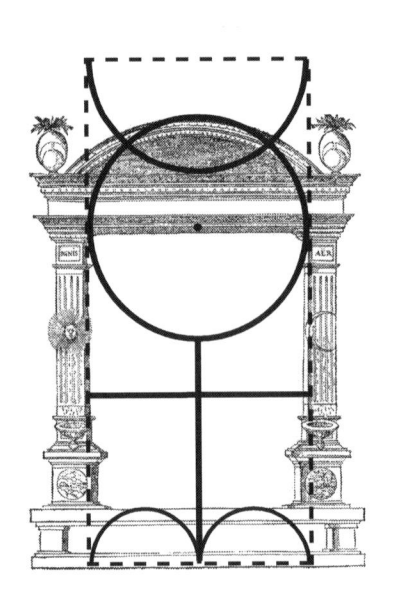

I also noticed that when Dee's cherished Monas symbol fit between the columns, the top of the sun circle was tangent with the top of the architectural dome.

(Hovever, the top part of the Moon half-circle stuck up above the dome).

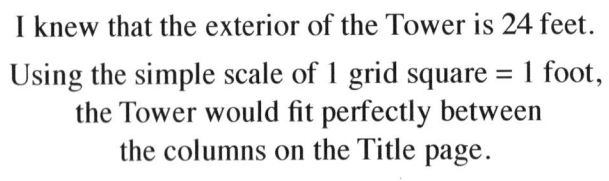

Title page and Monas symbol
(But what about the Moon's half circle?)

I knew that the exterior of the Tower is 24 feet.

Using the simple scale of 1 grid square = 1 foot, the Tower would fit perfectly between the columns on the Title page.

142

More clues about what Dee's Tower might have originally looked like.

Vitruvius wrote a whole chapter (Book 4, Chapter 8) on "circular temples."
He says some circular temples are simply a circular colonnade
(a ring of columns), but others have a *cella* (or central room)..

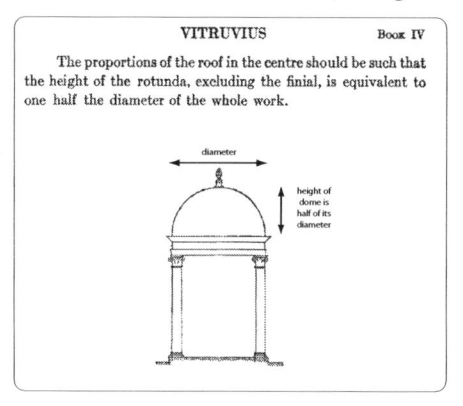

VITRUVIUS Book IV
The proportions of the roof in the centre should be such that the height of the rotunda, excluding the finial, is equivalent to one half the diameter of the whole work.

diameter
height of dome is half of its diameter

Vitruvius called circular temples with no cella *monopteral*.
Those with cellas in them were called peripteral.

As *peri* means "around" and *pteral* means "wings," *peripteral*
means a building with "wings" around it (having a circular colonnade).

Among his recommendations for proportions, Vitruvius writes
"the dome should be half the diameter of the whole work."
In other words, the dome should be a hemisphere.

Dee loved Vitruvius, that singular voice from antiquity who described classical architecture so thoroughly. In his library, Dee had translations and commentaries on Vitruvius by Cesare Caesarino (1522), Guilelmus Philander (1552), Daniele Barbaro (1567), and Jean Martin (1572).

(Roberts and Watson, *John Dee's Library Catalog*, p. 228)

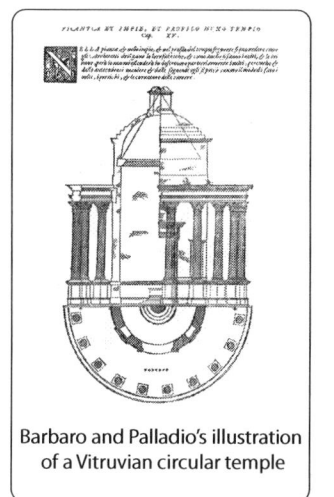

DANIELE BARBARO

In 1568, Daniele Barbaro published a book for artists and architects called the *Practice of Perspective* (Dee owned a copy of this as well). Barbaro's friend Andrea Palladio provided the illustrations. One of them is this cross-section of a Vitruvian circular temple.

Barbaro and Palladio's illustration of a Vitruvian circular temple

The central cella seems to be based on a "two circle plan."

Vitruvian Circular Temple

the "cella" or central room is based on a "two circle plan"

In 1570, Palladio wrote his own text, *Four Books on Architecture*, which included illustrations of three circular temples.

The first is San Stefano Rotundo (also known as the Temple of Hercules Victor, built around 475 AD) on the bank of the Tiber River in Rome. The twenty Corinthian columns exist today, but they have been capped by a conical roof. Palladio envisioned a circular cella that extended much higher than the colonnade. (Palladio, Book 4, chapter 16, plate 35 and pp.94-95)

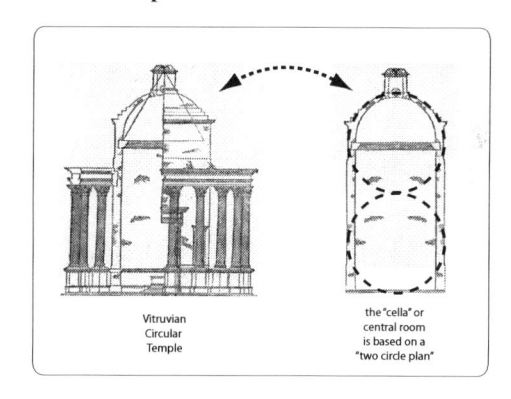

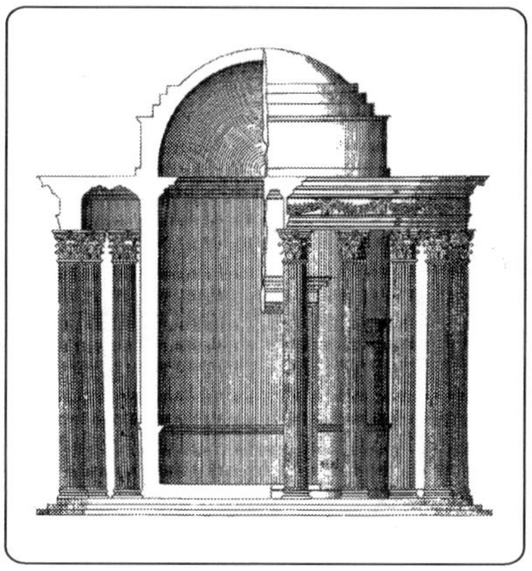

Andrea Palladio's illustration of San Stefano Rotundo Rome (ca. 475 AD)

143

Andrea Palladio's illustration of The Temple of Vesta 15 miles east of Rome in Tivoli (ca. 50 BC)

The second is the Temple of Vesta (the Roman goddess of the hearth) which sits proudly above a ravine and waterfalls in the more rural Tivoli, 15 miles east of Rome.

Back in 50 BC, the Temple of Vesta sported 18 Corinthian columns resting on a solid tribunal (a raised platform). About one-third of colonnade remains today, but the central cella disappeared long ago.

(Palladio, *Book 4*, chapter 23, p.103, and plate 66)

Temple of Vesta Tivoli, by Christian Dietrich (1750)

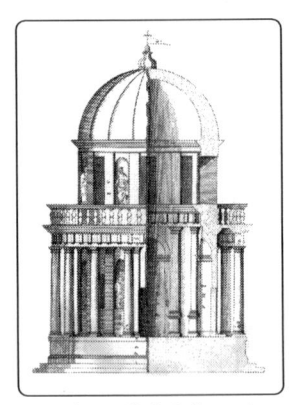

Palladio also illustrates a more "modern" classical building called San Pietro, which is in the district of Montorio, in Rome (in central Rome, a little west if the Tiber). It commemorates the location where Saint Peter was thought to have been crucified.

The "Tempietto" (Italian for "small temple") was built around 1502 by Donato Bramante (1444-1541) and still it stands today. The great Bramante also designed St. Peter's Basilica in the Vatican.

On a substantial platform, the domed cella extends well above the circular colonnade of 16 Doric columns. (Palladio, *Book 4*, chapter 17, p. 97 and plate 35)

Andrea Palladio's illustration of Donato Bramante's San Pietro 75 miles northwest of Rome in Montorio, (1502)

Bramante's 1502 San Pietro still stands today

Vitrivius discusses a third kind of circular temple in which the walls of the cellla run between the columns. He calls this kind of circular temple ***pseudo-peripteral*** (in other words, "false-building with wings-around-it")

Columns lose their freestanding splendor when they have walls interconnecting them. Construction wise, it's a lot easier to build a wall and attach pilasters to it (pilasters are flat columns that are only one quarter or one third the thickness of a full column). Even from up close, it's hard to tell the difference between a row of columns connected by short pieces of wall and a wall with pilasters attached.

In short, I think Dee designed the first Elizabethan building in the New World to be a ***pseudo-peripteral Vitruvian circular temple.*** He maintained the "two circle" proportion of the central cella and put the columns (pilasters) right on the building.

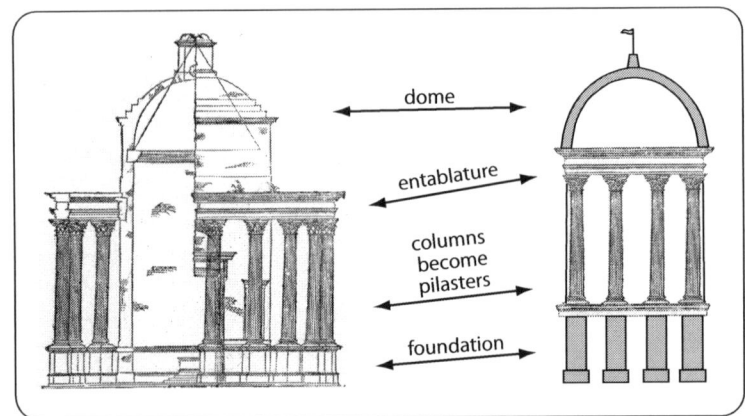

The eight sturdy pillars that still can be seen on the Tower today are most certainly **not** classical columns. They are 3 feet thick and 10 feet tall (including the drums) or a 3:10 width-to-height proportion.

Classical columns are much more slender. (In general, Doric columns are 1:8, Ionic columns are 1:9, and Corinthian columns are 1:10)

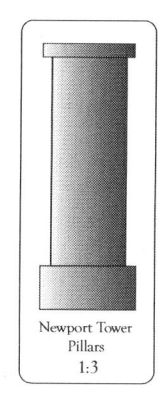

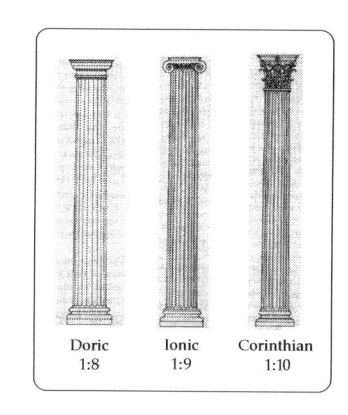

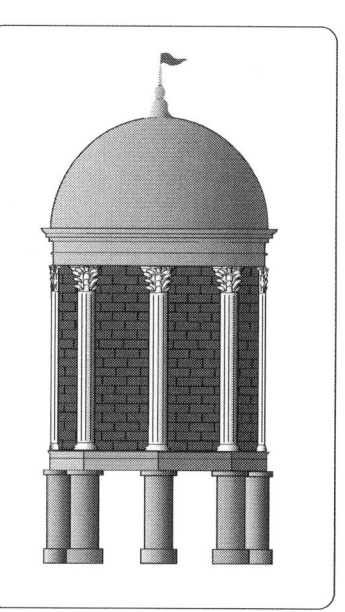

Newport Tower Pillars 1:3

Doric 1:8   Ionic 1:9   Corinthian 1:10

I believe the eight pillars originally supported a wooden entablature with eight Corinthian pilasters rising above it. In classical architecture, a vertical member is usually topped by a horizontal member called an **entablature.**
(From the word "entablature" we get our word "table," a horizontal top sitting on vertical legs).

I suggest that the crudely-constructed arches we see today were purely structural and were hidden behind the wooden entablature. Arches are structurally more supportive than lintels. Shaping long, thick stones to span the tops of the pillars would have been very labor intensive. Besides if a lintel ever broke, a large section of the cylinder wall above might fall down.

I also think there was an entablature above the columns that appeared to support a hemispherical dome. This "dome of the heavens," I believe, was made the same materials the cylinder wall was made from: stone and mortar, then plastered and painted gold. The pilasters and two entablatures could have been made from wooden planks and painted white to look like polished marble.

It's known that the tower was once plastered inside and outside. Would they have left it to be a white elephant? In Medieval and Renaissance days, they used a technique called *sgrafitto*, in which plaster was faux-painted to look like stone blocks. I suggest the walls between the columns were painted brick-red to complement the gold dome.

[Some of the plaster that originally covered the Tower can still be seen on the inside of the northwest pillar and the northeast pillar. True, this pargeting would cover the Sunstone and other key rocks, but I suggest these rocks were well-marked by sgrafitto designs on the outer surface of the plaster. Dee knew that if the Tower for some reason lost its outer skin (through long-term neglect, fire, or bullet marks, etc.) the clues would still remain, just as the windows, with their astronomical alignments, are forever embedded in the Tower.]

Dee illustrates Corinthian pilasters topped by an entablature on the Title page of his 1558 *Propaedeumata Aphoristica*.

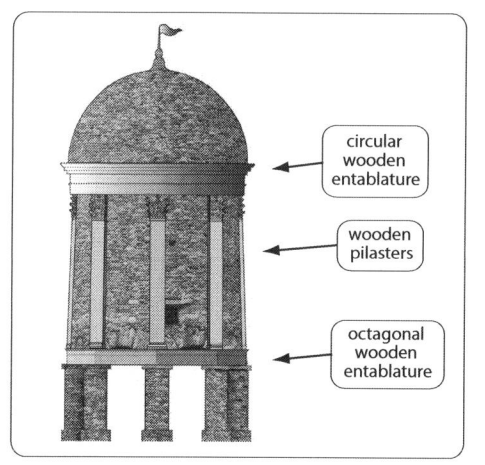

By using pilasters instead of columns, and faux entablatures instead of real ones, Dee's design was much easier to construct than the circular temples Palladio illustrated. But because of its to its harmonious proportions, from a distance it would still have a majestic, classical appearance.

From Leon Battista Alberti, Dee learned that it's not the material a building is made from that's important, it's the building's **lineaments** (its lines and proportions) that matter.

circular wooden entablature

wooden pilasters

octagonal wooden entablature

145

To look at more specific proportions, let's break the Title page architecture into 3 parts:

At the bottom, the Foundation Section is **12** grid squares in height.
[which includes the platform and two pedestals]

The Column Section is **24** grid squares in height.

And the Dome Section is **12** grid squares in height.
[which includes the entablature]

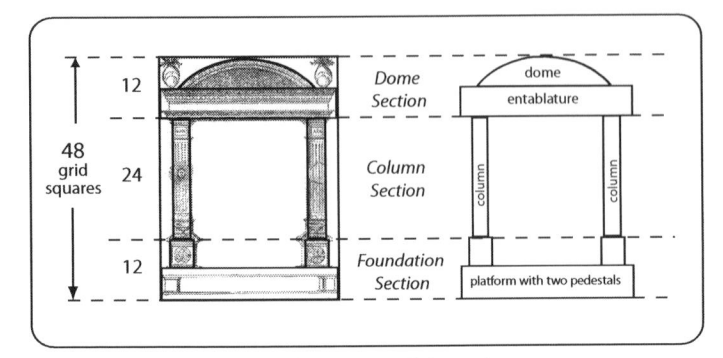

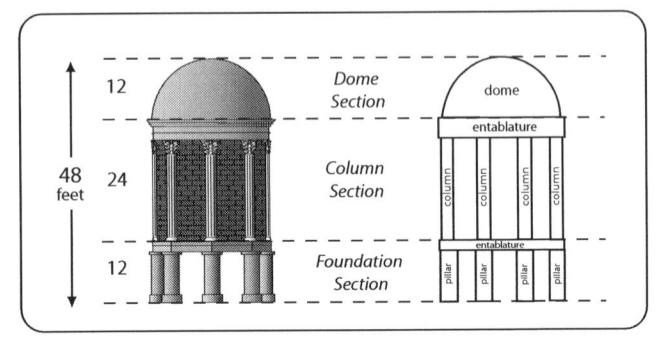

The architecture of the Title page has 3 main sections.

The Tower has 3 main sections.

My reconstruction of the Tower has 3 sections, which correspond to this same 12, 24, and 12 proportioning, with a few minor changes.

The Foundation Section rises to **12** feet above ground level
[which includes the pillars and the pillar entablature]

The Column Section is **24** feet in height.
[which includes the pilasters and the pilaster entablature]

And the Dome is **12** feet in height.

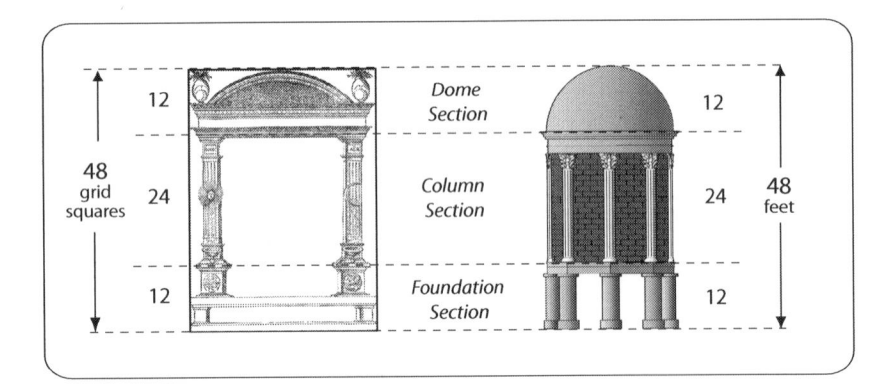

Dee has incorporated his numerological, geometrical, and astronomical cosmology in the design of his Tower.

The exterior proportions all involve **12's** and **24's**.

The first two Metamorphosis numbers are **12** and **24**.

The cuboctahedron has **12** vertices and **24** edges.

On the Equinox there are exactly **12** hours of light and **12** hours of darkness, totalling to **24** hours.

Indeed this "two-circle plan" echoes the Union of Opposites (like Dee's Sun and Moon). And each of the "two circles" is **12** feet in radius and **24** feet in diameter.

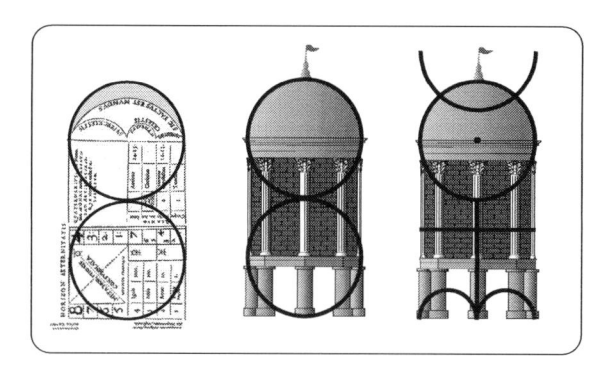

The **two circles** of the "ballooned Thus the World Was Created chart" is the overall plan of the 48-foot tall stone-and-mortar part of the Tower.

The Monas symbol is the same proportion.

(Another circle would fit perfectly under the Sun circle.)

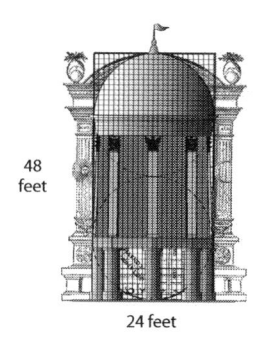

Plus, I think the 48 foot tall tower had a six-foot finial on top.

Geometrically, the spine of the Monas symbol has **10 key "points."** This means it has **"9 parts."**

To Dee, this uppermost ninth part (the top of the Moon half circle) corresponds like the "null nine" of number in Consummata.

And the "null nine" centerpoint of the cuboctahedron.

And the "epogdoon," an "octave plus one," in the "greatest and most perfect harmony."

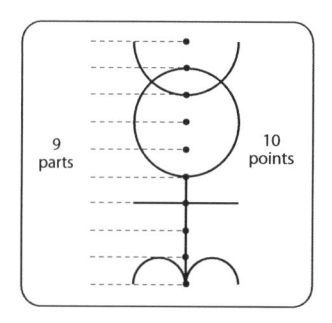

Dee creatively designed the left edge of the "Thus the World Was Created" chart as a scale.

(Though some numbers are typeset and some are engraved, all the digits from 1 to 8 are there.)

And the null ninth thing is at the top.
(the horizon number, nine)

This corresponds to the finial on top of the Tower

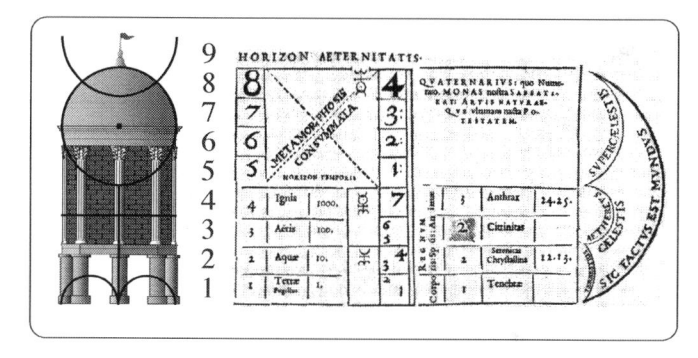

It appears to me that Dee must have been working on the Tower design at the same time his "mind was "pregnant" (as he puts it) with the *Monas Hieroglyphica*, the 7 years (2520 days), from 1557 to 1564.

The *Monas Hieroglyphica*, the Monas symbol, and his Tower all express the same thing: **Dee's cosmology.**

The clever Dee has woven the same ideas into a book, a geometrical figure, and a building.
Brilliant.

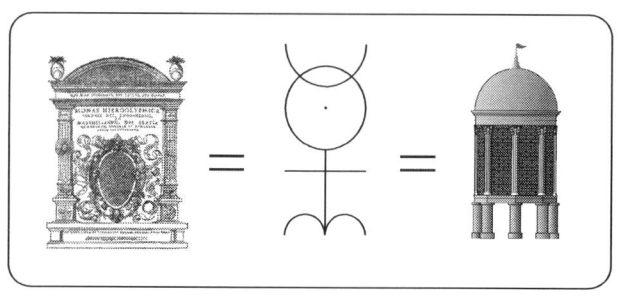

147

Another "hidden blueprint" indicating the "size" of the Tower

The "proportions" of the Tower are the same as the "proportions" of the Monas symbol.
But the Monas symbol can be any size, and it will always retains its same proportions.
(It could be an inch tall, or a foot tall, or 100 feet tall, etc.)

Dee gives us a hint about the "size" or "dimensions" of the Tower
by using the grid system on the Title page (48 units tall by 24 units wide).

But Dee is always courteous enough to leave a confirming clue.
This time he hid it in Theorem 22, disguised in the mystical-sounding

"secret Vessels of the Holy Art."

The clue involves *Gematria*, (letter/number code)
which Dee even informs us he is using in his book.

In Theorem 16, Dee explains,
"V" is the Latin letter 20, and "X" is the Latin letter 21.

In Theorem 24, he cryptically expresses
that "D" is the Latin letter 4.

So Dee's Latin alphabet code is as simple as it gets:
A is 1, B is 2, C is 3, etc.

ABCDEFGHIKLMNOPQRSTVXYZ

1	A Z	23
2	B Y	22
3	C X	21
4	D V	20
5	E T	19
6	F S	18
7	G R	17
8	H Q	16
9	I P	15
10	K O	14
11	L N	13
	M	
	12	

Thus, "M" is Latin letter 12.
(in the **M**iddle of the alphabet).

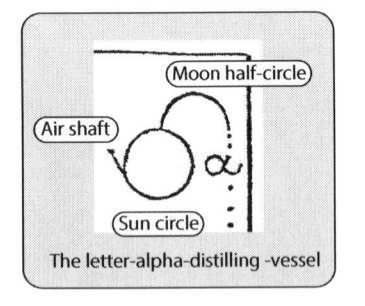

In Theorem 22, Dee explains that he has crafted a round
distilling vessel out of the lowercase Greek letter alpha (α).

To make this letter-alpha-distilling-vessel, Dee has combined
the Sun circle (the bowl part) and the Moon half circle, (the spout part).
He tells us they "**both have the same RADIUS, namely "M."**

He also notes that the "air shaft of the distilling vessel"
is "homologous to the part marked by the letter M..."

The letter-alpha-distilling-vessel
(Moon half-circle)
(Air shaft)
(Sun circle)

148

Using geometry, it's easy see that all of these lengths are "M."

Dee is cryptically saying they are all "12."

He has provided a "size" measurement for the various parts of the Monas symbol.

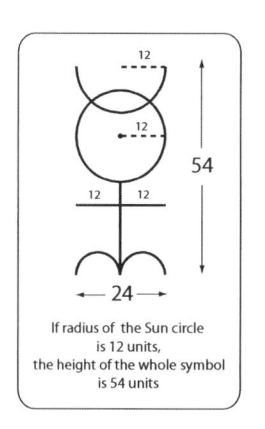

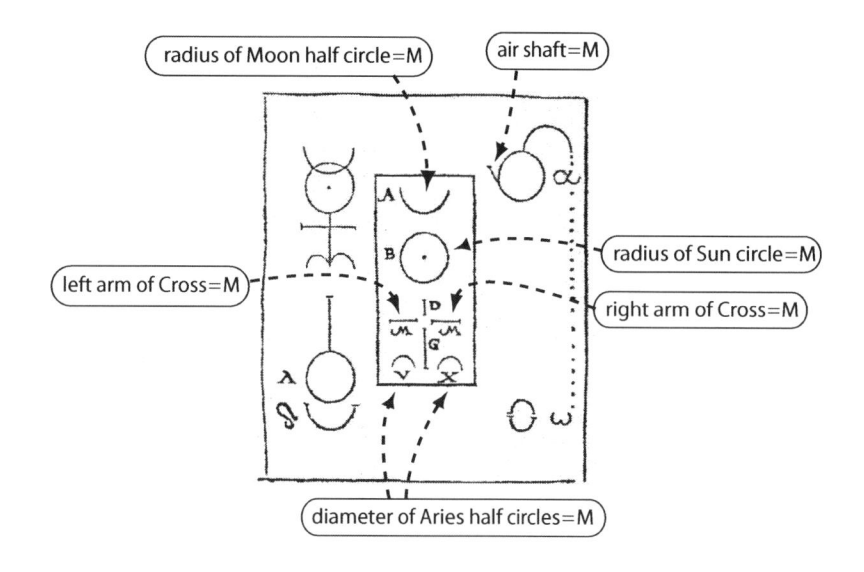

- radius of Moon half circle = M
- air shaft = M
- left arm of Cross = M
- radius of Sun circle = M
- right arm of Cross = M
- diameter of Aries half circles = M

If radius of the Sun circle is 12 units, the height of the whole symbol is 54 units

When these measurements are seen in terms of feet, they correspond to the size of the Tower.

Today, the Tower only about 28 feet tall, but you can still measure the width of the cylinder (where it sits on the pillars).

It's 24 feet in diameter, just as Dee prescribed back in 1564.

Thus, I think the Tower was originally 48 feet tall, with a 6-foot finial, totalling to 54 feet.

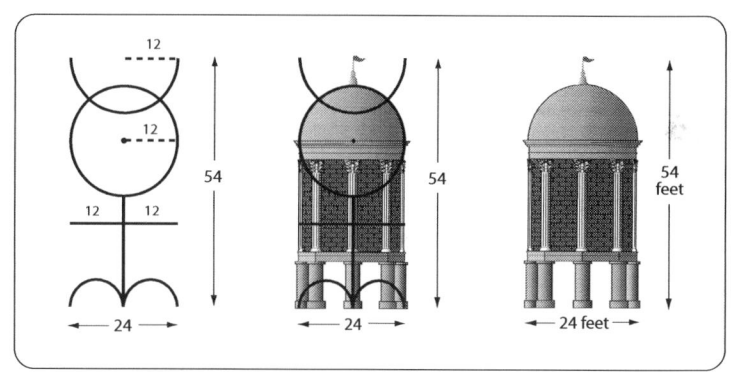

More specific details about the exterior of the Tower

Church of the Holy Sepulchre
Cambridge, England

The eight pillars celebrate the wonderful octave that Dee was aware of in number, geometry, and music. But Dee was incorporating another tradition as well. After the Crusades, the Knights Templar returned to their homelands and built round churches based on the design of the Church of the Holy Sepulchre in Jerusalem. Many of these round churches still stand today, all across Europe.

In England, only 4 have survived intact. The one most similar in scale to the Newport Tower is the Round Church of the Holy Sepulchre in Cambridge, England, built by the Templars around 1130.

This modern-day photo and old lithograph show the 8 pillars surrounding the nave.

149

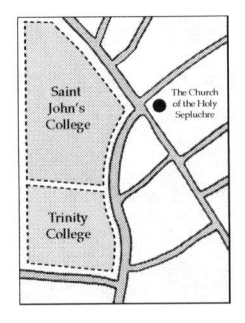

Dee would have been intimately familiar with this
beautiful church, as he spent six years in Cambridge
attending St. John's College and teaching at Trinity College.

[During some of those years, Saint John's College Chapel was under
repair and the college used the Round Church for services.]

There are important differences between the two structures.
The Round Church is ashlar (made of pre-shaped stone) and has ornate ribbing on its arches.
The Newport Tower is made from local slate and granite fieldstones
and its arches are made from randomly-sized flat fieldstones.

The top of each pillar of the
Newport Tower has an unusual
shelf that sticks out about 7 inches.

In my reconstruction, this is the
"capital" of the pillar. The shelves on
top support the a wooden entablature
that hides the crudely-made, but
structurally-stable arches.

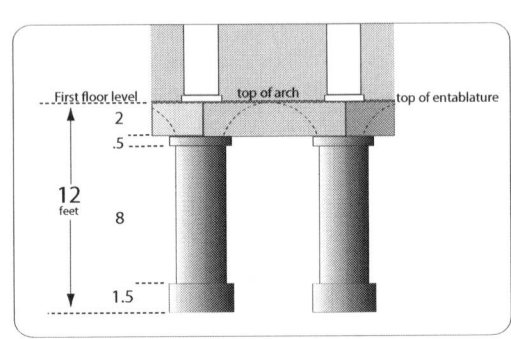

The 10-foot tall pillar and the 2-foot tall
entablature total to 12 feet in height.
(Inside the Tower, this corresponds
with the level of the first floor.)

In classical architecture, vertical members, like
pillars or columns, are generally surmounted
by a horizontal member, like an entablature.
[From which we get the word "table," a horizontal top on vertical legs.]

If the pilasters were twice the height of the pillars
(20 feet verses 10 feet), the upper entablature would
probably be twice the height of the lower entablature
(4 feet verses 2 feet).

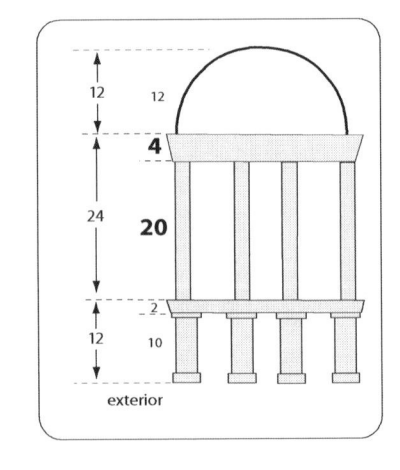

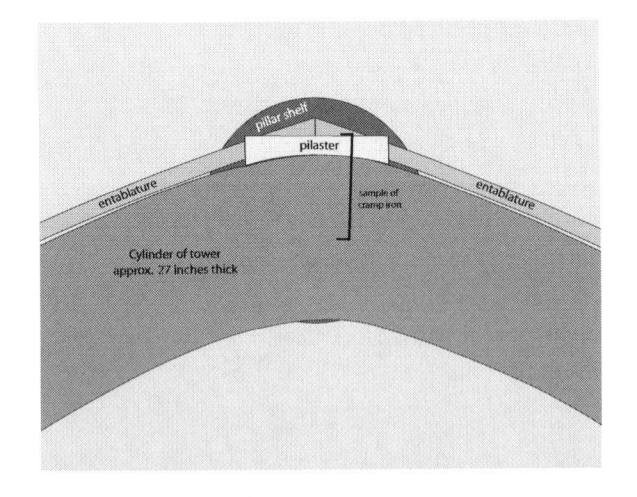

In this a bird's-eye, cross-section view,
the entablature rests on the pillar shelf.

The wooden entablature and pilasters could have
easily been attached with metal cramp irons, secured
into the stone and mortar wall during construction.

[The way anchor bolts stick up out of a
modern-day poured cement foundation.]

You might have noticed that the wooden pilasters would cover over parts of the windows.

Dee probably told the master mason to put the widows "where they needed to be" to make the astronomical alignments work.

Then, wooden shutters could be made to camouflage the windows.
(The shutters might be "part pilaster" and part wall facade, but this would be an easy projest for the master carpenters who had made the beams, floors, and scaffolding.)

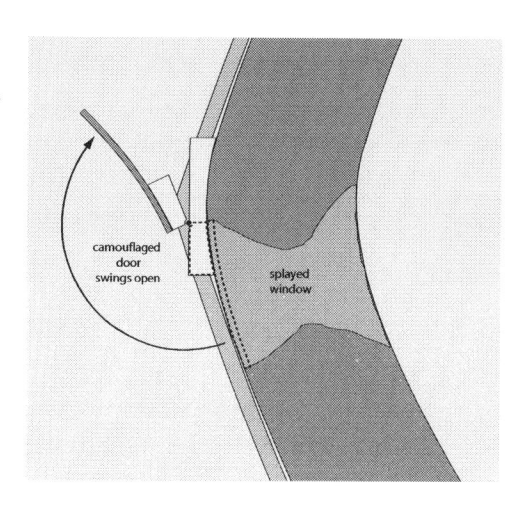

- camouflaged door swings open
- splayed window

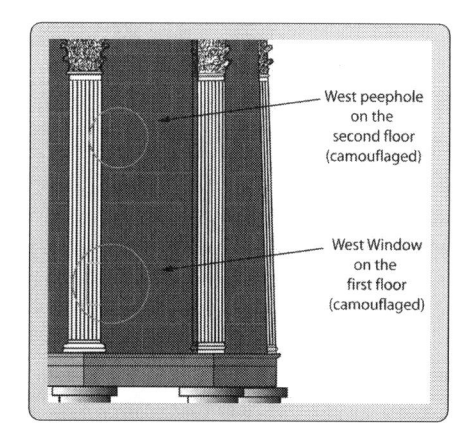

- West peephole on the second floor (camouflaged)
- West Window on the first floor (camouflaged)

In short, these astronomical alignments were not for the "general public"
(or, as Dee would say, the "vulgar").

The secrets of the Tower were for the cognoscenti, those "in the know."
(And, dear reader, as you have followed this strange tale so far, you are now a member of the cognoscenti)

The eight pillars, the classical columns, and the dome of the heavens all express aspects of Dee's world view.

The Latin word *mundus* can be translated as either "world" or "the dome of the heaven."

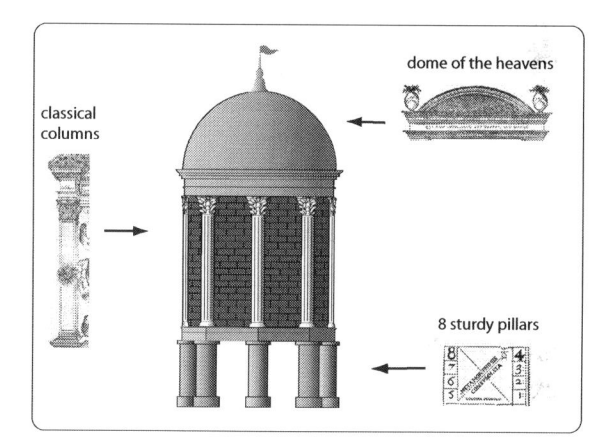

The "mundus" or the dome of heaven

- dome of the heavens
- classical columns
- 8 sturdy pillars

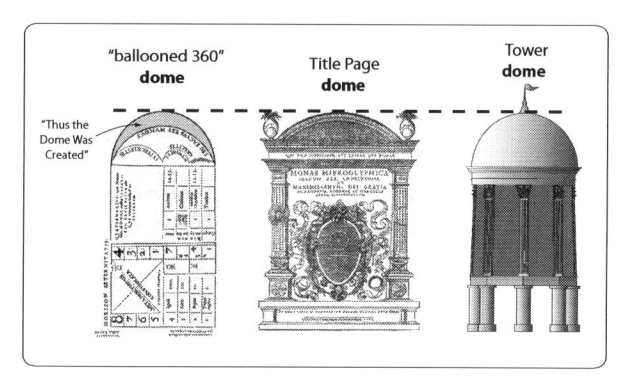

"ballooned 360" **dome** — "Thus the Dome Was Created"

Title Page **dome**

Tower **dome**

So Dee's phrase *"Sic Factus Est Mundi"* might be translated, "Thus the **dome** was made."

If superimposed, the "apex" points of these three domes would coincide.

[Ever since ancient nomads build yurts as a reflection of the celestial sphere of the heavens, domes have fascinated architects. Vitruvius writes the circular temples should have hemispherical domes. Brunelleschi engineered the huge dome of the Duomo in Florence. The state capitol buildings of 40 American states currently sport domes. And the 1900's, a new twist on the dome–the geodesic dome–a full sphere– invented by the great geometer Buckminster Fuller.

Dee's cosmology involves the relationship between the Above and the Below, the Celestial Sphere and the Earthly Sphere, like the two great globes his friend Mercator gave him, like the way an Astronomer's Ring functions, like the way a camera-obscura solar-disc calendar-room functions. To me, there's no way Dee would have designed his circular temple without a dome.]

Dee embedded the design plan of the Tower right into the facade of the Tower

As discussed earlier, Penhallow discovered that, on the winter solstice, the sun can be seen through the West window and through the south window. This happens around 7:30 AM, about a half an hour after sunrise.

After this event, the sun, coming through the south window, makes a small patch of light on the western interior wall. The patch moves slowly downward and to the right. And at 9:00 AM, a large egg-shaped rock in the west–north West arch is illuminated.
(It's very dramatic, as if a spotlight was focused on it.)

And guess what's on the exterior of the Tower, **directly behind** this egg-shaped rock:

The **Sun Stone** and the **Rock with Shoulders**.

I suggest that, combined, these stones represent the **Monas symbol**.

Admittedly, one is made from thin lines and the other is made from solid stones. But the Sun Stone is round like the Sun circle of the Monas symbol. Plus, the "hand-cut shoulders" align with the horizontal arm of Dee's offset cross.

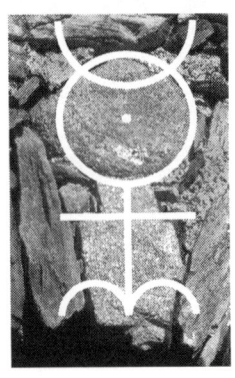

In other words, Dee had the stone masons embed the design plan of the Tower [the Monas symbol] right into the fabric of the building. And it's still there today, centuries later.
(The egg-shape and the Monas symbol were extremely important to Dee. He put them front and center on the Title page of his book.)

The **Sun's light show** inside the Tower corresponds with the **Sun Stone** outside ther Tower.
(Which is the **Sun circle** of the Monas Symbol).
Very clever, that Dee.

How did Dee incorporate his mathematical cosmology inside the Tower"

Measuring from the base of the beam sockets, I found the first floor room of the Tower is 10 feet tall (floor to floor).

However, only about 6 feet of the second floor room exists today. What was the original height of the second floor room?

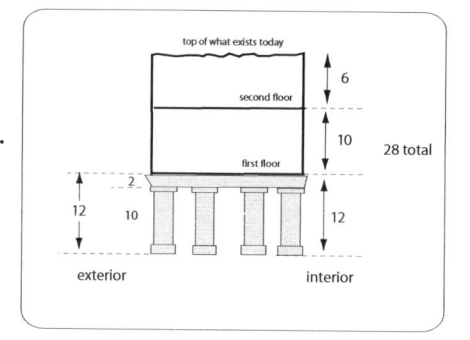

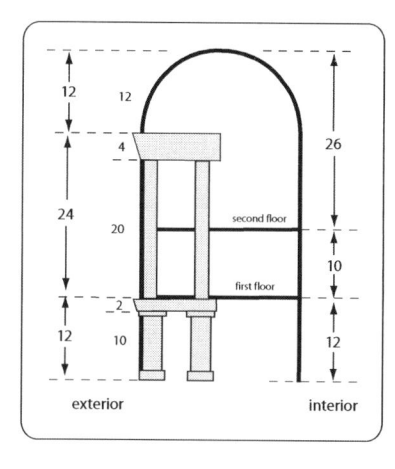

The exterior with the Tower today is about 24 feet. If the Tower was built on a "two circle plan," the height would be 48 feet.

Given that the first floor is 12 feet above the original ground level and the first-floor room is 10 feet tall, that means the second-floor room might have been 26 feet tall. Such a room would be nice and airy, but it doesn't seem to make maximum use of the interior space.

Adding a third floor would really increase the total square footage of available space inside the Tower. If the third floor was at the level of the bottom of the hemispherical dome, that would make the 14-foot tall second-floor room and a 12-foot tall dome room.

Having three rooms of different heights (10, 14, and 12) didn't feel very harmonious. And something else bothered me so much that my head hurt.

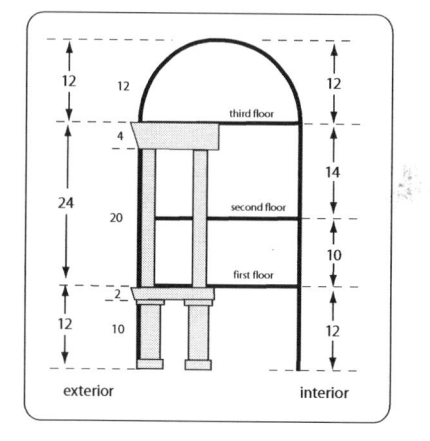

I visualized walking up the stairs that wound up the northern interior wall from the first floor to the second floor. After a small landing on the second floor, it seemed like the steps would continue, thus winding up the southern interior wall. But as I reached the top of the second flight of steps, I felt my head hitting the curved, lower part of the stone-and-mortar dome. Ouch!

For adequate head room, it seems as though the dome room should have at least 4 feet of vertical wall before arching to the 12-foot dome.

Yes, 16-foot tall dome room felt just right. Moreover, that made the second-floor room 10 feet tall—the exact same as the first floor room. The two rooms were like **twins**, only with spiral staircases on opposite walls. The Union of Opposites. Dee's Sun and Moon.

Also, the ratio of the foundation (the pillars and pillar entablature) to the height of the dome room is 12 feet:16 feet. This is the ratio 3:4, one of Dee's favorites. It's the ratio he chose for the overall proportions of the Title page of the *Monas Hieroglyphica*.

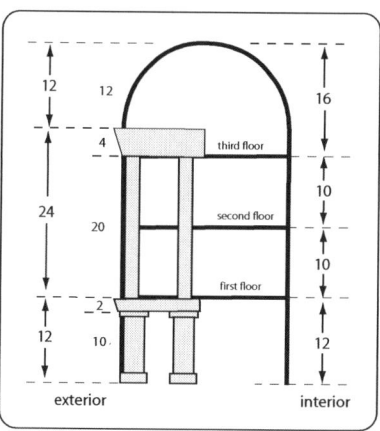

153

The three floors **inside** correspond with architectural features **outside**.

The first floor is level with the top of the pillar entablature.
The second floor is level with the midpoint of the columns.
And the dome room floor is level with the lower edge of the column entablature.

Admittedly, this is my conjectured reconstruction, but it sure felt like the type of harmonious proportioning Dee would have used.

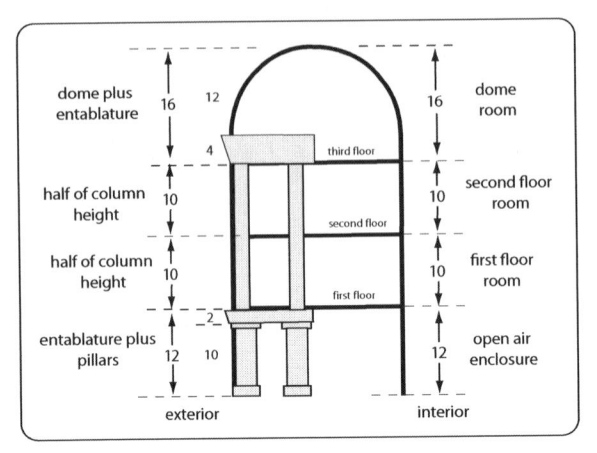

The Greek word *eurythmia* comes from *eu* (well) + *rhythmos* (proportioned)

I'm not the only person who senses the Monas symbol relates to arcitecture. In his 1995 Master of Architecture dissertation entitled *Stars, Stones and Architecture : An Episode in John Dee's Natural Philosophy*, Brent Wagler writes:

"The features of symmetry, orientation and circumscription expressed
in the Monas are fundamentally architectural... the Monas is in effect
a kind of architectural drawing."

"Dee constructs the hieroglyphic Monas upon principles
that are clearly resonant with the Vitruvian principles
of architectural order. In Chapter 2 of Book 1,
Vitruvius maintains that architecture depends
on arrangement, eurythmy, and symmetry.

His explanation might indeed serve without
any modification as the ground for Dee's Monas:
'Order gives due measure to the members of a work
considered separately, and symmetrical agreement
to the proportions of the whole...

Arrangement includes the putting of things
in their proper places and the elegance of effect
which is due to adjustments appropriate to the
character of the work... Eurythmy is beauty and
fitness in the adjustments of the members...
when they all correspond symmetrically."
(Brent Wagler, McGill Collections, online, p. 64-66,
quote from Vitruvius, Book 1, Chapter 2, p.1)

Having examined the harmonious proportioning of the Tower, let's next explore the Tower's **function**, which incorporates Dee's ideas about vision and time.

DEE'S IDEAS ABOUT VISION

Following Alberti, Dee used the idea of "Visual Pyramids" to describe how vision works. What are "visual pyramids"?

We saw earlier (in his *Preface to Euclid*) that Dee places the Art of Perspective **first** among all the Mathematical Arts which derive from Arithmetic and Geometry. Perspective means the Art of Optics or understanding vision and how light works.

Recall that Dee gave 3 compelling reasons for its importance:

First, without understanding Perspective,
Astronomical appearances cannot be easily comprehended.

Second, Perspective deals with **Light**, the first of God's Creatures.

Third, it deals with the **Eye**, the light of our body, and his Sense
most mighty, and his organ most Artificial and Geometrical.

We previously reviewed what Dee calls the Art of painting and sculpture: "Art of Zography." And within this Art, Dee includes the "odd Art of Althalmazat," Dee's term for the camera obscura. Let's take a closer look at Dee's definition of Zography:

**"Zographie, is an Arte Mathematicall, which
teaches and demonstrates, how the Intersection of
all visual Pyramids, made by any plane assigned,
(the Centre, distance, and light, being determined)
may be represented by lines, and due proper colours."**

Dee's definition of Zography is practically identical to Leon Battista Alberti's definition of painting written 135 years earlier [in a book which Dee had in his library.]
Alberti's [1435] definition of a painting:

**"A painting is the intersection of a visual pyramid at a
given distance, with a fixed center and a defined position of
light, represented by art with lines and colours on a given surface."**

For example, here Alberti is looking at a square object.
The visual pyramid has 4 sides plus a base.

Alberti called all those rays within the pyramid *intrinsico* (intrinsic or inner).
He called those rays that make up the outline or boundary
of the observed object *extrinsico* (extrinsic or extreme).

Combined, all these *extrinsico* or boundary rays form a "**visual pyramid.**"

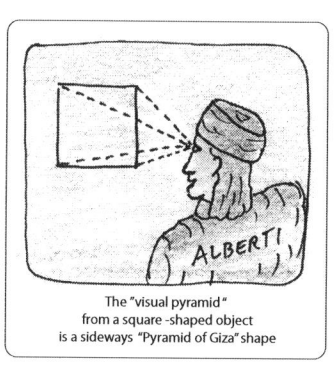

The "visual pyramid"
from a square-shaped object
is a sideways "Pyramid of Giza" shape

Nowadays, the word "pyramid" is generally envisioned as the "4 sides plus a base" kind, like the enormous Pyramids in Giza, Egypt. But, a geometric "pyramid" can actually have 3, 4, 5, 6, 7 … or any number of sides, all of which taper from a base to a single point at the apex.

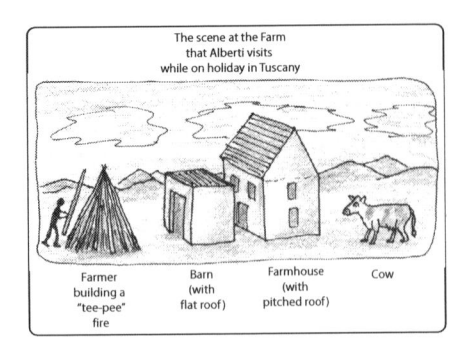

The scene at the Farm that Alberti visits while on holiday in Tuscany

Farmer building a "tee-pee" fire | Barn (with flat roof) | Farmhouse (with pitched roof) | Cow

Imagine that Alberti was on holiday, visiting a Tuscan farmhouse, which had a flat-roofed cow barn. The farmer was preparing a celebration for Alberti by building a huge tee-pee-shaped fire to ignite later that evening.

Viewing the scene face-on, Leon Battista Alberti would see the…

… wood for the fire as a 3-sided pyramid (plus a base)

… the barn as a 4-sided pyramid (plus a base)

… the farmhouse as a 5-sided pyramid (plus a base)

… and the cow as a many-sided pyramid (plus a base)

It's clear that the **simplest** pyramid is the "3-sided pyramid plus a base."

One might suggest that a pole in the ground (that looked at a **line**) might be simpler.

Geometrically-speaking, a line has no thickness. But a pole, even a thin rod, has a certain thickness.

Thus, to the viewer, a pole is just a tall, thin 4-sided pyramid (plus a base).

The "visual pyramid" from a pole or stick is actually a tall, thin four-sided pyramid (plus a base).

Note that all these examples of "visual pyramids" have triangular sides. Some are pretty skinny, but they all taper to the apex point, the eye.

However, only the **simplest** visual pyramid also has a base which is a triangle. This is the tetrahedron (meaning four-sided).

If the length of "one side of the base" equals the "distance from the base's corners to the eye," the visual pyramid is a "regular tetrahedron" (comprised of 4 equilateral triangles).

156

To simplify how this relates to the camera obscura, I've designed two rooms and a hole in their common wall.

In the left room, I've put 3 tall blocks in a triangle, cleverly spelling LVX, (or LUX, the Latin word for light).

If a light is turned on in the left room, an image of the LVX blocks will appear in the right room.

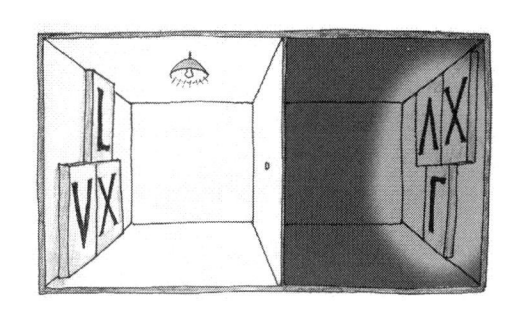

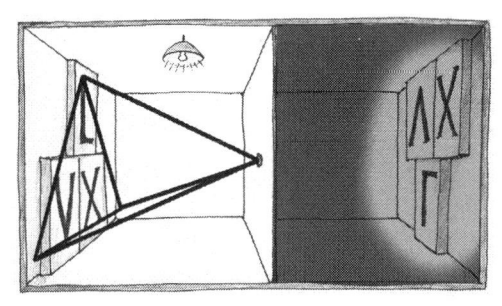

The visual pyramid in the left room (going from the 3 letters to the hole) is a tetrahedron.

In the right room is the "opposite" tetrahedron, (making letters which appear "upside-down" and "reversed left-to-right").

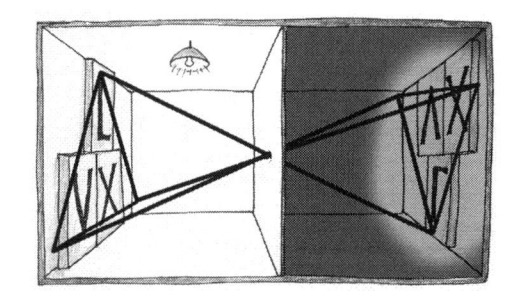

Here is my grand conclusion:
The simplest geometric shape that can be used to describe the behavior of light in a camera obscura is two tip-to-tip tetrahedra.

And of course you know what that is. It's a Bucky bowtie.

(And four Bucky bowties make a vector equilibrium, the shape Bucky considered to be Nature's operating system.)

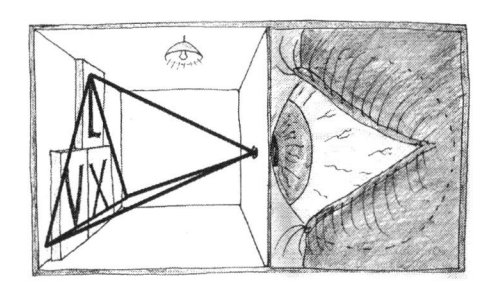

An **eye** is like that dark room.

Here is the tetrahedron of light coming from those three letters.

As the eye is a camera obscura, **the Bucky bowtie is the simplest geometric description of vision**.

It's all rather simple, isn't it?

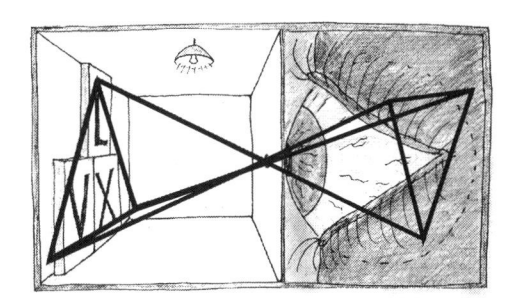

157

Dee was a top-rate geometer. He writes that the study of Perspective (optics, vision, how the eye sees) is the most important science. He knew about the vector equilibrium (or cubocta-hehron, or as he might have referred to it, the exoctahedron).

Thus, Dee saw "vision" as a Bucky bowtie. And he no doubt had a model just like the one I am holding here.

Drawing of a wooden model of a cuboctahedron by Leonardo da Vinci in Luca Pacioli's *De Divina Proportione*

How can I be so sure Dee had a model?

All Renaissance geometers had models (mostly made from pieces of wood glued together). Leonardo da Vinci probably worked from models to draw his fabulous illustrations for Luca Pacioli's *The Divine Proportion*.

There is no way Dee could have written the dozens of corollaries and addendums (many about 3-D shapes) to the first English translation of Euclid's *Elements of Geometry* if he wasn't working with models. (Most of the shapes Dee deals with are much more complex than a Bucky bowtie.)

Furthermore, Dee was the first Englishman to use the word "model" in a written work.
[The actual citation comes from the *Preface to Euclid*, in which Dee refes to a "Modell of a Ship."]

He obviously picked up the word from the many scholars he visited in France (who called it *modelle*) and Italy (who called it *modello*).   (*Oxford English Dictionary*, model; Dee, *Preface to Euclid*, p.c.iij.verso)

Here, I've added a dotted line that goes from the "place where the three blocks meet" to the "center of the retina." Alberti calls this the "**centric ray**." He writes that because it is the "most active and strongest of all the rays," it merits the name "Prince of Rays."

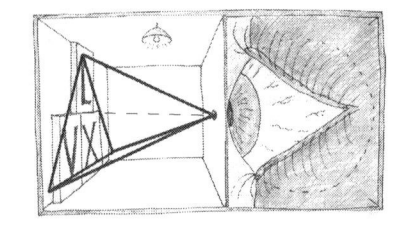

Nowadays, we know that the "fovea centralis" (or simply "fovea") of the retina has the highest density of rods and provides the sharpest vision.

Sure, you can hold a book open in your hands and see both pages. But if you are reading a sentence on the left page, you can't make out the words on the right page. When we read, our eyes move in order to maximize the use of that sharp central fovea.

We've already looked at a few of Dee's cryptic references to the camera obscura.

He recommends that "**with windows and Doors Shut on all sides, at any given Time,** astronomers are "**able to observe the movements of the heavenly bodies.**"

He cryptically refes to the movement of a solar disc in a camera-obscura calendar-room as " **A Perpetual Motion.**" (The solar disc is constantly in motion, and always on time.)

In the the *Monas,* Dee riddlingly tells "Experts on Weights," "**the Element of Earth can Float above that of Water.**"

158

Dee's advice to Opticians

But his clearest reference to the camera obscura in his advice to Opticians, or as Dee calls them in Latin, *"Perspectivus."* But still, he's a little cryptic in his description. He wants you to think about his metaphors.

"And won't the OPTICIAN condemn the Senselessness of his Ingenious work, laboring in all sorts of ways to make a Mirror according to a Line (appropriately curved in a circle) of a Parabolic Section of a Cone, which will attack any Matter (able to be burned by fire) with the incredible Heat from the Rays of the Sun.

Yet here a Line is presented, resulting from a Three-Cornered Section of the Tetrahedron, from which, when Made Full-Circle, a Mirror may be found that (even when the Sun is being blocked by Clouds) can reduce any kind of Stones or Metal into Impalpable Powders by the force of (truly the very strongest) Heat."

This might sound mysterious and mystical, but it's really quite scientific. In the first paragraph, Dee admonishes Opticians for wasting their time trying to find the most perfectly shaped concave mirror to focus the rays of the sun, when the behavior of light can best be understood in a different way.

To understand the second paragraph, let's look at Dee's original Latin words:

"... Cum, hic ex Tetrahedri Sectione Trigonica, Linea exhibeatur; ex cuiss Forma Circulata, fieri potest Speculum..."

(...Yet here a Line is presented, resulting from a Three-Cornered Section of the Tetrahedron, from which, when Made Full-Circle, a Mirror may be found ...)

Let's analyze this in sections:

...*a Three-Cornered Section of the Tetrahedron ...,*
Trigonica, in Greek means "three-cornered" or "a triangle"
(like the base of a tetrahedron).

...*a line presents itself ...*
The "line which presents itself" is Alberti's "centric ray." It emanates from the middle of the triangle (where the blocks labeled L, U, and X all touch each other) and extends to the apex of the tetrahedron, (at the pupil of the eye), then goes inside the eye (to the center of the fovea).

...*when Made Full-Circle...*
Dee's term "Forma Circulata" is a tricky one, but it is quite revealing. Dee is using the phrase "in Circular Form" metaphorically, in the sense of: "to make complete," "make whole," "come full circle," "round out," or "complete the circuit."

The visual-pyramid-tetrahedron on the left is "made complete" or "come full circle" when mated with its opposite, the "projected" visual-pyramid-tetrahedron on the right...

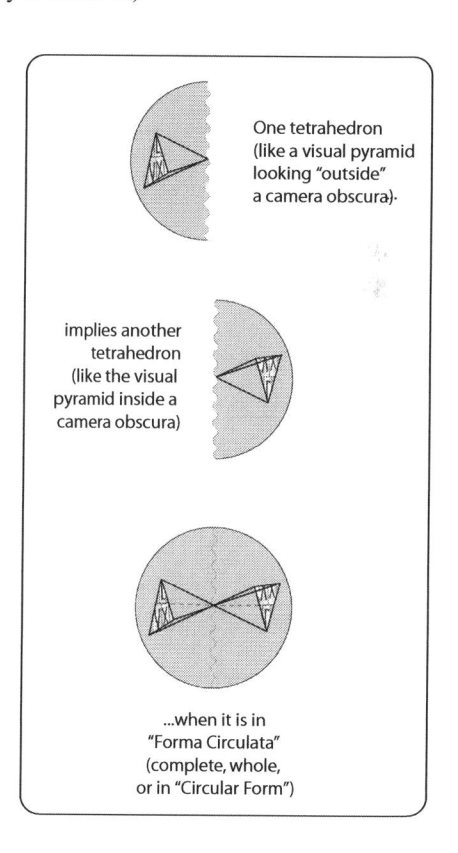

One tetrahedron (like a visual pyramid looking "outside" a camera obscura).

implies another tetrahedron (like the visual pyramid inside a camera obscura)

...when it is in "Forma Circulata" (complete, whole, or in "Circular Form")

...a mirror may be found...
Again, Dee is speaking metaphorically. He's not using the word "mirror" in the sense of "a silvery, reflective surface," but in the sense of a "copy," an "imitation," a "simulation," or an "echo."

He is using the term "mirror" (*speculum*) to metaphorically to describe that incredibly-accurate, full-color, live-action, projected-image seen in any camera obscura.

It really is much like a "mirror-image," a replication of every tiny detail in the "scene" on the other side of the aperture.

...(even when the Sun is being blocked by Clouds)...
This might be read as "A camera obscura even works on cloudy days."

...can reduce any kind of Stones or Metal into Impalpable Powders...
Inside a camera obscura, try touching the image of a stone wall or an iron cannon. Their images are like "powders, unable to be felt by touch."

...by the the force of (truly the strongest) Heat."
This is simply Dee's dramatic way of saying "the Sun."

Here's a visual summary.
How all these light rays pass through that teeny hole and simultaneously and come out the other side, so nicely organized, is indeed magical.

Dee is intentionally cryptic, but he has boiled down the camera obscura to its essence: a Bucky bowtie.

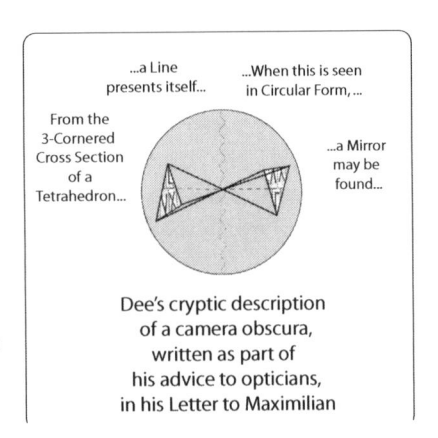

...a Line presents itself... ...When this is seen in Circular Form,...
From the 3-Cornered Cross Section of a Tetrahedron... ...a Mirror may be found...

Dee's cryptic description of a camera obscura, written as part of his advice to opticians, in his Letter to Maximilian

Another camera obscura reference found in "a dark place"

I searched long and hard to find a cryptic reference to the actual words "Camera Obscura" in the *Monas Hieroglyphica*. While researching, I found that Johannes Kepler was credited with first using the term around 1605. This was about 40 years after the *Monas Hieroglyphica* was written.

Exploring the Latin translation of Alhazen's groundbreaking studies on optics (which Dee owned), I noticed the camera obscura was called a *Locus Obscura*.

Locus means "place," so *Locus Obscura* means "a dark place." This made sense because Alhazen did his experiments in one room, using a screen for a wall. In the experiment shown here, Alhazen had his candle set-up on one side, and the other side was a "dark place."

So I searched through the *Monas Hieroglyphica* for the term "Locus Obscura."

locus obscura

In the emblem which follows Theorem 24, Dee writes,

"Intellect Judges Truth, Contact at a point, The eye of the Vulgar will, here, be Obscured and most Distrustful."
(Dee realized knew most people wouldn't have a clue what his book was all about.)

Translations are helpful, but all translations are approximations, and much can be lost. One should always refer back to the to the primary document, no matter what language it's in. So let's examine Dee's original Latin wording.

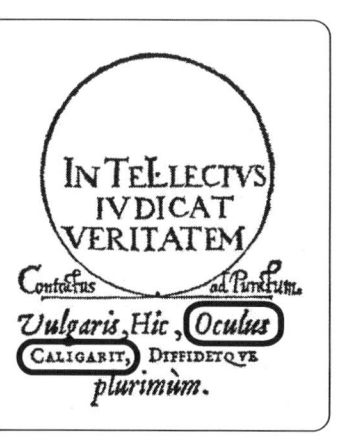

The word *oculus* means "eye" and *Caligibit* means "obscure." In Latin, the word *caligo* means "mist, vapor, fog, darkness, obscurity" and is synonymous with the Latin word *obscura*, meaning "dark, dim, dusky, or obscurity."

The word *oculus* means "eye," but you don't have to be a jumbled-letter genius to see the word *locus* among its letters.

Dee has cleverly hidden *locus obscura*, his term for "camera obscura," in the very sentence that says "the eye of the Vulgar will be obscured."
(No doubt Dee got a kick out of his own playful irony.)

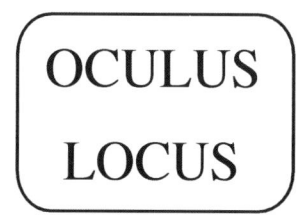

Dee always provides a confirming clue to let you know you're on the right track. Imagine his circle here is an eyeball or a spherical camera obscura. The "point of contact" with Dee's horizontal line is like the pupil or the aperture of a camera obscura.

If we follow the centric ray (Alberti's "prince of rays") of this eye looking downwards, it goes through the letters I, D, and M. Jumbling these letters, the word "dim" can be found. A "dim room" is like a "dark room."

[To make the clue less obvious, Dee has used several different typefaces, but the first letter of "Dim" is capitalized.]

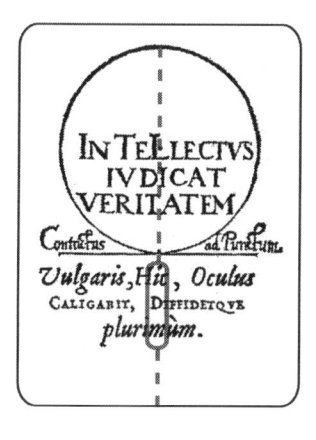

Dee provides other hints about the camera obscura, but the most front-and-center clue involves the " Two Mercuries" on the Title page. They are reflections of each other.

They are both looking at the same thing. They are each aiming their spears to that same thing. (One Mercury is even pointing at it.) The object of their attention is a "hole." I suggest his is a visual metaphor for that solitary hole in a camera obscura.

A hidden word clue about the camera obscura

Dee even put a "word reference" to the camera obscura in one of the flowing ribbons on the Title page page, in the form of what Dee calls "*Tzyruph,*" or a jumbled-letter code. Along the top of the ribbon he writes 1, 2, 3, and 4.

the right hand ribbon on the Title page

Taking one letter from STILBON, two letters from ACUMINE, three from STABILI, and four from CONSUMMATOS, the word ALHALAMOS, (a form of the word ALTHALMASAT) can almost be formed. (All that's missing is the letter H.)

Underneath the ribbon, Dee wants the reader to take one letter from STABILI and four from CONSUMMATA to find the word ATOMA.

Dee was an atomist and was encouraging the reader to explore atoms, especially spherical ones and how they close-pack.

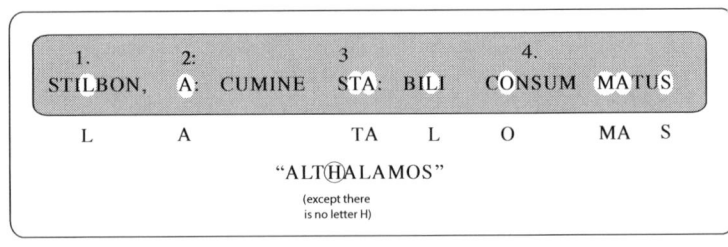

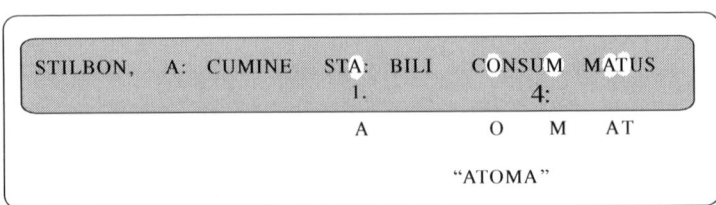

1.	2:		3		4.	
STILBON,	A:	CUMINE	STA:	BILI	CONSUM	MATUS
L	A		TA	L	O	MA S

"ALT(H)ALAMOS"
(except there is no letter H)

STILBON,	A:	CUMINE	STA:	BILI	CONSUM	MATUS
1.					4:	
A					O M	AT

"ATOMA"

Dee has added a twist to the puzzle. He put colons after the letter "A" in "A:CUMINE" and after the "A" in "STA:BILI."

In Greek, the letter "A" can have two completely opposite meanings. It can mean "**not**," as in Dee's word ATOMA, which means "**not**" cuttable. Or the "A" can mean "union, or being connected, or **likeness**."

The Greek word STILBON means "the Shining One" and is synonymous with the Roman god Mercury and the Greek god Hermes.

Dee wants the reader to see the "**likeness**" of STILBON as **HERMES,** thus providing the missing letter "H" for the word ALTHALAMOS.

The Monas symbol itself suggests a camera obscura

Dee sees the Sun and the Moon as sort of a mirror of each other.

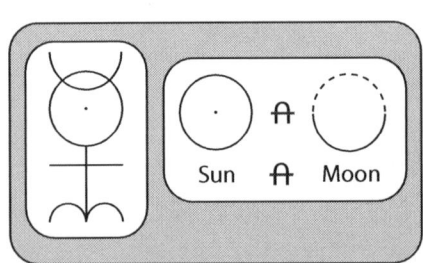

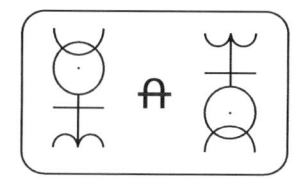

Several places in the *Monas*, Dee depicts the Monas symbol as inverted.

This is what the image of the Monas symbol would look like projected inside a camera obscura.

On a simplistic level, the Monas symbol looks like a squatting stick-figure with out-stretched arms (like a very skinny "Vitruvian man").

On the figure's head is a crown, or hair (on a bad hair day), or perhaps horns (though Dee would certainly not be presenting anything devlish to a King).

If the Sun circle represents a head, the single dot in it's center is like an **eye**. But why aren't their two eyes? This stick figure looks more like a **Cyclops**.

Can you think of something we've explored that acts like a Cyclops? (Someting Dee was quite fascinated by.)

The camera obscura!
It's a room that acts like a giant eyeball. Everything in the scene "outside," is projected "inside."

Mor evidence this was Dee's intent can be found in his "geometric construction" of the Monas symbol. Of the 17 letters he uses to label its various points, he "just happens" to use the letter "I" for the center-point of the Sun circle.

Even a kindergartener can hear that the letter "I" and the word "eye" sound the same. They are homonyms. Dee's revered Monas symbol is a visual joke about the "**one-eyed camera obscura.**"

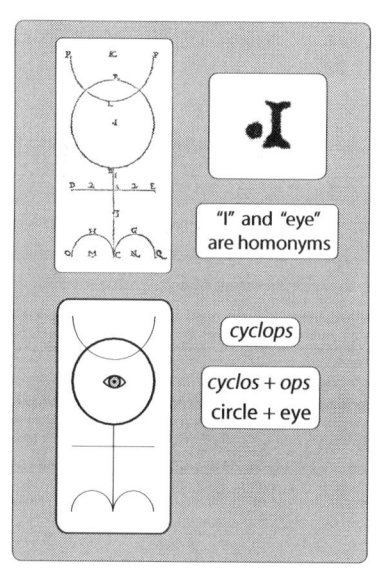

"I" and "eye" are homonyms

cyclops

cyclos + ops
circle + eye

But Dee's visual joke is a clever word joke on another level! The Greek word cyclops is a combination of the words *kuklos* (or *cyclos*), meaning "circle," and *ops*, meaning "eye."

Thus, **cy-clops** literally means "**circle eye**," which is just as Dee has drawn it in the Monas symbol!

Some modern renditions of Dee's joke

Two of my professional photographer friends, Eric Gould and Peter Goldberg, set up a portable "8-foot by 8-foot by 8-foot" camera obscura during Parents' Weekend at the Rhode Island School of Design.

Their friend, the talented Erminio Pinque, provided the colorful exterior décor.

Eric is pointing to the camera obscura hole in the center of the eyeball. This is the same joke Dee is telling, only 450 years later!

(Hold on, it gets even better)

Inside, a student looks at the inverted image of the RISD Art Museum.

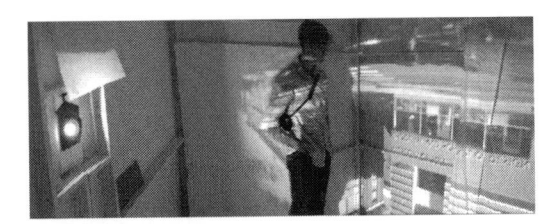

This photo gives you a sense of its overall box shape,
Let's zoom in for a close-up look of Erminio's artwork.

Looming over the tallest buildings
in Providence is **a giant Cyclops**.

Inside, a shocked woman points to the
inverted image of a one-eyed head on the wall.

This is exactly the is the same joke
Dee is expressing with his Monas symbol!

Here's another example of modern day artwork that expresses Dee' joke
(only using a completely different medium).

Every year Mike Wissman, who owns a farm near the Connecticut River in
Sunderland, Massachusetts, cuts a giant maze in his cornfield for children to explore.

Mike's friend, Will Sissin, had recently returned from visiting the camera
obscura room that overlooks Seal Rocks in San Francisco. Mike and
Will got the brilliant idea of cutting **a giant Cyclops** in the cornfield.

And right where the the eyeball of the
Cyclops is ... they put a camera obscura room!

They created a Cyclops with an eye that could actually see.
They're also expressing the same joke as Dee.

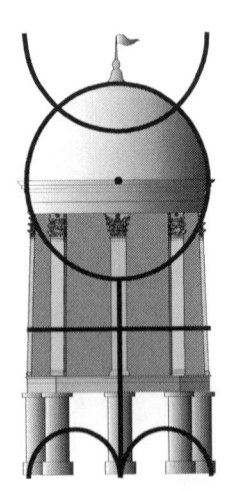

Dee's Monas symbol is the design plan of the Tower.

So, in a sense, the Tower is **a giant Cyclops**.

It's a building that can "see."

It's like a giant eyeball.

164

Actually, it's more like a "Tri-clops," as I suggest
each of its three rooms was a camera obscura room.

The rooms were like three eyes, each observing different
parts of the heavens (to the west, to the east, and upwards.)

[Or, as Dee might have called it, a "tri-locus obscura" or a "tri-althalmasat."]

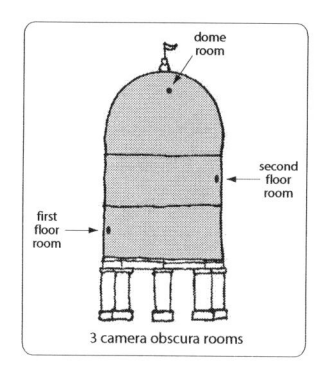

I think the first-floor room was accessed by a ladder
passing through a trap door where the 4 beams crisscross.

We've seen that a stairway once wound up the
northern interior wall to the second-floor room.
I suggest another stairway wound up the
southern interior wall to the dome room.

The first-floor room was a "camera-obscura
solar-disc-at-**sunset** calendar-room."

The second floor room was a "camera-obscura
solar-disc-at-**sunrise** calendar-room."

And the dome room was a "camera-obscura
solar-disc calendar-room for the **middle of the day**,"
(from around 10:00 AM to 2:00 PM).

[Interestingly, John Dee was the first person to use the phrase Ante Meridaim, (which later
evloved into "Antemeridian") in a book written in English. He used this term (meaning
"before midday") in his diary entry for September 8, 1563. (OED, ante meridiem)]

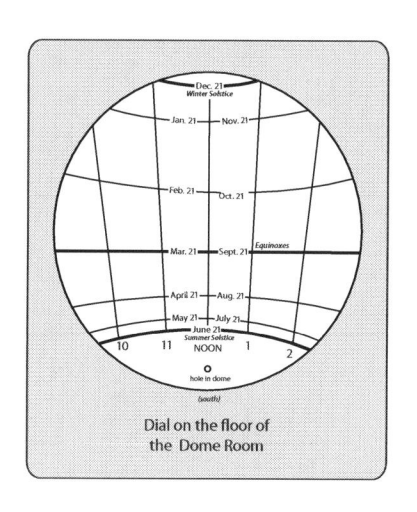

On the dome room floor, the "north-south line"
or the "meridiana line" (the noon-line)
was of utmost importance.

(Dee owned a very accurate "Dibley clock," and in his works,
he hints that he knew the solar-disc-at-noon actually traces
an analemma around the meridiana line. This figure-8 shape is
created because of the difference between clock time and solar time.

One of the uses of the dome-calendar-room woud be to study
this further, like making analemmas for all the hours.)

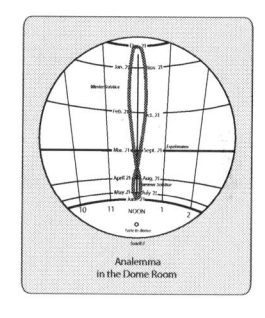

Incidentally, my reconstruction shows a ladder, about 16 feet tall. It wouldn't make
sense to store it outside. And it would be too cumbersome to fit in the first floor room.

I think the first floor, second floor and the Dome room floor each had a trap door in the middle.

Through a system of pulleys, the ladder could be raised up into the Dome room,
where it could be pulled aside to stay out of the way.

In 1558, Dee wrote a work in two books entitled *Trochillica Inventa* (meaning *Inventive Uses
for Wheels and Pulleys*) and he certainly used pulleys during his college days stage production
of Aristophanes' *Peace*, in which an actor on a giant dung-beetle flew up into the rafters of the theater.

To summarize, the Union of Opposites can be found in many things.

Bucky Fuller found the Union of Opposites in Geometry, in the Bucky bowtie and the Vector Equilibrium.

Bob Marshall found the Union of Opposites in the realm of number, called it "retrocity," and created a symbol to express it. It led to seeing the wonderful symmetries in Number like the Cycloflex and the Holotomes.

Bill Penhallow discovered that the Tower had important Sun and the Moon alignments and suggested the Tower might be a camera obscura.

Jim Egan saw that the most economical depiction of the behavior of light in a camera obscura is two tip-to-tip tetrahedra or a Bucky bowtie.

John Dee was as smart as all four of us combined.
(And then some.)

He saw the Union of Opposites in Geometry, Number and in the Camera Obscura.

This is what his *Monas Hieroglyphica* is all about.

And he summarizes the whole book with one multifaceted sign: his Monas symbol.

And he designed a three-dimensional, 48-foot tall sculpture, that also incorporates all these ideas.

Not only can the building still be seen today, **it still sees today**!

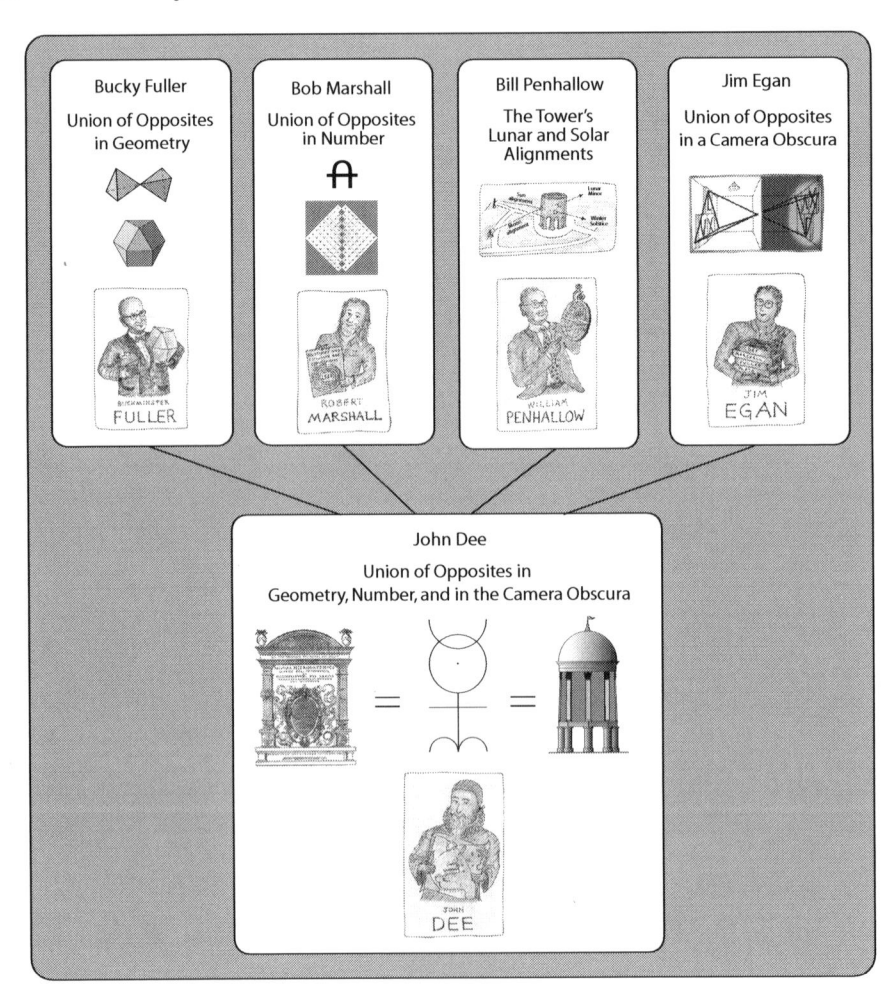

In short, the Tower was not just a fort,
it was to be the important city-center of the
first Elizabethan colony in the New World.

Not only did it have classical architectural features,
it was an example of perfect mathematical harmony.

Its 3 camera-obscura solar-disc calendar-rooms would keep the "New World"
in-sync with the sun at (what Dee thought would be) the beginning of the "New Time."

166

A BRIEF HISTORY OF CLOCKS IN CITY-CENTERS

To celebrate the concept of time, numerous cultures have put grand time-keeping devices right in the centers of their cities. Dee was well aware of the long tradition of **city-center horologia** when he designed the horologium at the first Elizabethan colony in the New World.

Over 4000 years ago, Stonehenge was built as a giant calendar-clock. The Sumerians, Babylonians, Egyptians and Chinese all built grand sundials.

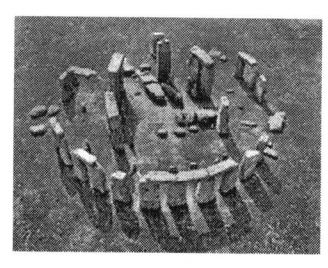

Solarium Augusti 10 BC — Tiber River, Mausoleum of Augustus, Via Flaminia (the road heading north from Rome), Ara Pacis (Altar of Peace)

In 44 BC, a year after instituting the Julian Calendar, Julius Caesar died. Rome was split by warring factions. In 10 BC, Caesar's nephew Augustus brought peace to the realm. To celebrate, he appropriated a 100-foot tall red granite **obelisk** from Heliopolis, Egypt and erected it as a gigantic sundial in central Rome.

To its north, the marble pavement was inlaid with an analemma (or dial) of gilded bronze. At sunset on Augustus' birthday (September 23), a shadow the tip of the obelisk crept up the stairs and into the *Ara Pacis Augustae*, the Altar of Augustan Peace.

One of Dee's inspirations to build a horologium was undoubtedly Vitruvius who describes the **Horologion** (now called the Tower of the Winds) built by Andronicus, around 75 BC, in the central marketplace of Athens.   (Vitruvius, Book1, Chapter 4)

This octagonal marble structure is 42 feet high and 26 feet in diameter. On the exterior are sundials and indicators of the eight winds. On the interior was a clepsydra or water clock, driven by water flowing down from the Acropolis. And amazingly, the structure still stands today.

Vitruvius wrote an entire chapter on the varius designs of sundials and water clocks used by the Greeks and Romans.

(Vitruvius, Book 9 chapter 8)

The Tower of the Winds still stands in Athens, Greece

In the Medieval era, mechanical clocks were installed town churches and monasteries. In 1292, a *"great horloge"* was installed in Canterbury Cathedral.

In 1330, the abbot Richard of Wallingford built a mechanical **"Horologium Astronomicum"** (Astronomical Clock) in St. Albans Church, Hertfordshire (about 22 miles north of London).

Around 1352, *L'Horoge Astronomique*, The Astronomical Clock, was built in Strasbourg, France.

Giovanni de Dondi designed an astronomical clock called the *Astrarium* (*Astralis* means "relating to the stars") around 1360, in the center of Padua, Italy (about 24 miles west of Venice).

In 1410, a clockmaker and an astronomy professor teamed up to make the *Orioj*, a large mechanical clock in the city center of Prague.

The clock, which still runs today, provides all sorts of astronomical data: the movement of the sun, the moon, and the stars of the ecliptic.

(The lower, circular dial, which is a calendar of the days and months, is a more recent addition).

The Astronomical Clock in Prague (built in 1410 and still running today)

In 1499, the famous *Torre dell' Orologio,* the Tower of Horology, was built in St. Mark's Square in Venice.

Galileo invented a pendulum clock, but Christiaan Huygens was the first to write about how to make one in his 1658 *Horologium* and his 1673 *Horologium Oscillatorium*.

Torre dell' Orologio (Tower of Horology) St. Mark's Square, Venice.

But Dee's horologium was different. It had "no mechanical parts." It was more accurate than a clock. It was always on time, as it displayed that "perpetual motion" of the earth/sun dance.

Royal Clock Tower Hotel under construction in Mecca, Saudi Arabia

Today the world's tallest clock tower is under construction in Mecca, Saudi Arabia, the place all Muslims turn towards when they pray. Millions of Muslims make an annual pilgrimage to Mecca to pray at the Kabba (Cube) in the Masjid al Haram (the Sacred Mosque).

Just south of this large open-air mosque is the Abraj Al Bait Towers, a massive hotel complex featuring **a giant clock tower** rising 1952 feet into the sky. (That's over six football-fields).

City-center clock towers can be found at small towns and large cities all over the United States. But perhaps America's "city-center-clock" in this digital age is the **Atomic Clock** at the National Institute of Standards and Technology laboratory in Boulder Colorado.

It might be hard for us moderns to perceive the value of a city-center clock. We have digital clocks by our bedside, watches on our wrists, and time shown on our computers and smartphones.

But throughout history, the chiming of city-center clocks notified the general populace of the times of work, public events, and church services. But just as important, it made the citizenry feel they were a part of the cosmos. The chiming of time helped connect their mundane lives to the splendor of the heavens.

In Dee's era, time was a huge fascination. As Mary E Hazard writes in *Elizabethan Silent Language*, "It has long been a truism among historians, including specialists in the history of art and technology, that a primary distinction between the Renaissance and earlier history was a new interest in the nature of **time** and especially in its more accurate scientific measurement."

(Hazard, p.174)

FROM VITRUVIUS TO VEGAS: THE LONG TRADITION OF CIRCULAR TEMPLES

A Greek or Roman "temple" was used differently than a Christian "church." The ancients used the interior to store religious artifacts sacred to the specific god of the temple. Religious services were held outside, in front of the temple. With most churches, the services take place on the inside.

Architects from the 1400's to the 2000's have "borrowed" the classical style and proportioning, but not generally to celebrate Greek and Roman gods.

In the Italian Renaissance, when Vituvius's *Ten Books on Architecture* were found and circulated, classical architecture became the rage. For space considerations, the majority of buildings were (and still are) rectangular. But circular temples made a comeback as well.

The influence of the Italian Renaissance drifted northward through Germany, France and the Low Countries, but it was slow to make the leap across the English Channel. John Dee, who had absorbed the energy of the Renaissance while studying travelling, and making friends abroad, helped bring cutting-edge ideas to England. Dee was instrumental in getting the English excited about Vitruvius and classical architecture. It didn't catch on as fast as he would have liked, but in the centuries after he died, the English and their colonies helped spread classical architecture around the globe.

Church domes (like St. Paul's in London and Rome), round churches, and Christian baptistries all evolved from the classical circular temple tradition. But let's look at some buildings that are even **closer replicas of Greek and Roman circular temple**s.

The **Tour de l'Horolge** in Aix-en Provence (Southern France) is a good example of a small Roman circular temple. Above a foundation topped by with an entablature rise ten Ionic pilasters (with a fancy geometric pattern between them). Above the upper entablature is a short conical roof.

(This relief of the original Tour de l'Horloge was carved in the wall of the Hospital of Saint John Laterno, in Rome, but is now in the Uffizi Gallery in Florence.)

relief of the
Tour de l'Horloge
(Timekeeping Tower)
Aix-en Provence, France

In 1504, Raphael painted *Lo Sposalizio* (*Marriage of The Virgin*), a depiction of the wedding between Mary and Joseph. The temple in the background came from Rafael's imagination (inspired by his teacher Pietro Perugino). It is an elegant Renaissance version of a **Vitruvian circular temple**. Up a tall series of steps are 16 columns, joined by arches and surmounted by an entablature. Buttresses join the colonnade to the central cella. And on top is a by a dome with a finial.

"Tempietto" at San Pietro
by Donato Bramante
Montorio, Italy, 1502

In 1502, Donato Bramante designed the **Tempietto** (Italian for "small temple") in the courtyard of **San Pietro in the Montorio**, district of Rome.

Steps lead to a colonnade of 16 Tuscan columns. Above a Doric entablature is a short railing. The tall, central cella has a dome and an ornate finial.

The first Renaissance church in Venice was built in 1468 on the small island of San Michele (Archangel Michael). Only five-minute water taxi ride from the main island of Venice, this island became the city's cemetery and is the final resting place for modern greats like Ezra Pound and Igor Stravinsky. Mario Codussi's design was influenced by the works of by Leon Battista Alberti.

Church of San Michele in Venice Italy

In 1530, Gugliemo Beramasco designed an addition to the San Michele called the **Chapele Emiliani.**

Sitting atop pedestals are six Corinthian pilasters topped by an entablature. Above the hexagonal building is a hemispherical dome, topped with a finial.

Capele Emiliani at the
Church of San Michele
Venice, 1530

The Rotunda, Stowe,
Buckinghamshire, 1720

Lord Cobham's Landscape Garden, in Stowe, Buckinghamshire, 50 northwest of London has two circular temples. In 1720, **The Rotunda** was built at the southern end of a long walkway. Its Ten Ionic columns support a round entablature capped by a dome, but it has no cella.

That same year, Jacques Rigaud featured **The Rotunda** in the foreground of this panoramic painting of the Garden.

The Rotunda, in a painting by Jacques Rigaud, 1720

Also in Stowe Gardens, in 1737, William Kent designed the even grander **Temple of Ancient Virtue**.

Above a short podiom rise sixteen Ionic columns spanned by a round entablature. The central cella has a hemispherical dome.

The Temple of Ancient Virtue, Stowe Landscape Gardens, Buckinghamshire, England, 1737

In 1747, Royal physician John Radcliffe engaged James Gibbs to design the **Radcliffe Library** to house science books. Gibbs was influenced by the Andrea Palladio, who had drawn illustrations of classical circular temples.

Above a 16-sided base rise 16 pairs of Corinthian pilasters, topped by a round entablature. At the top is a dome, supported by buttresses and capped with a lantern. When it became the reading room for the Bodleian library in 1860, the name was Latinized to **Radcliffe Camera.** [As you know, *camera* means "room."]

Radcliffe Camera, Oxford, 1747

In 1765, the architect Henry Flitcroft built a circular Temple for a large estate in Stourhead Estate, in Wiltshire, England.

The **Temple of Apollo** has a tall cella and a hemispherical dome, 12 freestanding Corinthian columns, as well as 12 pilasters attached to the outer wall of the cella.

circular temple on an estate in Stourhead, Wiltshire, England, 1765

In 1785, the 4th Earl of Bristol built the **Mussenden Temple** on a cliff overlooking the Atlantic in County Derry, Northern Ireland. It was modeled after the Temple of Vesta in Rome.

(Which Vitruvius wrote about, and Andrea Palladio later illustrated).

But instead of having a colonnade, there are 16 pilasters around a wide, domed cella. Around the upper entablature is a quote from the Greek atomist Lucretius:

"Tis pleasant safely to behold the shore,
The rolling ships and hear the tempest roar."

Mussenden Temple, Derry, Northern Ireland, 1785

Mausoleum of
Henry and Arabella Huntington
San Marino, California

In the 1920's, John Russell Pope used a circular temple design for the **mausoleum of the antiquarians Henry and Arabella Huntington** in San Marino, California.

It has a domed cella which has two side openings. The marble colonnade is echoed by pilasters on the outer wall of the cella.

Later, in 1943, John Russell Pope designed the **Jefferson Memorial** in Washington DC. Above the marble steps is a colonnade with Ionic columns. It has a dome and a prominent front portico, but no central cella.

Jefferson Memorial, designed by John Russell Pope, Washington DC, 1943

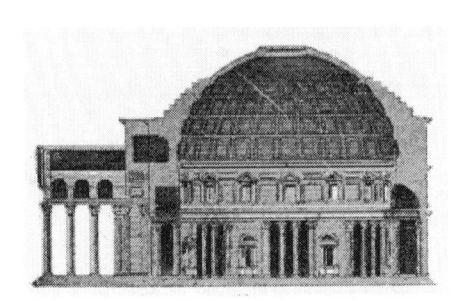

Pantheon, Rome, 126 AD

John Russell Pope writes that he was inspired by the **Pantheon** in Rome and Thomas Jefferson's design for **The Rotunda** built at the University of Virginia in 1826.

The Rotunda, University of Virginia, by Thomas Jefferson, 1826.

In 1966, a circular temple (with a dome, but no cella) was built as the centerpiece of a circular swimming pool at Caesar's Palace in Las Vegas.

Classical circular temple at Caesar's Palace, Las Vegas, 1966

Replicas of the Choragic Monument of Lysikrates

In the early 1750's, Englishmen James Stuart and Nicolas Revette journeyed to Athens to study the monuments of the ancients.

Starting in 1762, they published several volumes of *Antiquity of Athens*. Their books sparked the Greek revival architectural movement of the late 1700's and early 1800's in Northern Europe and the US.

(Thomas Jefferson owned a copy of the first volume. of *Antiquity of Athens*.)

Besides illustrating the Parthenon and the buildings on the Acropolis, they depicted smaller classical works like the Tower of the Winds and the **Choragic Monument of Lysicrates**.

James Stuart and Nicolas Revette's 1762 drawing of the Athenian Choragic Monument of Lysicrates

In 334 BC, a wealthy parton of the arts named Lysicrates had this small bulding erected to commemorate a choreography (dance-chorus) contest his troupe had won. It has a high, squared foundation and a tall, central cella surrounded by Corinthian pilasters. Its flat dome was originally crowned by the prize they had won, an ornate bronze sculpture.

Though it's more of a monument than a building, it does have a foundation, Corinthian pilasters, a cella, and it honors Dionysius, the god of the theater. Thus, it's a mini-circular temple.

Choragic Monument of Lysicrates Athens, 334 BC

Over the years, numerous replicas of the Choragic Monument of Lysicrates have been built in England and in the US.

In 1826, Archibald Simpson put one on the top of on the tower of **St. Giles Church** in Elgin, Northern Scotland.

Another replica is the **Dugald Stewart Memorial** built on a hill top overlooking Edinburgh, Scotland, in 1831.

replica of the Choragic Monument of Lysicrates, atop Saint Giles Church, Elgin, Scotland, 1826

Dugald Stewart Memorial, Edinburgh, Scotland, 1831

173

In 1859, famed architect William Strickland designed one for top of the **Tennesee State Capitol Building** in Nashville. He also put one at the top of the **Merchants' Exchange Building** in Philadelphia.

reproduction of the Choragic Monument of Lysicrates atop the Tennesee State Capitol, Nashville, 1859

The 1875 the design of **Portland Breakwater Light** in Maine was inspired by Lysicrates' monument. The architect Thomas U. Walter (who also designed the US Capitol dome) used six curved cast-iron plates for the walls and hid the seams with Corinthian pilasters. The top of the thick entablature is crenellated.

The design for the 1855 Portland Breakwater Lighthouse was based on the Choragic Monument of Lysicrates

In 1902, the **Soldiers' and Sailors' Memorial Monument** was erected in New York City (in Riverside Park at 89th St.) to commemorate those who fought for the Union Army. Its inspiration was the Choragic Monument of Lysicrates. This white marble circular temple has a high base, 12 Corinthian columns, and a tall cella with a conical roof.

Replicas of the Athenian "Tower of the Winds"

When James Stuart and Nicolas Revette visited the actual Tower of the Winds in Athens, they found it had a house abutting it.

They were intent on making accurate drawings and measurements, so they got permission to tear the house down. In the center of this illustration, they are seen negotiating with the houseowner.

The Tower of the Winds in Athens, from *Antiquity of Athens* by James Stuart and Nicolas Revette, 1762

As we saw previously, the **Tower of the Winds in Athens** is a horologium with sundials and a clepsydra (water clock) for keeping track of time.

It looks as great today as it did to Stuart and Revette in the mid-1700's, and almost as good as it did to its architect Andronicus of Cyrrhus, around 100 BC.

The Tower of the Winds, Athens, as seen today

In 1765, James "Athenian" Stuart built a **replica of the Tower of the Winds** in Shugborough, just north of Birmingham, England (the plaster friezes of the "eight winds" and weathervane have long since disappeared.

James Stuart's replica of the Athenian Tower of the Winds, Shugborough, England, 1765

Later, in 1782, James Stuart designed another **replica of the Tower of the Winds** for the Marquess of Londonderry at his Mount Stewart estate in Northern Ireland.

James Stuart's replica of the Athenian Tower of the Winds at Mount Stewart, County Down, Northern Ireland

In 1794, the Radcliffe Observatory was constructed in Oxford. At the very top is a **replica of the Tower of the Winds.**

The architect, James Wyatt had seen the Athenian tower in Stuart and Revett's *Antiquities of Athens*. The replic tower has large glass doors so the astronomers could roll their instruments onto the roof of the semicircular building below.

Radcliffe Observatory Oxford, 1794

In the 1930's, Albert Weilben designed a **replica of the Athenian Tower of the Winds** for the mausoleum of Joseph and Lucca Laccaro, in Metarie Cemetery, in New Orleans.

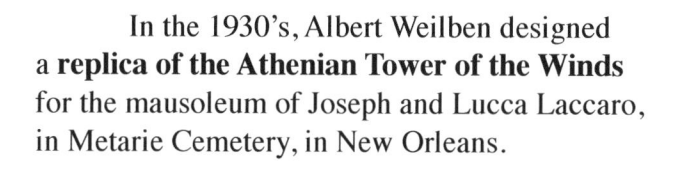

Mausoleum of Joseph and Lucca Laccaro, Metarie Cemetery, in New Orleans, ca. 1935 (replica of the Athenian Tower of the Winds)

Dee's variation on the theme: a circular temple for the "New Time"

Like the Italian Renaissance architects of the 1400s and 1500s, and like the Greek Revivalists of the 1700's and 1800's, and like the owners of Caesar's Palace (Las Vegas) in the 1900's, John Dee got the classical architecture bug. And he wanted Elizabethan England to catch it too. In the *Preface to Euclid*, he proclaims that his favorite architects are Vitruvius and Leon Battista Alberti.

In the previous sampling, all the buildings are similar, as they are all basically circular. But each one is slightly different from the others. They are each "variations on the theme."

Some have cellas, others don't. What they ***do*** have in common are a foundation area, column area, an entablature, a dome (or roof), and a finial.

Dee's 1583 Tower was also a "variation on the theme." It had an octagonal foundation of pillars, a cella, Corinthian pilasters, a thick entablature, a dome, and a finial.

In this sampling, many of the buildings were built to "commemorate" something. But some had special functions (like a library, lighthouse, burial chamber, swimming pool ornament, etc.).

Dee's circular temple was "commemorative," in the sense it was built to memorialize the birth of the British Empire.

But it also had a special function.
It was a horologium used to keep track of time.
This made it "commemorative" in another way. It celebrated (what was to have been) the English Calendar Reform of 1583.

Dee had designed what I call a "*templum tempus*" or a "temple of time."

Knowledge about the building somehow got "lost in time."

(But the Tower has an amazing story it has to tell.
It's "about time" we recognize and appreciate it.)

Dee's Tower was a temple of time

The Tower as a beacon of freedom

To Dee, the *Monas Hieroglyphica*, (the words and illustrations on paper),
the Monas symbol, (a composite of geometric shapes),
and the John Dee Tower, (a stone-and-mortar sculpture)
are all the same thing.

They are all echoes of Dee's synthesis of the "Laws of Nature" which he gleaned from intense study of natural things like shapes, numbers, light, and the movements of the earth, sun, moon, and stars.

But the John Dee Tower shines in another way. It was a symbol of hope and freedom for the first Elizabethan colony in the New World at the Dee River and Port, which had been granted total religious freedom by Queen Elizabeth.

Besides being a sculpture of mathematical harmony and a timepiece aligned with the Sun and Moon, it was also a beacon of freedom. It was to be a radiant symbol in the city-center of the new colony that would inspire generations.

Unfortunately, the colonizing effort failed. But in the next century, Benedict Arnold owned the Tower and he saw it as a symbol of freedom as well.

Newport was one of the most open-minded and tolerant of all the cities on the East Coast. And Governor Benedict Arnold was one of the main defenders of this freedom. As President of the Colony in 1657, he responded to his old comrades in Massachusetts when they demanded that Quakers not be allowed to settle in Newport:

> **"We have no law among us whereby we punish any for declaring by words their minds and understandings concerning the things and ways of God as to salvation and external condition."**

Quakers, Jew, Baptists, Sabbatarians, and others, all found a safe haven in Newport.

If the Tower was such an important beacon of freedom, why hasn't this been recognized by historians? Why didn't either the Elizabethans or the Colonials write about it? To put it briefly, its knowledge was **lost in the folds of the cloak of secrecy**.

Here's a brief overview of what transpired from the 1500's until now.

The Act of Supremacy, making Henry VIII the Head of the Church of England, led to decades of religious turmoil in England. When Walshingham and Queen Elizabeth finally agreed to a colony in the New World in which English Catholics would be granted freedom of religion, they insisted the details of the mission be kept secret. Until a well-defended foothold was established, the citizens of the small colony would be sitting ducks for the Spanish. The Spanish had completely wiped out a similar French colony in Florida.

When Sir Humprey Gilbert drowned, and Sir George Peckham was thrown in jail, and the frustrated Dee traveled to the Continent, the spirit for the colony was dead.

Sir Walter Raleigh revived the colonizing effort a few years later, but felt the mid-coast area (what is now Virginia and the Carolinas) was a more suitable location than the northern coast area. Because of its warmer climate, the growing season is longer.

When Roger Williams, the Arnold Clan, and others settled around Narragansett Bay in the 1630's, the last thing they would want known was that a building still existed from an earlier colonizing effort. Some influential courtier in England might use this as evidence of a previous land claim and the colonists would be forced to leave their new homelands they risked their lives to settle.

Furthermore, if this building was built for a colony of Elizabethan Catholics, some of the 1600s colonists might consider it Papist, and demand that it be torn down.

Benedict Arnold had the ability to keep the knowledge of who built the Tower "under wraps." He was a big-wig who could tell people it was just his "Stone-Built Wind Mill," and they wouldn't dare challenge him.

But something else happened in the 1600s, back in England. Around 1620, the antiquarian Sir Robert Cotton had decided to do some digging in John Dee's garden in Mortlake. He uncovered a pile of documents, somewhat damaged, but still legible.

It was Dee's handwritten diary of Dee and Edward Kelley's conversations with the angels. Sir Robert's son, Thomas, gave the papers to the scholar Meric Casaubon to copy, and in 1659 Casaubon published them under the title *A True and Faithful Relation of What Passed for Many Years Between Dr. Dee and Some Spirits*. Dee was branded as an occultist and his reputation as a scholar was tarnished for the next few centuries.

Based on the fact that the Redwood Library was built on the "summer-solstice-sunrise line" from the Tower and the Trinity Churches were built on the "summer-solstice-sunset" line from the Tower, it's clear to me that in the mid 1700s at least some of the Anglican leadership of Newport knew the history of the Tower and how it functioned.

Before retreating from Newport, the British Army ignited the gunpowder they had been storing in the Tower

In 1775, on the eve of the American Revolution, anyone loyal to the Crown was chased out of town. In the Fall of 1776, the British Forces took over Newport and occupied it for three years. Supposedly, they stored gunpowder in the Stone Tower. After losing the Battle of Rhode Island the Brits had to hightail it out of town. So the American forces wouldn't have access to their gunpowder, they ignited, and blew off the top part of the building. The ensuing fire compromised even the solid wooden beams. The British also took with them most the early town records, that later got lost when the ship that was carrying them was sunk by American forces.

Another repercussion of the American Revolution was that the name Benedict Arnold became synonymous with the word "Traitor."

After the war the population of Newport had dwindled to 4000 people. Nobody wanted anything to do with things "British." And most everyone who might have had knowledge of the Tower was long gone. The hard drive of knowledge had been erased.

In the 1800s Dee was still categorized as a misguided occultist, and no one would ever have suspected he was the architect of a building in the New World. The Tower became a mystery to be solved.

And in 1837 when the Danish antiquarian, Carl Christian Rafn, proposed it was built by the Vikings, the rumor spread far and wide that it was true. Indeed, Rafn never actually saw the Tower, only some not-very-accurate illustrations of it.

In his 1942 book *Newport Tower,* Philip Means debunks the Benedict Arnold Theory and the Viking Theory. After excavating at the base of the Tower in 1949, William Godfrey of Harvard concluded the Tower was Governor Benedict Arnold's "folly." A folly is a "costly structure considered to have shown folly (foolishness) of the builder."

In 1994, Bill Penhallow discovered important clues by studying the astronomical alignments through the various windows of the Tower.

In the late 1900s and the early 2000s scholars like Nicholas Clulee, William Sherman, Ken MacMillan, Jennifer Abeles, Benjamin Wooley and Stephen Clucas have shed new light on the key role Dee played not only in Elizabethan exploration and the birth of the British Empire, but in the whole intellectual revival of the English Renaissance.

Drifts in the sands of time have a way of covering up history, but fortunately many pieces of the puzzle remained: the whole lower-half of the Tower, the records of the attempted colonization in the Elizabethan State Papers, Benedict Arnold's chair, and of course the biggest puzzle piece of all, the *Monas Hieroglyphica*. All I did was piece them together. But I stand on the shoulders of the observant astronomer Bill Penhallow, great thinkers like Buckminster Fuller and Robert Marshall, and of course the great riddler himself, John Dee.

As all of these puzzle pieces were coming came together, I recognized another puzzle piece. And it has to do with the "Rhode Island" part of the state where the building is located: Rhode Island and Providence Plantations.

GIOVANNI DE VERRAZZANO'S VOYAGE OF 1524

The gentle Queen Claudia and the domineering Queen Mother, Louise (or Aloysia)

On maps from the 1500's, why is Verrazzano's "triangular island the size of the Isle of Rhodes" sometimes called **Claudia** and sometimes called **Aloysia**?

King Charles VII and Anne of Brittany could not produce a male heir, but they had two daughters, Claudia and Renee. The conniving Louise of Savoy (Aloysia in French) convinced the king that Claudia should marry her son Francis. Louise attained her goal and Francis was crowned king in 1515.

Claudia became the Queen when she was only 15 (Francis was 21). She was short in stature and had a small hunched back due to scoliosis (abnormal curvature of the spine). She had no political power, and became "one of the least prominent Queens of France."

Over the next 9 years, she and Francis had 7 children. At age 24, she died suddenly.

(During those years, Francis had many mistresses, including Mary Boleyn, Anne Boleyn's sister).

Claudia had been totally eclipsed at court by the powerful "Queen Mother," Louise of Savoy. Even King Francis revered (or feared) his mother so much that he knelt whenever he spoke to her.

[King Francis was a great patron of the arts. He convinced Leonardo da Vinci to move to France in his later years, which is why the *Mona Lisa* is in Paris, not Rome. His purchases of works by Michelangelo, Titian, and Raphael were the beginning of the great collection that can be seen today in the Louvre.]

King Francis sends Verrazzano off to explore America.

In 1523, King Francis helped the citizens of Lyon, France finance the expedition of Giovanni Verrazzano to search the New World's seacoast from Florida to Newfoundland) and find a short cut to the Pacific Ocean.

Verrazzano had been born around 1485 at Castello Verrazzano, his family's castle, about 30 miles south of Florence. But the sea was in his blood. In 1507, at age 22, he moved to Dieppe, France to pursue a maritime career.

He went on several trips to the eastern Mediterranean (the port of Rhodes, on the Island of Rhodes being a main trading center). He also was a "corsair," attacking Spanish boats, and had even crossed the Atlantic to Newfoundland.

This seasoned Italian navigator, with 50 French crewmen aboard *The Dauphine,* set off across the Atlantic on January 17, 1524.

Verrazzano's ship La Dauphine
(the Dolphin)
(based on a ship drawn on the 1529 map by his brother, Giralmo Verrazzano,

Verrazzano's 1524 Voyage

After traveling west for 25 days, they reached a "new land never seen before by anyone, ancient or modern."

He reports reaching the coast at "34 degrees north latitude," which places him at what is now Cape Fear, near Wilmington, North Carolina.

In honor of King Francis, he named the new land **Francesa**. (A name that never really caught on).

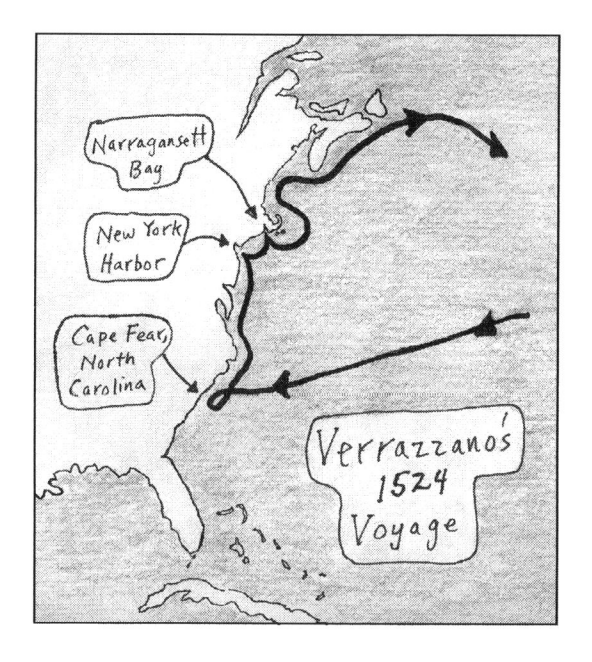

At first he headed south, along what is now the South Carolina coast. But he soon became concerned he was getting too close to Spanish Florida, so he turned around and headed north.

Passing by the Outer Banks, he could see the 25-mile-wide Pamlico Sound on the west of the barrier beach, and mistook it for an ocean. He searched for a passageway through the narrow strip of land, but was not successful.

After traveling north about another 125 miles, he landed on what is now called the Delmarva Peninsula. (Now the state of Delaware, plus parts of Maryland and Virginia.)

In his journal, Verrazano wrote about the native population and described the flora and fauna. He named several natural features after French dignitaries:

(1) Coast "diLorenna" (after the Cardinal)
(2) Promontory "Lanzone" (perhaps Cape Henlopen, Delaware)
(3) Promontory "Bonivetto" (perhaps Cape May, New Jersey)
(4) Large river "Vandoma" (perhaps Havesink Highlands, New Jersey)
(5) Small mountain "di S. Polo" (after the Count)
(Wroth, p. 85.)

About 250 miles further up the coast they found a "very agreeable place where a very wide river flowed out into the sea," thought to be (what is now) Staten Island at the mouth of the Hudson.

He named this area **Angleme** after the part of France in which Francis was born as a duke. He named the bay **Santa Margarita** after Francis' intellectual sister Marguerite.

Incidentally, Verrazzano has been commemorated in the names of two bridges that span two of the harbors he chose to explore.

The Verrazzano-Narrows Bridge connects New Jersey to New York.

The Jamestown-Verrazzano Bridge connects South County RI with the island of Jamestown.

Verrazzano reaches Southern New England

Let's hear from Verrazzano himself, as he travels from
New York Harbor, along the coast of Long Island, to Narragansett Bay:

We raised the anchor and sailed eastward since the land turned in that direction, and we went 80 leagues, always keeping in sight of land.

We discovered a triangular shaped island 10 leagues from the mainland, similar in size to the island of Rhodes.

If was full of hills, covered with trees and highly populated judging by the fires we saw burning continually along the shore.

We baptized it in the name of your illustrious mother Aloysia [Luisa or Louise], but did not anchor there because the weather was unfavorable.

We reached another land 15 leagues from the island where we found an excellent harbor.

Which we call Refugio, on account of its beauty

This country is situated on a parallel with Rome at 40 and two thirds degrees, but is somewhat colder, by chance and not by nature, as I will explain to your Majesty elsewhere.

I will now describe the position of the previously mentioned port. The shore of the land runs from west to east. The mouth of the port, faces south, and is a half a league wide.

From its entrance it extends for 12 leagues in a northeasterly direction and then widens out to form a large bay of about 20 leagues in circumference.

In this bay are five small islands, very fertile and beautiful, full of tall and spreading trees, and any large fleet could ride safely among them without fear of tempest or other dangers.

Then, going southward towards the entrance of the harbor, there are very pleasant hills on either side, with many streams of clear water flowing from the highlands to the sea.

In the middle of the mouth is a rock of Petra Viva formed by nature, which is suitable for building any kind of machine or bulwark for the defense of the harbor.

We called this rock "La Petra Viva" on account of both the nature of the stone and the family of a gentlewoman

On the right side of the harbor mouth is a promontory, which we will call "Jovius Promontory."   (Wroth, pp.127 and 137)

[Note: Petra Viva means a "very hard, nonporous rock." He is probably referring to the promontory where "Fort Dumplings" was built in the 1800's (shown here). Verrazzano named what is now Sakonnet Point for his friend "Jovius."]

182

Based on this account, most historians feel Verrazzano sailed eastwards along the Long Island coast, past the triangular-shaped Block Island, then veered northeast to the mouth of Newport Harbor, then around the islands of Narragansett Bay.

Verrazzano and his crew were so welcomed by the generous Narragansett Indians that they stayed for 15 days studying the native's culture. He remarked on how they lived on straw mats in round houses made of bent saplings and that they relocated according to the season. After making more observations on the types of trees, fruits, animals, and rocks, Verrazzano was off again.

He sailed way around sandy Cape Cod to the rocky shores of Maine. There, the natives weren't quite as friendly. They fired arrows and mooned the boat from the shore.

He skirted Nova Scotia, saw 32 islands off Newfoundland, and then headed back to France. He ended his 6-month trip around July 8, 1524, and submitted his report to King Francis in 1525.

Verrazzano later ventured on a voyage to Brazil where he and his men cut down huge trees for French shipbuilders. It's not known where his final voyage was, some historians suggest that he was captured by a Spanish boat and hanged. Others say he was killed (and maybe eaten) by natives in the Lesser Antilles.

Five Versions of Verrazzano's Report to King Francis

Verrazzano's original letter to King Francis, was probably written in Italian, then translated into French. This French translation has not survived, however several Italian versions have. In the late 1800s, the Italian historian Alesso Bacchiani tracked down **five** of them (all written in the 1500s).

The Cèllere version
Lawrence Wroth who wrote *The Voyages of Giovanni da Verrazzano* (1970) based his translation on this manuscript.

The Magliabechian version
Now in the National Library of Florence.

The Ramusio version
Giovanni Battista Ramusio, a Venetian scholar, published the letter in his
1565 *Delle navigationi et viaggi raccolta* (Collection of navigations and voyages)
John Dee had a copy of this book in his library (and it traveled with him to Prague)
(Roberts and Watson, #273).

The Cimento Fragment
The Accademia del Cimento (Academy of Experiment) was an early
scientific society in Florence that only lasted 10 years, from 1657 to 1667.
This fragment has Ramusio's mark on it, but includes only the last few pages of the letter.

The Vatican version
This manuscript (Ottoboniano 2202) is in the Vatican Library and has never been published.

The island of "Luisa" on two Italian Maps

There are also two maps that were complied from Verrazzano's data.

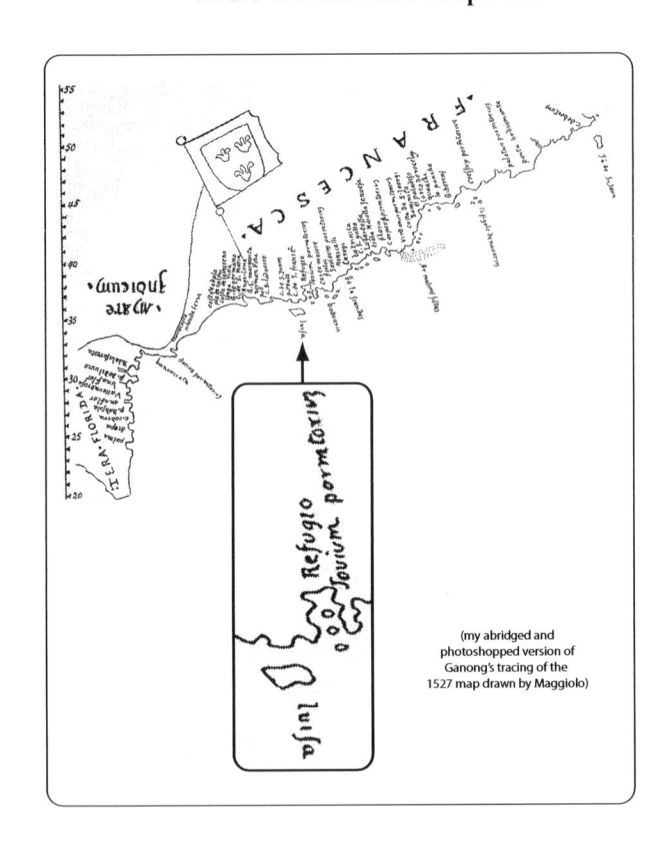

The 1527 Maggiolo Map

The Italian cartographer Visconte Maggiolo assembled the details of Verrazzano's trip (and more) on a map of "Francesca."

He even shows the *Mare Indium* (Sea of India) as covering present day South and North Carolina, Kentucky, Tennessee, and points west.

Zooming in on present-day Southern New England, one can can see **Refugio** (with three islands shown), the **Jovium Promontory** (Sakonnet Point) and the island of "**Luisa**," just off shore (but not very triangular).

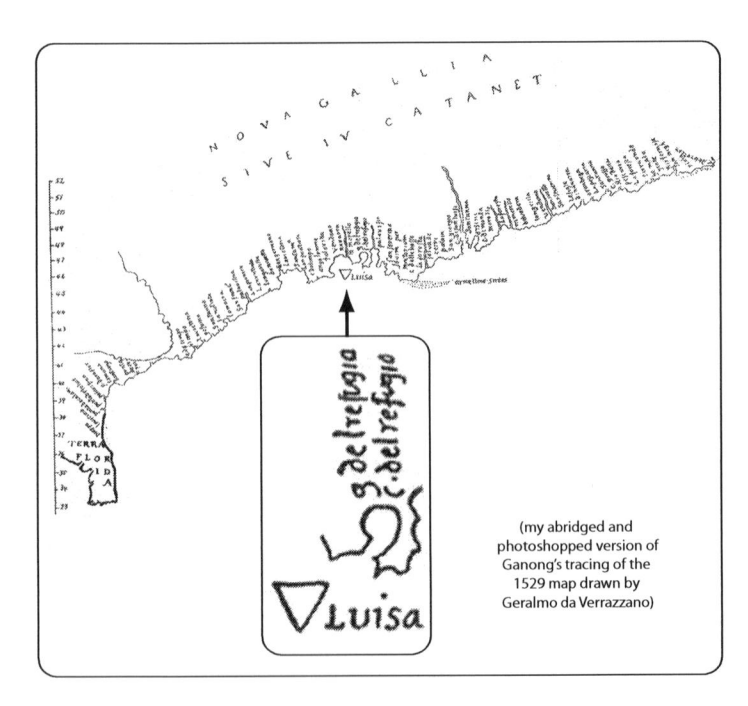

(my abridged and photoshopped version of Ganong's tracing of the 1527 map drawn by Maggiolo)

The 1529 Geralmo da Verrazzano Map

Giovanni's brother Geralmo reshaped the coastline, added some rivers, and changed a few names, but the two maps are essentially the same.

A close inspection shows the "**g del Refugio**" (Gulf of Refugio) and also the "**c del Refugio**" (Cape of Refugio or the Jovium Promontory).

On Geralmo's map, the island of **Luisa** is shaped like a perfect equilateral triangle. Even though the tip of the triangle is pointed south instead of north, it stands out as the most prominent graphic feature from Florida to Newfoundland.

(my abridged and photoshopped version of Ganong's tracing of the 1529 map drawn by Geralmo da Verrazzano)

The switch from Luisa to Claudia.

Forty to fifty years later, why did these Dutch and English navigators refer to the island of Luisa as Claudia?

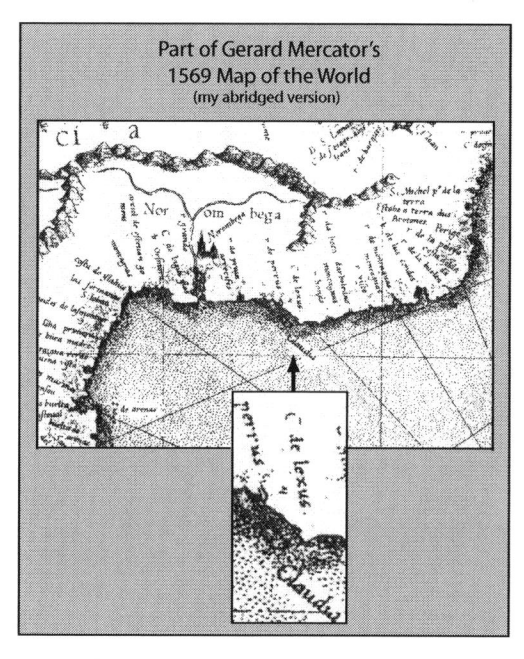

As early as 1569, Mercator identified Claudia as one of the few islands off the coast of North America.

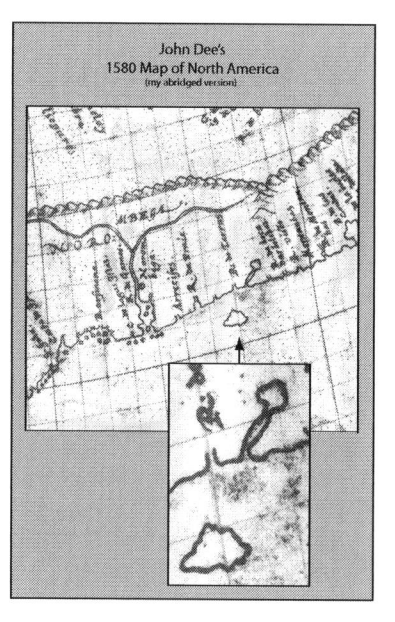

In John Dee's 1580 *Map of North America*, the triangular island is not labeled, but the round bay has been drawn headed in a northeast direction, just as Verrazzano described.

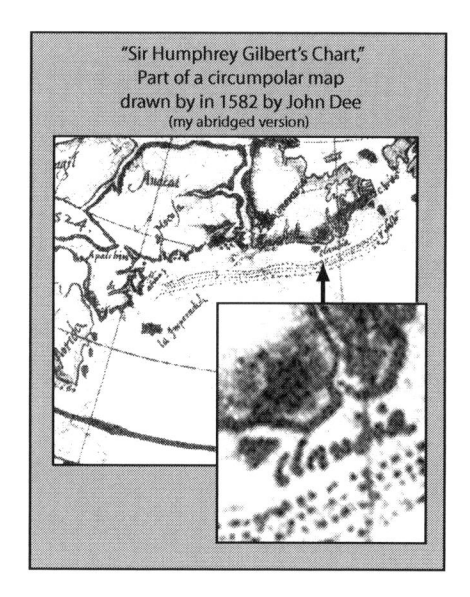

In 1582, Dee drew a circumpolar projection of the Northern Hemisphere and called it *Sir Humphrey Gilbert's Chart*. The triangular island of Claudia is one of the few landmarks listed from Florida to Newfoundland.

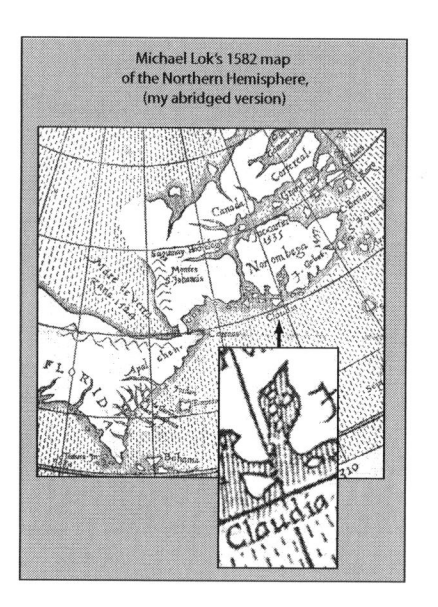

In Michael Lok's 1582 *Map of the Northern Hemisphere* (dedicated to Sir Philip Sidney), the triangular Claudia and the bay with a cluster of islands are clearly illustrated.

But why is it called Claudia on these later maps?

If Verrazzano named the triangular island **Aloysia**, or **Luisa** and his brother and Maggiolo both identify it on their maps as **Luisa**, where does the name **Claudia** come from?

New clues suddenly appear

In 1992, another version of Verrazzano's report was found in the archives of the McGill College Library in Montreal by researchers Dionysius Hatzopoulous and Richard Virr. This version contains words, phrases, and descriptions that are different (or spelled differently) than all of the other versions.

What's interesting is that the description of Southern New England in the "McGill version" differs from all the other versions. Most noticeably, it refers to Block Island as **Claudia** instead of **Aloysia**.

The description of Refugio in the McGill version

Sailing forward about what seems to be 100 leagues we found a beautiful River.

We had followed the shoreline towards the east and proceeded about 50 leagues where we discovered an island which was triangular in shape, lying 50 leagues from a mainland, full of mountains, dense with trees, and well inhabited, which we named Claudia.

Fifty leagues further we found a good port where we found very hospitable people who had a King, that was dressed in a deer skin, artfully wrapped around him, we found among them broken pieces of copper, with which they adorn themselves.

This land was already above the latitude of 41 2/3 and so extends eastward. We turned towards the meridian at the mouth of the port, which lies open towards the west, a half a league wide, which within heads northeast for 12 leagues.

It becomes wider and longer becoming a good sized gulf of 20 leagues, in which there are 5 small islands, which have very beautiful, fruitful trees, in the midst of the port is a very hard rock, suitable for building a castle or fortress to defend the port.

By comparing the distances given, the wording, and certain details,
Hatzopoulous and Virr concluded
"that all the extant versions seem to descend from different copies of the original."

(Hatrzopoulos, Dionysius and Richard Virr, *The Voyage of Giovanni da Verrazzano, A Newly Discovered Manuscript*, Fontana V. 1992.)

Studying all the details closely, archaeastronomer and naval architect James W. Mavor concluded

**" This may imply that Verrazzano mentioned two islands in his manuscript,
one of which was Block Island, and the other was Martha's Vineyard.
Scribes who copied the various versions of Verrazzano's letter may
have combined the two islands into one or the other."**

(Mavor, James W. Jr. *Bartholomew Gosnold's Voyage to Cape Cod in
Verrazzano's Wake*, NEARA Journal Volume 36, Number 2, Winter 2003.)

In 1582, Richard Hakluyt knew about several versions of Verrazzano's report
(plus he might have had first-hand info from someone who had been there)

Richard Hakluyt's 1582 English rendition of Verrazzano's letter seems to be a **combination** of the "McGill version" and one or more "other versions." Like the McGill version, it says they traveled 50 miles east from New York (and does not include the name "Refugio,").

But like the like the "other versions" it provides the key details describing the bay including the "triangular island ... about the bigness of the Islande of the Rodes."

Curiously, Hakluyt reports that the triangular island is 3 leagues from the mainland, **a distance found in none of the extant manuscripts**.

(This 3 leagues is 7 1/2 miles, not too far off from the actual distance of 10 miles).

> **The description of Claudia Island.**
>
> **Claudia was wife of King Francis.**
>
> We weied Ancker, and sayled towarde the East, for so the coast trended, and so alwayes for 50. leagues being in the sight thereof wee discouered an Ilande in forme of a triangle, distant from the maine lande 3. leagues, about the bignesse of the Ilande of the Rodes, it was full of hilles couered with trees, well peopled, for we sawe fires all along the coaste, wee gaue the name of it, of your Maiesties mother, not staying there by reason of the weather being contrarie.

Hakluyt also follows the "other versions" by saying that the triangular island was named after "your Majesty's mother," but then doesn't include her name, Aloysia. Instead, Hakluyt writes in the margin of the text *"The description of Claudia Island."* and *"Claudia was the wife of King Francis."*

So it appears that Hakluyt knew Aloysia and Claudia were both mentioned by Verrazzano. Instead of the tyranical Aloysia, he went with frail Claudia, whose name would be more palatable to his fellow Englishmen.

This certainly makes it seem as though Hakluyt had additional insight into the true lay of the land. I suggest he gleaned it from Simon Fernandez, who made a voyage of reconnaissance for Sir Humphrey Gilbert (from March 25, 1580 to around June 30, 1580).

Dee writes that Fernandez visited him at Mortlake on November 20, 1580 so Dee could copy his "sea-carte" or map. No doubt Dee, Hakluyt, and Gilbert all shared information.

> And wee came to another lande being 15. leagues distant from the Ilande, where wee founde a passing good hauen, wherein being entred we founde about 20. small boates of the people which with diuers cries and wondrings came about our shippe, comming no nerer then 50. paces towards vs, they stayed and behelde the artificialnesse of our ship, our
>
> *The Country of Sir H. G. voyage.*

Hakluyt printed one more very revealing comment in the margin of his text describing the "good haven" with the five small islands. He calls it, **"The Country of Sir H. G. voyage."**

Here is that February 28, 1583 agreement between Sir Humphrey Gilbert and Sir George Peckham. The author (most likely John Dee himself) even admits to using Verrazzano's description. Yet he curiously omits any reference to the "triangular island the size of the Isle of Rhodes, or Claudia, or Luisa or even Refugio.

> *"...all that river or port called by Master John Dee, Dee River,*
>
> *which River, by the description of Giovanni Verrazzano, a Florentine, lies in the Northerly latitudes about 42 degrees and has its mouth lying open to the South, half a league broad or thereabout,*
>
> *and entering within the said Bay between the East and the North increases its width and continues 12 leagues or thereabouts,*
>
> *and then makes a gulf of 20 leagues in circumference or thereabouts, and contains within it 5 small Islands, newly named the Cinque Isles..."*

Indeed, on page 3 of Hakluyt's book, he lists,

"The names of certain late travelers, both by sea and land, which also for the most part have written of their own travels and voyages."

Note that final entry on the list:

1582
Humphrey Gilbert Knight,
Edward Heyes,
Antonie Brigham,
Englishmen

Gilbert and Hayes didn't actually depart until 1583, but Hakluyt was anxious to get his timely book to the printer, thus the 1582 date.

But who is this Anthony Brigham?

(It's known that Brigham did **not** go on the Gilbert's expedition with 5 ships in 1583.

> The names of certaine late trauaylers, both by sea and by lande, which also for the most part haue written of their owne trauayles and voyages.
>
> The yere of our Lorde.
> 1178 Beniamin Tudelensis a Iewe.
> 1270 Marcus Paulus a Venetian.
> 1300 Harton an Armenian.
> 1320 Iohn Mandeuile knight, englishman.
> 1380 Nicolaus and Antonius Zeni, venetians.
> 1444 Nicolaus Conti venetian.
> 1492 Christopher Columbus a Genoway.
> 1497 Sebastian Gabot, an englishman the sonne of a venetian.
> 1497 M. Thorne and Hugh Eliot of Bristowe, englishmen.
> 1497 Vasques de Gama a portingale.
> 1500 Gasper Corterealis a portingale.
> 1516 Edoardus Barbosa a portingale.
> 1519 Fernandus Magalianes a portingale.
> 1530 Iohn Barros a portingale.
> 1534 Iaques Cartier a Briton.
> 1540 Francis Vasques de Coronado Spaniarde.
> 1542 Iohn Gaetan Spaniarde.
> 1549 Francis Xauier a Spaniarde.
> 1553 Hugh Willowbie knight, & Richard Chauncellor Eng.
> 1554 Francis Galuano a portingale.
> 1556 Stenen and William Burros Englishmen.
> 1562 Antonie Ienkinson Englishman.
> 1562 Iohn Ribault a Frenchman.
> 1565 Andrewe Theuet a Frenchman.
> 1576 Martin Frobisher Englishman.
> 1578 Francis Drake Englishman.
> 1580 Arthur Pet, and Charles Iackman Englishmen.
> 1582 Edwarde Fenton, and Luke warde, Englishmen.
> 1582 Humfrey Gilbert knight, Edward Heyes, and Antonie Brigham Englishmen.

188

Historians have known about the "Dee River" since 1934

Historians have known of the attempted English settlement at the Dee River for 75 years. It's not new news. But apparently no historian (until me) ever pieced it together that this might have something to do with the Tower.

In 1934, William B. Goodwin wrote an article Rhode Island Historical Society journal entitled,

"The John Dee River of 1583 (Now called Narragansett Bay) and its Relation to Norumbega"

(*Collections* 27:2, pp. 38-50),

In the next issue, October of 1935, Fulmer Mood wrote a follow-up article entitled,

"Narragansett Bay and the Dee River, 1583."

(*Collections* 28:4 pp. 97-100)

[In the late 1960's, Horace Sillman wrote two articles in the NEARA Journal about Sir Humphrey Gilbert, suggesting an "Elizabethan Connection" to the Newport Tower, but he does not mention John Dee.]

Here's how D. B. Quinn puts it (in 1974), writing about Sir George Peckham's July 16, 1582 meeting with John Dee at Mortlake:

"Eventually, Dee assured Peckham that Spain had no rights in the area; on the maps it was New France, having been claimed for Francis I by Verrazzano in 1524, but not occupied.

Moreover, Dee was able to point out to them on the large map of North America he had drawn in 1580 the precise place he thought their settlement should lie.

Verrazzano had stayed for some time on Narragansett Bay in modern Rhode Island, which he called his "Refugio," and there it was decided that Peckham should lay out his seignory."

(Quinn, *England and the Discovery of America*, p. 376)

In 1971, Samuel Eliot Morrison writes,

"And in 1582-83 Sir Humphrey deeded to Sir George Peckham and his son a modest patrimony of 1,500,000 acres. Guided by Verrazzano's Letter (which Hakluyt is had printed), the grant begins at the "Dee River" (Narragansett Bay) with its five islands, and extends 60 English miles "along the sea coast westwarde towards the ryver of Norumbeague."

(Samuel Eliot Morrison, *The European Discovery of America: The Northern Voyages AD 500-1600*, p. 570)

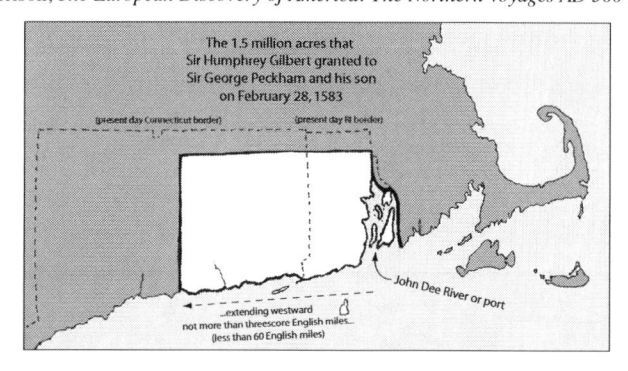

The 1.5 million acres that Sir Humphrey Gilbert granted to Sir George Peckham and his son on February 28, 1583

(present day Connecticut border) (present day RI border)

John Dee River or port

...extending westward not more than threescore English miles... (less than 60 English miles)

Mavor felt Gosnold was looking for Refugio during his 1603 Voyage.

Bartholomew Gosnold (1572-1607) was a protégé of Richard Hakluyt (1552-1616). According to James Mavor, it's likely that Hakluyt "had a major influence on the selection of Bartholomew Gosnold to lead the voyage of 1602."

Mavor suggests that Gosnold might have been destined for Refugio, but because he approached the region from the north, he missed the right clues.

Gosnold's landfall was in Maine. Heading south, he got caught in the arm of Cape Cod Bay. He went ashore and climbed the highhest hill he could find. To the south saw the triangular Martha's Vineyard, so sailed out around the Cape and settled just north of the triangular island. [It appears as though he didn't know his Luisa from his Claudia.]

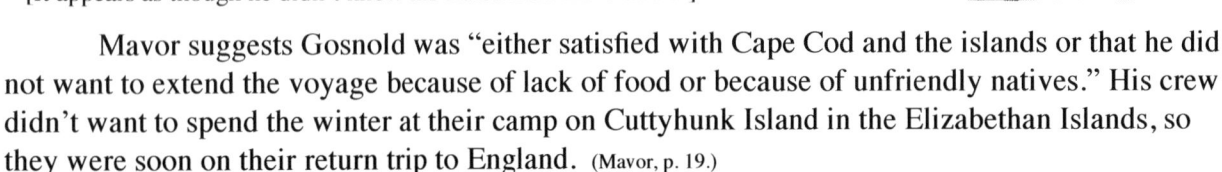

Mavor suggests Gosnold was "either satisfied with Cape Cod and the islands or that he did not want to extend the voyage because of lack of food or because of unfriendly natives." His crew didn't want to spend the winter at their camp on Cuttyhunk Island in the Elizabethan Islands, so they were soon on their return trip to England. (Mavor, p. 19.)

Quinn notes that one of the investors in the Gosnold Expedition was Henry Wriothesley, (1573-1624) the 3rd Earl of Southampton, the patron of Shakespeare. Wriothesley [pronounced Risley] was deeply involved in the Essex Rebellion and sentenced to die, but Cecil intervened and his sentence was reduced to life inprison. Fortunately, King James shortly took the throne and brought Henry back to court.

Quinn suggests that Wriothesley was the "catalyst who brought the American idea to life again for the English Catholics." Quinn also believed that Gosnold's mission **"was a reconnaissance to the area, which had already in 1582 been thought of as a site for settlement."**

(Quinn, p. 382-3)

Wriothesley was also a friend of Sir George Peckham, so he knew all about the ideal siting of Refugio. As Queen Elizabeth died in 1603, and a new regime was in power, it seems he was ready to claim the land that had so eluded the Elizabethans.

Verrazzano's "Size of Rhodes" later becomes Rhode Island.

Most historians agree that the reason colonial settlers named Aquidneck Island "Rhode Island' stems from Verrazzano's island-size comparison. I suggest their knowledge of Verrazzano came by way of Hakluyt's text, and thus the colonial settlers were well aware that Narragansett Bay was Sir Humphrey Gilbert's destination, the site of the Peckham "Catholic Colony," the Dee River.

Roger Williams used the term "Rode Island" in 1637, and in 1644 it was used as part of the name of the official name of the colony. (More on this later).

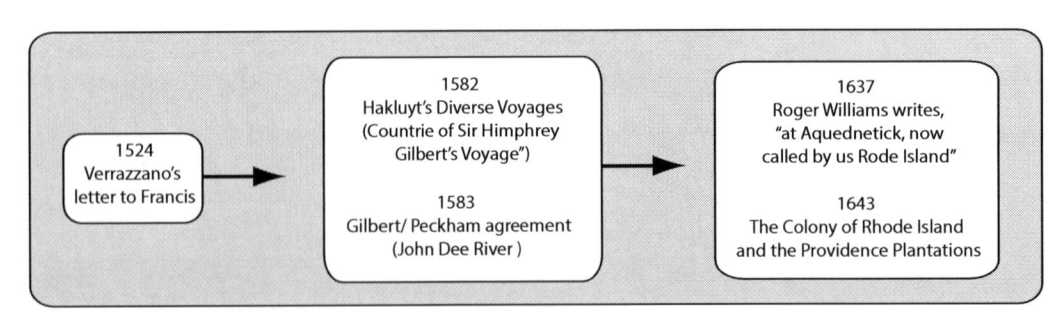

1524
Verrazzano's letter to Francis
→
1582
Hakluyt's Diverse Voyages
(Countrie of Sir Himphrey Gilbert's Voyage")
1583
Gilbert/ Peckham agreement
(John Dee River)
→
1637
Roger Williams writes, "at Aquednetick, now called by us Rode Island"
1643
The Colony of Rhode Island and the Providence Plantations

The Dutch theory about the origin of the name Rhode Island

Some historians suggest the name Rhode Island was coined by Adrian Block, a Dutch trader who visited Narragansett Bay in 1614. In an account of Block's expedition (printed by De Leat in 1625), Adrian Block describes "*een rodlich Eylande*" which has been translated as "**an island of reddish appearance**." It is claimed that "Rhode in "Rhode Island" came from this word *rodloch*.

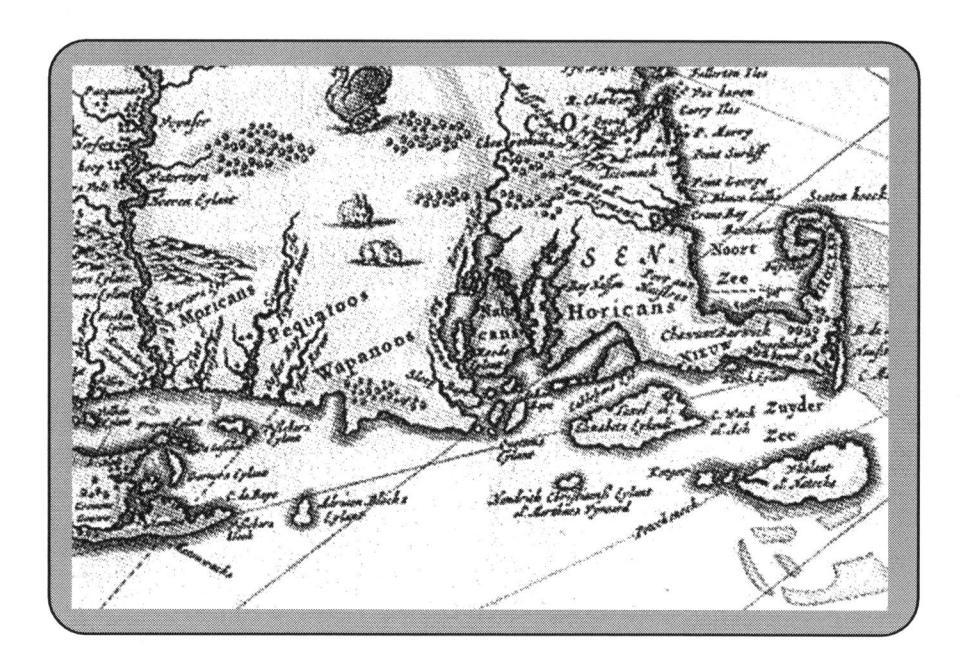

Dutch maps from the 1650's that label Aquidneck Island as "**Roode Eylant**" are used to support this theory. However, these maps were made after the English settlers officially named Aquidneck, "Rhode Island" (in 1647), and well after Roger Williams referred to it as "Rode Island" (in 1637),

191

Here is the part of De Leat's report that describes
Narragansett Bay, which they called the Bay of Nassau:

"Beyond these lies also an island which our countrymen have given the name of Block's Island, from Captain Adrian Block. ... Within the mainland, is situated the River or Bay of Nassau, which lies from the above named Block's Island east-northeast and west-southwest.

This Bay or River of Nassau is apparently very large and wide and according to the description Captain Block must be full nine miles in width. It has, in the midst of it, a number of islands, which one may pass on either side. It extends east-northeast about 24 miles, after which it is not more than two petard shots [two cannon shots] wide and has generally seven, eight, nine, five, and four fathoms of water except in a straight in the uppermost part of the day, at a petard's shot distance from an island in that direction, where there is but nine feet of water. Beyond this straight we have again three and a half fathoms of water [a fathom is 6 feet].

The land in this vicinity appears very fine, and the inhabitants seem strong of limb and of moderate size. However, they are somewhat shy, since they are not accustomed to trade with strangers, who would otherwise go there in quest of beaver and fox skins, for which they resort to other places in that quarter.

From the westerly passage into this Bay of Nassau to the most southerly entrance of Anchor Bay, the distance is twenty one miles, according to the statement of our skippers, and the course is southeast and northwest. Our countrymen had given two names to this bay as it has an island in the center and discharges into the sea by two mouths, the most easterly of which is a call Anchor Bay [now called the East Passage] and the most westerly Sloop Bay [West Passage]. The southeast shore of this Bay runs north-northeast.

In the lower part of the Bay dwell the Wapenocks, a nation of savages like the rest. Captain Adrian Block called the people would inhabit the west side of this Bay Nahicans, and their Sagamore Nathattozv. Another chief was named Cachaquant.

Towards the northwest side there is a sandy point with a small island, bearing east and west, and bending so as to form a handsome bay with a sandy bottom. On the right of the sandy point there is more than two fathoms of water, and farther on three and three and a half fathoms, with a sharp bottom, where lies "*een rodlich Eylande*."

From Sloop Bay, or the most westerly passage, it is twenty four miles to the Great Bay [Long Island Sound] which is situated between the mainland and several islands, that extend to the mouth of the Great River [Hudson]."

(emphasis mine, translation in NYHSC 2, I, p. 293)

Some historians have translated the phrase "*een rodlich Eylande*," as "a reddish Island," explaining it might refer to either "the red autumn foliage" or "red clay on portions of the shore." But there are several problems with this interpretation.

First, when Aquidneck Island is ablaze with autumn color, all of southern New England is ablaze with the same color. Secondly, I have scoured the coast of Aquidneck Island and have yet find any red clay. The rocks are shades of gray and the beaches are light tan.

Second, in Dutch the word "roede" means a "rod, wand, or pole." The English word "rod" is derived from this Dutch word. From this we get the measuring stick called the "rod," which was used in early surveying. Thus, "een rodlich Eylande," might be translated as "a rod-like Island" or one that is straight, like a stick or a wand.

Third, the "sandy point on the **northwest** side of the bay" Adrian Block is referring to is nowhere near Aquidneck Island (which is on the **southeast** part of the bay). Block was describing the sandy point that is now called Conimicut Point, in Warwick.

Though hurricanes have changed its shape many times throughout the years, the sandy point still prominently juts out into the bay.

As the passage through this tight section of the bay is dangerous, lighthouses is have been built on both sides. (The passage has been dredged in modern times so Block's depth estimates are outdated).

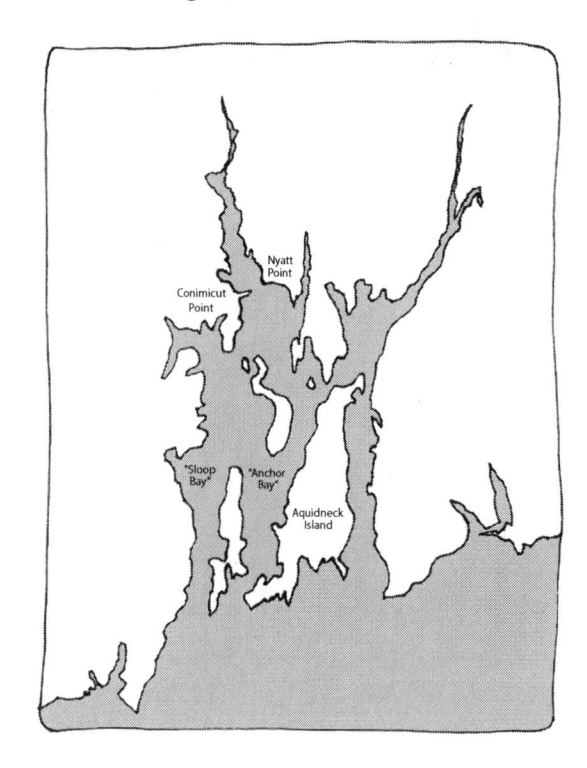

Conimicut Point Lighthouse still operates on a small rocky island near the western shore.

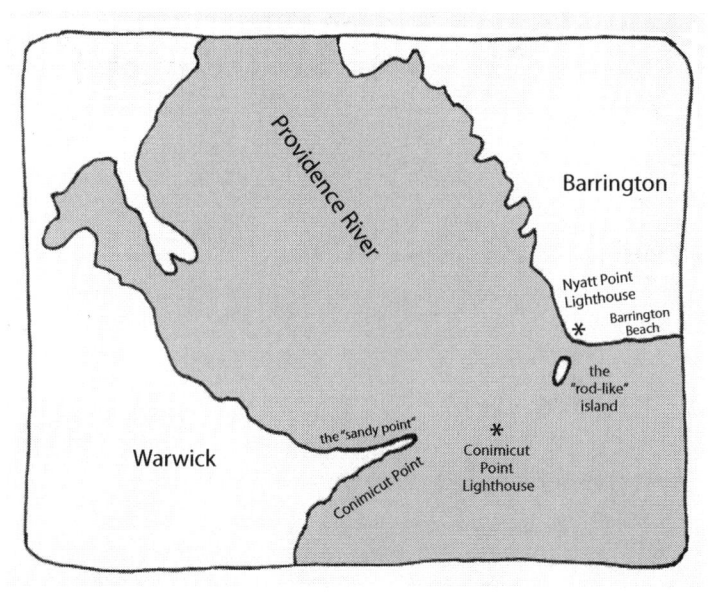

On the eastern shore (where the coast makes a right angle) is Nyatt Point Lighthouse in Barrington. Right off the coast of the lighthouse is a "*rodlich*" or "rod-like" island. It is most apparent at low tide.

By following the line of Conimicut Point, its lighthouse,
the "rod-like island," and Barrington Beach, you can get
a sense of how the south-flowing river broke through
an east-west ridge here in glacial times.

As the main stream doglegs to the southeast,
sand gets deposited in the crescent of
Conimicut Beach and its pointy spit.

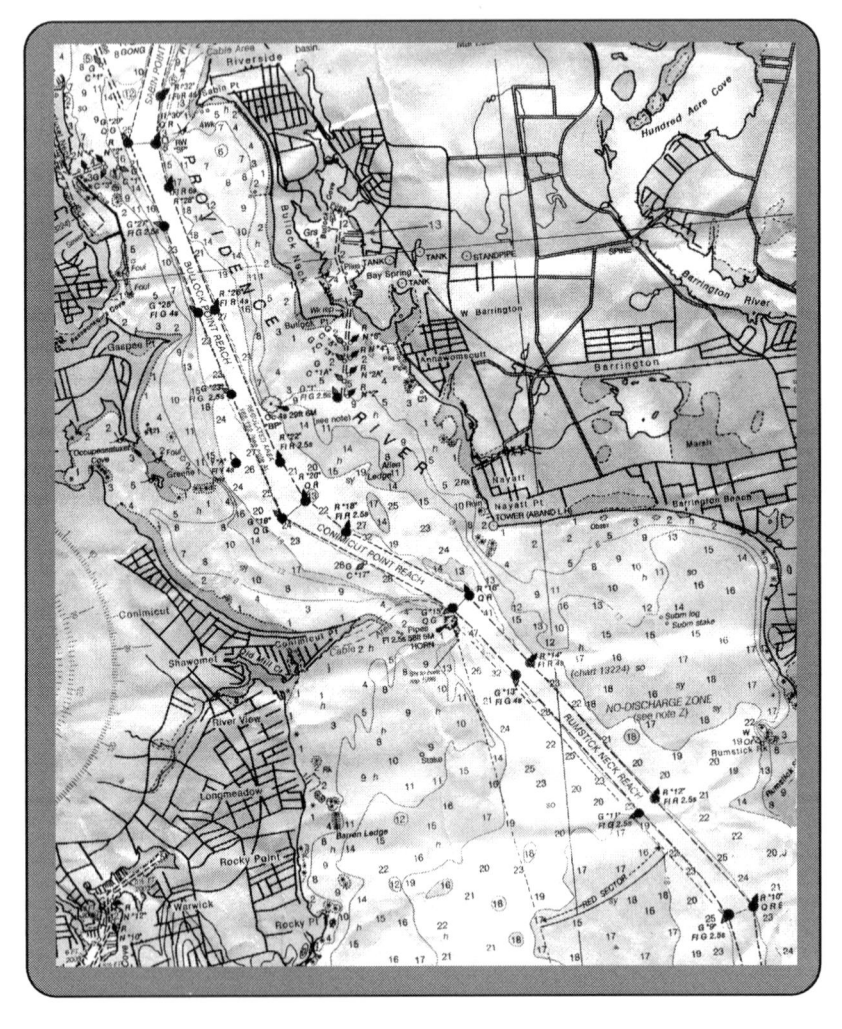

This small "rod-like" island is not reddish,
nor is it even close to Aquidneck Island.

Thus, it has nothing to do with the origin of the name Rhode Island.

"Mad Jack" Oldham and Narragansett Bay in 1634

> The Rebecka came from Narigansett with five hundred bushels of corn given to Mr. John Oldham. The Indians had promised him ‖one thousand‖ bushels, but their store fell out less than they expected. They gave him also an island in the Narigansett Bay, called Chippacursett, containing about *one thousand acres,* six miles long, and two miles broad. This is a very fair bay, being above twelve leagues square, with divers great islands in it, a deep channel close to the shore, being rocky. Mr. Peirce took the height there, and found it forty-one degrees, forty-one minutes, being not above half a degree to the southward of us. In his voyage to and fro, he went over the shoals, having, most part, five or six fathom, within half a mile and less of the shore from the north part of Cape Cod to Natuckett Island, which is about twenty leagues—and, in the shallowest place, two and an half fathom. The country on the west of the Bay of Naragansett is all champain for many miles, but very stony, and full of Indians. He saw there above one thousand men, women and children, yet the men were many abroad on hunting. Natuckett is an island full of Indians, about ten leagues in length east and west.

(Winthrop's Journal, History of New England, 1630-1649: Volume 1, p.189-191)

In 1634, two years before Roger Williams, the Arnold clan and others settled Province, the Narragansett Indians had made an offer to the English trader John Oldham. They traded him 500 bushels of corn and told him he could have Prudence Island if he would set up a trading post there.

Oldham never set down roots there, but for a few years, he was the "middleman" in the flourishing trade between the Narragansett Indians and the Massachusetts Bay Colony. He was quite familiar with the New England coast, as he had traveled it extensively for 11 years.

Oldham was an independent thinker, very much his own man. He had sailed aboard the ship Anne to the Plymouth Colony in 1623. As he was not a "Separatist" (like the Pilgrims), they made him sign an agreement to abide by the rules of the colony.

In 1624, the Reverend John Lyford arrived in Plymouth. He was vocally "non-Separatist." Lyford and Oldham led a group of dissidents working secretly to replace the authorities of the Plymouth church.

The pair wrote letters to a group of Adventurers in England who were opposed to the interests of the Pilgrims. A suspicious Governor Bradford boarded their ship, found the letters, and learned that Lyford and Oldham were intending to start their own church.

One night, the argumentative Oldham refused to report at his scheduled time for his duties as night watchman. When Captain Myles Standish confronted him, Oldham drew his knife, calling the captain a "beggarly rascal."

Governor Bradford ordered his men to subdue Oldham, but he "only ramped more like a furious beast than a man, and called them all traitors and rebels and other such foul language." Oldham was thrown into jail until he cooled down.

Lyman and Oldham went right ahead with their plans to establish their own church. Governor Bradford had had enough. When the pair were brought to trial, Bradford testified that he had secretly read the letters. Oldham flew into another rage.

Oldham was immediately banished, but his family was allowed to stay in Plymouth until he found them a new home. Two months later, Oldham returned and started yelling at the authorities again. Again he was tossed in jail and forced to walk out of town through a "guard of musketeers," who were each ordered to give him "a thump on the breech with the butt end of his musket." He acquired the nickname "mad jack in his mood."

Oldham moved to Hull, Massachusetts, then later to Cape Ann where he traded with the Indians. He took a ship to Virginia and even to London on trading missions. In 1629, he bought an island in the Charles River at what is now Watertown, Massachusetts. In 1634, Oldham led a group from Massachusetts Bay colony to settle Wethersfield, Connecticut (near Hartford).

In July of 1636, Oldham and his crew were murdered by Indians off the coast of Block Island. Oldham's death was one of the main factors that precipitated the Pequot War. There is reason to suspect the argumentative Oldham was asking for trouble in some business deal with the Indians (who responded more forcefully than with simply a "butt in the breeches.")

(*American National Biography*, Oldham, p. 672)

John Oldham opened trade relations between the Narragansetts, the largest tribe in New England, and the Mass Bay Colony.

When Oldham suddenly died in 1636, that left **a huge opportunity for some other Englishman to take over his trading business.**

(I suggest that, on his trading missions, Oldham made use of the Tower that overlooked the mouth of Narragansett Bay.)

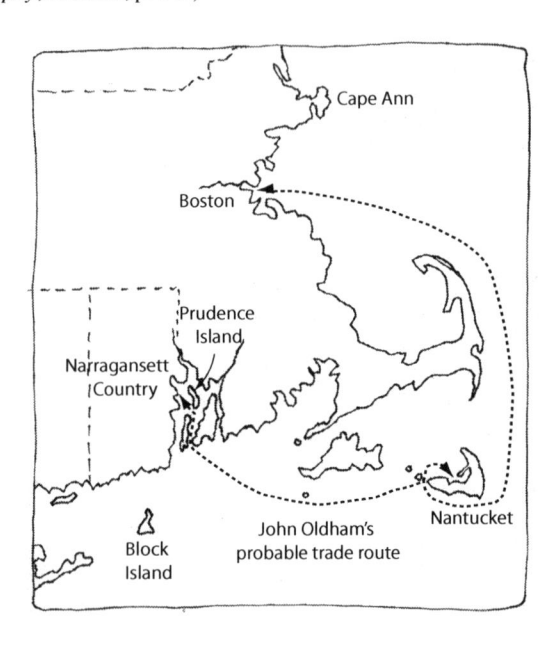

How Rhode Island got its name?

In the early days of Providence there were two main groups:

Roger Williams and his associates

William and Benedict Arnold and their associates.

Roger Williams and the Arnolds were both excited about their new home, but their backgrounds, motivations, and ambitions were quite different.

Roger Williams and his associates

William and Benedict Arnold and their associates

Most early Rhode Island history books focus on Roger Williams and his story:

As a teenager, Roger had been the stenographer for the famous judge, Sir Edward Coke, at the Star Court in London. Roger took the Holy Orders to become a minister in the Church of England, but while at Pembroke College in Cambridge, he became a Puritan.

Regarding the Church of England under Archbishop Laud as corrupt, Williams sailed to Massachusetts, where he became an assistant minister. He soon found the Puritans of Boston were not "separatist" enough, so he became a pastor of the church in Salem. But his "diverse, new, and dangerous opinions" were not appreciated there, and he was banished from the entire Massachusetts Bay Colony.

In the spring of 1636, Williams and a few followers purchased land from the Wampanoag Indian Sachem Massasoit. Williams was soon notified that he was on land claimed by Plymouth Colony, so he moved west across the Seekonk River to lands owned by the Narragansetts.

Roger was following his dream of developing in a community where men could have liberty of conscience and there was separation of church and state. Many of his followers had likewise been banished (or self-exiled) from Salem and Boston.

But most Rhode Island historians neglect to relate the story of William and Benedict Arnold and their family and associates. In the development of early Rhode Island, the Arnolds' role was just as important as that of Roger Williams.

For fifty years, William Arnold's father, Nicholas, had been a member of the influential Merchant Taylors' Guild (clothing merchants) in Ilchester, Somerset, (about 120 miles west-southwest of London).

When Nicholas died in 1622, his son William (then 35 years old) took over the successful business. Over the next 14 years, William gained "considerable wealth" before deciding to move to New England.

(E.L. Arnold, *Arnold Family*, p.5).

The Arnolds lived in Hingham for about ten months. But they disapproved of Hingham's form of government, which was changing from "West Country Leadership" to "East Anglican Oligarchy."

Hingham's new leaders were enforcing strict "presbyterianism and political exclusiveness." William Arnold was more interested in "worldly advancement and godly reformation." (O'Toole, p.275-276).

The Arnold Clan in 1635 — William Arnold 48, Christian Peake Arnold 52, Benedict Arnold 19, Thomas Hopkins 19, Stephen Arnold 12, Joanne Arnold 17, Frances Hopkins Man 21, William Mann 21, William Carpenter 24, Elizabeth Arnold Carpenter 23.

In short, William Arnold was a salesman, and a darned good one. And his eager-beaver, fresh-out-of school, eldest-son Benedict was just like him. They were here to pick the ripe fruits of the New World. They were focused more on acquiring wealth and land than on religious matters. They had a keen eye for opportunity, and had the ambition to grasp it.

Indeed, a mere three months after their April arrival in Narragansett Bay, opportunity came knocking at their door. As we've seen, on July 20, 1636, John Oldham and five crewmen were on a trading mission to Block Island when they were murdered by hostile Indians. The middleman between the Narragansetts (the largest tribe in New England) and the Massachusetts Bay Colony (the largest colony in New England) was dead.

William and Benedict took advantage of the circumstances and took over Oldham's trade route. Sure, it was risky business, but Benedict had learned the native Algonquin tongue and was well-respected by the two Narragansett Sachems, Canonicus and Miantonomi. (Roger Williams had a trading post in Wickford, and traded with the Narragansetts, but having been banished from Boston, he couldn't travel there even if he wanted to.)

Eager to pursue his own land deals with the Indians, William Arnold and several associates moved south from Providence, to the banks of the Pawtuxet River (in what is now Cranston). In 1640, provoked by the cantankerous Samuel Gorton, William and Benedict Arnold actually seceded from Providence colony and put their lands and estates under the jurisdiction of the Massachusetts Bay Colony.

William Arnold remained part of the Massachusetts Bay Colony until 1658. [Thus for 18 years it was like "Cranston, Massachusetts."] But Benedict broke from the Massachusetts Bay Colony (and his father) in 1651 to become a key figure in the governance of the towns around Narragansett Bay.

Back in 1636, Roger Williams and Benedict Arnold and other leaders were involved in negotiations with the Narragansetts to determining the boundaries of Providence. Just west of Benedict Arnold's cattle ranch (just south of present-day Olneyville) looms Neutaconcanut Hill.

West of the hill, where the land starts to flatten out, is a 40-foot tall glacial erratic that sticks up out of the ground. (It's now in a wooded area in a suburban neighborhood of Johnston.)

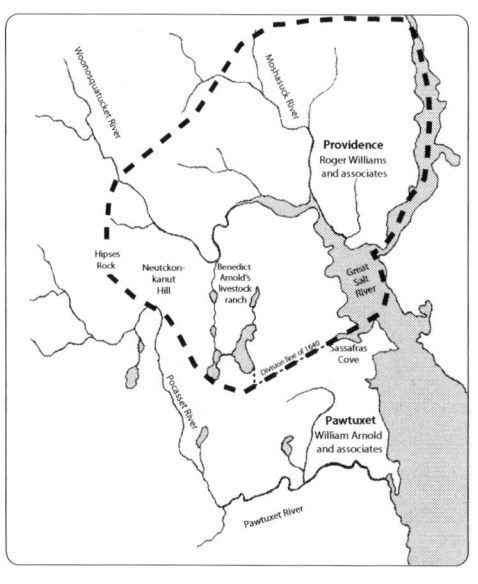

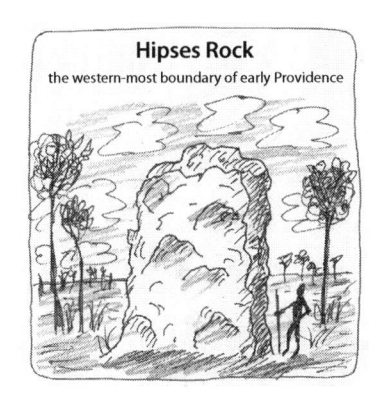

Hipses Rock
the western-most boundary of early Providence

What came to be known as **Hipses Rock** marks the western-most border of the early town of Providence. In his book on Rhode Island place-names, Sidney Rider suggests that the name comes from the word "**Hesperian**," which means "land of the West" in Latin and Greek.

According to Greek mythology, in the Hesperidian Garden, located at the **western extremity** of the ancient world, where the daughters of Hesperus guarded the golden apples.

[In alchemical texts, the Hesperidian Garden is where the philosopher's stone is found. In fact, John Dee refers to the "Hesperian Garden" in Theorem 22 of his *Monas Hieroglyphica*.]

Someone in early Providence had an affinity for place-names with classical symbolism. And it probably wasn't Roger Williams, as he preferred more theological names like Providence, Prudence (Island) and Patience (Island).

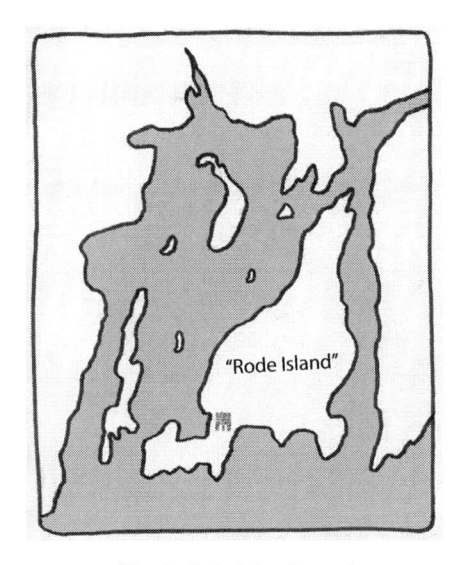

"Rode Island"

(I've included the Tower in this illustration, as I think it existed at this time.)

The first Colonial reference to the name "Rode Island"

Roger Williams made the first written reference to the name "Rhode Island" in his May 1, 1637 letter to Henry Vane and John Winthrop Sr.:

"They also conceive it easy for the English, that the provisions and munitions first arrive at Aquednetick, called by us Rode Island, at the Nanhiggontick's mouth..."

In 1637, Boston was abuzz with a controversy involving the independent-minded Anne Hutchinson. For speaking her mind at unauthorized Bible meetings held in her home, she was put to trial, found guilty and banished from the colony. A number of dissidents who sided with her, including William Coddington and John Clarke, decided to move away from Boston to settle their own new town.

Roger Williams took Coddington and Clarke to Plymouth to consult with Governor Bradford about settling at Sowams (now Barrington and Warren, RI). Bradford refused, claiming Sowams was part of Plymouth's territory, but they would be welcome to settle on Aquidneck Island, as that was beyond Plymouth's bounds.

On March 24, 1638, William Coddington, Anne and William Hutchinson, John Clarke and others (19 families in all) acquired the title to Aquidneck Island from the Narragansetts. But for some reason, they chose to settle in a rather nondescript part a of the northern end of the island. They called the new town Pocasset, (which is now Portsmouth).

Why didn't they settle in that beautiful natural harbor (now called Newport Harbor) that controls the entrance to Narragansett Bay?

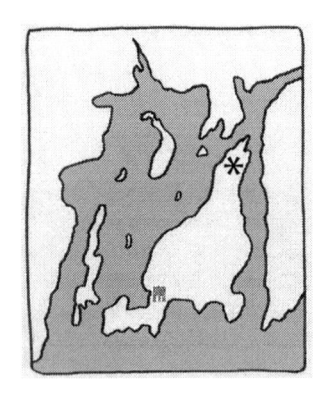

I contend it was because Benedict Arnold already had a presence in that choice harbor. Not only was he using the harbor as a trading outpost, but he had also claimed the Tower for himself. (First come, first serve.)

This might sound speculative, but there are more clues.

On June 14, 1638, Roger Williams penned another letter to John Winthrop Sr. in Boston, in which he writes:

"Sir, concerning the islands Prudence and (Patmos, if some had not hindered) Aquedenick..."

Patmos is the Island in the Aegean Sea where Saint John wrote the *Book of Revelation*. Roger Williams was passionate about Saint John's visions and felt they were not a thing of the past, but a prediction of what was about to happen in the near future.

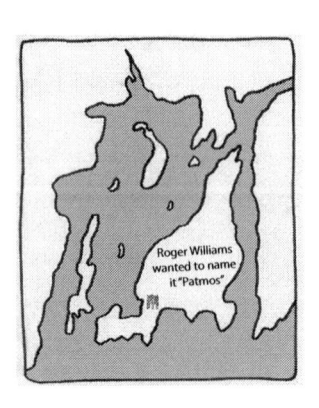

All these well-documented clues raise an important question:

Aquidneck was called "Rode Island" before Coddington's group had arrived.

Roger Williams wanted to name it Patmos.

So who insisted it be named "Rode Island"?

I suggest that Benedict Arnold had "staked a claim" to the Tower by using it a shipping outpost. To transport the hundreds of bushels of corn he purchased from the Narragansett Indians, he probably had a fleet of shallops that piled the coast on a three-day trading route.

The first day would be from Providence (or Pawtuxet) to Newport. The second day, from Newport to Nantucket. And the third day from Nantucket, around Cape Cod, to Boston. (And then back in three days.)

I think it was Benedict who insisted the island be named "Rode Island" to cryptically pay homage to the Elizabethan colonizing effort at the "Dee River and port."

After a dispute with the Hutchinsons in the new settlement of Pocasset, William Coddington, John Clarke and others move south to settle Newport on April 28, 1639. I think they said, in effect, "Move over Benedict, we want to use this splendid harbor too."

This might sound like a lot of conjecturing on my part. But, without making hypotheses, confirming clues will not become apparent. Here are two clues in the historical record that suggest **other** early leaders of New England knew about the Tower, John Dee, and the Elizabethan colonization effort of 1583.

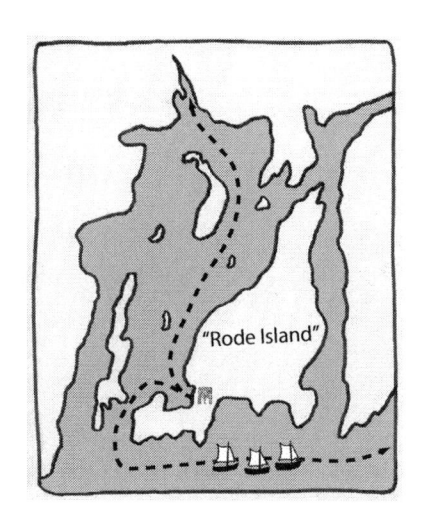

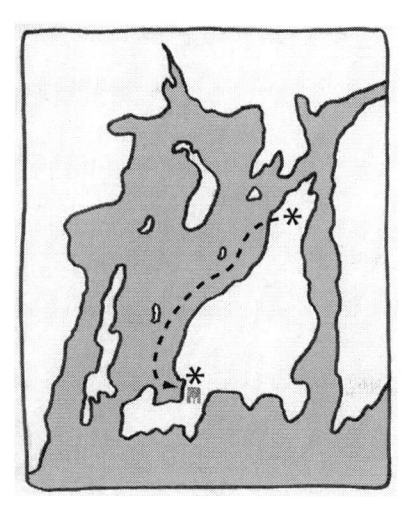

Bradford calls Aquidneck Island "Monachunte"

In a letter dated April 1638, William Bradford (Governor of Plymouth) wrote to John Winthrop Sr., (Governor of the Massachusetts Bay Colony),

"There was not long since, here with us, a Mr. Coddington and some other of your people, who brought Mr. Williams with them and pressed us hard for a place at or near Sowams, which we denied them.

Then Mr. Williams informed them of a spacious Island called Monachunte, touching which they solicited our goodwill, to which we yielded..."

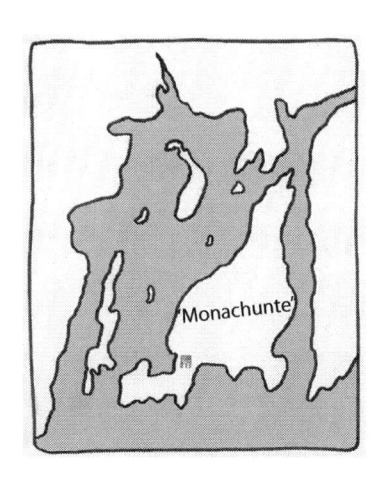

I think Governor Bradford was calling Aquidneck Island "Monachunte," to make a cryptic reference to (what I call) "the island with Dee's Monas Tower." (Monas + chunte)
And appears that Governor John Winthrop was in on the secret as well.

In all the Colonial records I have searched, this is the **only** instance in which I have seen Aquidneck called "Monachunte." I think Bradford made it sound like an Indian name to be cleverly cryptic.

A clue on William Wood's 1634 Map of Southern New England

The South part of New-England, as it is Planted this yeare, 1634.

old plymouth

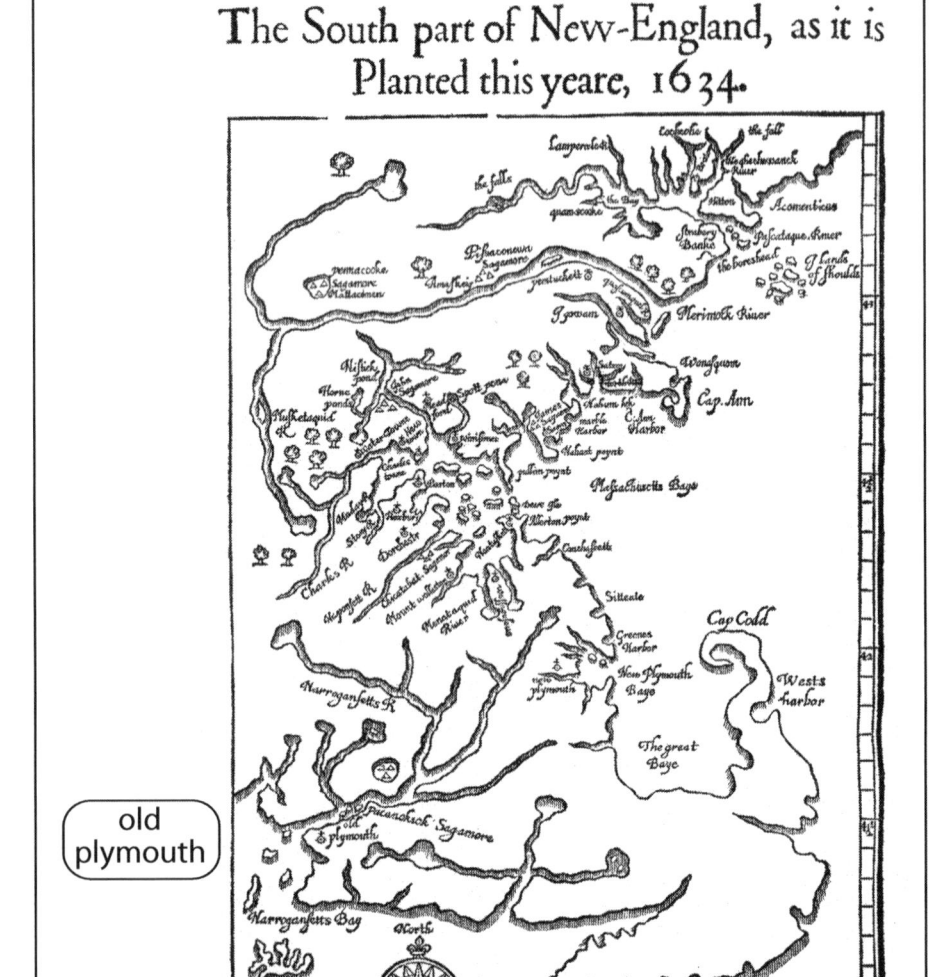

Map drawn by William Wood
(who lived in New England from 1629 to 1633)

William Wood lived in New England from 1629 to 1633 and wrote a report on the new land for curious Londoners. *New England's Prospect* and its map were published in 1634.

Judging from his map, it's apparent that he journeyed all around the Massachusetts Bay area from Strawbery Banke (now Portsmouth, NH) to Cape Ann to all the towns west of Boston. Notice that Plymouth is labeled **New Plymouth**.

[Wood might not have traveled to Cape Cod and southern New England, as his geography is a little bit off.]

But look closely at the eastern shore of Narragansett Bay. There is a place marked **"Old Plymouth."** Remember, this was two years before Roger Williams and the Arnold Clan had settled Providence. This has perplexed historians for years, but to me, its clear evidence that the early Colonials were aware of the Elizabethan colonization attempt of 1583.

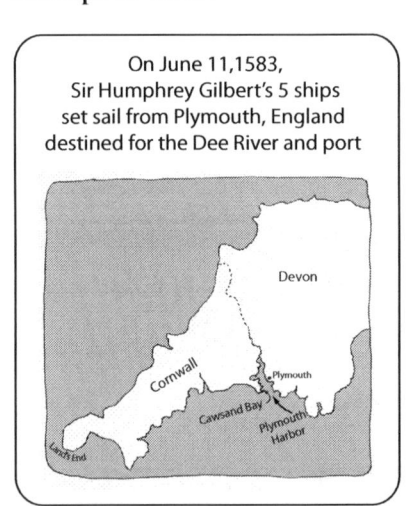

Remember that Sir Humphrey Gilbert's ill-fated 1583 colonizing expedition had departed from **Plymouth**, England.

I think "Old Plymouth" was a reference to Gilbert's intended destination, the Dee River (and the Tower that subsequently abandoned.)

On June 11, 1583, Sir Humphrey Gilbert's 5 ships set sail from Plymouth, England destined for the Dee River and port

202

John Winthrop Jr. used the Monas symbol as his personal mark

I had always envisioned the early Colonials as narrow-minded, conservative types. They were always banishing folks that fell out of line, going on witch-hunts, and locking people with loose lips in pillories. So I was surprised to come across Walter Woodward's 2010 book titled *Prospero's America: John Winthrop Jr., Alchemy, and the Creation of the New England culture, 1606-1676*. Alchemy in Colonial New England? It didn't make much sense.

Alchemy was the precursor of chemistry and related sciences like agriculture, metallurgy and medicine. John Winthrop Jr. was a noted Paracelcian physician, sometimes administering medicine to a dozen people a day in his journeys through the colonies. He was instrumental in setting up the first iron furnaces in Braintree and Saugus, Massachusetts. He also had planned an alchemical project to evaporate salt form the sea on large flats of land. In 1662, he was accepted into the Royal Society (or the Royal Society of London for Improving of Natural Knowledge), which had only been founded in 1660.

I was even more surprised to find out that John Winthrop Jr. was a big fan of John Dee. Winthrop owned at least 10 books that had once been part of Dee's library at Mortlake. In Dee's copy of Paracelsus' *Buch Meteororum I*, Winthrop wrote:

"I have divers of his bookes both printed
& some manuscript yt came out of his study,
in them he hath written both his name & notes,
for w[hi]ch they are farre the more precious."

(Wilkinson, p. 38)

John Winthrop Jr. not only owned a copy of Dee's *Monas Hieroglyphica*, he used the Monas symbol as his own personal mark in his books!

Winthrop's son (Wait Winthrop) and his grandson (John) both used the Monas symbol for their bookmarks as well.

(Roberts and Watson, p. 67-8)

Around 1630, Arthur Dee (John Dee's eldest son), gave John Winthrop Jr. a personally inscribed, author's copy of *Fascilus Chemicus (Chemical Collections)*.

John Winthrop Jr.'s signature and his Monas symbol mark

Besides being the leader of the effort to settle Connecticut, John Winthrop Jr. was an assistant in the Mass. Bay Colony from 1631-1649. During a 1645 journey from Connecticut to Boston, John Winthrop Jr. stayed with William Arnold (in Pawtuxet) one night and then with Benedict Arnold (in Providence) the next night.

Incidentally, many modern scholars believe Shakespeare modeled his character Prospero in *The Tempest* after John Dee. So Woodward's title *"Prospero's America"* is a subtle reference to Dee and his vision of the English colonization of North America.

Overlapping life spans of the characters in this story

Because all the Elizabethan colonies in America failed to take root, they seem to be relegated to a different chapter in American history books than the colonies of the Pilgrims and Puritans.

When Queen Elizabeth died in 1603, there was indeed a "changing of the guard." But the life spans of some of these Elizabethans, like Dee, Peckham, and Raleigh, extended into Jacobean times.

And some of the New England colonists, like William Arnold and John Winthrop Sr., had been born in Elizabethan times.

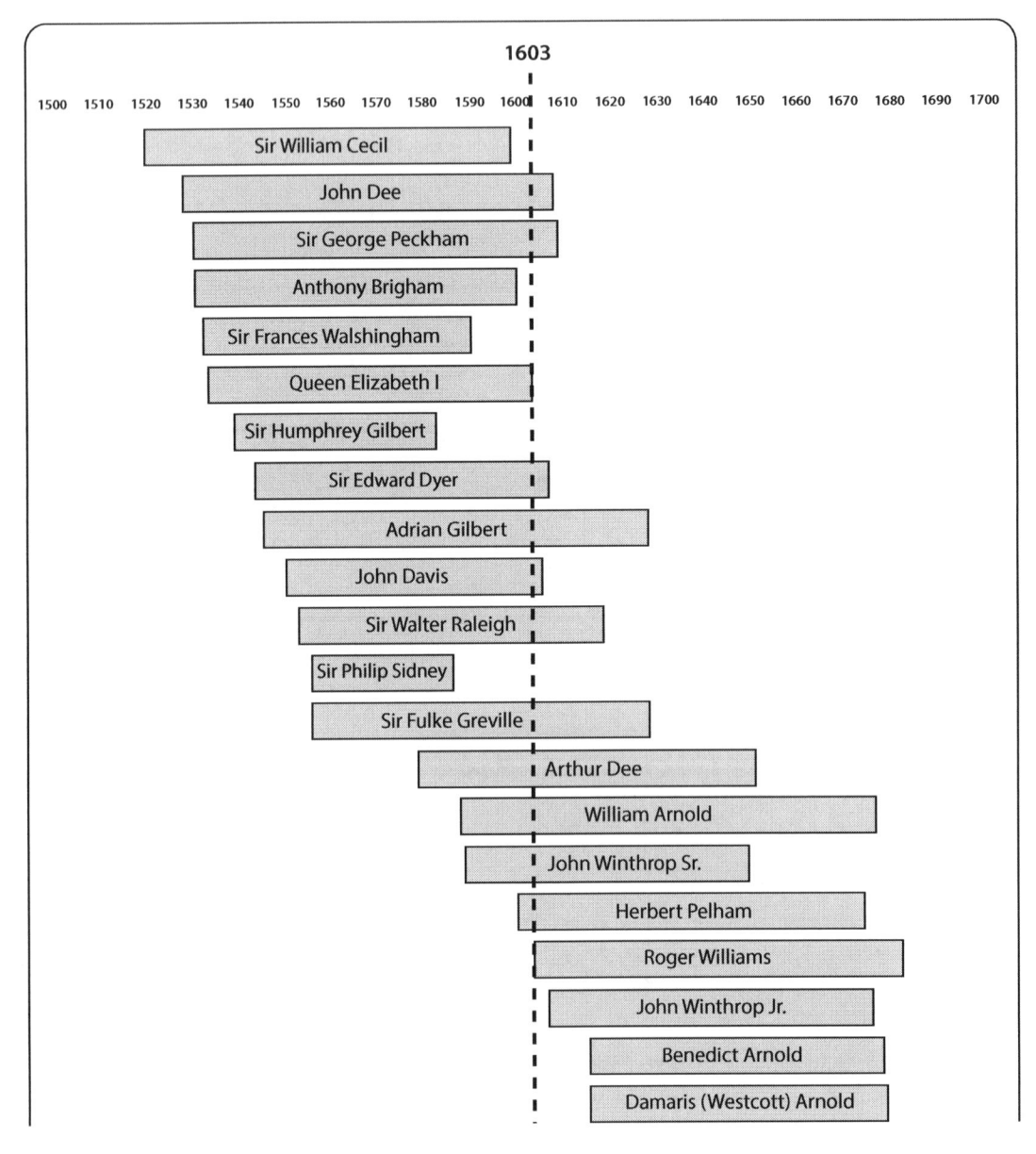

| 1500 | 1510 | 1520 | 1530 | 1540 | 1550 | 1560 | 1570 | 1580 | 1590 | 1600 | **1603** | 1610 | 1620 | 1630 | 1640 | 1650 | 1660 | 1670 | 1680 | 1690 | 1700 |

- Sir William Cecil
- John Dee
- Sir George Peckham
- Anthony Brigham
- Sir Frances Walshingham
- Queen Elizabeth I
- Sir Humphrey Gilbert
- Sir Edward Dyer
- Adrian Gilbert
- John Davis
- Sir Walter Raleigh
- Sir Philip Sidney
- Sir Fulke Greville
- Arthur Dee
- William Arnold
- John Winthrop Sr.
- Herbert Pelham
- Roger Williams
- John Winthrop Jr.
- Benedict Arnold
- Damaris (Westcott) Arnold

The point I'm trying to make here is that the colonial families
(like the Winthrops, the Williams, the Arnolds, etc.)
were quite familiar with the great Elizabethan families
(like the Gilberts and the Raleighs, the Peckhams, the Dees, etc.).

The name "Rhode Island" ultimately stems from Verrazzano's 1525 report

Why did Benedict Arnold specifically choose the name "Rode Island"?

The name ultimately derives from Verrzzano's 1525 report,
so let's briefly review some of the **key phrases** it contains.

quale per la beleza chiamamo **Refugio**.

Discoprimmo **una isola in forma triangulare**, lontana dal continente leghe dieci, **di grandeza simile a la insula di Rhodo** piena di colli, coperta d'albori, molto popolata per e continovi fuochi per tutto al lito intorno vedemmo facevano. Baptezammolla in nome de la Vostra clarissima genitrice Aloysia non surgendo a quella per la oppositione del tempo. Pervenimmo a una altra terra distante da la insula leghe XV, dove trovamio **uno bellissimo porto** et prima che in quello entrassimo vedemmo circa di XX barchette di gente che venivano con varii gridi et maravigle intorno a la nave…

Questa terra e situata **nel pararello di Roma in gradi 40 et 2/3**, ma alquanto piu fredda, per accidente et non per natura come in altra parte narrero a V. Mta, descrivendo al presente el sito di detto porto. Discorre el lito di detta terra da occidente in oriente. **La bocca del porto guarda verso l'Austro, angusta meza legha**, di poi entrato in quella **fra oriente e septemtrione si stende leghe XII**, dove allargandosi causa **uno amplo seno di circuito di leghe XX in circa**. Nel quale sono **cinque isolette** di molta fertilita et vagheza, piene d'alti e spatiosi alberi, fra quaili ogni numerosa classe, senza timore di tempesta o altro impedimento di fortuna sicuramente puo quiescere

Here is Lawrence C. Wroth's translation :

which we called **Refugio** on account of its beauty

We discovered a **triangular-shaped island**, ten leagues from the mainland, **similar in size to the island of Rhodes**; it was full of hills, covered in trees, and highly populated to judge by the fires we saw burning continually along the shore. We baptized it in the name of your illustrious mother, Aloysia, but did not anchor there because the weather was unfavorable. We reached another land 15 leagues from the island where we found **an excellent harbor**; before entering it, we saw about 20 boats full of people who came around the ship uttering various cries of wonderment….

This country is situated **on a parallel with Rome at 40 2/3 degrees**, but is somewhat colder, by chance and not by nature, as I shall explain to your Majesty at another point; I will now describe the position of the aforementioned port. The coast of this land runs from west to east. **The harbor mouth faces south, and is half a league wide**; from its entrance it **extends for 12 leagues in a northeasterly direction**, and then widens out to form **a large bay of about 20 leagues in circumference**. In this bay there are **five small islands**, very fertile and beautiful, full of tall spreading trees, and a large fleet could ride safely among them without fear of tempest or other dangers.

205

The deed from Sir Humphrey Gilbert to Sir George Peckham in 1583

Now, let's fast-forward about 60 years to the February 28, 1583, and look at the key phrases in the agreement between Sir Humphrey Gilbert and Sir George Peckham.

> "... all that ryver or porte **called by Master John Dee, Dee Ryver,** which Ryver by the **discripcion of John Verarzanus** a Florentyne lyeth in Septontrionall latitude **about fortye twoo degrees** and hath his **mouth lyinge open to the South halfe a league brode** or there aboute ...
>
> ... and enteringe within the saide Baye betwene the **Easte and the Northe** encreaseth his breadith and contynueth **twelve leagues** or there aboutes and then maketh a **gulf of twentie leagues compasse** or thereabouts and conteyneth in it selfe **five small Islandes** newlie named the Cinque Isles.

Here is my modernization of the 1583 Agreement:

> "... all that river or port **called by Master John Dee, Dee River,** which River, by the **description of Giovanni Verrazzano**, a Florentine, lies in the Northerly latitudes **about 42 degrees** and has its **mouth lying open to the South, about half a league wide** ...
>
> ... and entering within the said Bay increases its width and **continues about 12 leagues towards the Northeast,** and then makes **a gulf about 20 leagues in circumference,** and contains within it **five small Islands,** newly named the Cinque Isles.

Dee even tells us where he read about the beautiful bay which he selected for the colonizing site (and named after himself). Curiously, the only major descriptive detail this deed **omits** is that it is just north of "a triangular island similar in size to the island of Rhodes."

Richard Hakluyt's 1582 *Divers Voyages Touching the Discovery of America*

Next, let's look at another great promoter of English colonization, Richard Hakluyt and his book *Divers Voyages Touching the Discovery of America and the Islands Adjacent*. In 1582, Hakluyt was so anxious to get his first book to the printer, he even included Sir Humphrey Gilbert on his list of distinguished explorers.

Gilbert and his associate, Captain Edward Hayes, didn't actually depart until 1583. But Anthony Brigham had indeed left on his 1582 "preliminary voyage."

The names of certaine late trauaylers, both by sea and by lande, which also for the most part haue written of their owne trauayles and voyages.

The yere of our Lorde.
1178 Beniamin Tudelensis a Iewe.
1270 Marcus Paulus a Venetian.
1300 Harton an Armenian.
1320 Iohn Mandeuile knight, englishman.
1380 Nicolaus and Antonius Zeni, venetians.
1444 Nicolaus Conti venetian.
1492 Christopher Columbus a Genoway.
1497 Sebastian Gabot, an englishman the sonne of a venetian.
1497 M. Thorne and Hugh Eleot of Bristowe, englishmen.
1497 Vasques de Gama a portugale.
1500 Gasper Cortereal is a portingale.
1516 Edoardus Barbosa a portingale.
1519 Fernandus Magalianes a portingale.
1530 Iohn Barros a portingale.
1534 Iaques Cartier a Briton.
1540 Francis Vasques de Coronado Spaniarde.
1542 Iohn Gaetan Spaniarde.
1549 Francis Xauier a portingale.
1553 Hugh Willowbie knight, & Richard Chauncellor Eng.
1554 Francis Galuano a portingale.
1556 Steuen and William Burros Englishmen.
1562 Antonie Ienkinson Englishman.
1562 Iohn Ribault a Frenchman.
1565 Andrewe Theuet a Frenchman.
1576 Martin Frobisher Englishman.
1578 Francis Drake Englishman.
1580 Arthur Pet, and Charles Iackma Englishmen.
1582 Edwarde Fenton, and Luke warde, Englishmen.
1582 Humfrey Gilbert knight, Edward Heyes, and Antonie Brigham Englishmen.

206

Here is Richard Hakluyt's translation of Verrazzano's report

The descriptiō of Claudia Ilande.

Claudia was wife of King Francis.

wee discouered an Ilande in forme of a triangle, distant from the maine lande 3. leagues, about the bignesse of the Ilande of the Rodes, it was full of hilles couered with trees, well peopled, for we sawe fires all along the coaste, wee gaue the name of it, of your Maiesties mother, not staying there by reason of the weather being contrarie.

And wee came to another lande being 15. leagues distant from the Ilande, where wee founde a passing good hauen, wherein being entred we founde about 20. small boates of the people which with diuers cries and wondrings came about our shippe, comming no nerer then 50. paces towards vs, they stayed and behelde the artificialnesse of our ship, our

The Country of Sir H. G. voyage.

This lande is situated in the Paralele of Rome, in 41. degrees & 2. terces: but somewhat more colde by accidentall cause and not of nature, (as I will declare vnto your highnesse els where) describing at this present the situation of the foresaide countrie, which lyeth East and West, I say that the mouth of the hauen lyeth open to the South halfe a league broade, and being entred within it betweene the East and the North, it stretcheth twelue leagues: where it wareth broder and broder, and maketh a gulfe aboute 20. leagues in compasse, wherein are fiue small Ilandes very fruitfull and pleasant, full of hie and broade trees, among the which Ilandes, any great Nauie may ryde safe without any feare of tempest or other daunger.

In this transcription, I have emphasized the key phrases with bold type:

The description of Claudia Island

Claudia was the wife of King Francis

"...we discovered ***an island in the form of a triangle,*** *distant from the mainland 3 leagues, and* ***about the bigness of the Island of Rhodes,*** *it was full of hills covered with trees, well peopled, for we saw many fires all along the coast. We gave the name of it, of your Majesty's mother, not staying there by reason of the weather being contrarie.*

And we came to another land being 15 leagues distant from the Island, where we found ***a passing good haven,*** *wherein being entered we found about 20 small boats of the people which with divers cries and wonderings came about our ship.*

The Country of Sir H. G. voyage

This land is ***situated in the Parallel of Rome, in 41 degrees and two thirds,*** *but somewhat more cold by accidental cause and not of nature, (as I will declare to your highness elsewhere) describing at this present the situation of the foresaid countrie, which lyeth East and West, I say that* ***the mouth of the haven lies open to the South, a half of a league broad,*** *and being entered within it between the* ***East and the North, it stretches 12 leagues;*** *where it waxes broader and broader* and makes ***a gulf about 20 leagues in compass,*** *wherein are* ***5 small Islands,*** *very fruitful and pleasant, full of high and broad trees, among which Islands, any great Navy may ride safe without any fear of Tempest or other danger."*

Hakluyt faithfully translates all the key descriptions of the Bay.
And look what he writes in the margin!
" The Country of Sir H. G. voyage."

(Basically, what he's saying is, "This bay with five small islands was intended destination of Sir Humphrey Gilbert's colonizing expedition.")

Way back in 1890, in an article entitled *Origin of the Name of Rhode Island*, the noted Rhode Island historian Sidney S. Rider wrote:
"Hakluyt's Diverse Voyages was published in London in 1582, and republished several times, as late as 1600."
Then he adds:
"the first settlers here must have been familiar with it."
(Rider, *Origin*, RIHS, 1890)

By "*the first settlers*," Rider means Roger Williams, the Arnolds, and other early leaders. And by "*familiar with*," Rider means they knew of Hakluyt's translation of Verrazzano's term "Island of Rhodes."

And Sidney Rider, writing in 1890, was not even aware of the Gilbert-Peckham deed identifying the "Dee River." That deed wasn't brought to light until 45 years later, in 1935, by William Goodwin.

It appears as though Benedict Arnold named Aquidneck "Rhode Island" in 1636

Based on my studies of the very first years of the colonization of Narragansett Bay, its clear to me that the "*some who hindered*" Roger William's desire to name Aquidneck "**Patmos**" were **William and Benedict Arnold.**

I think that the bold Benedict, being one of the first and most ambitious settlers, claimed the Tower in 1636, the first year that Roger Williams, the Arnolds, and others arrived at the Bay.

It was in the summer of 1636 when John Oldham was murdered, and someone needed to handle the sale of the Narragansett Indians' bountiful corn harvest sometime between August and October. And the Indians were eager to obtain more English goods, like guns and gunpowder, cookware, cloth, and liquor. I suggest the opportunistic William and Benedict Arnold inherited this already well-established trading business.

Why wouldn't Benedict brag about the wonderful Tower he claimed? Why cryptically call it a "windmill"?

In the milieu of Puritan New England, Benedict would understandingly be reluctant to promulgate the idea that he owned a building once intended to be the centerpiece of a colony of Catholics. Puritans wanted nothing to do with anything Papist.

Furthermore, there might be certain Englishmen back in London who might use the Tower as evidence of an existing land claim made by one of their Elizabethan forebears. The early colonial settlers had risked their lives and estates to settle here, and they didn't want jeopardize losing it on some legal technicality. The bold Benedict probably made the message clear with something like, "Being the first ones here, my workers and I built this stone windmill. If you got a problem with that, come talk to me."

But Benedict wanted future generations to be aware of the importance of John Dee's masterpiece. Benedict recognized the Tower was not only an ingenious architectural expression of natural harmony, it was also symbol of freedom of religion and freedom of thought.

So Benedict insisted on the name "Rode Island," to incorporate (into the permanent name of this island) a cryptic reference to the Elizabethan colonization effort, and of course John Dee's mathematical harmonious timekeeping Tower.

To summarize visually, here is Benedict in front of the Tower he had recently claimed.

In the harbor is a fleet of shallops, well-protected by Goat Island.

Benedict is reading Hakluyt's popular travel book in which Narragansett Bay is described in detail, along with the footnote, "The Country of Sir H. G. voyage"

> Hey, my renaming Aquidneck Island the "Isle of Rodes" will forever hide a clever clue to the origin of the Tower I have claimed, which was designed by the great John Dee (Δ).

Hakluyt's 1582 Divers Voyages
...a triangular island...
the size of the Island of Rhodes...
...an excellent harbor...

The Country of Sir H. G. voyage

Benedict Arnold in 1636

My depiction of the colonial origin of the name: Rhode Island.

(my abridged version of Ganong's tracing of the 1529 map drawn by Giovanni da Verrazzano's brother, Geralmo da Verrazzano)

Hakluyt, following Verrazzano :
... a triangular Island ... about the size of the Island of Rhodes ...

Just north of the "Δ-shaped island" is the "Δ River"

There is a special clue in the shape of the "triangular island" of Claudia.

Have you deduced what it is?

Recall that Giovanni da Verrazzano's brother Geralmo drew the island as an equilateral triangle, and made it by far the most prominent island on the whole coast from Florida to Newfoundland.

209

Following the Verrazzano brothers, John Dee made the triangular island the most prominent island along the coast.

Where Geralmo made a perfect equilateral triangle, Dee made its shoreline slightly irregular (perhaps to make it seem more realistic).

You can clearly see the gulf of Refugio (or the Dee River), which heads northeast and then opens to a round bay.

But here's the clever part.
Dee's personal mark was an equilateral triangle.
He used it thousands of times and he even boasts about it at the very end of his *Monas Hieroglyphica:*

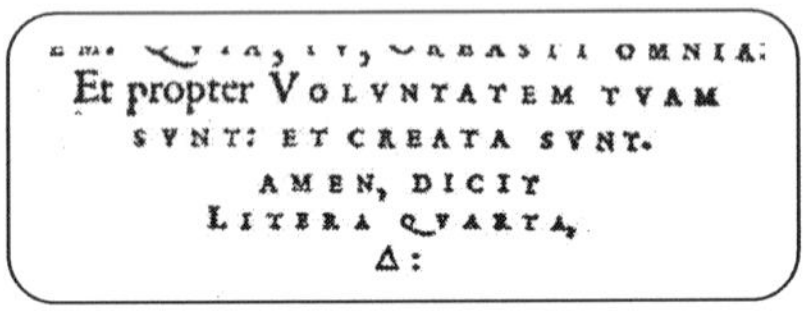

"Amen says the fourth letter."
(Δ = Greek Delta = D = Dee)

> Et propter VOLVNTATEM TVAM
> SVNT: ET CREATA SVNT.
> AMEN, DICIT
> LITERA QVARTA,
> Δ∴

> Because of THY WILL, THEY ARE, AND HAVE BEEN CREATED AMEN, SAYS THE FOURTH LETTER,
> Δ∴

John Dee's 1580 Map of North America
(my abridged version)

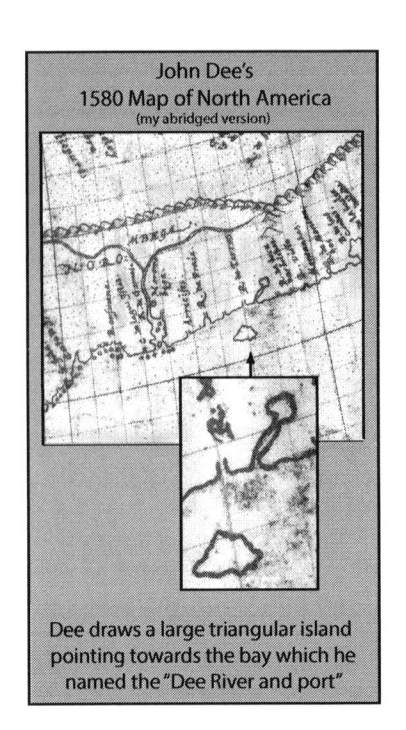

Dee draws a large triangular island pointing towards the bay which he named the "Dee River and port"

Thus, Dee doesn't even have to write the words "Dee River" on his map. The "triangular island" and the "northeast-heading river" are a rebus that says "Dee River."

(Rebuses, in which words are represented by pictures, were a popular form of word-game among the witty Elizabethans. Those in-the-know would get Dee's joke, but to most people it would be invisible.)

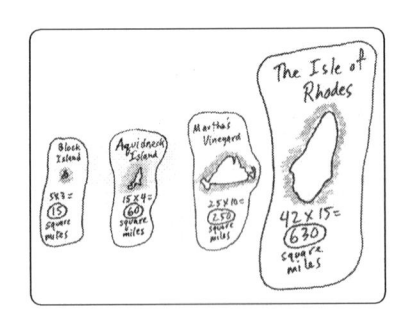

Verrazzano probably compared Block Island to the Isle of Rhodes to make it seem distinguished. Dedicating a **tiny** island to the Queen of France (or the Queen Mother) would be insulting.

In actuality, the Isle of Rhodes in the Aegean (630 square miles) is more than 40 times the size of Block Island (15 square miles).

Verrazzano had previously sailed throughout the Mediterranean. He realized that Block Island was strategically located in the middle of the Atlantic Coast, just as the Isle of Rhodes was in a strategically located in the northeast Mediterranean.

Also, the cliffs along southern New England coastal islands somewhat resemble the cliffs on the west coast of the Greek Isle of Rhodes.

In short, Verrazzano compared tiny Block Island to the ancient island of Rhodes give it a sense of prominence.

Kamiro Cliffs
Isle of Rhodes, Greece
(west coast)

Monhegan Cliffs
Block Island, RI
(south coast)

Aquinnah Cliffs
Martha's Vineyard, Mass.
(southwest coast)

To summarize, I believe the name of Rhode Island was born in the mind of Benedict Arnold, who was tying together Verrazzano, Hakluyt, Gilbert, and Dee.

But it doesn't stop there. Benedict was also probably instrumental in promoting the **Anchor of Hope** as the seal of the Colony.

Here's a quick visual quiz.

We've seen how prominently John Dee displays his **Monas symbol** on his Title pages and how he interprets it in inventive ways.

Here is the **anchor** from Benedict Arnold's official 1663 Governor's Seal.

Also inscribed are his initials, "BA," and the state motto, "HOPE."

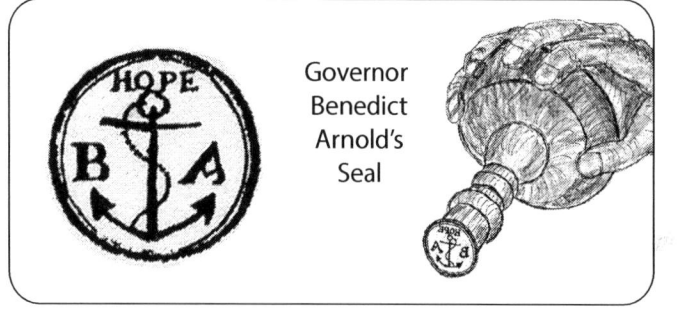

Governor Benedict Arnold's Seal

Notice any similarities?

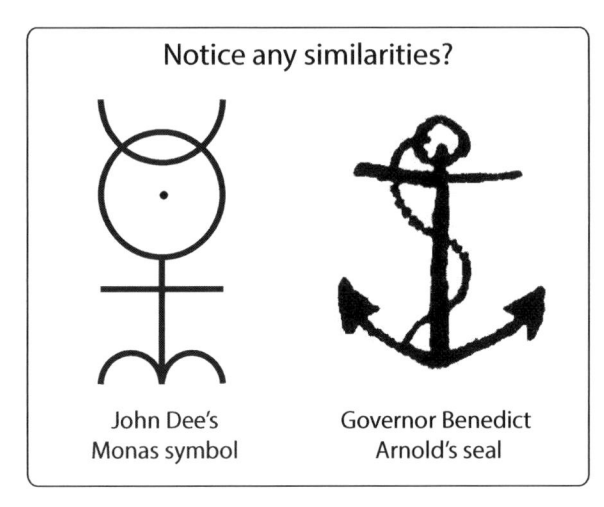

John Dee's Monas symbol

Governor Benedict Arnold's seal

Notice any similarities between the Monas symbol and the anchor?

1. The lower arms of the anchor are like Dee's Moon half-circle.
2. The ring at the top is like Dee's Sun circle
3. In the middle is Dee's offset Cross.
4. And what is called the "fouled rope" is made of two half circles, much like Dee's Aries symbol, only slightly reoriented.

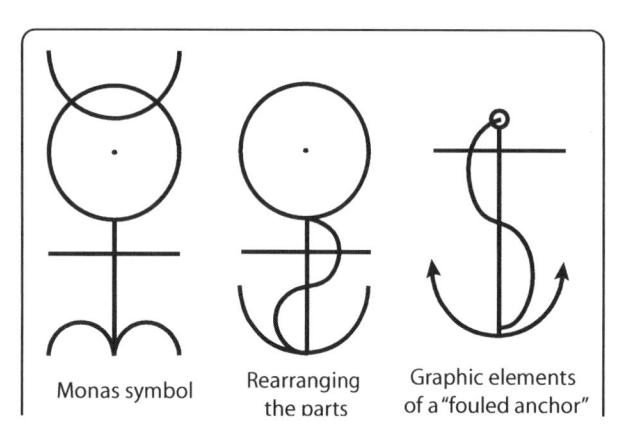

Here's one way to see the Monas symbol morph into the Anchor.
Basically, each of the symbols has 4 parts.

Monas symbol

Rearranging the parts

Graphic elements of a "fouled anchor"

A brief history of the *Anchor of Hope*

The expression "HOPE is an ANCHOR of the Soul" comes
from Hebrews, Chapter 6, Verses 18-20 of the Bible.

*"...the **hope** set before us, which we have as an **anchor** of the soul,
both sure and steadfast, and which entereth into that within the veil,
where the forerunner is for us entered, Jesus, made a high priest for ever..."*

To celebrate their faith in a way that would avoid persecution from the Romans, early Christians used a disguised cross (*Crux dissimulata*). The most frequently used disguise was to make it appear to be an anchor.

Anchor crosses dating from around 200 AD to 400 AD, can still be seen in the catacombs (the subterranean cemetaries) under Rome.

The **anchor cross** is often called the Saint Clement's cross after Pope Saint Clement. Around 100 AD, the Romans tied an anchor to Saint Clement, tossed him overboard, and left him to drown.

The Martyrdom of Saint Clement

Constantine's Chi Rho symbol

In 312 AD, to symbolize his conversion to Christianity, Emperor Constantine commanded his Armies display the "Chi Rho symbol."

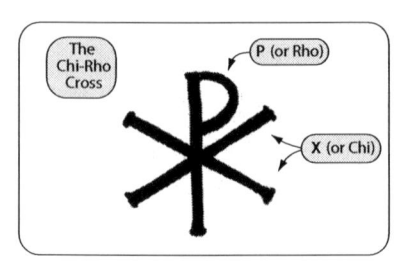

Chi (X) and the Rho (P) are the first two letters of the Greek word
ΧΡΙΣΤΟΣ
(XRISTOS or CHRISTOS)

The Chi-Rho Cross
P (or Rho)
X (or Chi)

Christians combined Christ's "Chi Rho initials" with the "Anchor of Hope" to make the **Chi Rho Anchor Cross**.

XRistos and the...
...ANCHOR of HOPE combined

And guess where two Chi Rho Anchor of Hope crosses appear...

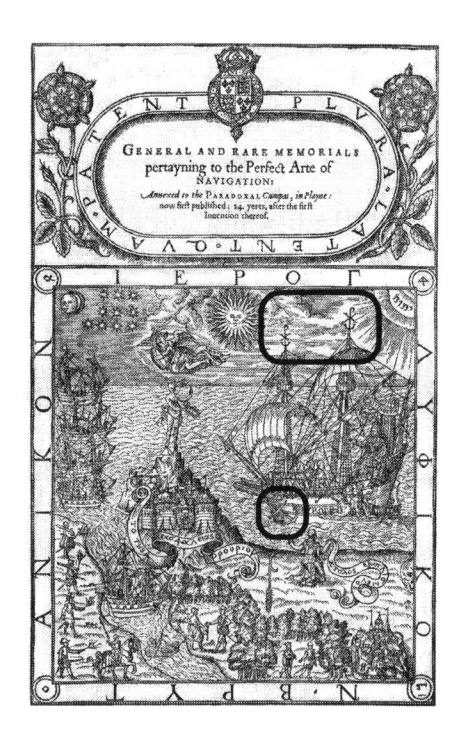

At the tops of the two masts of Dee's illustration of the "ship of state" with Elizabeth at the helm!

Does Dee also want us to see the prominent anchor, which is bound to the hull of this "ship of state," as an Anchor of Hope?

More cryptic references to the Anchor of Hope

A "word clue" that suggests Dee is making hidden references to the "Anchor of Hope" is the word *asphaleias*. This is the Greek word displayed prominently in front of the solid fortress on the hill.

asphaleias
(or steadfast)

"...the hope set before us, which we have as an anchor of the soul, both sure and steadfast, and which entereth into that within the veil, where the forerunner is for us entered, Jesus, made a high priest for ever..."

ἣν ὡς ἄγκυραν ἔχομεν
τῆς ψυχῆς ἀσφαλῆ
τε καὶ βεβαίαν καὶ
εἰσερχομένην εἰς τὸ
ἐσώτερον τοῦ καταπετάσματος

Hebrews 6:18-20 in the original Greek,
emphasizing the word *asphalê* (or steadfast)

The best translation of *asphaleias* is "steadfast. It is a form of the same word used in the Anchor of Hope quote in the original Greek Bible (*asphalê*).

To visually emphasize what Dee is implying, here is Dee's Greek word for "steadfast" in the English translation of the Hebrew 6:18-20 quote.

"...the **hope** set before us, which we have as an **anchor** of the soul, both sure and *asphaleias*, and which entereth into that within the veil, where the forerunner is for us entered, Jesus, made a high priest for ever..."

213

Well-versed in classical rhetoric and legal presentations, Dee knew the importance of concluding his argument with his main theme.

The **final paragraph** of his book comes "full-circle" and references the main points presented on the **Title page**.

Running vertically in the right margin are the words IEROGLYPHIKON BRYTANIKON.

These two words, which also surround the Title page illustration, mean a "British Hieroglyphic" or a "Sacred Symbol for Britain."

He mentions "ELIZABETH... at the HELM ...of the IMPERIAL SHIP, (just as he depicts on the Title page).

Dee then goes on to write in Greek *STOLOS EXOPLISMENOS* (Sending forth an expedition) ...may help us...to... *PHROURION TES ASPHALEIAS* (make a steadfast watch post). This is essentially the same quote that he used on the Title Page.

He references the HEAVENLY PROTECTOR, as illustrated in he upper right hand corner of the Title page.

And also "his GOOD ANGEL...with SHIELD and SWORD," a reference to Saint Michael, who hovers above Lady Occasion.

He also mentions "THE REPUBLIC OF BRITANNICA, on her knees...Soliciting ...ELIZABETH..."

> Forrein Neighbors, their vnaffured Frendfhip, being Confidered): Why fhould not we HOPE, that, RES·PVBL. BRYTANICA, on her knees, very Humbly, and erneftly Soliciting the moft Excellent Royall Maiefty, of our ELIZABETH, (Sitting at the HELM of this Imperiall Monarchy: or, rather, at the Helm of the IMPERIALL SHIP, of the moft parte of Chriftendome: if fo, it be her Graces Pleafure) fhall

But notice that he prefaces this collection of clues with the phrase, "Why should not we HOPE..."

To me, this is an obvious clue that Dee wants us to look for the idea of "HOPE" hidden in the Title page illustration.

Aside from the obvious "Chi-Rho Anchor-of-Hope Crosses" atop the masts, and the large anchor on Elizabeth's "ship of state," it seemed reasonable to expect the clever grammarian Dee might be hiding a **word clue** about HOPE as well.

Dee's cryptic expressions of the letters H, O, P, E

Dee breaks the words IEROGLYPHIKON BRYTANIKON into 4 parts.

The first part, IEROG, seems more prominent than the other parts because its letters are upright, not sideways or upside down.

An alternative form of the Latin word IEROGLYPHIKON is HIEROGLYPHIKON.

Dee is obviously aware of this, as he spells it with an H in his earlier book, the *Monas Hieroglyphica*.

If that implied H is added, all the letters on HOPE can be found.

[The Greek P (Rho) looks like a Latin P.]

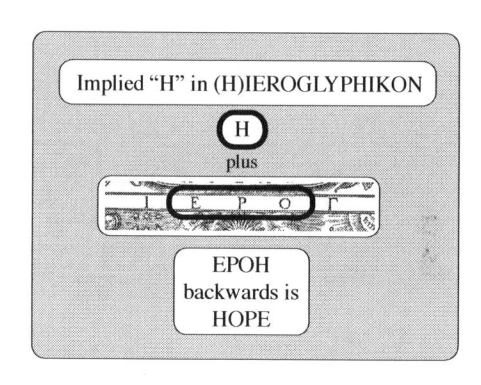

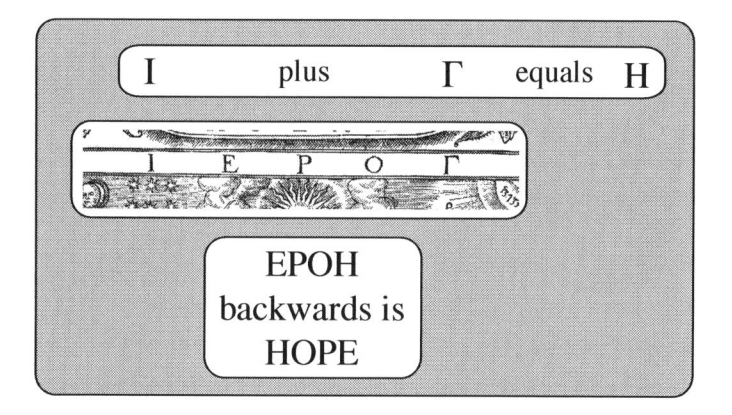

Implied "H" in (H)IEROGLYPHIKON

H
plus
I E P O Γ

EPOH backwards is HOPE

I plus Γ equals H

I E P O Γ

EPOH backwards is HOPE

Another way to make that missing H is to creatively combine the letters I (iota) and Γ (gamma).

In other words, two vertical lines and a crossbar can make the letter H.

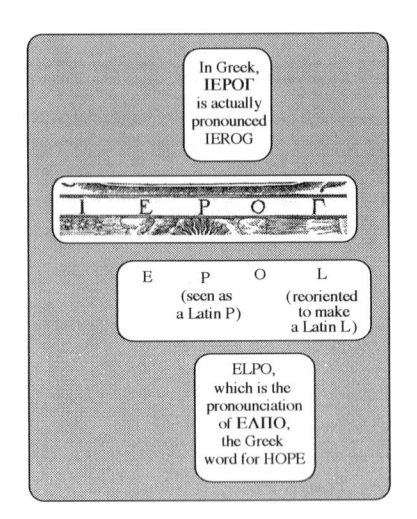

In Greek,
ΙΕΡΟΓ
is actually
pronounced
IEROG

Ι Ε Ρ Ο Γ

E   P   L
(seen as   (reoriented
a Latin P)   to make
            a Latin L)

ELPO,
which is the
pronounciation
of ΕΛΠΟ,
the Greek
word for HOPE

Greek scholars will see the word "ELPO," the Greek word for HOPE written in Latin Letters. (It's actually spelled ΕΛΠΟ.)

Dee also hid the word HOPE in the Greek spelling of the word EUROPH on the side of the ship of state.

Dee wanted England's allies in Europe to be partners in sharing the wealth of the New World.

If the Greek Omega is seen as an "O," all the letters in the word HOPE can be found in EUROPH.

ΕΥΡΩΠΗ
or
EUROPH
contains all the letters in the word HOPE

Λ Ε Ω Π

ΕΛΠΩ

ELPO,
Greek for
HOPE

Also, if the fluke of the anchor is seen as a Lambda, all the letters for ΕΓΠΩ or ELPO can be found.

Dee might not have explicitly written the word HOPE on the Title page, but he left plenty of "Dee style" visual clues that this was his intent.

The Anchor of Hope seems to be the symbol Dee devised for the Elizabethan colonization effort

Three months before Sir Humphrey set sail, Queen Elizabeth sent him (by way of his half-brother, Sir Walter Raleigh), a piece of custom made jewelry depicting **"an anchor guided by a lady."**

As Maurice Browne reports, " The device was an Anchor of gold set with 29 diamonds, with a Portrait of the Queen holding the ring of the Anchor in one hand and the fluke of the Anchor in the other."

Written on the back-side are the words :

"Tuemar sub sacra ancora"
"Be safe-guarded by the sacred anchor."

(Letter written by Maurice Browne to John Thynne, penned between April 25 and May 3, 1583, in David Beers Quinn and Neal Cheshire, *The New Founde Land of Stephen Parmenius*, U. of Toronto Press, 1972, p. 204-5)

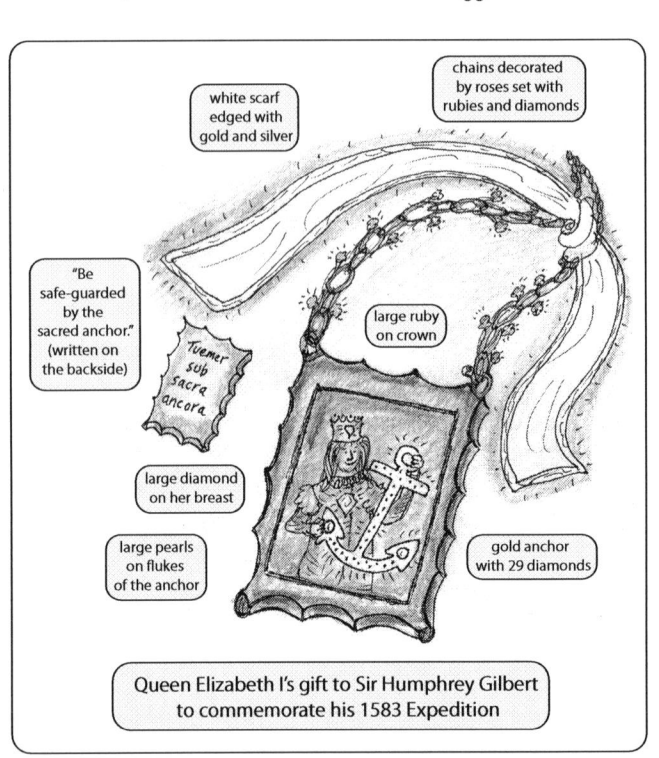

- white scarf edged with gold and silver
- chains decorated by roses set with rubies and diamonds
- "Be safe-guarded by the sacred anchor." (written on the backside)
- large ruby on crown
- large diamond on her breast
- large pearls on flukes of the anchor
- gold anchor with 29 diamonds

Queen Elizabeth I's gift to Sir Humphrey Gilbert to commemorate his 1583 Expedition

I suspect it was Dee who designed the brooch. The main graphic elements: **the Queen, the Anchor, and the idea of the sacred anchor (of Hope)** are all key elements on the Title page of *General and Rare Memorials*.

It seems as though Dee was writing the whole script for this real-life drama: the legal advice, the navigational advice, the maps, meeting individually with all parties involved, being given 10,000 acres of land, picking the destination, naming it after himself, choosing a symbol (The Anchor of Hope), and perhaps designing the commemorative gift (the brooch). In this light, it's not outlandish at all to suggest that he also designed the first building in this first British colony.

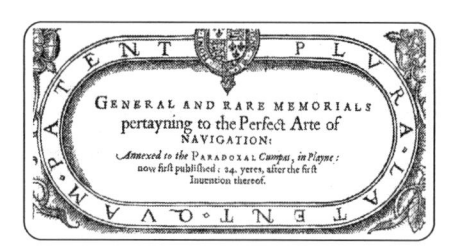

Am I being too creative with all this? Remember, Dee openly admits he's an inveterate clue-maker. The very title of the book is surrounded by the words:

PLURA LATENT QUAM PATENT, or
MORE IS HIDDEN THAN
IS OUT IN THE OPEN.

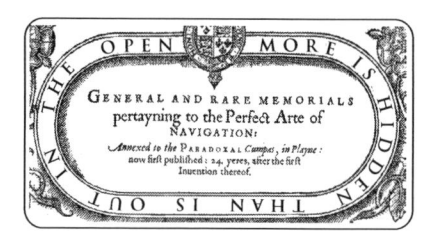

Indeed, even the lozenge shape in which he places the Title is a clue.

It's made from two tangent circles.
It's a geometrically-cryptic expression of the Sun and the Moon.
It's the Union of Opposites.

Which is also the design plan of his "Thus the World Was Created" chart.

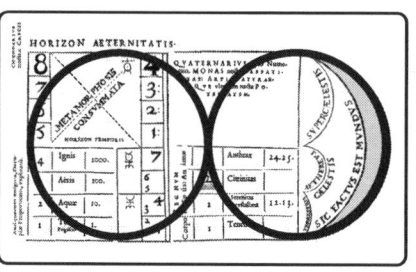

And I suggest that "two tangent circles" is the design plan for the Tower.

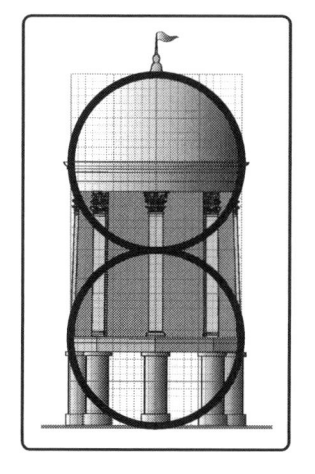

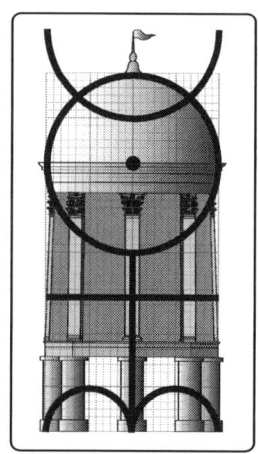

Which is the same proportion as the Monas symbol.

217

A quick way to read the story of the Title page is as a **spiral**.
[Start below, with the kneeling woman]

Across the top, the sun, the stars, and the moon are shining down beneficial rays over the vast ocean.

In the upper right-hand corner, God shines brightly on the whole endeavor.

The kneeling citizens of England are pleading to the Queen: "send forth a sailing expedition."

Down the left, four ships are at anchor near the mouth of a river in the New World. Another ship is anchored in the river.

Next, two men are walking through a clearing.

Four men are brandishing fire, one is riding his trusty horse, and another crosses the river in a small boat.

On the far shore, two men are trading goods.

And finally, in the lower right, two men are small silhouettes in a city which has blossomed.

Within the city walls, you can see housetops and church spires. At the very top is a domed building supported by columns.

Dee is cinematically advising the Queen that if she "sends forth an expedition," the heavens are aligned for all these great things to happen. A safe mission. Successful trading. A new thriving community. (All contributing to a flourishing economy for England and great wealth for the Crown.)

Dee has drawn a **storyboard** to present his vision for America the Queen. It apparently helped him make one hell of a good **sales pitch**, because the Queen approved his plan. One month later, Sir Humphrey Gilbert was given letters patent to discover all of North America north of Florida. Shortly thereafter, the grateful Gilbert gave Dee most of what is now Canada and Alaska.

Dee's Anchor of Hope symbol, from 1577 to today

Here is my conjectured history how the Anchor became a modern day symbol of the State of Rhode Island.

In his 1577 *General and Rare Memorials*, Dee introduces the Anchor of Hope as a symbol to safeguard the grand British Empire which he has envisioned.

I think the Anchor symbol is a cryptic representation of the Monas symbol, which itself is a summary of Dee's cosmology.

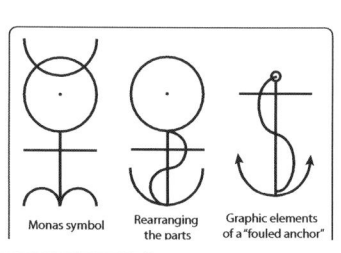

Monas symbol / Rearranging the parts / Graphic elements of a "fouled anchor"

In 1583, the Anchor of Hope is the symbol for Gilbert's expedition to settle the first English colony in the New World.

"Be safe-guarded by the sacred anchor"

In 1647, early leaders of Providence Plantations (Providence, Warwick, Portsmouth, and Newport) selected the Anchor as their official seal.

(I suggest that the enterprising merchant Benedict Arnold and others had already been using it for the previous 20 years as the unofficial seal for the growing port of Newport and the whole of Narragansett Bay in general.)

In 1663, The Colony of Rhode Island and the Providence Plantations, under first Governor Benedict Arnold, adopt the "fouled anchor and the word Hope" as the official seal.

And still today, the Anchor of Hope is the official seal of the State of Rhode Island and Providence Plantations.

219

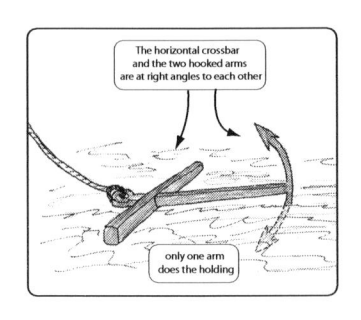

Incidentally, non-sailors might not realize the common anchor symbol is actually a "stylized representation" of a real anchor. On a real anchor, the thick, heavy crossbar is at "right angles" to the curved arms. When the heavy crossbar is dragged across along the bottom, one of the hooks will dig into the sand.

(The "upper hook" actually does nothing).

So realistically, when an anchor is drawn flat-on, the crossbar is hardly seen at all.

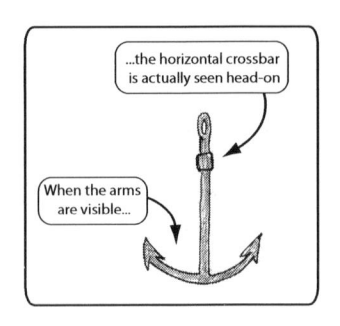

A summary of the numerous clues Benedict left behind.

I think Benedict knew it all. He knew that Narragansett Bay was the site of the first Elizabethan colonization effort of 1583. He knew that John Dee had designed the Tower. He knew it was to be the focal point of the new city. He knew how it operated as a giant calendar-clock. He knew its proportions incorporated John Dee's mathematical cosmology.

And even understood the *Monas Hieroglyphica* and the story it tells about optics, geometry, and number.

Clue 1: the name Rhode Island

The biggest clue is that Benedict appears to have been the person responsible for changing the name Aquidneck Island to Rhode Island. He knew from reading Richard Hakluyt's translation of Verrazzano that Narragansett Bay was the "Country of Sir H(umphrey) G(ilbert's) voyage."

Clue 2: Benedict Arnold's "east-west line" and the Metamorphosis numbers

We saw earlier how many of Benedict Arnold's properties align on what I call Benedict's "east-west line." The Tower, his cemetery, and his Mansion are on a line just slightly north of due west, but the Tower, Goat Island, his son's House on Beavertail in Jamestown, his Plains Ranch in West Kingston, and his "garrison house" in the Western border of Rhode Island are on a line that is due "east-west."

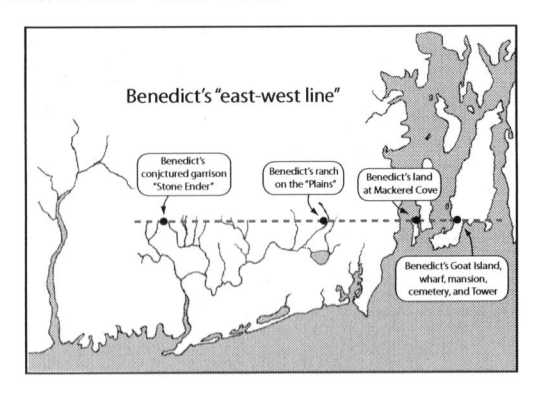

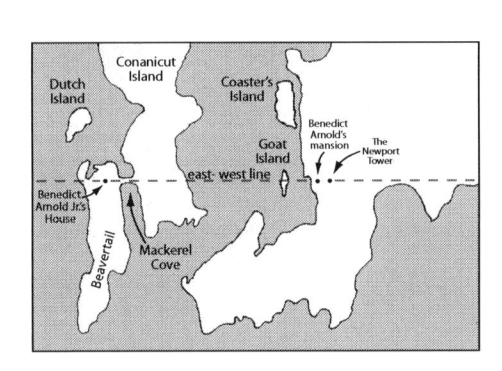

220

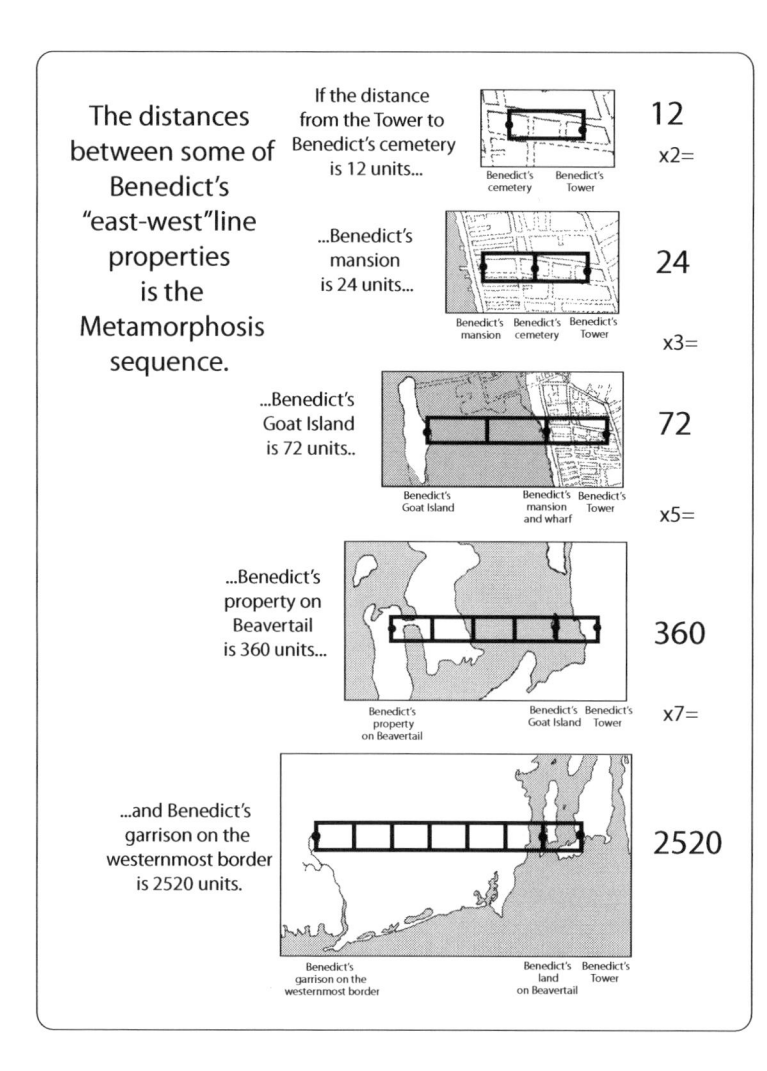

The distances between some of Benedict's "east-west" line properties is the Metamorphosis sequence.

If the distance from the Tower to Benedict's cemetery is 12 units...

12

x2=

...Benedict's mansion is 24 units...

24

x3=

...Benedict's Goat Island is 72 units..

72

x5=

...Benedict's property on Beavertail is 360 units...

360

x7=

...and Benedict's garrison on the westernmost border is 2520 units.

2520

Several of these properties have an interesting relationship: their distances express Dee's Metamorphosis number sequence: 12, 24, 72, 360, and 2520.

If the distance between the Tower and Benedict's family cemetery is **12** units, the distance from the Tower to his Mansion is double this, or **24** units.

(In his will, Arnold describes the cemetery as being "in or near ye line going from my Dwelling house to my Stone-Build Wind miln")

Using the same scale, the distance from the Tower to the highest point on Goat Island is **72** units.

(Benedict and one associate purchased Goat Island from the Indian leaders and later gave it to the City of Newport. This highest point probably had some kind of fortification, as it later became the site of Fort George.)

Using the same scale, the distance from the Tower to his son's house at the north end of Beavertail is **360** units.

And finally, the distance from the Tower to [what I believe to be] his "garrison house" on the westernmost edge of the lands of the Providence Plantations Charter [of 1644] is **2520** units.

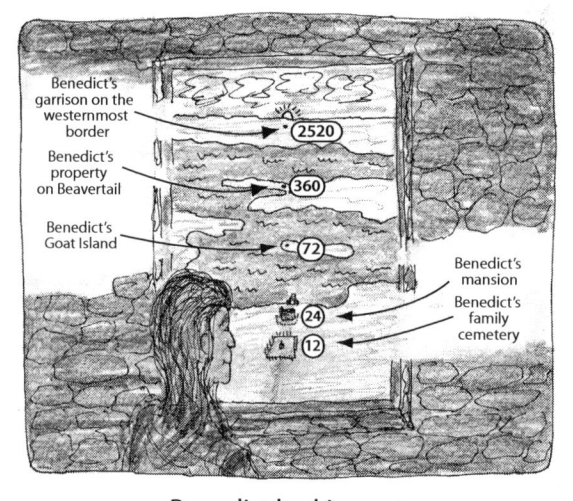

Benedict has woven the Metamorphosis numbers across Southern Rhode Island!

Benedict looking out the West window of the Tower at the "Metamorphosis" arrangement of properties

Could this all be accidental? Perhaps. But in light of some of his other cryptic clues, it's quite feasible that it was done with intent.

The positions of the Tower, Goat Island, and Beavertail were "givens," but Benedict himself decided where his mansion, his cemetery, and his western "garrison house" should be located.

But even if this "numbers game" is purely coincidental, the idea that he even had an east-west line of properties is enough to show that the Tower was important to him.

More about Clue 2:
The size of John Dee's intended colony was to be 2520 square miles

By hiding the Metamorphosis numbers in the overall landscape plan, Benedict is telling us he knows about Dee's mathematical cosmology. But it goes further than that. This suggests to me that Benedict was aware that the John Dee hid the number 2520 in the overall size of the first colony on the Dee River. To be more specific, Dee designed the colony to encompass 2520 square miles (in order to imbue it with mathematical harmony).

Dee hides the numerical clues of this math puzzle in the deed
between Sir Humphrey Gilbert and Sir George Peckham and his son:

*"... all that river or port called by Master John Dee, Dee River,
which River, by the description of Giovanni Verrazzano,
a Florentine, lies in the Northerly latitudes about 42 degrees*

*and has its mouth lying open to the South, half a league broad or
thereabout, and entering within the said Bay between the East and
the North increases its width and continues 12 leagues or thereabouts,
and then makes a gulf of 20 leagues in circumference or thereabouts,
and contains within it 5 small Islands, newly named the Cinque Isles.*

*And the said gulf and the 5 Isles at the choice of the said George and
George his youngest son, their heirs, deputies, or assigns or any of them."*

Further on in the document is this description of the whole parcel:

"... Fifteen hundred thousand [1.5 million] *acres of ground
extending along the sea coast westward towards
the River of Normbega* [probably the Hudson River]
not more that 60 English miles in length ..."

(my modernization; Quinn, *Voyages*, p. 343)

Here is a the Gilbert/Peckham/Dee colony, superimposed
on a map showing modern-day state boundaries.

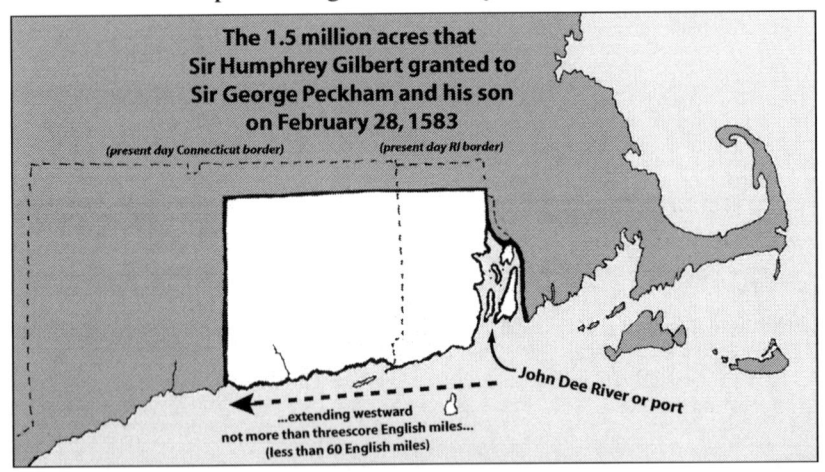

**The 1.5 million acres that
Sir Humphrey Gilbert granted to
Sir George Peckham and his son
on February 28, 1583**

(present day Connecticut border) (present day RI border)

John Dee River or port

...extending westward
not more than threescore English miles...
(less than 60 English miles)

For a simpler geometric analysis, let's convert these areas into rectangles and circles.

The gulf is a **circle**, its entrance way is a **vertical rectangle**, and the overall shape is a **horizontal rectangle**.

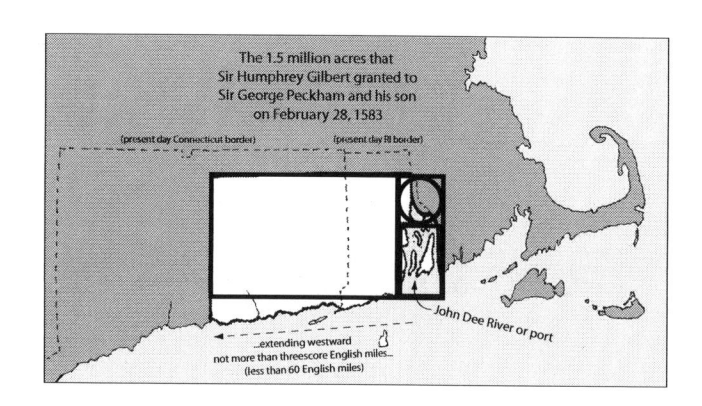

The 1.5 million acres that Sir Humphrey Gilbert granted to Sir George Peckham and his son on February 28, 1583

(present day Connecticut border) (present day RI border)

John Dee River or port

...extending westward not more than threescore English miles... (less than 60 English miles)

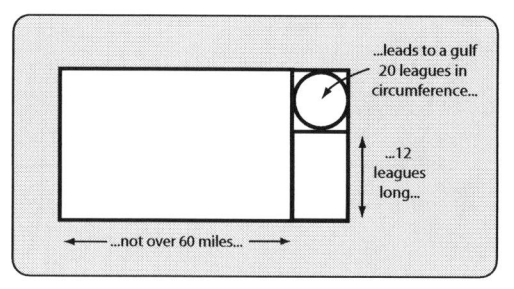

...leads to a gulf 20 leagues in circumference...

...12 leagues long...

...not over 60 miles...

Dee's boundary description in leagues (and miles)

Dee disguised the measurements by providing them in both "leagues" and "miles."

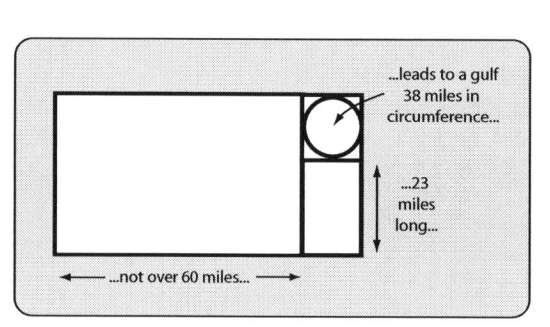

...leads to a gulf 38 miles in circumference...

...23 miles long...

...not over 60 miles...

Dee's boundary description converted into miles
1 French league =1.91 English miles

Using the conversion factor of
1.91 English miles = 1 French league (or *petit lieue*),
let's convert all the measurements into miles.

(Dee was using Verrazzano's measurements, and Verrazzano was on a mission for the King of France.)

As the gulf has a circumference of 38 miles, it has a diameter of 12 miles.

So the total height is **35** miles (23 + 12).
And the total width is **72** miles (60 +12).

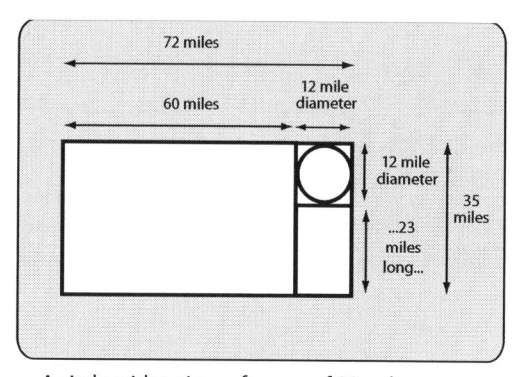

72 miles
60 miles
12 mile diameter
12 mile diameter
35 miles
...23 miles long...

A circle with a circumference of 38 miles has a diameter of approx. 12 miles

Multiplying 35 x 72 makes **2520**, Dee's "Sabbatizat"!

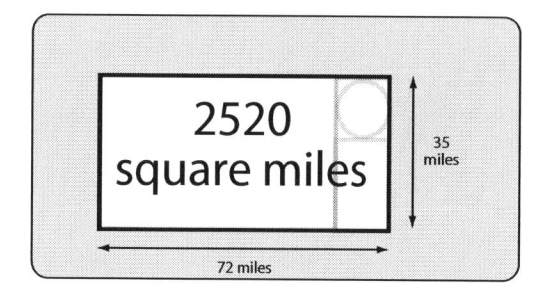

2520 square miles

35 miles

72 miles

35 miles x 72 miles = 2520 square miles

223

This particular "pathway" to 2520 (35 x 72 = 2520)
is quite important because it involves another
Metamorphosis number, 72.

The other number, 35,
combines the **5** from the (72 x 5 = 360) step
and the **7** from the (360 x 7 = 2520) step.

```
12 = 12
12 x 2 = 24
24 x 3 = 72
72 x 5 = 360
360 x 7 = 2520
5x7=35
```

(In another amazing correlation, Dee says the latitude is "about 42 degrees."
He also says that the width of the parcel of land is "not over 60 miles."
Admittedly these are both estimates, and also, one is in degrees and
the other is in miles. But multiplied together, 42 x 60 makes 2520.)

Certainly I have done some rounding off in my calculations, and the water-and land-forms involved are far from circular and rectangular. But this is how geometer Dee would have approached it. Dee had determined the colony's location. He named the main river after himself. To me, it's logical that he determined its overall size.

The colony was Dee's concept.
It was to be a Utopia designed by his mathematical mind.
His mathematical Tower sang perfect visual harmony.
His overall colony size was to be mathematically harmonious as well.

[As there are 640 acres in a square mile, 2520 square miles actually contains
about 1.6 million acres. This is pretty close to the deed's 1.5 million acres.

Expressed another way, 1.5 million acres is 2343 square miles,
which is only 177 square miles shy of 2520 square miles.]

But there is also a practical reason why Dee would want a colony of 2520 square miles. Just as 2520 is the lowest number divisible by 2, 3, 4, 5, 6, 7, 8, and 9, the colony would be the smallest-possible-size-colony that could be divided into halves, thirds, quarters, fifths, sixths, sevenths, eighths, or ninths (or even tenths or twelfths). This would allow for the maximum variety of options in governmental affairs like voting representation or land distribution.

Plato's ideal city (in Book 5, 737-8 of *Laws*) was to have 5040 citizens for the same reason. Plato explains he chose number 5040 (which is simply 2 x 2520) because it provides for many ways to divide the whole populace. And Plato was Dee's favorite philosopher.

Clue 3: Benedict's mark on the Charter Chair

The symbol in the 1663 Charter Chair
appears to have been carved by
Governor Benedict Arnold himself.

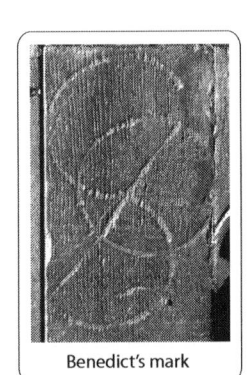

The Governor's chair
given to Benedict Arnold
by the King Charles II in 1663

Benedict's mark

Within the
"3 same-sized circles and a line"
design, Benedict's initials
(**BA**) can be found.

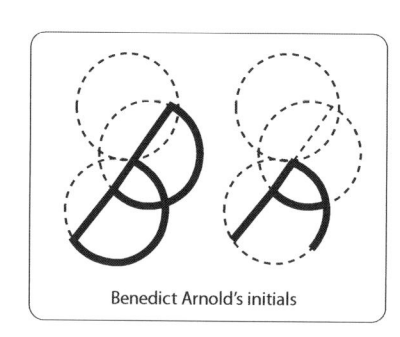

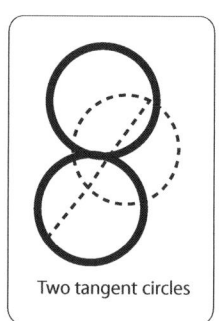

Benedict's mark

Benedict Arnold's initials

Two of the circles are "**tangent at a point**,"
thus depicting one of the main themes
of the *Monas Hieroglyphica*.

Benedict knew his **geometry**.
He knew how to divide a
circle into sixths and twelfths.
He knew how to make
a 30-60-90 triangle.

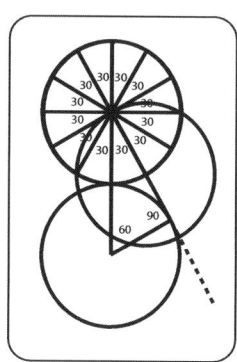

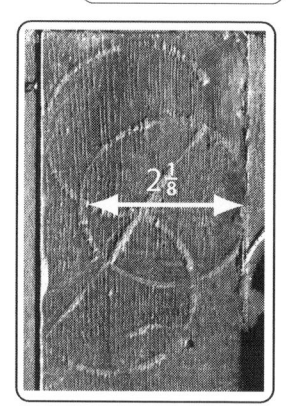

Two tangent circles

But most importantly, the 2 1/8 inch diameter
circles he used are the same size as the **solar disc**
in an 18 1/2 foot wide camera-obscura room.
And this is the width of the first-floor room of the Tower!

Benedict knew the Tower was a **horologium**,
and he knew how it worked.

(I was familiar with 2 1/8 inch diameter
solar discs because my photo studio was
18 1/2 feet wide. While tracking the
movement of the sun just before sunset
throughout the year, I had drawn
hundreds of these 2 1/8 inch circles.)

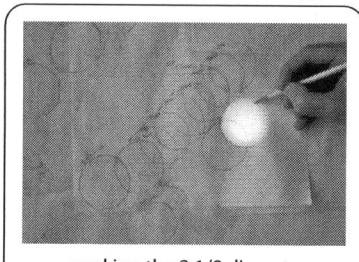

marking the 2 1/8 diameter
solar disc in my photo studio

Clue 4: An important agreement signed on the Equinox

There is another clue about Benedict's "east-west line" hidden in the historical record of the island of Jamestown, which was then called Quononaquutt (Conanicut).

The Narragansett Indians had allowed the colonists to use the island for grazing animals since 1637, so was presumably it was all clear, open pasture land. Twenty years later, on **March 10**, 1657, eighty colonists, (mostly from Newport) signed a 7-page agreement to purchase the island from the Narragansetts. On April 15, 1657, the local sachem Cojonoquant deeded them the land.

Benedict was the President of the Colony of Providence Plantations at the time. And he was clearly was a key player in this negotiation as well. He acquired more land than anyone else. He obtained the whole southern tip of the island, including Mackerel Cove and all of Beavertail. This parcel encompassed over 1000 acres, including all the island's coast bordering the Atlantic Ocean, and bordering the entrances to the two passages into Narragansett Bay.

[This strategically located land has been the site of many forts and lighthouses over the years.]

The special thing about **March 10,** is that it was the date of the Spring Equinox! The colonists were still using the Julian Calendar, which was out-of-sync from the sun by about 11 days. Thus, "March 10 in the Julian Calendar" equals "March 21 in the Gregorian Calendar".

It's the Spring Equinox. It's the first day of Aries.

(It's the day Dee was so excited about in the *Monas Hieroglyphica*, with its 12 hours of light and 12 hours of darkness, totalling to exactly 24 hours. And the Aries symbol is a key part of his Monas symbol)

If Benedict glanced out the West window of the Tower just before sunset on March 10, the sparkling reflections off the water's surface would silhouette the southern tip of Jamestown and Beavertail. These reflections would be too bright to look at.

(and Colonials didn't have sunglasses).

But if Benedict blocked up the West window, except for one small hole, the sparkling "fiery water" scene featuring Jamestown Island in silhouette would be projected on the back wall of the fireplace.

My conjectured illustration of Governor Benedict Arnold and fellow leaders watching the solar disc on the Governor's chair during an equinox sunset.

Helicopter view, looking west at the Tower, Goat Island, Jamestown, and the mainland of "South County."

Clue 5: Governor Benedict Arnold's Seal

It appears as though Benedict was unofficially using The Anchor of Hope motto as a symbol when he insisted Aquidneck be named "Rode Island" back around 1637. Once established, the other colonial leaders adopted the idea. The Anchor of Hope became the symbol for the Colony of Rhode Island and Providence Plantations in 1647, before Benedict's family moved to Newport.

But it seems like it was Benedict who embellished the anchor with the "fouled rope." The "fouled rope" version was the one Benedict made official in his first act as an elected Governor in 1664.

Governor Benedict Arnold's Seal

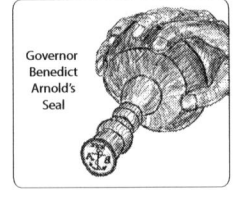

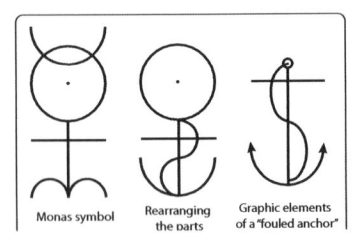

I call the anchor symbol a "Monas dissimulata," ["a Monas symbol in disguise"]. Dee came up with this "symbol of a symbol" idea. Benedict embellished it and brought it back into daily use.

Monas symbol | Rearranging the parts | Graphic elements of a "fouled anchor"

The main point here is that Benedict was enthusiastic about the motto "Anchor of Hope." It's pretty obvious to me that he knew it was the symbol Dee conceived for the 1583 colonization attempt. He probably was even aware of Anchor of Hope clues on the Title page illustration of Dee's *General and Rare Memorials*.

Some of the Narragansett Indians had been given metal rings stamped with an anchor design. The "fouled rope" has been changed into the shape of a heart [which is still sort of two semicircles]. It's thought that these rings might have been tokens of appreciation from Governor Benedict Arnold himself.

Ring thought to have been a gift from Benedict Arnold to an Narragansett sagamore

Clue 6: The nine children of Benedict and Damaris Arnold

A clue demonstrating how important the Tower and the "Anchor of Hope" were to Benedict Arnold can be found in the names he and Damaris chose for their children. All nine babies were born over a 19-year period, when Benedict Arnold was between 27 and 46 years old.

BENEDICT (JR.) 1642
CALEB 1644
JOSIAH 1646
DAMARIS 1648
WILLIAM 1651 (ONLY LIVED FOR 2 DAYS)
PENELOPE 1653
OLIVER 1655
GODSGIFT 1658
FREELOVE 1661

THE CHILDREN OF
DAMARIS AND BENEDICT ARNOLD

Benedict and Damaris named two of the early children after themselves. William is obviously named after Benedict's father. In 1651, Benedict was about to "break out of his father's shadow," and relinquish his loyalty to the Massachusetts Bay Colony in order to help the citizens of Newport combat Coddington's "Governor of Aquidneck for life" power grab.

Perhaps Benedict chose to name his son William to appease his father. [A cute, namesake baby would melt any grandpa's heart.] Unfortunately, only two days after being born, baby William died.

I've drawn a line after William because, a month after he died, the Arnold family moved to Newport. The first children born in Newport were **Penelope** and **Oliver**.

The Puritan leader Oliver Cromwell became Lord Protector of England in 1653 and held that position until 1658. Oliver Arnold was born in 1656, while Cromwell reigned. But there appears to be another good reason Benedict and Damaris chose this name.

With my American accent, when I pronounce the name **Oliver**, it sounds like it starts with an O. But with a British accent, especially 350 years ago, [and especially coming from someone in the Arnold clan, with their with a broad West-Country accent], it might be pronounced "**Holiver**." [Put on your best British accent and you'll see it sounds quite natural.]

Here's a quote from an 1856 short story that plays with the letter H.

"What was Holiver Cromwell but a brewer of good stout, and suckled on 'Untingdon ale? And did he not afterward cut off King Charles' 'ead, when he had pulled him by the ears out of the royal hoak where he was a hiding the Magna Charta from the people."

(The author has added an "H" to Oliver, oak, and Carta;
plus he has deleted an "H" from Huntingdon and head.)

(*The Old House of Dark brothers, Little's Living Age*, Boston 1856)

Holiver and Oliver have both been common last names in Kent, England for generations. Kent is on the coast opposite France so it's most likely the French "H" got dropped. It's much like the name Arnold itself, which comes from "Arnault," or another version, "Harnault," which also descended from French ancestry. ("Arnault" means "eagle power.")

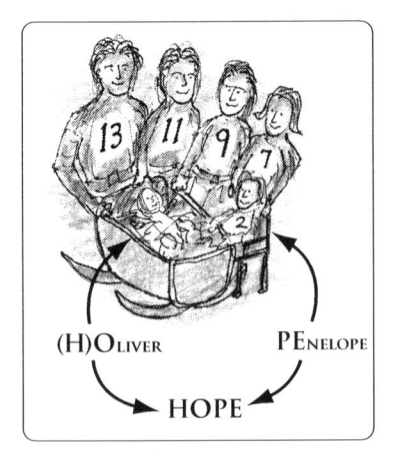

Picture the scene in Benedict Arnold's household in 1655. Four children (ages 13, 11, 9, and 7) are fawning over newborn Oliver and two-year-old Penelope.

Combine the beginning sounds of the two babies' names and you've got the word HOPE.

A (willi**A**m)
Benedict
Caleb
Damaris
E (p**E**n**E**lop**E**)
Freelove (1661)
Godsgift (1658)
H (oliver)
Josiah

Benedict and Damaris were playing another game with the names of their children. If the baby William Arnold (who died) is considered "A" and Penelope (which contains three E's) is considered "E" and (H)oliver is considered "H," the names start with all the letters of the alphabet from A through G.

[Support for this idea comes from the fact that he gave the **last** two children born names starting with G and F, the two letters that would have been "missing" in the sequence.]

This "name game" might not seem like solid evidence, but in light of Benedict's enthusiasm for the "Anchor of Hope," it's additional circumstantial evidence.

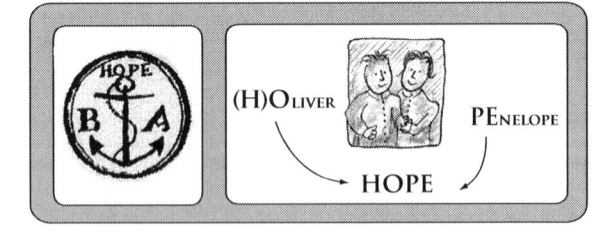

With this Oliver/Holiver riddle, Benedict is playing around with the letter H. John Dee also enjoyed riddling with a letter H. The Hieroglyphica (in *Monas Hieroglyphica*) starts with an H. But the Ieroglyphic (in "Ieroglyphikon Brytanikon," on the Title page of *General and Rare Memorials*) starts with the letter I. Dee also plays with the Greek letter I (Iota) and the letter Γ (Gamma) to make an H. And Dee used H is used to spell the exact same word Benedict was secretly spelling, HOPE.

Also, in a poem in that same book, Dee writes the word Jerusalem as Hierusalem. (In Dee's time the letter I and the letter J were the same letter. So the H is not essential, and each of spellings, Ierusalem or Hierusalem, were commonly used.)

As a further clue: in Dee's "Latin letter/number code," H is the eighth letter. And Dee loved the octave.

Clue 7: the date of Benedict's will

Benedict's Last Will was written on December 24, 1677.
(This was two days after Benedict's 62nd birthday).

The early Colonials didn't celebrate Christmas, but
12 and 24 are key numbers in John Dee's cosmology.

Month 12
Day 24

Clue 8: the five asterisks in Benedict's will

Governor Benedict Arnold's Will, December 24, 1677

In Benedict Arnold's entire 12-page Last Will and Testament, there are only 5 asterisks. They seem to encircle the words "my Stone-built Wind-Mill'n."

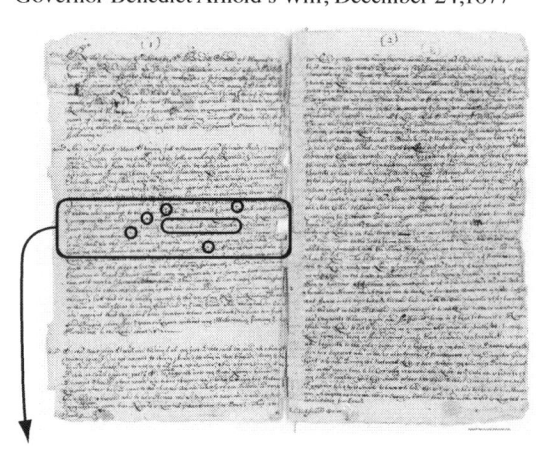

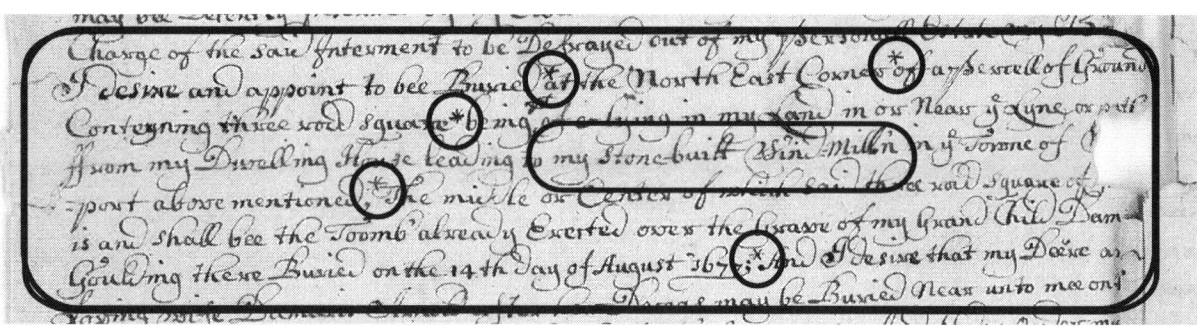

Nowadays, we use an asterisk as a *signe de renvoir* (French for a "sign of correspondence,") relating to a clarifying note in the margin. But this wasn't always the case. As M.B. Parkes explains in *Pause and Effect: An Introduction to Punctuation in the West:*

* is a *notea* [a symbol] originally used to mark omissions in the text, subsequently used as a *signe de renvoi* with more general application.

Around 650 AD, Isidore of Seville wrote about the
asterisk in his encyclopedic work *Etymologies*:

* a little star is put where things have been omitted, to indicate that something is lacking. In the Greek language, ASTER means star, from which ASTERISK is derived.

As Benedict has no corresponding asterisks in the margin. He's seems to be implying something is left out. And, as he drew 5 asterisks, that something must be important.

[Like the fact that the Tower was a not really a windmill, but something else.]

Benedict's clue functions on a deeper level. Even a kindergartner can see an asterisk looks like a star. And Benedict, who comprehended language well enough to speak Algonquin, definitely knew the basics of Greek. He no doubt knew the word "asterisk" came from the common Greek word *aster* or star.

Since ancient times, there were seven "asteres planetai" or "wandering stars," Sun, Moon, Mercury, Venus, Mars, Jupiter, and Saturn. (*Planetes* means "to wander.") But if Benedict was making some kind of **asterisk = star** joke, why didn't he use 7 asterisks instead of 5?

Remember the main theme of the Monas, the Union of Opposites, the Sun and the Moon. They are the the two tangent circles in Dee's "Thus the World Was Created" Chart. And they are was "two-tangent-circles" plan for the Tower.

Benedict saw his words "Stone-built Windmill" as the Tower, the Sun and the Moon. (Remember also it has solar and lunar alignments in its windows.)

If the words "Stone-built Windmill" are seen as the Sun and the Moon, the five asterisks are Mercury, Venus, Mars, Jupiter, and Saturn.

5 *asteres planetai* (wandering stars) + Sun and Moon = 7 planets

How can I be sure Benedict saw the Tower as two tangent circles, the Sun and Moon? Well, the first two geometric shapes he draws in his personal symbol (on his Charter Chair) are two circles. [They must be drawn before the center of the third circle can be located.]

And the size all those circles is 2 1/8 inches in diameter, the size of the solar disc inside the Tower! Benedict knew all about Dee's Tower and how it functioned as a horologium. He knew about the *Monas Hieroglyphica* and even understood Dee's mathematical cosmology. And here, in his final Will, he left a cryptic clue confirming he knew it all:

Clue 9: the date of Benedict's codicil to his will

In March of 1678, three months after writing his will, and even though he was housebound with illness, Benedict was re-elected as Governor.

On June 10, 1678, Benedict decided to add a codicil (an amendment) to his Will, clarifying to whom he had certain deeded properties. He must have been quite ill, as he died nine days later, on June 19, 1678. This might have been the last time he signed his name, but the clever Benedict was still sharp enough to hide one final clue about the origin of the Tower.

Recall that Sir Humphrey Gilbert was deeded his letters patent to discover North America on **June 11, 1578**.

And he finally departed with his five ships destined for the "John Dee River and port," on **June 11, 1583**.

These dates are exactly 5 years apart, and each is exactly on the **summer solstice**.

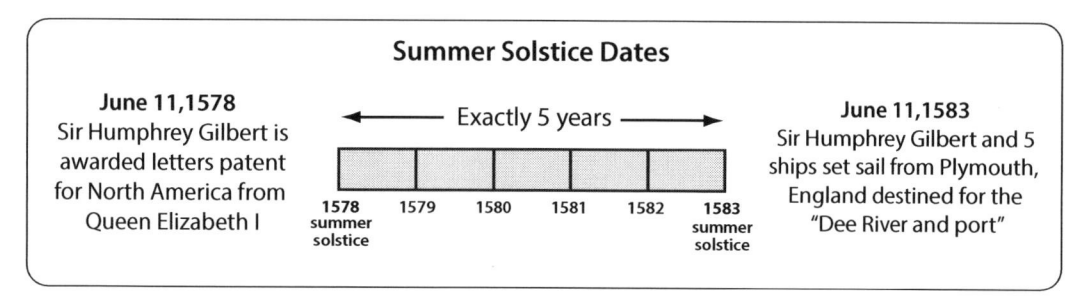

Summer Solstice Dates

June 11, 1578
Sir Humphrey Gilbert is awarded letters patent for North America from Queen Elizabeth I

← Exactly 5 years →

1578 summer solstice | 1579 | 1580 | 1581 | 1582 | 1583 summer solstice

June 11, 1583
Sir Humphrey Gilbert and 5 ships set sail from Plymouth, England destined for the "Dee River and port"

Here's the fascinating thing.
Exactly **one century** after the day Sir Humphrey Gilbert obtained his letters patent (**June 11, 1578**), Benedict Arnold signed the codicil to his will (**June 10, 1678**).

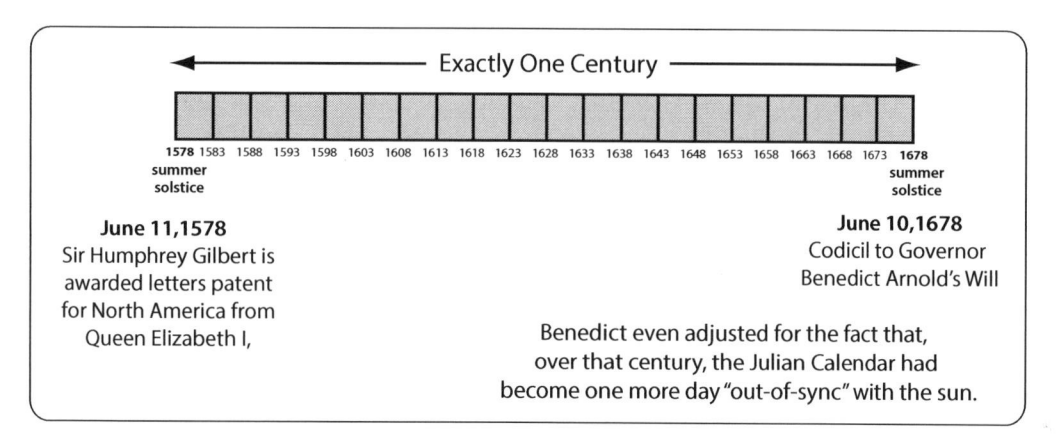

← Exactly One Century →

1578 summer solstice | 1583 | 1588 | 1593 | 1598 | 1603 | 1608 | 1613 | 1618 | 1623 | 1628 | 1633 | 1638 | 1643 | 1648 | 1653 | 1658 | 1663 | 1668 | 1673 | 1678 summer solstice

June 11, 1578
Sir Humphrey Gilbert is awarded letters patent for North America from Queen Elizabeth I,

June 10, 1678
Codicil to Governor Benedict Arnold's Will

Benedict even adjusted for the fact that, over that century, the Julian Calendar had become one more day "out-of-sync" with the sun.

It might appear as though Benedict was "off" by a day (June 10 as opposed to June 11). However, the Julian Calendar was still "drifting out-of-sync from the sun" by 1 day every 128 years. As 100 years had passed, the solstice would have occurred **June 10, 1678**, rather than **June 11, 1678**. Benedict seems to be telling us he was aware of this 1-day shift (as well as the "centennial" of Gilbert's letters patent).

To me this is all too coincidental to have happened by chance. It might seem strange to the modern mind to intentionally select the date of the solstice or the equinox for an important event. Likewise, it's hard for us to imagine that the 1583 Elizabethans would have built a huge time-keeping Tower celebrating celestial events instead of building shelters to live in.

But it doesn't matter if all this sounds strange to our modern day sensibilities. To understand what motivated Renaissance men, we must think like Renaissance men.

It should be added that when Benedict died on June 19, 1678, over 1000 people attended his funeral. It was probably the largest funeral ever held in Rhode Island up to that time. And yet Governor Benedict Arnold still gets ignored in most books about the colonial history of Rhode Island (because of his ancestor's actions).

GOVERNOR BENEDICT ARNOLD

Here's a brief summary of some of the clues Benedict left for us:

His insistence that Aquidneck be named "Rode Island."
His Anchor of Hope seal as first Governor.
His personal mark on the Charter Chair.
The word "Hope" in the names (H)oliver and Penelope.
His "east-west" line that starts at the Tower.
The agreement to purchase Jamestown Island, signed on the equinox.
His 12/24 Will, with 5 asterisks, and the "solstice-centennial" Codicil.

Benedict seemed intent on hiding cryptic clues about the origin of the Tower and its connection to John Dee and the Elizabethan colonization effort. Benedict saw himself as a pioneer in this second phase of making this New World Utopia a reality. He was well aware that was helping to build this "lively experiment" honoring freedom of thought, whose foundations were established in the written works of earlier Englishmen like Sir Thomas More, John Dee, and Richard Hakluyt.

Benedict wanted the future inhabitants of this land to remember how the very first seeds of the nascent British Empire were sown: by the boldness of Sir Humphrey Gilbert, the faith of Sir George Peckham, the hard work of Anthony Brigham and his stonemasons, the political-astuteness of Sir Frances Walsingham, the adventurous spirit of Queen Elizabeth, and most of all, the global-thinking of John Dee.

Why should we be concerned with history from the 1500's and 1600's?

First, the mathematical, optical, and astronomical principles that Dee built into the Tower will help teach our TV-Internet culture to be more attuned to Natural things.

Secondly, The "Anchor" is the "Hope" that "Rhode Island" has to become a World Heritage Site. In other words, "Dee's Monas Tower" is an opportunity for Narragansett Bay, in fact for all of New England, to be recognized by the world as the site of a Renaissance building, the birth of the British Empire.

(Whether you consider England's global expansion a good thing or a bad thing, the fact is, it has led to English being the second most spoken language on earth, after Chinese).

Thirdly, there is a well-known maxim among historians that "the past informs the future." Understanding where we came from and help us determine where humanity should be headed in the days to come.

And finally, as William Faulkner puts it, "the past isn't dead, it isn't even past." Visit Touro Park at sunrise on the Winter Solstice and see for yourself – the past is still alive!

(What I Call) The Riddle of the Royal Ring in John Dee's The Limits of the British Empire

As a one-man band trying to drum up imperial enthusiasm for what he calls the "British Empire," John Dee wrote 2 sets of books, each consisting of 4 volumes or documents.

What I call the "Riddle of the Royal Ring" is hidden in *Britanici Imperii Limites* (or *The Limits of the British Empire*). Dee's work is a compilation of 4 documents assembled under his supervision in 1593, intended to be placed in the Crown's Archives for posterity. It was only discovered in 1976, and now resides in the British Library.

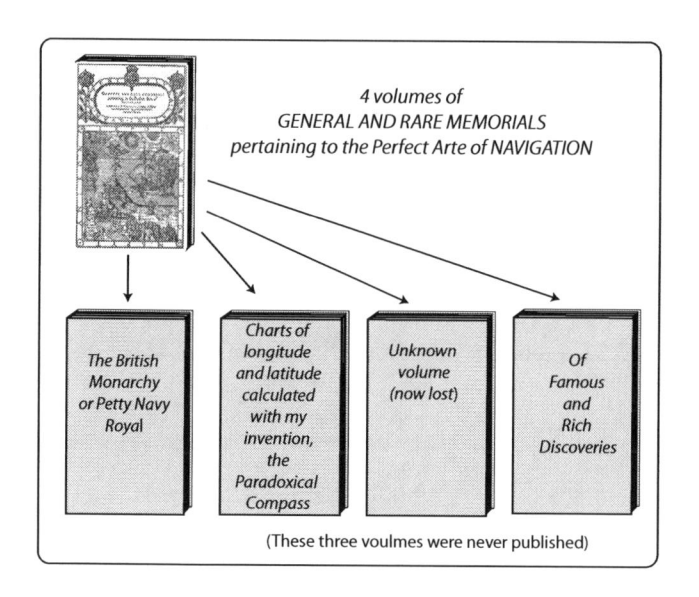

4 volumes of GENERAL AND RARE MEMORIALS pertaining to the Perfect Arte of NAVIGATION
- The British Monarchy or Petty Navy Royal
- Charts of longitude and latitude calculated with my invention, the Paradoxical Compass
- Unknown volume (now lost)
- Of Famous and Rich Discoveries

(These three voulmes were never published)

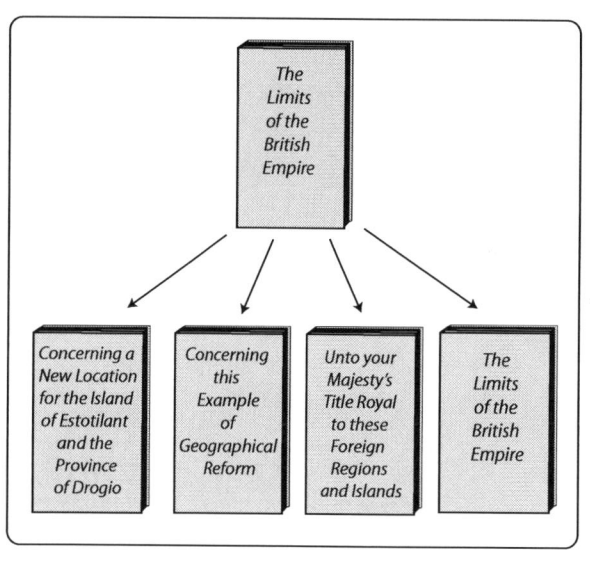

The Limits of the British Empire
- Concerning a New Location for the Island of Estotilant and the Province of Drogio
- Concerning this Example of Geographical Reform
- Unto your Majesty's Title Royal to these Foreign Regions and Islands
- The Limits of the British Empire

In the introduction to his comprehensive study of Dee's work entitled, *John Dee, The Limits of the British Empire*, Ken Macmillan points to numerous clues that suggest these 4 documents were originally written for the Queen Elizabeth I around 1577 or 1578. (MacMillan, Ken, with Jennifer Abeles, *John Dee, The Limits of the British Empire*, pp. 4-5)

During these years, London was abuzz with interest in the New World. Martin Frobisher had returned from his first voyage to what is now Baffin Island, Canada. Sir Humphrey Gilbert was applying for his letters patent to colonize all of North America north of Florida.

The second manuscript in Dee's 4 volume set was entitled *Concerning this Example of Geographical Reform*. Dee's term *"Geographical Reform"* refers to eight new refinements he has made to existing world maps. He is quick to offer his apologies to his cartographer friends Gerard Mercator and Abraham Ortelius, but "it is the burning love for the majesty of truth which inflames and impels me."

For example, Abrham Ortelius had estimated the difference between London to Baffin Island to be at about 30 degrees longitude. But after the recent voyage of Martin Frobisher, Dee had first-hand knowledge that it was closer to 50 degrees longitude.

At the beginning of the document, Dee refers to the "rare and novel features shown in our Diagram." Unfortunately, the "Diagram" which apparently accompanied his text has not survived. But Dee paints a detailed picture of it with his words.

Concerning Cambalu and Quinsay

However, what I said above – that both cities Cambalu and Quinsay, were situated on almost the same parallel as Venice – may be readily understood if we understand that the single little black circle shown on the left-hand side of your majesty's throne represents Cambalu, the capital of Cathay. But, by wonderful chance (as I hope) the City of Heaven (that is, of course, Quinsay) happens to be located at the middle joint of the index finger which encircles the hilt of your sword.

And there are other things, very noteworthy, which as if by Divine will, adorn the surroundings of your imperial seas.

For under your crown (the most glorious in the whole world), almost in the middle of it, is concealed an island, once known as Chryse, but now commonly called Japan (but incredibly, spoken of by the great M: Paulus Venetus as Zipangu), the object of easily the first voyages of this century, undertaken on the initiative of the princes of Castile.

Thirdly, at the right side of your majesty the coast of Atlantis is pleased to be found, almost opposite Quinsay.

But about the feet of your supreme highness lies the Strait of Arianus, which your British subjects, voyaging in the northern seas both to the east and the west, were the first to visit, and to sail through, to the honor of yourself and to the benefit of the commonweal.

And if these things are true which we have so far heard tell, those four places which I have named their own geographical symmetry.

But concerning these things, and others relating to them (which are known hitherto to have lain hidden under the shadow of your wings) many wonderful, surprising, secret, and very delightful facts will, if it pleases our august and blessed Empress, with God's will, be revealed within the next seven years.

[from John Dee, *Document II: Concerning this Example of Geographical Reform*, folios 8 and 9; from Ken MacMillan, with Jennifer Abeles, *John Dee, The Limits of the British Empire*, p. 41]

It's pretty clear that the
missing illustration was a map.

Ken MacMillan suggests
it was probably similar
to the map Dee later drew for
Sir Humphrey Gilbert in 1582.

This circumpolar projection
depicts the northern hemisphere,
from the North Pole down to
the Tropic of Cancer.

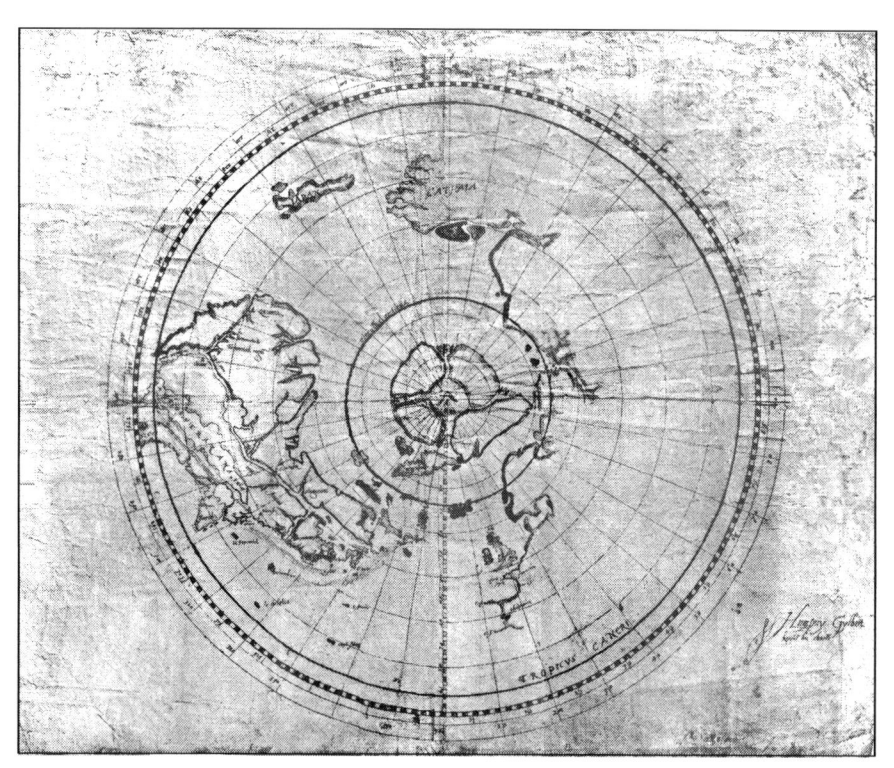

John Dee's 1582 Circumpolar Map of the Northern Hemisphere
(prepared for Sir Humphrey Gilbert)

But Dee's "diagram" was more than simply a map. It was a way for him
to graphically express his vision of a far-reaching British Empire.
Nowadays, most maps (like maps in atlases, road maps, and even Google Maps)
are technically accurate representations of land areas.
They aren't intended express moral or political beliefs.
But things were different in Dee's time.

As Mary E. Hazard writes in *Elizabethan Silent Language*:

***"Most known medieval and early Renaissance maps were designed, not to convey technical
geographical information, but rather for other kinds of didactic purposes."***

[Didacic means "intended to teach, particularly having a moral instruction as an ulterior motive."]

Hazard states that *"scientific accuracy"* was not *"the main motive in mapping."*

(Mary E. Hazard, *Elizabethan Silent Language*, p. 67)

Hazard even quotes from John Dee's chapter on Geography in his *Preface to Euclid*, summarizing,

***"As Dee suggests, aesthetics, nostalgia, sensationalism, and other motives
besides geographical accuracy generated interest in maps, and among
these, metaphorical expression was historically foremost."***

Dee cites two large cities in **Cathaia** (China): **Cambalu** (Beijing) and **Quinsay** (Hangzhou).
He calls Cambalu " the royal seat," and indeed, the name comes from the word
Khanbaliq, meaning "Great residence of the Khan."

Based on his readings of the Arab historian Ismael Abu al Fida (1273-1331)
and Marco Polo (1254-1324), Dee says these two cities in China lie on the
same parallel as Venice, Italy **(which is at 45 degrees north latitude)**.

235

Dee describes 4 places which have (what he calls) "**geographical symmetry**." In the middle of them, he has apparently drawn a picture of a Queen Elizabeth I, on her throne, holding a sword.

Here is a summary of the four places Dee describes:
1. Cambalu (Beijing) and Quinsay (Hangchou) in Cathay (China)
2. Chryse (Japan)
3. Atlantis (Dee's term for North America)
4. Strait of Arianus (the sea route to China)

As a picture is worth a thousand words,
I have attempted to recreate the image which Dee has described in words.
(In other words, this is my illustration of the Queen, and the place names Dee mentions, superimposed upon Dee's 1582 map).

It seems a bit unusual that Dee would put Queen Elizabeth in the middle of the North Pacific. She is way on the other side of the North Pole from her realm in England.

Why is Cambalu a "little black circle"?

And why is Quinsay the "middle joint" of the Queen's "index finger"?

[These smell like Dee-clues to me.]

236

One of the short-term goals for Dee's "sales pitch" to the Queen was to help his associate Sir Humphrey Gilbert obtain his "letters patent" for all of North America (north of Florida.) Indeed, Gilbert was successful on June 11, 1578.

And for all his help in the imperial negotiations, as well as for his cartographic and navigational advice, John Dee was granted all lands north of the 50 degree latitude by Sir Humphrey Gil-

This grant wasn't actually made until September 10, 1580, but it had probably been under negotiation between Gilbert and Dee for some time.

It's clear from John Dee's remarks about the **courageous Captain ...S.H.G.**" in Dee's 1570 *Preface to Euclid* that he and Gilbert had been working towards the same ends since the late 1560's.
(Dee, *Preface*, p. A.j, or 43, Egan, Book 2, *The Works of John Dee*, page 191)

Suddenly, the Queen doesn't seem so far from home. Now, right by her side, she has her courageous courtier, Sir Humphrey Gilbert, and her perspicacious philosopher, John Dee!

[Perspicacious is a good word to describe Dee. It means perceptive, astute, and wise.]

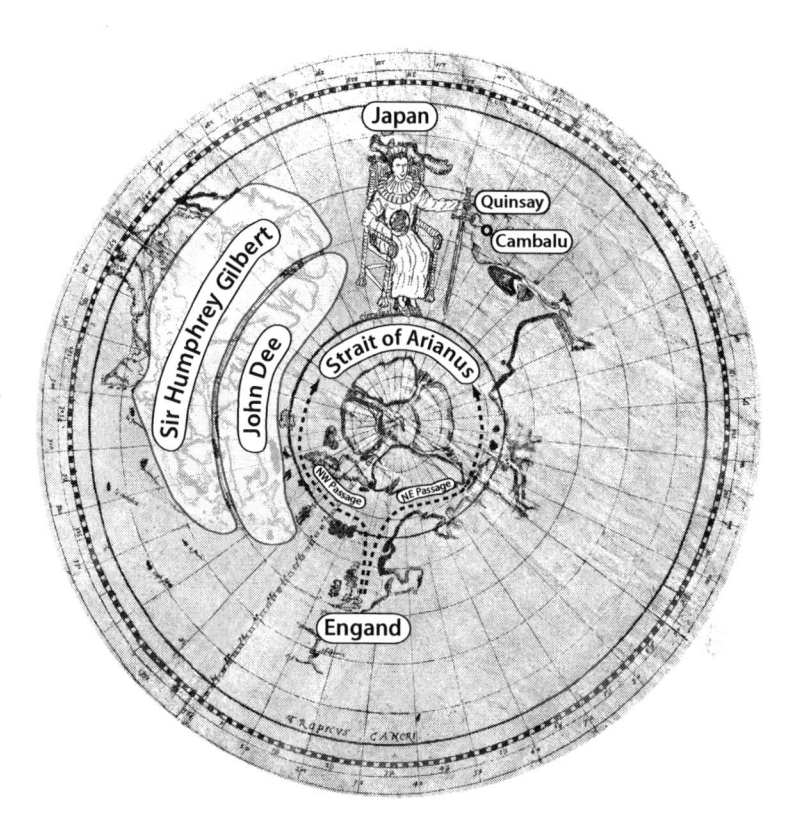

Dee was a visionary.
Here are a few things he envisioned way back in the mid 1500's:

1. British Empire extending around the World
2. British Colonization of North America
3. Global trade between the Orient and the West
4. Trade through the Northeast and Northwest Passages

Now let's look back on Dee's ideas from today's perspective:

1. Indeed, the British Empire grew to be the largest Empire the world has ever seen. By 1922, the British Empire held sway over on quarter of the world's population and covered one quarter of the Earth's total land area. It was so global, the expression arose: " The sun never sets on the British Empire."
2. The British ruled the East coast of America. (At least up until the American Revolution...and for a brief period in the 1960's during the British Invasion of Animals, Hermits, Beatles and Stones.)
3. Nowadays, China is the world's leading exporter. (For example, over 40% of consumer goods in the US now come from China.)
4. OK...maybe Dee was a bit too optimistic about these two sea passages. Centuries after Dee's time, they were both finally found to exist, but they have never become major trade routes.

Besides being a visionary, Dee knew the power of ***visual symbols***.
He knew illustrations and maps have the power express things
that can't be easily described in words.

(For example, Dee's simple Monas symbol encapsulates a number of his ideas about astronomy,
geometry, proportion, optics and even theology. Dee's Title-page illustration for *General and
Rare Memorials*, with Elizabeth at the helm of the ship of state, is chock-full of visual symbols.)

Similarly, Dee's map of Queen Elizabeth ruling the seaways of the Northern
Hemisphere tells a geographical story that is politcaly quite powerful.

Like Dee himself, his symbolism had a serious side,
but it also had a light-hearted, playful side. Dee had fun
with his toys: his symbols, his geometry, his numbers.

His imperial patroness, Elizabeth, had a serious side,
but fortunately, Bess loved clever riddles as well.

Dee loved putting things right in front of your eyes,
while still making them invisible... unless you took
the time and energy to reflect on his puzzle.

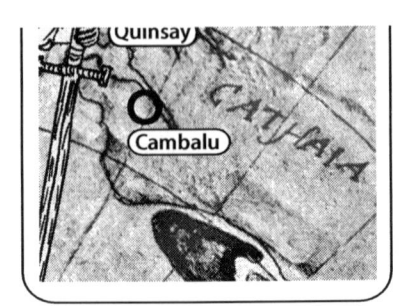

Queen Bess played the
lute and wrote poetry

Let's take a look closer at some of his clues:
It seemed curious that Dee had labeled China's royal city, Cambalu (or Beijing), with a "**little black circle,**" instead of something simpler, like large dot or an asterisk. And he associates Quinsay (Hangzhou) with the "**middle joint**" of the Queen's index finger.
Dee seems to be hinting that the "**little black circle**" is a **ring** that should go on the Queen's index finger.

The Elizabethans loved rings, and circular things.

Elizabethans would have picked up on Dee's ring metaphor right away. They were crazy about rings.
As Mary E. Hazard writes in *Elizabethan Silent Language*:
"More than any other widely used jeweled artifact, rings were valued for their talismanic and symbolic functions. Men and women both wore rings in profusion, sometimes several on one finger, sometimes between the first and second knuckle, or on the thumb, sometimes tied by ribbons around one's neck, elbow, or waist. Rings figure often in the complications of literary plots and in historical legend, and they are the subject of much speculative comment."

Hazard adds they had a *"fascination with the shape of a circle. Circular form was a comfort to Elizabethans, physical and metaphysical."*

Queen Elizabeth 1
at her Coronation
(attributed to
Robert Peake
the Elder)

Today, things like clothes, jewelry, artwork, and architecture can have a certain amount of symbolic meaning. But in Elizabethan times, these material objects were **super-symbolic**.

As Mary E. Hazard writes in *Elizabethan Silent Language*: ***"In all sizes of three-dimensional objects–from the smallest, whether coin or finger ring, the the largest, a great prodigy house– the shape and substance of Elizabethan artifacts work as units of nonverbal or extraverbal communication, grounding communication with the gravity of the things of this world."***

(Mary E. Hazard, *Elizabethan Silent Language,* p.112, pp. 59-61, and p. 139)

I noticed that Dee made a third cryptic reference to the idea of a "ring" in the place name "**Strait of Arianus**." The more commonly-used term for this body of water is the "**Strait of Anian**." The name probably derives from the Chinese province of *Ania*, which Marco Polo mentions in the 1559 edition of his book of travels.

On maps made by Giacomo Gastaldi (1562) and Bolognino Zalteri (1567), this "Strait of Anian" separates Asia and North America. But European cartographers started using the term to describe the whole open sea passage they thought connected Northern Europe with Northern China.

Dee implies that his "Strait of Arianus" includes **both** the Northeast and Northwest Passages, suggesting that explorers (like Stephen Borough and Martin Frobisher) had already entered it and even "sailed through" parts of it.

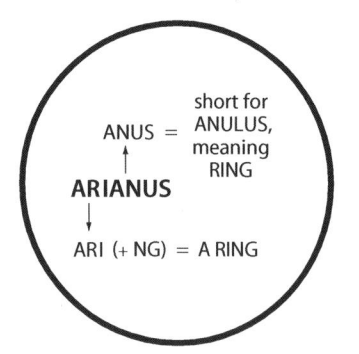

By concocting the term "Arianus," (instead of using the customary term "Anian,") I think Dee is making a word-riddle.

The Latin word *anus* (which is contained in "Arianus") is a shortened version of the word *anulus*, meaning "ring."

Furthermore, the beginning of Dee's term "Ari," sounds a lot like the beginning of the English expression, " A ring."

Dee plays the same "**anus = ring**" word-game in the *Monas Hieroglyphica*.

In his "Thus the World Was Created" chart, Dee hides the word *Anus* by associating the first part of the word *An-imae* with the last part of the word *Spirit-us*.

[As explained earlier, this is a hidden reference to the tale of the Ring of Gyges and the discussion of Glaucon's "two rings" in Plato's *Republic*.]

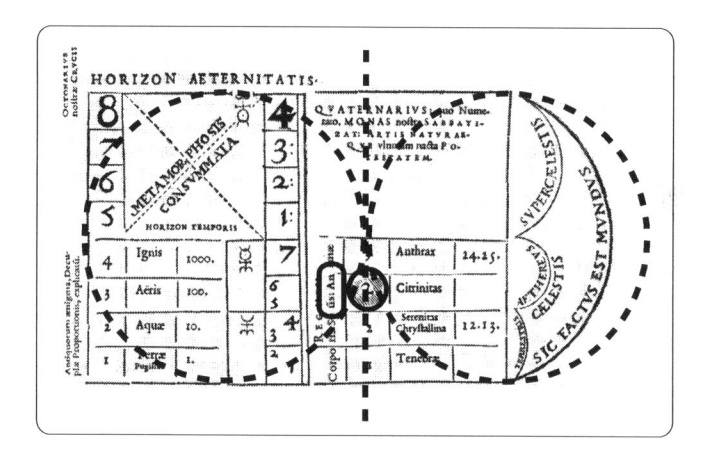

In Greek, the prefix *ari* strengthens the word with which it is combined. It comes from the same root as *aretê*, meaning excellence. If the creatve Dee was combining a Greek prefix and a Latin suffix, Arianus might mean "excellent ring," which corresponds with the importance Dee placed on this "ring" of water.

He seems to be describing the "strait" as the **whole ring of water** that goes around the ice cap of the North Pole, that is, the Northeast Passage, the Northwest Passage, **and** the North Pacific seaway to China and Japan.

239

Dee also explains that the four places he refers to have
"**their own geographical symmetry**."
It's pretty apparent that this "symmetry" is a square,
or in this case, a square rotated to be a **diamond**.

But there's another ring that Dee wants the reader to consider.
Twice in this document, Dee emphasizes that Cambalu and
Quinsay are "**situated on almost the same parallel as Venice**."
European cartographers knew Venice was on the 45° latitude line.

This 45° latitude line is important because it divides
the whole Northern Hemisphere in two parts:
From the equator (0°) to the 45° line.
And from the 45° line to the North Pole (90°).

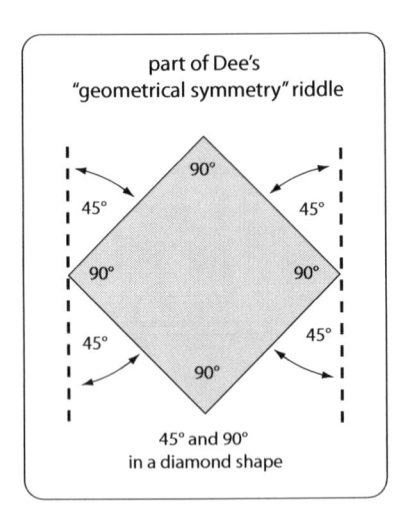

part of Dee's
"geometrical symmetry" riddle

45° and 90°
in a diamond shape

Let's return to the "geometric
symmetry" of the diamond-shape.

Its edges are each 45° from vertical
and there are four internal 90° angles.

In a circumpolar view of a globe,
45° and 90° are important as well.

Only here, the 45° is depicted as a circular
shape and the 90° is depicted as a point.

(Using number to show a connection between a "square"
and a "circle" would have been right up Dee's alley.)

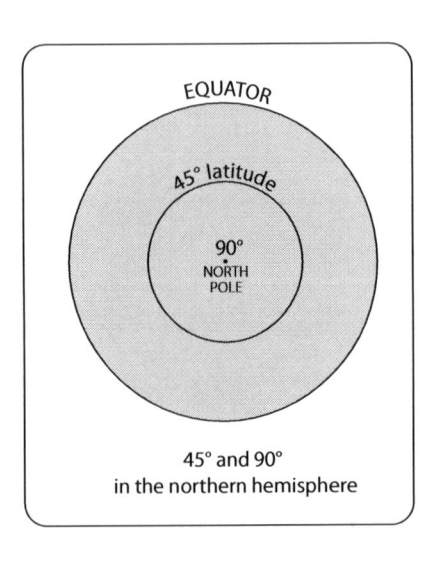

45° and 90°
in the northern hemisphere

Now, put the diamond shape and the circular band
together and what have you got?

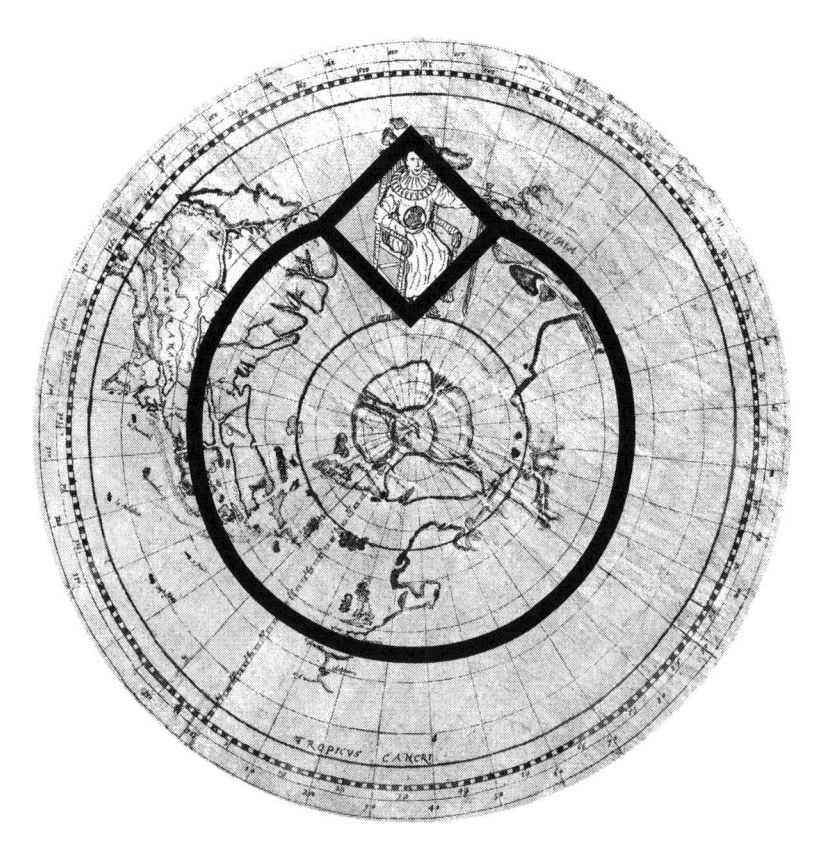

A Diamond Ring!

What a fitting symbol to depict Elizabeth's "imperial seas"
and the riches she will obtain from international trade!

Dee is hinting about this big, cryptic, "ring-shape" with his references to smaller "rings,"
like Quinsay (or Hangzhou) being located at the "**middle joint**" of the Queen's index finger
and China's royal city, Cambalu (Beijing) being depicted as a "**little black circle**."

One of the main themes of Dee's cosmology is **two rings**,
like the Sun and Moon, or the two Rings of Glaucon in Plato's
Republic, which Dee cryptically refers to in the *Monas Hieroglyphica*.

Thinking globally, the the Tropic of Cancer's "matching" ring to is the Tropic of Capricorn.
Though this map only shows a view of the Northern Hemisphere, cosmopolite Dee would
have been well aware that the two "Tropic" rings tell the story of the Earth/Sun dance.

Today, most brides get diamonds for wedding rings, but in Elizabethan times
only the Queen and her rich courtiers could afford diamonds. In portraits of
Queen Elizabeth I, she is usually depicted festooned with diamonds
either on her crown, brooch, collar, or necklace.

After explaining the "geographical symmetry" of the "four places," Dee begins his concluding sentence this way: "But concerning these things and others relating to them…"

Dee is certainly emphasizing the importance of England's discovery of the Northeast and Northwest Passages, but the "other" main thing he was pushing for was for England to get a foothold in the New World. He is encouraging Elizabeth to "make a steadfast watch post," as he puts it on the Title page of *General and Rare Memorials*.

This "watch post," (he later specifies) is one of the most well-protected natural bays on the east coast of America:

It's the one Verrazano called Refugio.

It's the one Dee named the Dee River and port.

It's Narragansett Bay in present-day Rhode Island.

As we've seen. the Anchor brooch Elizabeth gave Sir Humphrey Gilbert just before his 1583 expedition sparkled with diamonds.

Here again is my conception of what this brooch might have looked like, based on a description given by Maurice Browne (one of the sea captains on Gilbert's expedition).

A large diamond is prominent on the Queen's bosom, which is close to her heart.

And the 29 diamonds certainly made this sacred Anchor of Hope twinkle in the light!

(Letter written by Maurice Browne to John Thynne, penned between April 25 and May 3, 1583, in David Beers Quinn and Neal Cheshire, *The New Founde Land of Stephen Parmenius*, U. of Toronto Press, 1972, p. 204-5)

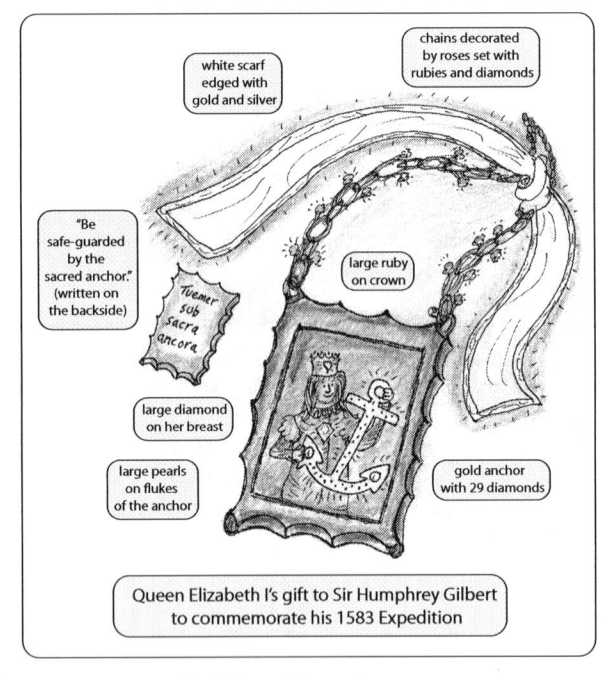

Dee's circumpolar map only has a few dozen place-names on it. It's telling that among them is Claudia, the triangular island at the entrance to the John Dee River and port.

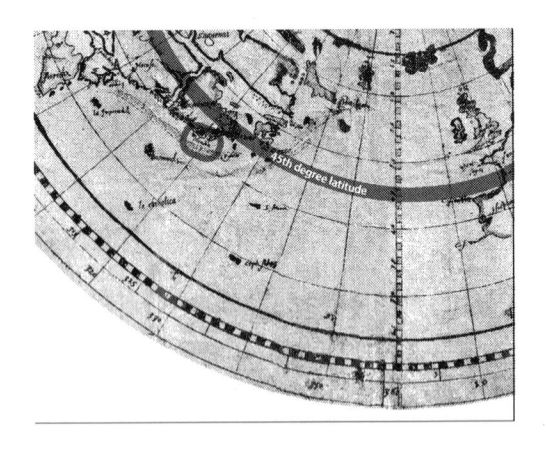

In actuality, the tiny island of Claudia (Block Island) is only about 15 square miles.

And Dee's map covers about 80 million square miles. Realistically, the island should only be a speck, instead of a discernable triangle. But in Dee's mind, Claudia was that important key that unlocked the door to the Dee River.

Dee's "45-degree-latitude diamond-ring" comes pretty close to Claudia. But doesn't quite touch it. Dee was well aware that Claudia was located at "about 42 degrees" latitude.

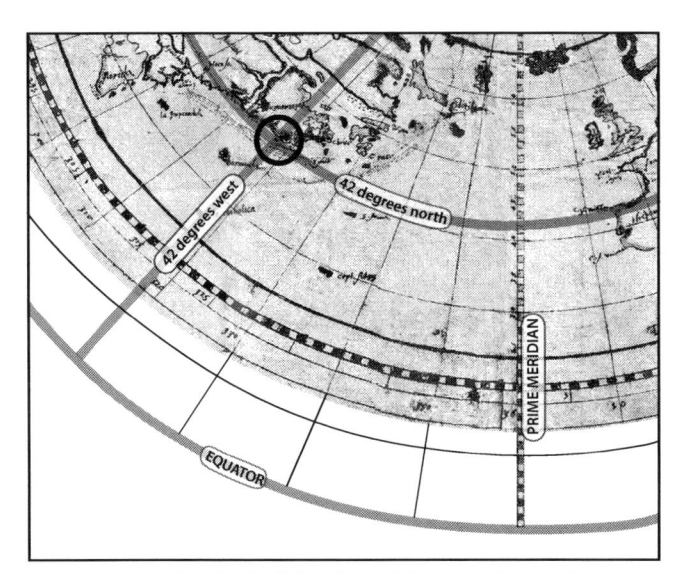

On Dee's map, the island of Claudia and the "Dee River and port" are located at 42 degrees north latitude and 42 dagrees west longitude.

Besides the "geometrical symmetry" of the "four places," Dee wants us to see the same "geometrical symmetry" in the location of the Claudia as well! Not only is Claudia
**42° latitude
north of the Equator,**
it is also
**42° longitude
west of the Prime Meridian!**

(In Dee's day, the Prime Meridian went through the island of Santa Maria in the Azores. More on this in a moment.)

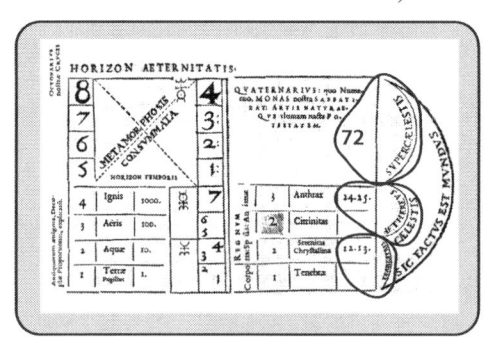

In the Title page illustration of *General and Rare Memorials*, Dee placed archangel Michael above the "steadfast watch post."

We've seen how Dee associates 72 with the "Super-Celestial" realm in his "Thus the World Was Created" chart.

Dee was quite familiar the Hebrew *Shemhamphorasch*, or 72 names of God, or the 72 Angel-names.

In this famous list of the Angels, **Michael is number 42.**

Right in front of our eyes, Dee is pinpointing the **exact location of the Dee River** (its 42° latitude as well as its 42° longitude).

The names of the 72 angels in the Shemhamphorasch

Fire Trine		Water Trine		Air Trine		Earth Trine	
1.	VHV : Vehuiah	19.	LVV : Levoiah	37.	ANI : Aniel	55.	MBH : Mabehiah
2.	ILI : Yeliel	20.	PHL : Paheliah	38.	ChAaM : Chaumiah	56.	PVI : Poïel
3.	SIT : Sitael	21.	NLK : Nelakel	39.	RHAa : Rehauel	57.	NMM : Nememiah
4.	AaLM : Aulemiah	22.	III : Yiaiel	40.	IIZ : Yeizel	58.	IIL : Yeilel
5.	MHSh : Mahasiah	23.	MLH : Melahel	41.	HHH : Harayel	59.	HRCh : Harachel
6.	LLH : Lelahel	24.	ChV : Chahuiah	42.	MIK : Mikael	60.	MTzR : Metzerel
7.	AKA : Akaiah	25.	NThH : Nethahiah	43.	VVL : Veualiah	61.	VMB : Umabel
8.	KHTh : Kahathel	26.	HAA : Haaiah	44.	YLH : Yelahiah	62.	IHH : Yehahel
9.	HZI : Heziel	27.	IRTh : Yerathel	45.	SAL : Saeliah	63.	AaNV : Aunuel
10.	ALD : Eladiah	28.	ShAH : Sheahiah	46.	AaRI : Auriel	64.	MChI : Mechiel
11.	LAV : Laviah	29.	RII : Riyiel	47.	AaShL : Aushaliah	65.	DMB : Damebiah
12.	HHAa : Hahauah	30.	AVM : Aumel	48.	MIH : Miahel	66.	MNQ : Menaqel
13.	IZL : Yezalel	31.	LKB : Lekabel	49.	VHV : Vehuel	67.	AIAa : Aiauel
14.	MBH : Mebahel	32.	VShR : Vesheriah	50.	DNI : Daniel	68.	ChBV : Chebuiah
15.	HRI : Hariel	33.	IchV : Yechoiah	51.	HChSh : Hachashiah	69.	RAH : Raahel
16.	HQM : Haqemiah	34.	LHCh : Lehachiah	52.	AaMM : Aumemiah	70.	IBM : Yebemiah
17.	LAV : Leviah	35.	KVQ : Keveqiah	53.	NNA : Nanael	71.	HII : Haïaiel
18.	KLI : Keliel	36.	MND : Menadel	54.	NITh : Neithel	72.	MVM : Moumiah

"... all that river or port called by Master John Dee, Dee River, which River, by the description of Giovanni Verrazzano, a Florentine, lies in the Northerly latitudes about **42 degrees**..."

(Agreement between Sir Humphrey Gilbert and Sir George Peckham, February 28, 1583)

...to make a steadfast watch-post

Send forth a sailing expedition...

243

Dee also drew an extremely detailed map of North America in 1580. Here I have drawn a dashed line to show what I call the "Claudia square."

(This perspective makes Claudia and the Dee River seem pretty close to England.)

Dee seems to be using the same Prime Meridian that his cartographer friends Gerard Mercator and Abraham Ortelius used: the north-south line passing through the islands of Sao Miguel and Santa Maria in the Azores.

But Dee tells us he has placed the east coast of America further west than his friends placed it on their world maps.

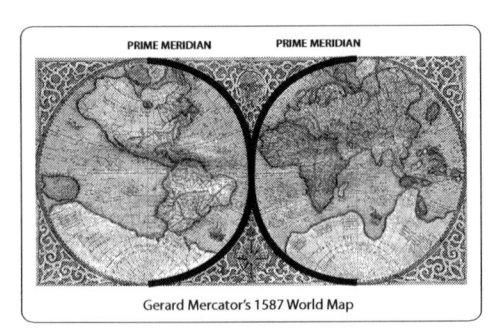

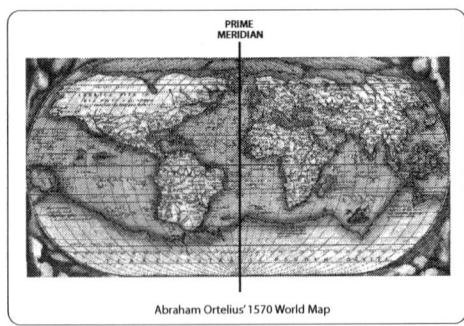

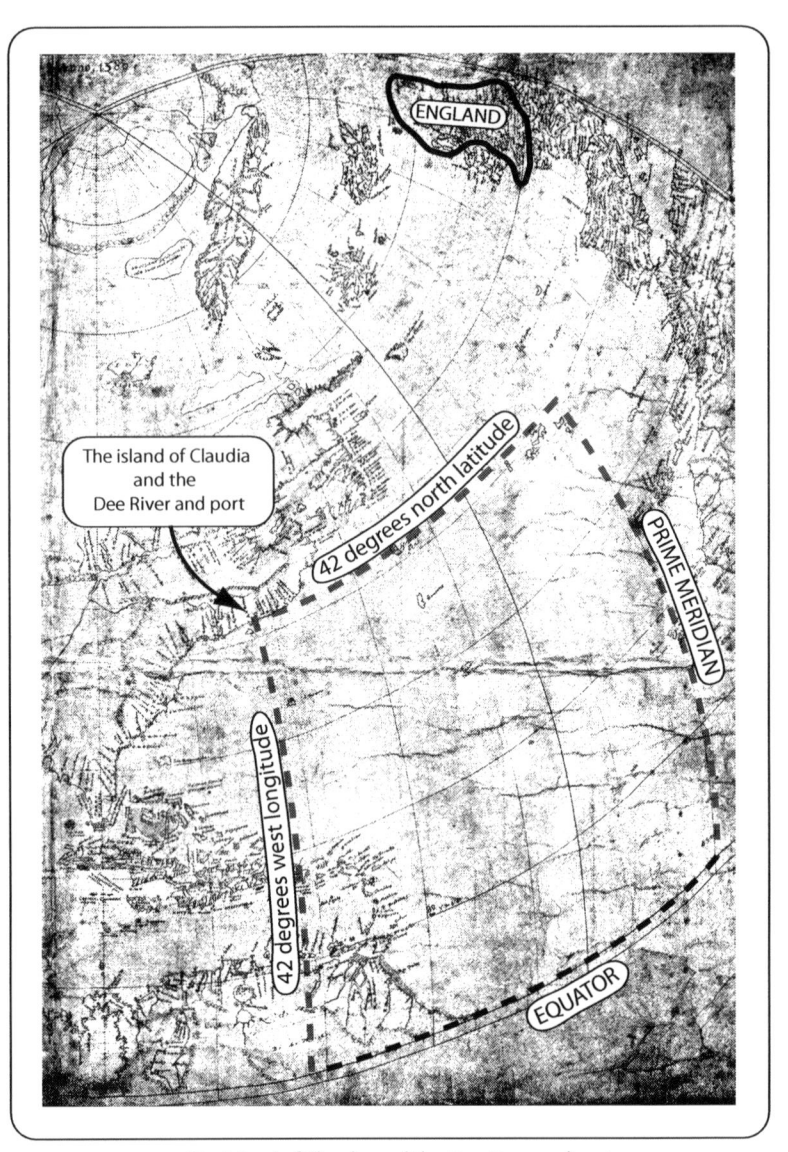

Gerard Mercator's 1587 World Map

Abraham Ortelius' 1570 World Map

The island of Claudia and the Dee River and port is located at 42 degrees north latitude as well as 42 degrees west longitude (as seen on part of Dee's 1580 map of North America)

Because Dee was estimating the longitude, he had a little flexibility in making things work out so well. (Still, it turns out that Dee was pretty close; Block Island is actually 44 degrees longitude west of the Azores.)

This "Diagram" of Elizabeth ruling the "imperial seas" provides a new perspective on the Newport Tower, which I claim Dee designed.

In one respect, the Atlantic Ocean is wide, and it's a long way from England to the island of Claudia and the Dee River. But in another respect, when seen in comparison to the distance from England to Japan, China, or to the West Coast of America, Claudia and the Dee River are not really very far from England at all. As Dee thought globally, he would have probably considered the trip to settle the Dee River as the relatively simple, first, baby-step for the infant British Empire.

Dee selected what is now Narragansett Bay to be the first Elizabethan colony in the New World. He named the bay after himself: the Dee River and port.

He designed the first building to be a symbol as well. Not just a symbol of his mathematical cosmology, but as a city-center, a welcoming beacon, a focal point for the English colonization of the East Coast of America. (The whole settlement process just took a lot longer than he had anticipated.)

We've seen that the 42° latitude of Claudia is close to the 45° latitude of Venice, Beijing, and Hangzhou. But there's another connection.

If we take (what I call) "the Claudia Square" of Dee's circumpolar projection, and flatten it out, it becomes a square. Though different in size and orientation, this square is essentially the same shape in which Dee has placed the Queen.

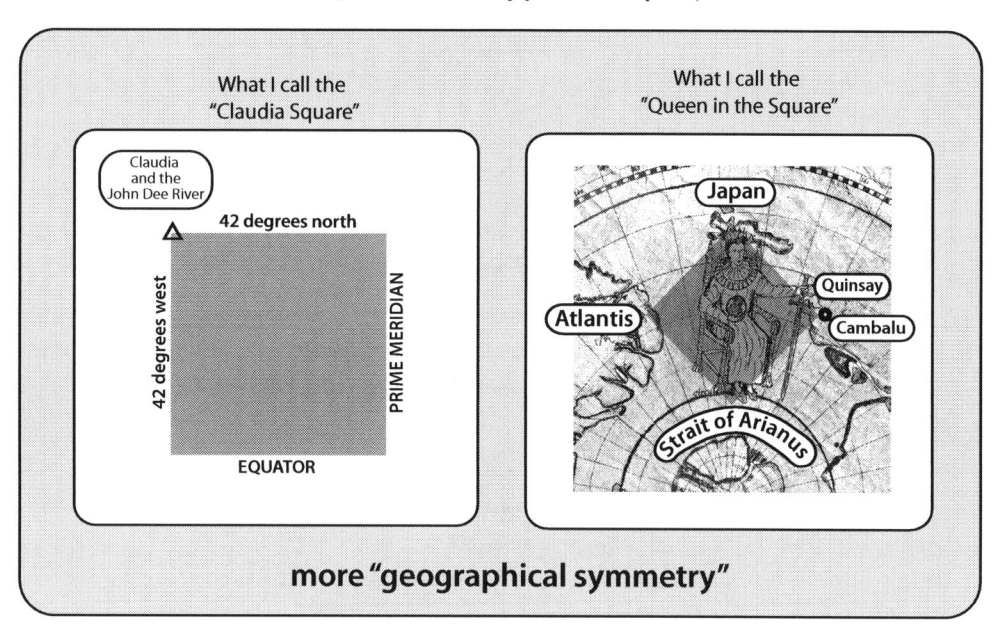

(A diamond is simply a rotated square.)

What I call the "Claudia Square"

Claudia and the John Dee River
42 degrees north
42 degrees west
PRIME MERIDIAN
EQUATOR

What I call the "Queen in the Square"

Japan
Atlantis
Quinsay
Cambalu
Strait of Arianus

more "geographical symmetry"

I'll admit that my analysis of a map that doesn't even exist (only described) might seem a little bit imaginative. If I was analyzing anyone other than the clever John Dee, such an analysis would indeed sound overreaching. But Dee was a geometric humorist. Having a brain hardwired with an understanding of geometry, his humorous riddle-games naturally involve navigational geometry, geometric shapes, and number.

The idea of drawing a circumpolar projection of the earth is a challenging geometric puzzle in itself (Dee seems to have been the first Englishman to do it). It's obvious that the distance between longitude lines varies greatly (they are very close together in the region around the North Pole), but the distances between the latitude lines are the same all over the map.

Dee certainly made some geometric riddles to keep his presentation to the Queen lighthearted. (We might hear the amused Queen, "Oh, dear John, aren't you clever.") But in a serious vein, Dee also wanted to portray the Queen's legal right to most the Northern Hemisphere seem "geometrically ordained" by nature.

Dee was a geometric spin doctor. And his spinning worked. Somehow he managed to wheedle (for free) most of Canada and Alaska.

What I call Dee's "Claudia Square" relates to another main
theme of Dee's mathematical cosmology, as espoused
in his *Propaedeumata Aphoristica* (1558 and 1568)
and his *Monas Hieroglyphica* (1564).

It has to do with the relationhip between
"four-ness and "three-ness." Or as Dee puts it:

"Quaternarius In Ternario Conquiescens."
or
"The Quaternary Rests in the Ternary."

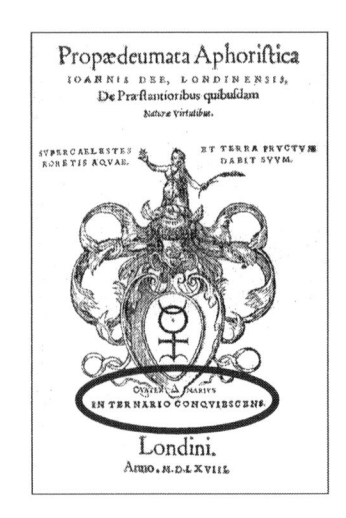

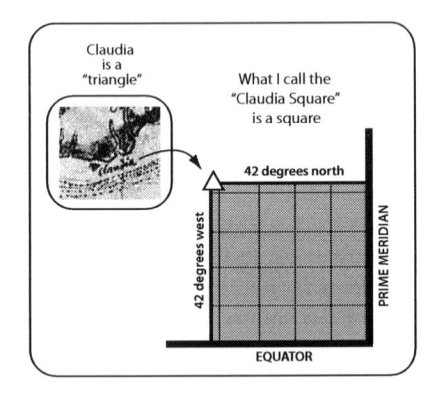

Here, the "Quaternary" (the "Claudia square") is
created by that **single reference point**, which
has a "Ternary" shape (the triangular island of Claudia).

Because the horizontal axis of the square (the Equator)
and the vertical axis of the square (the Prime Meridian)
are the basis or grid of the whole map, **only one point**
(Claudia) is needed to define the whole "Claudia Square."

And as we have seen, Dee uses the equilateral triangle (Δ) as a personal
symbol of his name: Dee (the Greek Delta or the Latin letter D).

And, this "Delta-shaped" island **points** towards the mouth of the Dee River.
One can almost hear Bess giggling with delight at the cleverness
of Dee's well-woven grand plan for the nascent British Empire.

In his book *Geometrical Landscapes, The Voyages of Discovery and the Transformation of Mathematical Practice*, Amir Alexander explains that the great Elizabethan geometers were also the great Elizabethan geographers.

Alexander writes extensively on the views John Dee and Thomas Harriot held about the British Empire. Thomas Harriot (1560-1621) was much younger than Dee (1528-1608), but Harriot actually visited the New World on Sir Walter Raleigh's mission to Roanoke Island in 1585-86. (Harriot visited with Dee in Mortlake and they were friends.)
In Chapter 3, entitled "Mathematical Empires," Alexander writes, ***"John Dee was known to his contemporaries as the foremost promoter of exploration and discovery in his time."***

Alexander summarizes, ***"English mathematicians, it is shown, were active and enthusiastic participants in the exploration enterprise. They not only lent their technical expertise to support the voyages, but also promoted and publicized them using the familiar narrative of geographical exploration. Most importantly, the mathematicians adopted this imagery and applied it to their own trade, describing themselves as daring voyagers on the uncharted mathematical oceans."*** (Alexander, Amir, *Geometrical Landscapes*, pp. 72-73 and p.3)

To these Elizabethan math-explorers, "geography and geometry" went hand-in-hand.
And the quick-witted Dee even integrated "geography and geometry" with the Queen's hand.

A Deeper Look at the Title of John Dee's Work:
The Limits of the British Empire

John Dee had a geometrical mind. He could speak extemporaneously on each on the 465 propositions of Euclid's *Elements*. He was perhaps England's best cartographer. He advised most of the great Elizabethan explorers on the geometry of navigation.

It's not unusual he would see **geography** through the eyes of the **geometer**.

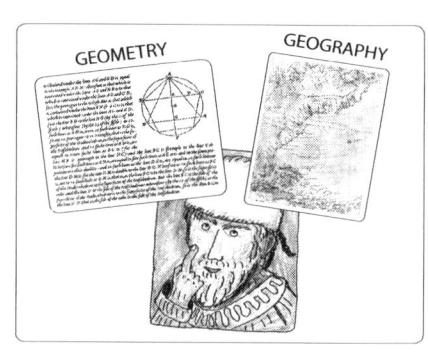

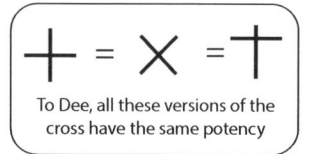

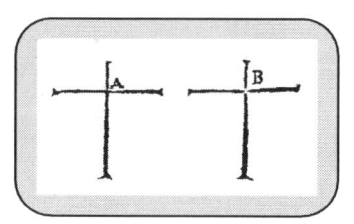

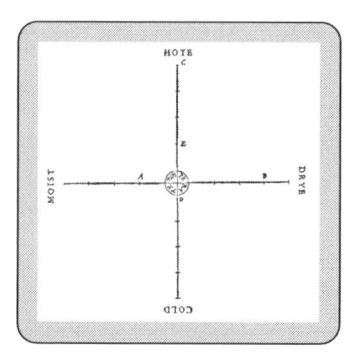

Beyond the "point, line, and circle," the 2-D geometric figure which fascinated Dee the most was the Cross. He writes extensively on the Cross in his *Monas* and it is one of the 4 parts of his Monas symbol.

Dee sees the equilateral cross and the saltire cross (tilted, to form an X) and his offset cross as having the same meaning or potency. All three versions symbolize the "Union of Opposites."

In Theorem 6, Dee visualizes the Cross several ways: as **3** things (two lines and a point), or as **4** things (four lines), or even as **7** (as 3+4=7), or as **8** (two crosses, X, X, or 4+4=8), or as **10** (Roman numeral X, which he even relates to the Pythagorean tetraktys, 1+2+3+4 = 10).

In his *Preface to Euclid*, Dee's "Art of Graduation" illustration is based on the shape of a Cross.

On another level, the Cross represented Christianity and Jesus– at the core of Dee's theology and the theology of most of Europe at the time (whether Protestant or Catholic).

So it should not be surprising to find a cryptic visual reference to a Cross in the text and illustrations in his presentation to the Queen. To find it, we must match wits with the clever Dee, who still speaks to us through his writings and illustrations.

247

Dee gave his work a powerful title:
Brytanici Imperii Limites
(The Limits of the British Empire)

British Empire

The very idea of a British Empire is a bold concept that seems to have sprouted from Dee's polymathic and patriotic mind. But to him, it was not a brand-new vision for Britain's future. It was a recouping or continuation of an ancient British Empire. In Dee's mind, the British Empire dated back to the days of King Arthur and Saint Brendan (around 550). It also extended through the times of Prince Madoc (around 1170) and John and Sebastian Cabot (around 1500).

By using the potent word "Empire," Dee might have been thinking of the Persian Empire or the Greek Empire. But its more likely he was thinking that the British Empire someday would become as great as the Roman Empire (or the Holy Roman Empire, which followed it).

However, Dee's "Empire" was a little different from all these earlier Empires, which were primarily "land empires." Dee's envisioned "British Empire" was more of a "maritime empire."

Limits

Let's focus on the remaining word of this powerful title, the word "Limits." It's a much deeper word than it might appear at first glance.

Obvious synonyms for "Limits" might be "boundary, bounds, outer edge, or perimeter." Nowadays, "limits" actually implies a "boundary that restricts or confines." But this is a modern meaning of "limits," so it's probably not what Dee had in mind.

Dee is not thinking in terms of a "restricting," a "confining" or a "contracting." In fact he's thinking just the opposite. He's thinking big. He's thinking of an expansive area. He's trying to get the Queen to think outside the box of her little island-realm. He's encouraging her to think globally.

"Ancient Bounds and Limits"

To Dee, "limits" was not simply a "boundary." In his *General and Rare Memorials,* several times he refers to Britain's "Ancient Bounds and Limits." It would be unlike the scholar Dee to be redundant. He wouldn't use two synonyms connected by the word "and." If they were synonyms, he would have picked just one of them. Thus, in Dee's mind "Bounds" and "Limits" seem to mean two different things.

"Sea Limits"

Dee provides more clues about what he means by "Limits." At least ten times throughout his text, he uses the more specific term "Sea Limits," suggesting a maritime empire.

To the Romans, "Limites" meant "in the shape of a cross"

Dee's Latin word *Limites* is the plural of the word *limes* (pronounced like "lie-mess.")

The Romans borrowed the word *limes* from the Greek word *lexris* meaning "in the shape of a cross."

Greek:	lexris	"in the shape of a cross"
Latin:	limes (singular) limites (plural)	"in the shape of a cross"

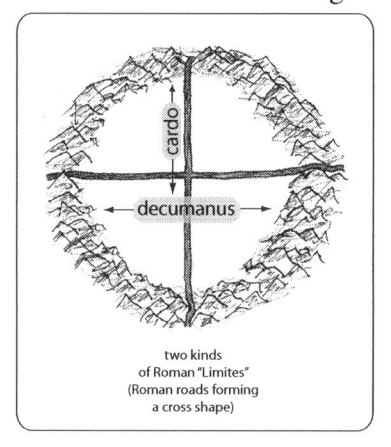

two kinds of Roman "Limites" (Roman roads forming a cross shape)

As the Roman Empire expanded into the hinterlands of Europe, paths or roads were built to allow for the swift transport of trade goods and armies.

Roman engineers would make two main *Limites* across a large field or region.

The path that ran north-south was called ***cardo** limes*.

The path that ran east–west was called ***decumanus** limes*.

The Romans quickly learned that too much chariot and cart traffic led to rutted paths (dusty when dry and full of puddles when rainy). Roman engineers soon became adept at building roads.

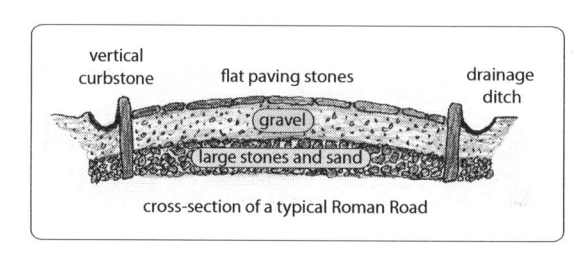

cross-section of a typical Roman Road

First, workers would dig out the roadway, fill it with a solid base of large stones, then add about a foot of gravel. They would finish the surface with artfully-fitted, flat paving-stones. Along the edges were vertical curbstones and drainage ditches

The Roman roads were so well-constructed, many can still be seen throughout Europe today.

tightly fitted paving stones of a Roman road

When "path *limites*" were upgraded to "Roman Road *limites*," they were called *Limites Maximi*.
The *cardo maximus* was the great north-south road through a region.
The *decamanus maximus* was the great east-west road.

(Peterson, JWM., *Computer aided Investigation of Ancient Cadastres*, thesis paper, University of East Anglia, England, January 1993, p.12)

As these roads were used as boundary lines for the distribution of lands, the word *limites* took on the meaning of "boundary." Modern historians extended the meaning of "limites" to mean "marked and fortified frontiers of the Roman Empire."

In the north of England, Hadrian's Wall is sometimes referred to as *Limes Britannicus*. The northern edge in Europe is called *Limes Germanicus*, and the eastern edge, bordering Arabia, is called the *Limes Arabicus*.

But I don't think either of the definitions,
"boundary line" or **"fortified frontier,"**
is precisely the meaning Dee had in mind for his word *"Limites."*

As Isidore of Seville writes in *Etymologies:*

"The two largest limites in the fields are the cardo and the decumanus.

The cardo is directed from the northern pole (cardo) of the sky:

without doubt the sky is turned in a northern cycle."

Etymologies is an etymological encyclopedia with excerpts from classical texts compiled by the Archbishop of Seville, Spain, around 600 AD. Dee had a copy of this important work in his library. (Roberts and Watson, book #1375)

In Latin, *cardo* means "a hinge" or "a point about which something turns," hence, "the North Pole."

(From cardo we get "cardinal" points of the compass and Catholic "cardinals," around whom church life "pivots.")

cardo
(the north-south Roman road, oriented to the North Pole)

decumanus
(the east-west Roman road, that makes an X with the cardo)

Isidore of Seville continues:

"The decumanus is across it, from the east to the west.

Because it makes the shape of an X, it is called decumanus.

A field twice divided makes the shape of the tenth number."

decumanus = decimal = 10 = X = +

In Latin, *decumanus* (pronounced "dek-eu-manus") or the more recognizable version of the word, *decimanus*, means "belonging to the tenth part," or "ten-fold." From *decumanus* we get the term "decimal," as in the Base 10 system used in mathematics.

In Theorem 8 of his *Monas Hieroglyphica*, Dee expounds upon this very idea:

"It is not without reason that the Oldest Latin Philosophers decided to signify the number TEN [DENARIUM] by the Rectilinear CROSS [CRUX] made from 4 Straight lines…"

(Dee, *Monas*, Theorem 8, page 13)

Roman numeral for ten = cross = X

In Theorem 16, Dee further divides the X (or 10) into two V's (or 5's), and also into two L's (or 50's.)

(Dee, *Monas*, pp. 15 verso and 16)

250

In short, Dee would have been well aware that *cardo limites* relate to the **North Pole** and *decumanus limites* derives from the form of an **X**, the Roman numeral for 10.

To navigator Dee,
cardo limites are essentially "longitude lines"
and *decumanus limites* are like "latitude lines."

So in a general sense, when Dee refers to Britain's "Ancient Bounds and Limits" or its "Sea Limits" he seems to be referring to what I call:
"the pathways through the seas to various destinations."

An even more specific meaning for the word "Limites"

But, wordsmith and geometer Dee seems to have had an **even more specific meaning** in mind for word that loaded term "*Limites*."

The first English translation of Euclid's *Elements* is credited to Henry Billingsley. But John Dee wrote the lengthy *Preface* and provided many detailed *Corollaries* and *Addendums* to Euclid's *Propositions*. Based on the content and style of writing, it's also apparent to me that Dee wrote the commentaries and clarifying remarks about Euclid's *Definitions*. In Definition 3 of the very first chapter of Book One, Dee uses the word "limites":

"The endes or limites of a line are points."

(In the original Greek, Euclid had written: **Grammês de perats sêmeia**. This sentence literally translates: "Lines drawn" + "opposite ends" + "mark or limit"

With this in mind, let's review the first two Theorems of Dee's *Monas Hieroglyphica*:

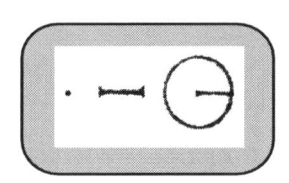

"The first representation of things in nature is made by means of a straight line and a circle.

But the circle cannot be made without the line and the line cannot be made without the point…"

(Dee, *Monas*, Theorems 1 and 2, my paraphrasing)

Strictly speaking, the "boundary or circumference of a circle" is the same thing as "the outer limits of all the radii of the circle."

But there is a shade of difference between the "**boundary**" and the "**limits**" (as in Dee's expression "Ancient Bounds and Limits").

Boundary means "the edge."

Limits means "the endpoints of the lines that lead to the edge."

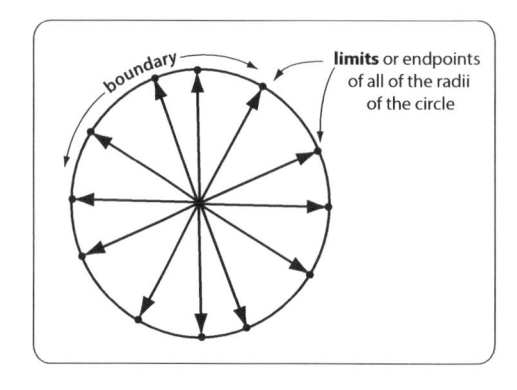

This may seem like splitting hairs. But think of the endpoints of the metal **spokes** of a bicycle wheel. They form a circle. Now think of the "metal rim of the wheel." The "**endpoints of the spokes**" and the "**metal rim**" both describe the same circle, but in slightly different ways.

Isidore of Seville also wrote:

"Transverse lines are called by an old word, limites, for the ancients called all crosswise things lima.

From this word the thresholds of doors, by which one goes in and out of are limina, and one goes into the fields through the limites."

So is Dee using the term "*Limites*" of the British Empire to indicate "transverse lines making a cross" **or** the "endpoints of those lines"?

He probably envisioned **both** these definitions combined, in the sense that **"Sea limits"** are **"Sea Routes to a particular destination."**

Let's explore how Dee might have envisioned "Sea Limits" on what he calls the "Diagram" or his map-illustration depicting the Queen on her throne the north part of the Pacific Ocean. Dee even informs the reader that he has included the words "*Imperij Brytanici Limites*" (*Limits of the British Empire*) on his map-illustration, as he begins Document 4 this way:

"For as much as one parte of the title prefixed to the litle charte (of geographij to be reformed) was Imperij Brytanici Limites, which phrase, without farder advertisement, given unto your Majesty, what is mente therby may seme either improperlie or to darkly annexed.

I thought it convenient therefore to add here **a fewe * lynes** sufficient both to give light to the meaning of that phrase and also to make somewhat manifest the veritie therof.

*(the above said phrase of **a fewe lines** of a few lines to be written hereof May seem undewly applied yf your Majesty considere the great booke ensuinge,...)

(MacMillan and Abeles, *The Limits of the British Empire*, p. 50; my bold)

Here is my modernization of these introductory sentences:

"Part of the title on the little chart given to your Majesty (of geography to be reformed), was Limits of the British Empire. But this phrase, without further explanation about its meaning, might seem too obscure or even improperly annexed.

So, I thought it helpful to add a **few * lines** to shed light on the meaning of that phrase and also to make its truth more evident.

* (the above phrase of **a few lines** which follow may seem insufficient if your Majesty considers the great book on this subject that is still a work-in-progress)."

Note that Dee used an asterisk to highlight the phrase "**a few * lines**" and he repeated the words " *... a few lines ..." in his footnote.

Dee seems to be punning with the word *Limites*, which his geometrical mind saw as the "**endpoints of lines.**"

252

If you think I am stretching for a connection here,
consider Dee's title to Document 3:

**"Unto your Majesties Tytle Royall
to these Forene Regions & Islands
do appertayne 4 poyntes"**

Here is my modernization of that title:
**"There are 4 points that pertain
to your Majesty's Royal Title to these
Foreign Regions and Islands."**

Dee actually lists 4 points:

1 The claim in particular
2 The reasons for the claim
3 The credit of the reason
4 The value of the credit by force of law

(MacMillan, with Abeles, *John Dee,
The Limits of the British Empire*, pp. 42-43)

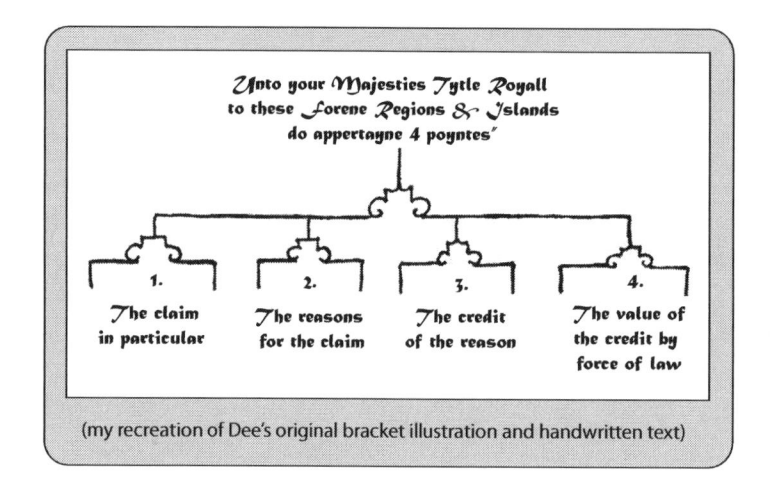

(my recreation of Dee's original bracket illustration and handwritten text)

And Dee even graphically displays the "4 poyntes"
with four brackets connecting to a single bracket.

I suggest that Dee is punning again. He is dropping a hint that the 4 "**discussion points**"
in his legal argument might also be seen as the 4 "**end-points**" of the lines of a cross.

In Document 2, when Dee describes where the image of the "Queen Elizabeth
on her throne" is situated on his map, he describes 4 different places:

**"And if those things are true which we have so far heard tell, those four
places which I have named have their own geographical symmetry."**

(MacMillan and Abeles, *John Dee, The Limits of the British Empire*, p. 41)

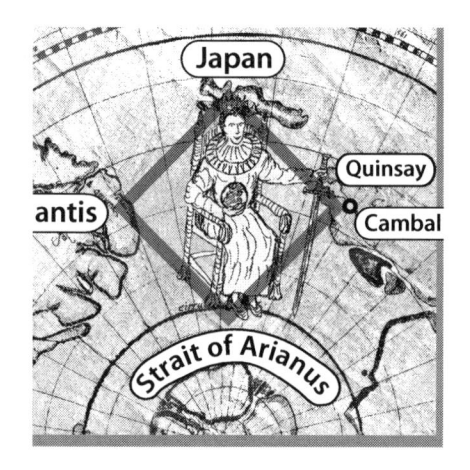

Dee's "**four places**" are:

1 Cambalu (Hangzhou) and Quinsay (Beijing) in Cathaia (China)
2 Chryse (Japan)
3 West Coast of Atlantis (America)
4 Straight of Arianus (the whole area between
    England and what is now the Bering Sea)

253

Where does Dee want us to see these *Limites* (or lines that form a cross)?

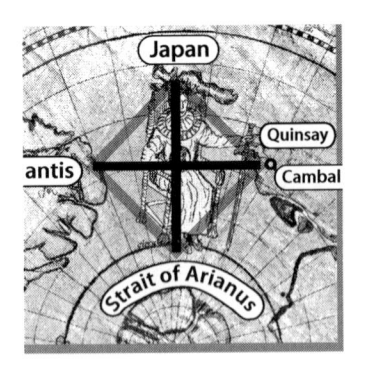

Putting together all these ideas,
"*Limites*" (lines in the form of a Cross),
"a few * lines" (pun),
"4 poyntes" (pun),
and "4 places,"
it's easy to imagine a large cross, superimposed
on the diamond-shaped image of the Queen.

Remember, the "diamond connecting the
four places," plus and the "45° latitude circle"
make what I call "The Riddle of the Royal Ring."

This idea has another, deeper level of meaning.
The X in the diamond-shape is or tenness or "*decum-*"
and the circular ring is *anulus*, or the short version, "*anus.*"

Together they make the word *decumanus*,
which is exactly what the ring is!
It's the *decumanus* (or latitude line) that runs through Venice.
(Dee is having too much fun.)

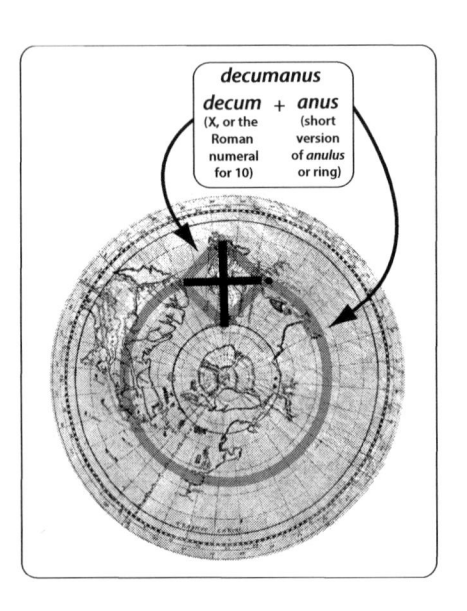

decumanus
decum + **anus**
(X, or the Roman numeral for 10) (short version of *anulus* or ring)

On a typical road map, the decumanus is a straight horizontal line.
But on a circumpolar projection, the decumanus is a circle.

As this is one of England's first polar projection maps,
Dee knew his fellow Elizabethans would have
to do some thinking to solve his rebus.
(in a rebus, words are represented by pictures)

In addition to the cross superimposed upon the Queen, Dee appears to be hiding another cross in different location on his map. Dee has divided the lands around the North Pole into four distinct parts by making a (somewhat disguised) "cross" of passageways between them.

Obviously, Dee had no idea what the region around the North Pole really looked like, so this was his own imaginative interpretation.
(Indeed, it's odd that the all the water in the immediate vicinity of the pole is not frozen.)

Close-up view of the "cross" of "pathways" in Dee's depiction of the lands surrounding the North Pole

254

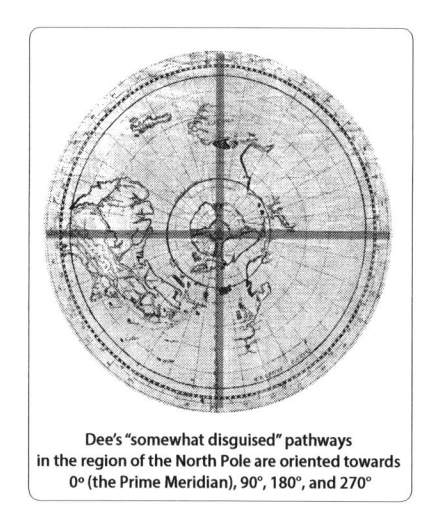

Dee's "somewhat disguised" pathways in the region of the North Pole are oriented towards 0° (the Prime Meridian), 90°, 180°, and 270°

Extending those lines outward, they seem to align with Dee's Prime Meridian (which goes through the Eastern Azores).

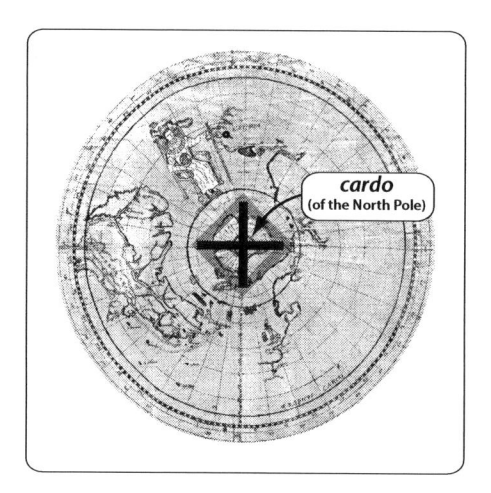

Remember, in Latin, *cardo* means "the point about which something turns," hence, "the North Pole."

So Dee seems to be hinting at **another** cross. This one is centered on the North Pole of his circumpolar projection.

cardo (of the North Pole)

I suggest that Dee did this to provide another cryptic hint about the "Cross" or "*Limites*." Remember Isidore of Seville's definitions:

"Transverse lines are called by an old word, *limites*, for the ancients called all cross-wise things *lima*."

"The two largest limites in the fields are the *cardo* and the *decumanus*.

"The cardo is directed from the northern pole (*cardo*) of the sky..."

"The *decumanus* is across it, from the east to the west."

Dee has made two interrelated puns about the two kinds of *Limites*.

First, he has made a visual pun out of "*decum-anus*" or the "Tenness-ring" or "X-ring."

Second, he has made a visual pun by making a cross of four waterways centered on the North Pole which is the "*cardo*."

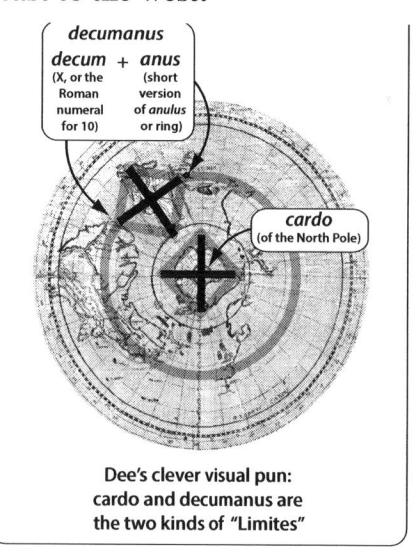

decumanus
decum (X, or the Roman numeral for 10) + *anus* (short version of *anulus* or ring)

cardo (of the North Pole)

Dee's clever visual pun: cardo and decumanus are the two kinds of "Limites"

Dee is having wordplay fun. Queen Bess would have loved it. But Dee is also discussing serious business about what he truly visualized as the "Limites" of the British Empire.

255

What are the actual "Sea Limits" Dee is hinting about? There seem to be 4 of them.

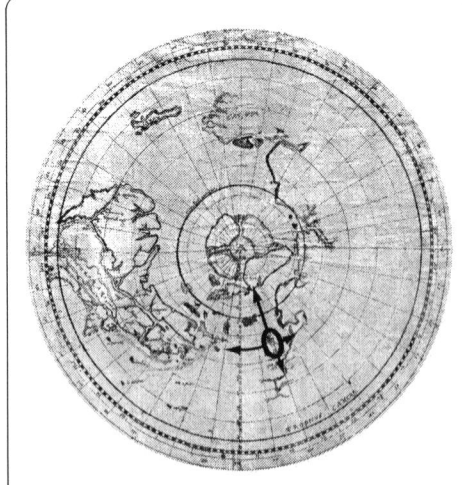

Does Dee want the reader to envision a *"cardo* and *decumanus* intersection" centered over England, where all British expeditions start from? Does he want us to look North, South, East, and West from London?

North: towards the North Pole.
South: to France
East: to Scandinavia
West: to lands across the Atlantic

This hardly seems him to be what Dee is getting at by the word "***Limites***" in the sense of
"Sea Limits to a particular destination."

Some of these Limits are vague and others aren't particularly distant. Remember, Dee has been encouraging the Queen to think globally.

North, East, South, and West lines emanating from England
(this doesn't quite seem like what Dee means by the "Limites" of the British Empire)

But I think the "Sea Limits" or "Sea Paths to a destination" that Dee is hinting about are much simpler to see.
I see Dee's whole map as a "child's maze" with
4 "Sea Limits" or 4 "Main Sea Routes" (like Dee's "4 poyntes").

Two of them are obvious:
the **Northeast Passage** and
the **Northwest Passage**.

As for the third "Sea Limit," even a kindergartener can see, Dee has made a **"waterway maze"** extending all the way across **North America**.

(Dee has placed the city of Quivera near the West Coast of North America. This was the important trading center the Spanish explorer Coronado unsuccessfully sought to find during his 1540-42 journey north from Mexico.)

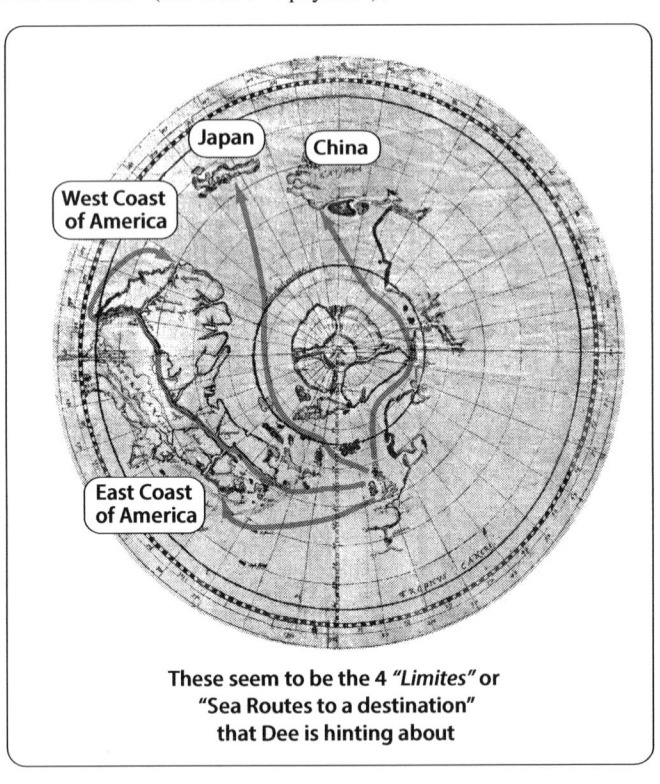

These seem to be the 4 *"Limites"* or *"Sea Routes to a destination"* that Dee is hinting about

256

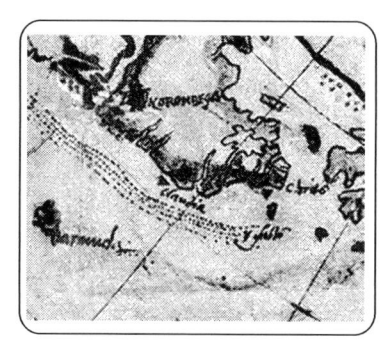

Dee illustrates and labels Claudia on his 1580 map of the Northern Hemisphere

This leaves one obvious place for the fourth Sea Limit: **the East Coast of North America.**

And the one place Dee was most enthusiastic about was Verrazzano's "Refugio," which Dee renamed the "**Dee River.**"

On the Title page, Dee implores the Queen to "Send forth a sailing expedition...to build a steadfast watch post" to this site, which he had selected.

Claudia is the **only** island on the coast from Newfoundland to Florida that Dee depicts and labels on his map.

[That's about 1800 miles, and tiny Block Island is only about 15 miles tall by 4 miles wide.]

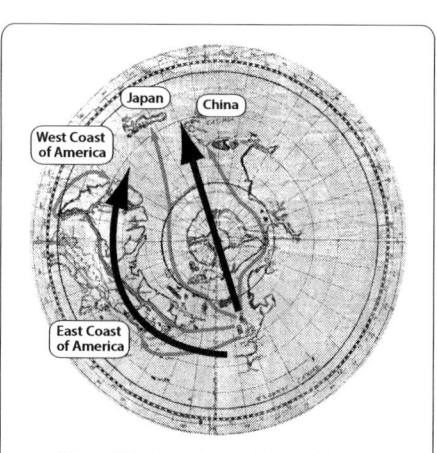

To summarize, Dee's four "Sea Limits" limits seem to be:

1 Northeast Passage (to China)
2 Northwest Passage (to Japan)
3 West Coast of North America
   (via an inland waterway to Quivera)
4 East Coast of North America
   (specifically, Claudia and the Dee River and port)

Two *"Limites"* roughly follow *cardo* (north-south) Sea routes and two roughly follow *decumanus* (east-west) Sea routes (approximately the 45° latitude line of Venice, Italy that Dee refers to)

While these 4 Sea "*Limites*" (or lines with endpoints) don't exactly form a Cross, two are basically running north-south, (roughly following longitude lines) and two are basically running east-west (roughly following latitude lines).

Both of Dee's east-west "Sea Limits" (Claudia and Quivera) are quite near that important 45 latitude line, the band of the "Royal Ring," which goes through Hangzhou, Beijing, and Venice.
(And is 3° degrees from the 42° degree Dee River and port).

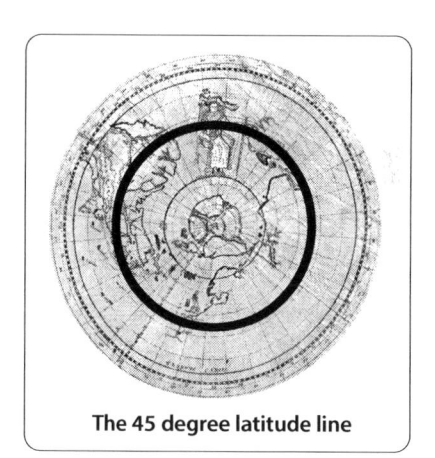

To conclude, it's probably more appropriate to see Dee's title, "**Limits of the British Empire,**" as "**Sea Paths to special destinations of the new British Empire.**"

Dee felt that travel to and from these special places would bring great wealth to the Queen and her island realm."

The 45 degree latitude line

To an ordinary Elizabethan in 1577, Dee's grand vision of British Empire might have seemed wildly outrageous. But it's interesting that the British Empire actually **did** grow to four similar "Limits":

1 The 13 British Colonies on the East Coast of America (at least until 1776)
2 All of Canada, (including British Columbia, which is on the West Coast of America)
3 Well, not Japan, but New Zealand and Australia
4 And not China, but least Hong Kong (from 1842 to 1977), and most of India (from 1856 to 1947)

To summarize this busy chapter:

Historically, the word *Limites* means "in the form of a cross," 2 lines connecting **4 points.**
On his map-illustration, Dee lists "**4 places**" surrounding Queen Elizabeth. He emphasizes
"**4 poyntes**" or 4 rationales for the Queen's "Royal Title" to various "Foreign Regions"
Dee seems to be emphasizing 4 "**Sea Limits**" or 4 "**endpoints**"
at important destinations in Dee's vision of the Empire.

There are **4 works** in Dee's *The Limits of the British Empire*.
And there are **4 works** in Dee's *General and Rare Memorials*
That makes an octave of books.

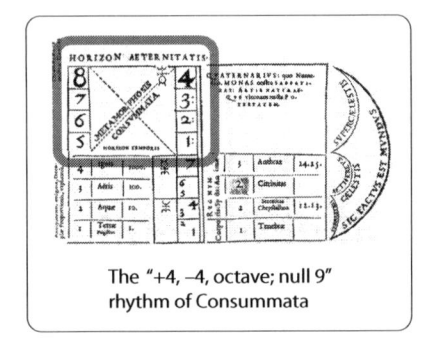

Dee loved the octave. He loved its nature as two quaternaries. He saw
the octave of the **number realm** in what he calls CONSUMMATA.
(in the *Monas Hieroglyphica;* Or what Bucky calls the "+4, −4, octave; null 9" rhythm of number.)

Dee expresses this by his octave in his final chart.
(In the largest typeface on the chart, he writes 1, 2, 3, 4,
then 5, 6, 7, 8, surmounted by 9, the Horizon number.)

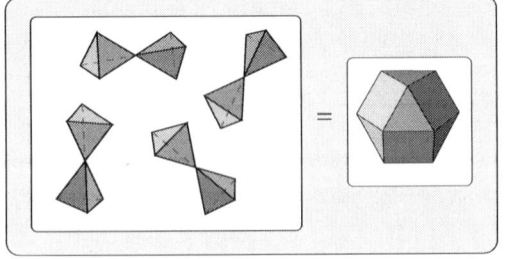

The "+4, −4, octave; null 9" rhythm of Consummata

Dee saw the octave in **geometry**, in the four pairs of
tetrahedra that combine to make a cuboctahedron.
(Or what Bucky calls a vector equilibrium).

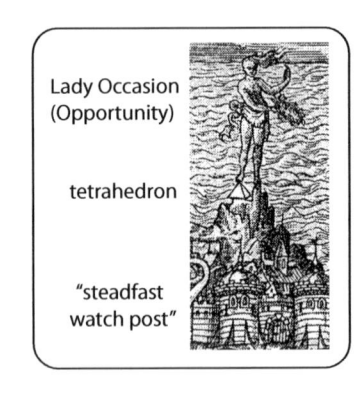

4 pairs of tip-to-tip tetrahedra assemble into a cuboctahedron

If you think its a stretch it to suddenly involve a 3-D polygon in this
discussion of the geography of the British Empire, look closely below
the foot of Lady Occassion (Lady Opportunity) who stands proudly above
the "steadfast watch post" on Dee's Title page. She is resting her foot on
a **tetrahedron**, nature's most basic shape, which connects "4 poyntes."

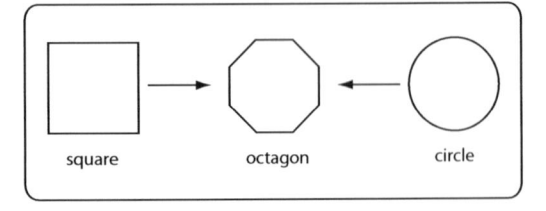

Lady Occasion
(Opportunity)

tetrahedron

"steadfast
watch post"

square → octagon ← circle

In 2-D geometry, eightness is best expressed by the octagon.

Even the ancients saw the octagonals as a nice "middle
ground" between the square and the circle. It is somewhat
round, yet also has some characteristics of squareness.

And eightness is particularly evident if you walk around the
Newport Tower, which morphs from "eight pillars forming
an octagon," into "an upper cylinder that forms a circle."

eight pillars of the
Newport Tower

DID THE ENGLISH NAME FOR THE STATE OF "RHODE ISLAND" COME FROM THE MIND OF JOHN DEE?

More specifically:
Did Dee conceal a hidden reference to "**Rhode Island**" in the Title page illustration of his *General and Rare Memorials pertaining to the Perfect Art of Navigation*?

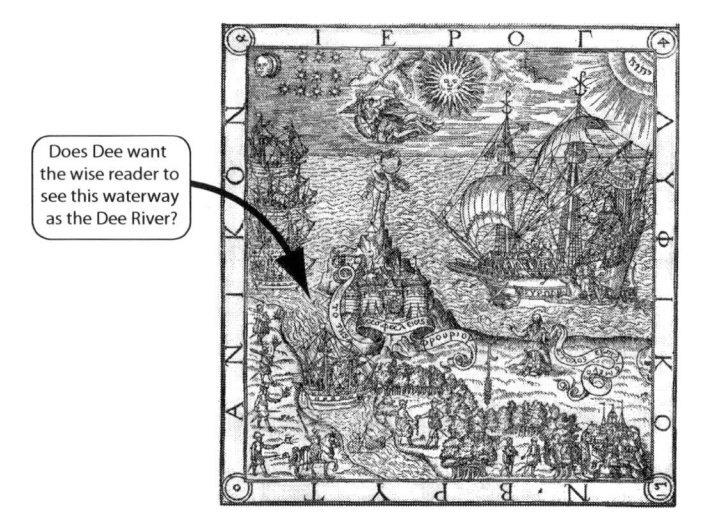

> Does Dee want the wise reader to see this waterway as the Dee River?

Even more specifically,
Was Dee depicting the entrance to the specific waterway Verrazzano called "**Refugio**," Dee called the "**Dee River**," and which is now called "**Narragansett Bay**, Rhode Island"?

Yes. Yes. Yes. Dee's provided a plethora of clues that his drawing was stylized depiction of the place he envisioned for the first Elizabethan colony!

On the right side of the drawing, the kneeling woman (representing the citizens of England) is imploring the Queen to "**Send forth his sailing expedition …**"

And on the left-hand side of illustration Dee continues "**… to make a steadfast watch post**."

Above that last half of the sentence, Dee depicts a well-fortified structure protecting a mountainous promontory.

Just to its left is a **flowing river** in which one of the ships is moored.

This is be one of the **five ships** in the "**sailing expedition**" Dee is graphically encouraging the Queen to "Send forth."

(Later, in 1583, Sir Humphrey Gilbert actually did leave England with a fleet of five ships.)

259

Beyond the defensive wall, on the summit of the craggy pinnacles, stands "Lady Occasion" (or Lady Opportunity, or Lady Luck). She is balanced precipitously with one foot on a sharp peak and the other on a tetrahedron.

In a footnote on page 64 of his text, Dee writes

*"**FRONTE** Capillata, post, est Occasio, Calva."*

This translates:

"ON THE FOREHEAD, Occasion has hair, but on the back part, she is bald."

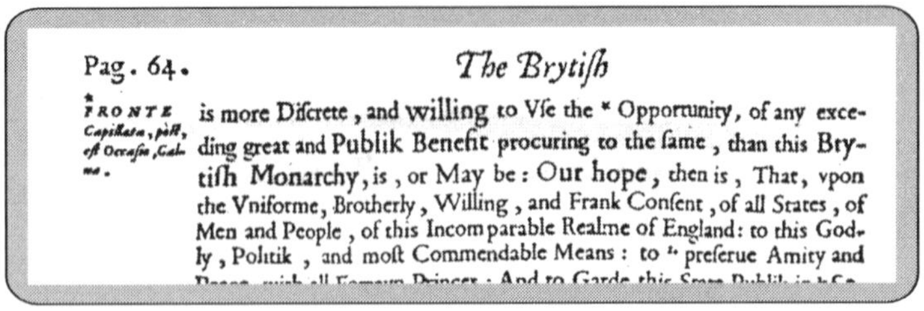

> Pag. 64.   *The Brytish*
> **FRONTE** is more Discrete, and willing to Vse the * Opportunity, of any exceeding great and Publik Benefit procuring to the same, than this Brytish Monarchy, is, or May be: Our hope, then is, That, vpon the Vniforme, Brotherly, Willing, and Frank Consent, of all States, of Men and People, of this Incomparable Realme of England: to this Godly, Politik, and most Commendable Means: to preserue Amity and

The proverb, "Seize opportunity by the forelock" goes back to the Greek and Roman poets like Phaedrus, Ausonius, and Cicero (Lady Occasion is the Greek goddess *Tyche* or the Roman goddess *Fortuna*). In Dee's era, Marlow and Shakespeare both used the "Lady Occasion's forelock" metaphor.

In Dee's drawing, Lady Occasion is partially bald, but has one flowing lock of hair. Dee even depicts her gesturing to her forelock as if she was saying to the Queen, "seize this opportunity and you will win the Crown of Victory."

Lady Occasion's other arm offers the Queen a "corolla" (a wreath worn as a crown). And the Queen, on her throne at the stern of the boat, seems to be gesturing back, reaching out towards the corolla.

All Lady Occasion is wearing is an apron secured at the waist by a belt strap that flows in the breeze behind her. **Curiously, the top of her head, the flowing locks, and the tip of her pointing finger, all coincide with the horizon line behind her.**

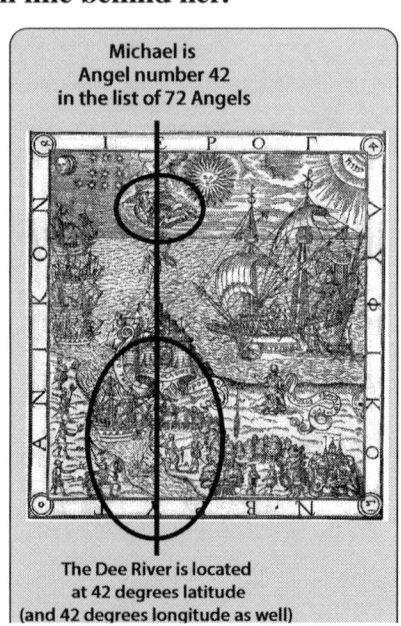

Hovering above her is the Archangel Michael, the angelic warrior, armed with sword and shield (Michael is written in Hebrew on his trailing robe). As we've seen, in the 72 Names of the Angels, **Michael is Angel number 42.**

To me, this was a clue that Dee was specifically depicting the Dee River.

In the 1583 land grant from Gilbert to Peckham, the Dee River is described as being "about 42 degrees" latitude. The Dee River was named by Dee. And, based on the style of composition, the land grant [now in the *Elizabethan State Papers*] appears to have been written by Dee.

Michael is Angel number 42 in the list of 72 Angels

The Dee River is located at 42 degrees latitude (and 42 degrees longitude as well)

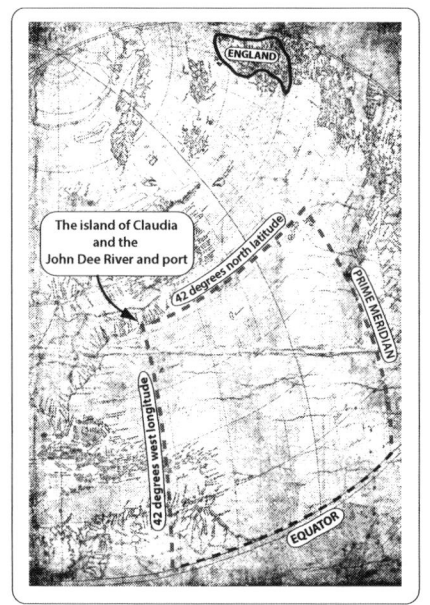

The island of Claudia and the John Dee River and port at 42 degrees north latitude and 42 degrees west longitude on part of Dee's 1580 map of North America

On Dee's 1580 map of North America, the Dee River appears to be at **42 degrees north latitude and also at 42 degrees west longitude** (based on Dee's Prime Meridian, which goes through the Eastern Azores).

The "River opening to the Ocean" and the cryptic reference to "42 degrees" are good clues. However, the "steadfast watch post" doesn't really resemble the Newport Tower.

It has several well-fortified towers with crenellations (notches at the top of the wall) and a main doorway. Its sturdy facade contrasts visually with the graceful, feminine Lady Occasion perched above it.

Earlier in my studies, I had deduced that the anchor on Elizabeth's ship and the Chi-Rho anchor symbols atop the masts (and some cryptic letter-play) were Dee's clues implying "Anchor of Hope." This was the symbol and motto for Sir Humphrey Gilbert's expedition, and later became symbol and motto for the state of Rhode Island.

I had a gnawing suspicion that Dee was hiding more clues identifying the Dee River in his illustration. But there was another obvious problem: **There is no "triangular island" in the ocean pointing to the entrance of the Dee River.**

I think Dee probably considered putting in a triangular island, but he knew it would make the secret site of the colony way too obvious. When such a juicy opportunity like this arose, Dee preferred to leave clues that were cunningly subtle...and ingenious.

**Agreement between Sir Humphrey Gilbert and Sir George Peckham
February 28, 1583**

"...all that river or port called by Master John Dee, Dee River, which River, by the description of Giovanni Verrazzano, a Florentine,

lies in the Northerly latitudes about 42 degrees, and has its mouth lying open to the South, half a league broad or thereabout,

and entering within the said Bay between the East and the North increases its width and continues 12 leagues or thereabouts,

and then makes a gulf of 20 leagues in circumference or thereabouts, and contains within it 5 small Islands, newly named the Cinque Isles."

In the 1583 land grant from Gilbert to Peckham, Dee used over a half dozen descriptive details about the bay that come right from in Verrazzano's report. But curiously, Dee he **omits** two important details form Verrazzano's description: the island is a **triangle** and it's about the size of **Rhodes**.

(As we'll soon see, this is an example of Dee's crypto-technique which I call a "clue by omission".)

In hindsight, we now know that the first Elizabethan colony at the Dee River failed to take root.

But remember, way back in 1577, Dee not only expected it to fully blossom, but he anticipated that it would grow by leaps and bounds, eventually seeding English colonies up and down the whole east coast of the New World.

Dee expected that his Title page illustration would become a famous, iconic British image – not just the curious visual footnote in history it has become.

To me, Dee's cover is the visual spark that ignited the British Empire, which, over the next few centuries, grew to be the largest empire the world has ever known.

But still, it wasn't immediately obvious to me how Dee might be expressing "**Rhodes**."

[On the right is my depiction of what was **supposed** to happen. However, Sir Humphrey Gilbert and his 5 ships never actually made it this close to the Dee River.]

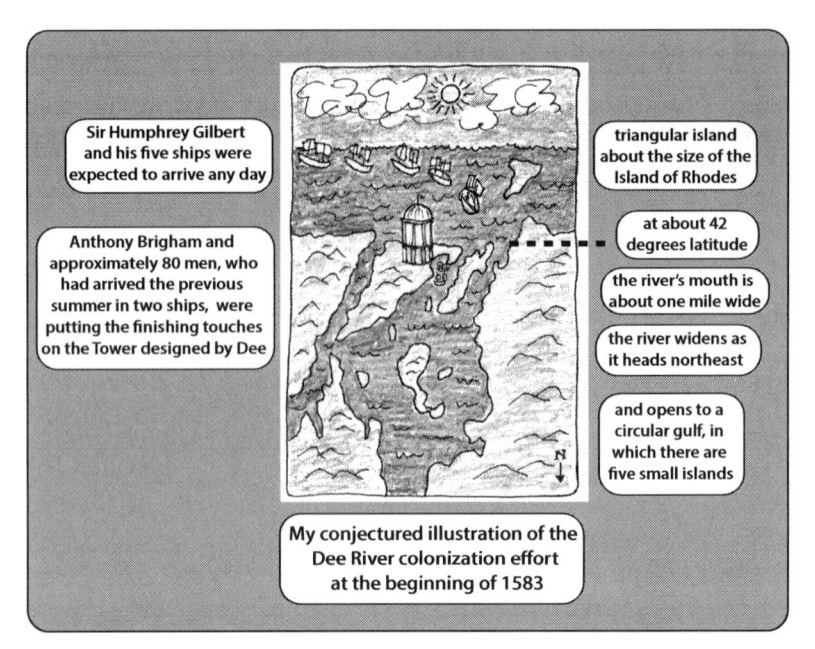

- Sir Humphrey Gilbert and his five ships were expected to arrive any day
- Anthony Brigham and approximately 80 men, who had arrived the previous summer in two ships, were putting the finishing touches on the Tower designed by Dee
- triangular island about the size of the Island of Rhodes
- at about 42 degrees latitude
- the river's mouth is about one mile wide
- the river widens as it heads northeast
- and opens to a circular gulf, in which there are five small islands

My conjectured illustration of the Dee River colonization effort at the beginning of 1583

John Dee: wordsmith, punster, and riddler

Remember, to understand Dee's clever visual puzzles, one must think like Dee. He delighted in making clever visual and word puns in his other texts. He coined (or was the first author to use) over 140 words in the English language. On this long list are these words: calculate, marketable, master key, meteorological, model, optical, tactical, unit, vertex and watch clock.

Also remember, Dee had taught Greek at Trinity College in Cambridge. He was fully versed in ancient Greek culture, mythology, and literature. He refers to his favorite philosopher as "Divine Plato."

Dee also wanted to convey information publicly, but he only wanted only the "**worthy**" among his countrymen to know what he was expressing. His work was not written for the "**vulgar**," and especially not for the Spanish spies who had infiltrated London. He could do this by using cryptic clues. With this in mind, let's take closer look at several of the clues in his illustration. But first, here's a little background information about the original Isle of Rhodes in the Aegean Sea.

Rhodes and Patmos, two of the twelve islands of the Dodecanese

I had already learned Roger Williams wanted to name the island of Aquidneck "Patmos," but it seems as though Benedict Arnold had insisted that it be named "Rode Island" [an early spelling of Rhode Island].

And I had already seen that that the Rhode Island state motto and emblem, the Anchor of Hope, seemed to have derived from Dee's *General and Rare Memorials*.

Could it be that the clever **Dee himself** was the person responsible for shifting the name "Rhode" from a description of Claudia (Block Island), to the name for Aquidneck? And Benedict was simply following Dee's lead?

I wanted to get a first hand understanding of what these Greek islands were all about, geographically and culturally. So, prior to a photo assignment I had in Barcelona, Spain, I took a side trip to Patmos and Rhodes.

The Dodecanese are cluster of 12 large islands and about 150 smaller islands in the eastern Aegean Sea. They are actually much closer to Asia Minor than to the mainland of Greece.
(Dodecanese literally means "12 islands").

(They are favorite destinations for vacationing Europeans, especially rock stars and actors who prefer the less-frequented Greek Islands for getaways.)

The charming island of Patmos is the northernmost of the Dodecanese. From north to south it's only about 8 miles long, and from east to west it's only about 2 miles wide. In ancient times it was called *Palmosa* because it was once covered by a lush forest of palm trees.

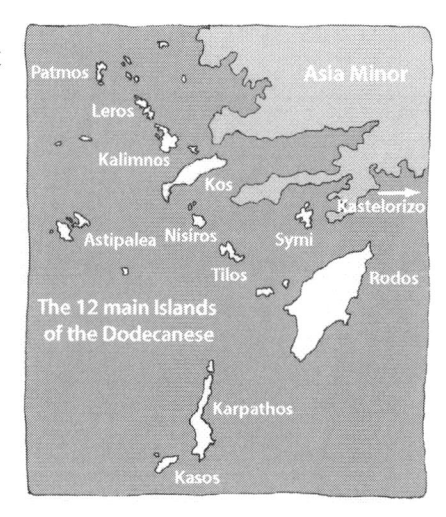

Every year, thousands of Christians pilgrimage to tiny Patmos, where St. John wrote *Revelation*, the last book in the New Testament. Saint John, who had been exiled to this remote island by the Roman Emperor Domation, wrote to the seven Christian churches in Asia Minor about two intense spiritual visions that he had experienced.

The ferry boat dropped me off in the main harbor town of Skala. A husky ex-fisherman cab driver in a tiny taxi took me southwards, up the winding road to the town of Chora, the highest point of the island. The view looking back north towards port of Skala was enchanting.

I walked through a maze of narrow lanes lined with whitewashed townhouses to the Monastery of Saint John. Around 1100, Christian monks built this abbey to honor Saint John the Evangelist.
(Saint John lived from around 1 AD to around 100AD).

Devout pilgrims venture about a quarter of a mile down the hill towards Skala to the much smaller Church of Agia Anna. This white church was built on top of the Holy Cave of the Apocalypse where Saint John supposedly wrote the *Book of Revelation*.

It is said that Saint John heard the voice of God coming through a rock in the ceiling. The hovering rock is divided into three parts, symbolizing the Holy Trinity. The grotto is adorned with religious artifacts. A short bronze fence protects the indentation in the rock wall where Saint John supposedly rested his head. The original cave opening, now converted to a window, has a fine view looking north towards Skala.

[I thought about how much Roger Williams would have loved this mystical cave.]

Around the island there are folk museums, convents, and pebbly beaches, but the main attraction is still Saint John. Aside from tourism, the chief industry on the island is sponge fishing.

263

The ferry ride from Patmos to Rhodes (heading southeast) follows the Asia Minor coastline, and makes short stops at several of the other *Dodekanisos* (ΔΩΔΕΚΑΝΗΣΟΣ).

The Dodecanese Express Ferry runs along the coast of Asia Minor, from Patmos (on the north) to Rhodes (on the south)

Do you know what the Isle of Rhodes is most famous for?
(Hint: It's one of seven.)

Rhodes is the largest of the Dodecanese, with a population of about 100,000.

About 50,000 people live at the extreme northern tip of the diamond-shaped island, in and around the capital city, which is also called Rhodes (or Rhodes Town). In Greek, Rhodes or RODOS (ΡΟΔΟΣ) means Rose.

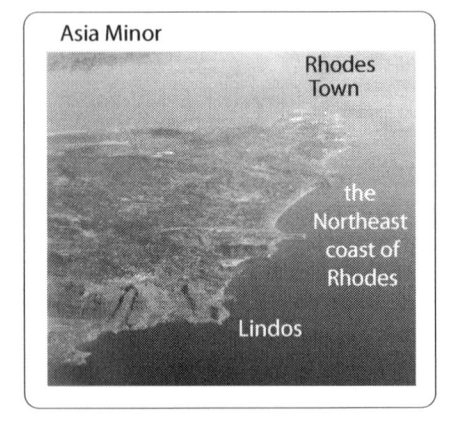

After checking into a small pensione in the medieval Old City, I negotiated with the cab driver to take me on a circuit of the island, which is about 50 miles long and about 25 miles wide.

We went south along the east coast to "Anthony Quinn Bay." The Rhodians loved Quinn for his starring role in Zorba the Greek.
(Even though he was born in Mexico and was a US citizen)

Further south, in Lindos, you can take a donkey ride to the top of an ancient acropolis.

Then we headed west across the island to Monolithos, a castle perched dramatically on a 700-foot tall cliff overlooking a turquoise sea. Heading back north along the coast, we visited shoreline cliffs and white sandy beaches at Kalavarda and Paradisi.

Most of the island is quite rural. All the action is in the bustling main port or the "City of Rhodes," sometimes called "Rhodes Town." Because of its prominent location in the northeastern Mediterranean, over the centuries Rhodes has been ruled by Greeks, Romans, Muslims, the Knights Hospitaller and the Turks.

264

The city of Rhodes is at the northernmost tip of the Island of Rhodes

The Greeks have always called Rhodes the "Island of the Sun." It was dedicated to the sun god Helios, who pulled the sun across the sky with his chariot during the day and travelled back to the east in a golden cup at night.

According to Greek mythology, Helios had fallen in love with a nymph named Rodos and when he shined his bright light on her, she became transformed into an island. Helios gifted the island with perpetual sunshine. [Indeed, it's sunny over 300 days a year.]

Ancient Rhodes

Now, let's step back in time,... to 323 BC.

After conquering most of the ancient world, **Alexander the Great** died of a sudden illness. He was only 32 and he had failed to appoint a successor. After considerable infighting, four of his generals divided up the great empire Alexander had amassed.

Antigonus ruled most of Asia Minor.

Ptolemy I ruled Egypt and most of northeast Africa.

Even though Rhodes was much closer to Asia Minor, the Rhodians formed an alliance with the Ptolemy I. Together they controlled trade in the eastern Mediterranean.

Antigonus was not pleased. In 305 BC, he sent his son, Demetrius Poliocretes, armed with 40,000 men, to capture Rhodes. (Poliocretes means the "besieger of cities.")

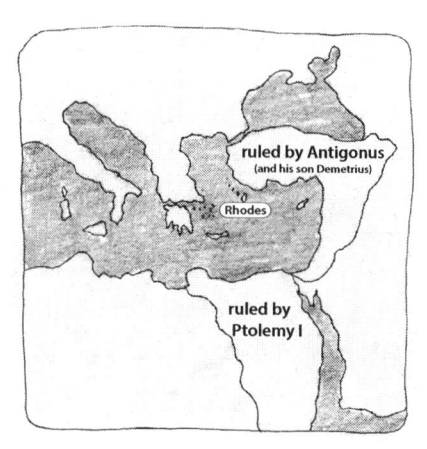

The city of Rhodes was well defended by huge city walls, so Demetrius ordered his men to build a tall, wooden siege tower called a *Helepolis* (which means a "taker of cities"). This massive structure was about 130 feet tall, about 65 feet square at its base, and rolled on eight 12-foot diameter wheels.

The front and sides were covered with thick iron plates. Inside there were seven stories connected with two broad sets of stairs, one set for ascending and one for descending.

The defending Rhodians managed to blast a fiery hole in Demtrius' *Herepolis* (or movable siege wall)

It took 3400 men to move the massive siege tower, which was well-stocked with projectile-hurling weapons. As the *Herepolis* approached the defensive wall, the Rhodians let loose with their own catapults.

They managed to blast away a large section of the protective iron plates on the front of the *Herepolis*. Then they launched fireballs into the open holes.

Before the seige tower became totally engulfed in flames, Demetrius ordered his men to back it away from the wall.

265

Soon Ptolemy's reinforcements arrived to help the besieged Rhodians. Demetrius was forced to hightail it back to Asia Minor, leaving the *Herepolis* and many armaments behind.

The Rhodians sold the siege equipment and used the profits to erect a giant statue of the sun god *Helios*. The reknowned local sculptor, Chares of Lindos, was commissioned for the project.

His monumental work became known as the **Colossus of Rhodes**, one of the Seven Wonders of the Ancient World.

Although the exact method of construction is still unknown, it is thought that the Colossus was made from a framework of iron bars with bronze plates individually formed to fit the contour of the skin. To make it solid, the interior was filled with stone blocks. It took a year just to build about 8 feet of height. Huge dirt ramps were built to facilitate the transport of materials for the chest, arms, and head.

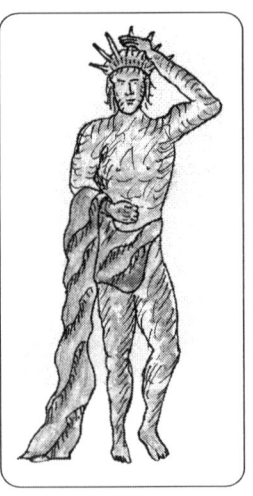

my depiction of Colossus of Rhodes

Ancient accounts indicate that the Colossus was naked, with one arm shading his eyes from the sun and the other holding a Greek robe. Some modern scholars suggest the robe draped all the way to the ground behind the sculpture to provide a triangular support.

It's also thought the statue of Helios wore a "*corona radiata*" or a "radiant crown." Lucian describes such a crown as a "chaplet studded with sunbeams." (A chaplet is a wreath for the head.)

A scaled-down replica at the entrance to the Colossus Restaurant (in a suburb of Rhodes Town)

Some sources claimed the Colossus straddled the entrance to the harbor, but modern engineers claim this would be structurally impossible (never mind it being an unflattering pose for a god). It probably stood right next to the harbor, or atop a nearby hill overlooking the harbor.

Artist's conception of the Colossus of Rhodes (done around 1700, by Fischer von Erlach)

The Colossus was the pride of Rhodes. But a mere 56 years later, things weren't so rosy on Rhodes. The great earthquake of 226 BC shook the eastern Mediterranean. The giant sculpture rocked back and forth. It's head and arms probably broke off first and then it snapped at the waist or knees and tumbled to the ground.

The superstitious Rhodians felt they had somehow offended their god *Helios*, so they decided not to rebuild the statue.

The historian Strabo writes that the remains of the Colossus could be seen for the next 800 years. Pliny the Elder reports that the thumb on the fallen hand was so large, few men had arms long enough to embrace it. Each finger was taller than a regular statue. Finally, in 654 AD, all the remaining metal was sold to a Syrian merchant to be recycled.

When the Knights Hospitaller moved to Rhodes in the 1300's and 1400's, they built even taller city walls, wide moats, and eleven gates to the city. The gates were each well-defended by pairs of tall, crenellated towers.

The Gate of Eleftherias built by the Knights Hospitaller

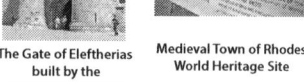

Medieval Town of Rhodes World Heritage Site

cannonballs and catapult balls by the sturdy city wall

The Gate of Milon built by the Knights Hospitaller

Crenellations are the short upper-walls, cut out at intervals, through which defenders shot arrows and poured hot oil on their ememies. (In chess, the rook is a crenellated tower)

The "**steadfast watch post**" Dee illustrates on the Title page bears a striking resemblance to the walls, gates and tower of Rhodes. While other cities in Europe have walls, gates and towers the ones surrounding the city of Rhodes are among the most famous.

A modern-day Mrs. Colossus

Now let's flash forward to the year 1886.

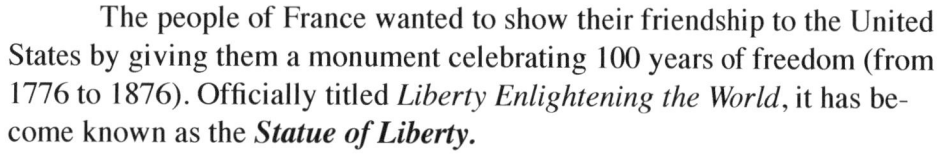

The people of France wanted to show their friendship to the United States by giving them a monument celebrating 100 years of freedom (from 1776 to 1876). Officially titled *Liberty Enlightening the World*, it has become known as the ***Statue of Liberty.***

This American icon is a depiction of the Roman goddess *Libertas*, who represents liberty and freedom. She is wearing a long stola (a long, pleated Roman dress). Around her head is a *corona radiata*, with its spikes of sunbeams. Beneath her sandals is a broken chain. Her raised right arm holds a torch and cradled in her left arm is a tablet inscribed July 4, 1776 (in Roman numerals).

Standing proudly on Liberty Island in New York Harbor, she has welcomed millions of immigrants, visitors, and Americans returning to their homeland.

The inner framework of the tower is steel. The outer sheeting is copper, which now has a verdigris (bluish-green) patina.

My depiction of the Statue of Liberty, by Frederic Auguste Bartholdi, in 1886

"The New Colossus"
by Emma Lazarus

Not like the brazen giant of Greek fame,
With conquering limbs astride from land to land;
Here at our sea-washed, sunset gates shall stand
A mighty woman with a torch, whose flame
Is the imprisoned lightning, and her name
Mother of Exiles. From her beacon-hand
Glows worldwide welcome; her mild eyes command
The air-bridged harbor that twin cities frame.
"Keep ancient lands, your storied pomp!" cries she
With silent lips. "Give me your tired, your poor,
Your huddled masses yearning to breathe free,
The wretched refuse of your teeming shore.
Send these, the homeless, tempest-tost to me,
I lift my lamp beside the golden door!"

The French sculptor Frederic Auguste Bartholdi clearly had the Colossus of Rhodes in mind when he designed the Statue of Liberty. They're both about the same size, approximately 110 feet from head to toe. But Bartholdi of Paris beat Chares of Lindos in the height competition by adding the upwards-reaching right arm holding the torch. Gustav Eiffel (who later designed the Eiffel Tower) engineered the skeletal framework.

In the entryway of the pedestal is a bronze plaque with a sonnet entitled, *The New Colossus* by Emma Lazarus, a local poet from New York City. The "brazen [bronze] giant" in the first two lines refers to the Colossus of Rhodes:

"Not like the brazen giant of Greek fame,
With conquering limbs astride from land to land; ..."

We've finished a brief a trip to the island of Rhodes and heard the story behind the Colossus and its modern reflection, the Statue of Liberty. Let's take a fresh look at Dee's Title page.

Near the center of all the activity in Dee's busy illustration is Lady Occasion. Because she is a mythological figure, so feminine, so involved with her gesturing, so precariously positioned at the mountains apex, so dramatically silhouetted against the wavy sea, that she seems ethereal, like a dream image.

But, looking at her in another way, she is actually a giant statue. She is as tall as the solid walls of the "watch post" or as tall as the mast of the ships.

Then it struck me.

Lady Occasion is quite tall compared to the ships or the sturdy city walls

Sun (like the sun god Helios)

Lady Occasion (like the Colossus of Rhodes)

Lady Occasion is Dee's "Colossus of Rhodes." Only disguised as a female!

It might seem odd to switch genders like this, but remember, Dee needed to be cryptic. And after all, Bartholdi made a similar "gender switch" when he designed Mrs. Colossus (the Statue of Liberty).

The actual Colossus of Rhodes was a depiction of the **Greek sun god Helios**. And look what Dee has drawn above and to the right of Lady Occasion: the radiant Sun, anthropomorphized with a confident countenance!

Just as the Colossus once stood overlooking the harbor of Rhodes, Dee's "Lady Occasion-Colossus" stands overlooking the entrance to the Dee River.

At her feet are the city walls that protected the Rhodians from Demetrius' siege tower on wheels. And just underneath the wall, Dee has cleverly positioned the word ασφαλειας, or *asphaleias*. And the city walls were indeed "steadfast." (They repelled the determined Demetrius.)

steadfast

my depiction of John Dee's

Here are a few more minor clues.
The Colossus and Lady Occasion are each naked, except for a small robe.

The Colossus wore a corolla on his head.
Lady Occasion is holding one in her right hand (and offering it to the Queen).

(By the way, these clues are typical of Dee's style of visual cryptography. He loves to put clues right in front of your eyes, yet they still can't be seen without a little creative contemplation.)

A riddle-clue involving the word Rhode?

If Dee really was using the visual metaphors of "**Lady Occasion represents the Colossus of Rhodes**" and "**the steadfast watch post represents the strong walls of Rhodes**," it seemed likely to me that he would toss in a word-clue or letter-clue as well. Besides being a visual punster, Dee was a master wordsmith.

What spelling of "Rhodes" should we look for?
In 1524, Giovanni Verrazzano spells it **"la insula di Rhodo."**
In 1582, Richard Hakluyt spells it **"the Island of Rodes."**
In 1637, Roger Williams spells it **"Rode Island."**

If Dee was hiding the word **RODE** he might have written it in Greek, which would be: ΡΟΔΕ.

The Greek letter "Ρ" (pronounced Rho) resembles the shape of the Latin letter P.

The Greek letter Δ is Delta, or the Latin D.

And look!
Centered symmetrically above the Sun are three of those Greek letters, Ε, Ρ, and Ο (or E, R, an O in English) as part of the spelling of the words ΙΕΡΟGLYPHIKON BRYTANIKON

I had already deduced that Dee used those letters ΙΕΡΟΓ to cryptically conceal the word HOPE. But Dee wasn't afraid to get double-duty work out of a clue.

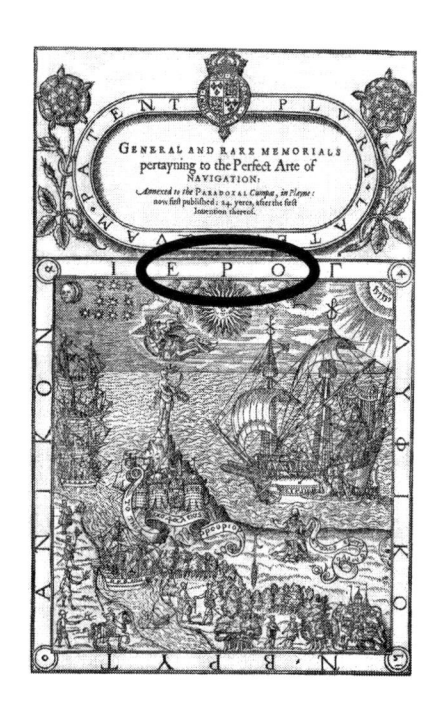

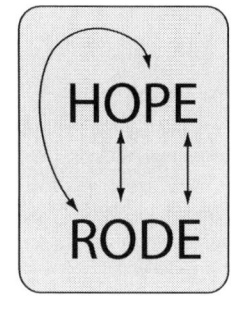

Dee made use of the fact that the word HOPE and the word RODE share three letters, the O, the E, and the "P and R"

(if you consider that the Greek P, or Rho, is pronounced like the English R).

One way that I had previously found the word HOPE was to combine the "I" and the "Γ" (Gamma) to make the shape of an "H."

I thought Dee might also be suggesting that the "I" and the "Γ" might also be combined to make a triangle Δ (Delta).

But the ace geometer Dee knew that equilateral triangles have three internal angles of 60° each.
And the Γ (Gamma) is a 90° right angle.

Where else might Dee be hiding the missing triangle?

I didn't have to look far. Lady Opportunity was standing on a tetrahedron, the most basic of 3-dimensional shapes.

It is comprised of 4 equilateral triangles. Any one of its four triangular sides could be the **missing Δ needed to spell the word ΡΟΔΕ** (RODE).

Furthermore, any of the triangle's other sides might be expressing the idea of the "**triangular island**" (which is the "size of Rhodes").

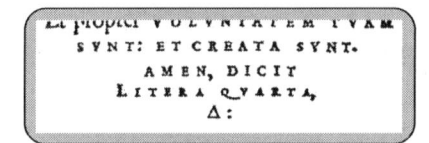

And further furthermore, any of the "triangular faces of the tetrahedron might be seen as **Dee's personal symbol**, the triangle. Dee uses the triangle as his personal symbol hundreds of times in his public and private writings. He seems to have used it more frequently than he does his own initials, I. D.

Could Dee be hiding a **fourth** "visual riddle" or "word clue" involving a triangle, in order to make a "multifaceted clue" or a "tetrahedron of clues"? Is this why Dee had Lady Occasion standing on a tetrahedron rather than simply a triangle?

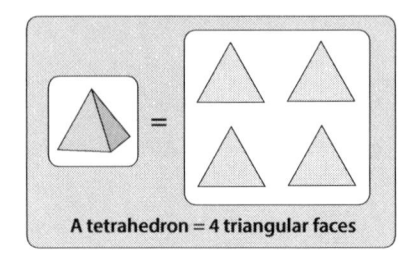

"AMEN, SAYS THE FOURTH LETTER"
(this is the last line of the last Theorem of Dee's *Monas Hieroglyphica*)

A tetrahedron = 4 triangular faces

Incidentally, in his original sketch for the Title page, Dee only had the letters "IEPO" along the upper border of the illustration.

But in the finished engraving for Title page, he changed it to "ΙΕΡΟΓ."

(Dee obviously put a great deal of thought into the most effective way to present his subtle clues. Aside from some redistribution of letters, the finished illustration is remarkably similar to Dee's preliminary drawing shown here.)

Dee's **preliminary drawing** for the Title page of *General and Rare Memorials*

Dee hides a clue in his page-numbering system

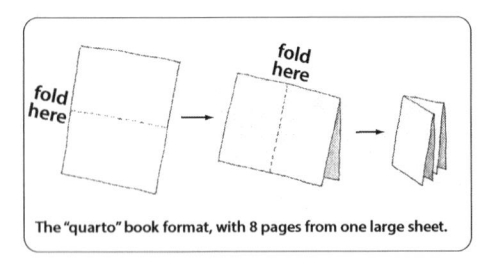

Dee leaves a clue about the "4 triangles" in the "numbering system" of the pages of *General and Rare Memorials*, which was printed and folded as a group of "quartos."

In the "quarto" book format, 8 pages of text are printed on one large sheet, which is folded twice to make 4 leaves.

The "quarto" book format, with 8 pages from one large sheet.

The "front" of each leaf is a right-hand page, which is called a *recto* page.
The "back side" of each leaf is called a "*verso*" page.
(Thus, *verso* pages are always left-hand pages).

In most Elizabethan texts, *recto* pages have numbers and *verso* pages are left unnumbered.

The main section of text of Dee's work is numbered in a common English fashion: Using upper-case letters (A, B, C, etc.), followed by (i, ij, iij, iiij)

				page numbering system in Dee's main text					
A.i.	B.i.	C.i.	D.i.	E.i.	F.i.	G.i.	H.i.	I.i.	K.i.
A.ij.	B.ij.	C.ij.	D.ij.	E.ij.	F.ij.	G.ij.	H.ij.	I.ij.	K.ij.
A.iij.	B.iij.	C.iij.	D.iij.	E.iij.	F.iij.	G.iij.	H.iij.	I.iij.	K.iij.
A.iiij.	B.iiij.	C.iiij.	D.iiij.	E.iiij.	F.iiij.	G.iiij.	H.iiij.	I.iiij.	K.iiij.

Preceding that main text, Dee has written a section entitled, *A necessary Advertisement* [or notice] *by an unknown friend.*

But instead of using the alphabet letters (A, B, C, etc.) in this section, strangely, he uses these symbols: Δ, s, and s*

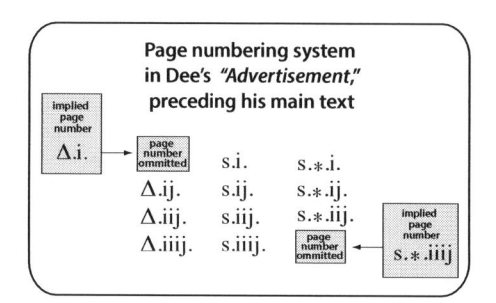

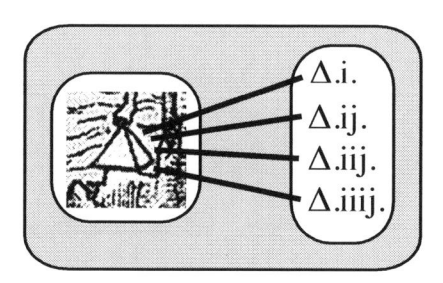

Page numbering system in Dee's "Advertisement," preceding his main text

implied page number Δ.i.	page number omitted	s.i.	s.*.i.	
	Δ.ij.	s.ij.	s.*.ij.	
	Δ.iij.	s.iij.	s.*.iij.	implied page number S.*.iiij
	Δ.iiij.	s.iiij.	page number ommitted	

On the very first page of his *Advertisement*, Dee writes a *Brief Note Scholastical,* which is not numbered. But it's pretty obvious its number would be Δ.i.

Δ.i.
Δ.ij.
Δ.iij.
Δ.iiij.

Thus, the page-numbering of the first "quarto" of Dee's book starts out with **4 triangles.** That's enough to make a **tetrahedron!**

Dee's ΔΔΔΔ page-numbering clue echoes the shape under Lady Occasion's foot, the tetrahedron, with its 4 triangular faces.

This reinforces the idea that there is **a fourth clue** involving a triangle.

(besides 1.Dee's name Δ,,,,,,, 2. the triangular island Δ, ... and 3. the missing Δ needed to spell RODE or POΔE)

Have you figured out what it is?

The fourth triangle seems to be used to spell RODE (or POΔE) is yet another riddle involving Lady Occasion.

Recall that in a footnote of his text, Dee writes:
"*FRONTE Capillata, post, est Occasio, Calva.*"
"**ON THE FOREHEAD**, Occasion has hair, but on the back part, she is bald."

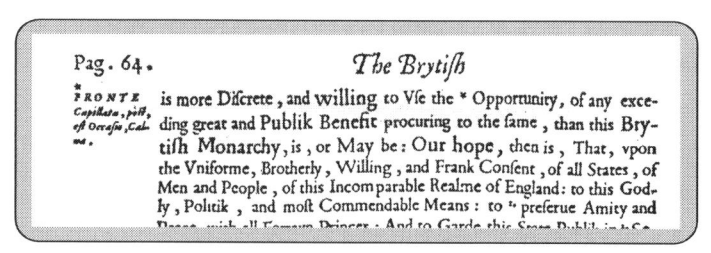

Pag. 64. *The Brytiſh*
FRONTE Capillata, poſt, eſt Occaſio, Calva. is more Diſcrete, and willing to Vſe the * Opportunity, of any exceeding great and Publik Benefit procuring to the ſame, than this Brytiſh Monarchy, is, or May be: Our hope, then is, That, vpon the Vniforme, Brotherly, Willing, and Frank Conſent, of all States, of Men and People, of this Incomparable Realme of England: to this Godly, Politik, and moſt Commendable Means: to " preſerue Amity and

Notice that Dee has only capitalized one word in this Latin sentence: "*FRONTE.*"

Among the letters of this word we can find R, O, and E. Simply borrow one of those triangles (Δ) from the tetrahedron and the word RODE (or ROΔE) can be made.

Thus, the four-sided tetrahedron holds four clues to four separate riddles!!!!

Hidden letters attest to Dee's love of the Queen
(and spell a top-secret code word)

Dee was a consummate riddler. If you're on the right track, you'll find that Dee is considerate enough to leave a confirming clue

Notice that Lady Occasion is pointing towards her forelock. But she is not grasping it. It appears to be blowing in the wind towards the **right side** of the illustration.

Now look at the sails of the Queen's ship. They are filled with wind, which seems to be blowing towards the **left side** of the illustration.

This smells like a "Dee clue," involving Lady Occasion's long hair.

Also, notice that Lady Occasion's arm, which is pointing to her flowing hair, appears "rounded" instead of having a 90-degree angle at the elbow.

Her arm and the hair seem to be forming a **letter "D,"** which has been rotated so it's resting on its rounded side.

Indeed, Dee has even positioned the straight, horizon-line to coincide with Lady Occasion's hair.

(Lady Occasion is acting out the letter "D" the way the Village People acted out the letters "YMCA.")

Was Dee really thinking all this? To confirm that indeed he was, he left another clue. It involves what Lady Occasion is standing on.

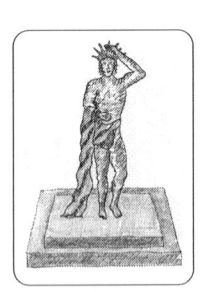

The Colossus was on a solid base.

The Statue of Liberty is on a solid base.

Why does Dee draw Lady Occasion so precariously balanced on a tetrahedron and a peak?

If Dee wanted Lady Occasion to seem like the Colossus, **why didn't he put her on a solid base**?

Chares put his Colossus of Rhodes on a 60-foot wide marble base.

Bartholdi put the Statue of Liberty on a foundation about 150 feet tall.

Then why does Dee draw Lady Occasion so precariously balanced on the sharp tip of a tetrahedron and the **pointy pinnacle of a mountain**?

The reason is: it's another riddle. It's a rebus that Dee's buddies in this Elizabethan exploration business would have gotten right away. Here's a little background information.

In the 1560's, a group of London merchants called the Muscovy Company (Muscovy refers to Moscow) made several successful trading missions to Russia. They had no interest in heading "Northwest" when "Northeast" had become so profitable.

The independent Martin Frobisher had set his sights on finding the Northwest Passage through northern North America, so he made an appeal directly to the Queen. At the Queen's request, the powerful Muscovy Company acquiesced to Frobisher's expedition, but under two conditions: The Muscovy Company was to share in any profits and their representative, Michael Lok, was to be the treasurer of the venture. Together they raised the equivalent of million dollars for this new coalition called "The Company of Cathay."

The Muscovy Company wanted to be assured of a successful mission, so who did they hire to "examine and instruct" the leaders of the expedition on "rules of Geometry and Cosmography"?

John Dee. In May of 1576, Dee brought his maps, charts, and instruments to Muscovy House and met with Michael Lok, Steven Borough, Sir Lionell Duckett, Martin Frobisher, and Christopher Hall (who had earlier been one of Dee's students).

After Dee's intensive 2-week cram course on mathematics and navigation, the mission set sail.

(Woolley, *The Queen's Conjurer*, p. 103)

Off the coast of Scotland, one of the ships started taking on water, so they went ashore for repair work. Christopher Hall had used Dee's navigational methods to calculate their latitude.

Frobisher sent a letter [by land messenger] with the accurate latitude measurement to "**the worshipful and our approved good friend M. Dee**," in which he writes, "we do remember you, and hold ourselves bound to you as your poor disciples." Clearly they held Dee in high esteem.

Underway again, they headed northwest and eventually came to the island we now called Greenland. As they approached the coast, they saw a group of huge snow-covered peaks, which Frobisher named, "**Mr. Dee his Pinnacles**." Frobisher even drew a sketch of the tall, pointed peaks.

Frobisher's 1576 mission went on to collect mineral samples from the shores of what was later named the Davis Strait. Upon their return, one black rock they collected seemed to have assayable quantities of gold in it.

Martin Frobisher names the first mountain peaks he sees in Greenland "Mr. Dee his Pinnacles"

This sparked another mission in 1577, and another in 1578. These missions returned with boatloads of rocks. Unfortunately the rocks didn't contain any gold or valuable minerals. They were worthless. The Company of Cathay went bankrupt.

However, during 1577, when Dee was working on *General and Rare Memorials*, London was abuzz with the great news about Frobisher's first voyage. Frobisher had named other geographical features after other dignitaries, but Dee was undoubtedly quite flattered to have the "first landmark sighted" named in his honor.

Four "D's" ("or Δ's") + pinnacles =
"D's" pinnacles =
Dee's pinnacles

(in the final, printed
Title page illustration)

Let's review what Lady Occasion is standing on:

One foot is on the tetrahedron,
which is four Δ's or four **D's**.

The other foot is on a **pinnacle**,
which is surrounded by other pinnacles.

Combining the two parts of this rebus makes,
"Dee's pinnacles"

Four "D's" ("or Δ's") + pinnacles =
"D's" pinnacles =
Dee's pinnacles

The pinnacles are actually more evident in Dee's **preliminary sketch** for the Title page. Notice that Dee switched the tetrahedron from under her left foot to under her right foot so it would "read" more clearly as "D's pinnacles," instead of "pinnacles D's."

(I don't think Dee was suggesting that Lady Occasion was standing on a Greenland pinnacle. But remember, Greenland was also a part of the "New World," which was the main subject of Dee's proposal to the Queen.)

(in Dee's preliminary sketch
for the Title page illustration)

In short, Dee's rebus, "Δ's + pinnacles" or "Dee's Pinnacles" relates to the riddle that the tetrahedron is an assemblage of four D's (Δ's) or 4 separate clues:

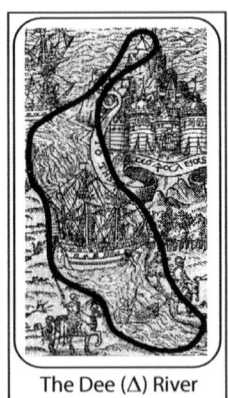

1. The "Dee River"
(near the triangular island Δ)

The Dee (Δ) River

2. Dee's personal symbol
(the triangle Δ)

Δ is Dee's
personal symbol

3. The Delta (Δ) plus the letters
EPO from IEPOΓ
spell the word RODE (POΔE).

"FRONTE"
RO E

ROΔE
RODE

4. The Delta (Δ), plus the letters
ERO, from FRONTE, spell
the word RODE (POΔE).

POΔE or RODE
(Rode Island)

Another clue : the word Greek for ROSE is RODE

Dee seems to be providing another "RODE" clue for us in the upper section of his Title page. On each side of the lozenge-shape of the title is a "**Tudor rose**," the renowned symbol of all the Tudor kings and queens. But also, the word for "rose" in Greek is "rode"

But in light of Dee's other clues, it seems as though he chose include these large "Tudor roses" to make another cryptic reference to the "Isle of Roses" or the "Isle of Rhodes."

When used as a emblem of the Tudor reign, the Tudor Rose is usually drawn as a solitary, five-sided flower with no stem. But here, Dee depicts two roses. And he has added a stem with thorns, and branches with buds and leaves. This suggests that Dee is implying more than just "Tudor Reign."

I think he's using them to cryptically express the **two** "Isles of Rhodes (Roses)," the ancient one in the **Aegean** and the soon-to-be colony on the Dee River in **America**.

A very brief history of the Tudor Rose

The Wars of the Roses were a series of battles between two rival branches of the House of Plantagenet. England's thirty-year internal conflict ended in 1485 when Henry Tudor defeated King Richard III of York at the Battle of Bosworth Field (about 100 miles northwest of London.) Richard was killed and Henry became the last English King to win the throne in a battle.

Henry Tudor, crowned as Henry VII, was from the House of **Lancaster**, whose badge was a **Red Rose**.

To bring the two factions together, Henry married Elizabeth from the House of **York**, whose badge was the **White Rose**.

To symbolize the reunification of England, Henry combined both badges into a Tudor Rose, sometimes called a Union Rose.

(This "double rose" has five **red** petals on the outside and five **white** petals on the inside.)

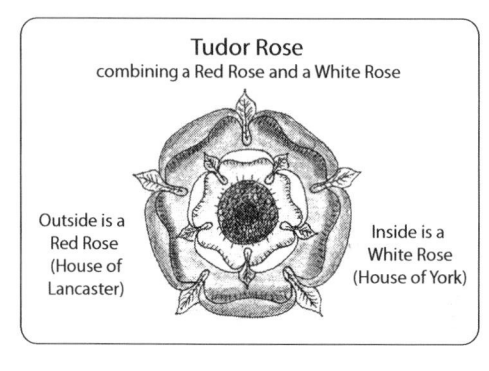

Tudor Rose
combining a Red Rose and a White Rose

Outside is a Red Rose (House of Lancaster)

Inside is a White Rose (House of York)

The rose is also an important symbol in alchemy. A white rose symbolizes the "albedo or pure white stage" and the red rose symbolizes the "rubedo or final, red stone which has the power to transmute all base metal into pure gold and earthly man into the illuminated philosopher."

(Lindy Abraham, *A Dictionary of Alchemical Imagery*, p.173)

(Dee placed what appear to be roses in the urns on the Title page of his *Monas Hieroglyphica*.)

Interestingly, Roger Williams makes a "Rhode-Rose" reference in a letter dated January 1, 1666, addressed, "To the Town of Warwick":

"Rode Island (in the Greeke language) is an Isle of Roses, and so the Kings Matie [Majesty] was pleased to resent [represent] it."

Roger Williams is referring to the Royal Charter of 1663, granted 3 years earlier by King Charles II. Regardless of whether or not Roger Williams is making a cryptic reference to Tudor roses or alchemical roses, it's clear he knew that "Rode" meant "Rose."

(Quote from LaFantasie, Glenn W., *The Correspondence of Roger Williams*, Vol. 2, p. 538)

Three levels of meaning for Dee's Lady Occasion

On one level, Lady Occasion means "opportunity," and the sturdy, city walls at her feet represent the "steadfast watch post" Dee is encouraging Elizabeth to establish in the New World.

On a second level of meaning, Lady Occasion is the Colossus of RHODES and the sturdy city walls are the defensive walls of RHODES.

On a third level of meaning, Lady Occasion and the "sturdy city walls" represent the grand architectural-sculpture Dee designed for the first Elizabethan colony at the Dee River: what I call the "John Dee Tower of 1583."

Like the "sturdy city walls," the Tower is solidly built from stone and mortar.

And just as Lady Occasion was the focal point of Dee's illustration, the Tower was meant to be the focal point of the new colony.

Three levels of meaning for Dee's "Lady Occasion"

1 Lady OPPORTUNITY

2 Colossus of RHODES

3 The MONUMENTAL SCULPTURE Dee designed for the first Elizabethan colony at the Dee River

There is a reason why the Colossus of Rhodes, the Statue of Liberty, the John Dee Tower, and even Lady Occasion are all located at **important ports that border on the sea**.
They are all symbolic "**greeters**."

My stylized depictions of these 4 symbolic "greeters"

In 300 BC, when sailors approached the harbor of Rhodes, Greece, they were greeted by the 110-foot tall colossal bronze statue of Helios.

The Colossus of Rhodes greets merchant ships entering Rhodes Harbor around 300 BC.

When immigrants coming to America entered New York Harbor in the early 1900's, they were greeted by the 110-foot tall, proud statue of freedom and liberty.

The Statue of Liberty greets immigrants and visitors entering New York Harbor (from 1886 to today)

As per Dee's Title page illustration, when the sailing expedition of the "five ships" approach the Dee River, they are greeted by a tall statue of Lady Occasion.

My stylized interpretation of the Title page of Dee's 1578 *General and Rare Memorials*: Lady Occasion greets one of the five ships destined for the Dee River.

If the Elizabethan colony had taken root, the thousands of anticipated new settlers would have been greeted by the harmoniously-proportioned, 48-foot tall, Vitruvian circular temple designed by John Dee.

What I call the John Dee Tower of 1583 was built not only to welcome Sir Humphrey Gilbert's expedition, but to also greet the thousands of Elizabethan colonists who were expected to follow.

The Colossus of Rhodes, the Statue of Liberty and the Tower at the Dee River. Beyond being "greeters," each represented freedom and liberty of conscience.

The Tower was intended to have been a source of inspiration and pride as the colony grew from small village, to major city, to (most likely) the capital of Virginia.
(Virginia was the English name for the whole east coast of America, named after Queen Elizabeth I, the Virgin Queen.)

[Indeed, in the 1700's Newport actually did become one of the five largest ports on the East Coast, along with Boston, New York, Philadelphia, and Charleston, South Carolina.]

Is there a "Dee triangle" (Δ) built into Dee's stone-and-mortar Tower?

Dee used his personal symbol Δ in all of his written works.
Dee drew the island of Claudia as a triangle Δ in his maps of North America.
Dee makes a "four-way" riddle, ΔΔΔΔ, by putting a tetrahedron on his Title page.

Is it too much to expect that Dee might have instructed the builders of the Tower
to put a triangle Δ in the Tower overlooking the mouth of the Dee Δ River?

West Window

"Sun Stone" symbol in the W NW arch   "Triangle" Rock in the W SW arch

The thousands of rocks used to construct the stone-and-mortar tower are primarily gray slate and tan granite fieldstones, both of which can be found locally.
The stones are all different shapes and sizes. However, a few of them look as though they were specifically selected and placed to make a visual statement.

For example, we've seen the circular "Sun Stone," a round, reddish rock in the arch between the West pillar and the Northwest pillar.

And just below the Sun Stone is a tall rock with distinctive "shoulders" that appear to have been shaped by chisel. Together, these two rocks are clearly an intentional symbol.

(I claim they represent Dee's Monas symbol, the overall design plan of the Tower.)

"Sun Stone" symbol in the W NW arch

The neighboring arch, just to the south,
(the arch between the West pillar and the Southwest pillar),
has a tall rectangular stone in the keystone area.

And above it is a rock with a triangular face!

The sides of the triangle are each about 7 inches long.
The upper right edge appears slightly chipped.

Given its prominent placement, and the fact that few other rocks in the Tower have faces which are triangular in shape, this one seems special.

"Triangle" Rock in the W SW arch

278

This triangular rock can be read in several ways.
In one respect, it is the "architect's signature":
Δ or Delta or "D" or "Dee."
But more significantly, because it's on the exterior
southwest arch, the triangular rock "**faces**" or
"**points towards**" the mouth of the Dee River!

This whole spectacular river-mouth waterway
was once visible from Touro Park
(before the houses were built on the west end of the park).

And there would have been an even better view of the mouth
of the Dee River from higher up in the 48-foot tall Tower.
(The view out the West window might have looked something like this:)

All these natural features would be visible:
(using modern place-names)
In Newport, Goat Island, Brenton Cove,
Fort Adams State Park, Castle Hill, and Brenton Point.

In Jamestown, the numerous rocky-islands called the
Dumplings, Bull Point, and Fort Wetherill State Park.

(And these features would be in sharp silhouette by the sparkling
waters of the river as the sun lowered to the west in the afternoon.)

My stylized depiction of the view out the West Window
looking west-southwest towards the entrance of the Dee River
(using modern place-names)

Looking out to sea, the triangular-shaped Block Island was probably visible on a clear day.
As Verrazzano recognized, its upper tip points towards the mouth of the port he called "Refugio."

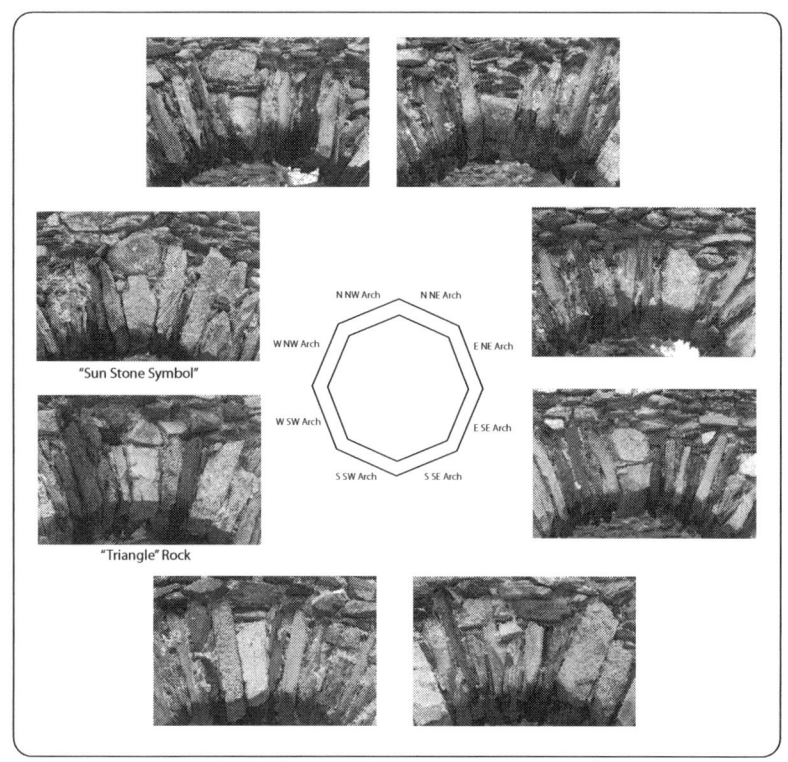

The centers of the eight arches
(on the exterior of the Tower)

I hesitate to refer to the the the combined "Sun Stone and the Rock with Shoulders" as a "keystone," because they are not exactly in the center of its arch.

In the neighboring arch, the "triangle rock" can't really be considered part of a keystone either. (Indeed, keystones should taper downwards, not upwards.)

The "keystone area" rocks in the other 6 arches don't appear to contain intentionally-shaped rocks (except the east-southeast arch, which has a roughly square rock in the bottom part of its central area).

Each of the 8 "keystone areas" of the 8 arches is different from the rest.

(This could be written of as casual construction
technique, but as we'll see shortly, other
keystone areas contain symbolic clues).

279

To someone who is visiting the Tower for the first time, that triangular rock might appear to be just random rock among thousands.

But, to me, someone who has studied the Tower closely, explored Dee's his pivotal role in the Elizabethan colonization effort, who is well-versed in Dee's clever clue-making skills, and who has deciphered Dee's *General and Rare Memorials* Title page rebus, that triangular rock shines like a neon light.

Δ says John Dee.
Δ says Dee River
Δ says "triangular Island,
the size of the Isle of Rhodes"

Sure, it's easy to be skeptical of this claim. There's no way I can definitively prove that this rock has any connection to Dee's signature or the Dee River.

If you take a "That can't be true" attitude, you'll never find any further clues. But if you take a "What if it's true" attitude, suddenly more clues may become apparent. No hypothesize, no prize.

And wouldn't it be just like Dee, so wise,
to hide a clue in front of your eyes!

My conclusion about who named Rhode Island:

In 1524, Verrazzano used the place-name **Rhode Island** in a metaphor about Block Island

In 1577, John Dee named gave **Rhode Island** its name.
(In other words, I believe Dee was the one responsible for transferring the name Rhode Island from a metaphorical description of Block Island to the actual name of Aquidneck Island.)

In 1637. Benedict Arnold followed Dee's lead
and insisted Aqiudneck be called **Rhode Island.**
(Even though Roger Williams wanted it named Patmos)

In 1644, the early Colonial leaders followed Benedict's lead
and made **Rhode Island** the official name of Aquidneck Island

Today it is still in the state name:
State of **Rhode Island** and Providence Plantations
(Which is proud have the longest name, yet be the smallest state.)

More fun.
Dee hid another riddle in the Title page:
his initials, **I.D.**

Dee's tetrahedron relates to the "four men brandishing fire" in the lower-left-edge of the picture (which are are echoed by the "four ships" above them.)

Dee seems to be hinting that these men are **pyrologians**.

(Dee also uses this "pyrologian" wordplay in Aphorism 18 of his *Propaedeumata Aphoristica*).

To Dee, "pyrologians" weren't people who set fires to houses. They are those who study the Element of Fire. Dee's favorite philosopher, Plato, associates the Element of Fire with the tetrahedron.

So, by "pyrologians," Dee means "those who study tetrahedra." (The first syllable of the words **pyr**ologian and **pyr**amid is *pyr*, the Greek word for fire.)

four ships

four "Pyrologians"

If the "pyrologians" represent 4 tetrahedra, and the four ships represent 4 more tetrahedra, this is an expression of the "+4,–4, octave" Dee shows in his "Thus the World Was Created" chart.

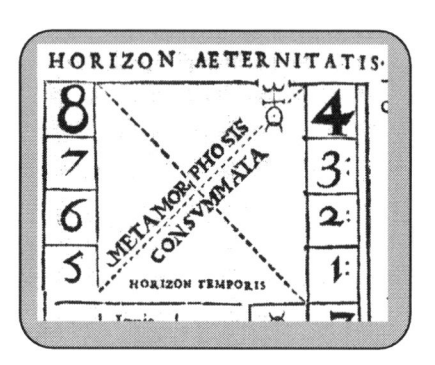

It is also an expression of the composition of the cuboctahedron, or Buckminster Fuller's "vector equilibrium," the shape that Dee and Fuller each recognized as "Nature's Operating System."

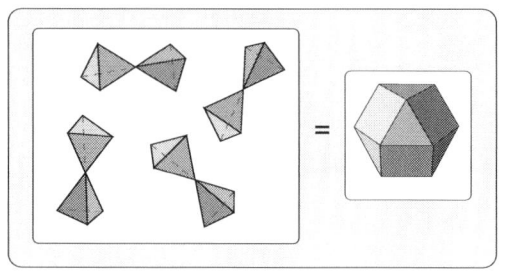

4 pairs of tip-to-tip tetrahedra assemble into a cuboctahedron

[Without knowledge of the number and geometry concepts Dee is referring to in the *Monas Hieroglyphica*, these 4 aligned ships and 4 pyrologians would just seem strange. But Elizabeth would understand because Dee explained his book to her in 1564, shortly after it was published.]

John Dee, Buckminster Fuller, and Robert Marshall all saw that in number and geometry, the "+4, –4, octave" is followed by a "null 9."

In Dee's "Thus the World was Created" chart, the **Horizon of Eternity** represents the **number 9**.

On the Title page, the horizon line of the ocean is similarly just above the "4 men and 4 ships" octave. Dee saw the **horizon** line as the **number 9**.

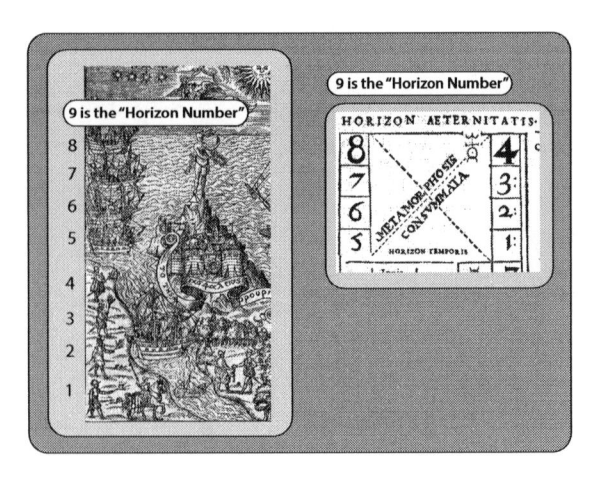

There is actually an alternative way to see the octave in Dee's "Thus the World was Created" chart: with all the numbers running up the left edge.

This is the exact same design Dee used with the men and the ships!

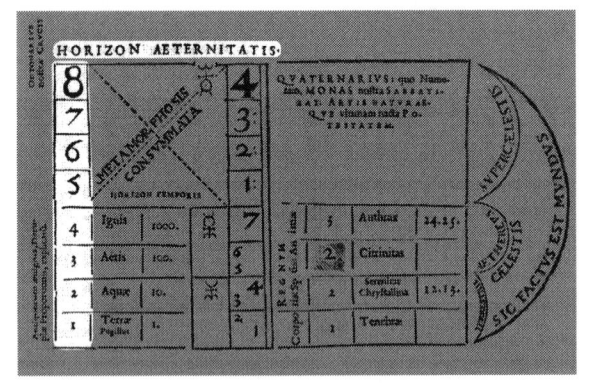

Another way to see "the octave and null nine"

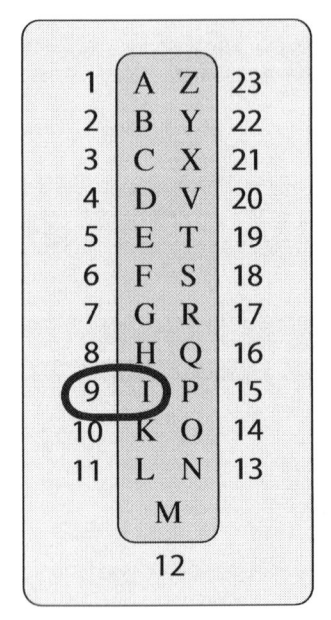

Throughout the *Monas Hieroglyphica* Dee displays his fascination with the sequence of the Latin alphabet. His hidden "alphabet/number code" couldn't get much simpler. (A=1, B=2, C=3, etc.)

As the 9th letter of the Latin alphabet is **I**, Dee saw the horizon in his illustration as the letter **I**.

We've also seen how Dee uses the horizon line, along with Lady Occasion's gesturing arm, to make the letter **D**.

Combine the **I** and the **D** and you have Dee's initials, **I.D.**

$$I + D = I.D. = \text{Ioannes Dee}$$

About 20 years earlier, in 1558, Dee had proudly displayed his initials (I.D.) on the Title page of his *Propaedeumata Aphoristica*.

I and **J** were the same letter in Dee's era, so, **I.D.** might just as easily be seen as **J.D.**

I.D. (Ioannes Dee) = **J.D.** (Johannes Dee)

Dee put his initials, **I.D.**, on the Title page of his *Propaedeumata Aphoristica* (1558 edition)

My associating the ocean "horizon" with **9**, and also with the letter **I**, may sound strange, but Dee uses this concept in several places in the *Monas Hieroglyphica*.

In his Artificial Quaternary chart, Dee lists 9 alchemical processes. He leaves number 4 and number 8 blank, and he labels the ninth process *Imb*. (for Imbibition). It's no accident that 9th process just happens to begin with the letter **I**.

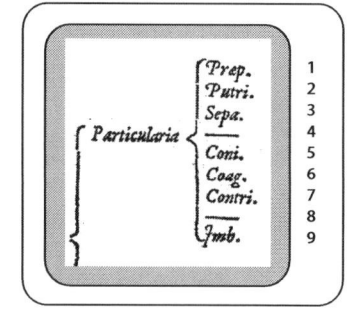

Dee also employs the letter **I = 9** trick" in the emblem which follows Theorem 24. In the word "INTELLICTUS," the large **I** represents **9**, the large **L** represents **11**, and the letters in between them spell the word "**Ten**."

(The numbers 9, 10, and 11, are the "transpalindromizer," the "base number," and the "palindromizer," respectively, in our Base Ten numbering system.)

As a hint, Dee emphasizes the letters **I**, **T**, and **L** by making them **super-sized** (in comparison to the other capitalized letters.) And the first 5 letters are somewhat isolated from the rest of the word (...LECTUS) by a dot.

It's interesting to note that Dee similarly isolated the first 5 letters of another long word starting with the letter **I**. That word is IEROGLYPHIKON, in the expression IEROGLYPHIKON BRITANIKON.

In this instance, he isolated the first five letters by running "IEROG" horizontally and running "LYPHIKON" vertically.

(And IEROG is a very important clue, as it is part of the word game involving the key words RODE and HOPE.)

Dee loved to play with the idea that his first initial, I, was the ninth letter, and it was also a geometric line. And Dee was consumed with the idea of the "+4, -4, octave, null nine, rhythm of Consummata. To me, all Dee's riddles shown above are "variations on a theme," thus they reinforce each other.

Having devised this clever visual riddle using his initials,
you can be certain that every time Dee looked at his illustration
he saw his own name, loud and clear. (**I**= horizon and **D**=curved arm)

He knew a clue this involved would be invisible to most eyes.

But he knew it would serve as a confirming clue to anyone who
understood that he was both math whiz and profound punster.

Why did Dee he go to such great lengths to hide his initials?

Dee hid his initials because his whole text of
General and Rare Memorials is written **anonymously**!

Look at the front cover. It doesn't say anywhere who the author is.
Nor is the author's name written anywhere in the text.

(It certainly seems as though Dee's "hiding of his
initials" is his cryptic way of signing his work.)

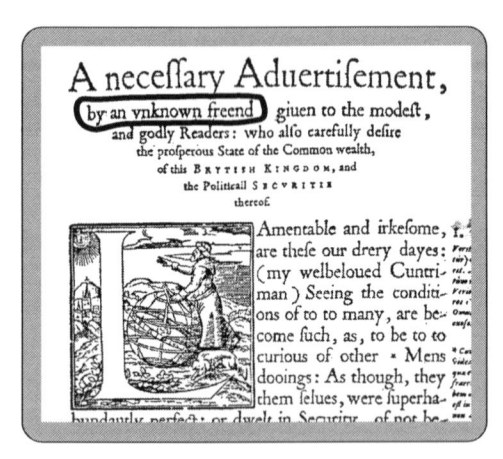

In both his "*Brief Note*" and his "*A necessary Advertisement*,"
Dee uses the rhetorical device of writing under the pen name of
an "**Unknown Friend**."

(It would have been pretty obvious to prominent
Elizabethans that Dee was the author of this work.
It's even obvious to modern-day historians.

Given the sentence structure, language, grasp
of subject matter, and the use of marginalia,
this text was unquestionably penned by Dee.)

But Dee uses this "anonymity" as a rhetorical device.
(Also, he could deny authorship in a court of law
if he somehow got in trouble for writing it.)

By writing from the point of view of an "Unknown Friend," Dee
portrayed himself an anonymous "voice of the people of England."

In this light, the kneeling woman, who is imploring to the Queen to
"Send forth a sailing expedition...," is not just the citizens of England.

She is **Dee**, acting as a **spokesperson** for the citizens of England.

(kneeling woman= Unknown Friend=Dee)

Is the
"kneeling woman"
actually Dee,
the "Unknown Friend,"
acting as a spokesperson
for the people of England?

284

The faces of practically everyone in the illustration are visible (either face-on or in profile). Even the Sun and Moon have faces. But, we only see the back of the kneeling woman's head, not her face. And if we could see her face, **it would probably look like John Dee**.

In this very book, Dee supplies all the legal and economic reasons for the Queen to broaden her horizons and allow England prosper by spreading its influence to the New World. In short, **Dee is the "kneeling woman."**

But, in another sense, **Dee is also "Lady Occasion."**
The Queen is lucky to have someone as
forward-thinking as Dee in her realm.
Dee is Lady Luck.

The flip side of Lady Luck is Danger and even Death!

A huge theme in Dee's *Monas Hieroglyphica* is the **Union of Opposites**
(*coincidentia oppositorum*, like Dee's Sun and Moon, or the transpalindromic
pair 12 and 21, which multiply to Dee's Magistral number, 252.)

The "opposite" of Lady Occasion (or Lady Luck or **good luck**) is **bad luck**.

And the ultimate of "bad luck" is death—whether it be the death of one's self, the death of a loved one, or even the death of a whole country (for example, if it's conquered by an enemy).

Without "bad luck,"
there would be no such thing as "good luck."

They are opposites, but they are similar, in
the sense that they are both just aspects of fate.

And sure enough, Dee portrays "bad luck" along the
lower right-hand edge of the illustration as a **skull**.

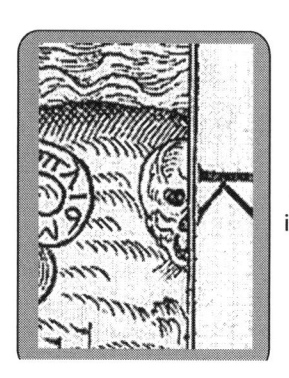

Danger,
or even Death,
is always lurking

The horizon line goes through Lady Occasion's skull

A line through the danger-skull
is the same distance from
the bottom edge as the
Lady Luck-horizon is
from the top edge.

Note that the skull is the same
distance from the **bottom** of the page,
as the horizon is from the **top** of the page.
(The horizon goes through Lady Occasion's
"skull" and aligns with her blowing hair.)

This seems to graphically connect
the unlucky head and the lucky head.

And curiously, Dee doesn't show the entire
skull. Using the edge of the illustration,
he chops the skull in half vertically.

285

Just as Lady Occasion's **arm and hair** form the letter **D**,
the outline of the **half-skull** also forms a (backwards) letter **D.**

(And as sort of a confirming clue, the word **D**eath starts with the letter **D**.)

Another "D-shape"

Geometrically speaking, two **D**'s combine
to form a circle with a vertical diameter in it.

It might seem like I'm stretching a good clue too
far, but this is a shape Dee cryptically refers to
(in several different cryptic ways) in the text of the *Monas*.
I call this shape the "**double-D**."

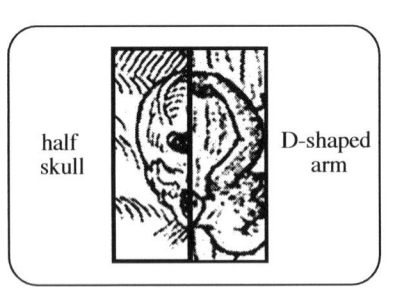

half skull   D-shaped arm

In Theorem 1, Dee writes, the "very First and most
Simple Representation" of things in Nature "is
made by means of a straight Line and a Circle."

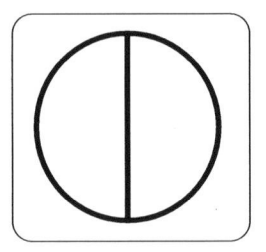

In his *Letter to Maximilian*, Dee writes about the:

**"Oneness of the IOD itself;
that Trinity being Formed from one straight line
and two different parts of the circumference**."

Even the very letters I, O, and D can
be found in this "double-D" shape.

(Dee, *Monas*, p..5)

If the two D's are seen as just two half circles
(without the vertical line between them), they
are like the two half circles in the Aries symbol.

And in Theorem 21, Dee describes closing up the
2 half circles (as if hinged) to make a complete circle.

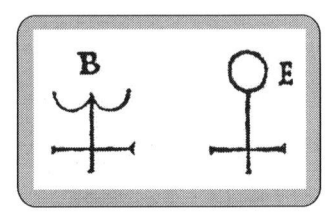

Two halves of the Aries symbol
closing-up to make a circle

286

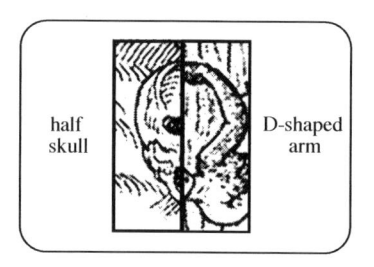

In short, the subliminal message here is:

Seize the lock of Lady Occasion's hair
(**D**'s or **Dee**'s sage advice)

or

"the opposite" will result
(bad luck or death).

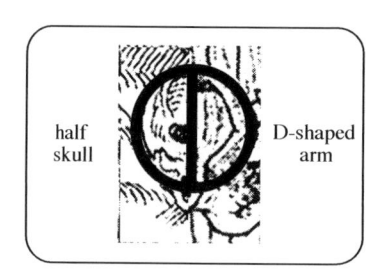

Another representation of IOD
(or the Union of Opposites) on the Title Page

Dee hides another letter-clue about the IOD, or the Union of Opposites, in the 4 Greek letters which are in the 4 corners of his illustration.

Three of the letters are the lowercase Greek letters "α, ς, and o," or the Latin letters **A**, **S**, and **O**."

In Aphorism 18 of his *Propaedeumata Aphoristica*, Dee cryptically suggests that (**A**, **S**, and **O**) represent (point, line, and circle) respectively.

> **A** is the first letter, like the **point** is the "first thing" in nature
>
> **S** is a **line** (which happens to be curved, but it's still a line)
>
> **O** is an obvious **circle**.

(A more thorough explanation of Aphorism 18 can be found in: Egan, James Alan, *Book 5: The Story of 1, 2, 3, 4 and the Proportions of the John Dee Tower*, pp. 35–46)

    In the first two Theorems of the *Monas*, Dee discusses how "all things" derive from the point, the line, and the circle.

    Then, he combines them all in the word **IOD**, and cryptically describes a circle with a vertical diameter.

    This "**double-D**" is his code symbol for the Union of Opposites, like the Sun and the Moon combined.

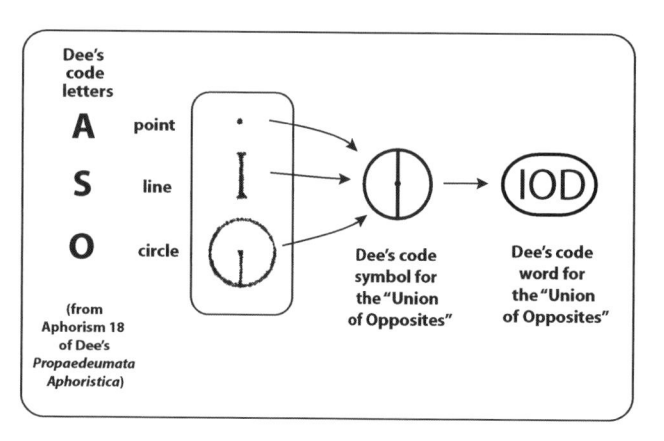

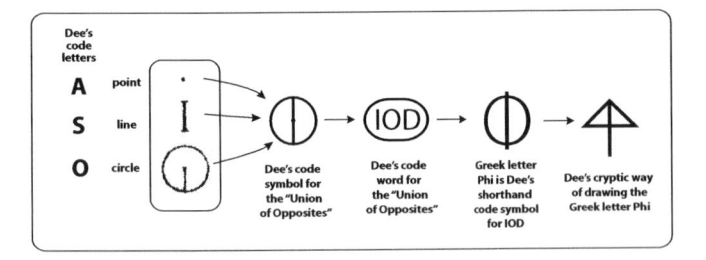

Dee's code letters		
A	point	•
S	line	I
O	circle	○

Dee's code symbol for the "Union of Opposites" → Dee's code word for the "Union of Opposites" (IOD) → Greek letter Phi is Dee's shorthand code symbol for IOD (Φ) → Dee's cryptic way of drawing the Greek letter Phi

In the extreme upper right hand corner of his illustration, he represents the IOD with the Greek letter Phi, Φ, the only Greek or Latin letter that closely resembles his code-symbol.

To further disguise the Phi, Dee makes it look like a "tree shape" (a triangle with a vertical line).

As a way of hinting about all this, Dee uses both a **tree-shaped Phi** and a **regular Phi** in the words written on on the flowing ribbons.

In the word ASΦALEIAS, he uses a **tree shaped Phi**, but in the word ΦROURIOM he uses a **regular Phi**.

(ASPHALEIAS means "steadfast" and PHROURIOM means "watch post")

Close-up view of the Greek letter Φ

Further proof of this can be seen in Dee's preliminary sketch for the Title page (drawn by Dee's own hand) where **he actually uses the letter Φ (Phi)** in the upper right-hand corner.

Dee's preliminary drawing for the Title page of General and Rare Memorials

To summarize, "point, line, and circle combined" or "A, S, and O combined" make Φ (Phi), Dee's code symbol for the Union of Opposites

(or "coincidentia oppositorum" or "retrocity").

This explanation might seem like a sidetrack, but as we'll see shortly, Dee's Union of Opposites theme unites an important male and an important female:

John Dee and Queen Elizabeth!

Strangely enough, most Elizabethans did not use the word "road" in the sense of a "path, way, or street."

In Medieval times, the word **road** (generally spelled **rode** or **rood**) meant the "act of riding on horseback." Shakespeare was the first author to use the word "road" in the sense of "path, way, or street."

In his 1598 play, *Henry IV,* the great bard refers to "London road." Most Elizabethans used the words "way, highway, trail, track, trace, and street," but not the word "road." You won't even find the word road (in the sense of "path or street") anywhere in the King James version of the Bible (which was translated from 1604 to 1611).

In Elizabethan times, the word "road" meant:
"a sheltered piece of water near the shore where vessels may lie at anchor in safety."

In 1518, Alexander Barclay writes,
"Lyke wise as shyppes, be docked in a **rode**."

In his 1617 *Itinerary,* Fynes Moryson writes,
"the Town of Gravesend is a known **Roade**."
(Situated at the mouth of the River Thames, Gravesend is a well-protected natural harbor.")

In 1824 *Tales of a Traveler*, Washington Irving writes
"the tide contrary, the vessel anchored far off in the **road**." (*OED*, road)

And "sheltered harbor" is still one of the meanings of road today.

Today's *Random House Dictionary* defines this nautical meaning of rode as, "a partly sheltered area of water near shore in which vessels may ride at anchor."

In 1996, U.S. Army Corps of Engineers correspondent N. D. Mulherin writes, "There are also anchorage areas...at the inner **roads**. The outer **roads** are exposed to winds."

This "sheltered harbor" meaning is still in the dictionaries, even though in modern usage it is decidedly overshadowed by the "path or street" meaning.

A ship "at road" is "at anchor" in a safe harbor

The phrase "**at road**" refers to a vessel that is
"in a road" or "safe in a sheltered waterway."
The phrase is synonymous with the phrase "**at anchor**."
This expression goes way back to Medieval days as well.

Henry VII's 1495 *Naval Inventories* read,
"The seid ship lying **at Rode** in the Kynges haven."

In 1596, the Elizabethan writer Robert Southwell writes in *Triumphs Over Death*, "God...casteth your anchor where your thoughts should lie **at rhode**."
(*OED*, road, phrases; emphasis mine)

A ship "at rode" or "at anchor"
in a sheltered harbor

The purpose of this in-depth etymological explanation is to help you to envision the Title page of Dee's *General and Rare Memorials* with Elizabethan eyes.

Safely at anchor in the protected waterway is a ship "**at rode**." Four more ships lie "**at rode**" lined up just off the coastline. You can see the anchor lines and the sails are furled. By contrast, Dee has depicted the Queen's ship under full sail.

In short, these 5 anchored ships are a pun on the word "Rode," the "code-name" for the first Elizabethan colony at the Dee River.

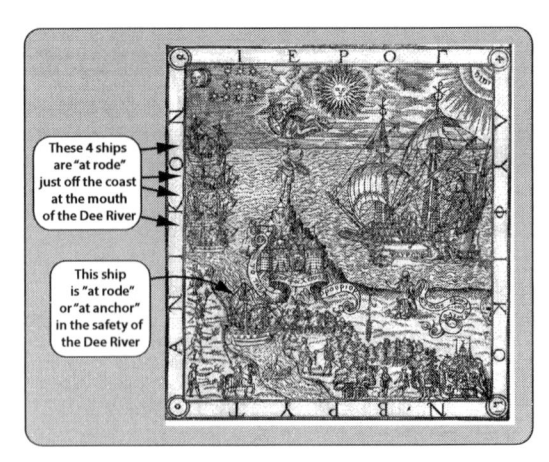

These 4 ships are "at rode" just off the coast at the mouth of the Dee River

This ship is "at rode" or "at anchor" in the safety of the Dee River

In the 1600s, a "rode" also meant an "anchor rope"

In the 1600s, the strong rope used to stay "at rode" or "at anchor" came to be called a "rode."

The *Boston Records of 1679* make a reference to "A **roade** taken out of his boat in the time of ye fire & made use of to pull down houses."

The 1883 *Fisheries Exhibition Catalog* refers to "12 Manilla Trawl **Rhode**, a large yarn."

"Rode" or "anchor rope"

This meaning is still in use today. In her 1950 *Candlemas Bay*, Ruth Moore writes, "His anchor and **rode** were stowed down under the stern." (OED, rode, note 2; emphasis mine)

(However, as this "cable or rope" meaning came about in the 1600s, the actual ropes securing the five ships in Dee's illustration should **not** be seen as another cryptic representation of the word "Rode.")

But, when the early colonial leaders of Rhode Island adopted the "fouled anchor" as the symbol of the state in the mid-1600s, I think they included a small piece of the anchor rope because that rope **actually expressed the name of the state.**

The state symbol of Rhode Island, the Anchor of Hope, has an "anchor rope" attached. So this "**rode**" or "**anchor rope**" visually expresses the word "**Rhode**," as in the name Rhode Island.

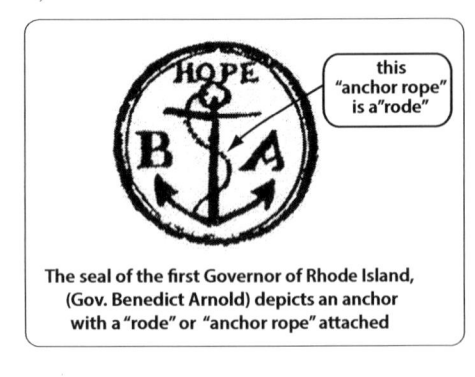

this "anchor rope" is a "rode"

The seal of the first Governor of Rhode Island, (Gov. Benedict Arnold) depicts an anchor with a "rode" or "anchor rope" attached

Yet another cryptic representation of the word "Rode" on the Title page: ER + DO= RODE

Queen Elizabeth I rules the Title page.

Her hand is on the rudder guiding the Ship of State through (what Dee considered to be) Elizabeth's Oceans of the North Atlantic to the first Elizabethan colony at the Dee River.

On the canopy above her head is her name, ELIZABETH.

On the rudder is the English Royal Coat of Arms.

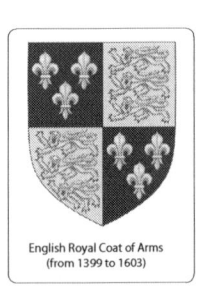

English Royal Coat of Arms (from 1399 to 1603)

The Queen's Initials are ER

Queen Elizabeth I's real name is Elizabeth Tudor, but she didn't use either the initials QE or ET. She used the initials **ER**, which stand for *Elizabetha Regina*.

(*Regina* is Latin for "Queen").

The initials ER can be found on many coins, engravings, and portraits of the Queen.

She even signed her name **Elizabeth R**.

The signature of Queen Elizabeth I, signed as Elizabeth R (for Regina)

The Queen's initials, ER, on Elizabethan coinage

The initials ER embroidered on the cushion of Queen's throne.
(This painting was done in the early 1580's, after an earlier painting by Nicholas Hilliard.)

In this 1590s engraving by William Rogers, Queen Elizabeth I is surrounded by roses.

She is the "Rosa Electa" or "The Choice Rose," who will "Flourish Forever."

Above her are the initials ER, which are also first two letters in **R**osa **E**lecta.

(Elizabethans loved initials, wordplay, and symbolism.)

Queen Elizabeth I as ROSA ELECTA (The Choice Rose), surrounded by flowing roses.

Above her is written FLOREAT, IN AETERNUM (Flourish Forever)

On the top left and right are her initals, ER.

(Engraving done by William Rogers in the early 1590's)

Now, four centuries later, her namesake, Queen Elizabeth II, also uses the initials ER,
(along with a "II," just to keep things clear.)

This modern Queen Elizabeth II also signs her name Elizabeth R.

Queen Elizabeth II

ER II or Elizabeth Regina II

The signature of Queen Elizabeth II. Notice the R at the end, for Elizabeth Regina

291

So even though Dee hasn't actually drawn these initials next to the Queen, they are such a common symbol for her, let's assume for a moment that they are implied.

Notice that the letters **ER** are two of the letters in the word **RODE**, which is cryptically referred to in so many ways.

To spell the word "RODE," all that is needed is find an "**O**" and a "**D**." And we've already seen that Lady Occasion's arm forms a **D**-shape with her hair and the horizon.

With this in mind, it's not hard to locate the other missing letter, the O. Lady Occasion is holding a corolla or a crown of victory in her other hand.

Seen obliquely (as it has been drawn) it looks like in a ellipse or egg-shape.

But this is because of "perspectiva" or "point of view." When viewed straight-on, a corolla is actually a perfect circle. **It's the missing "O."**

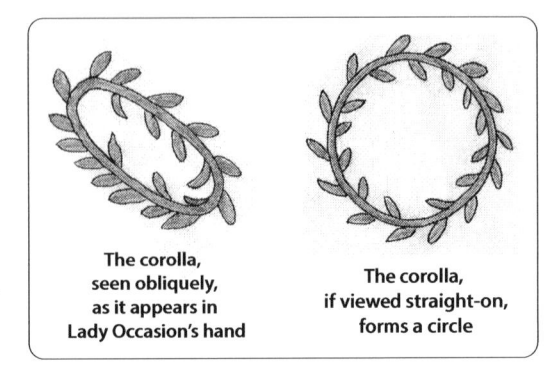

The corolla, seen obliquely, as it appears in Lady Occasion's hand

The corolla, if viewed straight-on, forms a circle

Just as Lady Occasion is gesturing (with the corolla) towards the Queen, the Queen is gesturing back, as if reaching out for the crown of victory.

To me, these gestures connect that **D** and **O** of Lady Occasion's gestures to the Queen, who might be identified as **ER**. Another cryptic **RODE**!

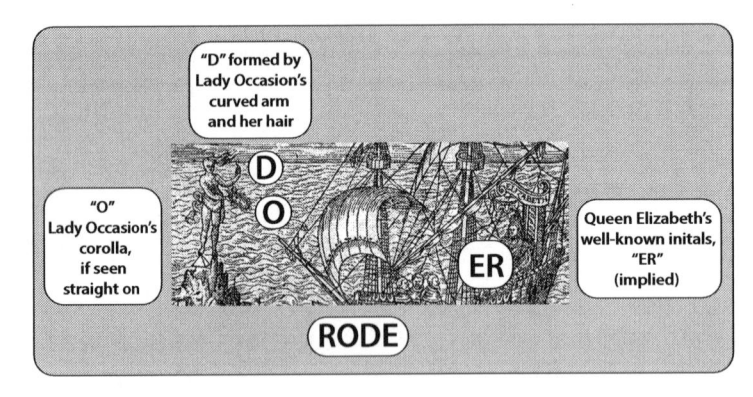

"D" formed by Lady Occasion's curved arm and her hair

"O" Lady Occasion's corolla, if seen straight on

Queen Elizabeth's well-known initals, "ER" (implied)

(RODE)

As the letters E and R do not actually appear on Elizabeth, or on her pennant or on her rudder, I will admit that this cryptic RODE is an imaginative solution.

But if Dee had drawn the initials ER in big letters, it would have confused all the other word-puzzles on the Title page.

Being familiar with Dee's subtle clue-hiding techniques, I think he intended this "RODE" to be seen. It's Dee's way of dramatizing his personal connection with the Queen.

One of the things that Dee was most proud of in life was that the Queen referred to him as "my Philosopher."

And here's how I think Dee expresses this royal relationship visually on the Title page:

The Union of Opposites: Ioannes Dee and Elizabetha Regina

As we've seen, John Dee expresses the initials of his Latin name, Ioannes Dee with the horizon line (**I** = ninth letter) and **D**-shaped arm of Lady Occasion.

The Queen's name is *Elizabetha Regina*.

Dee, **ID,** portrays himself as Lady Occasion, offering a corolla to the Queen, **ER**, who in turn is reaching out for it. And the corolla represents the letter **O**.

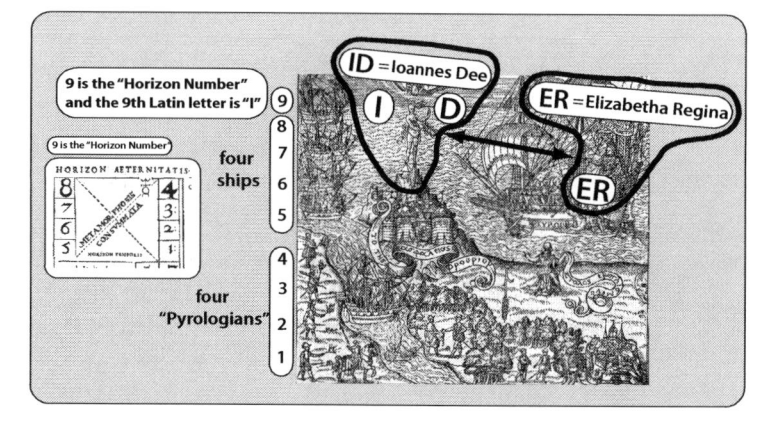

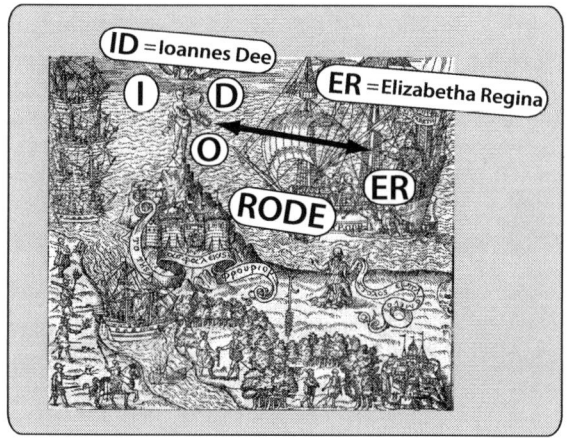

Among these letters (**ID**, **ER** and **O**) are the 4 letters used to spell that secret-code-word **RODE**,

(That perfect location Dee chose for the birthplace of the British Empire.)

John Dee conceived the whole plan of action.

The Queen had the power to authorize it.

Dee is portraying himself and the Queen as a unified team, the Union of Opposites, like the Sun and Moon.

Dee was full of hope. Dee was an inveterate optimist. He expected this seed colony at RODE to fully blossom, bringing unimaginable riches to the Queen (and of course to himself).

This first spark of the British Empire at RODE would be their bonding connection. In a sense it was to be their child.

Dee was the father and Elizabeth was the mother about to give birth to a infant that would one day grow to be quite powerful.

There is a confirming clue that Dee intended himself and the Queen to express the Union of Opposites.

The letters he cryptically associates with Lady Occasion are **I**, **O**, and **D**, which spell **IOD**, his shorthand word for the Union of Opposites.

Could Dee have really conceived of this web of clues?

Yes. His other works demonstrate he had the mind of a master puzzlemaker.

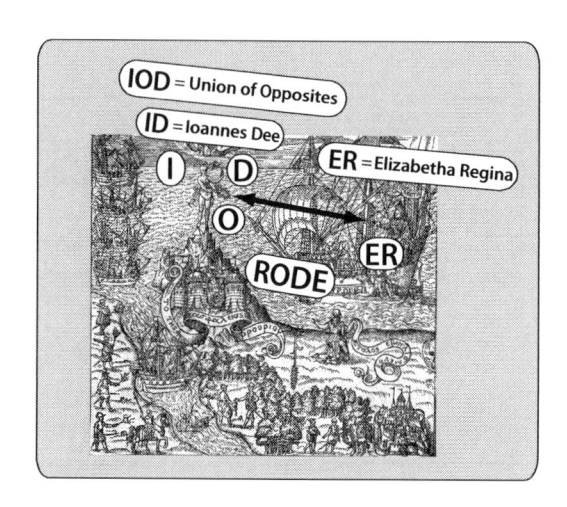

293

Dee's Title page is an Elizabethan Nike ad: "JUST DO IT"

In short, Dee is pleading to the Queen: "Make it or break it!" or "Go for it, before it's too late!" On bended knees, Dee is imploring the Queen to take this "Opportunity" to "Send forth a sailing expedition to make a steadfast watch post," or else it might be the "death" of England.

That's a pretty strong statement to make to the Queen. Encoding this dire warning in a fun-illustration at least makes it a bit more palatable. And once understood, it perhaps made the message more memorable. With this "Do or Die" message, it's also a little more understandable why Dee would have written this text "anonymously," as if it was advice from a "Unknown Friend."

Dee's language might be strong, but he was right. Unless an organization, state, or person is proactive, changing, exploring and evolving, it risks becoming obsolete. This is why Constitutions have Amendments, why corporations have Research and Development departments, why people take continuing education classes.

It's strange how it seems like I'm hearing these stories from Dee's mouth 450 years after he wrote them down. Dee was not only writing to the Queen, he was writing for posterity. He knew the birth of the British Empire would be a landmark moment in English history.

Dee was a visual thinker. He knew that one symbolic image could express 1000 words. And his Title page illustration contains dozens of symbolic images.

RODE (or Rhode) seems to be the "code name" for the first Elizabethan colony at the mouth of the Dee River

To summarize, Dee, the Queen, the Privy council members, and the courtiers involved probably used the word **RODE** (or Rhode) as a code name for the settlement at the mouth of the Dee River.

Dee was cryptic for a reason. Even if the Spanish ambassador got his hands on a copy of the book, decoders in Madrid never be able deduce the code-name or the hints about the colony's location.

A brief visual summary of Dee's **RODE** *clues*

Dee's Title page is a panoply of visual puzzles and word riddles involving the the code-name, "RODE,"

There are so many clues that they can get confusing.

First of all, Dee tells us right up front that he is hiding clues.

More is hidden than meets the eye.

A British Hieroglyphic

294

What Dee writes in Greek on his Elizabethan
"word balloon" (or his flowing ribbon of words)
is exactly what he depicts in his illustration:
a sailing expedition and
a watch post on the Dee River.

To express it in modern-day lingo,
Dee is selling something to the Queen,
(A sailing expedition to make a steadfast watch post).

And, as is done in strategic advertising,
Dee made the product the "hero" of the ad.

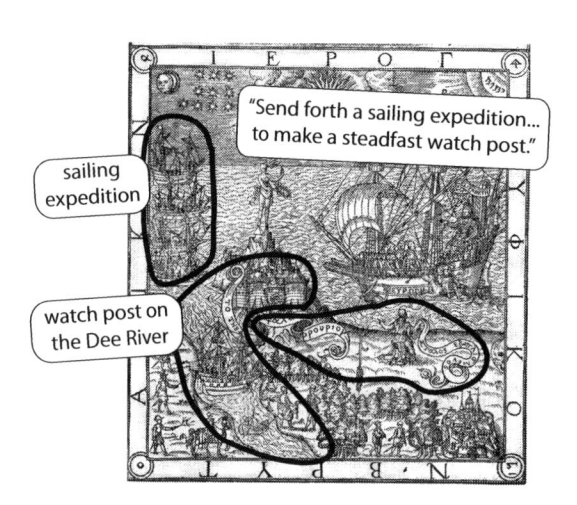

"Send forth a sailing expedition... to make a steadfast watch post."

sailing expedition

watch post on the Dee River

Dee's use of the archangel Michael (42) helps confirm
that he is depicting the Dee River (42° north and 42° west).

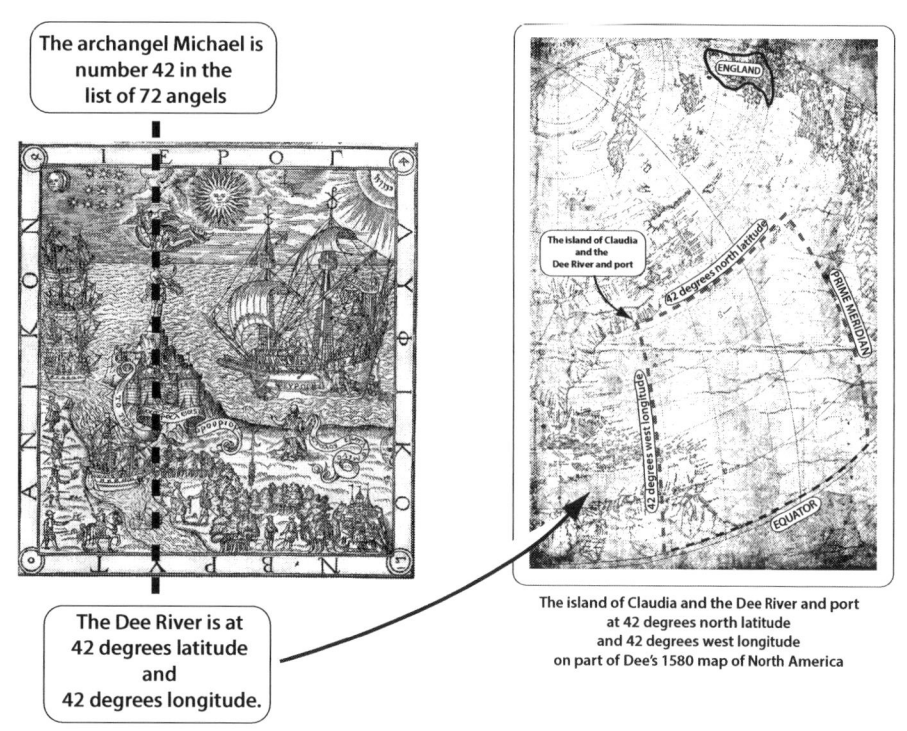

The archangel Michael is number 42 in the list of 72 angels

The Dee River is at 42 degrees latitude and 42 degrees longitude.

The island of Claudia and the Dee River and port

42 degrees north latitude

PRIME MERIDIAN

42 degrees west longitude

EQUATOR

ENGLAND

The island of Claudia and the Dee River and port
at 42 degrees north latitude
and 42 degrees west longitude
on part of Dee's 1580 map of North America

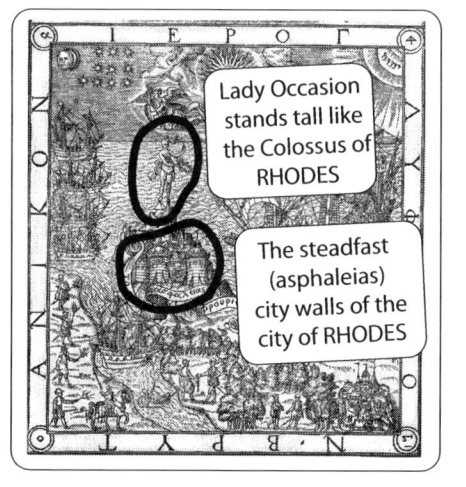

Lady Occasion stands tall like the Colossus of RHODES

The steadfast (asphaleias) city walls of the city of RHODES

Dee makes several
strong (yet cryptic) visual
references to the word **RODE**.

Tudor Rose
In Greek,
ROSE=RODE

295

A summary of the "4 clues-in-1"

Dee's tetrahedron is "4-clues-in-1," each clue involving a triangle

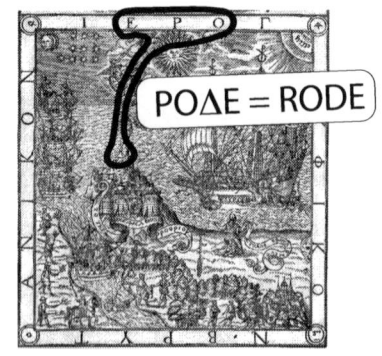

PO∆E = RODE

1. One triangle, ∆, plus the letters OPE, spells PO∆E, or RODE

2. With another triangle, the author Dee is signing his work with his pen name, ∆.
(or "pen symbol")

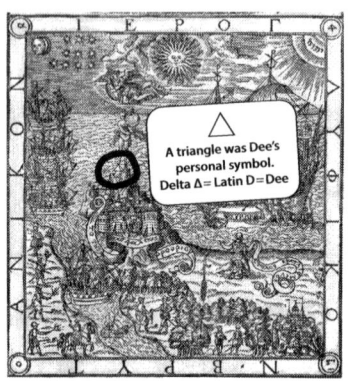

△
A triangle was Dee's personal symbol.
Delta ∆ = Latin D = Dee

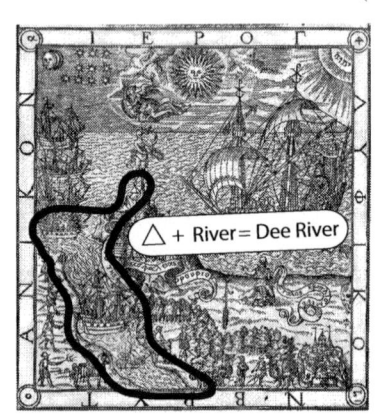

△ + River = Dee River

3. Another triangle, ∆, identifies the name of the river that John Dee named after himself.
(Which is near the "triangular island")

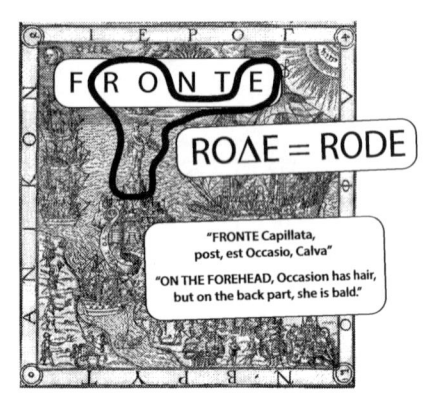

FRONTE
RO∆E = RODE

"FRONTE Capillata, post, est Occasio, Calva"
"ON THE FOREHEAD, Occasion has hair, but on the back part, she is bald."

4. The final triangle ∆, along with the letters ROE from the Latin word FRONTE, spells RODE

Cleverly, one of ships is "**at rode**" (at anchor) in the safety of the Dee River. And 4 more ships are "**at rode**" near the coast, at the river's mouth.

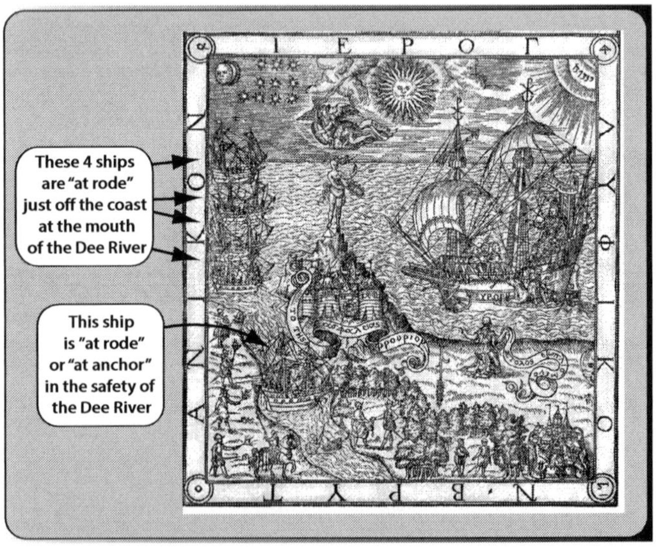

These 4 ships are "at rode" just off the coast at the mouth of the Dee River

This ship is "at rode" or "at anchor" in the safety of the Dee River

If you understand Dee's "CONSUMMATA," or the "+4, −4, octave; null 9" rhythm found in geometry and number, you can see another way the author John Dee has signed his work with his initials, **ID**.

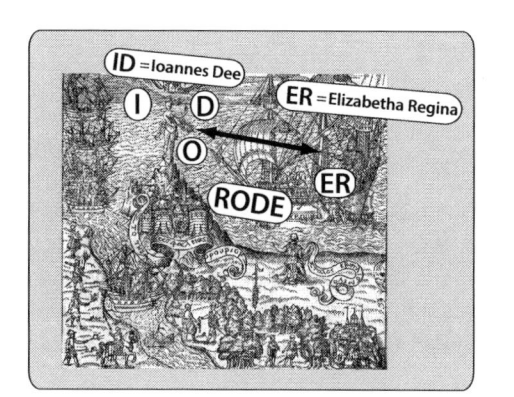

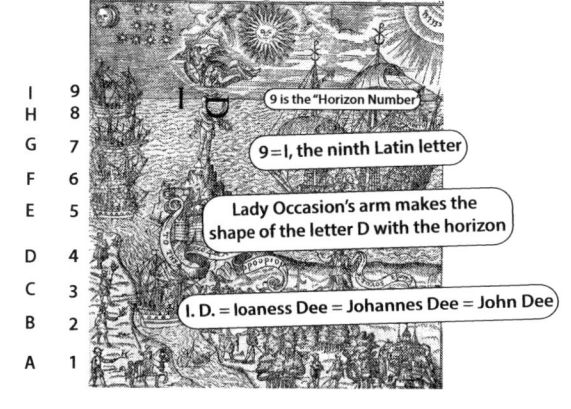

I	9
H	8
G	7
F	6
E	5
D	4
C	3
B	2
A	1

- 9 is the "Horizon Number"
- 9 = I, the ninth Latin letter
- Lady Occasion's arm makes the shape of the letter D with the horizon
- I. D. = Ioaness Dee = Johannes Dee = John Dee

ID = Ioannes Dee
ER = Elizabetha Regina

Lady Occasion offers the Queen the circular corolla. When this **O** is added to the mix of the Latin initials **ID** and **ER**, the word **RODE** can be spelled once again.

Even this summary can sound confusing, so here are Dee's main clues related to "RODE," shown in one diagram.

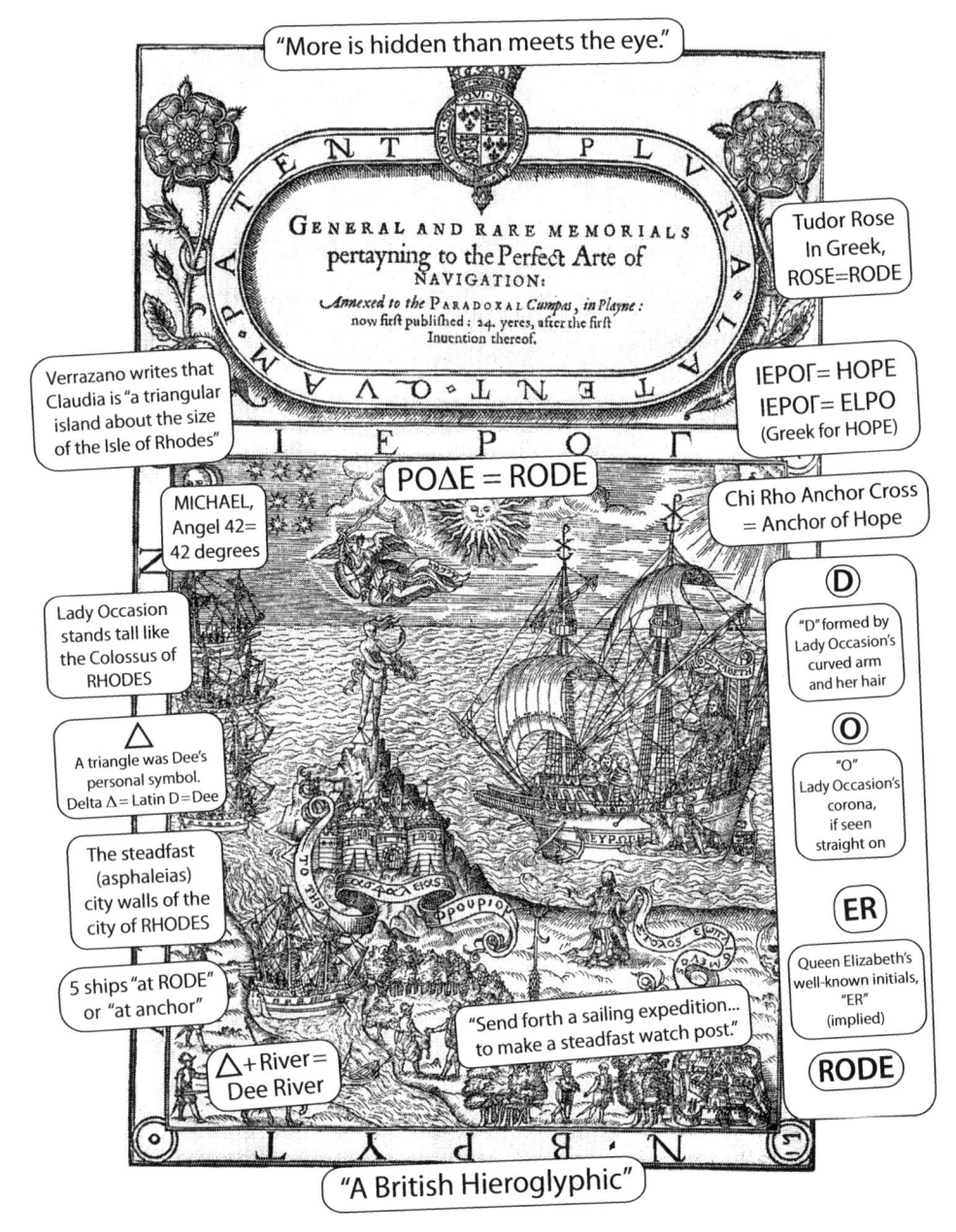

"More is hidden than meets the eye."

- Tudor Rose In Greek, ROSE=RODE
- Verrazano writes that Claudia is "a triangular island about the size of the Isle of Rhodes"
- ΙΕΡΟΓ = HOPE ΙΕΡΟΓ = ELPO (Greek for HOPE)
- ΡΟΔΕ = RODE
- MICHAEL, Angel 42 = 42 degrees
- Chi Rho Anchor Cross = Anchor of Hope
- Lady Occasion stands tall like the Colossus of RHODES
- **D** "D" formed by Lady Occasion's curved arm and her hair
- △ A triangle was Dee's personal symbol. Delta △ = Latin D = Dee
- **O** "O" Lady Occasion's corona, if seen straight on
- The steadfast (asphaleias) city walls of the city of RHODES
- **ER** Queen Elizabeth's well-known initials, "ER" (implied)
- 5 ships "at RODE" or "at anchor"
- △+River = Dee River
- "Send forth a sailing expedition... to make a steadfast watch post."
- **RODE**

"A British Hieroglyphic"

297

Historians have always been puzzled about how the name "Rhode" got "shifted" Block Island to (Aquidneck Island) which was over 15 miles away. It seems like a long jump. And island names don't usually switch to other nearby islands.

But from the viewpoint of John Dee, sitting in his London library, concocting plans for the first Elizabethan colony, Claudia (Block Island), the Dee River, and Aquidneck Island **are virtually all the same place.**

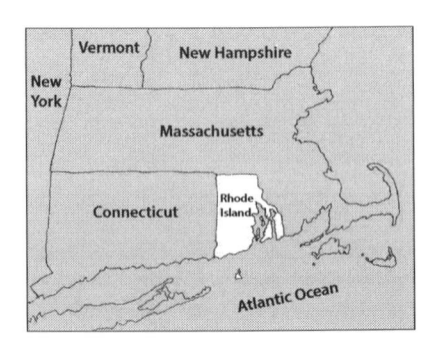

Thus, I believe the state name RODE originated in the mind of John Dee.

It was John Dee who took part of Verrazzano's "size-metaphor" about Block Island and used it to name the site of the first Elizabethan colony.

Benedict Arnold simply followed suit.

And the other early Colonial leaders went along with Benedict's name.

And today, **RODE** is still a part of the state name: "**RhODE** Island and Providence Plantations."

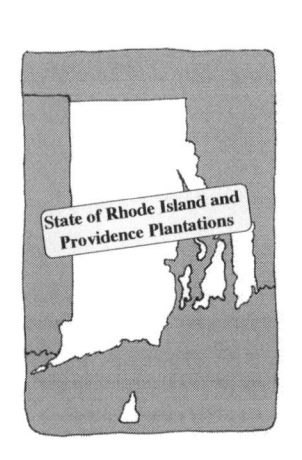

A summary of how this all relates to the Tower?

There are recognizable symbols in the "keystone areas" of the west-facing arches in the Tower.

The triangular rock (Δ) or (Dee) is oriented towards, (or "points to) the mouth of the Dee River.

"Triangle" Rock in the W SW arch

These rocks in the "keystone area" suggest another hidden clue in the Tower. Do you know what I'm referring to?

298

The "Shibboleth" (or "watchword") for the first Elizabethan colony in America, at the Dee River

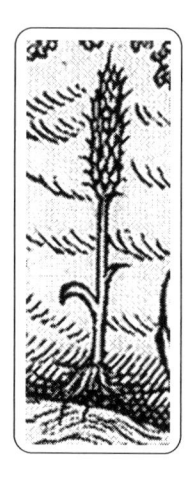

One of the most puzzling details in the Title page illustration for *General and Rare Memorials* is this "upside down plant."

To examine it, let's rotate it 180 degrees so it's upright.

It has roots, a stalk with two leaves, and a head containing several dozen seeds that have spiked tips.

It could be any of several species of the grass family: wheat, barley, or rye.

Upper-class Elizabethans ate "Manchet," a loaf of bread made from wheat. The lower classes ate bread made from barley or rye.

But barley was the most common grain for making beer, which was a staple at Elizabethan meals. In the cities, water wasn't clean enough to drink, so the average Elizabethan drank about a gallon of beer a day.

(But they weren't tipsy all the time, as their beer had a lower alcohol content than ours does today.)

What is Dee trying to express with this "stalk of grain"?

He may be implying that the colony at the Dee River
(which he is depicting in the whole Title page illustation)
will be the "seed" of the new British Empire.
Indeed the roots of the plant are right on the shoreline.
(And some roots even extend into the sea.)

There are several problems with this solution.

First, wheat doesn't grow on the shoreline.
It needs rich soil and fresh water.

Secondly, it's not really just a
"seed" that is shown here.
It's a whole plant.

Given Dee's devout Christianity, the plant might symbolize "bread,"
as in the "bread and wine," or "body and blood" of the Eucharist.
But if this was Dee's intent, where is the wine represented?

> Lauda HIERUSALEM Dominum,
> Lauda Deum tuum SION.
> Quoniam confortauit Seras Portarum tuarum:
> Benedixit filijs tuis in te.
> Qui pofuit fines tuos PACEM,
> Et adipe Frumenti fatiat te. &.
> Non fecit Taliter omni Nationi.

Dee makes a reference to "wheat" in
the prayer included in the text of
General and Rare Memorials.
(Dee, *Memorials* p.64)

He also provides a
translation of the prayer:

> O HIERUSALEM, prayfe the Lord:
> Prayfe thy God, O Syon.
> For, he hath Strengthened the Barres of Thy Gates,
> And hath bleffed thy Children within thee:
> He hath made all thy Borders PEACE:
> And with the good Nutriment of wheat,
> doth fatiffy thee. &.
> He hath not done thus, to euery Nation, els :
> Prayfe we all, the Lord therefore.
> Amen.

Dee's term, "Nutriment of wheat" suggests a bounty
or an abundant harvest that would sustain the nation.

But the grain from the single plant shown here won't
even make a loaf of bread, never mind feed a realm.

Only after decoding many of the other clues on the Title page was able to
deduce what Dee meant by this inverted plant. And, strange as it may seem,
it's actually an "ear of corn" which expresses Dee's code-word: RODE.
Let me explain.

An Elizabethan's "ear of corn" isn't our "ear of corn"

To modern day Americans, an **ear of corn** means that sweet, golden-colored, butter-slathered, summertime treat.

But what we call corn is actually **maize**, a plant North American Indians have grown for centuries.

In the 1500's, the only maize plants in Europe were a few specimens that had been brought back by explorers.

When Elizabethans used the term **ear of corn**, they were referring to an ear of **wheat, barley or rye**.
(OED., corn, p. 559)

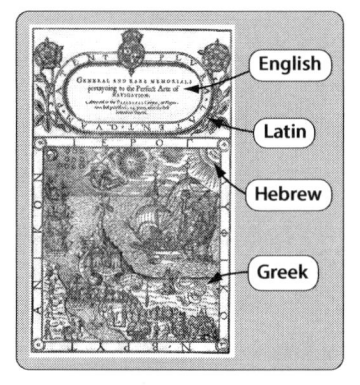

Dee was multilingual.
How many Title pages or book covers can you think of that contain words written in four languages: English, Latin, Greek, and Hebrew. **Dee uses them all**:

English: "General and Rare Memorials..."
Latin: "PLURA LATENT, QUAM PATENT"
Hebrew: "MYKAL" (Michael) and "YHVH" (Yahweh)
Greek:"Stolos explisMenos TO TES asphaleias phrouriom"

Dee was also well-versed in the **Bible**. In his library, he had versions of the Old Testament written in the original **Hebrew**, the **Greek** Septaugint, St. Jerome's **Latin** Vulgate, and **English** versions like John Wycliffe's 1395 translation.

Dee would have known the **Hebrew** word for an **ear of corn**: *shibboleth*.

He would not have become aware of this word by happening upon it in a Hebrew dictionary, but because it is of its importance in a well-known verse in the Bible.

The seventh book of the Old Testament, *Judges*, covers the main events that took place in the Holy Land from 1410 BC to 1050 BC:

In a fierce battle, Jepthtath and his Gileadites soundly defeated the neighboring Ephriamites, many of whom fled westward across the River Jordan.

After things had settled down, the refugees yearned to return east to their homeland.

But they were forbidden to return. The Gileadites set up sentries at the ford, the shallow crossing place.

Anyone who wanted to travel back east across the river was given a test. The sentries ask them to pronounce the Hebrew word for an **ear of corn**.

The Gileadites pronounced it *SHibboleth*, but the Ephriamites had no *SH* sound in their dialect, so they would pronounce it *Sibboleth*.

Over time, 42,000 Ephriamites failed the test and were slaughtered at the ford.

Over the years, different Bible translations have
used different spellings of these two words.

> Sei thou therfor 'Sebolech,'
> which is interpretid 'an eer of corn'
> which answeride 'Thebolech'

In St. Jerome's 405 AD
Latin Vulgate translation, uses
Sebboleth and *Tebboleth*.

John Wycliffe's 1395 English translation
uses *Sebolech* and *Thebolech*

The 1535 Bible translation by
Miles Coverdale uses the terms,
Schiboleth and *Siboleth*.

The 1611 King James Bible
uses *Shibboleth* and *Sibboleth*.

> *Judges 12:5-6*
>
> And the Gileadites took the passages
> of Jordan before the Ephraimites:
>
> and it was [so], that when those Ephraimites which
> were escaped said, Let me go over; that the men of
> Gilead said unto him, [Art] thou an Ephraimite?
>
> If he said, Nay; Then said they unto him,
> Say now Shibboleth: and he said Sibboleth:
>
> for he could not frame to pronounce [it] right. Then
> they took him, and slew him at the passages of Jordan:
>
> and there fell at that time of the
> Ephraimites forty and two thousand.

Even though *shibboleth* originally meant "an ear of corn," over time it has come
to mean a "test word, code word, catchword, password, byword, or countersign."

However, all these are terms were popularized **after** Dee's time.
Dee have probably called it a "**watchword**."

A little history of the term "Watchword"

As early as 150 BC, Polybius describes the Roman military's system for
distributing new passwords to the various sentinels guarding the city.

The English have used the word "**watch**" since around the year 1000.

(Both "watch" and "wake" derive from the Old English word *woc*,
meaning "to remain awake when most people normally are asleep.")

Tudor authors like Sir Thomas More, Sir Philip Sidney,
and William Shakespeare all use the term **watchword**.

Eventually **watch** took on the meaning of a small timepiece
carried in the pocket, then one worn on the wrist. (OED, watchword, p.155)

In short, a **watchman** would keep **watch** over a community from a **watch post**
(perhaps even a **watchtower**), and all the officials would know the **watchword**.

Dee's shibboleth was RODE

By depicting an "ear of corn," Dee is saying,
"I'm hiding a **watchword** on the Title page."

And that watchword is **RODE**, the code word for
the first Elizabethan colony on the Dee River, the
place Dee chose to "make a steadfast watch post."

> The
> watchword
> is RODE

It's possible Dee even intended RODE to be a shibboleth, which enemies
might incorrectly pronounce ROAD. Whereas, allies would know the "correct"
pronounciation was the ancient Greek pronounciation: "HRO-DEE."

(We'll explore this Greek pronunciation more in a moment.)

But it's more likely that Dee was keeping his name for the colony secret
until the settlement had become well-fortified and more fully-established.
Only then would it be safe to make RODE the permanent name of the colony.

(And indeed, RODE eventually did become the permanent name.)

Confirming clues

If Dee intended his inverted "ear of corn" to mean "shibboleth,"
he definitely would have left some confirming clues.

Perhaps one clue is that he inverted it. If it was upright, it might have looked like
a normal wheat plant growing in the land. Its inversion emphasizes that it's a **symbol**.

In the *Monas*, Dee devotes all of Theorem 21 to cryptically
explaining the (theological) virtues of the **inverted Monas symbol**.

In Dee's **Union of Opposites** way of perceiving the world,
upright and inverted are simply two sides of the same coin.

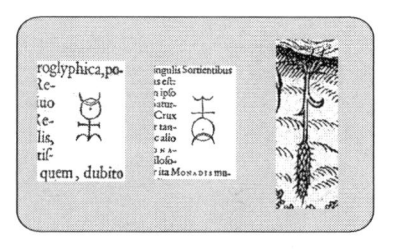

If you look closely, the gentleman in the small boat
crossing the Dee River provides another confirming clue.

He appears to be using a pole instead of an oar,
suggesting he is crossing **a shallow part of the river**
(like Ephriamites crossing the River Jordon at the **ford**).

(If he was rowing, realistically he would have
two oars, and be facing in the opposite direction.)

In addition, the two shorelines of the river bulge
towards each other at the very place he is crossing.

(Perhaps the "man with the outstretched arm" is asking the visitor for the "watchword," RODE,
which echoes across the illustration in so many loud, yet cryptically silent ways.)

But the best confirming clue is in the Greek letter which
is nearest to the "ear of corn." It's the Greek letter mu
(or **m**), the last letter in Dee's word *phrourio***m**.

Phrouriom, meaning "watch post," is also the last word in Dee's plea
"Send forth a sailing expedition...to make a steadfast watch post."

But there is something unusual about Dee's spelling of *phrouriom*.
In every Greek dictionary that I have consulted, this word
ends with an **n** (*phrourio***n**), not with an "**m**" (*phourio***m**).

Curiously, in the text of *General and Rare Memorials*, Dee even spells the word proprerly with an **n**, (*phrourio**n***).

To someone who doesn't know Greek, the difference between ***phrouriom*** and ***phrourion*** might not seem significant.

But it would be as strange as spelling the English word **idiom** as **idion**.

(This is a technique that Dee has employed elsewhere: He makes an "intentional error" in order to hide a clue.)

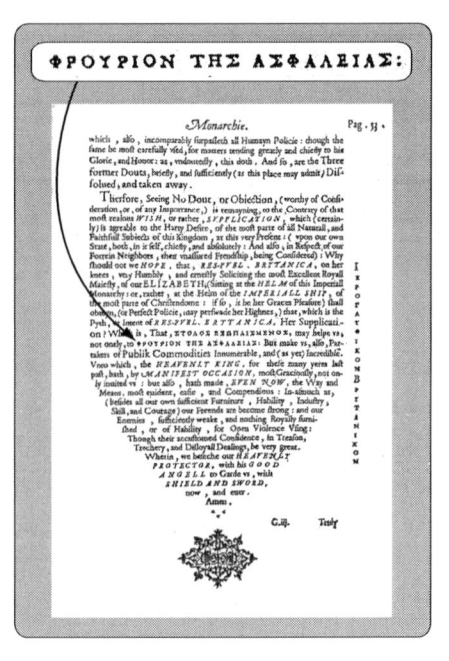

And Dee is this little riddle game with very special letters:

To most people the letters M and N might seem just like two of the 26 letters of the alphabet. But to grammarians who study the history of letters, **M and N are quite closely related**.

(And I'm not just talking about being neighbors in the middle of the alphabet.)

The letters M and N are the **only two nasals** the alphabet.

They are the only two letters that use the nose as a sound box.

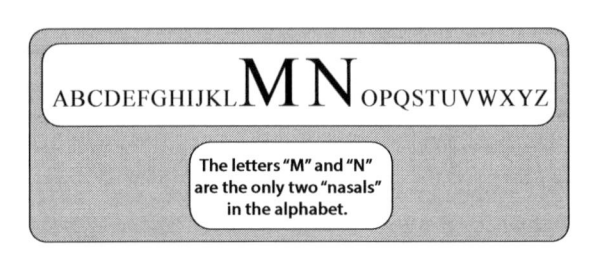

ABCDEFGHIJKL **M N** OPQSTUVWXYZ

The letters "M" and "N" are the only two "nasals" in the alphabet.

When you say **M**, your mouth is totally shut.
The air and sound comes out of your nose.

(Hold your nose and try to say **M**, and you'll see what I mean.)

To pronounce the sound **N**, your mouth may be open, but your tongue blocks all air from escaping, forcing it up into your vibrating nasal cavity and out your nose.

(Again, try holding your nose and you'll have to strain to make an **N** sound.)

In his book *Letter Perfect*, David Sacks notes how some letters have been "paired off" since Roman times, "letters like (C and G), (B and P), and (S and Z)."

But he adds,
"**Two letters could hardly be closer than N and M**, fraternal twins in shape, name, sound and position... Basically, N is three quarters M, and the two letters have had this sort of visual kinship since at least Phoenician times 3000 years ago."

(David Sacks, *Letter Perfect*, p. 240–241)

To the Phoenicians, M and N were the
letters *mem* (water) and *nun* (fish).

The Greeks borrowed them for their **M**
(pronounced *mu*) and **N** (pronounced *nu*).

Then the Etruscans borrowed them from the
Greeks for their **me** (may) and **ne** (nay).

Then the Romans borrowed them from the Etruscans.
In early Latin, **M** was probably pronounced
emmay and the **N**, **ennay**.

(Sacks, *Letter Perfect*, p.242-3, illustration after Sacks, p 229-245)

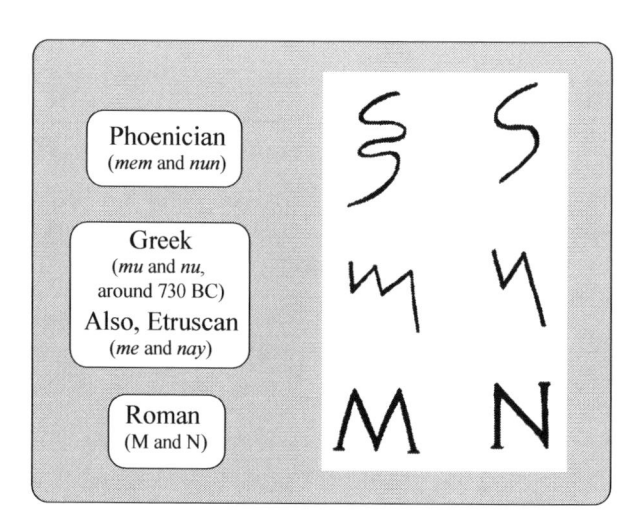

A summary of Dee's **M** *and* **N** *"intentional mistake"*

To summarize, there are several ways this phourio**m**/phourio**n** "intentional mistake" acts as a clue:

1   This mistake involves the **last letter** of the
last word of Dee's plea to the Queen,
"Send forth a sailing expedition...
to make a steadfast *phouriom*."

2   In the illustration, it is the **nearest letter** to
the **ear of corn**, or the *shibboleth*.

3   The M and the N have been perhaps the **two most closely
allied letters** in various alphabets for over 3000 years.

I'm not suggesting that *phouriom* is Dee's
secret code word. The secret code word is RODE.

Dee is simply employing this M/N switcheroo in
phouriom as a subtle reference to the Sh/S switcheroo
in the *shibbileth* "ear of corn" drawn right next to it.

4   The only other Greek letter **M** (Mu) in Dee's "plea
on the flowing ribbons" (in *exoplisMenos*), which should
be lowercase, like its neighboring letters.

But instead, it's uppercase. Dee seems to be hinting that
"something's up" with both the **M**'s in his sentence.

(The Σ in the word Στολος or Stolos is also capitalized, perhaps
because it is the beginning word of Dee's "sentence," or maybe
because it resembles an M, turned 90 degrees).

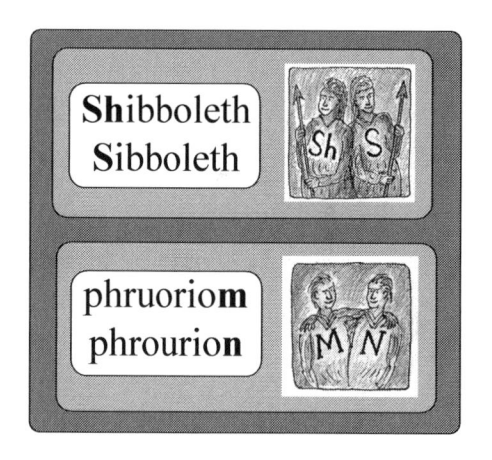

305

5   Dee has **inverted** the "ear of corn" to make it appear more like a **symbol**. In the *Monas*, Dee uses the upright Monas symbol and the inverted Monas symbol to express the Union of Opposites.

A *shibboleth* is a watchword that acts as a "sorting filter" between two opposites, like the Gileadites and the Ephriamites.

phrouriom or *phrourion* means WATCH-POST

The "ear of corn", or "shibboleth" means WATCHWORD

6   The word *phrouriom* (or *phrourion*) means "**watch post**," and the "ear of corn" or *shibboleth* means "**watchword**."

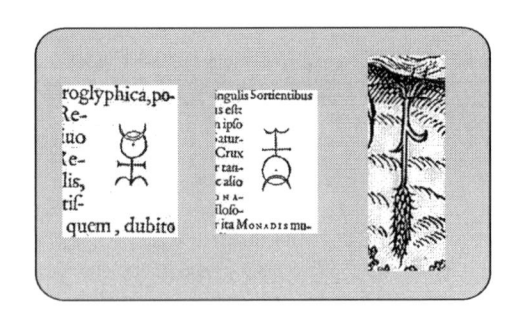

7   And that **watch post** was to be the **watch tower** built as the first building in the new colony on the Dee River, whose **watchword** was RODE.

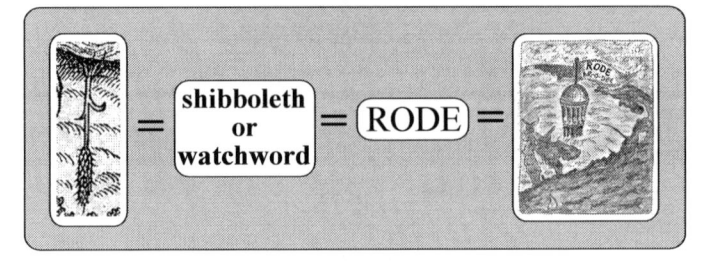

= shibboleth or watchword = RODE =

8   Let's go a step further and connect all the links. If you are a modern-day Rhode Islander looking at Dee's 1577 drawing of an upside down "ear of corn," you might very easily see the name of your state: R(h)ODE (Island)

Dee's "ear of corn" represents the Elizabethan watchword RODE, later adopted by the early Colonial leaders in the 1630's as the name of Aquidneck Island, and then made part of the state name in 1663. And RODE remains in the state name today.

Furthermore, Dee is hiding another code word in the illustration. Actually it's more of a code phrase or a code symbol: **Anchor of Hope**.

Thus, looking at Dee's "ear of corn" we might also see the current day symbol and motto for the state of Rhode Island.

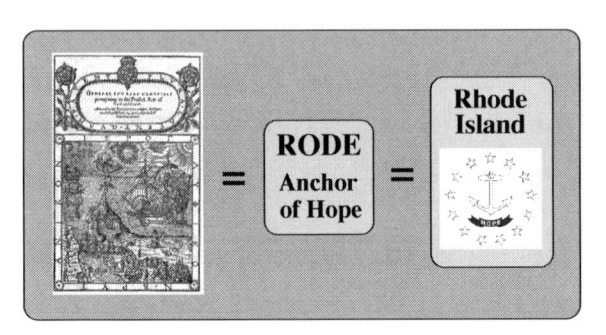

= RODE Anchor of Hope = Rhode Island

Yet another confirming clue: 42 thousand

Dee managed to work in another confirming clue that
all this "watchword business" is what he had in mind.

Recall the final line of Judges 12:6, "and there fell at that time of the Ephraimites **forty and two thousand**."

This **42,000** is a curious echo of the coordinates of the Dee River: **42° north latitude and 42° west longitude**.

> "And there fell at that time of the Ephraimites forty two thousand."
>
> 42 degrees is the latitude (and also the longitude) of the Dee River on Dee's 1582 Map of North America

Michael is Angel number 42

"Send forth a sailing expedition...
to make a steadfast watch post."

As we've seen right on Title page, the number **42** is expressed by the Archangel Michael, who is Angel number **42** in the list of the "72 Names of the Angels."

Some famous shibboleths

The idea of a *shibboleth* or watchword is not just a Biblical story.
These "identifying code words" have been used in battles throughout the centuries.

In London, during Tyler's rebellion of 1381, the English arrested Dutch infiltrators who used the expression **cheese and bread** instead of the British expression **bread and cheese**.

During World War II, at the beginning of the battle of Normandy,
if an American soldier shouted out word "Flash," the proper response
was "Thunder." Then the first man would reply "Welcome."

The Germans soon caught on to the Flash part, but when they replied Welcome, it sounded like **Velcome** and gave away their true identity.

The modern meaning of shibboleth

The word *shibboleth* is still in most modern dictionaries, but its meaning has broadened. Over time, *shibboleth* has come to mean **slogan**, **motto**, **nickname** and even **handle**.

And now it doesn't necessarily just mean a "test word" to distinguish two antagonistic groups. A *shibboleth* can be any **in-crowd word** or an **inside joke** that others don't "get."

Dee's *shibboleth*-watchword, RODE, is an "inside joke" that only well-connected and well-educated Elizabethans would "get." And apparently Benedict Arnold "got it" too.

(And now you are "in" on the joke, too)

In short, by putting the **inverted ear of corn** on the Title page, Dee cryptically saying,

"Psst! There is a secret watchword hidden here."

Remember, Dee forewarned us,

MORE IS HIDDEN THAN MEETS THE EYE.
(PLURA LATENT, QUAM PATENT)

"Psst! there is a secret watchword hidden here"

308

Did John Dee have the word "Rode" cryptically concealed in the stone-and-mortar fabric of the Tower?

Dee has woven together his *Monas Hieroglyphica* cosmology, the birth of the British Empire, the Elizabethan colonization project, and the Tower into one grand riddle. Dee loves to put clues in front of your face yet have them invisible. Realizing all this, I wondered if he had hidden any cryptic clues in the Tower. (Clues that would be undetectable unless seen through "Dee glasses.")

Dee takes a theme and runs with it. He concealed the word RODE in many subtle and clever ways on the Title page of *General and Rare Memorials*. Could Dee have hidden the word RODE in the Tower?

Dee was a Greek scholar and even taught Greek at Trinity College. How would he have pronounced the word RODE in Greek? Or even in Elizabethan English?

How to pronounce RODE

About one fifth of the world speaks English. Most people in the United States speak what is called "American English." But even American English has many dialects.

In the Northeast, many speak with a "New England accent." And there's special kind of New England accent called a "Rhode Island accent." Local comedians joke that we pronounce our state name **Roe Dyelan** or even **Vho Dilan'**.

Despite this local accent, most people pronounce the word **Rhode** the same way they would pronounce **road** or even **rode**, (Say this sentence aloud to hear the three homonyms.)

"Joe **rode** his horse down a dirt **road** in **Rhode** Island."

Even Roger Williams dispensed with that "silent h," spelling "RHODE" as "RODE." (Though it's not known exactly how he pronounced the word.)

The pronunciation of RODE in Greek is quite different than it is in American English. In Greek it's much more musical. Where we pronounce RODE with one syllable, the Greeks pronounce it with two syllables **RO** and **DE**, with the accent on the final syllable, **DE**.

Furthermore, where Americans see the final letter E as silent, in Greek it is pronounced it as a **long E.** In other words, our word **rode** is pronounced **ro-DEE** in Greek. But even this is an oversimplification. Each of the letters in RODE is actually pronounced slightly differently from the way you probably just pronounced **ro-DEE**.

We'll review each letter, one at a time, but first let's look at how RODE is spelled in Greek:

᾿ΡΟΔῆ

You're probably saying, "This looks Greek to me." Fear not. Don't be concerned that this looks too weird to be pronounced RODE.

Even after having learned the correct Greek pronunciation, it still looks to me like "**apostrophe P, O, triangle, and H with a squiggly worm on top.**"

But in several minutes you'll be pronouncing it like Aristotle did in 350 BC.

It helps to convert the Greek letter into English letters equivalents. Seeing the Greek capital letter **P** (Rho) as an **R**, and the **Δ** as a **D**, sure makes it a lot easier to look at.

᾿ΡΟΔῆ
᾿RODẼ

P

Let's take it one letter at a time. In Greek, the **R** is trilled, or pronounced with a little tongue vibration.

Pretend you're a Scotsman, **rrrr**olling his **arrrr**s:

Rrr

"**Rr**ound the **rr**ugged **rr**ock the **rr**agged **rr**ascal **rr**an."

Next, let's deal with the **apostrophe** in front of the R.

᾿P

This diacritical mark (distinguishing mark) indicates that an H sound should be pronounced in front of the R.

Thus, it sounds like **hRrr**.

hRrr

Technically speaking, this "apostrophe" or "single quotation mark" is called *dasy pneuma* (in Greek), or *spiritus asper* (in Latin), both of which mean "rough breathing."
(From the Latin word *asper* we get our word "aspirate" which means "to begin with a breathing sound.")

This "apostrophe indicating an H sound" can be used with any of the Greek vowels (῾Α, ῾Ε, ῾Η, ῾Ι, ῾Ο, ῾Υ, ῾Ω).

(For example, the name of the great poet ῾*Omer* is pronounced *Homer*)

But there is **only one consonant** that can take this "apostrophe indicating an H sound."

And that happens to be the **P** (or Rho), the very letter we are investigating here.

Incidentally, a "reversed apostrophe" in front of any of the vowels (Ἀ, Ἐ, Ἠ, Ἰ, Ὀ, Ὠ) or ’Ρ (’Rho), indicates what is called *psilon pneuma* (in Greek) or *spiritus lenis* (in Latin),

<small>(Both of which mean "mild or smooth breathing." From the Latin word *lenis*, we get our word "lenient," meaning "mild or tolerant punishment.")</small>

In other words, this "reversed apostrophe" indicates there is "no H sound" preceding the letter.

This idea of the "pronounced H" versus "un-pronounced H" is found in American English. In front of a "pronounced H," we use the indefinite article "**an**": an hour, an honor, an heir.

But in front of an "un-pronounced H," we use the indefinite article "**a**": a history, a heaven, a hair.

[O]

[(g)O(t)]

Next, the **O** sound should be pronounced more like the **O** in the word "**ought**" (or "got"), rather than the **O** in "owe" (or "Ohio").

With your best British accent, pretend you are Professor Henry Higgins, thrilled about Eliza Doolittle's new upper-class way of speaking:

"Aye thenk she's **got** it!"

(Open your lips really tall with that "oh" sound, as in "got".)

Next, the **D** sound in Greek is much different than the American English **D** sound. It's more of a **Dh** sound, like the way Zsa Zsa Gabor would say, "Thank you, **Dharling**." Or an Indian guru would pronounce **Dharma**.

But the "**dh**" sound should actually have a hint of the "**th**" sound in it, so **Dharma** should sound more like **THarma**.

To get the right mix, pronounce it **DTHarma**.
In other words, Greek letter Δ, is pronounced *Dthelta*.

[Δ]

[Dth]

The Greek letter E (or Epsilon) is a "short E," as in "bet."
But the Greek letter H (or Eta, pronounced or "eeta") is a "long E," as in "meet."

[H̃]

So, the final Greek letter, H, should not be pronounced like an English "H," but more like "**ee**."

However, when the H (eeta) has a **tilde** (that squiggly worm) on top of it, the "ee sound" is much more melodious!

First, there is a **rise** in pitch, which is immediately followed by a **fall** in pitch.

[eEee]

It's like the Doppler effect of a train passing by while blowing its horn.

Say this out loud: eeeEEEeeeeee.

Except the train is going *really* fast: eeEEeeee

Now, even *faster* : eEee.

Now let's practice each letter separately:

(Pronounce the h)   (O like "ought")   (eEee has a rise in pitch, then a fall in pitch)

| hRrr | O | Dth | eEee |

(Roll the Rrr)   (Dh is more like Dth)

Next, flow all the sounds together: hRrr O – Dth eEee

Now, a little faster: hRrO-DEe

This time, remember to accentuate the second syllable: **DEe**.   hRrO-**DEe**

Now, repeat that pronunciation while looking at Greek symbols which looked so strange before.

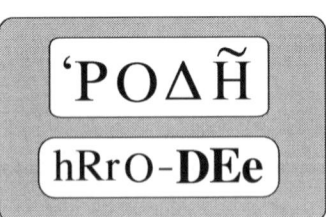

ʽΡΟΔῆ
hRrO-DEe

And of course, the pronunciation is the same in lowercase Greek letters, so say it again:

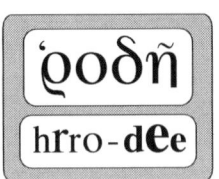

ῥοδῆ
hr̃ro-dee

I think you've got it!

(Now let's explore how Greek teacher John Dee used this Greek pronunciation and Greek spelling to hide more clues.)

A brief history of the word "river" (as in the "Dee River")

The word "river" comes from the Latin word *ripa*, "meaning the "bank of a river." Trade goods coming from around the Mediterranean up the Tiber to Rome unloaded at the *Ripa Grande* (or the Great Embankment). Trade goods coming from inland Italy, traveling down the Tiber to Rome, were unloaded at the *Ripetta* (or the Small Bank).

In British English the final "r" in river is generally not pronounced.
The River Thames is pronounced the "**Rivah** Temmes."

In American English, the final letter "r," is generally pronounced as a hard **r**, like Mississippi Rive**r**.

Only around Boston has the British accent remained, as the Charles River is still pronounced "Charles Riv**ah**."

From the Latin word *ripa* comes the word *riuss*, meaning "a brook." In both Spanish and Portuguese, *ruiss* became **rio**, as in the **Rio** Grande or **Rio** de Janeiro.

In French, *ripa* became *rive*, as in the **Rive** Gauche, the Left Bank of the Seine in Paris. The coast (or sea bank) of Southern France is called the **Riv**iera.

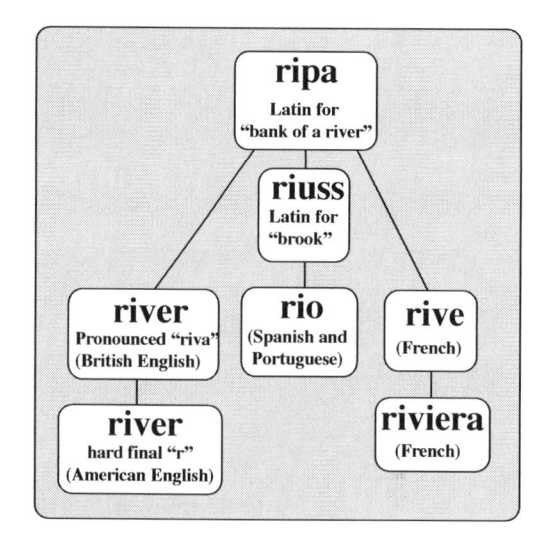

Why does John Dee call it the "Dee River" and not the "River of Dee"?

The 1583 land grant from Sir Humphrey Gilbert to Sir George Peckham describes, "all that ryver or porte called by Master John Dee, **Dee Ryver**..."

The spelling of Ryver, might seem odd, but Elizabethans were flexible when it came to spelling. However, there is something else that's unusual.

When the British say the name of a river, they generally put the word "river" **first**, not **second**:

the River Thames,
the River Severn,
the River Exe,
the River Trent,
and even the River Dee
(which is on the border between England and northern Wales.)

However, way back in Elizabethan times, the word "**of**" was used in the middle:

the Ryver **of** Thamys,
the Ryver **of** Severn,
the Ryver **of** Exe,
the Ryver **of** Trent,
the Ryver **of** Dee

In the late 1600s, the word "of" was dropped.
For example, the **River of Thames** was just called the **River Thames**.

[Colonial settlers in **North America** adopted a differnt way to name rivers rivers. By 1650, the style of putting the proper noun **before** the word "river" became the predominant style in North America.

For example, John Smith's 1614 map of New England lists "the **River Charles**." William Woods's 1634 map of New England calls it the "**Charles River**."]

There are some exceptions, but this is the general metamorphosis of the way the British named rivers. To demonstrate, this flow chart uses the fictitious example of the "River Joe."

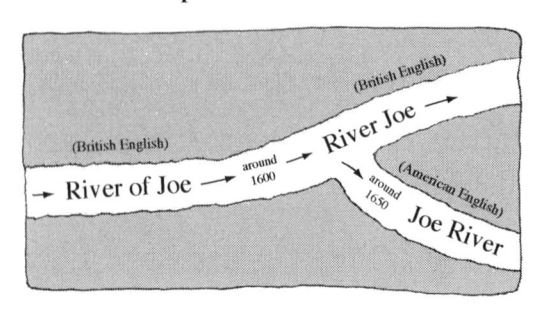

in this noble Riuer of Thames

in this Incomparable Riuer of Thames

John Dee lived in the 1500's, when most rivers still had the "**of**" in their names. In Dee's 1577 *General and Rare Memorials*, he refers to "this noble **River of Thames**" and "in this Incomparable **River of Thames**."

Dee's 1580 map of North America lists over 50 rivers along the East Coast.

For space considerations, Dee abbreviates most of them, in the style of "R. Joe." (So it's unclear if he meant to include the word "of.")

However, in several Portuguese or Spanish-sounding names, he uses the style of "R. de José" where the "de" means "of."

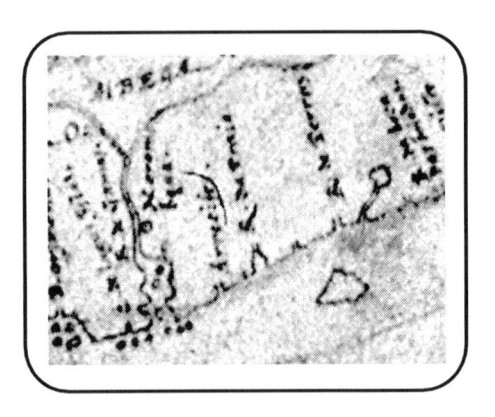

Then why does the 1583 deed from Gilbert to Peckham refer to the "**Dee River**" with the word "River" **after** the proper name "Dee"?
(… all that ryver or porte called by Master John Dee, **Dee Ryver**…")

Is Dee kind trying to hide a clue?
In Dee's era, the more common expression would be "River of Dee."
Spoken with a slight slur, **River of Dee** sounds an awful lot like **RODE** or **hRr-O-DEe**.

(Saying it in Spanish helps you to hear the interconnection.
Say "Rio de Janeiro." without the Janeiro:
Rio de……. River of Dee…… hR-O- DEe)

River of Dee =
RODE =
"hRr-O-DEe"

314

This homophone would most certainly not
go unnoticed by the master-wordsmith,
multiple-language-speaker,
and clever-clue-concealer
John Dee.

I think he made the **River of Dee** to **Dee River** switcheroo"
to hide all the clever clues about the "code name" for the
first Elizabethan colony, **RODE** (or Rhode or hRrO-DEe).

Dee wasn't a part of an organization, association or a law firm that
was recommending the Queen spark the fire of the British Empire.
He was acting alone. He was the mastermind of the whole project.
Sure there were others involved, but Dee was conducting of the symphony.

Sure, Dee is was a bit of an egomaniac to name the river after himself,
and to portray himself a spokesperson for the citizens of England,
and to visually link himself with the Queen.

But this only helps reinforce the idea that he was also the architect of the Tower.

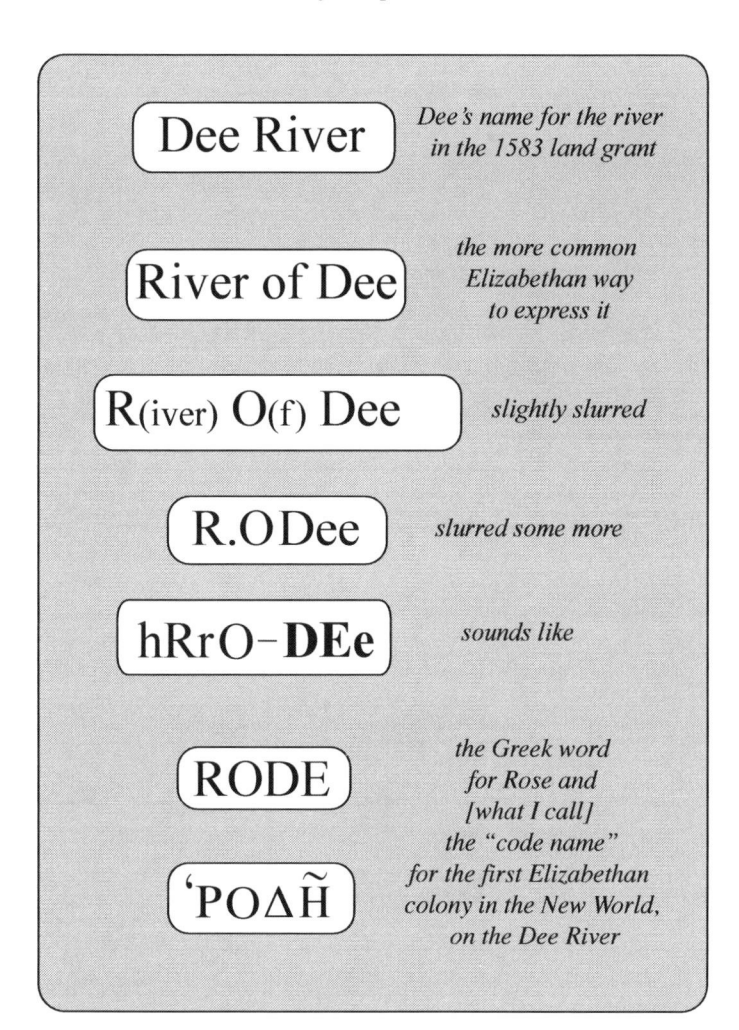

Dee River	*Dee's name for the river in the 1583 land grant*
River of Dee	*the more common Elizabethan way to express it*
R(iver) O(f) Dee	*slightly slurred*
R.ODee	*slurred some more*
hRrO-DEe	*sounds like*
RODE	
'POΔH̃	*the Greek word for Rose and [what I call] the "code name" for the first Elizabethan colony in the New World, on the Dee River*

You don't have to be a classical linguist to
hear that that the accentuated syllable
of 'POΔE or "hRro-**DEe**"
is pronounced is like
Dee's last name.

While pondering Dee's homophone
game, something else rang a bell!

I remembered another place I had
seen those two middle letters,
O and Δ,
side-by-side,
in the same sequence.

Do you know where?

West Window

"Sun Stone" symbol in the W NW arch

"Triangle" Rock in the W SW arch

Greek letters on the Tower

One of the "keystone areas" of the arches in the Tower has a **circular** rock in it.

And the arch just to the right of it has a **triangular** rock in it.

These are the middle two letters of ‹POΔH.

I raced over to the Tower to look for more letters. The arch just to the left of the **O** and **Δ arches** had two rocks that somewhat resembled a **P** (Rho) shape.

However, the rock forming the vertical line of the **P** was not exactly vertical. And the rock that formed the circular part of the **P** was not exactly circular. Still, it was pretty close to looking like a **P** (Rho).

If it was, that would account for three of the four letters.

P (Rho)

N NW Arch

P — N NW Arch

O — W NW Arch

Δ — W SW Arch

I zipped around to the other side of the tower. Unfortunately, the arch just to the right of the **O** and **Δ arches** did **not** look like an **H** (Eta).

This arch had a pair of adjacent granite rocks in the "keystone area." The rock on the left was taller.

The one on the right had several small horizontal flat rocks mortared on top of it.

At first I thought the small rocks might be forming the letter **E**. But ‹POΔH ends in an **H** (Eta or long e) **not** an **E** (Epsilon or short e).

(It seemed unlikely, though not out of the question, that Dee would have used **three** Greek letters followed by **one** English letter.)

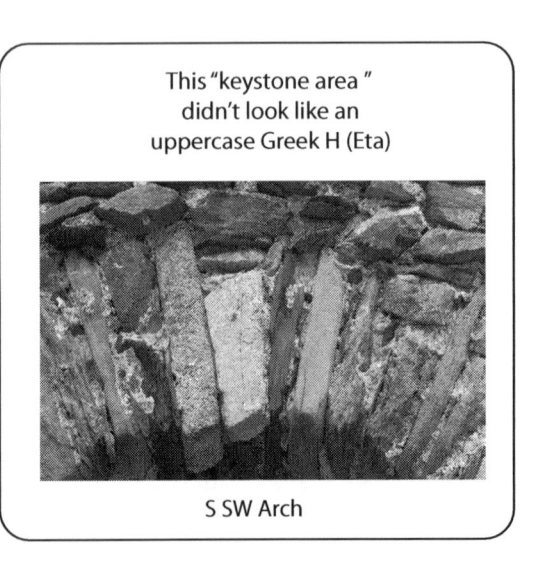

This "keystone area" didn't look like an uppercase Greek **H** (Eta)

S SW Arch

316

So I thought about this problem from the point of view of both Dee and the master mason who was given the responsibility of actually shaping these rock-letters.

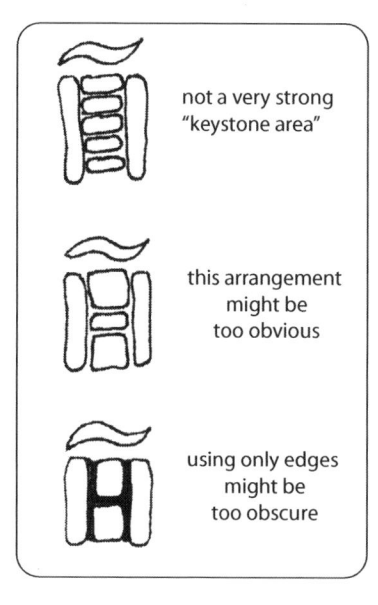

not a very strong "keystone area"

this arrangement might be too obvious

using only edges might be too obscure

The **P**, **O**, and **Δ** were simple to make, compared to making an **H**.

An **H**-shaped arrangement of rocks might be either too obvious or too obscure. If he was to put a "crossbar-rock" between two vertical rocks, how would he fill the remaining spaces?

If he filled them with similarly-shaped horizontal rocks, that wouldn't make for a very sturdy "keystone area."

If he filled the space with two square rocks, the **H** might be too apparent.

If he just used the "edges" of rocks, the letter might be too well-concealed.

(Not to mention that it would be hard to a find a rock that bends in two different directions to make a long "squiggly-worm" tilde mark on top.)

But as I stared at the arch, it occurred to me that Dee might have used a lowercase η (eta) instead of an uppercase **H** (Eta).

While the "keystone area" didn't look like an uppercase **H** (Eta) with a tilde, it did look like a lowercase η (eta) with a tilde.

The two large vertical keystone rocks form this lowercase Greek letter η.

The upper part of the left piece of granite is like the serif of the η shape.

And now the "squiggly-worm" tilde doesn't have to "squiggle" as much. It can be smaller and can fit into the "nest" formed on top of the letter.

(In modern Greek typefaces, the right leg of the η (eta) is a bit longer than the left leg, but this was not the style in Dee's time.)

S SW Arch

lowercase Greek letter η (eta), with tilde on top

S SW Arch

two examples of a "lowercase eta with a tilde on top," from Dee's *Monas Hieroglyphica*

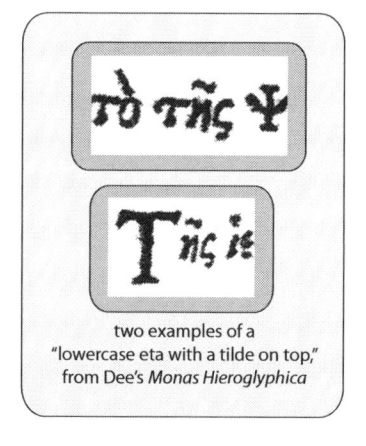

In the *Monas Hieroglyphica*, there are several examples of Dee's use of a "lowercase eta" with a tilde above it.

But in this instance, because the letters are so small, the tilde goes over the whole letter.

Would Dee have mixed uppercase and lowercase letters in the same word?

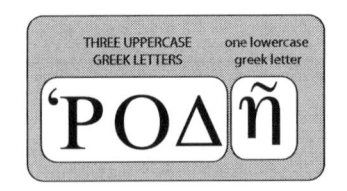

I recalled noticing that Dee had "mixed his cases" on the Title page of *General and Rare Memorials*.

In his Greek word **exoplisMenos** (meaning to "send forth"), Dee had put an uppercase **M** in the midst of lowercase letters.

(An uppercase Greek Mu is written a **M**, but the lowercase mu is written as **μ**.)

And in his Greek phrase, **TO TES asphaleias phrouriom** ("to build a steadfast watch post"), two of the words are in uppercase and two are in lowercase.

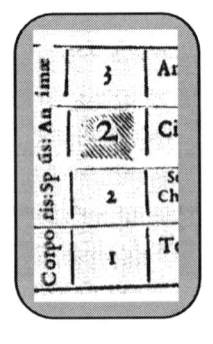

Dee used this same clue-technique of grouping "three similar items" with "one oddball item" in his "Thus the World Was Created" chart.

Three of the numbers in his Artificial Quaternary are printed using letterpress type, and one is printed by an engraved plate

(Dee even crosshatched the surrounding area make it seem like a printer's error. But it's not a mistake. Dee did it intentionally to emphasize the 2.)

Meanwhile ... back at the Tower

If Dee was using this "squiggly worm" diacritical mark above the lower case eta (η̃) in this arch, perhaps he was using an "apostrophe" in front of the **P** (Rho) in the other arch.

I raced back to the other side of the Tower.

There was a small black rock that looked somewhat like an "apostrophe," but it wasn't totally convincing.

The masons had used small rocks like this as "filler" between larger rocks all over the Tower.

I suspected there was more to the story of Greek pronunciation, so I researched the **history of Greek diacritical marks**.

I found that the "apostrophe indicating an h-sound" and the "reverse apostrophe for no h-sound" were used during the Hellenistic period, from about 300 BC to about 300 AD.

But earlier, during the Classical period (from around 500 BC to 300 BC), the Ancient Greeks **sliced the letter H in half vertically** to distinguish between the two types of "breathing."

The left vertical line and most of the horizontal line on the H indicated "rough breathing" or the **presence** of an "h-sound" (or *spiritus asper*).

The right vertical line and most of the horizontal line of an H indicated "smooth breathing" or the **absence** of an "h-sound" (or *spiritus lenis*).

These marks are sometimes referred to as the "**tack-like**" **breathing marks** because they look like side views of a thumb tack.

(Liddell and Scott, *Greek-English Lexicon*: Eta)

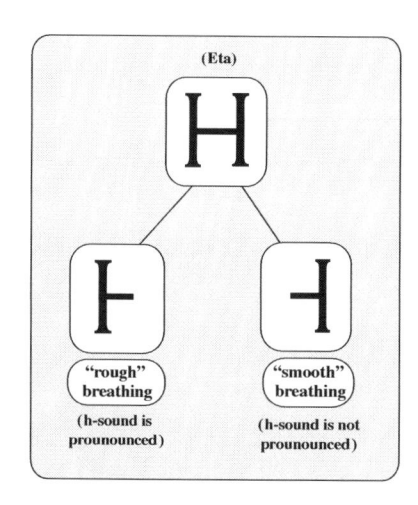

(Eta)
H
⊢ "rough" breathing (h-sound is pronounced)
⊣ "smooth" breathing (h-sound is not pronounced)

As an example, let's take the name of that great epic poet credited with writing the *Iliad* and the *Odyssey*: with a rough breathing mark it's **Homer**, with smooth breathing mark it's **Owe-mer**.

(The Ancient Greeks actually referred to him HOMEROS, but I have simplified his name and converted the final letter, P (Rho), to an English **R**.)

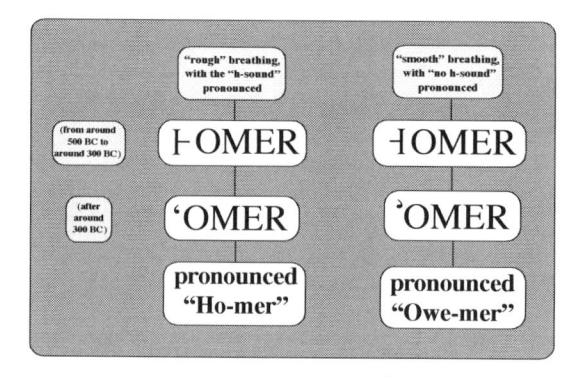

ὍΜΗΡΟΣ
HOMEROS
HOMER

"rough" breathing, with the "h-sound" pronounced / "smooth" breathing, with "no h-sound" pronounced

(from around 500 BC to around 300 BC) ⊢OMER / ⊣OMER
(after around 300 BC) 'OMER / ʼOMER
pronounced "Ho-mer" / pronounced "Owe-mer"

(Incidentally, in order to make Modern Greek easier to write and type, these "rough breathing and smooth breathing apostrophes" were officially abolished by a presidential decree in 1982)

Back at the Tower, I reinspected the arch with the **P** (Rho) in the "keystone area." There didn't appear to be a "right-facing thumb tack shape" to the left of the rocks forming the P-shape, **so I slid over one arch to the left.**

Sure enough, there was a prominent vertical granite rock with horizontal rock at its midsection, which was pointing to the right!

N NE Arch ← one arch to the left   N NW Arch, with the P (Rho)

" rough breathing" mark, indicating the presence of the h-sound

N NE Arch

It certainly wasn't perfect looking. The horizontal rock was somewhat weathered because it's a piece if slate.

But it certainly seemed odd that the master mason would use a horizontal rock in such a structurally important "keystone area."

Slate has a high compressive strength when squeezed from top to bottom but when squeezed from side to side, it's more likely to fracture along its plate lines.

Here is a summary chart of the 5 rock letter-sounds.

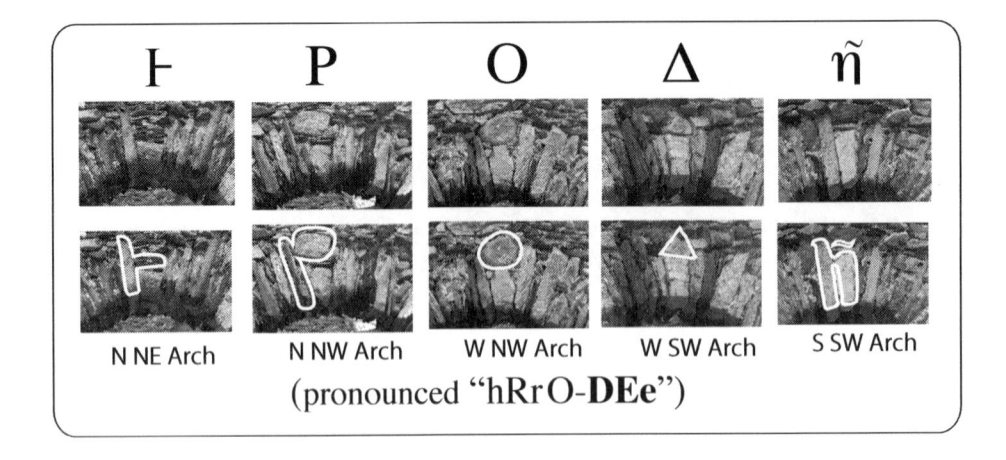

Ͱ　Ρ　Ο　Δ　ñ

N NE Arch　N NW Arch　W NW Arch　W SW Arch　S SW Arch

(pronounced "hRrO-DEe")

No wonder Benedict Arnold was so insistent Aquidneck Island be called **Rode Island**.
The word **Rode** itself is an integral part of the Tower!

This bird's-eye view clarifies the compass orientation of the 5 letters.

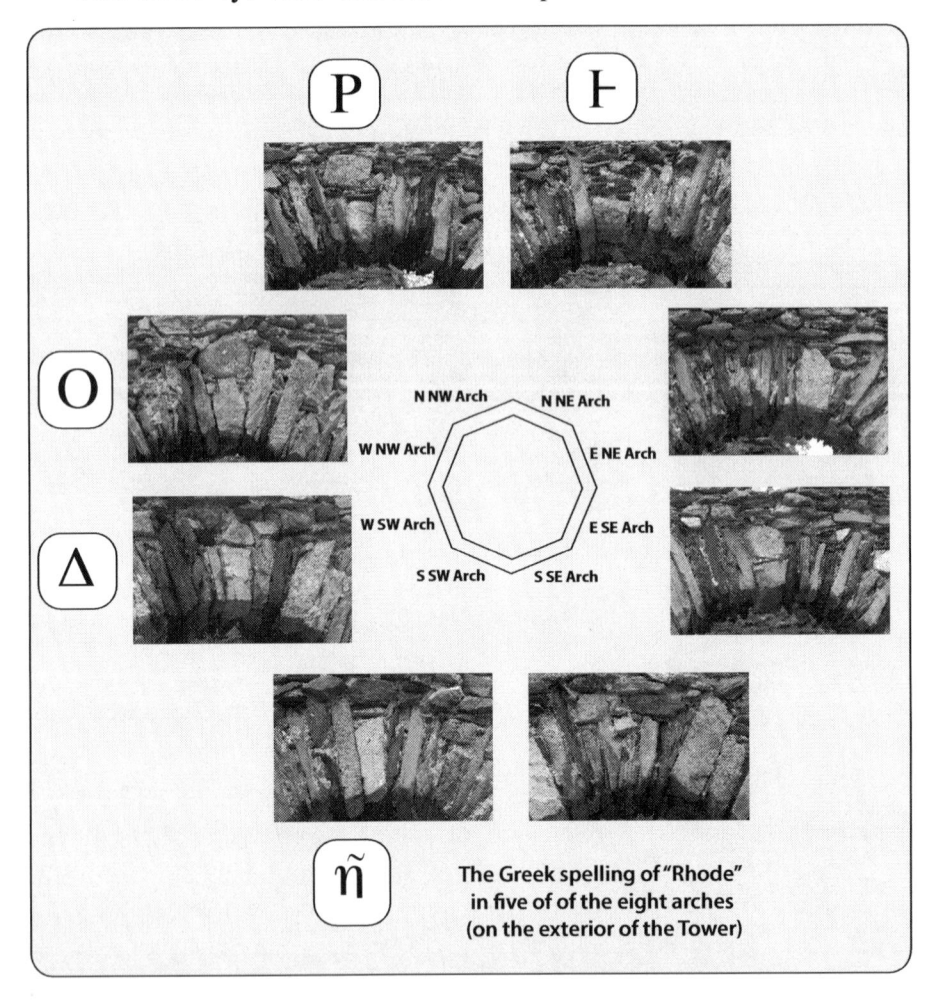

Ρ　Ͱ

Ο

Δ

ñ　**The Greek spelling of "Rhode" in five of of the eight arches (on the exterior of the Tower)**

320

To Dee, ʹΡΟΔΗ̃ *and* ⊢ΡΟΔΗ̃ *would be pronounced differently*

The final letter H̃ is pronounced "eEee" in Modern Greek and also in Ancient Greek,
but for several centuries (from about 1500 AD to about 1800 AD) it was pronounced "AYEee."
Sort of like the way the Fonz on the old TV sitcom *Happy Days* would say the word Heyyyy :
In other words, like **AYEeeee!**
But not exactly. Pronounce it shorter, not as drawn out.
More like: **AYEe**
(The **AY** is the rise in pitch, and the **Ee** is the fall in pitch.)

This is called the Erasmian pronunciation, after the humanist Erasmus (1466-1536) who (with others, around the year 1500) was trying to make Ancient Greek sound more like Latin.

In England, Sir John Cheke (1514-1577), a teacher at St. John's College in Cambridge, was a big fan of the Erasmian pronunciation and even wrote a book about it entitled, *The Right Way Speaking Latin and Greek: A Dialogue.*

John Dee was a student of Sir John Cheke. After graduating, Dee taught Greek at Trinity College, so he was well aware of the Erasmian pronunciation.

In the Tower, if Dee used the word ʹRODH̃, he would
pronounce it in the Erasmian manner: hRrO-**DAYEe**
But instead he writes the word ⊢ΡΟΔΗ̃,
which is pronounced: hRrO-**DEe.**

Why does changing the first symbol from an "apostrophe" to a
⊢ (ancient, tack-like H) change the pronunciation of the last letter, H̃ ?

Because it indicates the **whole word** should be
pronounced in the Ancient manner (not the Erasmian manner)

Dee wants us to use the Ancient pronunciation,
so we will hear his name at the end: "**Dee**"

H barely makes it as a letter

Roman and Renaissance grammarians considered H to be an oddball among the letters.
Geofroy Tory, in *Champs Fleury,* his 1529 book about the letters of the Lain alphabet wrote:

" *The aspirate* [**H**] *is not a letter; nonetheless, it
is by poetic license given the place of a letter.*"

ABCDEFGHIKLMNOPQRSTUXYZ

Tory quotes the Roman grammarian Priscian:
"*H is the symbol of the breathing, and has nothing else
pertaining to a letter save the figure of one and* [the fact]
that by custom it is written among the other letters."

(Geofroy Tory, *Champs Fleury,* p.108; This is a book which Dee owned)

Dee's switches the **last** letter from uppercase **H** (Eta)
to lowercase **η** (eta) to bring attention to the letter **Eta**.

This is the exact same letter that is at the **beginning** of the word RODE.
(The tack-like diacritical mark, ⊢, is "half of an Eta")

In other words,
the first and last rock-letters are related.

They are both variations of the letter **Eta**.

And in the Tower, their arches are exactly 180 degrees apart! They are exactly "opposites."

To me, Dee's use of the lowercase **η** along with the uppercase letters **POΔ** is actually a confirming clue.

He's cryptically saying, "Pay attention to the letter **Eta**! The Ancient Greek diacritical mark, (⊢), at the beginning of this word indicates it should be pronounced **in the Ancient manner**: hRrO-DEe"

For a letter that doesn't count much, Dee certainly gets a lot of clue-mileage out of **H**. Dee also plays with it in the word **IEROGLYPHIKON**, where it is implied before the beginning letter **I**.

(And the word itself, HIEROGLYPHIKON, even means an "**enigmatic symbol**.")

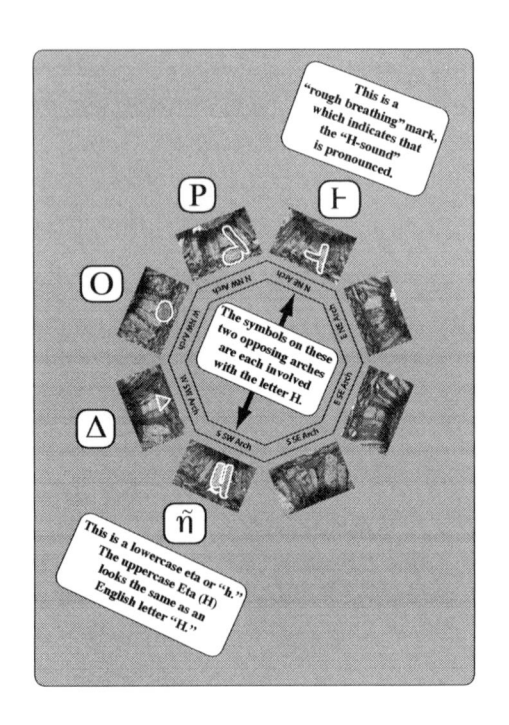

Dee used the same riddle in the Tower's stone-letters that he used in the Title page!

I'll admit that finding hidden Greek letters in the rocks of the centuries-old building sounds a bit far-fetched.

But remember, we're dealing with Dee here.

He creatively designed the astronomically oriented windows and the mathematically harmonious proportions of the Tower.

He was an expert in Greek, and served as a Greek Reader (teacher) at Trinity College.

And he incorporated Greek word clues in the Title page of *General and Rare Memorials*.

In fact, some of his hidden clues involve this very word: RODE.

322

Γ — The Greek letter Gamma
Simply slide the horizontal line down a bit

⊢ — "Rough" breathing Eta diacritical mark

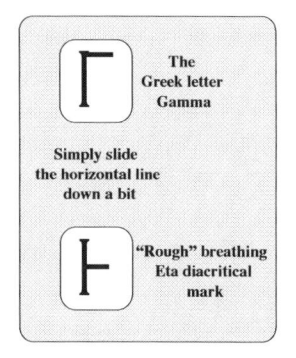

Indeed, the Greek letter Gamma, (Γ), which is used in the ΙΕΡΟΓ part of Dee's Greek word, ΙΕΡΟΓΛΥΦΙΚΟΝ (IEROGLYPHIKON), closely resembles the "rough-breathing, right-pointed thumb-tack symbol."

Just slide the short, middle line down a little bit.

Now the word ⊢ΡΟΔΕ can be found, which sounds like "hRrO-DEe"

⊢ΡΟΔΕ = hRrO-DEe

(Alternatively, an "H" can be made by combining the I and the Γ. Or an "H" might be implied by the word IEROGHYPHIKON, which might also be written as HIEROGLYPHIKON.)

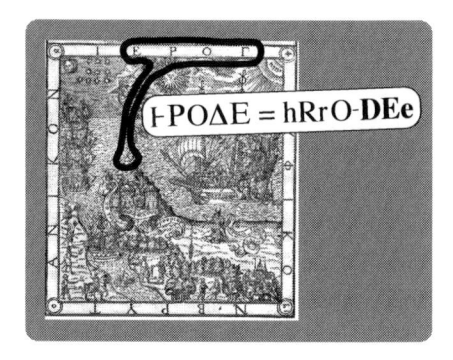

Now we have all of the 5 symbols or sounds that are on the 5 arches of the Tower!

(It's interesting how, some four centuries later, a weathered, old, 1583 stone Tower can still provide a clue to interpreting a 1577 Title page illustration-riddle.)

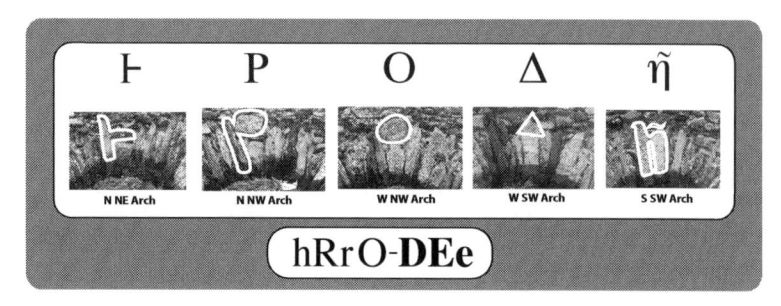

⊢	Ρ	Ο	Δ	ñ
N NE Arch	N NW Arch	W NW Arch	W SW Arch	S SW Arch

hRrO-DEe

Finding the same letter-riddle in the arches of the Tower and in the Title page illustration helps confirm that this is what Dee had in mind.

You can sense Dee's mind, spinning with possibilities about how to express his **RODE letter-riddle game**.

One method had to work using ink and paper, the other had to be created from field stones.

These hidden rock-letters are in keeping with Dee's style of clue making: Right front of your eyes, yet invisible, unless you are on his wavelength.

(Indeed, thousands of eyes have looked at the Tower over the years and not seen these Greek letters.)

⊢ Ρ Ο Δ ñ   hRrO-DEe

I suggest that Dee probably sketched out the size and shape of the stones he wanted used in making the letters and included the drawing along with the blueprints of the Tower.

Far from being far-fetched, to me these rocks help prove John Dee designed the Tower.

323

Summary of Dee's fun riddles

Just like the Title page of *General and Rare Memorials*, the John Dee Tower is designed to be a "British Heiroglyphic," in which "More is hidden than meets the eye."

Dee's superb orchestration of clues is evident when they are all are assembled in one chart:

All these "little riddles" are part of one "grand riddle."

The "code name" for the first Elizabethan colony in the New World was RODE (hRrO-**DEe**).

The same name we use today.

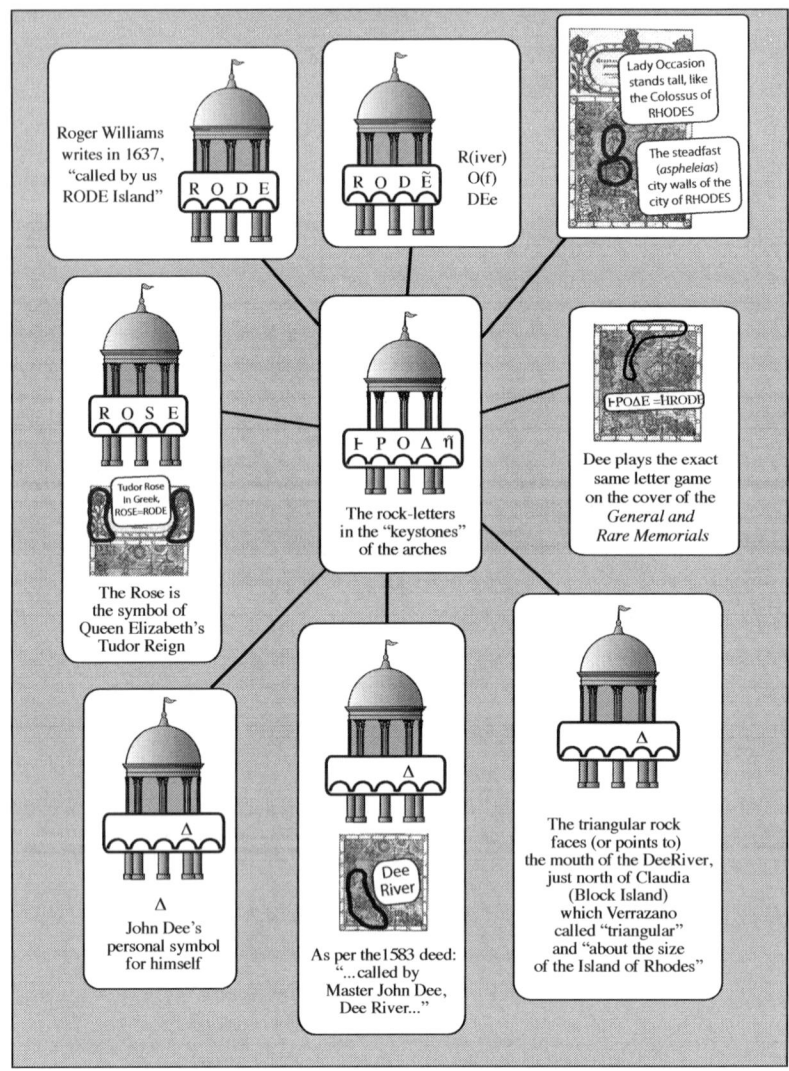

Vitruvius tells us circular temples were usually dedicated to a specific god. If Dee had a one of the Ancients gods in mind for his Tower, I suspect it would have been **Helios**, because of the way the Tower keeps track of time by using the sun.

(Helios was a Greek Titan, whose equivalent in Roman mythology was Sol or Sol Invictus)

And remember, **Helios** was the god of the Greek island of **Rhodes**.

(the Colossus of Rhodes was a sculpture of **Helios**.)

And **Rhodes** is the code name for Dee's first colony on the **Dee River**.

It's all one big riddle.

A DEEPER CLUE ABOUT THE SYMBOLS IN THE ARCHES OF THE TOWER:

IN ANCIENT GREECE, THE LOWERCASE ETA MEANT **EIGHT**

Ancient Greek Numerals

The lowercase *eta* relates to the Tower and to Dee's mathematical cosmology in a very important way. In Ancient Greece, **the lowercase *eta* meant the number "eight."** And I don't mean *eta* sounds like "eighta." Here's a little background:

Around 350 BC, the Ancient Greeks adopted a system of representing numbers using Greek letters. These numerals were called alphabetic numerals, Ionian numerals, or the Milesian numerals.

(They were invented by the Greeks who lived in the town of Miletus in Ionia, the eastern part of Greece that was actually in Asia Minor.)

The digits 1 through 9 were each assigned a separate letter.

The multiples of 10 (10, 20, 30… 90) were different letters.

The multiples of 100 (100, 200, 300 … 900) were different letters.

1 = α	10 = ι	100 = ρ
2 = β	20 = κ	200 = σ
3 = γ	30 = λ	300 = τ
4 = δ	40 = μ	400 = υ
5 = ε	50 = ν	500 = φ
6 = Ϝ	60 = ξ	600 = χ
7 = ζ	70 = ο	700 = ψ
8 = η	80 = π	800 = ω
9 = θ	90 = ϙ	900 = ϡ

This system requires 27 letters. But as the Greeks only had 24 letters in their alphabet, three new symbols were adopted:

The *digamma* represented the number 6.
The *quoppa* represented the number 90
The *sampi* represented the number 900.

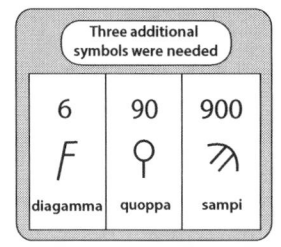

Three additional symbols were needed

6	90	900
Ϝ	ϙ	ϡ
diagamma	quoppa	sampi

So that numerals wouldn't be read as letters, the Greeks put an accent mark following a group of letters that was meant to be a number.

This *keraia* (Greek for "a hornlike projection") looked like an "acute accent" mark. The number 888 would be written like this:

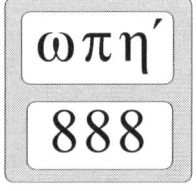

ωπη´

888

325

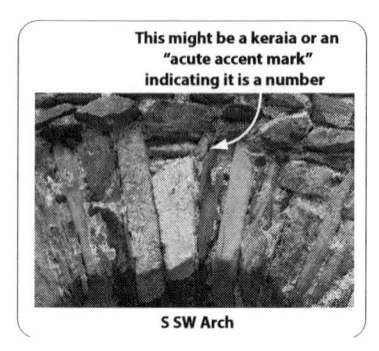

This might be a keraia or an "acute accent mark" indicating it is a number

S SW Arch

To the right of the stone "eta" letter in the Tower, there is a small vertical rock. But there are so many small stones on the face of the Tower, its hard to say definitively that this stone was intended to be a *keraia* or accent mark.

Eta is the actually seventh letter of the Greek alphabet. But because the *digamma* was used to represent 6, that pushed the "eta" up one spot so that it represented 8.

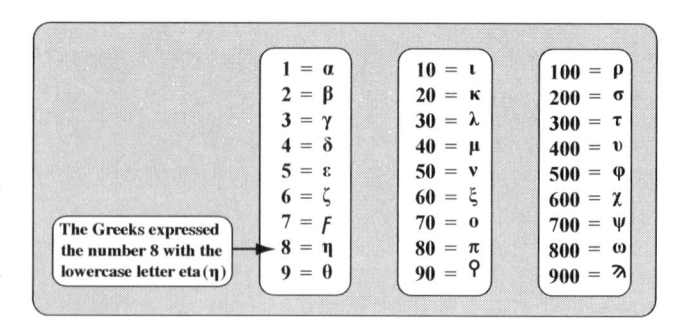

The Greeks expressed the number 8 with the lowercase letter eta (η)

1 = α	10 = ι	100 = ρ
2 = β	20 = κ	200 = σ
3 = γ	30 = λ	300 = τ
4 = δ	40 = μ	400 = υ
5 = ε	50 = ν	500 = φ
6 = ζ	60 = ξ	600 = χ
7 = Ϝ	70 = ο	700 = ψ
8 = η	80 = π	800 = ω
9 = θ	90 = ϙ	900 = ϡ

[Why the Geeeks used a new mark for numeral 6 instead of 9 (like 90 and 900) is not known. The Greek Eta (H) derived from the Phoenician letter Heta which was the eighth letter of the Phoenician alphabet. Curiously, the Phoenician Heta looks like a "square 8-shape" (日). However, not much should be read into this because the Phoenicians used groups of slashes for numbers and our modern figure-8 derived from Arabic numerical symbols. The Etruscans also used this "square 8-shape" for their letter Heta.].

Of course, the modern Greeks use Arabic numerals like we do.
But for ordinal numbers (numbers which order things)
modern Greeks use the letter=number system.
(Except modern Greeks use uppercase letters instead of lowercase like the ancients did.)
For example, in modern Greek, "Philip the 8th" would look like this:

Φιλιππος Η′

Philippos the 8th

The key point here is that the ancient Greeks used **lowercase letters** for their numbers.
To me, this is another reason why John Dee used the lowercase letter **eta**
instead of an uppercase **Eta** in the arch of the Tower: The lowercase *eta* says "**eight**."

And Dee loved the octave.
It was at the heart of his mathematical cosmology.

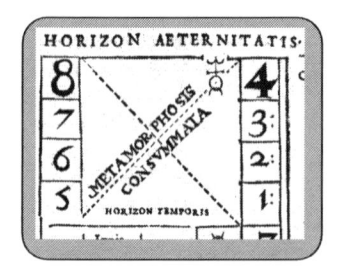

It's the octave in the "octave, null nine" rhythm of Consummata.

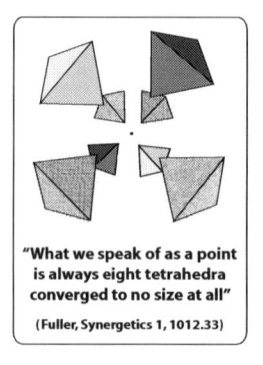

"What we speak of as a point is always eight tetrahedra converged to no size at all"
(Fuller, Synergetics 1, 1012.33)

It's the 8 tetrahedra that make a cuboctahedron.

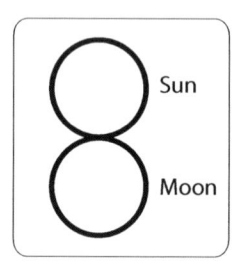

Sun
Moon

In Arabic numerals, the 8 is made from two tangent circles, like the "Sun and Moon," a main theme of Dee's *Monas Hieroglyphica*.

The octave is pretty obvious to anyone who looks at the Tower.

Not only is it proudly perched on eight solid pillars, there are eight semicircular arches bridging those pillars.

Imagine two ancient Greeks time-traveling to visit the Tower.

One might tell his friend, "this tower has **η′** arches in it."

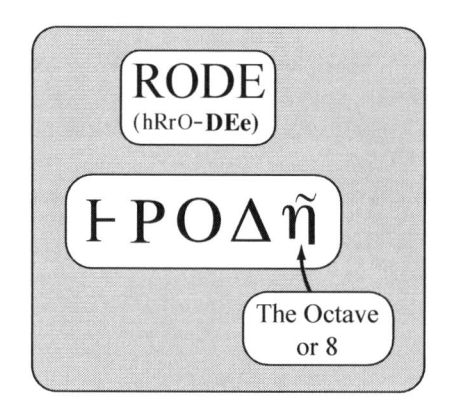

RODE
(hRrO-**DEe**)

⊢ P O Δ η̃

The Octave or 8

In short, Dee didn't use the lowercase eta (**η**) simply because it was a little more obscure-looking than the uppercase Eta (**H**).

The lowercase eta (**η**) brings a mathematical dimension to the word RODE. And Dee loved numbers.

If he had used an uppercase Eta (**H**), it would **not** have implied "8-ness."
Only the lowercase would do.

Remember, several of the stone-letters in the other arches have multiple meanings as well.

The triangle not only represents the Δ in "ROΔE," but it also represents Dee's name, the triangle Δ.

And it faces the mouth of the Dee River (**Δ River**), which is just north of the triangular Δ island of Claudia.

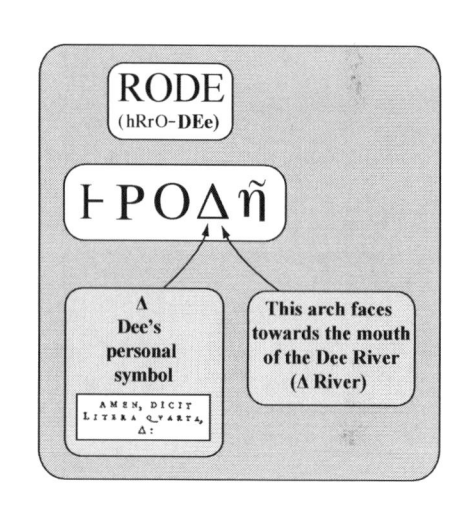

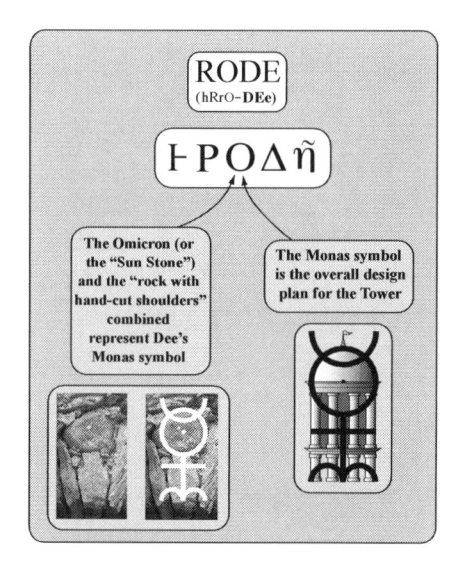

RODE
(hRrO-**DEe**)

⊢ P O Δ η̃

Δ
Dee's personal symbol

AMEN, DICIT
LITERA QVARTA,
Δ:

This arch faces towards the mouth of the Dee River (Δ River)

RODE
(hRrO-**DEe**)

⊢ P O Δ η̃

The Omicron (or the "Sun Stone") and the "rock with hand-cut shoulders" combined represent Dee's Monas symbol

The Monas symbol is the overall design plan for the Tower

Underneath the "O" shaped "Sun Stone" is the rock with hand-chiseled "shoulders."

Combined, I think they represent the **Monas symbol**, which is not only Dee's graphic summation of his mathematical cosmology, it's also the blueprint for the whole Tower.

Dee liked to play around with the idea that the Greek P (Rho)
was pronounced like the Latin or English letter R.
His bilingual mind saw P and R as interchangeable. **P=R**

He also liked the word **PYR**, as in **pyr**ologian.
In Greek, **PYR** means "fire," as Plato associates the
Element of fire with the tetrahedron (or **PYR**amid).

I think Dee instructed the builders of the Tower to use a parallelogram-shaped rock to make the circular part of the P (Rho), so the **letter Y** might also be seen.

The left edge of the parallelogram, combined with the tall "vertical-line" rock seem to make a Y shape.

(Perhaps this is why the "vertical line" rock is slightly slanted. It helps make a more convincing letter Y.)

In other words, these "keystone area" rocks express the letters **P** (Rho), **Y**, and **R** which spell the key word **PYR**.

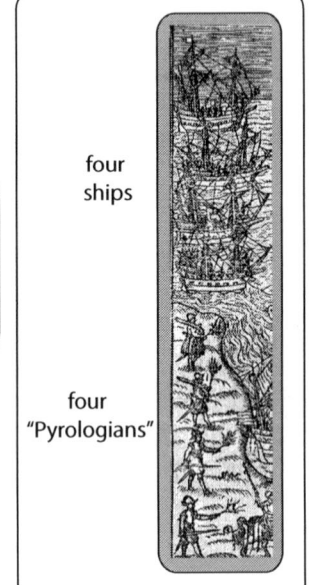

RODE
(hRrO-DEe)

⊢ Ρ Ο Δ η̃

The N NW arch

| The Greek letter P (Rho) looks exactly like the Latin or English letter P | The edge of the parallelogram-shaped rock, combined with the tall, slanted-line rock might be seen as the letter Y | The Greek P (Rho) is pronounced like a Latin or English "R" |

P   Y   R

PYR = "Fire" (in Greek) = Plato's word for a tetrahedron

four ships

four "Pyrologians"

Remember that Dee drew a tetrahedron on the Title page of *General and Rare Memorials*.

He drew 4 "**pyr**ologians," or men brandishing fire," again hinting at a tetrahedron.

Not only does the word PYRO contain both a P and an R it also contains the sound "Rho."

(You can be sure Dee would have been enchanted by a word containing "equivalent" Greek and Roman letters, and that also meant "tetrahedron" to his favorite Greek philosopher. As mentioned earlier, in Dee's cryptically mathematical Aphorism 18 of his *Propaedeumata Aphoristica*, where he writes, "Pyrologians will understand what I mean," he is referring to geometers who study tetrahedra.)

Thus, the arch with the **P** (Rho) in it relates to the arch with the **Δ** (delta) in it.

(In 3 dimensions, this rock with the 2-D triangular face might be visualized as a tetrahedron.

Perhaps it really is a tetrahedon with most of it hidden in the mortar behind it.)

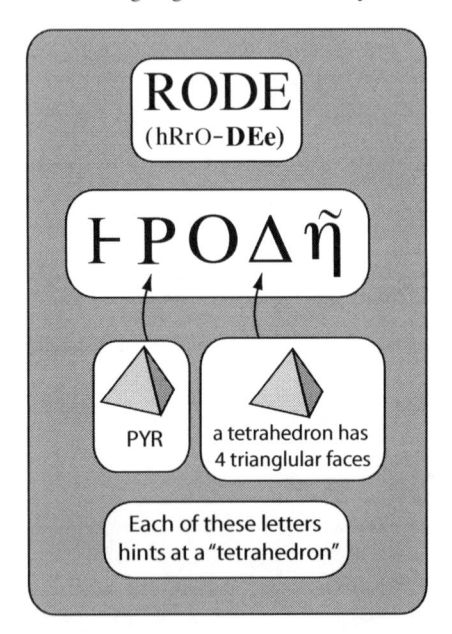

RODE
(hRrO-DEe)

⊢ Ρ Ο Δ η̃

PYR   a tetrahedron has 4 trianglular faces

Each of these letters hints at a "tetrahedron"

328

In a similar fashion, the first and last symbols might also be "paired up." As we've seen, they each involve the Greek letter Eta (**H**).

The first symbol is made from the left half of the letter Eta. The last symbol is the lowercase eta, which represents the number 8.

RODE
(hRrO-DEe)

Ͱ P O Δ η̃

the "rough breathing" mark is made from the left half of the Greek letter Eta (H)

the lowercase eta represents the number 8

Each of these letters involves the Greek letter Eta (H)

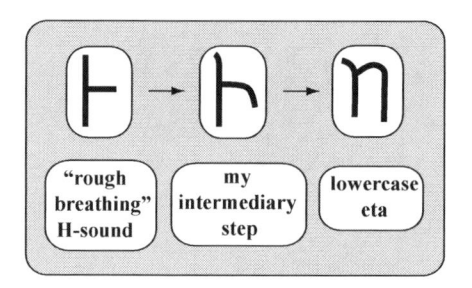

Ͱ → ђ → η

"rough breathing" H-sound

my intermediary step

lowercase eta

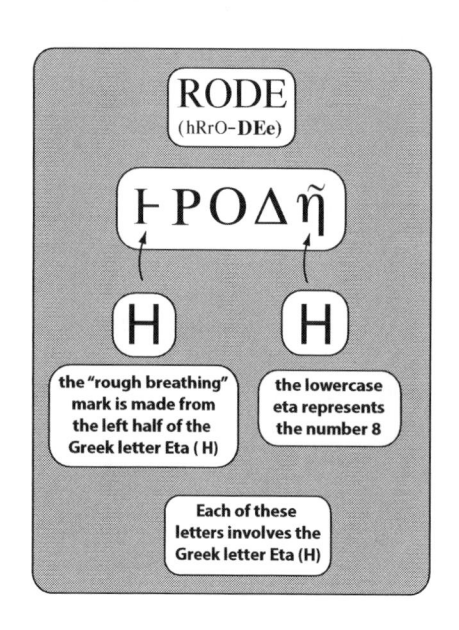

[Besides being both involved with the letter Eta, the first and last symbols are related in other ways.

To see their graphic connection, here I have drawn an intermediary step.

I'm not suggesting that one morphed from the other.

I'm merely visually emphasizing how they are close cousins, each being a variation of the uppercase H-shape.]

To summarize, there is a certain symmetry to Dee's clue-scheme.

It is centered around the circular Omicron (**O**), which I have depicted as a point. As Dee tells us, **"the circle could not exist without the point."**

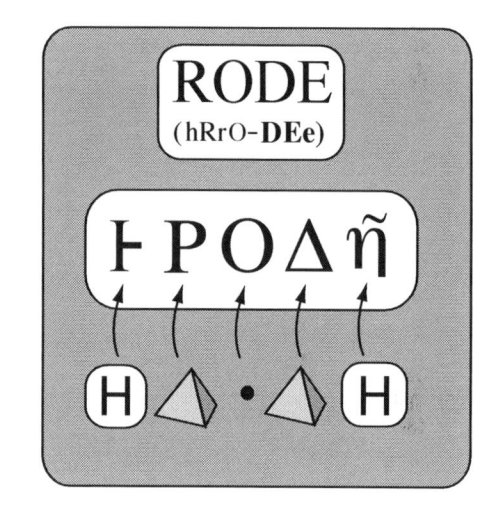

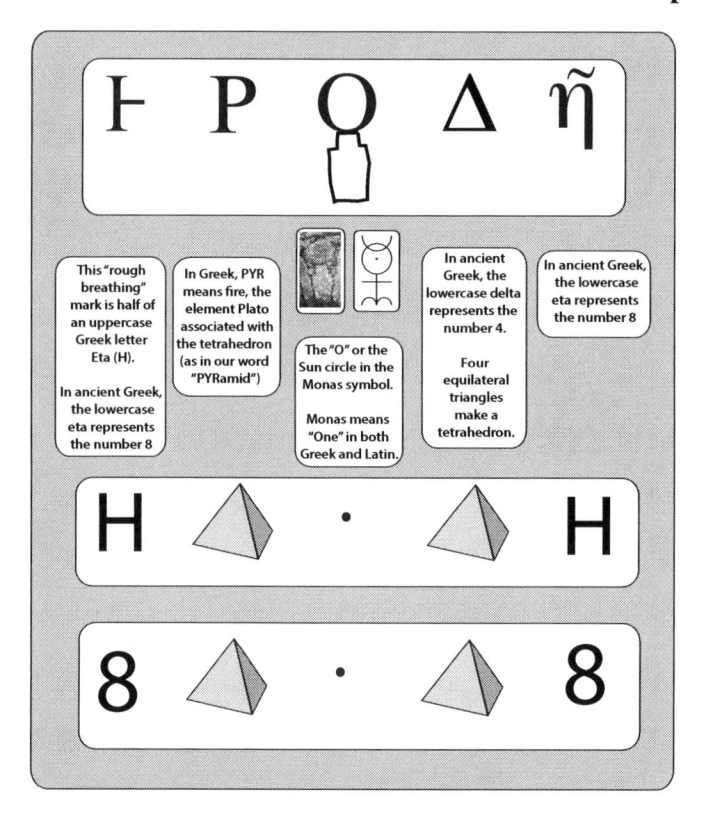

Ͱ P O Δ η̃

This "rough breathing" mark is half of an uppercase Greek letter Eta (H).

In ancient Greek, the lowercase eta represents the number 8

In Greek, PYR means fire, the element Plato associated with the tetrahedron (as in our word "PYRamid")

The "O" or the Sun circle in the Monas symbol.

Monas means "One" in both Greek and Latin.

In ancient Greek, the lowercase delta represents the number 4.

Four equilateral triangles make a tetrahedron.

In ancient Greek, the lowercase eta represents the number 8

H △ · △ H

8 △ · △ 8

RODE
(hRrO-DEe)

Ͱ P O Δ η̃

H △ · △ H

As the η (or **H**) represents the number **8** in ancient Greek, a picture emerges that is an echo of Dee's cosmology.

It involves the octave, two tetrahedra, and the idea of "oppositeness."

329

If the two tetrahedra are reoriented, they form the "Bucky bowtie" or the two tip-to-tip tetrahedra arrangement.

In **Geometry**, this is a representation of the "+4, –4, octave," and the "null 9" is the point of intersection.

In **Optics**, this is the most economical depiction of the behavior of light in a camera obscura.

And in **Number**, this is the +4, –4, octave; null 9" rhythm found in the "9 Wave, the 99 Wave, the 1089 Wave, etc." of what Dee calls CONSUMMATA.

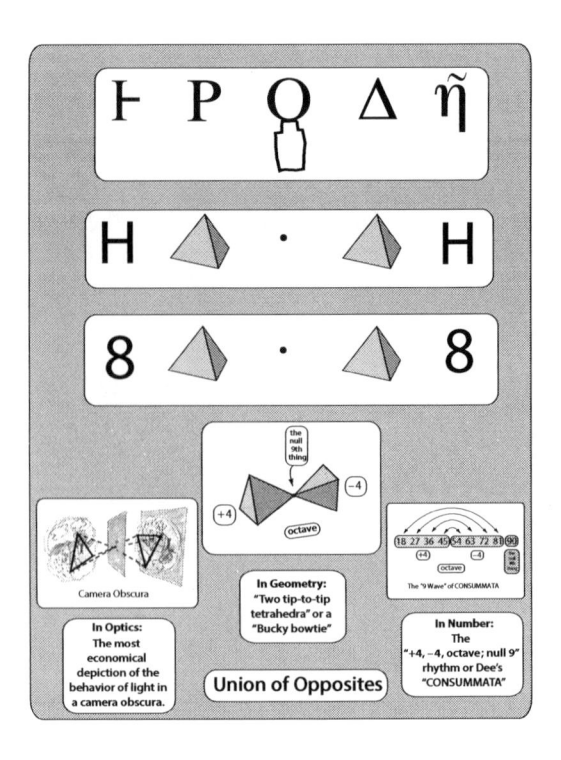

This arrangement of "H's" and "tetrahedra" expresses Dee's cosmology in another mathematical way.

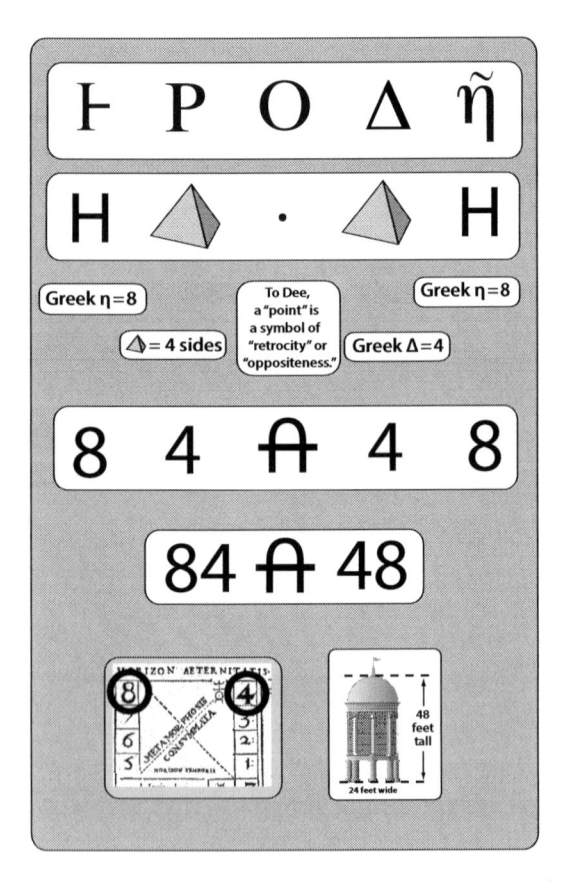

The triangle in the word "ROΔE" can be seen as Dee's personal symbol, which he proudly asserts is the "**Fourth Letter**"(in Hebrew, Greek, and Latin). In Dee's mind, **Δ=4**

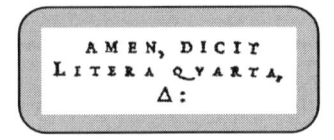

AMEN, DICIT LITERA QVARTA, Δ:

The *tetra* in tetrahedron means 4, and the *hedron* means sides. So, numerically, Dee's arrangement might be seen as **4**'s (the tetrahedra) and **8**'s (the **H**'s).

Merging these digits makes the numbers **84** and **48**. Suddenly, we have a transpalindromic pair that is important in Dee's mathematical cosmos.

The digits **8** and **4** are the boldest, most prominent digits on Dee's "Thus the World Was Created" chart.

And **48** feet is what I consider to be the original height of the John Dee Tower.

(And the Title page of the *Monas Hieroglyphica* appears to have been made on a matrix **48** grid-squares tall by 36 grid-squares wide).

(Mathematicians might want to explore this clue further: The ratio 48:84 is equivalent to 4:7 (4 and 7 are the boldest numbers in the "Below" half of Dee's "Thus the World Was Created" chart). And 48:84 is a ratio Dee cryptically refers to as one of the 4 *Gradus* (or Grades), which are, 12:21, 24:42, 36:63, and 48:84. These four pairs are the only 2-digit transpalindromes that reduce down to fractions that have a single-digit numerator and a single-digit denominator. Furthermore, this key 4:7 proportion can also be seen in important ratios 144:252 and 252:441 in Bob Marshall's "Syndex pretzel."

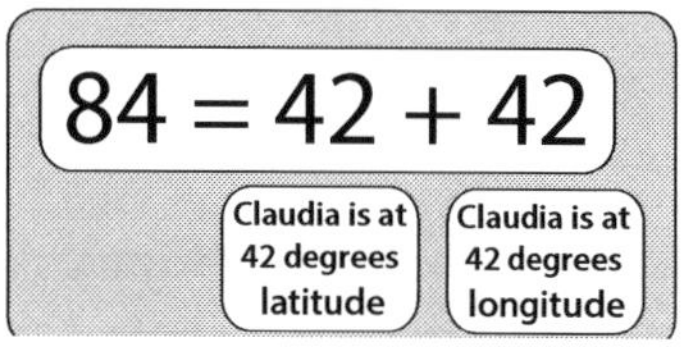

$84 = 42 + 42$

Claudia is at 42 degrees latitude | Claudia is at 42 degrees longitude

Here's another related curiosity. Dividing 84 in half results in 42+42.

This pinpoints the island of Claudia and the Dee River on Dee's maps: 42 degrees latitide and 42 degrees longitude!

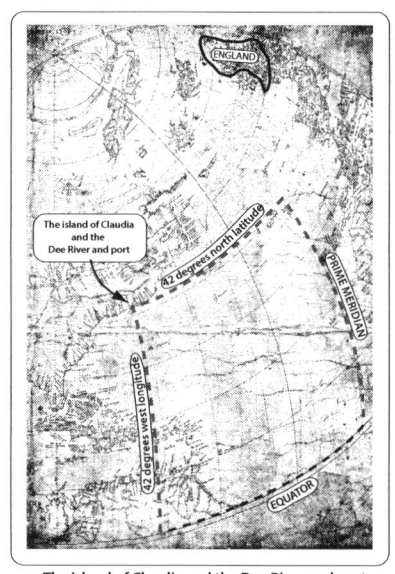

The island of Claudia and the Dee River and port at 42 degrees north latitude and 42 degrees west longitude on part of Dee's 1580 map of North America

RODE
(hRrO-**DEe**)

Ƕ P Q Δ η̃

8 △ · △ 8

Bucky Bowtie

The "9 Wave" of CONSUMMATA

Camera Obscura

Union of Opposites

To visually summarize, the "hRrO-**DEe**" written in the stone-and-mortar Tower expresses the Union of Opposites, the main theme of Dee's *Monas Hieroglyphica*.

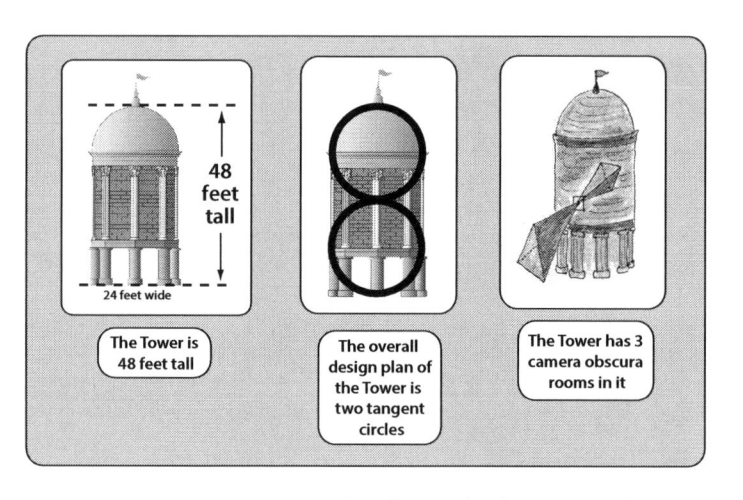

Not only was the Tower originally 48 feet tall, its overall design plan is "two circles," like Dee's classic opposites, the Sun and the Moon.

And "two tangent circles" just happen to form a figure-8, the octave.

Furthermore, the Tower's function incorporates the "Union of Opposites." It contains 3 camera obscura rooms!

The Tower is 48 feet tall — 48 feet tall, 24 feet wide

The overall design plan of the Tower is two tangent circles

The Tower has 3 camera obscura rooms in it

In short, the letters (RODE), which is the name of the location of the building, also explain how the building works!

That Dee was a master web-weaver.

[Dee uses this arrangement of "a central thing surrounded by several pairs of things" cryptically in his "Testamentum," a short poem written to his friend John Gwynn to help clarify the meaning of the *Monas Hieroglyphica*. In a series of word and letter clues, Dee cryptically refers to the numbers 8, 9, 10, 11, 12. The central thing, 10, is our Base number. The closest surrounding pair is 9 and 11. They represent the 9 Wave and the 11 Wave of Consummata. The outer pair, 8 and 12, are each "cuboctahedral numbers." A cuboctahedron is made from 8 tip-to-tip tetrahedra and has 12 vertices. Dee also relates 8 and 12 in his Artificial Quaternary, where 1+2+3+2 =8 and 1x2x3x2 =12.]

If my analysis of the "secondary meanings" of the 5 symbols in the arches of the Tower is correct, we should expect to find **similar clues in the Title page** of *General and Rare Memorials*, which is Dee's "visual paean" to the word RODE.

(A paean is a "song of praise." I see the Title page as Dee's "graphic tribute" to the name "RODE.")

The pair of tetrahedra in the Title page

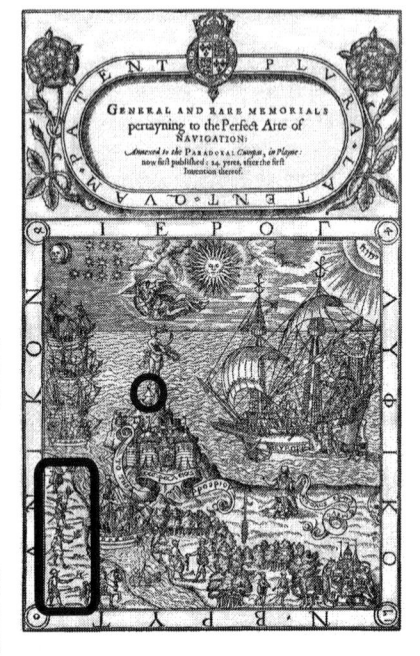

Finding one tetrahedron is pretty easy. It's under Lady Occasion's foot.

And the "4 pryologians" are a cryptic representation of another tetrahedron.

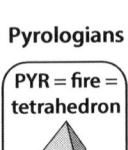

The pair of 8's in the Title page

The 4 "pryologians," plus the 4 ships "at rode" off the coast" constitute one representation of the number 8.

Another representation is the "two circle or the "sideways figure-8" design framework of the lozenge-shape surrounding the title.

332

The pair of H's in the Title page

There are two prominent Eta's or "**H** shapes" in the Greek words of Dee's illustration, each with a strong hint that Dee has intentionally planted them there.

Most of the letters of Dee's plea, **"Stolos explisminos TO THS asphaleais phrourion"** are lowercase Greek letters.

But oddly, the letters in the words **TO THS** are uppercase.
(The detailed-oriented, Greek-scholar Dee would not have done this by accident.)

On the final, printed Title page

This should be...
τ ο τ η ς

...but Dee writes:
T O T(H)S

And Dee partially hides another letter H with the leg of Europa's bull:
Ε Υ Ρ Ο Π (H)

TO TES written in lowercase letters from the text of Dee's Monas Hieroglyphica

By contrast, in the text of the *Monas Hieroglyphica*, Dee spells these words in **lowercase**.

By making them **uppercase** on the Title page of *General and Rare Memorials*, Dee seems to be intentionally disguising the **H** in T**H**S, which, in lowercase (η), expresses the number **8**.

Another "disguised" **H** appears in the word ΕΥΡΟΠ**H**,
(running along the side of the Queen's ship.)

Dee graphically obscures part of the **H** by hiding it behind the leg of Europa's bull.

As can be seen in Dee's preliminary drawing for this Title page,, this "hiding the **H** with the leg of Europa's bull" is a refinement made later on, in the finished illustration.

However, in the original sketch, he had already decided to make the **H** in TO T**H**S uppercase.

On Dee's preliminary drawing for the Title page

This should be...
τ ο τ η ς

...but Dee writes:
T O T(H)S

Here the letter H is visible:
Ε Υ Ρ Ο Π (H)

Dee cleverly concealed yet another **pair of H**'s in the Title page.
Radiating out of the upper right hand corner are the letters Yod–He–Waw–He.
This is the *Tetragrammaton*, or the 4-letter name of God in Hebrew.

These Hebrew letters correspond to the Latin letters YHVH, which just happens to have **two H**'s in it.

(Leave it to Dee to hide a clue in the name of God)

On the final, printed Title page

In his original sketch, Dee must have had some other word in mind.

He crossed it out, and for some reason wrote the four Hebrew letters left-to-right-reading instead of the customary Hebrew right-to-left-reading.

On Dee's original sketch for the Title page

The "point" in the Title page

To graphically conceal the idea of a "point" is challenging.
In the *Monas Hieroglyphica*, Dee writes at great length about the "point" in the center of the cross.

Making a giant X from the 4 corners of the illustration, the "point" of intersection coincides with the front tip of the bow the of Elizabeth's ship of state.

Metaphorically, this is very important "point."
It's like the "cutting edge" or the "directional point" that aims England into the future.

Note that the two lines of this giant X
are not exactly perpendicular to each other.

The overall shape of the finished illustration
is not a square, it's slightly rectangular.

It seems Dee employed a grid that was
42 grid-squares tall by 40 grid-squares wide.

(Dee appears to be is hiding yet another clue alluding to
the fact that the Dee River is at "42" degrees latitude.)

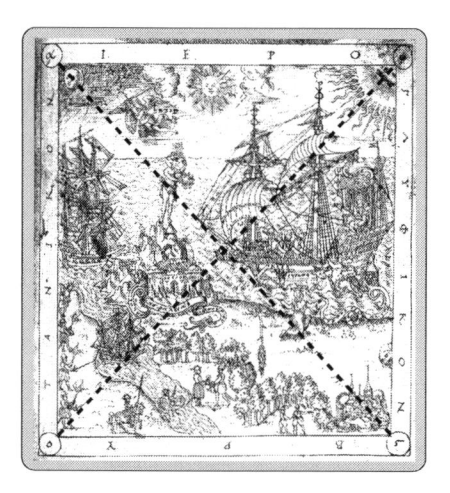

Interestingly, the tip of the prow is not exactly in the
center of Dee's preliminary drawing for the Title page.

He seems to have had originally envisioned
a different cryptic reference to a "point."

A line connecting the center of the **O** (or Omega)
and the **X** in the Chi-Rho atop the forward mast,
also intersects with the "pointy" tips of bowsprit
and two of the upper wooden yards.

This "line" from the
"O... to the "pointy" bowsprit tip... to the X"
can also be seen in the finished illustration.

It no longer touches the (now single) wooden yard arm,
but it does run parallel to the bowsprit's support rope.

335

As can be proven geometrically, the front tip of the ship's bow is also on the "vertical midline" of the Title page. This midline passes through several other prominent "points."

It runs through the center of the circular Order of the Garter emblem, the point of tangency of the two circles in the lozenge shape, and the center point of the "Sun circle."

The midline also passes through 3 Greek letters,
and they are all the letter Ρ (Rho).

It passes through the only two Greek Ρ's (Rho's) in
ΙΕΡΟΓΛΥΦΙΚΟΝ ΒΡΥΤΑΝΙΚΟΝ
(or HIE**R**OGLYPHIKON B**R**YTANIKON)

It also passes through the Greek letter ρ (lowercase rho),
in the Greek word on the flowing ribbon,
φρουριομ (*phrouriom*, meaning "watch post").

Dee even spells out the word "POINT"

If Dee really wanted us to see these "points,"
he would most likely leave a confirming clue.
And indeed he does.

In Theorem 3 of the *Monas*, Dee emphasizes
that the Sun circle of his Monas symbol
"is represented by a Complete Circle with a Visible Center."

He calls it,
"the central Conspicuous Point of the Hieroglyphic Monad."

The clever Dee has arranged things so the vertical midline passes through
five letters that spell the word **POINT**. Let's start from the bottom.

Starting at the bottom, first, the midline goes right
through the "central Conspicuous Point" of
the Sun circle, which is a pretty obvious **O**.

Next, it goes through the **P** in ΙΕΡΟΓΛΥΦΙΚΟΝ.
(which is actually a Greek Rho, but in Dee code it can be a English P)

Next, through the **T** in LATENT.
(which is Latin for "hidden," and the T is inverted to make it more "hidden"

Then, through the **n** in Invention.
(Dee was inventive for sure, he even made this letter be lowercase to disguise it)

And finally through the **I** in QUI.
(*Honi soit qui mal y pense*, the motto of the English chivalric
Order of the Garter means, "Shame on him who thinks ill of it")

Would Dee really have gone through all
this trouble to conceal the word **POINT**?

336

Yes. Dee loved the point.
And as a deep thinking geometer-philosopher, he loved to talk about it.

In his cosmology, it was the very first thing to exist. In the *Monas,* he frequently refers to the "sharp, stable point." In Theorem 2, he declares that, without the point, neither line nor circle could be crafted, concluding,
"... things came into being by way of a point..."

(Dee provides a lengthy discussion of the history of the definition of a "point" at the very beginning of Book One of the 1570 first English translation of Euclid's *Elements*.)

These symbols, which are implied by...

8 △ · △ 8

Ͱ P Q̧ Δ η̃

RODE
(hRrO-DEe)

... letters in the arches of the Tower

...can also be seen in the the Title page.

To summarize, thinking like Dee, the various letters in the arches of the Tower have symbolic meanings: the number 8, the tetrahedron, and the "point."

Representations of these symbolic meanings can also be found on the Title page of *General and Rare Memorials*.

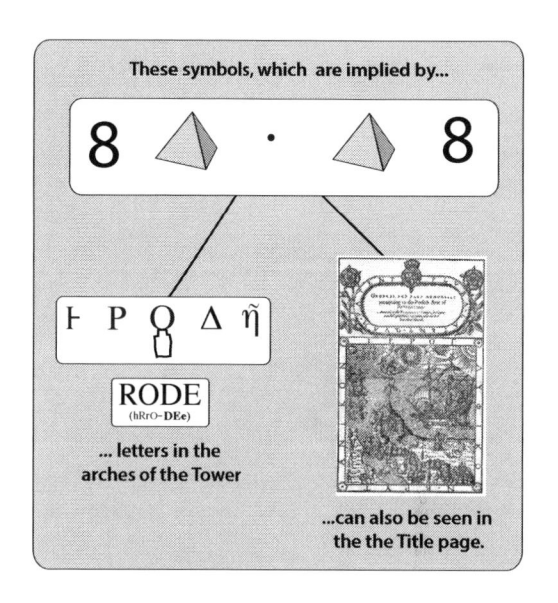

Let's analyze this idea of "8-ness" a bit further.

If we were to number the arches starting at the beginning of Dee's 5-letter/symbol word, it might look like this:

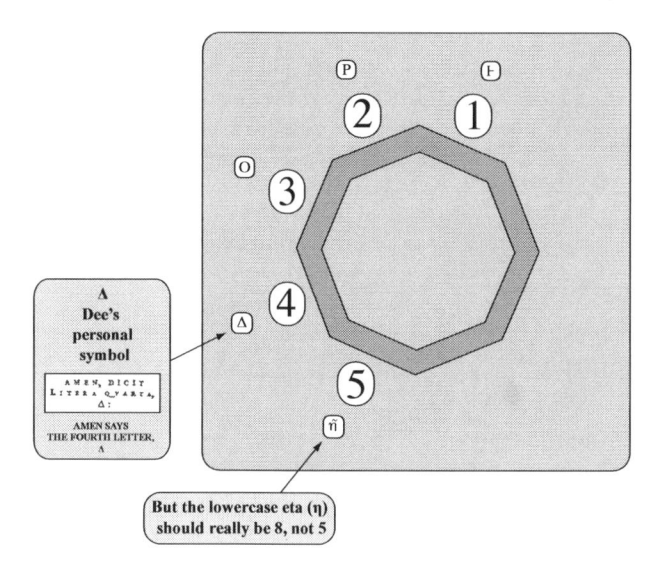

Δ
Dee's personal symbol

AMEN, DICIT
LITERA QVARTA,
Δ:
AMEN SAYS
THE FOURTH LETTER,
Δ

But the lowercase eta (η) should really be 8, not 5

Propitiously,
Greek letter Delta (Δ) is in the fourth arch.

Dee was quite enthused that his name, "Dee," was the 4th letter in Greek, Latin, and Hebrew.

(At the end of the *Monas* he simply calls himself "THE FOURTH LETTER, Δ.")

You can be certain Dee was aware the Δ was the FOURTH symbol in his 5-letter/symbol word.

However, the arch containing the lowercase eta (**η**), really **shouldn't** be labled with the numeral **5**.

As per the Greek numbering system, Dee would have seen the lowercase eta (**η**) as an **8**.

337

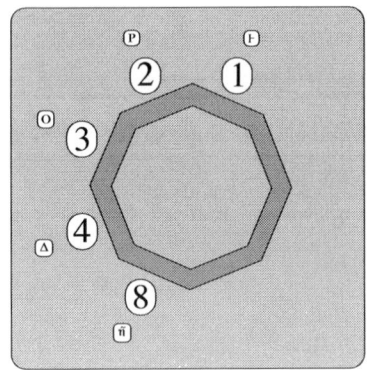

So let's make replace the numeral 5 with the numeral 8.

Now, the most logical way of placing the "missing numerals" would be this:

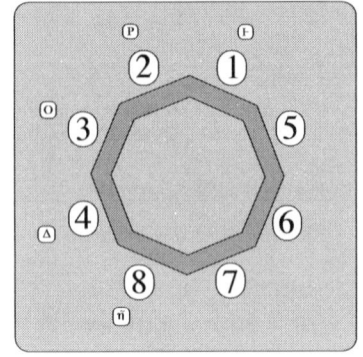

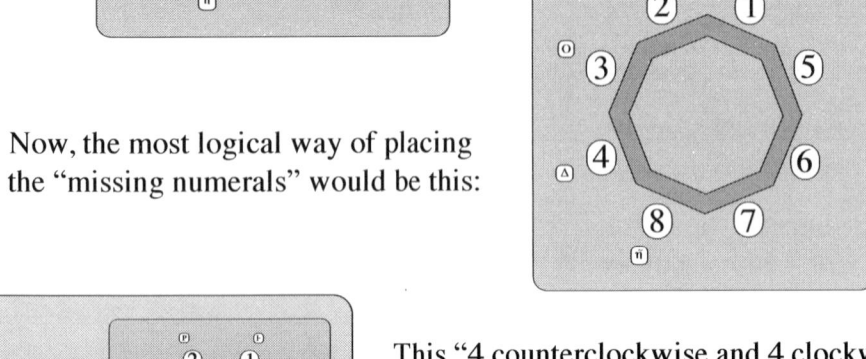

This "4 counterclockwise and 4 clockwise" arrangement perfectly expresses the "+4, −4" nature of the octave.

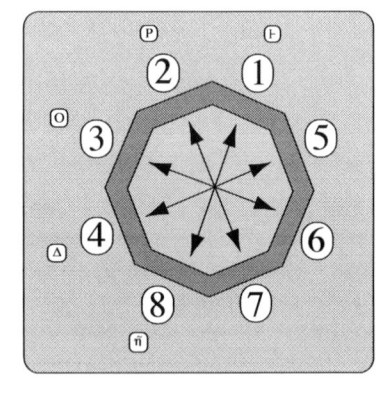

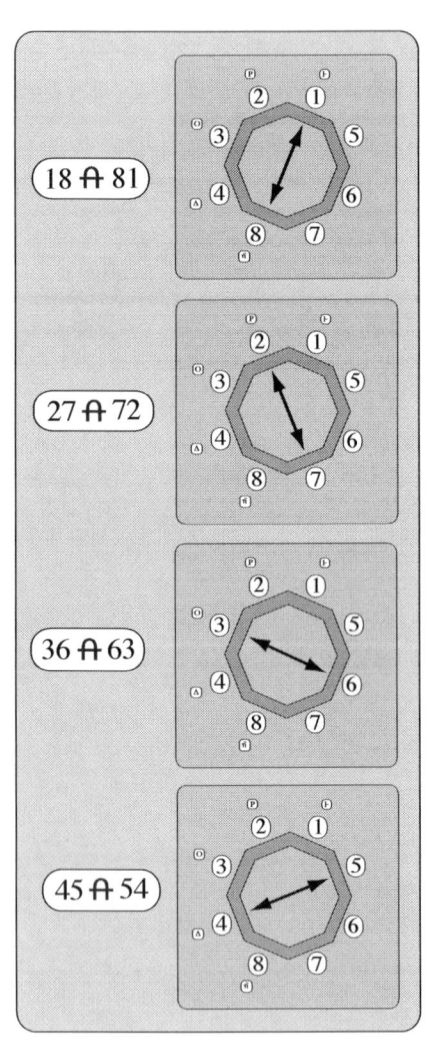

The interconnected 1 and 8 imply the transpalindromes 18 and 81.

The 2 and 7 imply 27 and 72.

The 3 and 6 imply 36 and 63.

And the 4 and 5 imply 45 and 54.

In short, this arrangement displays all four of the transpalindromes in the **9 Wave** (in the **two-digit range** of number).

The 9 Wave of Consummata

These same 4 pairs of transpalindromes can be seen in Dee's "Thus the World Was Created" chart.

With the help of Dee's watchword (RODE), the arches of the Tower express what Dee calls CONSUMMATA.

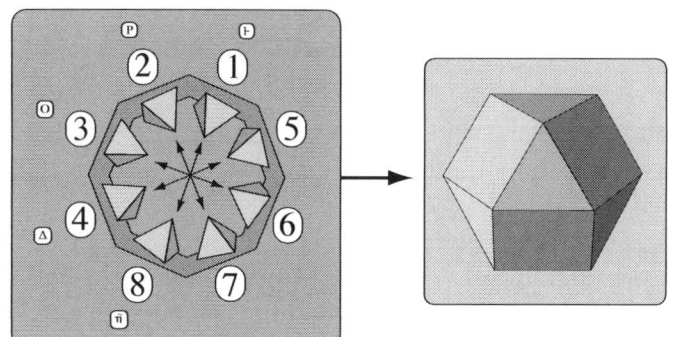

Using this same arrangement, let's imagine that each of the arches is a tetrahedron.

Suitably arranged, they could make a cuboctahedron.

(As noted previously, in the arch with the triangular rock, we can only see one face of that rock. Perhaps it really is a tetrahedron!)

Here's how the **9 Wave** (in number) and the **cuboctahedron** (in geometry) can be as interrelated:

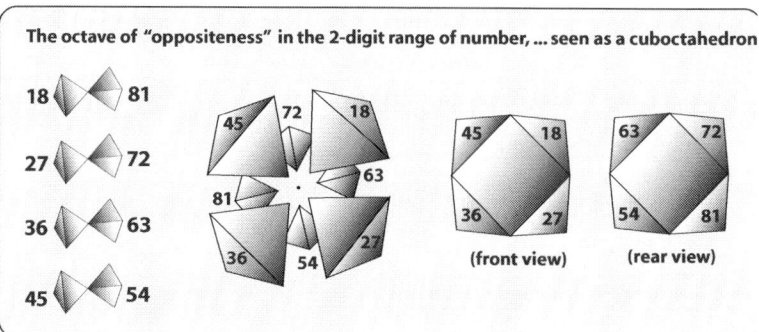

The octave of "oppositeness" in the 2-digit range of number, ... seen as a cuboctahedron

18 ◁▷ 81
27 ◁▷ 72
36 ◁▷ 63
45 ◁▷ 54

(front view) (rear view)

Am I being over-inventive?

I don't think so. It's not me who's being clever here. It's John Dee. He is the genius who conceived this letter-number-game. He loved mixing letters and numbers together to conceal clues.

In the *Monas Hieroglyphica* he uses a **Latin alphabet–number code**. He remarks "X is the 21st letter," and that "V is the 20th letter," and that his own personal symbol, "Δ (Delta) is the 4th letter."

Here, in the arches of the Tower, he is simply using a **Greek alphabet-number code** instead of the Latin alphabet-number code.

Would Dee really have written the word **RODE** in Greek, made one of the letters lowercase to indicate the number 8, and have the whole thing sculpted out of rock?

Most certainly. He was a multidisciplinary-creative-whiz-Renaissance man. And he loved to plant clues. And he was meticulous and thorough in creating them.

Most modern people see numbers and letters as mundane and utilitarian. Dee felt they were **spiritual** or **holy**. Here's his advice to grammarians in his *Letter to Maximilian*:

"We admonish them, as friends, that the first Mystical letters of Hebrew, Greek, and Latin were issued by God alone and handed down to Mortals. Furthermore, (despite what may be the custom of human arrogance to boast) the shapes of all those letters derive from points, straight lines, and circumferences of circles (by wonderful and most wise artfulness)."

(Dee, *Monas*, p.5)

Dee's clues are as interrelated as his cosmology.
He intermingles geometry, number, and letters with architecture, optics, and even with name of the first colony in the British Empire.

Now that's creative!

Dee's Message is Simple

All this detailed clue-finding and mathematics should not cloud the simple message of Dee's cosmology:

The Union of Opposites

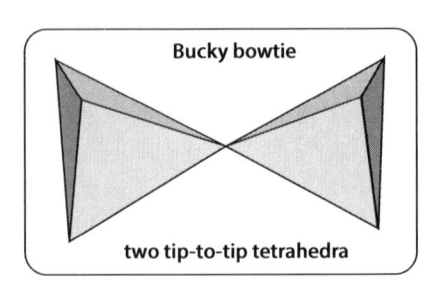

Geometrically, Dee sees the "Union of Opposites" as 2 tip-to-tip tetrahedra. It's the "Bucky bowtie."

This is the "energy event" Buckminster Fuller called, **"the tuned in or tuned out minimum structural experience of Universe."**

It's the most economic description of the behavior of light in a camera obscura.

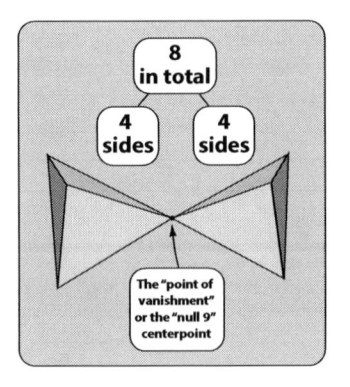

Bucky bowtie

two tip-to-tip tetrahedra

This simple idea is at the heart of Dee's most cherished work, the *Monas Hieroglyphica*.

It's at the heart of the design of the Tower. (Not just the octave of 8 pillars, but also the three camera obscura rooms, which are each "Bucky bowties of light.")

Each of the tetrahedra has 4 sides, totaling to 8 sides.

8 in total
4 sides   4 sides

The "point of vanishment" or the "null 9" centerpoint

And strangely enough, the "Union of Opposites" is at the heart of the name Dee chose for the first English colony of the British Empire: "RODE" or as Greek teacher Dee creatively expressed it:.

Ͱ P O Δ η̃

Which, seen in Dee's symbolic way is:

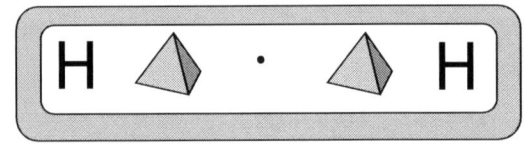

H △ · △ H

or

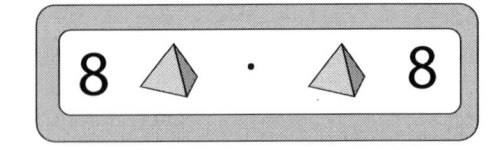

8 △ · △ 8

340

A fun way to see Dee's "Union of Opposites" symbolism

To simplify even further, let's look at these symbols in
terms of something thoroughly modern: **a football game**

It's going to be a great game.
There is a long-standing rivalry between the **Rho Team (P)** and the **Delta Team (Δ)**.
We've got 50-yard line seats, so each of the H-shaped goalposts will be visible.

Just before kickoff, **four players from each team** come to midfield.
The referee tosses a coin in the air. Even though it's only one
coin, it has a form that expresses the Union of Opposites.

Heads and tails are truly **opposites**. But in another sense
they are truly **united**, as they are each parts of the same coin.
When the coin finally settles on the ground will only be one team
who will get to choose whether they will kick or receive.

It's a symphony of opposites.
Two sides of the coin.

The Rho Team (in **white** jerseys)
verses the Delta Team (in **black** jerseys).

The impartial referee wears
a **black and white** shirt.

Each team, while defending its own territory,
attempts to penetrate into the opponent's
territory ... all the way to the goal line.

Close-up view of the coin toss

Even with all this oppositeness, there is still Unity. The rival teams are different,
but they are also similar, as they are each comprised of football players.

And both teams are needed in order to play a game.

Football teams wear many different colored jerseys.
But there's one color that they cannot wear.
You know what that is?

The answer is: the color the other team is wearing.

If they did, there would be no visual oppositenesss. Every play would be pandemonium.
Despite this, there is still a sense of unity: all of the players on the field are wearing jerseys.

341

How does a football game say: $\vdash P O \Delta \tilde{\eta}$

The first and last letters are forms of (**H**), or the two goal posts.
The second letter (**P**) and fourth letter (**Δ**) each symbolize a
"tetrahedron" (**PYR**) of football players that come out for the coin toss.

The middle letter, **O**, symbolizes the point of retrocity, the point of vanishment,
the hole in the camera obscura, or the null 9 in number.

The average guy in the street might consider a "point" to be
unimportant, but to geometer Dee, it was of supreme importance.
As Dee puts it, "... things came into being by way of a point..."

Admittedly, it seems *wildly* creative to say that the symbols in the rocks
on the western facade of the Tower are like a football game coin-toss.

I am merely trying to help the you visualize the idea of the **Union of Opposites**.
The more ways you visualize **retrocity**, the easier it is to grasp.

The Union of Opposites is are easier to
visualize with tangible objects.

For example, the opposites "hot and cold"
are both expressed in the same thermometer.

The opposites of the "inside and outside" are simply
different locations in relation to the same open door.

In between the opposites of white paint and black paint,
one can find light gray, medium gray, and dark gray paint.

White and black may be opposites, but they are united as
they are both simply different degrees of brightness.

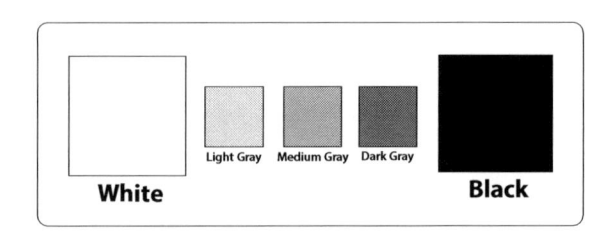

A pencil expresses the Union of Opposites.
The sharp, graphite end is a mark maker.
The blunt, eraser end is a mark deleter.
Yet they are united as parts of the same pencil

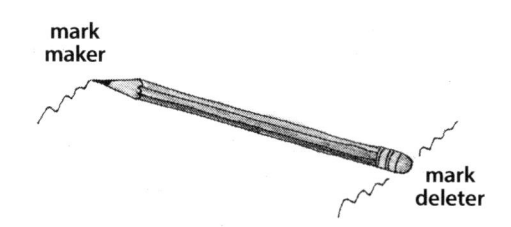

Other examples of the Union of Opposites are more abstract and harder to depict visually. Like war and peace. Or happy and sad.

The Union of Opposites can be recognized in many fields:

rich and poor	yin and yang
wet and dry	sweet and sour
day and night	gold and silver
young and old	light and dark
acids and bases	victory and defeat
backwards and forwards	synonym and antonym

(Try to come up with a few more.
Listen for them in music lyrics.
See them in the world around you)

Dee hid his guiding principle of the Union of Opposites everywhere.

Dee was very thorough. He buried the idea of the Union of Opposites in the name of the colony.

(And he even buried name of the colony in the stone-and-mortar arches of the Tower.)

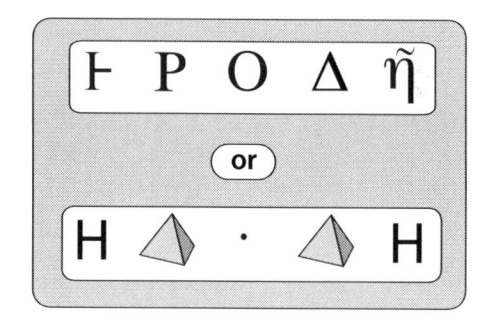

He buried the Union of Opposites
in the function of the Tower
(as a camera obscura).

The Tower has 3 camera obscura rooms in it

Dee's clever Monas symbol is the epitome of **oppositeness**:
The Sun and the Moon.

The two perpendicular lines of the Cross of the Elements.

Or the two half circles of the Aries symbol.

(In the *Monas Hieroglyphica*, Dee emphasizes the fact that on the first of Aries, the Spring equinox, there are exactly 12 hours of light and 12 hours of darkness.
Light and dark are opposites.)

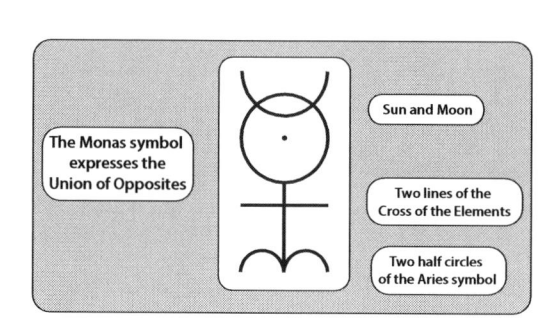

The Monas symbol expresses the Union of Opposites

Sun and Moon

Two lines of the Cross of the Elements

Two half circles of the Aries symbol

343

And the Monas symbol is the overall plan for the Tower.

Dee's architectural wonder is a three dimensional stone-and-mortar Monas symbol.

The Monas symbol is also the overall design plan of the Tower

Another way to visualize this design plan is two tangent circles.

These might be seen as the Sun and the Moon.

And indeed, even the shape of the number 8.

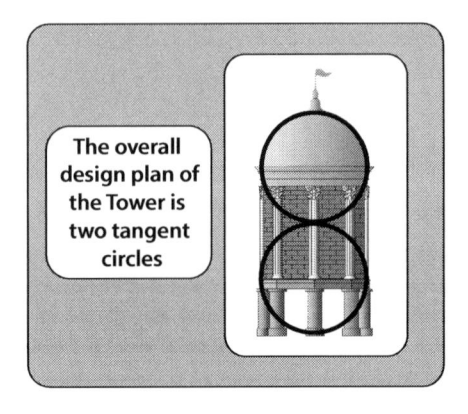

The overall design plan of the Tower is two tangent circles

John Dee wanted the settlers of the new land to be cognizant of the Union of Opposites for moral reasons

Throughout Dee's lifetime, England was plagued by bitter infighting among its citizens.

Henry VIII split from the Catholic Church of Rome.
Under Edward VI, Protestants persecuted Catholics.
Under Mary I, Catholics persecuted Protestants.
Under Elizabeth I, Protestants persecuted Catholics.

By the time Dee was 35, he had been Catholic, Protestant, Catholic, and then Protestant again.

He saw this infighting as futile, and he travailed ardently to come up with a solution.

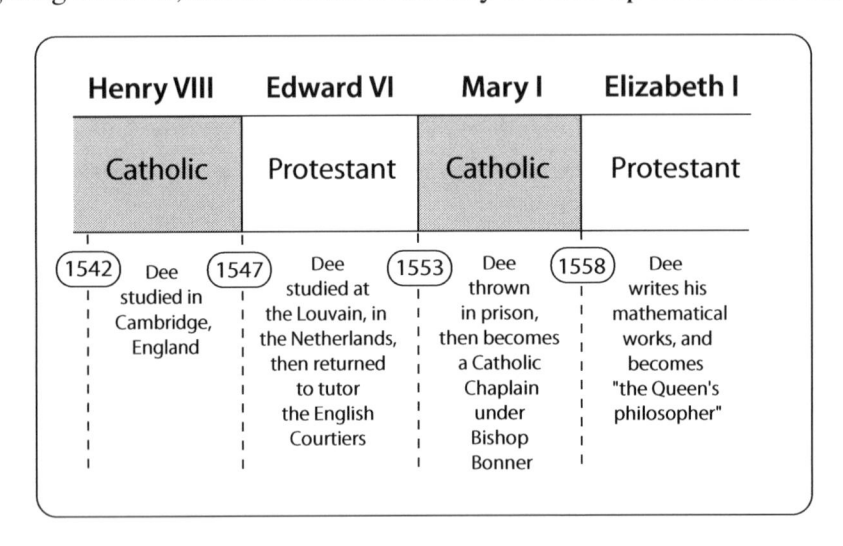

Henry VIII	Edward VI	Mary I	Elizabeth I
Catholic	Protestant	Catholic	Protestant
(1542) Dee studied in Cambridge, England	(1547) Dee studied at the Louvain, in the Netherlands, then returned to tutor the English Courtiers	(1553) Dee thrown in prison, then becomes a Catholic Chaplain under Bishop Bonner	(1558) Dee writes his mathematical works, and becomes "the Queen's philosopher"

John Dee was instrumental (legally, politically, navigationally, and cartographically) in orchestrating this new colony where the English Protestants and English Catholics could each worship as they pleased.

The new colony on the Dee River, RODE, was itself to be a "Union of Opposites." (Protestants and Catholics)

It was to be the seed for other colonies up and down the coast, and eventually inland, across the vast continent.

RODE was to be a place of complete religious toleration.

The people of this Utopia could believe whatever they wanted, and would be free to speak their minds.

Not only does the building still exist, but the concept it symbolizes lives on

The masons and carpenters who actually constructed the Tower knew they were planting an important seed. They were aware of the potent symbolism of Dee's Tower.

Benedict Arnold also was aware of the symbolism of the Tower. He knew all about Dee's colonization effort that had taken place a scant 43 years earlier (the time between 1583 and 1636).

Benedict knew about the camera obscura rooms. (As can be deduced from his personal mark inscribed in the first Governor's chair). Benedict knew that the Tower symbolized freedom of thought and the union of opposing viewpoints. Benedict (and his comrades) insisted that this tolerance be woven into the fabric of their new colony.

The best way to carry forward what the Elizabethan Dee had begun was to use the same name that Dee had chosen for the colony: **Rhode Island**. They also adopted Dee's symbol for the colonization effort: the **Anchor of Hope**. The tradition of tolerance planted by John Dee gained momentum under Benedict Arnold and the early leaders of Rhode Island.

This state might have been the smallest, but it was the **most religiously tolerant** of all the 13 original colonies. Religious sects of all sorts were welcomed in the City by the Sea. In the late 1700's, Rhode Island leaders insisted that the Bill of Rights be amended before they would agree to ratify the US Constitution. (Rhode Islanders didn't want to be losing rights they already had.)

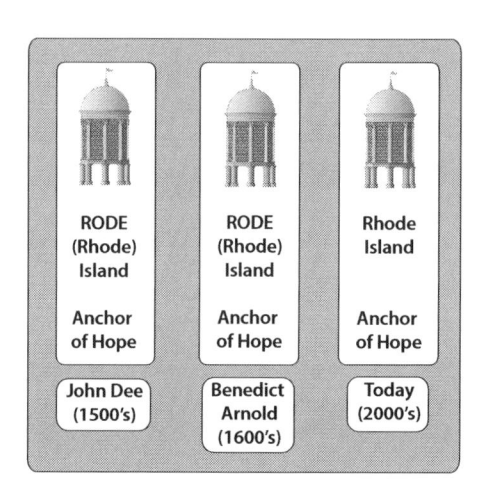

RODE (Rhode) Island	RODE (Rhode) Island	Rhode Island
Anchor of Hope	Anchor of Hope	Anchor of Hope
John Dee (1500's)	Benedict Arnold (1600's)	Today (2000's)

Still today, a wide variety kinds of churches, synagogues, and places of worship can be found throughout Newport (and all over Rhode Island.)

The name of the state **still** contains the words: Rhode Island. And state symbol is **still**: The Anchor of Hope.

And the John Dee Tower of 1583 **still** stands in Touro Park, silently expressing: The Union of Opposites.

The Tower was the first English building in America.
And the 13 original English colonies formed the United States.

In a sense, the Tower represents "Union of Opposites concepts,"
which are at the core the United States government,
(things like like the balance of powers in the 3 branches of government,
the multi-party system, the separation of Church and State, etc.).

The Tower represents the concepts of liberty
and freedom – all men are created equal
and have certain inalienable rights.

United States of America is a Union of Opposites.

From this acorn of a Tower the sturdy
oak tree of America has sprouted.

Dee would be pleased.

Moreover, the Tower is important on a global scale.

John Dee coined the term: **British Empire**. He convinced Queen Elizabeth
that she had a legal right to all of North America north of Florida.

He chose "Narragansett Bay," as the site of the first Elizabethan colony.
And he named it after himself: the **Dee River** (or River of Dee or RODE).

Because Sir Humphrey Gilbert made the mid-ocean decision to land at Saint
John's Bay in Newfoundland before heading to the colony at the Dee River,
Saint John's proclaims their city to be the birthplace of the British Empire.
(Technically they are right, but Saint John's was only intended to be a stop-over point for
Sir Humphrey Gilbert. The ultimate destination of his expedition was the Dee River.)

Dee wanted his Tower of mathematical harmony, his Renaissance Vitruvian temple,
his celestial horologium, to be the first English building built in the New World.

It was to be the focal point, the city center, the timekeeper, and
the "greeter" for future settlers – an architectural Statue of Liberty.

This was to be the **birthplace of the British Empire**, which
Dee envisioned would spread along the East Coast of
America, and eventually span the Northern Hemisphere.

And this "seed" was to have sprouted in 1583, at the beginning
of the **New Time**, the start of the new "Elizabethan Calendar,"
when the "civil year" was to be realigned with "heaven."

Dee envisioned Elizabeth reigning over a **vast Sea Empire** whose
"Limits" went all the way to Japan and China in the Pacific.

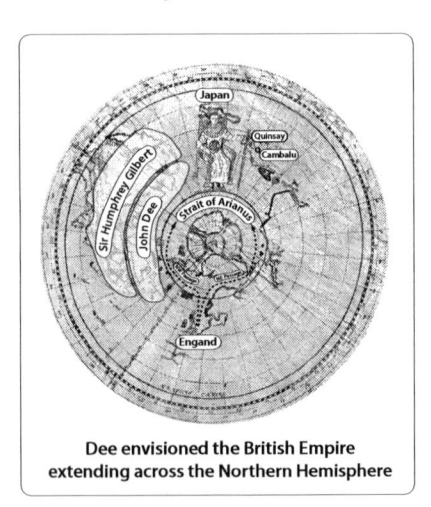

**Dee envisioned the British Empire
extending across the Northern Hemisphere**

Granted, the new colony at the Dee River never took root, the Archbishop of Canterbury
vetoed the Calendar Reform, and the Elizabethans never opened trade routes with China.

But, the John Dee Tower of 1583 **did** actually get constructed,
and over the next few centuries, the British Empire **did** grow
to become the largest empire the world has ever known.

At its height, the British Empire covered one quarter of
all the land mass of earth and one quarter of the earth's population.

At various times there were colonies on every continent–Australia, Asia,
Africa, Europe, North America, South America, and even Antarctica.

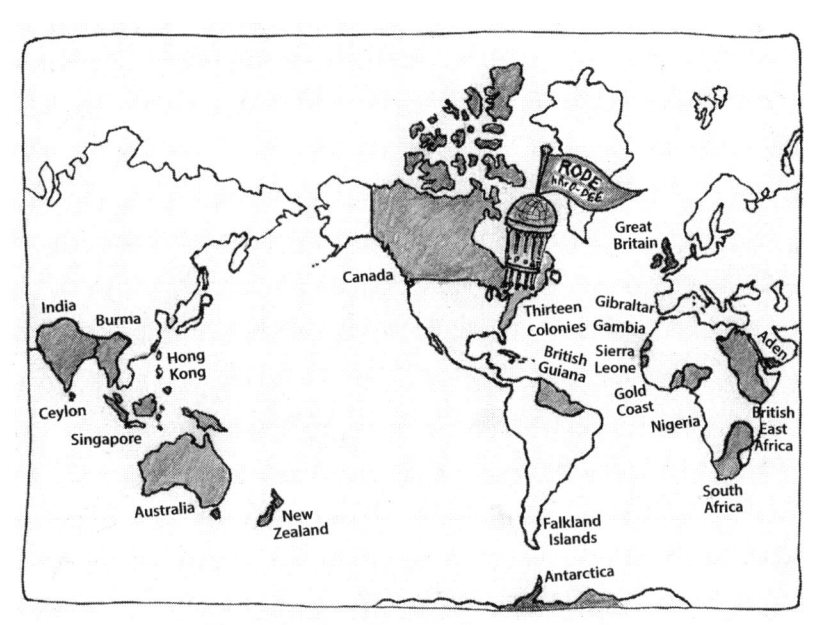

**The John Dee Tower of 1583 was the
first building in the British Empire, which
later grew to include all these colonies.**

**The Anchor of Hope on
Benedict Arnold's seal
as the first Governor
of Rhode Island**

As Benedict Arnold (who claimed the tower for himself) adopted the same name
(RODE) and the same symbol (Anchor of Hope) of the Elizabethan venture, he
saw his 1600's colony as an **extension** of the Elizabethan effort of the 1500's.

Thus, Dee's "seed" of the British Empire **did** actually sprout in what is
now Touro Park, Newport, Rhode Island, at the mouth of the Dee River.

The John Dee Tower of 1583 might justifiably be considered
the first building of the British Empire. This isn't just a Newport story,
or a New England story, or even an American story, or even a British story.

It's a global story.

*Moreover, Dee designed his Tower to be even **beyond** global*

Not many building have windows that pair-up to that align with celestial events involving the Sun, Moon, and Stars,

The John Dee Tower of 1583 might even be seen as connecting earth with the sky, the **Earthly Realm** with the **Heavenly Realm**.

Because of the celestial alignments through the various windows, the John Dee Tower connects the

Would Dee have envisioned it this way?
Most definitely.
Who would be so bold as to construct a chart for the Holy Roman Emperor entitled "Thus the World Was Created."

The bottom half is the **Earthly Realm** and the top half is the **Heavenly Realm**.

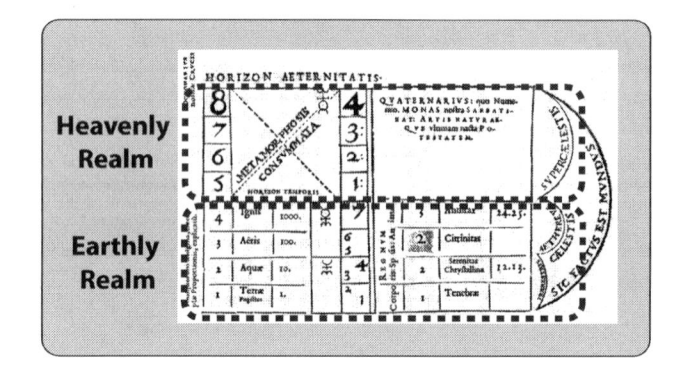

And the chart itself is a blueprint for his Tower.

Dee ingeniously tied all his projects together with the same mathematical cosmology.

He was truly a Renaissance man.

348

Epilogue

I realize that this story of the Newport Tower sounds like fiction, but it's all based on historical fact. As Lord Byron wrote, and Ripley's "Believe It or Not" confirms,

"Truth is always strange. Stranger than fiction."

However, the story of the Newport Tower does have a curious association with a great work of fiction: the 1941 movie ***Citizen Kane***, starring Orson Welles.

In the opening scene, the wealthy newspaper magnate Charles Foster Kane is on his deathbed. As he dies, his final word is **"Rosebud."**

The movie is a series of flashbacks about the great successes as well as the great misfortunes of Kane's tumultuous life.

Only in the final scene do we learn that "Rosebud" was the name of the sled from Kane's childhood, the only time in his life when he was truly happy.

In this history-mystery about the Newport Tower, the name **Rhode** Island is right in our noses from the very beginning.

In 1524, Verrazzano wrote that Claudia was, "about the size of the Isle of **Rhodes**."

Around 1637, Aquidneck Island was called "**Rode** Island."

And in 1663, when Benedict Arnold was made the first Governor, **Rhode** Island officially became part of the State name.

..called by us Rode Island...
(1637)

Further clues indicate **RODE** was actually coined in the mid-1500s by John Dee, as the code name for the first Elizabethan colony.

Finally, the Greek letters spelling "**Rhode**" are found in the stone-and-mortar of the Tower, tying all the clues together.

The curious parallel here is not simply that Citizen Kane and the story of the Newport Tower both revolve around a one-word clue. The uncanny thing is that the clue is virtually **the exact same word**!

Rosebud is simply a "rose" that is not yet blossomed.

And in Greek, **Rhode** means "rose."

349

Both John Dee and Orson Wells probably chose "**rose**" because it's a colorful, yet generic object with many connotations: red, fragrance, purity, beauty, love...

Brides, leading actresses and beauty queens, and Valentine all sweethearts receive bouquets of **roses**.

The petals and rose hips (the fruit at the base of the **rose** flower) are edible and have been used in medicines since ancient times.

The Greeks saw the beauty of the rose and they gave that name to the Isle of **Rhodes**, a strategically important sunny island in the eastern Mediterranean.

The **rose** was the symbol of Venus, the Roman goddess of love and beauty.

Many European cathedrals have "**rose windows**" dedicated to the Virgin Mary, as one on her titles is "The Mystical **Rose**."

Around 1593, (when Dee was 66), William Shakespeare wrote in *Romeo and Juliet*:

> *"What's in a name? That which we call a rose,*
> *By any other name would smell as sweet."*

The **rose** has been the National Flower of England since Henry Tudor won the War of the Roses in 1485.

The **rose** became the National Flower of the United States in 1986.

Every every year before the **Rose Bowl** there is a **Rose Parade** featuring **rose**-covered floats.

With so many connotations, the **rose** can be right in front of your face, yet its intended meaning might be invisible.

Dee had fun with this idea of **RODE** (ROSE) on the Title page of *General and Rare Memorials*.

By writing the Greek for **RODE** in stone-and-mortar Tower, he put it right in front of the eyes of everyone who has ever visited Touro Park. Yet it has been invisible for centuries.

ROSE IS THE ROSEBUD OF RHODE ISLAND

Why John Dee selected JANUARY 15 to be the CORONATION DATE for Queen Elizabeth I

Dee infused his mathematical ideas into everything he did—from books, to geography, to cartography, to architecture. When summoned by the Crown to perform a momentous task, again he was guided by his views about number

When Queen Mary I died in November of 1558, Robert Dudley asked the wise John Dee to select the most auspicious day for the coronation of Elizabeth I.

Historians have been unable to explain why Dee chose January 15, 1559 as the Coronation Day. But after understanding the *Monas*, one can easily see the reason.

This particular date involves Metamorphosis numbers 12, 24, and 360.

Can you figure out how?

First, let's turn the clock back 3000 years.
The ancient Babylonians counted the days
of the year and came up with 365.
(They were pretty close; it's actually 365.2425).

Unfortunately 365 doesn't have many divisors.
(They knew 5 x 73 = 365, but 73 days was too large a time period to deal with. And, being a prime number, 73 is not divisible any further.)

So instead, **they rounded 365 off to 360**,
a number divisible by many factors,
including all the single digits except 7.

They chose to have 12 months of 30 days each and
tagged on the five extra days at the end of the year.
(This use of 360 could be what led them to use the Base 60 for their arithmetic. Several of the authors of the Bible rounded the year off to 360 days as well.)

The many factors of 360

2 x 180 = 360
3 x 120 = 360
4 x 90 = 360
5 x 72 = 360
6 x 60 = 360
8 x 45 = 360
9 x 40 = 360
10 x 36 = 360
12 x 30 = 360
15 x 24 = 360
18 x 20 = 360

Here is the 365.24-day-year broken up into 12 parts of 30 days (plus a 5.24 snippet at the end).

(As fewer and fewer people can read Babylonian these days, I've used the more familiar Roman names, despite the fact that they're not all 30 days long.)

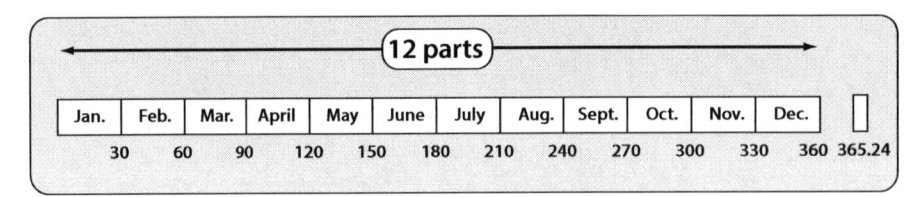

Jan.	Feb.	Mar.	April	May	June	July	Aug.	Sept.	Oct.	Nov.	Dec.	
30	60	90	120	150	180	210	240	270	300	330	360	365.24

⟵ 12 parts ⟶

Next, let's divide the 30 day months in half, making 24 periods of 15 days each.
Dee's selection for the for the Queen's coronation date **is exactly one twenty-fourth of a year!**

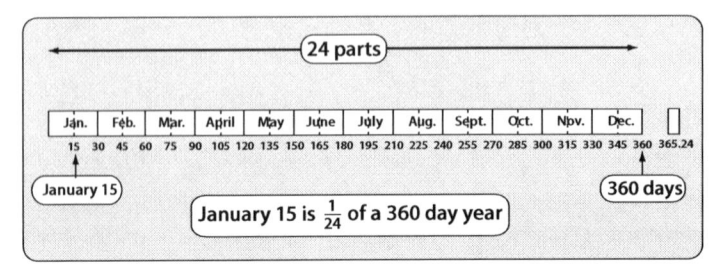

⟵ 24 parts ⟶

Jan.	Feb.	Mar.	April	May	June	July	Aug.	Sept.	Oct.	Nov.	Dec.	
15 30	45 60	75 90	105 120	135 150	165 180	195 210	225 240	255 270	285 300	315 330	345 360	365.24

↑ January 15

January 15 is $\frac{1}{24}$ of a 360 day year   360 days

Let's visualize this another way, using what Dee calls "Circular Arithmetic."

Let's bend the calendar into a circle and slice it into 24 parts.

(like the "24 Wheel" discussed earlier.)

Each part has 15 degrees (or 15 days) in it.

In total, 24 parts of 15 degrees each, make a full 360-degree circle.

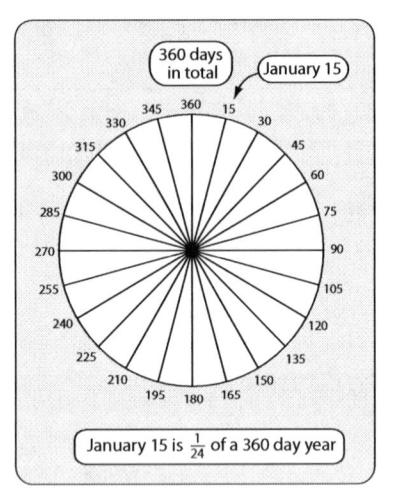

360 days in total   January 15

January 15 is $\frac{1}{24}$ of a 360 day year

The importance of this is that January 15 involves the first three Metamorphosis numbers: **12** (months), **24** (half-months), and **360** (days).

But wait, there's more!

Let's enlarge the January 1 to January 15 section of this calendar.

Multiplying 15 days, times 24 hours a day, **totals to 360 hours!**

The Queen was to be crowned **360 hours** after the beginning of the new year. And 360 is a Metamorphosis Number.

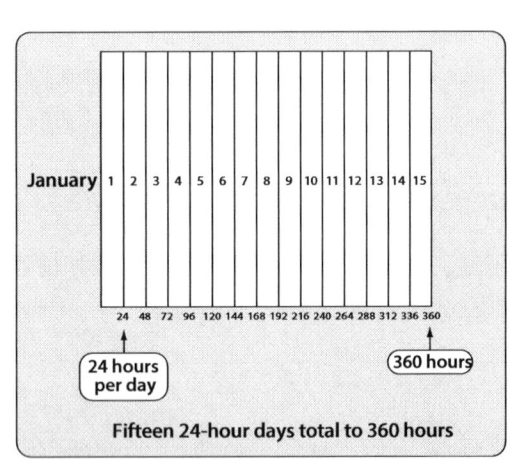

January | 1 | 2 | 3 | 4 | 5 | 6 | 7 | 8 | 9 | 10 | 11 | 12 | 13 | 14 | 15 |

24 48 72 96 120 144 168 192 216 240 264 288 312 336 360

↑ 24 hours per day   ↑ 360 hours

Fifteen 24-hour days total to 360 hours

To see this another way, we might envision a different "Circular Arithmetic" wheel with 15 parts (or 15 days).

As each section is 24 hours, the full circle has 360 degrees (or 360 hours). This involves the three first Metamorphosis numbers in a new way:
12 (hours in a half day), **24** (hours in a day), and **360** (hours in 15 days).

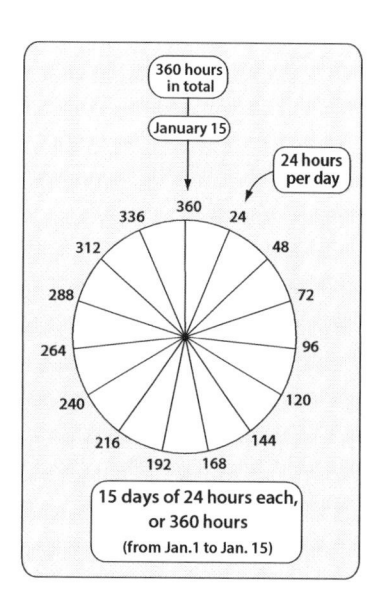

Another reason Dee chose the month of January

January is named after the Roman god **Janus**, the Roman God of Beginnings. Janus is depicted with two heads facing opposite directions:
one looking **back at the old** and
one looking **forward to the new**.
(Just as January 1 ends the old year and starts the new one.)

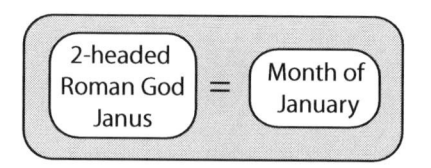

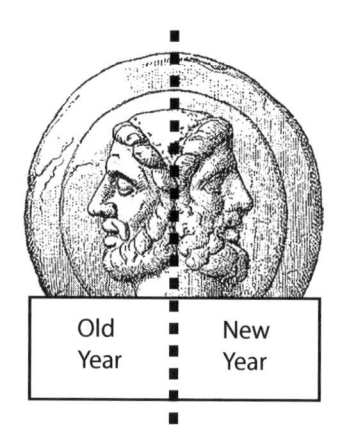

2-headed Roman God Janus = Month of January

When Queen Mary died and the throne went to Elizabeth, Dee saw that a whole new era in English history was about to begin.

(How right he was.)

Out with the old, in with the new.
Exactly what Janus (or January) expresses.

(However, if Dee had selected January 1 for the Coronation Day, it wouldn't actually be perceived as very special. Anybody could have picked January 1. The Queen would not be impressed)

Let's envision Janus another way–as expressing the **whole month** of January. The day that best marks the **middle** of the month would be January **15,** the very date Dee chose!
(January 14 or January 16 just don't feel quite right)

If the left face is the beginning of the month, and the right face is the ending of the month, and the midline runs straight through January 15. The Coronation day denotes the **Union of Opposites** (left face and right face).

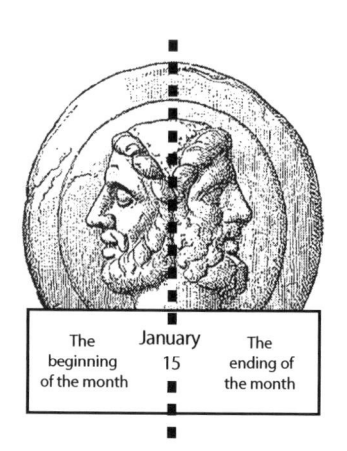

353

When Dee was asked to select the date for the Queen's
Coronation, I don't think he had to think about it for too long.
By 1558, he had fully developed his mathematical cosmology.

(As he had incorporated it in his 1558 *Propaedeumata Aphoristica*).

But there is more evidence suggesting Dee considered
January 15 to be a special day, even prior to 1558.

The date of Dee's Royal Library proposal

When Mary became Queen in 1553, Dee was tossed in jail. To save his skin he became a Catholic priest under Bishop Bonner. Over the next few years, Dee got more comfortable with Mary's regime and became bold enough to even present a proposal to her. With the dissolution of the monasteries under her father, Henry VIII, many of the books and manuscripts from monastic libraries had been dispersed. And many were lost.

In 1556, Dee presented Queen Mary I his "*Supplication for the recovery and the preservation of ancient Writers and Monuments*," recommending the establishment England's first Royal Library. Here is an excerpt:

"But albeit that in those days many a precious jewel and ancient monument did utterly perish (as at Canterbury did that wonderful work of the sage and eloquent Cicero de Republica, and in many other places and like)."

(Dee, *Supplication*, in Roberts and Watson, p. 194)

Dee volunteered to assemble the library, donate books, and even to scour the Continent in search of rare texts.

"And the whole project was to be carried out "without any penny charge unto your [Majestie]."

In 1556, Dee writes a "Supplication" to Queen Mary, recommending the establishment of a Royal Library

Dee's proposal fell on ears as deaf as the ones Bloody Mary
and her henchman Bishop Bonner were busy cutting off.

But the important thing about the "*Supplication*" is the date on which Dee chose to submit it.

You guessed it,
Dee presented his "*Supplication*" to Queen Mary on
January 15, 1556

Dee undoubtedly felt the proposal would be accepted and this would be a mathematically propitious "creation date" for an institution that would grow over the centuries to become an vital repository of wisdom.

(Which the British Library actually became in 1753. Dee was about 200 years ahead of his time.)

(Incidentally, this date, January 15, 1556 involves the cosmologically important number 24 in a different way. If the digits of the month (1), the day (1+5) and the year (1+5+5+6) are added, they sum to 24.)

Having the numerical power of the cosmos on his side probably emboldened Dee to approach the Queen on this day.

To Dee, the idea of preserving the great written works of the ages in a permanent national library was a no-brainer. Unfortunately, this seems to be what Mary had.

A quick review of Dee's use of 12, 24, and 360

Dee hints about the importance of 12, 24, and 360 in many places.

In the Vessels of the Holy Art diagram (in Theorem 22) he applies 12 and 24 to the Monas symbol.

Each arm of the Cross is labeled M, which is the **12**th Latin letter.

Both arms sum to **24**, which is also the diameter of both the Sun and the Moon.

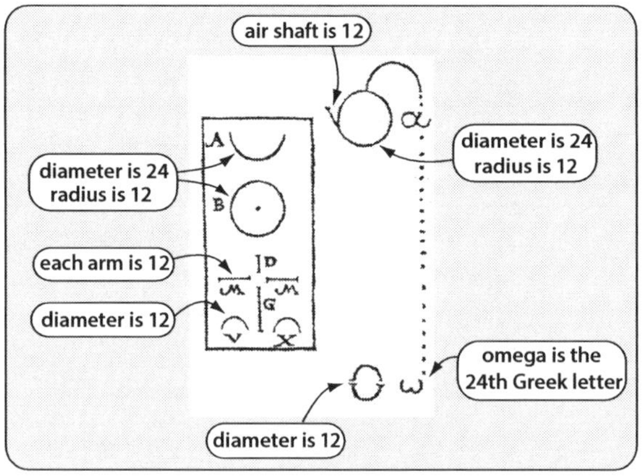

We can see 12, 24, and 360 in the "Thus the World Was Created" chart, when it has been "ballooned to **360**" (making the two circle design).

Also, **12** and **24** are displayed prominently within the chart.

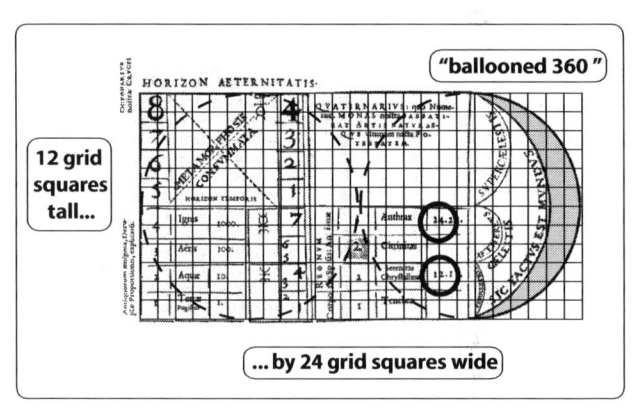

We can see it on the Title page where the theater is **24** x **24** grid-squares, which puts the center point **12** grid squares in from each of the 4 sides.

In the "restored" Title page, that point is also the center point of the Sun Circle, which is a **360** degree circle.

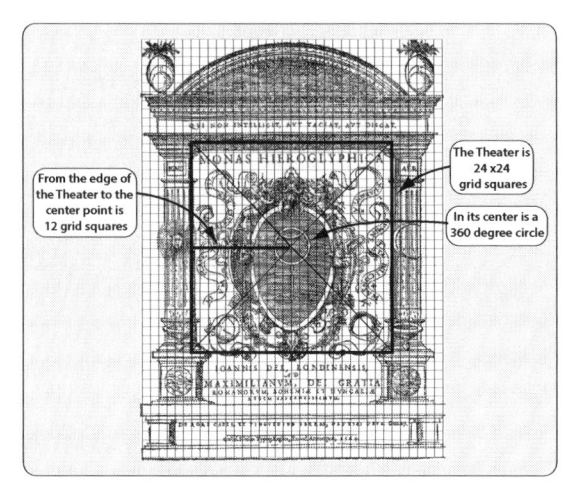

355

> 12252240
>
> 12 252 24 O

A graphic way to see 12, 24, and 360 in Dee's "Exemplar number," 12252240, is to envision the final zero as a **360°** circle.

But a more mathematical way is to add the first three Metamorphosis numbers. (12+24+72=108)

When 108 is added to the 252, Dee's Magistral number, **360** is obtained arithmetically.

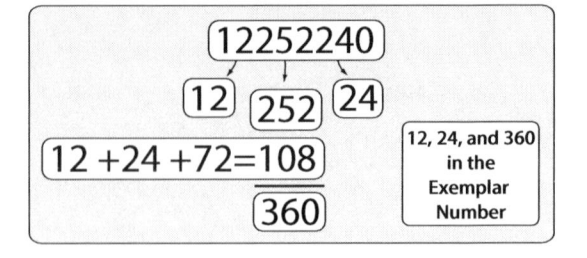

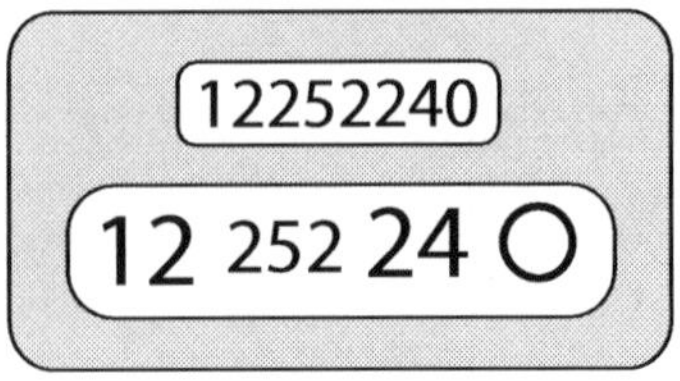

> 12252240
> 12 252 24
> 12 +24 +72=108
> 360

12, 24, and 360 in the Exemplar Number

The numbers 12, 24, and 360 are woven into the very fabric of Dee's book.

In the 24th and final Theorem, Dee tells us his book is "**like a Circle Completing Itself**."

> THEOR. 24
> "In the Beginning of this Little Book, we started with a Point, a Straight Line, and a Circle.
>
> Now, at the End,
> **like a Circle Completing Itself**,
> we have a POINT, LINE, and our ELEMENTS Flowing Out of our MONAD,
> which is Analogous to the Equinoctial when a Circuit is completed in 24 Hours."
>
> Exerpt from Theorem 24
> (p. 27 verso, emphasis mine):

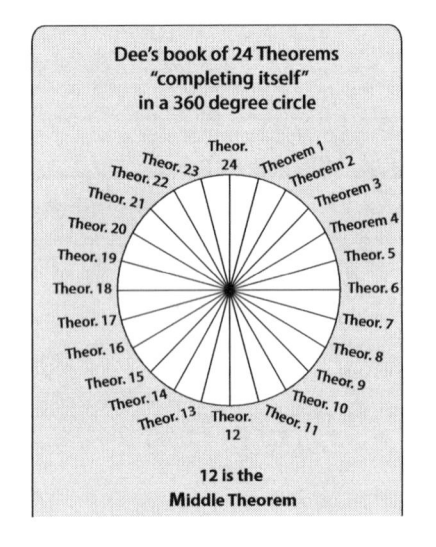

Dee's book of 24 Theorems "completing itself" in a 360 degree circle

(circlegram showing Theorems 1–24 arranged around a circle)

12 is the Middle Theorem

This "circlegram," with its 24 sections in a 360 degree circle, shows the book "Completing itself."

Theorem 12 is "half-way around."

(That makes Theorem 1 similar to **January 15**, the Queen's Coronation Date, one twenty-fourth of a circle).

Dee even informs us in his *Letter to Maximillian* that the "*Quality*" of his "*Theoretical gift*" is "*defined by its own limits.*"

> "...You may now Agree, O King Maximilian, ... that I have said enough... of the Rarity of this our Theoretical gift, whose Quality is defined by its own limits."
>
> Exerpt from the Letter to Maximillian
> (p. 8, emphasis mine)

He might be referring to either the Exemplar number (12252240), or the Monas Symbol, or the whole *Monas Hieroglyphica* book. They are all "defined" by their "own limits."

These "limits" seem to be the "fixed limits" Dee cryptically refers to in his Artificial Quaternary chart.

The "fixed limits" are the Metamorphosis numbers 12, 24, 72, 360, 2520..., which contain a perfect symmetry, unlike other numbers.

Also in Theorem 24, Dee is quick to add that this way of seeing the book is like the *"Equinoctial when a Circuit is completed in 24 Hours."*

In Theorem 11, Dee emphasizes that in the *"Mystical Sign of Aries"* there are *12 hours of lightness and 12 hours of darkness."*

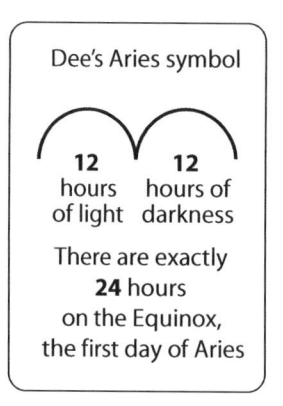

Dee's Aries symbol

12 hours of light **12** hours of darkness

There are exactly **24** hours on the Equinox, the first day of Aries

In several other Theorems, he shows graphically how the **two horns of Aries** can be morphed into a **360°** circle.

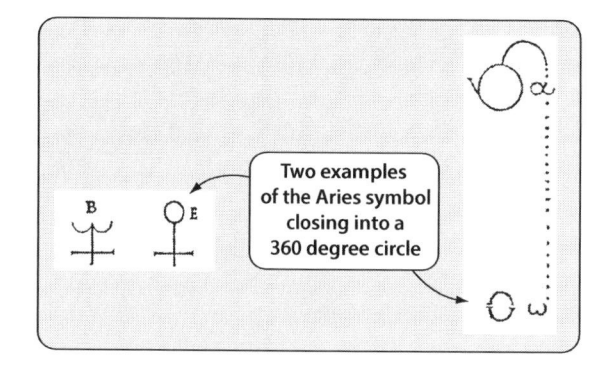

Two examples of the Aries symbol closing into a 360 degree circle

Thus the Equinox might be visually summarized by a circle that is half dark and half light.

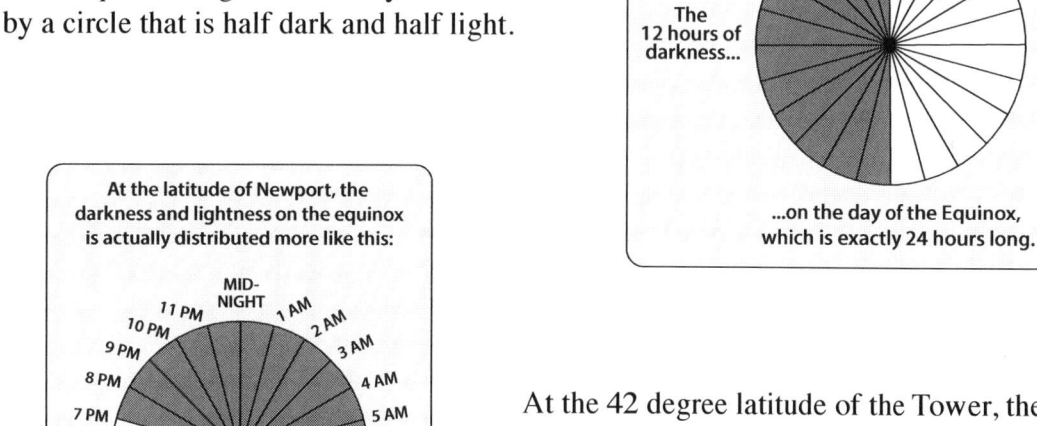

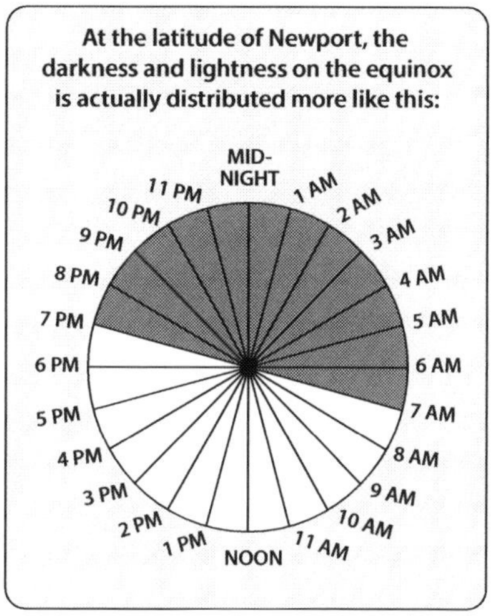

The 12 hours of darkness...

...and 12 hours of light...

...on the day of the Equinox, which is exactly 24 hours long.

At the latitude of Newport, the darkness and lightness on the equinox is actually distributed more like this:

At the 42 degree latitude of the Tower, the darkness/lightness dividing line is not actually a vertical line, but it still incorporates 12, 24, and 360.

357

And of course 12, 24, and 360 can easily be seen in the design for the John Dee Tower. Half of the 48-foot tower is **24** feet. Half of that 24 feet is the **12**-foot height of the "pillars plus the pillar entablature."

A bird's eye view of the Tower shows it has a **12** foot radius, a **24** foot diameter, and is round, like a **360** degree circle.

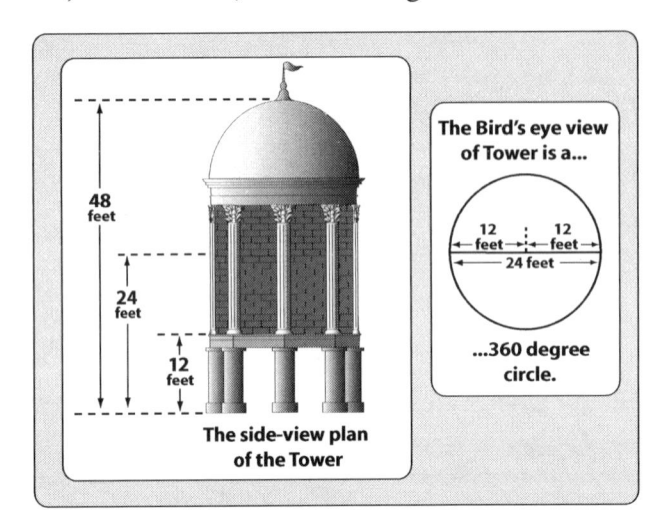

Standing in Touro Park, looking at the timeworn remnants of the **Tower**, it doesn't seem likely that it expresses the **Coronation Date** of Queen Elizabeth I.

But both of these things are constructions that come from Dee's mind, and he was consistent in applying his mathematical cosmology **all** his fields of interest.

As Gerald Suster begins his *John Dee: Essential Readings*: *"Until comparatively recently, John Dee was regarded as an isolated crank in the margin of Tudor history, beyond the pale of serious academic consideration, and of interest only to a small minority of antiquarians and occultists."*

Even today, the *Encyclopaedia Britannica* gives Dee just one small paragraph of scanty and under-researched information—a sad fate for a man who was revered in his time as one of the most learned men in all Europe."

Likewise, the stone-and-mortar Tower in Touro Park has been under-researched by historians, academia, and archeologists. Yet if you google the "oldest buildings in the United States," you'll see that it is the 22nd oldest.

(And it is the oldest standing structure in Rhode Island.)

To bring this 360 page tome "full circle" from page 1, here again is the conclusion Philip Ainsworth Means wrote in his 1942 book, *Newport Tower*:

"The circular arcaded tower at Newport continues to be the most enigmatic and puzzling single building in the United States, a building which may hold the very key to the early Christian history of the Western Hemisphere."

John Dee should be appreciated and given his due place in American, British, and World History. And the Tower should be recognized as the Renaissance Vitruvian circular temple that it is.

It's about time.

The watery Dew
of Heaven

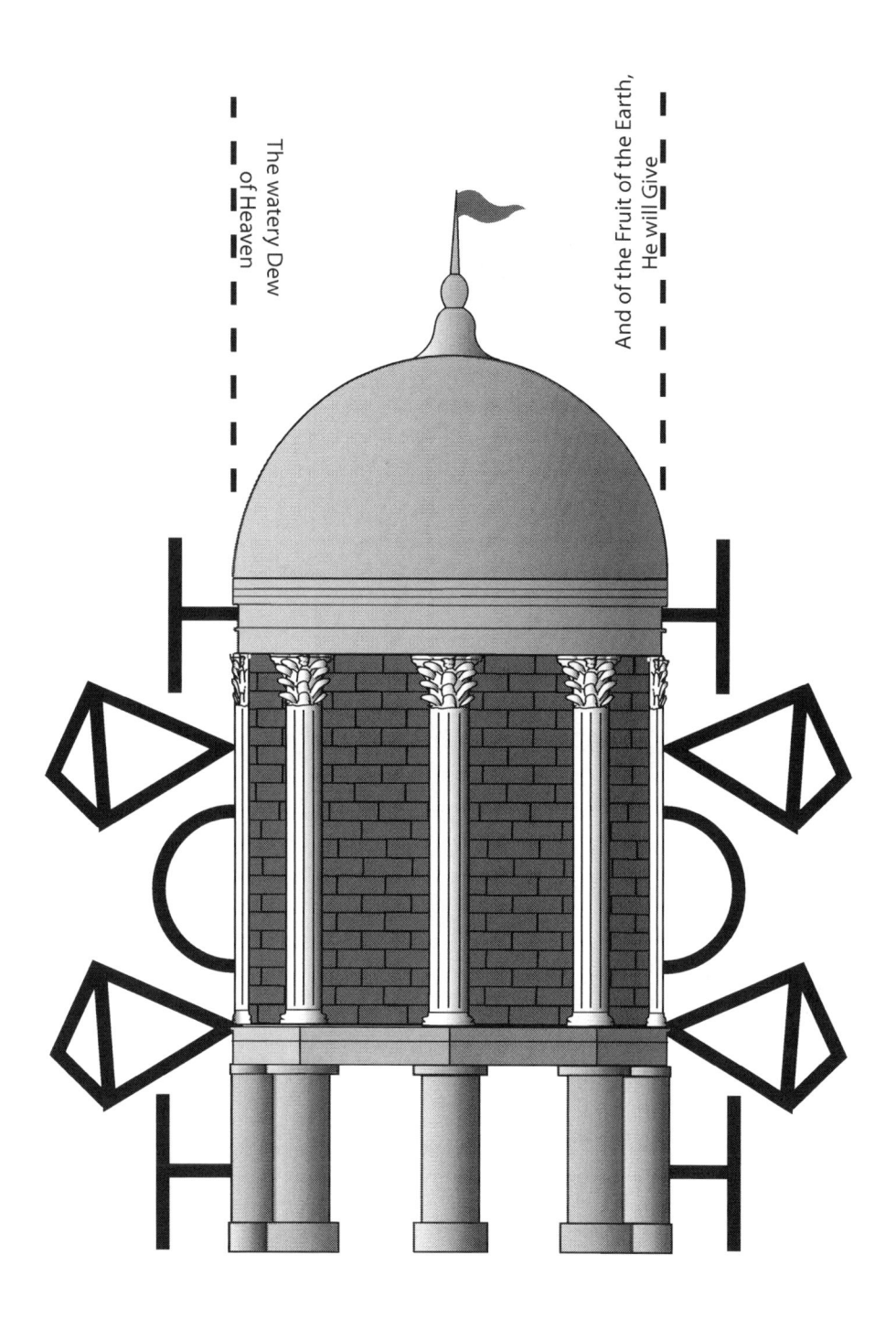

And of the Fruit of the Earth,
He will Give

Once you find what I consider to be Dee's cryptic graphic representation of the word ῬΟΔῆ (Rhode), you'll be able to find what Dee is hiding in the emblem he put on the back cover of his *Monas Hieroglyphica*.

(Which is reproduced on the flip side of this page)

[Answer: Fold the page so the two dotted lines match up and you'll see the pattern described in the previous chapter, on pages 325-343.]

359

The Watery Dew
of Heaven

And of the Fruit of the Earth,
He Will Give

[Answer: Re-fold this page the same way you folded the previous page (by matching up the lower baselines of the two blocks of type) and you will find (written by the strangely elongated acanthus leaves) the number of columns supporting the John Dee Tower.]

BOOKS WRITTEN BY JOHN DEE

(SOME PUBLISHED, SOME EXISTING ONLY IN MANUSCRIPT FORM, AND SOME NO LONGER EXTANT)

1528 [Dee is born]

1547 The Art of Logic
1548 The "13 Sophistocall Fallacias" [13 misleading arguments in rhetoric, as identified by Aristotle]
1549 Planet Mercury in the Heavens

1550 Speech on Euclid's Elements to the College of Reims in Paris
1550 The Uses of the Celestial Globe, dedicated to King Edward VI
1551 On the Distances of the Clouds, Sun, Moon, Planets, and Fixed Stars in Heaven
1555 *De Acribologia Mathematica* [16 books on "Precision in Mathematics"]
1553 300 Astrological Aphorisms
1553 The true Cause of the and Ebbs [of the tides] for Lady Jane, Duchess of Northumberland
1553 The Original Philosophical and Poetical Reason for the Configurations and the Names of the Asterims
    [prominent pattern of stars, but smaller than a constellation; the Big Dipper is an asterism in the Great Bear]
1553 The Astronomical and Logistical Rules, and Canons, to calculate the Ephemerides [tables of the
    positions of the planets] by Heavenly Motions, for Richard Chancellor on his last trip to Moscow
1556 Supplication to Queen Mary to Start a Royal Library
1557 On Burning Mirrors
1557 On Perspective, as it Pertains to Pictures
1557 A Defense of the Great Works of Roger Bacon
1557 The Many Uses for the Astronomer's Ring
1558 *Peri Anabibasmos Theologikon* [3 books on the "Theology of Ascendancy"]
1556 Invention of the Paradoxicall Compass
1558 The Inventive Use of Pulleys and Wheels
1558 *Propaedeumata Aphoristica* ["Preparatory Aphorisms"; also 1568, second edition]
1559 On the Refraction of Rays, the Third and Most Excellent Part of Perspective

1560 On Right Triangles
1560 On Subterranean Tunnels [for Mining]
1562 Compendious Table of the Hebrew Cabala
1564 *Monas Hieroglyphica* ["Sacred Symbol of Oneness"]
1565 A Synopsis of the British Republic

1570 Preface to the first European translation of Mohammed of Baghdad's *On the Division of Surfaces*,
     translated by Frederico Commandino of Urbano, Italy
1570 Mathematical Preface to the first English translation of Euclid's *Elements*
1573 A Renewing of a Tract by Hipparchus
1573 Essentials of Parallax
1574 Ten Sundry and Very Rare Heraldic Blazonings of a Crest or Coat of Arms
1576 Rich and Famous Discoveries [of early English explorers]
1577 General and Rare Memorials Pertaining to the Perfect Art of Navigation
1578 Her Majesty's Royal Title to Many Foreign Countries, Kingdoms, and Provinces
1579 On Imperial Name, Authority, and Power, dedicated to Queen Elizabeth

1580 Navigational Maps for the Northeast Passage, for Arthur Pitt and Charles Jackman
1580 Map of Atlantides [North America]
1581 The measure of the Evangelical Jesus Christ
1582 Advice and Discourse about the Reformation of the Vulgar Julian Year written by Her Majesty's
     Commandment and the Lords of the Privy Council
1583 The Original and Chief Points of our British History
1583 A Land and Water Map of the Northern Hemisphere [circumpolar projection]

1591 On the Body, Soul, Spirit in the whole Microcosm of Natural Philosophy
1592 Compendious Rehearsal [Dee's list of his written works]
1592 Certain Considerations and Conferrings on Three Ancient Sentences:
     Know thyself; Man is a God to Man; Man is a Wolf to Man.
1594 Discourse Apologetical [another list of Dee's works]

(1540's through-1590's The Diaries of John Dee (some written as notes in ephemerides.)

1608 [Dee dies at age 81]

Translations of the John Dee's *Monas Hieroglphica*

1691 Anonymous, *Monas Hieroglyphica of John Dee*,
     (Ferguson collection MS 21, Glasgow University Library, Glasgow, Scotland)
1925 Grillot de Givry, (French translation), *Le Monade Hieroglyphique*,
     (reprinted, Milan, 1975)
1947 J. W. Hamilton-Jones, *The Hieroglyphic Monad*,
     (York Beach, ME, Red Wheel/Weiser, 1975 and 2000)
1964 C.H. Josten, "A Translation of John Dee's *Monas Hieroglyphica* (Antwerp 1564),
     with an introduction and Annotations" (AMBIX, Vol. XII, No. 2 and 3, London)
2010 James A. Egan, *The Works of John Dee: Modernizations of his Main Mathematical Masterpieces*,
     (Book Two of Nine Books: Newport, RI, Cosmopolite Press, 2010)

BIBLIOGRAPHY

Agrippa, Henry Cornelius, *Three Books of Occult Philosophy*, annotated by Donald Tyson, (St. Paul MN, Llewellyn, 2000)
Alexander, Amir R., *Geometrical Landscapes, The Voyages of Discovery and the Transformation of Mathematical Pracrtices,* (Stanford, Stanford U. Press, 2002)
Allen, Dr. F.J., *The Ruined Mill, or Round Church of the Norsemen, at Newport, Rhode Island, USA, compared with the Round Church at Cambridgeshire and others in Europe,* (1921)
Allen, R. E., *Plato, The Republic*, (New Haven, Yale, 2006)
al-Haitham, Ibn, "Opticae Thesaurus: The Mechanistic Hypothesis and the Scientific Study of Vision," edited by . F. Risnero, in A. C. Crombie (Cambridge, MA: Heffer, 1967)
Abraham, Lindy, *A Dictionary of Alchemical Imagery,* (Cambridge, Cambridge U. Press, 1998)
Archibald, Raymond Clare, *Euclid's Book on Division of Figures* (Cambridge, University Press, 1915)
Arnold, Elisha Stephen, *The Arnold Memorial: William Arnold of Providence and Pawtuxet 1587-1675*, (Rutland, Vt., Turtle Pub., 1935)
Arnold, Ethan L., *An Arnold Family Record*, (Elkhart Ind., Bell Printing, 1958)
Ashmole, Elias, *Theatricum Chemicum Brittannicum*, (London, J. Grismond, 1652)
Aslaksen, Helmer, *Guide to The Sun in the Church by Heilbron*, http://www.math.nus.edu.sg/aslaksen/teaching/heilbron.html
Aubrey, John, (edited by Oliver L. Dick) *Aubrey's Brief Lives* (Ann Arbor, U. of Michigan, 1962)

Bailyn, Bernard, *The New England Merchants of the Seventeenth Century*, (Cambridge, Harvard University, 1955)
Barone, Robert W., *A Reputation History of John Dee 1527-1609*, (Lewiston, NY, The Edward Mellen Press, 2009)
Berg, Yehuda, *The 72 Names of God: Technology for the Soul*, (Los Angeles, The Kabbalah Center, 2003)
Biedermann, Hans, *Dictionary of Symbolism*, (New York,, Meridian,1989)
Bridenbaugh, Carl, *Peter Harrison, First American Architect*, (Chapel Hill, UNC Press, 1949)
Brann, Eva, *What, Then, Is Time?* (Lanham MD, Rowman and Littlefield Publishers, Inc.,1999)
Bridenbaugh, Carl, *Fat, Mutton, and Liberty of Conscience: Society in Rhode Island, 1636-1690*, (Providence, Brown U. Press, 1974)
Bridenbaugh, Carl, *Vexed and Troubled Englishmen:1590 to 1642*, (NY, Oxford, 1968)
Black, Robert C. III, *The Younger John Winthrop*, (New York, Columbia University Press, 1966)
Bloom, Allan, *The Republic of Plato*, (NY, Basic Books: Perseus, 1960)
Bond, H. Lawrence, *Nicholas of Cusa, Selected Spiritual Writings* (New York, Paulist Press, 1997)
Briggs, John, *Fire in the Crucible: Understanding the Process of Creative Genius*, (Grand Rapids, Phanes Press, 2000)
Brunner, G. O., "An Unconventional View of Closest Sphere Packings,"(1971, *Acta Crystallographica*, A, Part 4, 1971, p. 27)

Caljori, Florian, *A History of Mathematical Notations*, (Mineola, NY, Dover, 1993)
Carlson, Suzanne, "Loose Threads in a Tapestry of Stone" in *The Newport Tower: Arnold to Zeno*, (Edgecomb, ME, NEARA, 2006)
Clauson, J. Earl, "Pages from Rhode Island's Album 1636-1936," (*Prov. Journal Bulletin*. February 12, 1936)
Clausen, J. Earl., "Benedict Arnold was elected 12 times Governor of Colony," (*Prov. Journal Bulletin*, Feb 12, 1936)
Clausen, J. Earl., *These Plantations*, (Providence, Roger Williams Press, 1937) (see page 3 for reference to "Dee River)

Clucas, Stephen, editor, *John Dee: Interdisciplinary Studies in English Renaissance Thought,*
    (Dordecht, Netherlands, Springer, 2006)
Colket, Meredith B. Jr., (editor) *The American Genealogist* (Dallas, TX, American Society of Genealogists)
Clulee, Nicholas H., *John Dee's Natural Philosophy; Between Science and Religion,* (London and NY, Routledge, 1988)
Crombie, Alistair Cameron, *Science, Art, and Nature in Medieval and Modern Thought,* (London, Hambledon, 1990)
Curl, James Stevens, *Classical Architecture,* (New York, W. W. Norton and Company)

Dantzig, Tobias, *Number: the Language of Science,* (New York, Pi Press, 2005)
Della Porta, Giambattista, ed. Derek Price, *Natural Magick in 20 Books,* (translated into English in 1658), (New York, Basic
    Books, 1957)
Downing, Antoinette F. and Scully, Vincent J. Jr., *The Architectural Heritage of Newport R.I. 1640-1915,*
    (New York, American Legacy Press, 1967)

Edmondson, Amy C., *A Fuller Explanation: The Synergetic Geometry of R. Buckminster Fuller,*
    (Pueblo Colorado, Emergent World, 2007)
Egan, James A., "Highlights of Research on the Newport Tower," in *The Newport Tower, Arnold to Zeno,*
    (NEARA, Edgecomb, ME, 2006)
Egan, James A., Nine Books: (Newport, RI, Cosmopolite Press, 2010)
    Book One: The John Dee Tower of 1583: A Renaissance Building in Newport, Rhode Island
    Book Two: The Works of John Dee: Modernizations of his Main Mathematical Masterpieces
    Book Three: The Meaning of the *Monas Hieroglyphica* with Regards to Geometry
    Book Four: The Meaning of the *Monas Hieroglyphica* with Regards to Number
    Book Five: The Story of 1, 2, 3, 4, and the Proportions of the John Dee Tower
    Book Six: The Coronation Date of Queen Elizabeth I and More *Monas* Mathematics
    Book Seven: Dee's Decad of Shapes and Plato's Number
    Book Eight: John Dee, Governor Benedict Arnold and the Anchor of Hope
    Book Nine: John Dee's British Empire was to be born at "Rode" on the River of Dee
Euclid, *Euclid's Elements,* (Santa Fe, Green Lion Press, 2003)

Fenton, Edward, *The Diaries of John Dee,* (Oxfordshire, Day Books, 2000)
Fernando, Diana T., *The Dictionary of Alchemy: An A-Z of History, People, Definitions,* (London, Vega, 2002)
Fischer, David Hackett, *Albion's Seed: Four British Folkways in America,* (NY, Oxford, Oxford U. Press, 1989)
Fisher, Dennis, *Latitude Hooks and Azimuth Rings: How to build 18 Traditional Navigational Tools,*
    (Camden, ME, International Marine, 1995)
Forshaw, Peter, "The Early Alchemical Reception of John Dee's *Monas Hieroglyphica*," (Ambix 52:3, 2005, pp. 247-269)
French, Peter J., *John Dee: The World of an Elizabethan Magus,* (London, Routledge and Kegan Paul, 1972)
Fuller, *Synergetics 1: Explorations in the Geometry of Thinking,* (NY, Macmillan, 1975)
Fuller, *Synergetics 2: Explorations in the Geometry of Thinking,* (NY, Macmillan, 1979)
Fox, Robert, editor, *Thomas Harriot: An Elizabethan Man of Science,* (Aldershot, Ashgate, 2000)

Goodwin, William B., "The Dee River of 1538 (Now called Narragansett Bay) and its relation to Norumbega."
    (R. I. Historical Society, *Collections,* April 1934, pp. 38-50)
Gernsheim, Helmut, *The History of the Camera Obscura* in *The History of Photography.* (NY, McGraw-Hill, 1969)
Gilbert, Sir Humphrey, *A New Passage to Cataia, 1576,* (Menston, England, Scolar, 1972)
Godfrey, William S. Jr., "The Archeology of the Old Stone Mill in Newport, Rhode Island,"
    (*American Antiquity,* 1951-2, pp. 120-129)
Gorton, Samuel Adelos, *Samuel Gorton,* (Philadelphia, Ferguson, 1907)
Grafton, Anthony, *Cardano's Cosmos: The Worlds and Works of a Renaissance Astrologer,*
    (Cambridge, MA, Harvard University Press, 1999)
Gullberg, Jan, *Mathematics: From the Birth of Numbers,* (NY, Norton, 1997)

d

Hakluyt, Richard, *The Principal Navigations, Traffiques and Discoveries of the English Nation*, (London, Penguin, 1972)
Hales, Thomas C., "Cannonballs and Honeycombs," (Providence, American Mathematical Society, April 2000)
Hammond, John H., *The Camera Obscura: A chronicle*, (Bristol, Adam Hilger Ltd., 1981)
Hammond, Mary Sayer, "The Camera Obscura: A Chapter in the Prehistory of Photography; Pinhole Photography,
    Astronomy, Drawing Machines, Kepler, Perspective," (Ph.D. Thesis, Ohio State University, 1986)
Hattendorf, John B, *Semper Eadem: A History of the Trinity Church in Newport 1698-2000*,
    (Newport, Trinity Church, 2001)
Hazard, Mary E., *Elizabethan Silent Language*, (Lincoln, University of Nebraska Press, 2000)
Heath, Sir Thomas, *A History of Greek Mathematics* (New York, Dover, 1927)
Heilbron, J. L., *The Sun in the Church: Cathedrals as Solar Observatories* (Cambridge, Harvard University Press, 1999)
Hendrix, John, *Platonic Architectonics: Platonic Philosophies & the Visual Arts*, (New York, Peter Lang, 2004)
Hendrix, John, *The Relation Between Architectural Forms and Philosophical Structures in the Work of*
    Francesco Borromini in Seventeenth-Century Rome, (Lewiston NY, Edward Mellen Press, 2002)
Hertz, Johannes, "Round Church or Windmill? New light on the Newport Tower,"
    (Newport History: Journal of the Newport Hist.Soc., Vol 68, Part 2, 1997, No. 235, pp. 55-111)
Hett, W.S, translator, *Aristotle: in 23 Volumes*, (Cambridge, MA, Loeb Classical Library, Harvard University, 1936)
Hopkins, Charles Wyman, *The Home Lots of the Early Settlers of Providence Plantations*, (Providence, 1886)
Hockney, David, *Secret Knowledge, Rediscovering the Lost Techniques of the Old Masters* (New York, Penguin, 2001)

Iamblichus, *The Theology of Arithmetic*, trans. by Robin Waterfield, (Phanes Press, Grand Rapids, 1988)
Ifrah, Georges, *The Universal History of Numbers*, (NY, Wiley, 2000)
Innes, Stephen, *Creating the Commonwealth The Economic Culture of Puritan New England*,
    (New York, W.W. Norton and Co., 1995)

James, Sydney, V., *Colonial Rhode Island: A History*, (New York, Charles Scribner's Sons, 1975)
James, Sydney, V., James, *The Colonial Metamorphoses in Rhode Island: A Study of Institutions in Change*
    (Hanover, NH, University Press of New England, 2000)
Kargon, Robert Hugh, *Atomism in England from Hariot to Newton*, (Oxford, Clarnedon Press, 1996)
Kenner, Hugh, *Bucky: A Guided Tour of Buckminster Fuller*, (New York, William Morrow and Co., 1973)
Kepler, Johannes, *The 6-Cornered Snowflake*, translated by Colin Hardie, (Oxford, Clarendon Press, 1966)
Kuin, Roger, *Querre Mahau: Sir Philip Sidney and the New World*

Lafantasie, Glenn W. (editor), *The Correspondence of Roger Williams, Vol. I and II*,
    (Hanover and London, Brown U. Press/University Press of New England 1988).
Lindberg, David C., *The Beginnings of Western Science* (Chicago, University of Chicago Press, 1992)
Lindberg, David C., *Theories of Vision: Al Kindi to Kepler* (Chicago, University of Chicago, 1976)
Lippincott, Bertram, *Indians, Privateers, and High Society*, (Philadelphia and New York, Lippincott, 1961)
Lippincott, Bertram, *Jamestown Sampler*, (Flourtown, PA, GO Printing, 1980)
MacMillan, Kenneth, *Sovereignity and Possession in the English New World; The Legal Foundations*
    of Empire, 1576-1640, (Cambridge, Cambridge University, 2006)

MacMillan, Kenneth, with Jennifer Abeles, *John Dee The Limits of the British Empire*, (Westport, CT, Praeger, 2004)
Mancall, Peter C., *Hakluyts Promise: An Elizabethan's Obsession for an English America* (New Haven, Yale U. Press)
Mann, A.T., *Sacred Architecture* (Rockport, MA, Element Books, 1993)
Marshall, Robert, (personal correspondences about Syndex, 2000-2010)
Martin, James Kirby, *Benedict Arnold, Revolutionary Hero*, (New York and London, NewYork University Press, 1977)
Masi, Michael, *Boethian Number Theory: A Translation of De Institutione Arithmetica*
    (Amsterdam, Editions Rodopi B.V., 1983)
McCann, Franklin T., *English Discovery of America to 1585* (New York, Octagon, 1969)
McCluskey, Stephen C., *Astronomies and Cultures in Early Medieval Europe* (Cambridge, Cambridge University Press, 1998)
McDermott, James, *Martin Frobisher: Elizabethan Privateer*, (New Haven, Yale University Press, 2001)
McKeon, Richard, editor, *The Basic Works of Aristotle*, (New York, Modern Library, 2001)

Means, Philip Ainsworth, *Newport Tower,* (New York, Henry Holt and Co., 1942)
Means, Philip Ainsworth, "The Riddle of Newport Tower," (*The Christian Science Monitor*, Boston, 1943)
Merriman, R.B., "Some Notes on the Treatment of the English Catholics in the Reign of Elizabeth II"
    American Historical Review, (London, Macmillan, 1908)
Miller, William Davis, *The Narragansett Planters*, (Worcester American Antiquarian Society, 1939)
Mood, Fulmer., "Narragansett Bay and the Dee River, 1583," (R.I. Historical Society, *Collections*, October, 1935, p. 97-100)
Monahan, Tom, *The Do-It-Yourself Lobotomy: Open your Mind to Greater Creative Thinking,*
    (New York, John Wiley and Sons, 2002)
Morison, Samuel Eliot, *The European Discovery of America: The Northern Voyages AD 500-1600,*
    (New York, Oxford University Press, 1971) (see p. 570 for "Dee River")

Navarrete, Fernandez., *de Documentos,* (Letter from Bernadino Mendoza to Philip II, July 11, 1582)
Nicomachus of Gerasa, *The Manual of Harmonics,* trans. by Flora R. Levin, (Grand Rapids, MI, Phanes Press, 1994)
Nicomachus of Gerasa, *Introduction to Arithmetic,* trans. by Martin L. D'Ooge (Chicago, Encyclopedia Brittanica, 1978)

Omar, Saheh Beshara, *Ibn al Haytham's Optics; A Study in the Origins of Experimental Science,*
    (Minneapolis, Bibliotheca Islamica, 1977)
O'Toole, Dennis Allen, "Exiles, Rogues and Refugees," (Ph.D. Thesis, Brown University, 1973) (and also as a book: Newport,
    Cosmopolite Press, 2014)

Penhallow, William S., "Astronomical Alignments in the Newport Tower," in *The Newport Tower, Arnold to Zeno,*
    (NEARA Publications, Edgecomb, ME, 2006)
Poole, Robert, *Time's Alteration,* (London, University College of London Press, 1998)
Potonniee, Georges, *History of the Discovery of Photography,* (New York, Arno Press, 1972)
Pyle, Andrew, *Atomism and its Critics: From Democritus to Newton*, (Bristol, Theommes Press, 1997)

Quinn, David Beers, *The Voyages and Colonizing Enterprises of Sir Humphrey Gilbert*
    (Vol. I and II, London, Hakluyt Society, 1940)
Quinn, David Beers, *Sir Humphrey Gilbert and Newfoundland*. (St. Johns, Newfoundland Hist. Society, 1983)
Quinn, David Beers, *England and the Discovery of America 1461-1620*, (London, George Allen & Unwin Ltd, 1974)

Reeds, Jim, "Solved–The Ciphers in Book III of Trithemius' Steganographia,"
    (AT&T Labs, NJ, 3/26/98 26, *Cryptologia* 22, 10/98, pp. 291-319)
Renner, Eric and Nancy Spencer, "Pinhole Journal: A Tour of Renaissance Pinhole Sites in Italy,"
    (Vol 14, #1, April 1998)
Renner, Eric and Nancy Spencer, *Pinhole Photography,* (Boston, Focal Press, 2000)
Rider, Sidney S., *The Lands of Rhode Island as they were known to Caunaunicus and Miantunnomu*
    when Roger Williams came in 1636, (Providence, Chronicle Printing, 1903).
Robson, Lloyd, *Newport Begins,* (Newport Historical Society, Newport RI, 1964)
Roberts, Julian and Watson, Andrew, *John Dee's Library Catalogue,* (London, Bibliographical Society, 1990)
Rohr, Rene R. J., *Sundials: History, Theory, and Practice,* (NY, Dover, 1996)
Rowland, Ingrid D. and Thomas Noble Howe, *Vitruvius: Ten books on Architecture*, (Cambridge, Cambridge University
    Press, 1999)
Rykwert, Joseph, Neil Lynch, and Robert Tavernor, *Leon Battista Alberti: on the Art of Building in Ten Books* (1486)
    (Cambridge, The MIT Press, 1997)

Sacks, David, *Letter Perfect: The Marvelous History of Our Alphabet from A to Z,* (New York, Broadway Books, 2003)
Savage, James, *Genealogical Register of RI*
Schumaker, Wayne, *Renaissance Curiosa* (Binghampton, New York, Center for Medieval and Renaissance Studies, 1982)
Schumaker, Wayne and J. L. Heilbron, *John Dee on Astronomy: Propaedeumata Aphoristica, 1558 and 1568,*
    (Berkeley, University of California, 1978)

Schneider, Michael S., *A Beginner's Guide to Constructing the Universe: The mathematical archetypes of Nature, Art, and Science,* (New York, Harper Perennial, 1994)
Sherman, William H., *John Dee, The Politics of Reading and Writing in the English Renaissance,* (Amherst, University Mass. Press, 1995)
Sherman, William H., "Putting the British Seas on the Map: John Dee's Imperial Cartography" (*Cartographica*, 35, 1998, pp. 1-10)

Shirley, John W., *Thomas Harriot: A Biography,* (Oxford, Clarendon Press, 1983)
Sieden, Lloyd Steven, *Buckminster Fuller's Universe: His Life and Work,* (Cambridge, Perseus Publishing, 1989)
Singman, Jeffrey L., *Daily Life in Elizabethan England,* (Westport, CT and London Greenwood Press, 1995)
Smith, Charlotte Fell, *John Dee, 1527-1608,* (Berwick, ME, Ibis Press, 2004)
Smith, George, editor, *Dictionary of National Biography,* (London, Oxford, 1917)
Staiger, Ralph C., *Thomas Harriot Science Pioneer,* (N.Y. Clarion, 1998)
Straker, Stephen M., "Kepler's Optics: A study in the Development of 17th Century Natural Philosophy" (Unpublished doctoral thesis, Indiana University, 1971)
Szonyi, György, *John Dee's Occultism,* (Albany, NY, SUNY, 2004)
Strong, Donald, *Leonardo on the Eye* (dissertation, NY, Garland, 1979)
Suster, Gerald, *John Dee: Essential Readings* (London, Aquarian Press, 1986)
Smith, D.E., *History of Mathematics,* 2 Volumes, (New York, Dover, 1923)
Smith, E. Baldwin, *The Dome: A Study in the History of Ideas,* (Princeton, Princeton U. Press, 1950)
Smith, Thomas Gordon, *Vitruvius on Architecture,* (NewYork, Monacelli Press, 2003)
Szpiro, George G. PhD, *Kepler's Conjecture,* (Hoboken, John Wiley and Sons, 2003)
Szulakowska, Urszula, "John Dee and European Alchemy," (Occasional Paper 21, Durham, Thomas Harriot Seminar, 1995)

Tavernor, Robert, *On Alberti and the Art of Building,* (New Haven, Yale University Press, 1998)
Taylor, E.G. *The Two Hakluyts* (Oxford University, 1935)
Tompkins, Hamilton B., *Benedict Arnold: First Governor of Rhode Island,* (Newport, Mercury Print, 1919)

Vaughn, Alden T., *New England's Prospect* (Amherst, University Mass Press, 1977)

Wade, Nicholas J., *A Natural History of Vision,* (Cambridge, MIT Press, 1998)
Waugh, Albert E., *Sundials: Their Theory and Construction,* (New York, Dover, 1973)
Waterfield, Robin, *Herotodus, The Histories,* (New York, Oxford University Press, 1998)
Waterhouse, James, *Notes on the Early History of the Camera Obscura,* (*The Photogrpahic Journal*, May 31, 1901)
Welch, Dan, *Report of the Ground-Penetrating Radar Survey, Touro Park, Newport, RI, June 12, 2001* (Sponsored by NEARA)
Wheelock, Arthur K., *Perspective, Optics, and Delft Artists Around 1650.* (New York: Garland, 1977)
White, Elizabeth N., *Christian Peake, Mother of Governor Benedict Arnold,* (Providence, National Society of Colonial Dames of RI, 1939)
Wier, Alison, *The Life of Elizabeth I,* (New York, Ballantine, 1998)
Wilkinson, Ronald Sterne, *The Alchemical Library of John Winthrop Jr. 1606-1676* (Ambix, 1963, Vol II, pp. 33-51)
Willison, George F., *Saints and Strangers: The Lives of the Pilgrim Fathers and their Families, with their Friends and Foes,* (Orleans MA, Parnassus Imprints, 1971)
Wilson, Derek, *Sir Francis Walsingham: A Courtier in an Age of Terror,* (New York, Carroll and Graf, 2007)
Woodward, Walter William, *Prospero's America: John Winthrop Jr., Alchemy, and the Creation of New England Culture 1606-1676* (Chapel Hill, University of North Carolina.Press, 2010)
Woolley, Benjamin, *The Queen's Conjurer,* (New York, Henry Holt, 2001)
Wroth, Lawrence C., *The Voyages of Giovanni da Verrazzano: 1524-1528,* (New Haven, Yale University Press, 1970)

Yewbrey, Graham, *John Dee and the Sidney Group,* (1981, British Thesis Service, Hull)

Who is Jim Egan?

Born in 1950, in Belmont Massachusetts, I majored in Business and Art at Franklin and Marshall College and was a professional photographer for 30 years in Providence, RI. My wife and I raised two sons, Alex and Eric in a 1726 farmhouse in the woods of Foster, RI.

I became fascinated by the interesting stone walls, cairns, and chambers I came across while hiking in the woods, so I joined the New England Antiquities Research Association. One of the most unusual stone structures the amateur historians in NEARA were studying was the Newport Tower.

We had put men on the moon, but historians still hadn't figured out who built this stone-and-mortar Tower. After learning about the Elizabethan colonization effort of 1583, I took a five-year sabbatical to research, write, and illustrate nine books (over 2000 pages) on my thesis. (Followed by this 360 page synopsis). In 2010, I opened the Newport Tower Museum to share my discoveries with others.

Why was I able to solve a mystery that has baffled historians for so many years?

I humbly submit these six reasons:

1. I tried harder. Having studied the Tower for 25 years, I noticed that many theorists came to the Tower with preconceived ideas (the Scandinavians think the Vikings built it, Portuguese researchers think the Portuguese built it, etc.) I kept an open mind about who built it. I worked like a detective, studying all the suspects, digging in libraries for clues, following leads, forming hypotheses, and studying in Rhode Island History, Elizabethan History and the History of Mathematics and Optics.

2. I'm a visual thinker, and the solution to the Tower just happens to involve how we see. The Tower works in the exact same way our eye works. In the Renaissance, this art and science of vision was called *Perspectiva*. Nowadays, it's called Optics. Over the course of 30 years, I had made over one million camera obscura images (photographs). Many were made with a view camera, in which the image on the groundglass is upside down. Also, one of the photographer's main tools is light, which also happens to be a key clue in solving the Tower history-mystery.

3 I learned how to think creatively. I studied the writings of Renaissance men like Michelangelo, Raphael, Leon Battista Alberti, Leonardo da Vinci, and Luca Pacioli, and Albrecht Dürer. These great thinkers were polymaths, skilled in mathematics, science, architecture, astronomy, writing, painting, sculpture and music. But most importantly they saw how all these fields were interrelated.

I call John Dee's *Monas Hieroglyphica*, "The book of 100 riddles.
I needed to think like a Renaissance polymath (as well as brush up on my Latin and Greek) in order to figure it out.

4. I had tools which were not available to researchers in the 1900's. They didn't have Google, Amazon, or Wikipedia. Around the year 2000, journals, genealogies, research databases and card catalogs started coming online. The world's database of knowledge suddenly came right into my computer. E-mail made communications a snap.

In addition, new manuscripts have come to light and scholars have begun to recognize Dee's importance in British History.

5. I live in Rhode Island and I'm fascinated by its rich history and architecture. In 1995, my wife and I purchased the beams, girts, rafters and chimney-stones of a 1709 Rhode Island Stone Ender and reassembled it as an addition to our 1726 farmhouse.

6. I stand on the shoulders of great thinkers like astronomer William Penhallow (whose incredible findings have been largely under-appreciated for over a decade), Buckminster Fuller (one of the greatest thinkers of the 20th century), Robert Marshall (who saw amazing symmetries in the realm of number), and of course John Dee (who masterfully boiled down geometry, number, and optics to its essence.).

Regardless of how confident I am that my thesis is correct, I still allow for you and others to have your own opinions about who built the Tower. Indeed, to me, that is precisely what the Tower represents: freedom of thought.

(the octave)

Made in the USA
Middletown, DE
20 May 2025

75811007R00210